Julia Child's Menu Cookbook

by Julia Child

In collaboration with
E. S. Yntema

Photographs by
James Scherer

WINGS BOOKS
NEW YORK

JULIA CHILD'S
Menu Cookbook

A new one-volume edition combining the complete texts of
Julia Child & Company and *Julia Child & More Company*

Also by Julia Child

Mastering the Art of French Cooking, Volume I
(with Simone Beck and Louisette Bertholle)

The French Chef Cookbook

Mastering the Art of French Cooking, Volume II
(with Simone Beck)

From Julia Child's Kitchen

The Way To Cook

The titles in this edition were originally published under the titles: *Julia Child & Company*, Copyright © 1978 by Julia Child; *Julia Child & More Company*, Copyright © 1979 by Julia Child.

This 1991 edition is published by Wings Books, distributed by Outlet Book Company, Inc., a Random House Company, 225 Park Avenue South, New York, New York 10003, by arrangement with Alfred A. Knopf, Inc.

Photographs (*Julia Child & Company*), © 1978 by James D. Scherer.

"Lo-Cal Banquet," "Dinner for the Boss," "Birthday Dinner," "UFOs in Wine," "Soup for Supper," and "Butterflied Pork for a Party," all appeared in somewhat shorter form in *McCalls*.

Printed and bound in the United States of America

Library of Congress Cataloging-in-Publication Data
Child, Julia.
    (Julia Child & company)
    Julia Child's menu cookbook/by Julia Child.
       p.   cm.
    "Originally published under the titles: Julia Child
      & company . . .
Julia Child & more company—T.p. verso.
    Includes bibliographical references and index.
    ISBN 0-517-06485-5
    1. Cookery. 2. Menus. I. Child, Julia. Julia
Child & more company. 1991. II. Title. III. Title:
Menu cookbook.
TX715.C5455 1991
641.5—dc20
                               91-19172
                                CIP

ISBN 0-517-06485-5
8 7 6 5 4 3 2 1

Contents

Foreword and Acknowledgments

The two books that this volume combines into one were originally issued by Alfred A. Knopf, Inc. to accompany the two television series, *Julia Child & Company,* and *Julia Child & More Company.* Since shows and book were to appear simultaneously, it was hard to be television cook as well as writer. How wonderfully fortunate we were, then, to find a fast working professional collaborator with literary style and dash, E. S. Yntema. She fitted in beautifully with our cooking team, being a fine cook herself.

I am always inclined to the "we" form when writing about this book since "we" were a team, a family of intimates during the shooting of these Company shows. We worked intensely, ate wonderfully, and had a very good as well as always interesting time. Our leader was Russell Norash, Producer-Director, with whom I've very much enjoyed working since our very first show. Second leader and dear friend was Ruth Lockwood, close collaborator in the planning and execution of the programs. Photographer James Scherer, and Food Designer/Cook Rosemary Manell, were essential members of the team, as was Executive Chef Marian Morash and Executive Associate Elizabeth Bishop.

Members of our cooking team at one time or another were Gladys Christopherson, Bess Coughlin, Wendy Davidson, Bonnie Eleph, Jo Ford, Temi Hyde, Sara Moulton, Pat Pratt, John Reardon, and Bev Seamans. Our able make-up artist was Louise Miller, and office managers were Avid De Voto and Marilyn Ambrose.

It takes a particular peck of people to put on a menu-type cooking show, and I've not even mentioned the production team including cameras, lights, tape editors, and so forth. Nor have I put in a word of deepest appreciation to Chris Pullman, book designer, and to my own dear, unique, and only editor at Knopf, Judith Jones. I thank them all profoundly!

Introduction

This is a book of menus. The first half consists of those for special occasions—the special kind that most of us run into most of the time. For example, you suddenly find that your guest list has swelled to 19 people. You can't sit them down at your table; you'll have to serve them buffet style. Anyway, stand-up or sit-down, what do you feed to 19 people when you're the cook and butler combined? How do you shop for the meal? What staples do you have on hand? How do you time the cooking and then, of course, how do you cook everything?

Or, on another occasion, you are to have a comfortable family-style Sunday night supper, with both grown-ups and children. What would be fun for all? What do you have ready, and what can everyone join in on? Or you've planned a barbecue but it looks like rain, or you just want a cozy and delicious meal for intimate friends.

The second group of thirteen menus is concerned more with special foods than special occasions. What to do with mussels, for instance. Or can the classic way with onion soup be better still? How about making a *pâté en croûte,* or an old-fashioned chicken dinner? These menus keep a thrifty budget in mind, but allow for an occasional splurge, like a rack of lamb, or a lobster soufflé.

This book tells you the whole story for every dish on each of the menus—how to buy, how to cook, and how to serve. Because the best food is the freshest, other choices are available for almost every dish, in case ingredients are not available or a particular item of food does not appeal to you. Finally, since the occasions I have chosen are those that frequently crop up in life, there is an appendix of alternate menus for the same situations, made up of recipes drawn from other books (mostly my own!). Thus you should never be at a loss for what to serve.

Words are not enough, however, when one is reading about a meal rather than seeing it being prepared. Here, therefore, you will find beautiful close-up color photographs of the food before, during, and after its cooking, as well as displays not only of the finished dish, but the look of it when presented in a whole menu.

How-to illustrations are of prime importance in describing complicated procedures: exactly where do you grip the stem when you are to rip it off from a leaf of fresh spinach? Where do you cut to remove a chicken thigh from its attachment to the small of the back? What does a half-finished roll-out of puff pastry look like? Thanks to the patient devotion and talent of our photographer, James Scherer, and of our food designer, Rosemary Manell, you can see exactly how, and you'll see it from the cook's point of view.

This menu book combines into one volume the two *Julia Child and Company* books that appeared with the television series of the same name, and I am delighted they are together at last.

J.C.
Cambridge, Mass., March 26, 1991

Note: throughout this book, ❶ indicates a stopping point in the recipe, and ▼ indicates further discussion under Remarks.

JULIA CHILD'S
Menu Cookbook

A menu designed around duck, with a special roasting method which guarantees perfect cooking and easy carving. Herewith, also, a sumptuous apricot and hazelnut cake.

Birthday Dinner

Whenever anyone asks me what I want for a birthday dinner, I always say, "Roast duck and a big gooey cake." I love to eat duck when the skin is crisp and mahogany red-brown, the legs and wings just tender through, the breast meat moist, rosy, and tender. And guests always feel it's a special treat. You don't see duck too often at dinner parties. It does pose problems, and I've been giving them some thought.

Even a carver as adept as my husband finds that the docile duck becomes as stubborn as an ostrich on the carving board; that's the first problem. Second is the fact that roasted the usual way the breast meat is done much sooner than the leg and wing. Fat is problem number three: for perfect flavor, the fat must be drained off during cooking. But if you want a crisp skin, you can't cook it in the normal manner because the meat will be overdone. Many a cook is resigned to ruining the meat in order to enjoy a crackling skin.

A famous Chinese solution to these problems is Peking duck, the glory of Mandarin cuisine, for which one starts way ahead by forcing air between the duck's skin and flesh and hanging up the inflated carcass to dry. For the fine Norman ducks of Rouen, which are a cross between wild and domestic strains and are sold unbled, the French have thought up the duck press and produce a carnal feast indeed. Here the partly roasted bird is peeled of its skin, the breast is carved, the legs and wings are removed, and the carcass is crushed for its juices. The breast is then warmed in these juices, a rich dark red, laced with Burgundy wine. The legs and wings finish cooking while you eat the more delicate breast, and they come in as an encore. This requires expert servers, a chafing dish, and a duck press. But when we filmed the process at the Dorin brothers' restaurant in Rouen, I also showed a less elaborate alternative. With that in mind, I decided to continue with the roast-peel idea that I used then to produce another and simpler dish.

This way of dealing with duck involves neither sideboard antics nor fancy paraphernalia; and it solves all three of the problems I mentioned. The duck can be beautifully presented, since it is carved in the kitchen, and served before its redolence evaporates. I like to contrast its rich flavor, crisp skin, and succulent meat with a velvety purée of parsnips. Their very special flavor, earthy and sweetish—so compatible with duck—is transformed by puréeing. People who think they don't like parsnips are almost always enchanted with them this way, wondering happily, "What can it be?" I like to serve the parsnip purée in baked zucchini shells—chosen for their unobtrusive taste and their jade and emerald color—an easy and elegant vegetable accompaniment. I'd hate to disturb the rapport of these congenial flavors with anything else, so I serve another vegetable as a separate course.

Like opposite primary and secondary colors, fruit flavors seem to balance duck. So I've chosen a fruit-layered cake for the birthday dessert: crisp strips of nut meringue spread with a luscious apricot filling flavored with orange liqueur and a touch of Cognac, plus a discreet amount of butter cream, just enough to mediate the contrast in taste and texture.

I like this luxurious menu; and I also like to feel rested as well as hospitable when I call my best friends in to the table. No damp brow or hot hands for the birthday cook! I prepare most of this very posh dinner well in advance, and the work itself isn't difficult. The gorgeous cake is not only more fun to make than the sponge-layer kind, it's easier. And in the privacy of my kitchen, nobody can see me subduing the duck.

Preparations

Marketing and Storage:
Staples to have on hand

Salt
Peppercorns
Sugar (both granulated and confectioners)
Pure vanilla extract
Almond extract
Cream of tartar
Stick cinnamon
Bay leaves
Thyme or sage
Mustard (the strong Dijon type or
  Düsseldorf)▼
Apricot preserves or jam (optional)
All-purpose flour
Olive oil and cooking oil
Wines and liqueurs: dry white French
  vermouth, Cognac or rum, dry Port or
  Sercial Madeira, orange or apricot
  liqueur
Vegetables and fruits: a few carrots, onions,
  shallots or scallions, an orange, and
  lemons
Eggs (12)
Cream (½ pint [225 g] or so)
Fresh bread crumbs (in the freezer) ▼

Specific ingredients for this menu

Crab (enough for 6 as a first course;
  see recipe) ▼
Ducklings (two 4- to 5-pound or 2- to
  2½-kg) ▼
Zucchini (6, about 6 inches or 15 cm long)
Parsnips (1½ to 2 pounds or ¾ to 1 kg)
Broccoli (2 bunches)
Parsley (1 bunch; or 1 or 2 of watercress)
Unsalted butter (about 1 pound or 450 g)
Dried apricots (1 pound or 450 g)
Whole shelled hazelnuts and blanched
  almonds (about 4 ounces or 120 g of
  each) ▼
Shaved (thinly sliced) almonds, toasted (about
  8 ounces or 240 g)

► *Remarks:*

Staples

Mustard: always store prepared mustard in the refrigerator, otherwise it goes off in flavor; most supermarkets carry several varieties of strong European-type mustard, and the ballpark variety is not meant here. *Bread crumbs:* it's useful to have these always on hand in the freezer, and crumbs from fresh bread are best. To make them easily, cut crusts off nonsweet white bread, such as French, Italian, and Viennese, and crumb either in the blender or with the grating disk of a food processor; store in a plastic bag in the freezer where they will keep for weeks.

Specific ingredients for this menu

Crab: if you buy frozen crab, allow a day for it to defrost in the refrigerator, and see notes on crab in "Fish Talk," page 111.) *Ducks:* frozen ducks, like all frozen poultry, should be defrosted in the refrigerator to minimize juice loss since too quick defrosting can cause the ice crystals to pierce the flesh. Your best alternative is to defrost them in a sinkful of water. In either case, leave ducks in their plastic wrapping, and allow 2 to 3 days in the refrigerator, several hours in water. *Hazelnuts and almonds:* nuts are perishable, especially hazelnuts (called filberts by some people); taste them to be sure they are fresh, and store them in the freezer. To skin hazelnuts, place in a roasting pan in a 350°F/180°C oven, tossing about every 5 minutes or so, for 15 to 20 minutes, or until the nuts are lightly browned; rub in a towel to remove as much skin as you easily can. Toasting also gives them added flavor. Toast whole blanched shaved almonds in the same manner.

Chesapeake Lump Crabmeat Appetizer

Since how much you season your crabmeat depends entirely on its quality, I can only make suggestions. Freshly boiled crabmeat needs nothing on it, I think, only lemon, salt, and a peppermill passed at the table, and to each his own. Frozen and canned crab are very much up to you and your tastebuds as you fix your appetizer. Lemon juice, certainly, and often you will need very finely minced shallot or scallion, sometimes a little minced celery, and fresh minced dill or fragrant bottled dill weed, plus salt and pepper, and perhaps a tossing with good olive oil; I like to pass mayonnaise separately, for those who wish it. Arrange the crab on a bed of either shredded lettuce or romaine, or surround it with watercress, or wreathe it in seasoned ripe tomato pulp or red pimiento. You could also include quartered hard-boiled eggs, but that would be dictated by how much crab you were serving per person—and since crab is a luxury, ⅓ cup (¾ dL) for each guest is generous enough, even for a birthday party.

Roast Duck with Cracklings

In this method, the duck is given a preliminary or partial roasting, then a skin peeling and carving; half an hour before serving, the legs finish cooking along with the skin, cut into strips which render their fat and crisp in the oven. The breast meat is warmed briefly in wine and seasonings just before being arranged on the platter with the browned legs and crackling skin. All but the final cooking may be done in advance.

For 6 people

Two 4- to 5-pound (2 to 2¼-kg) ducklings
1 Tb cooking oil
1 medium-size carrot, roughly chopped
1 medium-size onion, roughly chopped
Salt, thyme or sage, 1 bay leaf, ½ cup (1 dL) strong prepared mustard, Dijon type
Generous 1 cup (¼ L) lightly pressed down, fresh nonsweet white bread crumbs
2 Tb duck-roasting fat or melted butter
1 Tb minced shallots or scallions
Pepper
¼ cup (½ dL) or so dry Port or Sercial Madeira

Preliminaries to roasting

Chop the ducks' wings off at the elbows and brown them in cooking oil with the neck, gizzard, and vegetables, in a heavy saucepan, then simmer in water to cover and ½ teaspoon salt for an hour. Drain, degrease, and reserve liquid for sauce later; you should have about ½ cup (1 dL) strong meaty liquid.

Meanwhile, here's a good trick for easy carving (you won't be carving at table with this recipe, but it still makes the duck easier to disjoint): working from inside the duck, sever ball joints where wings join shoulders (as illustrated opposite, top left) and second joints join small of back (opposite, lower left). Again for easy carving, remove wishbone from inside of neck opening and add to duck stock.

Sprinkle inside of duck with ¼ teaspoon salt and a pinch of thyme or sage, and tuck in the bay leaf. Pull out any loose fat from inside neck and cavity. Prick the skin all over on the back and sides (where you see the yellow fat under the skin) with a sharp-pronged fork or trussing needle, but do not go too deep where rosy flesh shows through skin, or the duck juices will seep out and stain the skin as the duck is roasting. To truss the duck, first, push needle through carcass underneath the wings, then come up around one wing, catch the neck skin flap against the backbone (upper right picture); come out over opposite wing, and tie. For the second truss (middle right picture), push needle through underside of drumstick ends, catching the tail piece as you go, come back over tops of drumsticks, and tie. The neatly trussed duck will look like the one in the bottom picture.

🕐 May be prepared for roasting a day in advance.

A preliminary roasting
Preheat oven to 350°F/180°C. Place ducks breast up in roasting pan and set in middle level of preheated oven. Roast 30 to 35 minutes, or until breast meat is just springy to the touch (rather than squashy like raw duck)—this means the breast meat is just rosy and easy to carve, but the legs and thighs (which will cook more later) are still rare.

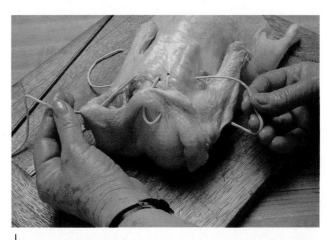

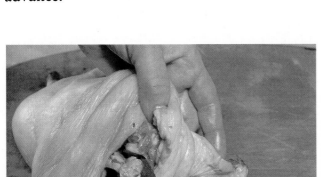

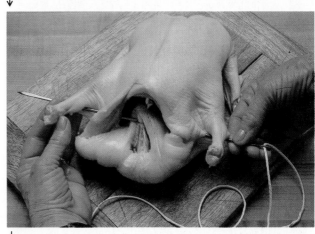

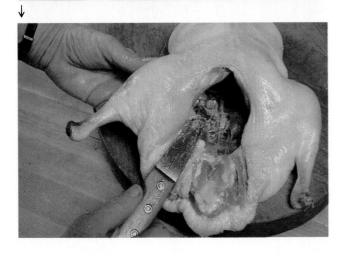

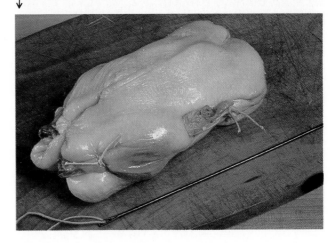

**Skinning and carving—preliminaries
to final cooking**

While the duck is still warm, peel off its skin as follows: cut a slit down the length of the duck on either side of the breastbone, as I've done in the picture below, and remove skin from breast and thighs.

Then cut up the duck as shown in the lower right picture. Remove leg-thigh sections and separate legs from thighs; peel as much skin off them as you easily can, and cut off visible fat. Cut fat and skin into strips ¼ inch (¾ cm) wide and place in a baking dish. Paint legs and thighs with a thin coating of mustard, roll in crumbs, and arrange in another baking dish; sprinkle tops with a dribble of duck-roasting fat or melted butter.

Film a frying pan (not of cast iron) with duck fat or melted butter, sprinkle in half the shallots or scallions, carve the breast meat into neat slices, as illustrated, and arrange in the pan. Season lightly with salt and pepper and sprinkle with the remaining shallots or scallions. Pour in the Port or Madeira and the duck stock from the first paragraph. (You may wish to roast the carcasses and wings—which have little meat—a few minutes more and save for the cook's lunch the next day; that's what I do, at least.)

🕐   May be prepared to this point several hours before serving.

Finishing the ducks

Preheat the oven to 400°F/200°C, and half an hour before you plan to serve dinner, set dishes with crumbed legs and thighs and skin strips in the upper-third level. Roast skin until the pieces have browned nicely and rendered their fat; remove with a slotted spoon to a plate covered with paper toweling to drain; then toss with a sprinkling of salt and pepper. Roast legs until just tender when pressed—about 20 to 25 minutes. Keep both warm in turned-off oven, door ajar, until you are ready to serve. Between courses, as you are changing plates, bring the pan with the duck breast slices barely to the simmer, to poach the meat but keep it the color of a deep blush. Then arrange it on a hot platter and rapidly boil down the cooking juices until syrupy while you arrange the legs and the skin cracklings on the platter; pour the reduced pan juices over the breast meat and serve at once.

Remarks:

I was discussing duck the other day with a restaurant owner who serves a lot of duck to his clientele. He says he puts his in a 250°F/130°C oven and lets them roast slowly for 3 or 4 hours, pricking them several times to drain out the fat. The meat emerges a nice medium rare, the birds exude a lot of fat, and when he is ready to serve he pops them back in the oven, at 550°F/290°C, to brown and crisp the skin. I haven't tried the final crisping, since I fear so hot an oven and its effect on the rosy meat, but the slow roast is certainly easy and painless.

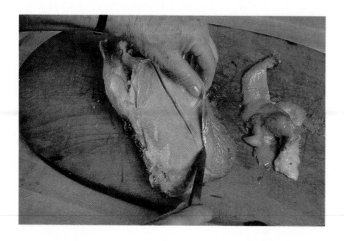

Purée of Parsnips

To go with roast duck, goose, pork,
or turkey

For 4 to 6 servings (more than you need
for the zucchini boats, but the purée is so
good and reheats so well, I am suggest-
ing almost double the necessary amount)

2 pounds (1 kg) parsnips

Salt

5 Tb cream

2 Tb butter

Pepper

Trim and peel the parsnips and cut into slices about ⅓ inch (1 cm) thick. Place in a saucepan with water barely to cover and a teaspoon of salt. Bring to the boil, cover pan, and boil slowly 20 to 30 minutes or until parsnips are tender and water has almost entirely evaporated. Using a vegetable mill or food processor, purée, and return to saucepan. Beat in the cream and butter, and season to taste with salt and pepper. Set pan in another containing simmering water, cover, and let cook 20 to 30 minutes more—note the subtle change in taste that takes place. Correct seasoning before serving.

🕐 May be cooked in advance and reheated over simmering water.

Zucchini Boats

To hold a purée of parsnips or other
cooked filling

6 zucchini of uniform size, about 6 inches
(15 cm) long

Salt

2 to 3 Tb melted butter

Pepper

Trim stem ends off zucchini and cut zucchini in half lengthwise. Hollow out the centers with a grapefruit knife, leaving a 3/16-inch (scant ¾-cm) border of flesh all around. (Save removed centers for soup.) Drop the boat-shaped zucchini in a large pan of lightly salted boiling water and boil slowly 4 to 5 minutes, or until barely tender—they must hold their shape. Brush with melted butter, season lightly with salt and pepper, and arrange in a roasting pan. Shortly before serving, pour in ¼ inch (¾ cm) water, and bake 4 to 5 minutes in the upper third of a preheated 425°F/220°C oven—to give them a little more flavor, but without letting them overcook and lose their shape.

Assembling

Arrange the hot zucchini boats in a serving dish, and with a pastry bag and cannelated tube, rapidly pipe the hot parsnip purée into them—much more attractive than when they are filled with a spoon. Serve at once.

Broccoli Flowerettes

For 6 people have a good 2 quarts or 2 liters of prepared broccoli—1½ bunches

This doesn't need a full-scale recipe, since broccoli is so easy to cook, but for the freshest-tasting, greenest, slightly crunchy, beautiful broccoli, you do have to peel the stems. Then the broccoli cooks in less than 5 minutes. Here's how to go about it: cut the stems off the broccoli, leaving the bud ends about 2½ inches (6½ cm) long; quarter the bud ends to make them all about 3/16 inch (scant ¾ cm) in diameter. From the cut end, pull off the skin up to the bud section. Peel the stems with a knife, going down to the tender white. Refrigerate in a covered bowl until you are ready to cook the broccoli.

To cook, you may blanch the broccoli ahead, and plunge into boiling water just before serving; or boil between courses, since it cooks so quickly. Bring a very large kettle with 5 to 6 quarts or liters lightly salted water to the rapid boil, drop in the broccoli, cover the kettle, and bring to the boil again over highest heat; as soon as the water boils, remove cover and boil slowly 4 to 5 minutes, just until broccoli is cooked through, slightly crunchy, and a beautiful bright green. Remove at once from the boiling water—a large perforated scoop is useful here. If you are serving immediately, arrange quickly on a platter, seasoning lightly with salt and pepper, the Brown Butter Sauce (see following recipe)—or use melted butter—and drops of lemon juice. (Or you may pre-cook the broccoli until barely tender before dinner and spread it out on a towel to cool rapidly; keep a kettle of fresh salted water at the boil between courses, and plunge the broccoli into the boiling water just before serving, to reheat for a moment; then dress it on the platter as described.)

Brown Butter Sauce:
For 6 servings

Cut 1 stick (4 ounces or 115 g) butter into fairly thin slices—for even melting—and place in a small saucepan over moderate heat, bringing the butter to a boil. Skim off foam as it collects and cook until butter turns a nice nutty brown—this will take only 2 to 3 minutes in all. If serving immediately, spoon over the food, leaving speckled particles in bottom of pan. For later serving, spoon into a clean pan and either reheat or keep over hot water.

The Los Gatos Gâteau Cake

A Dacquoise type of apricot-filled torte

For a 12-by-4-inch cake about 2 inches high, serving 12 to 14

The Meringue-Nut Layers:

¾ cup (1⅓ dL) each toasted and skinned hazelnuts and blanched toasted almonds

1 cup (¼ L)sugar

¾ cup (1¾ dL or 5 to 6) egg whites

Pinch salt and ¼ tsp cream of tartar

3 Tb additional sugar

1 Tb pure vanilla extract

¼ tsp almond extract

Equipment

A blender or food processor; 2 pastry sheets about 12 by 15 inches (30 x 37 cm) each (nonstick recommended); a 14-inch (35-cm) pastry bag with ½-inch (1½-cm) tip opening (recommended); a flexible-blade spatula

Using a blender or food processor, pulverize the hazelnuts with half the sugar, then the almonds with the remaining sugar. Preheat oven to 250°F/120°C, placing racks in upper- and lower-third levels. Butter and flour the pastry sheets, and trace 4 rectangles on them 12 by 4 inches (30 x 10 cm), as I have done here.

Beat the egg whites at slow speed until they have foamed, then beat in the salt and cream of tartar; increase speed gradually to fast, and beat until egg whites form stiff shining peaks. Immediately sprinkle in the remaining 3 tablespoons sugar while beating, add the vanilla and almond extracts, and continue for 30 seconds more. Remove beater from stand and at once sprinkle on the pulverized nuts and sugar, folding them in rapidly with a rubber spatula as you do so. Scoop the meringue into the pastry bag and squeeze out onto the traced rectangles, starting at the edges of each and

working inward; smooth with a flexible-blade spatula. (Or spread and smooth with a spatula.) Set in oven and bake about an hour, switching levels every 20 minutes or so. The meringue layers are done when you can gently push them loose; do not force them, since they break easily and will budge only when they are ready to do so. Remove to a rack.

🕐 If not used within an hour or so, keep in a warming oven at 120°F/50°C, or wrap airtight and freeze.

The Apricot Filling:

About 2½ cups (6 dL)

1 pound (450 g) dried apricots

1 cup (¼ L) dry white French vermouth

2 cups (½ L) water

1 stick cinnamon

Zest (colored part of peel) of 1 orange

⅔ cup (1½ dL) sugar

2 Tb orange or apricot liqueur and 1 Tb Cognac or rum

Place the apricots in a saucepan and soak in vermouth and water several hours or overnight until tender. Then simmer with cinnamon and zest of orange for 10 minutes; add the sugar and simmer 10 minutes more or until very tender. Drain thoroughly and purée, using food processor or vegetable mill. Boil down cooking liquid (if any) to a thick syrup, and stir into the purée along with the liqueur.

🕐 May be completed a week or more in advance; cover and refrigerate.

Confectioners Butter Cream:
For 1 to 1½ cups
Make just before using

8 ounces (225 g) unsalted butter

10 ounces (285 g; 2 cups sifted directly into cup) confectioners sugar

2 egg yolks

1 Tb pure vanilla extract

3 to 4 Tb orange or apricot liqueur, Cognac, or rum

Equipment

An electric mixer

Beat the butter in a bowl over hot water just until softened, then beat in the sugar and continue for a minute or so until light and fluffy. Add the egg yolks, beating for 1 minute, then beat in the vanilla and liqueur. If too soft, beat over cold water until of easy spreading consistency.

Assembling the cake
(and additional ingredients)

About 1 cup (¼ L) confectioners sugar in a sieve or shaker

2 cups (about 8 ounces or 240 g) shaved almonds, lightly toasted

Lightly whipped and sweetened cream to pass with the cake (optional)

Equipment

A serving board or tray to hold the cake; wax paper; a flexible-blade spatula; rubber spatulas

The meringue layers break easily, but don't worry if they do; breaks—or San Andreas faults, as one California friend terms them—can be disguised. Save the best one for the top of the cake, 2 more for layers, and the final one is there just in case. Place double layers of wax paper strips on the serving board in such a way that they can be slipped out from sides and ends of cake after icing.

Set the least attractive of the meringue layers on the board, adjusting the wax paper to fit just under its edges. Reserving almost two thirds of the butter filling to ice the sides of the cake, spread half of what remains on the meringue layer, then cover with half of the apricot purée. Set a second meringue layer on top, and repeat with a spreading of butter cream and the remaining apricot. Top with a final meringue layer, and if it is unblemished dust with a coating of confectioners sugar. (If it is irreparably cracked, too much so to be disguised with sugar, ice it with butter cream and later sprinkle with almonds.)

Spread butter cream all around the sides of the cake. Then, with the palm of one hand, brush almonds all around to make an informal decoration. (Scatter almonds also on top, if you have the San Andreas fault to deal with.) Chill the cake—you may wish to cover it with a long box.

🕐 May be refrigerated for a day or two; the meringue layers gradually soften as the cake sits. Cake may be frozen; thaw in the refrigerator for several hours.

Serving

Cut cake into serving pieces from one of the small ends; a dollop of lightly whipped cream on the side goes nicely with the tart apricot filling.

Remarks:

This recipe allows for a good amount of butter cream, and you may wish to set a little aside. Then, if a reasonable amount of cake is left over, you can refrost the cut end and present, for all the world, a fresh new cake for its next go-around. As an aid to keeping the meringue-nut layers more crisp, you could paint the top of the bottom one, both sides of the middle one, and the bottom of the top layer with the following apricot glaze, letting it set for several minutes before filling the cake.

Apricot Glaze:

Boil up the contents of a 12-ounce (340-g) jar of apricot preserves with 3 tablespoons sugar, stirring, until last drops from a spoon are thick and sticky—and glaze reaches 238°F/115°C. Push through a sieve and use while still warm; return any left over to jar and keep for future glazings.

The fourth meringue layer

If you are sure of your layer stability, you can pulverize this one and either stir it into your apricot purée, or save it for a dessert topping as in the Floating Island, page 58. Or freeze it, and when you want finger cookies, cut it into crosswise strips with a serrated knife, sawing gently; cover with a sifting of confectioners sugar, or the icing of your choice.

🕐 *Timing*

This is a relatively fancy meal and involves quite a bit of work, but not much has to be done at the last minute. You can accomplish most of your marketing days in advance. The meringue-nut layers can be baked months beforehand if you freeze them, and the apricots can be cooked a week or more ahead. Just don't forget to thaw your ducks.

You'll need only about five minutes between first and second courses to crisp the duck cracklings and warm the breast slices; and just a moment before the third course to finish the broccoli if you have blanched it in advance.

Not long before announcing dinner, slip the dishes containing legs and skin strips into the oven. They can have sat an hour all prepared, and so can the breasts in their frying pan. You should get your wine bottles ready for evening, chill your whites, two hours before dinner.

Pre-roast, peel, and carve the ducks, if you're doing them the slow way, in the afternoon.

Early on the day of the party, you can assemble the cake and refrigerate it, purée the parsnips, and blanch the broccoli and the zucchini boats.

Menu Variations

The appetizer: Rather than crab you could serve caviar, or any shellfish: mussels, oysters, clams, scallops, shrimp, lobster. (See "Fish Talk," page 111.)

The main course: The ragout with garlic (bonus recipe) is wonderful, and very easy to serve, but you'd have to change your vegetables accordingly, as the recipe suggests. With the roast, you could omit the zucchini boats and just serve a plain parsnip purée in a dish, but no other way of cooking parsnips would suit roast duck so well. You might substitute a purée of turnips, celery root, or potatoes for the parsnips.

The vegetable course: This is probably the ideal way to cook broccoli. Any sauce but butter and lemon would be too rich on this menu, and a Polonaise garnish of browned crumbs and sieved egg would repeat the crumbs on the duck parts.

The dessert: You could fill your baked layers with puréed dried prunes. Or you could use very stiff, wine-flavored applesauce.

Leftovers

The appetizer: Since the crab is already seasoned, I wouldn't try it in a hot dish, but it would make fine stuffing for hard-boiled eggs or delicious sandwiches.

The main dish: Duck scraps are good in soup, or in a pilaff, or sauced in cocktail puffs or patty shells with drinks. Paul and I like to make a cannibal lunch for ourselves, picking the carcass (which I've roasted 15 to 20 minutes after its bloody carving). Then it goes into the stockpot.

The vegetable course: If you passed the lemon and butter sauce separately, any remaining unseasoned broccoli would be nice in a salad, soup, or timbale.

The dessert: Since I make a rectangular rather than round cake, I save a bit of butter cream, then beat up the butter cream to soften it, refrost the cut end of the cake as described earlier, and serve it again.

Postscript

The keynote of this dinner is flavor, and the duck dominates. If you think about this menu, you'll see that every dish on it was carefully chosen to contrast, in taste and color, with the duck—except the parsnips, which are such a good accompaniment to the bird that the two flavors almost combine in the mouth. Duck deserves this sort of "feature presentation." Having devised a way of dealing with its eccentricities, I serve it much oftener now, as the centerpiece of a luxurious dinner—as well as the grand main course for a plain family dinner. Duck has so much natural flavor and succulence that it is really one of my favorite meat treats.

Post-Postscript: A birthday bonus recipe

The following recipe is totally different in flavor from the roast duck preceding, is very little trouble to do, and is quite good reheated. For a larger birthday party, say 10 to 12 people, I think this would be tidier to serve. I'd buy 3 ducks and increase all the recipe proportions to match. With it I'd serve broccoli flowerettes and baked baby tomatoes, and perhaps a purée of some sort (like the parsnips recipe above, or a purée of turnips or rutabagas, or the potato-and-turnip purée in *Mastering I*), or instead of a purée, a mixture of steamed rice sautéed with little mushroom *duxelles,* or plain mashed potatoes. You would never know how much garlic this lovely duck dish contains if the cook didn't tell you. I wouldn't even call this a "garlic sauce"—it's just a satiny, full-flavored nap for the duck meat.

Ragout of Duck with Twenty Cloves of Garlic

For 4 servings

A 4- to 5-pound (2- to 2¼-kg) duckling

1 head garlic, unpeeled, separated into cloves and roughly chopped

2 medium-size ripe tomatoes

1 Tb tomato sauce (if needed for taste and color)

Herbs and spices: 4 whole allspice berries, ½ tsp fennel seeds, ½ tsp thyme, 1 imported bay leaf

½ cup (1 dL) dry white French vermouth

1 cup (¼ L) brown duck stock or beef bouillon

Salt and pepper

Parsley sprigs

Preliminaries

Split the duck down the back on both sides of backbone and reserve backbone for duck stock, along with wing ends, which you sever at the elbows. Cut the peel off the gizzard and add to stock ingredients along with the neck. Cut the duck into 4 pieces, giving more breast

meat to the wing portions than to the leg portions to even things out. Cut off and discard fatty skin pieces and any interior fat. If you wish to do so—and it makes the best sauce—prepare a duck stock by sautéing the backbone, wing, neck, and gizzard peel with ½ cup (1 dL) each chopped onions and carrots; when lightly browned, drain off fat, add water to cover, salt lightly, simmer for an hour, strain, and degrease.

Browning and simmering the duck

Prick the skin of the duck pieces all over at ½-inch (1½-cm) intervals and brown very slowly on all sides in a heavy chicken fryer or casserole, concentrating especially on the skin sides to render out as much fat as possible. Then drain out fat, add the unpeeled garlic cloves, tomatoes and optional tomato sauce, herbs, spices, vermouth, and stock to the pan, and season lightly with salt and pepper. Bring to the simmer, cover, and simmer slowly for about an hour, turning and basting occasionally, until duck leg and wing meat is just tender when pierced with a sharp-pronged fork. Remove from heat and let cool for 10 minutes or so, basting occasionally.

Remove duck pieces from pan, cut off the skin, and cut skin into strips. Sauté the strips slowly in a covered pan until they brown lightly, crisp, and render their fat; drain on paper towels and reserve. Meanwhile, thoroughly degrease the cooking liquid and strain it, pushing the garlic against the sieve to purée it into the liquid; boil down rapidly until sauce is lightly thickened. Return duck pieces to sauce and heat briefly, basting, to warm them. Carefully correct seasoning of sauce, and the duck is ready to serve.

🕐 May be done somewhat in advance, if you keep the duck pieces barely warm in their sauce, and reheat to the simmer just before serving.

Serving

Arrange duck on a platter and spoon the sauce over it. Decorate with parsley sprigs and sprinkle cracklings over the duck (you may wish to include the duck's liver, sautéed as the cracklings cook).

For unspecified numbers, at unpredictable hours, a festive but practical menu. One of its minor components is the Perfectly Peelable HB Egg, on which there is new news.

Holiday Lunch

Menu

*Chicken Melon, or Poulet de Charente à la
Melonaise*
Rosie's Great Potato Salad
Mayonnaise in the Food Processor
Skewered Vegetable Salad
Boston or Butter Lettuce Salad

Apple Turnover

Suggested wines:
*Beaujolais, Côtes du Rhône, Zinfandel, or a
very good rosé*

The thing is, we'd forgotten tomorrow was a holiday when we started asking people to lunch. Naturally it turned out they all were expecting houseguests, or children back from college with friends and about four sets of plans apiece. "See, Ma, if Johnny can get his clutch fixed he'll give us a ride back, but if he can't we'll have to take the two o'clock if you could just give us a lift over" kind of thing. Of course I said to the distracted ma's, "Well, come when you can, and bring whom you please," and thought no more about it until yesterday, when Paul pointed out that what we propose to do is feed lunch to anywhere from 6 to 20 guests, any time from noon until three.

It therefore follows, with cast-iron logic, that I am now doing funny things with chickens. Like most cooks, I tot up the limitations first, then look at the remaining possibilities. Six to 20 guests may mean huge leftovers; mustn't waste. We blew ourselves to veal on Monday, so we can't spend the moon today. We want to feel free tomorrow, so we cook now. We don't know all these friends-of-friends or their tastes: what does everybody like? And what is nobody allergic to? So far, a "made dish" (as opposed to a roast or sauté) of chicken looks a good answer. *But* it can't be hot, or it would dry out in three hours; and it can't be chilled, like an aspic, because the non-melting kind is rubbery. And we want the serving platter to stay attractive while under attack during a three-hour span.

However: the possibilities. Our friend Rosie the salad whiz is visiting us. We do have our faithful food processor, and Paul says he'll shell pistachio nuts and peel apples. Most of our friends' kids, home from cafeterialand, appreciate fancy food as never before.

So, our menu. Nothing could be more classical, or classier, than chicken boned to make *pâté* and roasted to a lovely color, and it feeds a lot of people. One could do it in the traditional *ballottine* shape, like a log; but you don't need calculus to see that the optimum form, with most volume to least surface, is a sphere. So a round, melon-shaped *pâté* it will be. I'll do three, keep one in reserve, put one, uncut, in the middle of my big round platter, then slice the third and make a wreath of perfect, even sections. No carving, no mess; and, if only half the people come, I'll have another party.

It won't take the three of us long to fix this festive meal, and right now the kitchen is a hive of industry. Rosie, with an artist's eye and a potter's deft hand, is preparing the makings of her three salads, each the last word of its kind: vegetable, lettuce, and potato. Perched on a high stool with a bowl in his lap, Paul is briskly popping pistachio shells for the tiny green kernels that look so pretty and crunch so nicely in a *pâté.* Every so often he darts a glance out the window: one of the resident squirrels, extra lithe or extra smart, knows a way into the bird feeder. Sometimes we scold him, but mostly, I admit, we bribe him; and he loves pistachios. "Here, you rogue," and Paul flips one out.

I've boned and defleshed the chickens' skins and sewn each into a loose pouch. In goes the stuffing, nuts and all, while Paul starts peeling apples for the dessert. The chickens did look odd, bereft of shape; but now, tied in their cheesecloth corsets, they're firming up. Then the string: each loop, like a natural rib, reinforces the melon form. *Fathoms of string... can do most anything...* I find myself humming to "I Get a Kick Out of You," and realize suddenly that Cole Porter, as usual, got the tune right; but it took a cook to discover the real words. I have a Thing about String...

"So you have," says Rosie. "Why not decorate your turnover to look like a fat, well-tied parcel?"

Preparations

Recommended Equipment:
Knives and knife sharpening

To make Chicken Melon (see recipe), a sharp boning knife, white string, a trussing or mattress needle, and cheesecloth are essential. Especially important is the knife: if it won't cut like a razor, the boning and defleshing of a chicken are a horrendous if not impossible undertaking. You want a stout sharp-pointed knife, and I like a slightly curved 6-inch (15-cm) blade for this type of work. You should also have the proper sharpening equipment, since no knife, however fine its quality, will keep an edge—it will only take an edge. Get yourself, therefore, a proper butcher's steel, the kind with a foot-long (30-cm) rod of finely ridged steel set into a handle. To sharpen the knife, sweep its blade from its handle end to its tip down the length of the steel, holding the blade at a 20-degree angle—the movement is as though the steel were a long pencil that you were sharpening. Give a half-dozen swipes down one side, then down the other, and that should hone the blade to perfect cut-ability. For very dull knives, however, you should also have a carborundum oil stone, fine on one side and a little rougher on the other; use the same general technique first on the rough side, then on the smooth, and finish up on your butcher's steel.

Disagreement note

Some practitioners sharpen their knives in the other direction on the theory that this realigns the molecules in the steel. In my system you are pushing the steel back from the cutting edge to make it sharp. Both systems seem to work and if I have a particularly dull knife I sharpen it both ways, hoping for results.

Marketing and Storage:
Staples to have on hand
(*Quantities for 6 people*)

Salt
Black and white peppercorns (see Remarks, page 82)
Nutmeg
Fragrant dried tarragon
Optional: powdered cinnamon
Mustard (the strong Dijon type; see Remarks, page 5)
Cider vinegar and wine vinegar
Crisp dill pickles (1 small)
Canned pimiento
Chicken broth (½ cup or 1 dL)
Fresh olive, peanut, and/or salad oil ▼
Ingredients for a *vinaigrette* dressing ▼
Unsalted butter (12 ounces or 340 g)
Heavy cream (1 cup or ¼ L ; and more if desired to accompany dessert)
Eggs (12)
All-purpose flour (unbleached preferred)
Plain bleached cake flour
Granulated sugar

Lemons (1)
Onions (1)
Celery (1 stalk)
"Boiling" potatoes (3 pounds or 1½ kg)
Shallots or scallions
Curly parsley, chives, and/or other fresh herbs
Recommended: flat-leaf parsley
Cognac

Specific ingredients for this menu
(Quantities for 6 people)

Roasting chicken or capon (6 to 7 pounds or
    2¾ to 3¼ kg) ▼
Boned and skinned chicken breast (1, or
    possibly 2) ▼
Boiled ham (¼ pound or 115 g)
Pistachio nuts (4 ounces or 115 g)
Boston or butter lettuce (2 heads)
Cooking apples (4 or 5) ▼
For the skewered salad, select among the
    following:
Artichokes
Avocados
Cherry tomatoes
Cucumbers
Mushrooms
Onions (small white)
Peppers (bell type: green, red, or both)
Potatoes (small new)
Topinambours (Jerusalem artichokes or
    sunchokes)
Turnips
Zucchini

▶ *Remarks:*
Staples
Olive, peanut, and salad oils: These may be
used singly or in combination; just be sure
your oil is fresh and of best quality.
Homemade vinaigrette dressing: See page 205
for recipe.
Ingredients for this menu
Chicken: If you don't think yours is plump
enough to supply 4 cups (1 L) ground meat
after boning, buy an additional skinless,
boneless chicken breast. *Cooking apples:* See
recipe for varieties, and check page 40 for
background information.

Chicken Melon

*Boned and stuffed chicken formed, in its
own skin, into a pâté the shape of a
melon.*

You can perform this operation on a small
frying chicken, but it is far more impressive,
and serves far more people, when you find
yourself a large roaster or capon. In fact, there
is no reason why you could not use the same
system on a turkey—but heaven knows how
long a 20-pound (10-kilo) bird would take in
the oven. Not me! (My fanciful French title,
Poulet de Charente à la Melonaise, was
suggested by the small sweet spring melons
from the Charente district of France, plus a
corruption of *à la Milanaise,* a classical appel-
lation from the old school designating a cheesy
Italianesque concoction from the region of
Milan. Of course, this chicken contains neither
melon nor cheese, but it might describe to a
knowing gastronome some conception of the
dish. We have to have a little fun with this sort
of thing, I think!)

For 14 to 16 servings

A 6- to 7-pound (2¾- to 3¼-kg) roasting chicken or capon

For the stuffing
To make about 5 cups (1¼ liters)

4 cups (1 L) ground chicken meat—salvaged from the boned chicken, plus 1 or more skinless and boneless chicken-breast halves if needed

1 whole egg plus 1 egg white

1½ tsp salt

9 grinds of the pepper mill

2 Tb minced shallots or scallions

A big speck nutmeg

½ tsp fragrant dried tarragon

2 to 3 Tb Cognac

1 cup (¼ L) chilled heavy cream

Garniture for the stuffing

1 chicken breast, cut into ¼-inch (¾-cm) dice

⅔ cup (1½ dL) boiled ham, diced as above

5 Tb shelled pistachio nuts

Salt and pepper

1 Tb finely minced shallots or scallions

1 Tb Cognac

Pinch fragrant dried tarragon

Other ingredients

Salt and pepper

Drops of Cognac

Several Tb melted butter

Equipment

A very sharp boning knife; a large ball of plain white string (butcher's corned-beef twine); a trussing needle—a mattress or sail-makers needle; a square of washed cheesecloth about 20 inches (50 cm) to a side

Boning the chicken

Your object here is to remove the carcass from the chicken leaving the skin intact except at the openings at the back vent and the neck and along the backbone. The meat of the chicken will go into your stuffing, and the skin will be the container for the *pâté* mixture. Proceed as follows.

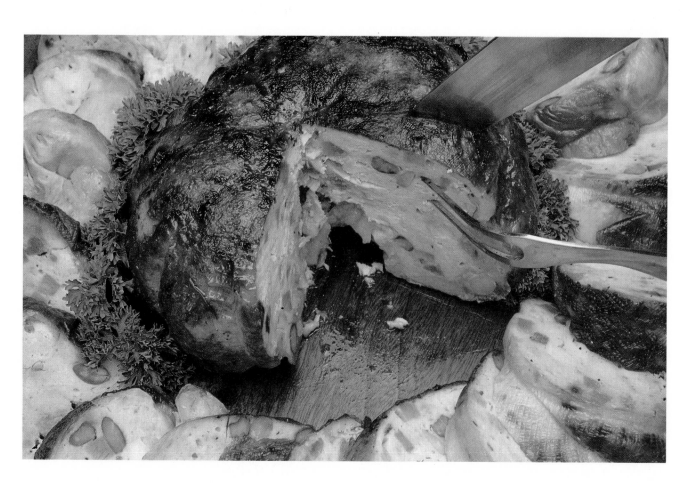

First, for easy removal of meat from skin after boning, slip your fingers between meat and skin at the neck opening, and loosen skin all around breast, thighs, and as far down the drumsticks as you can—being careful not to tear the skin.

Then turn the chicken on its side and make a slit down the backbone from neck end to tail end. One side at a time, scrape down backbone, severing ball joints of wings at shoulder and of thigh at small of back and continuing down rib cage and side of breastbone until you come near its edge, at top of breast. Stop! Skin is very thin over ridge of breastbone and easily pierced. Do the same on the other side. Finally lift carcass and scrape close under ridge of breastbone (not against skin) to free the carcass. To remove wing and leg bones easily, chop off wings above elbows and chop ball joints off ends of drumsticks. Then remove

wing, thigh, and drumstick bones from inside the chicken, poking their skin sleeves inside out onto flesh side of chicken. Carefully cut and pull as much of the meat as you can from the chicken skin without piercing it. Sprinkle inside of chicken skin with a little salt and drops of Cognac. Reserve bones and carcass for chicken stock. Dice one breast-meat half and reserve for stuffing garniture, using second breast half and rest of meat to grind up for stuffing.

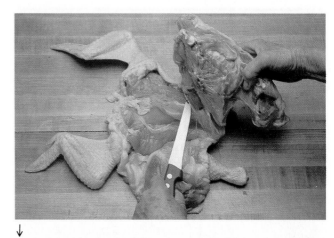

↓

↓

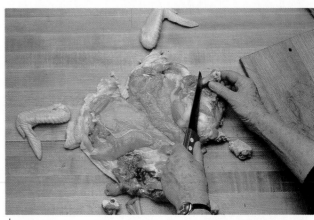

↓

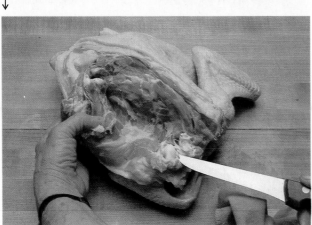

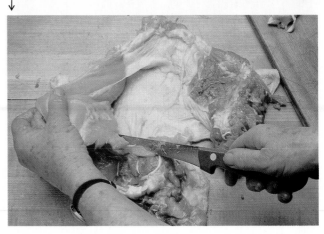

The stuffing

(If you do not have a food processor, grind up the meat, then beat in the rest of the ingredients.) Cut the meat into 1-inch (2½-cm) pieces and purée in the processor in 2 or 3 batches. Then return all to food processor, add the rest of the ingredients listed for the stuffing, and purée for a minute or so until finely ground. Sauté a spoonful in a small frying pan, taste, and add more seasoning if you think it necessary. Toss the garniture chicken, ham, pistachios, and seasonings in a bowl and let sit until you are ready to stuff the chicken, then fold into the stuffing.

Stuffing the chicken

Thread your trussing needle with a good 16 inches (40 cm) of string, and you are now ready to make a pouch, with drawstring, of the chicken skin. To do so, sew a loose basting stitch around the circumference of the chicken skin and draw up the two ends of the string slightly to make an open pouch. Fill the pouch with the stuffing (not too full), pull the string

taut, and tie. Dip the cheesecloth square into melted butter, spread out on your work surface, and place the chicken, tie side up, in the middle. Tie the 2 opposite corners of cheesecloth together over the chicken, then the other 2 ends, to enclose the chicken in a ball shape. Cut off extra cheesecloth. Then, always from the central tie, wind successive rounds of string around the ball to make the melon pattern. (Hold one end of string taut as a guideline and twist free end about it to secure each loop as you wind it around the chicken.) Chicken is now ready to roast.

🕐   May be prepared a day in advance and refrigerated; may be frozen, but thaw before roasting.

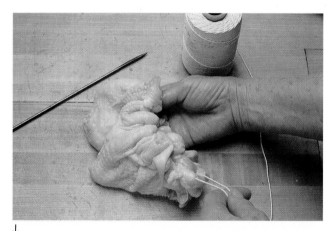

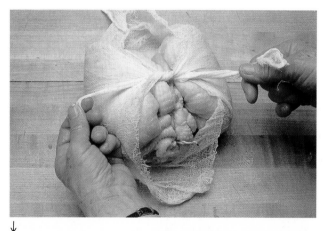

Roasting and serving

(So that chicken will brown nicely on the top as well as the bottom, but so that it will not lose its juices, start it tie side down and turn after 25 to 30 minutes, before any juices have managed to escape from that side.) Preheat oven to 350°F/180°C. Set chicken tie side down on a lightly buttered pie dish and roast in middle level of oven for 25 to 30 minutes to brown top nicely, then turn tie side up for the rest of the roasting. Baste occasionally with accumulated fat in dish. Chicken is done at a thermometer reading of 170°F/77°C. (Total cooking time is 1½ to 2 hours.) Remove and let rest 20 minutes, then carefully ease off the cheesecloth and string without tearing chicken skin.

Serve hot with pan juices and *béarnaise* sauce. Or let cool to room temperature, cover, and chill; serve as you would a *pâté,* as part of a cold lunch or as the first course for a dinner. To carve, cut into wedges, starting from the center, as though cutting a thick pie.

Rosie's Great Potato Salad

After Rosie had tried a number of off-beat combinations and additions, hoping that the best possible salad might be something unusual, she concluded that the thing to aim at was that old-fashioned taste where the potatoes dominate and where there is just enough onion, the right amount of celery for a bit of crunch, enough eggs for their subtle effect, plus a light but sufficient binding and melding with the best mayonnaise. Here is her recipe.

For about 2 quarts (2 liters),
serving 6 to 8

3 pounds (1½ kg) "boiling" potatoes, the type that will keep their shape when cooked and sliced—such as round red potatoes or new potatoes
½ cup (1 dL) chicken broth mixed with 2 to 3 Tb cider vinegar
Salt and pepper
1 medium-size to large mild onion, finely diced
1 medium-size stalk celery, finely diced
1 small crisp dill pickle, finely diced
3 hard-boiled eggs, diced
2 Tb minced fresh parsley, preferably the flat-leaf variety
1 canned pimiento, diced
½ to ¾ cup (1–1¾ dL) homemade mayonnaise (see next recipe)
For decoration
Strips of canned pimiento
Parsley and/or chives
Sliced or quartered hard-boiled eggs (see recipe at end of chapter)

Scrub the potatoes and boil in their jackets, in lightly salted water, just until tender (halve a potato and eat a slice to be sure). Then drain off water, cover pan, and let sit for 5 minutes to let them firm up and to make for easier slicing. Peel while still warm and cut into slices about ³/₁₆ inch (¾ cm) thick. Toss the still-warm potatoes gently in a large mixing bowl with the broth and with salt and pepper to taste. Salt the diced onion lightly and add to the potatoes along with the celery, pickle, eggs, parsley, and pimiento. Toss and fold gently to blend flavors. Taste carefully and correct seasoning. When cool, fold in two-thirds of the mayonnaise, saving the rest for decoration.

🕐 May be made a day in advance; cover and refrigerate.

An hour or so before you are ready to serve, taste again for seasoning and turn the salad into a nice bowl; mask the top with the remaining mayonnaise and decorate with pimiento, herbs, and eggs.

Remarks:

Rosie suggests, when you are making larger quantities, that you toss the equivalent of the above ingredients in a mixing bowl (or several bowls), turn that into a larger bowl, and continue with the same amount, adding each batch as you do it to the larger bowl. This way you can easily manage the potatoes and the perfection of the seasoning without breaking the slices.

Mayonnaise in the Food Processor

Certainly the easiest way to make mayonnaise is in the food processor, where in 2 or 3 minutes you have 2 or 3 cups (or ½ liter). Regardless of method, the best mayonnaise is made from the freshest and best ingredients, since nothing can disguise a cheap-tasting oil, a harsh vinegar, or a fake lemon.

For about 2 ¼ cups (½ liter)

1 whole egg
2 egg yolks
1 tsp strong prepared mustard (Dijon type)
½ tsp or more salt
1 Tb or more fresh lemon juice or wine vinegar
2 cups best-quality light olive oil, salad oil, or fresh peanut oil—all one kind or a combination
White pepper

Using the metal blade (I never use the plastic one for anything), process the egg, yolks, mustard, and ½ teaspoon salt for 30 seconds. Then add 1 tablespoon lemon juice or vinegar and process half a minute more. Finally, in a very thin stream, pour in the oil. When all has gone in, remove cover, check consistency, and taste for seasoning: you will probably want to beat in a little more lemon juice or vinegar, and salt and white pepper, but you can also beat in driblets of cold water for a milder and lighter taste and texture.

Remarks:

The purpose of the whole egg here is to dilute the thickening capacity of the yolks, since if you have all yolks the mayonnaise stiffens so much in the machine you cannot add the full amount of oil. However, you can thin the sauce with droplets of water rather than egg white. The proportions I use are 3 yolks for every 2 cups or ½ liter of oil, and, in the processor, 1 egg white.

Turned, or thinned-out, mayonnaise: I am not always successful with the processor when I have a badly thinned-out mayonnaise. (This sometimes happens when the mayonnaise has been kept in too cold a refrigerator: the emulsion property of the egg yolks has broken down, and they release the oil from suspension.) To restore the mayonnaise it has to be reconstituted bit by bit, and because the processor can't manage a small enough quantity initially to begin the homogenizing and reconstituting process, I've had more luck bringing the sauce back by hand or in an electric blender. I suggest that you start with a half tablespoon of Dijon-type prepared mustard and a tablespoon of thinned-out mayonnaise and beat vigorously in a bowl or blender until the mixture has thickened; then beat in the thinned-out sauce by driblets—it is the very slow addition of the sauce, particularly at first, that brings it back to its thick emulsified state.

Freezing homemade mayonnaise: It often happens to me that I've a nice jar of homemade mayonnaise in my refrigerator and then we go off somewhere on a vacation. I've found that I can freeze it, let it defrost in the refrigerator, and then reconstitute it just as though it were the thinned-out mayonnaise in the preceding paragraph.

Using frozen egg yolks for mayonnaise: Thaw the egg yolks at room temperature or overnight in the refrigerator. Then whip them in an electric blender or food processor (if you have enough for the food processor—4 or 5 at least), adding a tablespoon of prepared mustard and another of lemon juice or vinegar, and proceed as usual.

Skewered Salad

Vegetable salad en brochettes

This attractive way to serve salad vegetables makes it easy for guests, who pick up a skewered collection and bear it off on their plates. Use any combination of cooked and raw vegetables that appeals to you and will skewer successfully. Be sure, however, to use skewers with flat sides or double prongs, or two skewers per serving; the vegetables must hang in there, and the skewer must be solid enough to stay rigid from platter to plate. I find it best to prepare each vegetable separately and then marinate it in dressing long enough for it to pick up the desired taste, but not so long as to wilt it. Green vegetables and tomatoes, for instance, can wilt, while potatoes and topinambours will thrive in a dressing. Skewer the vegetables half an hour or so before your guests arrive, arrange in a platter, cover, and refrigerate. Just before serving, spoon on a little more dressing and sprinkle on finely minced fresh herbs, such as parsley and chives, or whatever other herbal delight your garden offers, like fresh chervil, tarragon, or basil. Here are some vegetable choices that have been successfully skewered in our house. (See index for various dressings.)

Artichokes: hearts or bottoms, cooked in a *blanc* (as described on page 203) and halved or quartered, depending on size. Toss in the dressing half an hour or longer before skewering.

Avocados: skewered at the last minute. However, avocado chunks will hold quite nicely if you dip them first for a moment in a solution of cold water and lemon juice, in the proportions of 1 tablespoon of lemon juice for 8 of water.

Cherry tomatoes: either impaled whole, as is, or halved and tossed in dressing just before skewering.

Cucumbers: peeled, halved lengthwise, seeded, and cut into chunks. I always marinate them first for 20 minutes or longer in a little salt, a pinch of sugar, and droplets of wine vinegar (¼ teaspoon salt, ⅛ teaspoon sugar, and ½ teaspoon vinegar per cucumber).

Mushrooms: use small caps or quartered large caps and drop for 1 minute in boiling water with lemon and salt to keep them fresh-looking. Toss in the dressing and leave for an hour, or more if you wish, before skewering.

Onions: the very small white ones. Drop into boiling water for ½ minute, then peel and simmer until just tender in lightly

salted water. Marinate for as long as you wish in the dressing.

Peppers: either green or red, halved, seeded, and cut into 1-inch (2½-cm) pieces. Drop them for 1 minute into boiling water just to soften slightly, then drain. Toss in dressing just before skewering.

Potatoes: small new ones. Boil in their skins in lightly salted water, just until tender. Peel or not, as you wish. Marinate while still warm in your dressing for as long as you like. (You wouldn't need potatoes when serving potato salad, of course, but they are good on skewers—be sure you have the waxy boiling kind or they will break up when pierced.)

Topinambours (Jerusalem artichokes or sunchokes): cook them in a *blanc* (as described on page 203) and toss while still warm in the dressing, letting them marinate for as long as you wish.

Turnips: white turnips or even the yellow rutabaga. Peel, cut into appropriate-size chunks, and boil in lightly salted water until just tender. Toss while still warm in the dressing, letting them marinate for as long as you wish.

Zucchini: scrub them, trim the two ends, but do not peel them. Boil whole in lightly salted water until barely tender. Cube them. Toss in dressing half an hour or so before serving.

Boston or Butter Lettuce Salad

Rosie very carefully separates each perfect leaf from the central stem, washes the leaves with care in a basin of water, drains them on a towel or in the dish drainer, then gently surrounds them with clean towels and a plastic bag, and refrigerates them. Half an hour or so before serving, she arranges them stem down and smallest leaves in the center in a big bowl, so that the salad looks like an enormous head of lettuce sitting there. She covers the bowl with plastic wrap and refrigerates it, and just before serving she dribbles a *vinaigrette* dressing, such as the one on page 205, all around and over the leaves. No tossing is necessary, and serving is easy since one picks up the leaves without disturbing the design—at least until near the end.

Apple Turnover

I am particularly fond of the free-form turnover, since one can make it any size and shape, from mini to gargantua. Round is pretty, but either square or rectangular is more practical because it uses less dough and the leftovers are evenly shaped and therefore easily turned into decorations.

For 1 large turnover about 9 by 9 inches (23 x 23 cm), serving 6 to 8

Sweet pie dough
Pâte brisée fine, sucrée

1½ cups (215 g) all-purpose flour, unbleached preferred

½ cup (70 g) plain bleached cake flour

1½ sticks (6 ounces or 170 g) chilled unsalted butter and 2 Tb shortening

2 Tb sugar

¼ tsp salt

½ cup (1 dL), more or less, iced water

Other ingredients for the turnover

4 or 5 apples that will keep their shape in cooking, such as Golden Delicious, Rome Beauty, Newton, Monroe, Northern Spy

3 Tb or more sugar

½ tsp, more or less, powdered cinnamon (optional)

The grated rind and the juice of ½ lemon (optional)

1 Tb or more melted butter

Egg glaze (1 egg beaten in a cup with 1 tsp water)

Equipment

A food processor is dandy for making the dough; a rolling pin; a buttered pastry sheet; a pastry brush for glazing the tart

The dough

Of course you can make the dough by hand or in an electric mixer, but the food processor is sensationally fast and foolproof using these proportions. Proceed as follows: with metal blade in place, measure the flours into the bowl of the machine, cut the butter rapidly into pieces the size of your little-finger joint, and drop into the flour, along with the sugar, shortening, and salt. Using the on-off flick technique lasting ½ second, process 7 to 8 flicks, just to start breaking up the butter. Then, with water poised over opening of machine, turn it on and pour in all but 1 tablespoon of the iced water. Process in spurts, on and off, just until dough begins to mass together but is still rough with some unformed bits. Turn it out onto your work surface and mass together rapidly with the heel of one hand into a somewhat rough cake. (Dough should be pliable—neither dry and hard nor, on the other hand, sticky. Pat in sprinkles more of all-purpose flour if sticky; cut into pieces and sprinkle on droplets more water if dry and hard, then re-form into a cake.) Wrap in plastic and refrigerate for at least an hour, to congeal the butter in the dough so that it will roll easily, and to allow the flour particles to absorb the water so that it will handle nicely and bake properly.

🕐   May be made 2 or 3 days in advance and refrigerated—but if you have used unbleached flour it will gradually turn grayish; it can still be baked at that point if only mildly discolored since it will whiten in the oven. Or freeze the dough, which is the best plan when you want to have ready dough available; defrost at room temperature or overnight in the refrigerator—dough should be cold and firm for easy rolling.

The apples

Quarter, core, and peel the apples, then cut into thinnish lengthwise slices. Toss in a mixing bowl with sugar and optional cinnamon and lemon rind and juice. Cover with plastic wrap and let macerate for 20 minutes or longer, so that apples will exude their excess juices.

Forming the turnover

(Always work rapidly from here on to prevent the dough from softening; if it becomes difficult to handle, refrigerate it at once for 20 minutes or so, then continue.) Roll the chilled dough into a rectangle 20 inches long and 10 inches wide (50 x 25 cm) and trim off the edges with a pastry wheel or a knife—refrigerate trimmings for decorations later. Lightly flour surface of dough, fold in half end to end, and center on the buttered pastry sheet. Place a piece of wax paper at edge of fold, and unfold top of dough onto paper. Paint a border of cold water around the 3 edges of the bottom piece and pile the apples onto it, leaving a ¾-inch (2-cm) border free at the 3 edges. Sprinkle on more sugar, and a tablespoon or so of melted butter. Flip top of dough over onto the apples, and press edges firmly together, to seal. Turn up the 3 edges all around, then press a design into them (to seal further) with the tines of a table fork and, if you wish, press a decorative edging all around those sides with the back of a knife.

🕐   If you have time, it is a good idea at this point to refrigerate the turnover (covered lightly with plastic wrap) for half an hour (or for several hours); it will bake more evenly when the dough has had time to relax, and you, in turn, will have time to turn your leftover bits of dough into a mock puff pastry which will rise into a splendid design.

Mock puff pastry decorations
(For massed scraps about the size of a half tennis ball)

Knead leftover raw pastry scraps briefly into a cake, roll into a rectangle, and spread 1 teaspoon of butter down two-thirds of its length. Fold into 3 as though folding a business letter; repeat with another roll-out, buttering, and fold-up. Wrap and refrigerate for 20 to 30 minutes, then roll and fold (but omit butter) 2 more times. For the simple decorations I used on this turnover, roll out again into a rectangle about 10 inches (25 cm) long, and cut into 5 strips about ¼ inch (¾ cm) wide. Refrigerate, covered, until ready to use.

Decorating and baking the turnover
Preheat oven to 400°F/200°C. Paint top of turnover lightly with cold water. To simulate wrapping ribbon for your turnover "parcel," crisscross 2 strips of dough, laying them from corner to corner; lay 1 crosswise from top to bottom, and a final one horizontally, as shown. Loop the final strip into a loose knot and place on top. Pierce 2 steam holes 1/16 inch (¼ cm) in diameter in top of dough with the point of a knife, going down through the dough to the apples. Paint top of dough and decorations with a coating of egg glaze, wait a moment, and paint on another coat. (Egg glaze goes on just the moment before baking.) Make crosshatchings in the glaze with the back of a knife or the tines of a table fork—to give it a more interesting texture when baked.

Set turnover in the middle level of preheated oven and bake for 20 minutes, then check to see if it is browning too much. It bakes 35 to 40 minutes in all, and does best at high heat so the pastry will crisp; if it seems to be cooking too fast, turn oven down a little and/or cover top of turnover loosely with foil. It is done when bottom has browned nicely and when juices begin to bubble out of steam holes. Remove from oven and slide it out onto a rack. Serve hot, warm, or cold. You may wish to accompany the turnover with vanilla ice cream, fresh cream, lightly whipped and sweetened cream, or custard sauce.

Remarks:
Other sizes, other fillings. You can, of course, make turnovers any size and shape you wish, and you can use all sorts of fillings as long as they are not too juicy. Always macerate fresh fruit first with sugar and lemon to force out their excess juices, and a very juicy fruit should first be cooked. Canned fruits or jams bake well in turnovers, as do all sorts of dried nut and fruit mixtures.

Pie and Quiche Dough:
Use the same proportions of butter, flour, and water for meat pies, turnovers, and quiches but omit the sugar and increase the salt to ¾ teaspoon in all.

⏱ *Timing*

Wait till you hear the doorbell ring before drizzling dressing on the lettuce salad. Your only other last-minute job is the pleasant one of arranging beautiful platters and setting them out. Part of the skewered salad and the dressing can be prepared that morning, but the skewering itself, and the brief marination of mushrooms, cherry tomatoes, zucchini, and peppers, is done half an hour before guests are due.

Otherwise, all your preparations can be made the day before; and the turnover dough can be frozen. While the Chicken Melon roasts, you can cook the hard-boiled eggs, make mayonnaise, and prepare some of the salad vegetables: artichokes, onions, potatoes, topinambours, and turnips.

If you've never boned a chicken before, it's wise to make your first attempt at a leisurely pace, giving yourself time to stop frequently and take a fix on your location in the sometimes bewildering mass of flesh and bone. Once you've done it and understood it, this job is a breeze ever after, and takes little more time than, for example, carving a cooked bird.

Menu Variations

The Chicken Melon: You can bone, stuff, tie, and roast almost any bird, or bake it in a pastry crust (see *Mastering II*), or poach it instead of roasting it and finish with an aspic glaze. Or simply pack the *pâté* stuffing into a terrine and bake it that way, or bake it skinless in a pastry case. But if you have a crust here, you will not want one for dessert!

The salads: If you omit the potato salad, a loaf or two of French bread will provide starch. For the lettuce salad, when perfect leaf lettuce is unavailable, substitute one of the mixed salads in this book. The make-up of the skewered vegetable salad will be determined by the season anyway.

The Apple Turnover: You could make little individual turnovers by the same recipe— but baking time will be only 20 to 30 minutes. Or use the same dough to make a tart or tartlets: bake the shell or shells, waterproof the inside with a melted jelly glaze, arrange the fruit (cooked or not, depending on type), and glaze again (see *Mastering I* for a basic method).

Leftovers

The Chicken Melon: You might plan to have a little extra of the stuffing mixture and save it for a special meal! Lightly formed into little cakes, dredged with flour, and sautéed, it is a charming luncheon or first-course dish, something between a *quenelle* or mousse and a chickenburger, and can be given extra savor by a creamy, full-flavored *béchamel* sauce (for which you'd save every drop of degreased roasting juice). You can freeze an uncooked *pâté* mixture or the raw chicken melon itself; but few *pâtés* take kindly to freezing after cooking. However, a cooked, finished "melon" will keep a week under refrigeration.

The salads: The potato salad will keep in the refrigerator for 3 or 4 days; but not if it has sat at room temperature for any length of time. That's because mayonnaise, like any egg mixture, is vulnerable to bacterial action. If you have marinated vegetables to spare, why not dice them, fold into a mayonnaise, and serve on lettuce next day as a *macédoine* salad?

The Apple Turnover: If you have extra dough, refrigerate it or freeze it (see recipe) and use again (see Menu Variations). Extra macerated fruit can always be cooked gently, then puréed and used as a sauce for custard or rice pudding. The cooked turnover itself will freeze and may be reheated in the oven.

HB Eggs

An unusual and successful way to boil and peel them

The perfect hard-boiled egg is one that is perfectly unblemished when peeled; its white is tender, its yolk is nicely centered and just set, and no dark line surrounds it. Excess heat toughens the egg, and excess heat also causes that dark line between yolk and white. To illustrate such a perfect estate, way back in the 1960s I did a whole television program on this earth-shaking subject, calling it "HB Eggs." No sooner was it aired than our French Chef office was flooded with suggestions, some of which were very useful indeed. As an example, one viewer suggested the use of an egg pricker, an instrument that pierces the shell at the large end to release the contents of its ever-present air pocket; if the air is allowed to remain it will expand when the egg heats, and that sometimes causes the shell to crack.

The most interesting idea came from the Georgia Egg Board, and the reason they got into the picture is that Georgia is a breeding ground not only for Presidents and peaches, but also for millions of eggs boiled and peeled by home cooks and especially by business enterprises. Because of the egg's commercial importance, scientists at the University of Georgia undertook a study involving over 800 of them and concluded that the best way of shrinking the egg body from the shell, to make for easy peeling, was to plunge the just-boiled eggs into iced water for one minute, meanwhile bringing the cooking water back to the boil, then to plunge the eggs into boiling water for ten seconds, and right after that to peel them. The iced water shrinks egg from shell, and the subsequent short boil expands shell from egg.

I tried out the Georgia method, found it good, and described it in my monthly column for *McCall's* magazine, thereby receiving even more new suggestions, including one from a testy 74-year-old asking if the U. of Georgia had nothing better to do! They should ask their grandmothers, said she who has been boiling eggs since she was a little girl: she boils them 12 to 15 minutes, plunges them into cold water, and has never had the slightest bit of trouble peeling them.

However, since an actual boil really does produce a tough egg, the Georgia people will just tolerate a simmer but prefer what I call "the 17-minute sit-in," where eggs are submerged in a pan of cold water, brought to the boil, then covered and removed from heat to remain for 17 minutes before their rapid cooling and peeling. I was therefore skeptical indeed when a letter came from the American Egg Board in Chicago outlining a series of experiments conducted by the Department of Poultry Science at the University of Wisconsin, using—of all things—the pressure cooker. How did they ever dream that up? I wonder. But it works very well indeed, and here is how to go about it.

HB eggs in the pressure cooker

1. Pour enough water into the pan of the cooker to cover the number of eggs you plan to cook—2 inches (5 cm) for 12 eggs is usually sufficient. Bring the water to the boil.

2. Meanwhile, wash the eggs in warm water with detergent to remove possible preserving spray from shells and to take the chill off the eggs. Rinse thoroughly. (Do not pierce them.)

3. Remove the pressure pan from heat, gently lower eggs into water, cover the pan, and bring rapidly to full (15 pounds) pressure. Immediately remove pan from heat and let sit under pressure for exactly five minutes.

4. At once release pressure, drain eggs, and cool them in cold water—or iced water.

5. Peel the eggs as soon as possible. I must admit that my first trial with this method gave me some qualms, but it worked—the eggs peeled beautifully. I kept at it, finding sometimes that the yolks were not entirely set at the very central point, but I never have had any trouble peeling. My last experiment was, I feel, pretty conclusive since I had managed to get some absolutely fresh eggs, laid by the young hens of a retired vicar on Cape Cod, each egg carefully dated on the large end. They were laid on a Sunday, boiled on a Monday,

and that's about as fresh a dozen eggs as I am ever likely to get. Here are the results:

1. Four eggs cooked by the coddle method (brought to the boil, removed from heat, covered, and let sit for 17 minutes). Two of these simply chilled in cold water—peeled with difficulty. Two of these chilled in iced water for 1 minute, plunged into boiling water for ten seconds, then chilled briefly and peeled—peeled with some difficulty but more easily than the first batch.

2. Four eggs done in the electric egg steamer/poacher. Peeled easily, but seemed a little tough. (And, by the way, mine poaches me a tough egg, too.)

3. Four eggs done in the pressure cooker. Peeled easily, and whites were tender.

Conclusion: The pressure cooker is great for HB eggs!

Peeling addendum

Two of my *McCall's* readers suggested a helpful peeling trick: after cracking the shells all over and peeling a circle of shell off the large end, slip an ordinary teaspoon between shell and egg and work it down the egg all around to the small end, manipulating the egg under a thin stream of cold water or in a bowl of water as you go.

The ugly dark line around the yolk on the left is due to excessive heat—the perfect HB egg is on the right.

*Don't try to fool a dieter's appetite. Excite it.
Beautiful, contrasting, full-flavored, this is
food, not fodder; and a little feels like a lot.*

Lo-Cal Banquet

Menu

Angosoda Cocktail

Appetizer of Shrimp, Green Beans, and Sliced Mushrooms

Chicken Bouillabaisse with Rouille, a Garlic and Pimiento Sauce

Steamed Rice

Caramel-crowned Steam-baked Apples

Suggested wines:
A hearty Pinot Blanc or
white Châteauneuf-du-Pape

When you're on a diet, do you feel you "just can't give a dinner party"? Or does it depress you to plan a menu for dieting guests? I sympathize, because "diet food," as such, is dismal food: no fun to plan, no fun to fix. Pure labor in vain. Fake food—I mean those patented substances chemically flavored and mechanically bulked out to kill the appetite and deceive the gut—is unnatural, almost immoral, a bane to good eating and good cooking. I'd rather look at it this way: nothing, except conscious virtue, can mitigate the groaning intervals between a dieter's meals; but why should the meals, too, be a penance? On the contrary. Light food for sharp appetites should stimulate, then satisfy, with calories allotted to bulk and balance and a few strategically disposed— like crack troops—where they'll be most telling: for flavoring, for unctuous or crackling texture, for mouth-filling opulence. The relish of it! Dieters are the best audience a cook ever has, for they savor and remember every morsel.

Of course Paul and I have to diet every now and then. It helps to have happy, busy lives and to get some exercise. Believing in the healthy body's wisdom, that what you want is what you need, we seek variety and practice moderation, eat less and enjoy it more than when we were young string beans. But sometimes we have absentminded or greedy spells, and the day comes when we start planning and get out the old notebook. All right: 1200 calories each per diem. Breakfast, 150; lunch, 200; dinner, 800. Fifty calories are left out, you'll notice; it's our error factor—a small one, since we are faithful about recording every stray bite or sample while cooking. Authorities vary in the calorie amounts they give, so we take the highest we can find for each item. Better, we think, to deprive than to deceive ourselves; but we soften the deprivation by allotting 100 of our dinner calories to a glass of good wine. It never tastes better!

At parties, we eat a bit of everything, but we are glad of the growing fashion for lighter, more savory menus. More thoughtful planning, more scrupulous preparation, are the modern cook's response to the challenge: make every calorie count. Don't hesitate to invite nondieters to the meal I'm about to describe, or even the lean and hungry young. You can double quantities, add bread or extras like cookies or cakes for dessert for them, or otherwise supplement or vary the menu (see Menu Variations); but it's certainly not necessary. This meal is so delicious, they'll take big helpings and return for seconds; but a moderate portion of each dish, though you'd hardly believe it, adds up to a sensible 678 calories. There's no trick to it, and no secret—only a well-considered application of the simplest principles of sound gastronomy: contrast, balance, beauty, savor, and style.

A subtle appetizer of shrimp, fresh green beans, and thinly sliced raw mushrooms arranged on watercress; a bouillabaisse of chicken, robust and aromatic, heaped on steamed rice and richly enhanced with a Provençal *rouille;* and a fresh, fragrant dessert of apples, steam-baked with wine, lemon, and stick cinnamon, then webbed with glistening caramel—this meal has everything. Everything plus. The ingredients aren't expensive; most of the work can be done in advance; and, since the dishes are all cooked on top of the stove, you won't waste fuel. And finally, the leftovers: delicious, elegant, and infinitely transformable. Sometimes I buy and cook the whole works in double quantities. Why not have two meals for the effort of one?

A Note on Alcohol and Calories:

As opposed to wine, which is a food as well as something to lift your spirits, liquor is full of empty but horribly real calories that don't nourish you. Only the most serious dieters need omit wine altogether, but instead of a cocktail I suggest you try

The Angosoda Cocktail:

In a large, handsome stemmed glass, place several cubes of ice, dash on a few drops of Angostura Bitters, add a slice of lime, and fill up with sparkling water. The fizz, the rosy color, and the dot of green are attractive, and it tastes like a real drink.

On Wine in Cooking:

Calorie counters can use a lot, and I do. The alcohol, which carries the calories, evaporates away in a moment of cooking. The flavor, now a bit softer and subtler, remains to give your dish complexity and depth of taste that make it more satisfying as well as more delicious.

Preparations

Marketing and Storage:
Staples to have on hand

Salt
Peppercorns
Granulated sugar
Pure vanilla extract
Hot pepper sauce
Whole fennel seeds
Dried thyme
Dried oregano (if you can't get fresh basil) ▼
Bay leaves
Saffron threads ▼
Stick cinnamon
Dried orange peel ▼
Angostura Bitters
Plain canned tomato sauce
Long-grain untreated white Carolina rice ▼
Onions (ordinary white or yellow)
Garlic
Fresh bread crumbs (in the freezer; see page 6)
Lemons (1)
Eggs (1)
Canned pimiento
Dry white wine or dry white French vermouth
Soda water

Specific ingredients for this menu

Shrimp (24 "large medium") ▼
Chicken (two fryers, or 16 pieces of cut-up chicken) ▼
Green beans (½ pound or 225 g)
Mushrooms (12)
Watercress
Parsley
Leeks (about 4)
Tomatoes (about 12)▼
Apples (6, Golden Delicious if possible) ▼

▶ *Remarks:*
Staples

Dried oregano: substituted for dried basil, because I don't think the latter has much flavor. *Fresh basil:* grow your own if you have a sunny spot; it's incomparable. *Saffron threads:* specified because powdered saffron may not be pure. The real saffron threads, which bear the pollen in a certain kind of crocus, are something of a luxury, but you use them sparingly. And you must, because too much saffron produces a medicinal taste which can't be corrected. *Dried orange peel:* to make your own, using a vegetable peeler take 2-inch-long (5-cm) strips of zest off an orange, let dry for a day or two on paper towels, then bottle—keeps indefinitely. *Long-grain untreated white Carolina rice* (see "Rice Talk," page 63): this is best

for steaming. The plump, nutty-flavored grains of Italian rice will too often degenerate into a gluey mass.

Ingredients for this menu

Shrimp: if you're lucky enough to live near the seacoast and to have a trustworthy market, you may be able to get them fresh and alive. Otherwise, your safest bet is to buy them raw in the shell, frozen solid in a block. Keep them that way until ready to cook; then thaw rapidly in lots of cold water and peel as soon as you can detach them from the frozen mass. Devein them: if you see a black line, it's the intestinal vein; you can usually pull it out from the large end without slitting the shrimp. (See "Fish Talk," page 111, for illustration.) *Chicken:* fryers are perfect for the fricassee method, which you employ in making this bouilla-baisse. It is easy to cut up your own.

But if you decide on ready-cut chicken, note that thighs are the best buy: they are cheaper than drumsticks and have more flesh and less bone. Before storing or cooking chicken, be on the safe side: rinse with warm water, inside and out, and dry before refrigerating. If you're going to keep it more than a day or two, refrigerate it in a plastic bag set in a bowl of ice cubes which you renew as needed. *Vegetables:* refrigerate unwashed beans in a plastic bag until ready to prepare; mushrooms and leeks ditto. Parsley and cress can be freshened by soaking several hours in cold water. Then drain; shake dry and roll up loosely in paper towels and refrigerate in plastic bags. Be sure your garlic is not dried out. Sniff your bottled herbs and spices for freshness—they should always be kept out of the light. *Tomatoes:* be sure you get in your tomatoes several days in advance to let them ripen properly. (See "Tomato Talk," page 159.) *Apples:* some of the most savory varieties turn into mush when steamed. Depending on where you live, try Golden Delicious, Rome Beauty, York Imperial, Greening, Newton, Monroe, or Northern Spy. The Golden Delicious, available in most regions, is always reliable, and its flavor will be enhanced by the spice and wine; its green-yellow skin is a nice pale topaz after cooking.

Appetizer of Shrimp, Green Beans, and Sliced Mushrooms

For 6 people
½ pound (225 g) green beans
12 large mushrooms
Fresh lemon juice
24 "large medium" shrimp
¾ cup (1¾ dL) dry white French vermouth or 1 cup (¼ L) dry white wine
1 Tb minced shallots or scallions
½ tsp salt
¼ tsp dried dill weed
Several grinds black pepper
Watercress or parsley
Garnish: lemon wedges; small pitcher olive oil

The beans

Several hours or the morning before serving, wash the fresh green beans. Snap off each end with your fingers, pulling down the bean's

seam to remove any lurking string. Plunge the beans into 3 to 4 quarts or liters of rapidly boiling salted water and boil uncovered 5 to 8 minutes (tasting frequently after 5 minutes) until beans are just cooked through. They are done when still a little crunchy and still bright green. (There has been a vogue for describing such beans as "crunchily underdone," but I do think such terms are used by those who have been brought up on frozen beans, which have no crunch, and little taste either, for that matter. Properly cooked beans are just cooked through; improperly cooked beans are either over- or underdone.) Once the beans are just cooked through, then, drain in a colander, run cold water into the kettle, and dump the beans back in to refresh them and stop the cooking—this also serves to retain their fresh texture and bright green color. Drain again, dry in a towel, and chill in a plastic bag.

The mushrooms

An hour before serving, trim the fresh large fine mushrooms, wash rapidly, and dry. Slice thinly and neatly, and toss in a little fresh lemon juice to prevent discoloration. Arrange on a dish, cover with plastic wrap, and chill.

The shrimp

Several hours or the morning before serving, simmer the raw peeled shrimp in the dry white French vermouth or dry white wine, minced shallots or scallions, salt, dried dill weed, and pepper. Toss and turn the shrimp in the liquid for 2 to 3 minutes, until shrimp curl and just become springy to the touch. Remove shrimp to a bowl, then rapidly boil down the cooking liquid to a syrupy consistency; pour it back over the shrimp, tossing several times. Chill.

To serve

An hour before serving, slice the shrimp in half horizontally—so they will look like more shrimp!—and arrange tastefully, either on individual plates or on a platter, with watercress or parsley, the beans, and the mushrooms. Cover with plastic wrap and chill until dinner time. Pass lemon wedges with the appetizer and a little pitcher of good olive oil for those who are permitted such luxury.

Chicken Bouillabaisse with Rouille

Fricassee of chicken with leeks, tomatoes, herbs, and wine, with a garlic and pimiento sauce on the side

For 6 people with ample leftovers

Two 3½-pound (1¼-kg) fryers, or 16 chicken pieces, such as thighs, drumsticks, breast halves

⅓ cup (¾ dL) olive oil

3 cups (¾ L) combination of thinly sliced white of leek and onions, or onions only

3 to 4 large cloves garlic

4 cups (1 L) fresh tomato pulp (about 2½ pounds or 1 kg tomatoes, peeled, seeded, juiced, sliced)

2 to 4 Tb plain tomato sauce, or as needed, for added flavor

½ tsp fennel seeds, 1 tsp thyme, large pinch saffron threads, two 2-inch (5-cm) strips dried orange peel, 2 imported bay leaves

Salt

2 cups (½ L) dry white French vermouth

Pepper

Fresh chopped parsley

Preliminary cooking of the chicken

If you are cutting up the chicken yourself, as I like to do, see illustrated directions in *J.C.'s Kitchen*, page 228. Dry the chicken pieces and place with the olive oil in a large skillet or casserole over moderate heat. Simmer about 10 minutes, turning the pieces several times in the hot oil until they stiffen slightly but do not brown. While the chicken is cooking, wash and slice the leeks, peel and slice the onion, and peel and chop the garlic.

When chicken has stiffened, remove it to a side dish, leaving oil in pan. Stir in the leeks, onions, and garlic; cook slowly 5 minutes or so, until fairly soft but not browned. Meanwhile, peel, seed, and juice the tomatoes (see "Tomato Talk," page 159); slice them roughly and fold into the leeks, onions and garlic along with the fennel, thyme, saffron, orange peel, and bay leaves. Taste, and if the tomatoes aren't flavorful enough, add a little tomato sauce as needed. Then salt the chicken on all sides. Arrange in the pan, basting with the vegetables. Cover and cook 5 minutes; turn, baste, cover, and cook 5 minutes more.

🕐   Recipe may be completed to this point several hours or even a day in advance. Let cool, then cover and refrigerate. Bring to the simmer again, covered, before proceeding.

Finishing the cooking

An hour before serving, pour in the wine, cover the pan, and simmer 15 to 20 minutes more, basting and turning the chicken several times just until the pieces are tender when pierced with a fork. Remove chicken to a side dish, tilt pan, and skim off all visible cooking fat; then rapidly boil down cooking liquid to thicken it. Taste very carefully for seasoning, adding salt and pepper to taste. Return chicken to pan, baste with the sauce, set cover askew, and keep warm (but well below the simmer) until serving time. When ready to bring to the table, arrange the chicken and sauce on a hot platter and decorate with parsley. Pass the special sauce (next recipe) separately.

Dieting Notes:

To cut down on calories, you can peel the skin off the chicken after it is cooked as described in the preceding paragraph and do a very thorough degreasing of the sauce before boiling it down—even pour it through a sieve, so that you can remove the fat more easily from the liquid. Then return contents of sieve and skimmed liquid to the cooking pan with the chicken.

Rouille

Garlic and pimiento sauce. To serve with a bouillabaisse, or with pasta, boiled potatoes or beans, boiled fish or chicken, and so forth

6 cloves garlic

1 tsp salt

12 large leaves fresh basil (or 1 tsp dried oregano)

⅓ cup (¾ dL) canned red pimiento

⅓ cup (¾ dL) lightly pressed down fresh white nonsweet bread crumbs

1 egg yolk

1 cup (¼ L) olive oil

Freshly ground pepper

Drops of hot pepper sauce

Equipment

A mortar and pestle are nice, but you can use the bottom of a ladle and a sturdy bowl, which, if not metal, should be set on a mat so it won't crack.

Purée the garlic cloves through a press into a mortar or bowl. Then pound the garlic with the salt into a smooth paste. Pound in the basil or oregano. When the mixture is smooth, add the pimiento and pound again; then add the crumbs, and finally pound in the egg yolk. Switch from pestle to wire whisk and, drop by drop at first, beat in the olive oil until mixture has thickened like mayonnaise, then beat in the oil a little faster to make a quite stiff sauce. Season highly with pepper and hot sauce.

🕐 May be made a day or two in advance. Refrigerate in a covered container; remove and let come to room temperature an hour before serving.

Remarks:

This redolent sauce, named for its rich rust color, is high in calories; but even a small dollop adds a voluptuous texture and hearty flavor to a serving of the bouillabaisse. I find it more satisfying to take one piece of chicken, rather than two, and enjoy it with the *rouille*.

Steamed Rice

For 4½ cups

1½ cups (3½ dL) plain raw white rice

2 tsp salt

In a large pot, bring 6 to 8 cups (1½ to 2 L) water to rolling boil, add rice and salt, and boil 7 to 8 minutes, or until *al dente*. Test by biting a grain. It should have a tiny hard core. Drain in a colander, and rinse under cold running water to remove all traces of starch—which would make the rice gummy.

🕐   Rice may be cooked ahead to this point even a day in advance, and its final cooking finished later.

About 15 minutes before serving, set colander of rice over a kettle of boiling water (bottom of colander should not rest in the water). Cover colander with a lid or a clean towel and steam just until rice is tender. Toss it once or twice to be sure it is steaming evenly. Do not overcook: ends of rice should remain rounded (splayed-out ends declare rice to be overdone).

Caramel-crowned Steam-baked Apples

1 cup (2 dL) white wine, or half wine or dry white vermouth and water, or water only

2 tsp pure vanilla extract

½ lemon

6 cooking apples (Golden Delicious or others that will keep their shape)

4 or more Tb sugar

Maraschino cherries

½ cup (1 dL) sugar

3 Tb water

Stick cinnamon

    Equipment

Get a steaming rack, now available almost anywhere. It's perfect for most fruits and vegetables, though not for rice. The kind I like doesn't work for pudding, either, since it is lifted out of the pot by a vertical center handle. It's made of stainless steel and consists of a round perforated bottom dish standing on folding legs an inch or so high. Hinged around the circumference of the disk is a series of perforated flaps that fold inward for storage and outward, against the edge of the saucepan, when the steamer is in use.

Into a saucepan large enough to hold steamer and apples comfortably with a cover, put the liquid, vanilla, cinnamon, and several strips of

lemon peel, adding water if necessary so you have ½ inch (1½ cm) liquid in the pan for the steaming operation. Wash and core the apples, and peel half the way down from blossom (small) end, dropping peel into saucepan with steaming-liquid—to give added flavor and body to it for later. Place steamer in pan and the apples, peeled ends up, upon it. Squeeze the juice of the half lemon over the apples, and sprinkle on as much sugar as you think appropriate for the apples you are using. Bring to the simmer, cover the pan closely, and regulate heat so that liquid is barely simmering—too intense a steam will cause the apples to disintegrate—and keep checking on their progress. They should be done in 15 to 20 minutes when you can pierce them easily with a small knife.

🕐 Apples may be cooked a day or more ahead and served cold.

Set the apples on a serving dish or on individual plates or bowls. Remove steamer from pan; boil down the cooking liquid rapidly until lightly syrupy, sweeten to taste, and strain over the apples. Decorate each with a maraschino cherry.

The caramel

Shortly before serving, prepare a caramel syrup. Bring ½ cup (1 dL) sugar and 3 table-spoons water to the boil in a small, heavy saucepan, then remove from heat and swirl pan until all sugar has dissolved and liquid is clear—an essential step in sugar-boiling operations, to prevent sugar from crystallizing. Then return to heat, bring again to the boil, cover, and boil rapidly for a minute or so until bubbles are large and thick, indicating that liquid has almost evaporated. Remove cover and boil, swirling pan gently by its handle but *never never* stirring, until syrup turns a nice, not-too-dark caramel brown. Immediately set bottom of pan in cold water and stir with a spoon for a few seconds until caramel cools slightly and begins to thicken. It should ooze off the spoon in lazy, thick strands. This is important, because if you put it on the apples too soon, when it's too hot or too thin, it'll just slide off onto the dish. Rapidly decorate the apples with strands of syrup dripped over them from tip of spoon, waving it over them in a circular spiral to make attractive patterns.

Remarks:

To clean the caramel pan and the spoon easily, simply fill pan with water and set to simmer for a few minutes to dissolve all traces of caramel.

⏱ *Timing*

This is an easy menu, and you can be leisurely getting most of it done ahead. If you want to do as much as possible in advance, start by deciding to serve the apples cold. Then look at the recipes for suggestions and for the point marked ⏱ . For this menu, you can start as much as two days ahead of time.

There's only one last-minute job: as your guests sit down to their appetizer, turn on the heat under the rice for its final steaming.

Half an hour before serving the main course, finish simmering the chicken.

An hour before your guests arrive, take the *rouille* from the refrigerator, but don't give it a final stir until it has reached room temperature. Slice limes for your Angosoda Cocktail, and place in a covered dish.

About two hours before the party, arrange the appetizer on a large platter or individual plates, cover with plastic wrap, and refrigerate. Chill white wine if you're serving it.

Several hours—but not the day—before, accomplish the second stage of the bouillabaisse, that of boiling down the sauce, tasting and correcting the seasoning. Wash, blanch, drain, and dry green beans. Clean and slice mushrooms, toss in lemon juice to keep white, and chill. Prepare and chill shrimp. Make a caramel sauce, let cool a bit, and decorate the apples.

Still on the day of your party, start cooking chicken.

A day or so before, you can steam the apples and start the rice.

The bouilla-"base," the concentrate of vegetables, herbs, and wine, though better flavored if made with the chicken in it, can in fact be made well in advance. It doesn't hurt to cook the vegetables the day before you make the "base." Keep them covered and chilled.

The *rouille* actually tastes better if you make it a day before serving and let its flavors marry in the refrigerator.

Menu Variations

The *appetizer* could be varied by substituting asparagus tips for the beans, or fine small spinach leaves for the cress, or almost any shellfish for the shrimp. Raw bay or sea scallops may be marinated in fresh lime juice and seasonings, which delicately cook them—see the *seviche* on page 183. Green beans and mushrooms on cress, without shellfish, are delicious, perhaps with cherry tomatoes and a scattering of finely chopped chives or scallions.

The *bouillabaisse,* as you know, is most familiar as a hearty soup containing a mixture of fish. In this more condensed form, which of course you eat with a fork, you could exchange chicken for a firm-fleshed fish, for scallops, or for salt cod (but allow time to freshen it). It makes a grand main dish for vegetarians if you use chunks of presalted, sautéed eggplant instead of chicken; or else one of the bulkier pastas, like *rotini* and *rigatoni.* Only steamed rice is a proper complement to the bouillabaisse, so I have no alternative to suggest.

The *dessert* can be made with pears instead of apples. It can be lightened by omitting the caramel, or enriched by passing, separately, a bowl of custard sauce or lightly whipped cream.

Rigatoni (left) and rotini.

Leftovers

Rice: if you have extra, make a cold rice salad, or serve it in a soup, or use it to thicken a sauce *soubise.* As for the *bouillabaisse,* you can reheat it, and it will still be delicious. But I love it cold as a luncheon dish. If I plan on that, I usually pull the skin off all the chicken pieces (don't like cold chicken skin!), then arrange the chicken in a nice serving dish and spoon the sauce over. After chilling, the sauce jells; before serving, I remove any surface fat and sprinkle a bit of fresh chopped parsley over all. Delicious just as it is, or arranged on a bed of lettuce and decorated with black olives. The rice could even accompany the chicken again as a cold salad.

Here's another idea I developed after the television show, when I had quantities of chicken in bouillabaisse to play with. After reheating batches of it twice, serving it cold once, and still having more, I decided to purée the sauce in a food processor. It turned into a kind of horrid pudding, so I simmered it with a cup of chicken broth and tried to strain it, with no success. Then I thought of my trusty potato ricer. I lined it with a double thickness of washed cheesecloth, filled it with a ladleful of my rosy pudding, gave it a squeeze, and out came a savory, translucent, satiny rose liquid which I spooned over my chilled and peeled chicken and chilled again. A happy discovery.

The rouille will keep for a week or more and is delicious as a spaghetti sauce, with boiled or broiled fish or chicken, with boiled or baked potatoes, or stirred into a minestrone-type soup.

The apples are excellent cold, and will keep several days refrigerated in a covered dish. Or you may slice the flesh and serve with a fruit sauce (frozen raspberries, thawed, puréed and strained, are good, though rather high in sugar). To make more juice, simmer a fresh apple with a cinnamon stick, a slice of lemon, and an ounce or so of vermouth, then strain.

Postscript

Here's your calorie count. I put it last so as not to deter nondieters from trying this excellent meal—for the bald numbers are so shockingly low you may not believe, before tasting, that I have been talking about real food all this time.

Salad of shrimp, green beans, and sliced mushrooms	66
Chicken bouillabaisse (2 sauced pieces)	250
Rouille (1 tablespoon)	75
Steamed rice (½ cup)	100
1 apple with syrup and caramel crown	187

The ingredients
(calories per 3½ oz or 100 g):

Raw shrimp		91
Cooked green beans		25
Raw mushrooms		28
Watercress		19
Fryer, light meat with skin, without	120,	101
dark meat with skin, without	132,	112
Olive oil		884
Leeks		52
Onions		38
Raw tomatoes		22
Tomato sauce		39
Bread crumbs		392
Egg yolk		348
Cooked rice		109
Raw apple		117
Sugar		385
Wine, dry, sweet	85,	137
Gin, rum, vodka, whiskey (80 proof)		231
Beer		42

The calorie counts are those given in an excellent handbook by Bernice K. Watt and Annabel L. Merrill, *Composition of Foods: Raw, Processed, Prepared* (Agriculture Handbook No. 8, U.S. Department of Agriculture, Washington, D.C., revised December 1963). For sale from the Superintendent of Documents, U.S. Government Printing Office, Washington, D.C. 20402. Price: $2.35, domestic postpaid, or $2.00, GPO Bookstore.

Beautiful ingredients prepared with loving care but little effort: this simple menu is an example of the wisdom and sane good taste of civilized cookery.

Informal Dinner

Menu

Asparagus Tips in Puff Pastry, Lemon Butter Sauce

Casserole Roast of Veal with Carrots and Celery Hearts
Wok Sauté of Grated Zucchini and Fresh Spinach

Floating Island

Suggested wines:
A light white wine with the first course, like a Chablis, Chardonnay, or dry Riesling; a red Bordeaux or Cabernet Sauvignon with the veal; a Champagne or sparkling white wine with the dessert

"Love and work," said Sigmund Freud when somebody asked him what he thought were the most important things in life. Not much work goes into cooking the ingredients for this simple, beautiful dinner. But in choosing them you acknowledge your guests' love of perfection and exercise your own.

You could spend half the money this menu demands and create a meal twice as impressive. There are several such menus in this book, and very good they are, too. But if your trusted butcher lets you know that he has been able to procure a veal roast of impeccable quality, wouldn't you plan to share it with friends who will appreciate its rarity? Wouldn't you go to market that morning for the freshest vegetables, imagining which ones would contribute to the flavor of the meat?

This serene, unpretentious perfection in dining is, indeed, the reward of love, expressed by care and respect for your guests and for the food you offer them. And if veal really is too expensive for you—or impossible to come by—try one of the less luxurious meats suggested in Menu Variations; the substitutes are perfectly suited to this kind of cooking method and will have a fine harmony of flavors.

A casserole is a very comfortable kind of informal cooking. You simply brown the meat, briefly blanch the vegetables, and put them all together with butter and seasonings. Then when you're ready to roast, you stick the casserole in the oven and let it cook quietly by itself, once in a while basting the meat and vegetables with their communal juices while you go about other things. The fresh, slightly crunchy spinach and zucchini, only lightly cooked at the last minute, will complete a pretty plateful and make a salad unnecessary.

What's a Chinese wok doing at this very traditional meal? Improving it, that's what, and reminding us not to be pedantic...but you could use a frying pan.

The main course doesn't include rice or potatoes, but it doesn't need to if you serve a loaf of French bread. And you may not even need that because of the appetizer. These crinkly little puff pastry "rafts" are all the rage these days in France; but puff pastry was never an everyday item there, any more than here, until recently. With a new fast method (page 98), puff pastry dishes are almost effortless, once you get the habit of making a batch of dough at intervals and cutting some of it into handy little rectangles to await your convenience in the freezer. Asparagus, formerly such a luxury, is available here from February through June at gradually decreasing prices. You need only three or four spears per person. Peel them, of course, or the dish is hardly worth presenting. And, to round out the delicate contrast of texture and flavor, whisk up a last-minute little sauce.

Be careful the butter doesn't overheat; be careful the asparagus doesn't overcook; be careful your oven thermostat is accurate. Cooking, I do strongly feel, expresses love more by fastidious everyday care than by festival bursts of effort. The effort, when you come to the dessert, can be left to your heavy-duty mixer. If you had to do this by hand, it would indeed be heavy duty.

Floating island, as the French do it, is a meringue soufflé about the size of Australia, floating on a sea of pale gold custard sauce. I like to serve it in archipelago form, cut into Greenland-size chunks. Don't be daunted at this point by the word "soufflé," in case you aren't yet confident with them: this meringue is so foolproof you can unmold it any time, or even put it in the freezer. The custard sauce, too, can be made well in advance, and it is very easy, provided you give it the few minutes' close attention (to prevent its curdling) that this lovely satiny confection deserves.

"Make every meal an occasion" sounds to me like "Live each day as though it were your last"—just plain overwrought. People do preach it, but does anyone practice? Not me! But to love your art as well as your audience does seem to make for pretty good living, day by pleasant day.

Preparations

Recommended Equipment:
A wok is not essential for the zucchini and spinach dish, just an attractive option. But I would not tackle 12 egg whites without a big electric mixer and an appropriate bowl (see recipe).

Marketing and Storage:
Staples to have on hand

Salt
Black and white peppercorns
Cream of tartar
Pure vanilla extract
Fragrant dried tarragon
Light olive oil or fresh peanut oil ▼
Granulated sugar
Optional but recommended: superfine
   granulated sugar

Butter (¾ pound or 350 g)
Milk (1 pint or 2 cups or ½ L)
Eggs (13 or more, depending on size)
Onions (2)
Lemons (1)
Puff pastry (from the freezer)
Shallots or scallions
Dry white French vermouth
Optional: dark Jamaica rum or
   bourbon whiskey

Specific ingredients for this menu

Boneless roast of veal (3 pounds or 1¼ to
   1½ kg); please read the recipe
   before marketing
Fresh pork fat (or beef fat) ▼
Fresh asparagus (18 to 24 spears)
Fresh celery hearts (3 to 6 whole)
Fresh carrots (6 to 8 or more)
Zucchini (6 medium-size)
Fresh spinach (1½ to 2 pounds or ¾ to 1 kg)
Optional: heavy cream (2 to 4 Tb)
Optional: sprinkles for meringue (see recipe)

► *Remarks:*

Staples

Fresh peanut oil: Peanut oil can get rancid, so sniff yours before using.

Ingredients for this menu

Fresh pork fat: "Barding" fat, to cover a lean roast, is not always sold; so whenever I see some I buy it and freeze it. And I trim scraps of extra fat off pork roasts before cooking, and save them. If the strips you buy are too thick, place between sheets of wax paper and pound with a rubber hammer, rolling pin, or bottle to flatten them out. You can substitute fat trimmed from a beef loin or rib roast; it does the work, although not as neatly since it shrinks and tends to break as it cooks.

Asparagus Tips in Puff Pastry, Lemon Butter Sauce

Petites Feuilletées aux Asperges, Sauce Beurre au Citron

For 6 people as a first course

18 to 24 fresh asparagus spears (depending on size)
2 to 3 Tb butter and 1 Tb minced shallots or scallions
Salt and pepper
6 puff pastry rectangles about 2½ by 5 by ¼ inches or 6½ by 13 by ¾ cm (the recipe for French puff pastry is on page 98)
Egg glaze (1 egg beaten with 1 tsp water)
Lemon butter sauce
2 Tb fresh lemon juice
3 Tb dry white French vermouth
Salt and white pepper
1 stick (115 g) chilled butter cut into 12 fingertip-size pieces

The asparagus

Trim ends off asparagus spears and peel from butt to near tip to remove tough outer skin. Choose a deep skillet or oval flameproof casserole large enough to hold asparagus flat; fill with water and bring to the rolling boil, adding 1½ teaspoons salt per quart or liter of water. Lay in the asparagus, cover until boil is reached, then uncover and boil slowly just until asparagus is cooked through—5 to 8 minutes or so, depending on quality (eat a piece off the butt end of one to make sure). Immediately remove the asparagus and arrange in one layer on a clean towel to cool. Cut the tip ends of the spears into 5-inch (13-cm) lengths; save the butt ends for a salad.

🕐 May be cooked in advance. When cold, wrap and refrigerate.

Just before serving (and when the following pastry is baked and ready), melt 2 to 3 tablespoons butter in a frying pan large enough to hold the tips in one layer, add the shallots or scallions and cook for a moment, then add the asparagus tips, shaking pan by handle to roll them over and over to coat with butter; season lightly with salt and pepper and roll again.

The puff pastry rectangles

Preheat oven to 450°F/230°C. About 15 minutes before serving, arrange the pastries (still frozen, if you wish) on a baking sheet and paint the tops (not the sides) with egg glaze; in a moment, paint with a second coat, then make decorative knife cuts and crosshatchings in the surface. Immediately bake in middle level of oven for 12 to 15 minutes, until pastries have puffed up and browned and the sides have crisped.

🕐 May be baked somewhat ahead and left in turned-off oven, door ajar—but the sooner you serve them the more tenderly flakily buttery they will be.

To serve

While they are still hot, split the pastries in half horizontally, arrange 3 or 4 hot and buttery asparagus spears on the bottom half, their tips peeking out one of the ends, spoon a bit of the following sauce over the asparagus, cover loosely with the top, and serve at once.

Lemon butter sauce: an informal *beurre blanc* (which takes only 3 to 4 minutes to make; if you are not familiar with it, I suggest you do so just before serving since it is tricky to keep). Boil the lemon juice, vermouth, and ¼ teaspoon salt slowly in a small saucepan until liquid has reduced to about 1 tablespoon. Then, a piece or two at a time, start beating in the chilled pieces of butter, adding another piece or two just as the previous pieces have almost melted—the object here is to force its milk solids to hold in creamy suspension as the butter warms and softens, so that the sauce remains ivory colored rather than looking like melted butter. Season to taste with salt and pepper.

🕐 Sauce can be held over the faint heat of a pilot light or anywhere it is warm enough to keep the butter from congealing, but not so warm as to turn the sauce into melted butter. However, if this happens you can often bring it back by beating over cold water until it begins to congeal and cream again.

Remarks:

Jacques Pépin, the able French chef and teacher based in Connecticut, has another version of the sauce where you bring 2 tablespoons each of lemon juice and water to the rolling boil and rapidly beat in 1 stick (115 g) of soft butter in pieces; bring the sauce to the rolling boil again for a few seconds, turn into a sauce boat, and serve at once. It produces the same effect of a warm creamy liaison of butter, rather than melted butter.

Puff pastry rectangle before and after baking.

Casserole Roast of Veal with Carrots and Celery Hearts

Rôti de Veau Poêlé à la Nivernaise

A fine roast of veal of top quality has no pronounced flavor of its own and no natural fat to keep it moist while it is cooking. I therefore like to tie my veal roast with strips of fat and to roast it slowly in a covered casserole with herbs and aromatic vegetables. As it cooks, the aroma of its savory companions seeps into the meat and the meat itself flavors the vegetables, both exuding a modicum of fragrant juices which combine to make a spontaneous sauce.

For 6 to 8 people

A 3-pound (1¼–1½ kg) boneless roast of veal, of the finest quality and palest pink (see notes on veal at end of recipe)

Strips of fresh pork fat (or beef fat) to tie around roast (about ⅛ inch or ½ cm thick and enough to cover half of the roast)

Light olive oil or fresh peanut oil, for browning meat

3 to 6 celery hearts

6 to 8 or more carrots

1 medium-size onion, sliced

Salt and pepper

1 tsp fragrant dried tarragon

2 Tb melted butter

Equipment

White butcher's string; a heavy covered casserole or roaster just large enough to hold meat and vegetables comfortably; a bulb baster; a meat thermometer

Preliminaries to roasting

Dry the veal in paper towels and tie the fat in place over it so you have strips on both top and bottom of veal. Film a frying pan or bottom of casserole with oil and brown the meat slowly over moderately high heat. Meanwhile cut the celery hearts into 5-inch (13-cm) lengths and reserve tops for another recipe. Trim celery roots, being careful not to detach ribs from them and trim any bruised spots off ribs. Cut into halves or thirds lengthwise and wash under cold water, spreading ribs carefully apart to force sand and dirt out from around root end. Set aside. Peel the carrots and cut into thickish bias slices about 2½ inches (6½ cm) long. Drop both celery and carrots into a large pan of boiling salted water and blanch (boil) for 1 minute; drain.

Arranging the casserole

If you have browned the meat in the casserole, remove it and discard browning fat. Strew the onion slices in the bottom of the casserole, season the veal with a good sprinkling of salt and pepper, and place in casserole, a fat-stripped side up. Sprinkle on half the tarragon, and arrange the celery hearts on either side of roast. Sprinkle hearts with salt and a pinch of tarragon, then strew the carrots on top, seasoning them also. Baste with the melted butter.

🕐 Casserole may be arranged several hours before roasting.

Roasting the meat

Roasting time: 1¼ to 1½ hours

Preheat oven to 350°F/180°C. About 2 hours before you wish to serve (reheat casserole on top of the stove if you have arranged it ahead), set casserole in lower-middle level of preheated oven. Roast for 20 minutes, then rapidly baste meat and vegetables with accumulated juices (a bulb baster is best for this) and turn thermostat down to 325°F/170°C. Baste every 20 minutes, and when an hour is up begin checking meat temperature. Meat is done at 165–170°F/75–77°C.

🕐   May be roasted somewhat ahead but should be kept warm; set cover slightly askew and keep in turned-off oven with door ajar, or over almost simmering water, or at a temperature of 120°F/50°C.

Serving

Slice the veal into thin, even pieces and arrange down the center of a hot platter, with the carrots bordering the meat and the celery hearts ringing them. Baste meat and vegetables with a little of the casserole juices. Spoon accumulated fat off remaining juices, correct seasoning, and strain into a hot sauce bowl.

Notes on Veal:

Veal is the meat of a young calf, and the best or Prime quality comes from an animal 10 to 12 weeks old that has been fed on milk or milk by-products. It is of the palest pink in color and has both texture and flavor—although the flavor of veal is never robust, like that of lamb or beef. Such veal is very expensive indeed but produces beautiful boneless cuts of solid meat from the leg (such as the top round) and from the loin and rib. Younger and less expensive veal, which should also be of the palest pink in color, is usually too small to furnish top or bottom round cuts, so one should take the whole leg and either roast it as is or have it boned and tied.

Wok Sauté of Grated Zucchini and Fresh Spinach

Sauté de Courgettes, Viroflay

In this attractive combination, the fresh spinach gives character to the zucchini, and the zucchini tenderizes the bite of the spinach, while a little onion lends its subtle depth. Although you can cook it all in a frying pan, the wok is especially successful here.

For 6 people

| 6 medium-size zucchini |
| Salt |
| 1½ to 2 pounds (¾–1 kg) fresh spinach |

2 to 3 Tb light olive oil or fresh peanut oil

3 to 4 Tb butter

1 medium-size onion, sliced

Pepper

Equipment

A food processor (optional) for grating the zucchini—or the coarse side of a hand grater; a wok (also optional), preferably with stainless-steel or nonstick interior so that spinach will not pick up a metallic taste

Trim off the ends and scrub the zucchini under cold water, but do not peel them. Grate either in a processor or through a hand grater and place in a sieve set over a bowl; toss with a teaspoon of salt and let drain while you trim the spinach.

Pull the stems off the spinach and pump leaves up and down in a basin of cold water, draining and repeating process if necessary to be sure spinach contains no sand or dirt. Drain in a colander.

🕐 May be prepared several hours in advance; refrigerate if you are not proceeding with recipe.

When you are ready to sauté, heat 1 tablespoon of oil and 1½ tablespoons butter in the wok (or frying pan). When butter has melted, add the spinach (if spinach is dry, add also 2 to 3 tablespoons water). Toss and turn for 5 minutes or so, until spinach is wilted and just cooked through, then remove it to a side dish. While spinach is cooking, by handfuls squeeze the juices out of the zucchini and set on a plate. When spinach is done and out of the wok, add more oil and butter and the sliced onion. Toss and cook for a minute or two, then add the zucchini, tossing and turning it for several minutes until just tender. Press any accumulated liquid out of spinach, and toss spinach with

zucchini, tossing and turning for a minute or two to blend and heat the two vegetables together. Taste carefully for seasoning, adding salt and pepper as needed, and you are ready to serve.

🕐 Most of the cooking may be done in advance, but in this case cook the spinach and set aside, then cook the zucchini until almost tender; finish the cooking just before serving, then add the spinach, tossing and turning for a moment or two.

Remarks:

You could add several tablespoons of heavy cream near the end of the cooking, or enrich the vegetables with more butter at the end of the cooking. Alternatively, you can cook with oil only, or use less of the amounts of both butter and oil specified in the recipe—that is the versatility of cooking in a well-designed wok.

Pulling the stems off spinach leaves.

Squeezing the juices out of grated raw zucchini.

Floating Island

Ile Flottante—A giant meringue soufflé floating on a custard sea

Here is a dramatic yet light and lovely cold dessert that is simplicity itself to make when you have a well-designed electric mixer that will keep the whole mass of your egg whites in motion at once, so that you get the lightness and volume egg whites should produce.

For 6 to 8 people

1⅔ cups (3¾ dL) egg whites (about 12)
½ tsp cream of tartar and 1/16 tsp salt
1½ cups (3½ dL) sugar (preferably the very finely granulated or instant kind)
2 tsp pure vanilla extract
3 cups (¾ L) Custard Sauce (see notes at end of recipe)
4 to 5 Tb decorative sprinkles for top of meringue, as suggested in Serving paragraph below (optional)
Equipment
(Besides the mixer): a 4- to 5-quart (4- to 4¾-L) straight-sided baking dish or casserole, interior heavily buttered and dusted with sugar; a round flat platter for unmolding

Cautionary remarks

Be sure that your egg-beating bowl and beater blades are absolutely clean and dry, since any oil or grease on them will prevent the egg whites from mounting. Also, because you are separating so many eggs, it is a good idea to break the whites, one at a time, into a small clean bowl and add each as you do it to the beating bowl; then if you break a yolk, it will ruin only one egg white, not the whole batch (since specks of egg yolk can prevent the whites from rising). Finally, chilled egg whites will not mount properly; stir them in the mixing bowl over hot water until the chill is off and they are about the temperature of your finger.

The meringue mixture

Preheat oven to 250°F/130°C. Start beating the egg whites at moderately slow speed until they are foamy. Beat in the cream of tartar and salt and gradually increase speed to fast. When the egg whites form soft peaks, sprinkle in the sugar (decreasing speed if necessary) by 4-spoonful dollops until all is added, then beat at high speed for several minutes until egg whites form stiff shining peaks. Beat in the vanilla. Scoop the meringue into the prepared baking dish, which should be almost filled (but do not worry if dish is only three-quarters full—it makes no difference).

Baking the meringue

Immediately set the dish in the lower-middle level of your preheated oven and bake 35 to 40 minutes, or until the meringue has souffléed (or risen) 2 to 3 inches (5 to 8 cm) and a skewer plunged through the side of the puff down to the bottom of the dish comes out clean. If necessary, bake 4 to 5 minutes or so more—a very little too much is better than too little. Remove from oven and set at room temperature for 30 minutes or until cool; it will sink down to somewhat less than its original volume, and will eventually shrink from sides of dish. When cool, cover and refrigerate.

🕐 May be baked several hours or even a day or two in advance; may even be frozen.

Serving

(You may unmold it onto a round platter, pour your custard sauce around, and serve as is, or use the following system.) Run a thin knife around edge of dish to detach meringue, then push the whole meringue gently with a rubber spatula all around to make sure bottom is not sticking. Turn a flat round dish, like a pizza pan, upside down over baking dish and reverse the two, giving a slap and a downward jerk to dislodge meringue onto round dish. Pour a good layer of custard sauce into a round platter, cut large wedges out of the meringue with a pie server, and arrange in the custard. Just before serving, sprinkle the meringue wedges, if you wish, with pulverized nut brittle, crumbled macaroons, toasted ground nuts, or something like the baked meringue-nut layers of a Los Gatos Gâteau Cake (page 11).

Custard Sauce:

You will need about 3 cups (¾ L), using the general outline of the recipe on page 73, with 6 egg yolks, ⅔ cup (1½ dL) sugar, 1½ cups (3½ dL) milk, 1½ tablespoons pure vanilla extract, plus an addition I like with this dessert—3 to 4 tablespoons dark Jamaica rum or bourbon whiskey—and 3 to 4 tablespoons unsalted butter beaten in at the end.

🕐 *Timing*

When we're "just family," or have invited guests to dine informally, we often eat in the kitchen so that last-minute jobs don't interrupt the conversation. With this menu, which does involve some final touches, we'd surely eat there. Before sitting down, one must turn the asparagus in butter; and, since the little sauce is tricky to keep warm, it's a good idea to make it at the last minute. And the spinach and zucchini dish is at its best if you finish its cooking, a matter of moments, just before eating it. The veal and vegetable platter takes only a minute to arrange, so do it on the spot.

The puff pastry is best when just baked, which takes no more than 15 minutes. I'd remove mine from the freezer and slip it into the preheated oven just about halfway through our apéritifs or cocktails.

Otherwise, this meal puts only slight demands on your time. Two hours before dinner, start cooking your casserole. You can arrange it in the morning; and that's when, ideally, you'd shop for the freshest asparagus, spinach, and zucchini. You can boil the asparagus then and precook the wok vegetables.

Both the custard sauce and the meringue, though the latter looks so ethereal, can be made and refrigerated a day or so ahead, and the puff pastry dough, any time at all.

Menu Variations

The appetizer: Inside a hot split piece of puff pastry, you can place a creamed shellfish mixture, sauced wild mushrooms or chicken livers, or—using the butter sauce—substitute peeled broccoli flowerets for the asparagus, or spears of peeled and seeded cucumber cooked in butter with chopped shallots and herbs. Instead of pastry, you can use hard-toasted bread (*croûtes*), and a nice way to make them crisp and rich is to butter sliced crustless bread on both sides and bake till golden in a moderate oven. Or hollow out two-finger-thick rectangles of unsliced white bread, butter tops, sides, and insides, and brown in the oven for *croustades.*

The casserole roast: A boned loin of pork roast works beautifully in this recipe, as does a boneless half turkey breast. Though the slices will be inelegant, you can keep that lovely veal flavor by using a cheaper cut, boned and rolled. Or substitute a boneless cut of beef; but use only meat of roasting quality, like *filet,* sirloin strip, or extra-fine rump.

For aromatic vegetables which will hold their shape and color, think of such roots as onions, turnips, rutabaga, celery root, or oyster plant to combine with the likes of fennel, leeks, or endive. These flavors are strong, so adjust your herbs accordingly.

The wok sauté: For something leafy and green combined with something soft and succulent, one could substitute very young beet or turnip greens, young dandelion leaves, kale, or stemmed chard for the spinach; and for the zucchini, summer or pattypan squash, pumpkin, cucumber, or slivers of white turnip, which are remarkably good with spinach.

The dessert: The American form of floating island has little islets of meringue poached in milk afloat on a custard sauce flavored with vanilla only. I wouldn't use any custard-and-meringue variant involving cake or pastry, since it would be a little heavy, considering the pastry appetizer; but that still leaves a vast range, from the elegant sabayons (of which Zabaione Batardo Veneziano on page 205 is a cousin on the Bavarian cream side). There are mousses and flans and unmolded custards, simple cup custards baked or boiled; and you could even bake a meringue case with a custard filling and decorate it with fruit. You can make a charming fruit soufflé by adding a thick purée of fruit like prunes or apricots to the meringue mixture, in the proportion of 1 cup (¼ L) purée to 5 egg whites; this, of course, you serve hot. And there are many delicious cold "soufflés."

Leftovers

The casserole: The leftover vegetables, and all the juice, will be good additions to a soup. Cold sliced veal is excellent with a piquant sauce; add any scraps to a creamed dish.

The wok sauté: One delicious by-product is the bright green juice extracted from the zucchini by the grater. If you add it to a soup, be careful with salt, as it contains a lot. Any leftover cooked zucchini and spinach would also be good in a soup; or use it as filling for omelets or quiche.

The dessert: You can refrigerate any leftovers and serve again the next day. Extra custard sauce can be frozen and is wonderful on all kinds of puddings, particularly Indian (see page 72). Or you can stir in any leftover sprinklings, add chopped nuts and chopped candied fruit, and freeze, for a sort of biscuit tortoni. Extra baked meringue is pleasant with a fruit sauce—raspberry, for instance.

Wok sauté of spinach with turnips.

Postscript

The French are given to classifying everything, usually on a scale of grandeur. In ascending degrees, cooking is divided into *la cuisine bonne femme* (goodwife), sometimes also termed *paysanne* or peasant; next step up, plain family cooking, or *la cuisine de famille;* then *la cuisine bourgeoise,* or fancy family cooking; and, finally, great, or high-class, cooking, *la grande* or *la haute cuisine.* The differences are not easy to define.

Perhaps some examples will help. If you have had dinner at midday and now make your supper on a hearty potato-and-leek soup taken with chunks of bread and a local wine and followed by a bowl of cherries, you are eating goodwife or peasant style—which I love to do. If your idea of a Sunday lunch is a starter of sliced tomatoes *vinaigrette,* then roast garlicky leg of lamb with green beans cooked in lard, then cheese, then perhaps an apple tart from the baker's, that's family cooking. Bourgeois cooking—a bit more sophisticated and expensive, but not showy and never eccentric—is exemplified by the menu in this chapter. Grand, or classy, cuisine really means the cooking of great chefs and grand restaurants: with its hierarchy of foundation stocks and sauces and flavored butters, its complexity, and, occasionally, its emphasis on display or on rare ingredients.

In her scholarly *Great Cooks and Their Recipes: From Taillevent to Escoffier* (New York: McGraw-Hill Book Company, 1977), Anne Willan cites Escoffier's turn-of-the-century recipe for Tournedos Chasseur as "a good example of the step-by-step preparation of *haute cuisine,* resulting here in a deceptively simple steak with wine sauce. The recipe requires four basic preparations—stock, demi-glace sauce, meat glaze…and tomato sauce—for the final sauce." *Demi-glace* and meat glaze, as she reminds us, are themselves cooked for hours and are composed of other, still more basic preparations. Nonetheless, the dish is "one of Escoffier's easier recipes for tournedos, with no elaborate garnish."

Cooking of such complexity will rarely be practical at home, though none of the four basic preparations is technically difficult; but other formerly *haute, grande,* and indeed formidable dishes are now perfectly manageable, thanks to the processor, the freezer, etc.

"In reality," wrote Escoffier, "practice dictates fixed and regular quantities, and from these one cannot diverge." He was writing about sauces, of which, in his *Guide Culinaire,* he described 136, not counting dessert sauces. The great codifier put enormous emphasis on correctness, hence predictability. In Escoffier's case, as in politics, his creativity and revolutionary work were succeeded by a long period of gradual rigidification; thirty years after his death in 1935, great chefs were following his dictates everywhere. If you ordered a dish in any great restaurant, you knew by its name precisely what you were getting. If, for instance, your *coulibiac* failed to contain *vesiga,* or a sturgeon's spinal marrow (a minor and almost unobtainable ingredient), then it wasn't *coulibiac* at all, and the chef had scandalously flouted the proprieties.

In the seventies, cooking was released from this straitjacket by the joyously anarchic *nouvelle cuisine,* whose most familiar exponent—to Americans—is Michel Guérard. Best known here for the ingenious diet recipes of *la cuisine minceur*—which is only one aspect of his work—Guérard is a classically trained chef of great sensitivity. His unprecedented combinations and piquant menus have inspired some bizarre travesties; but cooking has been liberated by his daring and original genius. Several of the recipes in this book are *nouvelles* in a restrained way, like the little composed salads which serve as appetizers, or the Choulibiac and the Chicken Melon, both of which, though classical in flavor, are untraditional assemblages.

A natural rightness rather than a pedantic correctness is my goal in cooking. And in composing a menu—or a dish—nobody's codes or classifications have any bearing whatever, so far as I'm concerned. One turns with relief from words to realities.

Essay

Four basic types of rice: (clockwise from upper left) Carolina long-grain, Italian Arborio, short-grain, and converted rice.

Rice Talk

Opening my Rice file is like entering the Tower of Babel. So many kinds of rice, so many recipes, so many cooking methods—and so many disagreements, including, as I experiment over the years, those between J.C. Past and J.C. Present. There is universal agreement, though, on the desired end result for general cooking: perfect rice is dry and fluffy, with every grain separate, and feels very slightly resistant to the tooth. If you encounter a tiny hard core, like a grain of sand, when you bite into a kernel, cook your rice a moment longer. If the kernels appear splayed out at each end, the rice has been cooked too long. Better luck next time.

Rice is so widely cultivated on this earth (we eat more of it even than wheat) that a great many types and cooking methods have evolved, adapted to different climates and cultures. But all rice cookery is based on the fact that rice can absorb at least twice its volume of liquid. It may do this before cooking, as in the Persian *chelo* (pronounced like ''hello'') with its lovely golden crust: the rice is first soaked for hours, then cooked in butter, without water, in a thick-walled pot. Or the rice may be boiled in a great quantity of liquid; it may be simmered in ''just its size'' of liquid until all is absorbed; or it may be braised—that is, warmed in oil or butter and then simmered; it may be steamed over (but not *in*) water; or it may be cooked in a combination of liquid and liquiferous substances, like fruits or vegetables.

As it is packaged in America nowadays, rice does not need the preliminary washing always called for in old recipes. This was intended to remove the coating of starch left on the grain after husking, since the starch, combined with moisture, turned into the equivalent of flour paste and made the grains stick gummily together. Brown rice doesn't need washing either: this is rice whose outer hull has been husked, but whose bran coating remains. It is cooked like white long-grain rice but takes twice as long to become tender. I like it, but its pronounced nutty flavor argues with the more delicate sauces. You may have to resort to a health-food store for brown rice, or to a gourmet-type shop for wild rice (which isn't real rice at all, but a grass).

For rice used as an accompaniment to a sauced dish, or rice which I want to serve cold in a salad, or in fact for 90 percent of the rice that we eat in our family, we buy the easily available white long-grain type grown in the Carolinas. You will find our favorite cooking method on page 44. For rice used as a main dish, as in the Italian risottos and the Eastern Mediterranean pilafs, I like a more absorbent rice and choose a shorter grain when I can get it, though the long-grain type will do. Long-grain is so much the easiest type to get here that most Italian cookbooks published in this country prescribe it. For Italian ways with rice, originally adapted to the delicious plump Arborio grain of the Po river valley, I refer you to Marcella Hazan's *The Classic Italian Cook Book* (New York: Alfred A. Knopf, 1976) or to Giuliano Bugialli, *The Art of Fine Italian Cooking* (New York: Quadrangle/The New York Times Book Company, 1977).

But for one especially pleasing main dish, the Spanish paella, you really can't use long-

Brown rice and wild rice.

grain rice. If you can't find the short-grained Spanish sort, or the fat Arborio, look for the patented packaged rice which is clearly labeled "parboiled enriched long-grain rice." The following recipe suggests an international medley of ingredients and equipment; though you don't have to use an electric wok, it does work nicely, and I'm all for being eclectic. Since a paella is essentially a peasanty family dish—although it is wonderful for a party—you can put into it anything you want as long as you have rice, saffron, garlic, and paprika as your base. The following features shrimp, chicken, sausages, and other easily found ingredients, but it could include rabbit, fish, lobsters, snails, mussels, and even squid.

An American Paella in a Chinese-Style Electric Wok

For 8 people

Adapted from *The French Chef Cookbook* and *From Julia Child's Kitchen.* Copyright ©1976 by Alfred A. Knopf, Inc. All rights reserved.

1 pound (450 g) fresh chorizos or Italian sausages, or fresh pork breakfast sausage
2 Tb olive oil
1 cup (¼ L) each sliced onions and green or red bell peppers
8 or more chicken thighs or drumsticks
½ cup (1 dL) dry white wine or dry white vermouth
3 cloves garlic, minced
4½ cups (1 L) chicken broth
½ tsp saffron threads
1 tsp paprika
¼ tsp ground coriander
1 bay leaf
2 cups (½ L) Italian Arborio rice, short-grain rice, or packaged parboiled rice
16 to 24 raw shrimp in the shell
3 medium-size ripe red firm tomatoes peeled, seeded, juiced, and roughly chopped
2 cups (½ L) fresh shelled green peas or diced fresh green beans blanched (boiled) for 5 minutes in a large pan of water, drained, and refreshed in cold water
1 cup (¼ L) chick peas (garbanzos), fresh cooked or canned
½ cup (1 dL) black olives
2 lemons, quartered
Parsley sprigs
Equipment
An electric wok or an electric frying pan, a chicken-fryer skillet, or even a paella pan

Preliminaries with sausages and chicken
Prick sausages in several places with a pin and place in the wok (or whatever you are using) with ¼ inch (¾ cm) water; cover and simmer slowly for 5 minutes and then drain, discarding liquid. Cut sausages into ½-inch (1½-cm) pieces and sauté in pan with the oil until lightly browned; stir in the onions and peppers. Cover and cook slowly until they are tender. Remove with a slotted spoon, leaving fat in pan. Dry chicken pieces with paper towels, heat fat in pan, and brown chicken on all sides. Drain fat out of pan; add the sausages, onions and peppers, and then the wine or vermouth, garlic, chicken broth, saffron, paprika, coriander, and bay leaf. Cover and simmer slowly 15 minutes—chicken will be half to two-thirds cooked and will finish later, with the rice.

🕐 May be cooked in advance; bring to the boil before proceeding.

Finishing the paella
About half an hour before serving, bring chicken-sausage mixture to the rapid boil. Sprinkle in the rice, mixing it down into the liquid with a spoon. Boil rapidly 5 or 6 minutes, uncovered—do not stir the rice. When it has swollen and begun to rise to the surface, rapidly push the shrimp tail-end down into the rice, strew on the tomatoes, peas or beans, chick peas, and olives. Again do not stir; simply push these ingredients down into the rice with a spoon. Carefully correct seasoning. Reduce heat and let paella simmer for another 8 or 10 minutes, or more, always uncovered, until rice is just tender—slightly *al dente*. (It is best not to cover pan, but if you feel rice is not cooking properly, cover for a few minutes, sprinkling on a few tablespoons or so of stock or water if rice seems dry; then uncover to finish the cooking).

At the end of the cooking, the rice will have absorbed the liquid. Serve the paella from its cooking pan, and decorate with the lemon quarters and parsley.

Paella for sharing
Like the dishes on pages 441-455, paella is a fine contribution to a friend's party. Although it may be fully cooked and reheated, it is infinitely better when freshly cooked. I would therefore suggest that you bring the paella to the party with the chicken-sausage mixture done, then add the rice, and finish with the rest of the cooking and the garnish there at the party—and with an electric wok, you can do all of this in public rather than being buried in the kitchen.

"Love in a cold climate" is the phrase for these hearty, comforting dishes from Down East. Great food when a gale is howling outside.

New England Potluck Supper

Menu

New England Fresh Fish Chowder

Cole Slaw

*Indian Pudding with
Vanilla Ice Cream or Custard Sauce*

*Suggested wines:
Cider, beer, or dry white wine*

You would think every northern region of the world would have a version of New England chowder: salt pork and potatoes and onions are everywhere, to combine with whatever fresh or salt fish—or even vegetables—might be handy. But it isn't so: chowder is as typical of New England as the Down East accent which pronounces it to rhyme with "howdah." Equally typical is Indian pudding, so called because it is based on "Indian Meal," the ground dried corn which the early settlers obtained from the Indians of the Bay Colony.

Born a Californian, I first tasted Indian pudding as an adult. It was made by—of all people—an Armenian chef in a restaurant in Lexington, Massachusetts. I loved that first Indian pudding. It was hearty and rich and elemental, deep in flavor, in texture almost like caramel, and I felt it was born out of a harsh climate and an economy of scarcity. I can't taste Indian pudding without thinking of it simmering all of an iron-hard January afternoon, slowly releasing its comfortable spicy scent into a cold dark little cabin. It must have hit the spot for frozen weary people who'd been hacking all day at the endless forest. Chowder, on the other hand, has a summery quality to me, perhaps because I associate it with July and August in Maine, with salty sun-baked granite around me and the sea crinkling below—and with the knowledge that a pail of wild berries is waiting in a cool purple cranny in the rocks. But it's a great dish any time, and a hearty one.

The name comes from *chaudière,* French for the big iron cauldron which was an all-purpose cooking vessel in early times. It could be hung from a fireplace crane, or, if of the footed type, be stood in the warm embers. We borrowed a beautiful old one from the ancient Wayside Inn at Sudbury, Massachusetts, for our television show on chowder, as well as showing forth some machines for grinding your own Indian pudding corn. Of course you can make chowder in any old pot, and of course you can buy cornmeal anywhere; it doesn't make much difference. But I wanted to make a point of the earthy, primal simplicity of these great American dishes. There are loads of recipes around for both fish chowder and Indian pudding, and many cooks insist their particular recipes are the only authentic versions; but the ones I'm giving here are the ones I like, so for me they're the best, the most genuine, indeed the only recipes worth cooking. I like my chowder with untraditional trimmings: croutons instead of pilot biscuits, and sour cream and parsley instead of a final blob of butter. My Indian pudding version is severely plain—unusual, though, in that it contains grated apple; but in fact it's a very old version.

It is adapted from the recipe of Lydia Maria Child (no relation to me), an early feminist of stern and rockbound character, who never, I suspect, threw away a scrap of paper or string and whose mission in life was to teach us all how to live sparely. Her book *The American Frugal Housewife* was first published in 1829, and went through many editions. (A facsimile of the twelfth, published in 1971, is available through the Office of Educational Services, Ohio State University Libraries, Columbus, Ohio 43210.) Mrs. Child's recipe for pudding involves long slow baking and two applications of milk, stirred in the first time, floated on top the second. The result is rich, redolent, and guaranteed to stick to your ribs. There are versions with eggs, or versions cooked quickly; but they don't have that primeval New England Puritan quality that I find so appealing in Lydia Maria Child.

In their journals and in letters home, the settlers gave touchingly fervent thanks for the variety of fish, game, and wild berries they found in New England; but they hadn't much choice of ingredients that kept well. Maybe, if put to it, some good wives occasionally had to use salt pork, onions, and molasses twice in the same meal. Mercifully, we don't, so my excellent recipe for authentic-tasting baked beans, adapted to modern methods, is not suggested for this menu, but placed at a discreet distance, as a bonus.

Lydia Maria Child.

Preparations

Marketing and Storage:
Staples to have on hand

Salt, regular and coarse or kosher (which is optional)
Peppercorns
Herbs and spices: sage or thyme; imported bay leaves; caraway or cumin seed; powdered ginger ▼

Wine vinegar
Mustard (the strong Dijon type; see Remarks, page 6)
Flour
Sugar
Butter
Milk
Eggs
Lemons
Celery, carrots, scallions, purple onion, green pepper
Fresh parsley

Specific ingredients for this menu

Fish: Several fish frames, if available, for fish stock, or bottled or canned clam juice (16 ounces or ½ L)
Fresh fish (2½ pounds or 1¼ kg), or see recipe for details ▼
Dark unsulphured molasses (½ cup or 1 dL)
Pure vanilla extract
Cornmeal (¼ cup or ½ dL), preferably stone ground ▼
Nonsweet white bread, for croutons
Milk (2 quarts or 2 L)
Sour cream (1 pint or ½ L) for chowder and cole slaw
Homemade mayonnaise (⅓ to ½ cup or 1 dL), optional for cole slaw
Fat-and-lean salt pork (6 ounces or 180 g) ▼
"Boiling" potatoes (4 pounds or 1¾ kg)
Onions (1½ pounds or 675 g or 6 medium-size)
Cabbage (1 small-medium)
Vanilla ice cream
Heavy cream
Tart apples (2 medium-size)

▶ *Remarks:*

Staples

Powdered ginger: you can season Indian pudding with a variety of spices, including cinnamon, nutmeg, allspice—alone or in combination—all of which the Puritans could get from the Caribbean Islands along with their molasses and their rum. But I like ginger alone, mostly for its taste but also for its eighteenth-century association with blue and white jars and the tall ships of the China trade.

Specific ingredients for this menu

Cornmeal: can be yellow or white, and I prefer it to be stone ground or home ground, although when it is cooked so long and with such strong flavors the regular supermarket kind is permissible. *Salt pork:* since this is an essential chowder ingredient it should be of top quality; I either use my own (page 250), or look and feel around in the supermarket display until I find a nice softish piece, meaning it is quite freshly salted. The blanching of the pork, in the recipe, not only removes excess salt but freshens the taste. *Fish:* certainly the beauty of a chowder resides in the quality of its fish, which must smell and taste as fresh as possible; see discussion in "Fish Talk," page 111. The clam-juice substitute for your own fresh fish stock is acceptable, although it cannot compare in beauty of taste to the real thing.

New England Fresh Fish Chowder

For 6 people, as a main course

Either—2 or more large meaty fish frames (head and bone structure of freshly filleted fish) from cod, hake, haddock, sea bass, or other lean fish (to provide fish meat and fish stock)

Or—2½ pounds (1¼ kg) fresh cod, hake, haddock, or other lean fish fillets, all one kind or a mixture, plus either 4 cups (1 L) fish stock, or 2 cups (½ L) bottled or canned clam juice and 2 cups (½ L) water

---

6 ounces (180 g) fat-and-lean salt pork (rind off), diced into ⅜-inch (1-cm) pieces and blanched (boiled 5 minutes in 2 quarts or liters water and drained)

About 4½ cups (1 L) sliced onions

---

3 Tb flour (optional, but I like a light liaison here)

About 5 cups (1¼ L) sliced "boiling" potatoes

½ tsp sage or thyme

2 imported bay leaves

¼ tsp peppercorns, roughly crushed

Salt (coarse or kosher preferred) and pepper

Fish stock, milk, or water as necessary

½ cup (1 dL), or more, sour cream

⅓ cup (¾ dL) roughly chopped parsley

2 cups (½ L) toasted croutons tossed in butter, salt, and pepper

Equipment

A pressure cooker, optional

Fish stock from fish frames

If you are using fish frames, remove gills (the feathery red tissue) from head and whack fish into pieces that will fit into a kettle; cover with cold water, salt lightly, and boil 3 to 4 minutes or until meat is just cooked on bones. Scrape meat from bones and reserve; return remains to kettle and boil 20 minutes, then strain, discarding bones; this liquid is your fish stock.

The chowder base

Sauté the blanched salt pork several minutes in a 3-quart (3-L) saucepan (or bottom of pressure cooker), to brown very lightly and render fat. Stir in onions and cook 8 to 10 minutes, stirring frequently, until tender and lightly browned (or pressure-cook 2 minutes and release pressure). Drain out fat. Stir in optional flour, adding a little rendered pork fat if too dry, and cook slowly, stirring, for 2 minutes; remove from heat. Bring fish stock or clam juice and water to the simmer, then vigorously beat 4 cups (1 L) into the onions and pork; add the potatoes, herbs, and peppercorns, but no salt until potatoes are tender (or pressure-cook 2 minutes, release pressure, then simmer slowly 5 minutes to bring out flavors). Correct seasoning; you wait until now to add salt because salt pork may still be a bit salty, and store-bought clam juice, if you used it, is bound to be.

🕐 May be completed in advance to this point; refrigerate, and cover when chilled. Will keep 2 days.

Finishing the chowder

Shortly before you are ready to serve, bring chowder base to the simmer. If you are using fresh fish, cut into 2-inch (5-cm) chunks and add to the chowder base along with additional stock, or milk, to cover ingredients; simmer about 5 minutes or until fish is just cooked— opaque rather than translucent and lightly springy. Do not overcook. If you are using cooked fish-frame meat, simply add it when chowder is at the simmer, along with more stock or milk, if you wish; it needs only warming through. Taste carefully and correct seasoning.

🕐 May be completed, chilled, then brought to a simmer again just before serving. Or you may keep the chowder warm for 20 minutes or so, loosely covered and set on an electric hot plate.

To serve

Ladle into wide soup plates, top with a dollop of sour cream, a sprinkling of parsley, and a handful of croutons.

Cole Slaw

For a low-calorie version, simply omit the mayonnaise and/or the sour cream (the liquid from the vegetables makes a natural dressing). Or, as a compromise, include the sour cream but pass a bowl of mayonnaise separately.

4 cups (1 L) thinly shredded cabbage

½ cup (1 dL) each diced green pepper, diced celery, grated carrot, minced scallions or purple onion

1 small apple, grated

3 Tb fresh minced parsley

2 Tb each wine vinegar and fresh lemon juice

1 Tb Dijon-type prepared mustard

1½ tsp each salt and sugar

2 pulverized imported bay leaves

½ tsp caraway or cumin seed

⅓ to ½ cup (¾ to 1 dL) homemade mayonnaise, or sour cream, or a mixture (optional)

Toss together the cabbage, vegetables, apple, and parsley. Combine the other ingredients to make dressing; toss with the cabbage mixture, taste carefully, correct seasoning, and toss again. Taste again; cover and refrigerate for several hours.

Indian Pudding

For about 6 cups, serving 6 to 8 people
Cooking time: 5 to 6 hours

¼ cup (½ dL) cornmeal, stone ground recommended

2 cups (½ L) cold milk, regular or low-fat

2 to 3 Tb butter or chopped fresh beef suet

1 tsp salt

2 tsp fragrant powdered ginger

Scant ½ cup (1 dL) excellent dark unsulphured molasses

1 tart apple, peeled, cored, and coarsely grated (scant 1 cup or ¼ L)

1 cup (¼ L) additional milk

To serve with the pudding: vanilla ice cream, or lightly whipped and sweetened cream, or Custard Sauce (see recipe), or heavy cream and sugar

Equipment

Corn grinder (see right)

Place the cornmeal in a heavy-bottomed 2-quart (2-L) saucepan and with a wire whip gradually beat in the milk. (Old recipes say to sprinkle cornmeal into boiling milk; do it this way if you prefer, but I find no need for it.) Set over moderately high heat and add the butter, salt, ginger, and molasses. Bring to the boil, stirring and beating with a wire whip to be sure all is smooth, then add grated apple. Boil 10 to 15 minutes, stirring frequently, until you have a thick, porridgelike mixture. Meanwhile, preheat oven to 350°F/180°C.

🕐 This preliminary cooking may be done ahead; set aside or refrigerate, and bring to the boil again before proceeding.

Turn the hot pudding mixture into a buttered 2-quart (2-L) baking dish and set uncovered in the middle level of the preheated oven for 20 minutes, or until bubbling. Stir up the pudding, blend in ½ cup (1 dL) additional milk, clean sides of dish with a rubber spatula, and turn oven down to 250°F/130°C. Bake 1½ to 2 hours longer.

Stir up again as before, and pour over surface of the pudding the remaining ½ cup (1 dL) milk, letting it float on top. Continue baking uncovered another 3 to 4 hours; the top will glaze over.

🕐 If you are not ready to serve by that time, cover the pudding and keep it warm, but not too hot or it will dry out.

Serve the pudding (which will look like a very thick caramel-brown sauce) warm, with the ice cream, whipped cream, the following sauce, or cream and sugar passed separately.

Custard Sauce (optional):
For 2 cups or ½ liter

Gradually beat 5 Tb sugar into 4 egg yolks and continue beating until mixture is pale yellow and forms the ribbon. By dribbles beat in 1 cup (¼ L) boiling milk. Set over moderately low heat and stir slowly with a wooden spoon, reaching all over bottom of pan and watching carefully as mixture slowly thickens: at first bubbles will appear on surface, and as they begin to disappear custard is about to thicken; a wisp of steam rising from the surface is another indication. Stir more rapidly, and as soon as custard lies in a creamy layer on the back of the spoon, it is done. Immediately remove from heat, stirring vigorously to cool. Beat in a tablespoon of unsalted butter and tablespoon of pure vanilla extract. Serve hot, warm, or cool.

🕐 May be made a day or two in advance and reheated carefully by stirring over hot water. May be frozen.

⏱ *Timing*

There is only one last-minute job in this menu: adding the fish to the chowder 5 minutes before you serve it. That's for A-Plus results. But there are alternatives, none of which gets less than A-Minus. You can keep chowder warm; you can reheat it; you can make the "base" 2 days in advance. Note—start early if you are using the salt fish suggested in the following variations: 2 or 3 days to soak a whole fish, depending on its size; 24 hours or more for packaged salt cod; a few hours for chopped or shredded salt cod.

Cole slaw must, of course, be made and chilled in advance: anywhere between a few hours to 2 days.

Indian pudding is prepared half a day before serving, since its cooking time is 5 or 6 hours. It can, of course, be made in advance and reheated over hot water; but then you will probably lose the glazed crust because you will need to stir it as it warms.

Menu Variations

The chowder: Using the traditional chowder base of salt pork, onions, and potatoes, you can vary the recipe in a number of ways. You might like to use frozen fish or soaked salt codfish instead of fresh fish, with a fish stock. Vegetarians could make a hearty main course of corn chowder, using butter for salt pork and fresh cream-style grated corn (see "Dinner for the Boss," page 127). I wouldn't use such delicate, expensive shellfish as lobster or crab; but

you could have scallops or mussels, and certainly clams. For mussels or steamer clams, because they can be terribly salty I always soak them an hour or more in several changes of cold water. Then steam them open with ½ inch (1½ cm) water in a covered kettle; the steaming liquid becomes the chowder stock, and the shellfish meat, now fully cooked, goes into the finished chowder. Since hard-shelled clams can be tough, I steam them open, chop the meat, and cook it until tender with the pork and onions. As to other chowder systems, some cooks thicken their chowders by running one-quarter of the cooked potatoes through the blender with a little stock and returning them to the pot before the fish goes in. Some garnish chowder with extra bits of fried salt pork, chips of onions fried till dry and brown, or chopped chives. It's all good, and, providing you stick to the traditional base, it's all chowder.

Cole slaw: This splendid stuff has almost as many variations as it does aficionados, as a tour through the basic cookbooks amply illustrates. There's another good cole slaw, based on my friend Avis DeVoto's version, in *J.C.'s Kitchen.*

Indian pudding: "Maybe it's sacrilege," says Anthony Athanas of the Boston waterfront restaurant Anthony's Pier Four, "but we use raisins." For a light, eggy Indian pudding, you couldn't do better than his: ½ cup (1 dL) light cream is brought to the simmer in a double boiler with 2½ cups (6 dL) whole milk; you then add 3½ tablespoons cornmeal and 4 tablespoons granulated sugar, whisking as you go, and let simmer while you beat together 3 "extra-large" eggs, 2½ tablespoons brown sugar, 4 tablespoons molasses, a good pinch each cinnamon and ginger, a pinch nutmeg, and a small pinch salt. Add the heated milk and cream, blend completely, and stir in 5 tablespoons raisins; then pour into a baking dish, set in a pan containing 1 inch (2½ cm) boiling water, and bake for 2 hours at 400°F/200°C.

Leftovers, or: Use it up, wear it out, make it do, or do without

Fish chowder: A completed chowder is good reheated and maybe frozen (once). In some thrifty New England households, part of the liquid is drained off and the solids are topped with buttered crumbs and baked until golden brown. The "base," with the stock added or not, is versatile indeed (see Menu Variations) and may be frozen. Extra fish stock, well strained and frozen, is a kitchen staple for sauces and soups. A very Yankee way of using extra cooked fish is to moisten it with cream or with a "cream" sauce (as they call it although it's usually creamless; the French would call it

Fish cakes and baked beans with English muffins.

béchamel if the liquid is milk, or *velouté* if it is stock) and bake it topped with crumbs or pastry; "fish pie" is a Sunday-night staple Down East, and very good if you add a bit of crab or lobster, dry Madeira, and a speck of nutmeg. Leftover salt cod and potatoes make deep-fried fish cakes (eaten with baked beans on Sunday morning), or, mixed with thick white sauce and crumbed, it becomes fish croquettes. If you made your chowder with smoked fish, it's not far to finnan haddie for a second round. If you used clams, and have a few too many, steam extra raw soft-shelled ones and eat with melted butter; or steam open the hard-shelled type, chop the meat and mix with crumbs, season highly, stuff in the shells, and bake. Or save the soft-shelled type, which, raw and un-opened, keep for 3 days in the refrigerator, and use them in the paella on page 64. (Steamer clams have rubbery black necks, which make them unappealing raw.) I really don't see much future (except reheating) for the remains of a corn chowder; but extra raw cream-style corn (see "Dinner for the Boss," page 133) is a treasure not to be wasted.

Cole slaw: A completed cole slaw will keep for several days, though you will want to drain its accumulated juices after a while. You wouldn't want to shred extra cabbage unless you planned to use it soon, because the cut edges wilt, though iced water helps. Cabbage wedges, however, are integral to a New England boiled dinner. Quickly boiled, shredded cabbage is nice with butter and a few caraway or poppy seeds. Braised, with chestnuts or apples, or with sausage and salt meat (as in a *choucroute garnie*), it is delicious. You can bake it with tomato sauce, or with cream or cheese or bits of ham or bacon; you can stuff a strudel with it; or, perhaps best of all, you can combine it with leeks and potatoes for a hearty peasant soup. Or you can save a few outside leaves and stuff them (see *Mastering I*).

Indian pudding: It can be eaten cold or it can be reheated—best done in a double boiler.

Postscript: Another way to bake beans

A few summers ago a friend of ours on the coast of Maine dug a deep hole in his back yard and lined it with big round rocks. Then, one early morning, he built a fire in it and let it smoulder for several hours, raked coals out from the center, and put in a big iron pot filled with pork and beans. He raked the coals back over the pot, piled seaweed on top, and covered that with a canvas tarpaulin which he anchored in place with more big round rocks. In a few hours we could smell those beans cooking, and at 7 o'clock in the evening he unloosed the tarp, raked the seaweed and coal ash from around the pot, and lifted it out, its hoop-shaped handle grasped by a hook-and-pulley contraption he had constructed over the bean hole. We sat out on the grass, in a circle, while he lifted the lid to release the aroma of those slow-cooked beans with the flavor of onions, molasses, and pork baked right into them. They were almost crusty although surrounded by thick juices, and we ate them with great helpings of cole slaw and homemade rye bread.

I thought to myself at the time that I loved the idea of the bean hole, and I loved the beans that came out of it, but why wouldn't an electric Crock-Pot give the same effect? While not quite the same, as I found from experiment, it does produce an easy-cooking meal of pork and beans, and to make things even more untraditional I precooked the beans in a pressure cooker. Anyway, as with a fish chowder, there is no set recipe for baked beans, from Fannie Farmer, Mrs. Rorer, Lydia Maria Child, and on up to the old Boston restaurant of Durgin Park. All the recipes have beans and pork, of course, but in differing quantities; some have molasses, or brown sugar, or even honey or maple syrup. Others include mustard, and vinegar, and tomato, while some have no onion at all, and so forth. I have therefore seasoned my beans to my own taste, which means more onions than usual, a little garlic, herbs, molasses, tomato, and mustard.

Manufacturing Notes:

The Crock-Pot, I find, is slow on cooking raw vegetables; thus I recommend precooking the onions separately with the pork before adding them to the beans. The beans themselves need precooking before they go in, and if they are not quite soft enough beforehand they may remain a little too crunchy even after several hours of crockery. As to the pork, I prefer to blanch it before cooking, to get rid of its salt; otherwise it can oversalt the beans. And whether or not to leave the pork whole or sliced is up to you; I like it cut into strips so that it distributes its considerable charms throughout the beans. Finally, if you don't have a Crock-Pot, just cook the beans in a casserole or bean pot in a 275°F/140°C oven, and if you've no pressure pan for the precooking, simmer the soaked beans in an open pot.

Baked Beans or Boston Baked Beans or Pork and Beans

For about 2 quarts baked beans, serving 6 people

1 pound (450 g) small white beans
6 cups (1½ L) water (more if needed)
8 ounces (225 g) fat-and-lean salt pork (rind included)
2 cups (½ L) diced onions (2 medium-size onions)
2 large cloves garlic, minced or puréed
¼ cup (½ dL) each: dark molasses, plain tomato sauce or purée, and Dijon-type prepared mustard
1 Tb minced fresh ginger (optional)
1 imported bay leaf
½ tsp dried thyme, or mixed herbs such as Italian or Provençal blend
1½ tsp salt

Quick soaking and precooking of the beans

Toss the beans in a sieve and pick over carefully to remove any tiny stones (I found 14 in a box of beans the other day!), rinse under cold water, and place in pressure pan (or saucepan) with the 6 cups (1½ L) water. Bring rapidly to the boil and boil uncovered exactly 2 minutes; remove from heat, cover pan, and let sit exactly 1 hour. Then cover with lid and pressure valve and bring rapidly to full pressure for exactly 1 minute; set aside for 10 minutes, then release pressure (or simmer an hour or so in partially covered saucepan until beans are almost tender when you eat several as a test).

The pork, onions, and other ingredients

Meanwhile cut the salt pork into slices (including rind) ⅜ inch (1 cm) thick and, if you wish, cut the slices into sticks; drop into 2 quarts (2L) cold water and simmer 10 minutes, then drain. Sauté for several minutes in a heavy-bottomed 10-inch (25-cm) frying pan until they start rendering some fat, then fold in the onions. Cover and cook over moderately low heat for 10 minutes or so, stirring up several times, until onions are quite tender but not browned. While onions are cooking, measure out the rest of the ingredients into the Crock-Pot (or a 3-quart or 3-L casserole).

Assembling and baking the beans

When the beans are done, drain them in a colander set over a bowl, and turn them into the Crock-Pot (or casserole), folding them together with the pork and onions and other ingredients. Pour in bean-cooking juices just to level of beans, adding additional water if you need more liquid. Cover Crock-Pot and set at "high" until contents are bubbling, usually 30 minutes, then cook at "low" for 6 to 8 hours, or until you feel the beans are done. (Or set casserole of beans in a 350°F/180°C oven for ½ hour or until bubbling, then turn oven down to 275°F/140°C and bake for 6 to 8 hours.) As they cook, the beans turn a brownish red—a more pronounced color in the oven than in the Crock-Pot—and the various flavors meld themselves into the beans while the juices thicken; their point of doneness is up to you.

🕐 May be baked several days in advance; let cool uncovered, then cover and chill. Reheat to bubbling either in Crock-Pot or in a casserole in a 325°F/170°C oven, and if they seem dry, add spoonfuls of water.

An exquisite and fanciful luncheon menu for your most sophisticated acquaintances, under the Sign of the Smiling Fish.

VIP Lunch

Menu

Apéritif: Kir au Champagne—Champagne with black currant or raspberry liqueur

Choulibiac—Fillets of sole and mushrooms baked in choux pastry

Watercress Salad with Endive and Cucumbers Melba Toast or Toasted Pita Bread Triangles

Sorbet aux Poires—Fresh pear sherbet

Suggested wines:
A fine white Burgundy or Pinot Chardonnay

This luncheon menu is elegant but not fussy, unusual but not eccentric, and eminently suitable for those occasions when you want to offer a charming surprise either to distinguished guests, or to friends well-versed in cookery who enjoy innovative food and good wine. The main course, the Choulibiac, is so spectacular a dish in both its composition and its presentation that it needs nothing accompanying it. I follow it with a bit of greenery, and then end the meal with fresh pear sherbet —a delight of the purest and most refreshing kind. Therefore I serve no first course, and offer only a glass of chilled Champagne before the meal. To give a stylish and colorful touch, Paul adds a few drops of black currant or raspberry liqueur to each glass.

Such a creation as the Choulibiac was unthinkable in all but the grandest houses and greatest restaurants until a few years ago, when the invention of the food processor brought such culinary fantasies right to the ordinary kitchen's doorstep. Almost anyone now may produce with ease many a classical preparation of the *haute cuisine* (such as a velvety, airy mousse of fish, which once took hours of labor with mortar and pestle, then beating over constantly renewed bowls of ice, then forcing the mixture through hair-fine sieves). In addition, the basic elements are easily available. So the modern cook's imagination is freed to devise original and fanciful assemblages like the Choulibiac.

In its rococo style, it is almost a playful dish. Even its name is a pun on the Russian *coulibiac,* an envelope of brioche pastry stuffed with salmon, mushrooms, and *kasha*... and a very good dish, too, though a heavy one in comparison to this. The Choulibiac is so much lighter because it rests on a giant crêpe rather than on a layer of brioche dough, and it is encased in the thinnest possible cloak of *choux* or cream puff pastry—just enough to protect its overall inside covering of fish mousse, under which rest layers of the freshest of sole fillets interspersed with wine-flavored minced mushrooms.

What you present to your guests as the finished dish is a plump golden-brown pillow topped with a fat flirtatious fish, wearing such a broad smile that one knows he is proud to have become a Choulibiac. When sliced it is dark brown, white, and daffodil yellow—the layering of mushroom *duxelles,* fish fillets, and fish mousse. Each serving is surrounded with a beautifully buttery yellow sauce.

After the salad, the silver-white pear sherbet seems to capture with icy intensity the flavor and perfume of a ripe pear at its fleeting peak. You can't always count on having perfect pears ready for a given day, and, if you do find some, you can't keep them. But this simple, artful recipe does seem to preserve their indescribable taste intact. You may discreetly enhance it with a touch of Williams pear brandy, which is sold by a few knowing shops to connoisseurs. (It comes with a plump pear lolling about in the bottle. When the pear tree buds, the bottle is slipped over a choice twig and acts as a little private greenhouse for the fruit which ripens inside it, and which will flavor the spirit.)

It seems a bit pedestrian, perhaps, for me to remind you that most of the elements of this meal—except for the final assemblage and baking—can be prepared long in advance, that it requires no novel or difficult techniques, and that it is not particularly expensive. Like so many delightful examples of the rococo, it is simply a happy combination of tried-and-true basic components; and, like them, it is sound and practical. It just happens to be great fun, too.

Filling ingredients
16 skinless and boneless sole fillets (each about 9 x 2 inches, or 23 x 5 cm), or about 2 pounds (900 g)
½ pound (225 g) skinless and boneless halibut, or more sole fillets
1 cup (¼ L) heavy cream, chilled
1 quart (10 ounces or 285 g) fresh mushrooms
Miscellaneous
Several shallots and/or scallions
A little Cognac and 3 Tb dry Port or Sercial Madeira
Salt, freshly ground white pepper, ground nutmeg
4 or more Tb butter (for greasing pans, sautéing, etc.)
4 funnels made of aluminum foil (twisted around a pencil), ⅓ inch (¾ cm) in diameter and 1 inch (2½ cm) long
Egg glaze (1 egg beaten with 1 tsp water in a small bowl)
3 cups (¾ L) white wine sauce (next recipe) or hollandaise, page 171, to serve with the Choulibiac

Equipment
You need a sturdy, level jelly roll pan, preferably with a nonstick surface. An old battered pan is going to produce an uneven crêpe since the batter is spread so thin—there may even be areas that are not covered, while other areas, where the batter settles, will be too thick. Also, your oven must be absolutely level. If you don't have reliable equipment, make two large, thin crêpes in your biggest frying pan, then piece them together to obtain approximately the dimensions called for in the final assembling.

The giant crêpe

Place the flour in a mixing bowl and beat in the milk, egg, oil, and salt; let rest for 10 minutes. Meanwhile preheat oven to 400°F/200°C, smear jelly roll pan with a tablespoon of soft butter, roll flour in it, and knock out excess. Pour crêpe batter into pan to a depth of about ⅛ inch (½ cm), and set in lower level of oven for 4 to 5 minutes, until batter has set. Then place pan 4 to 5 inches (10 to 13 cm) under a medium-hot broiler element to brown top of crêpe slowly and lightly—it will seethe and bubble a bit as it browns but do not let it overcook and stiffen. Remove from oven and with a flexible-blade spatula carefully loosen crêpe all around from edges to center of pan. If it sticks, it has not cooked quite long enough; return to lower level of oven 2 to 3 minutes more. Slide crêpe off onto a cake rack.

🕐 You may roll crêpe, when cool, between two sheets of wax paper and refrigerate, or wrap airtight and freeze.

Seasoning the fish fillets

Mince enough shallots or scallions to make 3 tablespoons and set aside in a small bowl, reserving half for the mushrooms later. Choose a rectangular or oval dish 10 to 12 inches (25 to 30 cm) long, sprinkle 1 teaspoon shallots on the bottom, and arrange over them a layer of overlapping sole fillets; season lightly with salt and pepper, a sprinkling of minced shallots or scallions, a few drops of Cognac, and continue with the rest of the fillets, making probably three layers in all. Cover with plastic wrap and refrigerate. (Set over ice if wait is more than a few hours.)

The pâte à choux

Bring the 1½ cups (3½ dL) water rather slowly to the boil with the cut-up butter and the salt. As soon as butter has melted, remove from heat and immediately dump in all of the cup (¼ L) of flour at once, beating vigorously with a portable mixer and/or wooden spoon. When smooth, set over moderately high heat and beat for several minutes until mixture begins to film the bottom of the pan—indicating excess moisture has boiled off.

When using a food processor, scrape hot paste into machine, activate it, and break in 5 eggs rapidly, one after the other, then stop the machine. (Do the same if you have a table model mixer, beating just until each egg is absorbed before adding the next. By hand,

make a well in center of hot paste in saucepan, then beat in 5 eggs one by one with either a portable mixer or a wooden spoon. Break sixth egg into a bowl, blend yolk and white with a fork, and how much to add to the paste depends on its thickness—it should just hold its shape in a spoon. Beat in as much of the final egg by droplets as you judge safe, remembering the more egg the more the pastry puffs, but you don't want the batter to thin out too much.)

Remove ½ cup (1 dL) of the *choux* pastry to a medium-size metal mixing bowl and reserve for fish mousse, next step. For the food processor, scrape paste back into the saucepan, and do not wash out processor; simply replace blade; cover pastry with plastic wrap, set in a pan of warm but not too hot water, and hold for final assembly.

The fish mousse

Set the reserved bowl of *choux* pastry in a larger bowl with a tray of ice cubes and water to cover them, and stir several minutes with a wooden spoon to chill; leave over ice. For the food processor, cut the halibut and one of the sole fillets into ½-inch (1½-cm) pieces and place in the processor with the cold *choux* paste, ¾ cup (1¾ dL) chilled cream, ½ teaspoon salt, several grinds white pepper, and a big pinch nutmeg; activate the processor for about a minute, until the fish is ground into a fine paste. If still stiff, beat in more cream by dribbles—mousse must be just firm enough to hold its shape for spreading; scrape out of food processor into *choux*-paste bowl; do not wash processor; simply replace blade and use for mushrooms, next step. (Lacking a processor, put fish twice through finest blade of meat grinder and beat resulting purée into the *choux* paste over ice; then, with a portable mixer, beat in the seasonings and, by driblets, as much of the cream as the mixture will take and still hold its shape.)

Cover bowl with plastic wrap and, still over ice, refrigerate.

🕐 Or cover airtight and freeze if wait is longer than 12 hours.

The mushroom duxelles

Trim the mushrooms, wash rapidly, and if you are using a food processor, chop by hand into ½-inch (1½-cm) pieces, then mince 1 cup (¼ L) at a time in the processor—flipping it on and off every second just until mushrooms are cut into ⅛-inch (½-cm) pieces; otherwise mince by hand with a big knife. To extract juices, either squeeze in a potato ricer or twist by handfuls in the corner of a towel. Sauté in a frying pan, in 2 tablespoons hot butter and 1 tablespoon minced shallots or scallions until mushroom pieces begin to separate from each other—4 to 5 minutes over moderately high heat, stirring. Season lightly with salt and pepper, pour in 3 tablespoons Port or Madeira, and boil down rapidly to evaporate liquid. Scrape the *duxelles* into a bowl and reserve.

🕐 If done in advance, cool, cover, and either refrigerate for up to 4 or 5 days, or freeze.

Assembling the Choulibiac

Spread the giant crêpe, browned side down, on a buttered baking sheet (nonstick if possible) and trim off any stiff edges with scissors. Spread ⅓ of the fish mousse in a rectangle about 12 inches (30 cm) long and 5 inches (13 cm) wide down the center, and over it arrange ½ of the fish fillets, slightly overlapping. On top of that spread ½ of the mushroom *duxelles,* then the rest of the fish fillets and remaining *duxelles.* Beat any fish-seasoning juices into reserved mousse, spread mousse over top and sides of fish structure, then bring the ends and sides of the crêpe (cutting out the corners) up over the fish. Trim off excess crêpe, leaving a side edging on top of only 1 inch (2½ cm). Reserve ½ cup (1 dL) or so of pastry for final decorations; then, using a flexible-blade spatula dipped in cold water, spread ⅛ inch (½ cm) *choux* pastry evenly over top and sides, masking the structure completely. Poke holes ⅛ inch (½ cm) across and ½ inch (1½ cm) deep, angled toward center of structure, in the lower part of each of the four corners, and insert buttered foil funnels (to drain out any juices during baking).

🕐 Refrigerate the Choulibiac if you are not continuing—but plan to bake it within a few hours.

Final decorations and baking

Baking time: about 45 minutes

Preheat oven to 425°F/220°C and set rack in lower-middle level. If *choux* pastry has cooled and stiffened, beat over hot water to soften and warm to tepid only; spoon it into a pastry bag with ½-inch (1½-cm) cannelated tube. Paint Choulibiac with a coating of egg glaze, then pipe *choux* pastry decorations onto it—such as the fanciful outline of a fish with mouth, eyes, fins; or a zigzag border all around the edges and a number of rosettes on top. Glaze the decorations, and the rest of the pastry, with two coatings of egg.

Immediately set in oven and bake for 15 to 20 minutes at 425°F/220°C, or until the pastry top has begun to brown and to puff slightly; turn thermostat down to 375°F/190°C and continue baking another 20 min-utes or so. Choulibiac is done when you begin to smell a delicious odor of pastry, fish, and mushrooms, and, finally, when juices start to exude onto baking sheet. (Pastry will not puff a great deal, just slightly.)

Plan to serve as soon as possible, although the Choulibiac will stay warm in turned-off oven, door ajar, for 20 to 30 min-utes—the longer it sits the more of its vital fish juices will exude. Loosen bottom of Chouli-biac carefully from pastry sheet, using a flex-ible-blade spatula, and slide it onto a hot platter or a serving board.

To serve, cut into crosswise pieces from one of the short sides and surround each por-tion with sauce—either the following, which can be made well ahead, or hollandaise (see page 171).

Sauce Vin Blanc:

White wine velouté sauce

For about 2½ cups

If you plan on this sauce for the Choulibiac, save out 5 to 6 tablespoons of the *choux* pastry (scrapings from the pastry bag, for instance), and the sauce is practically made, except for the white-wine fish stock. Here's how to go about it, in a rather free-form way.

2 cups (½ L) fresh fish trimmings (or extra sole or halibut)
1 small onion, chopped
½ carrot, chopped
1 small celery stalk, sliced
8 to 10 parsley stems (not leaves)
1 imported bay leaf
1 cup (¼ L) dry white French vermouth
1 cup (¼ L) water
½ tsp salt (and more as needed)
5 to 6 Tb ready-made *choux* pastry in a bowl
About 1 cup (¼ L) milk
About ½ cup (1 dL) heavy cream
White pepper
Drops of fresh lemon juice
Softened unsalted butter, as your conscience permits

Simmer the fish trimmings or fish with the vegetables, herbs, wine, water, and ½ teaspoon salt for 20 to 30 minutes; strain, then boil down rapidly to 1 cup. Gradually blend into the *choux* pastry, pour into saucepan and simmer, thinning out as necessary with spoonfuls of milk and cream. Sauce should coat a spoon lightly; season carefully with additional salt, pepper, and drops of lemon juice.

🕐 If made in advance, clean sauce off sides of pan and float a spoonful of cream over surface to prevent a skin from forming. Bring to the simmer before proceeding.

Just before serving, taste again carefully for seasoning, then remove from heat and beat in softened butter by spoonfuls. (Just a spoonful or two will enrich the sauce nicely, but you may beat in as many more, almost, as you wish, as though you were making a hollandaise.)

Watercress Salad with Endive and Cucumbers

The salad should really be served after the Choulibiac, but this depends on your table and service arrangements. Whether to serve it on a platter or in a big bowl, or arrange each serving individually—which can be very attractive—is also a matter of your choice and facilities. Pass the Melba toast or pita separately. For recipes, see page 124 for Melba toast and page 203 for homemade pita.

For 6 people

2 or 3 bunches watercress, depending on size
2 cucumbers
3 or 4 heads Belgian endive
1 tsp Dijon-type prepared mustard
1 Tb fresh lemon juice
4 to 5 Tb best-quality light olive oil or salad oil
Salt and pepper
Fresh minced dill weed or parsley, halved cherry tomatoes (optional)

Trim off tough stems from watercress, wash the cress, spin dry, and wrap loosely in a clean towel; refrigerate in a plastic bag. Peel the cucumbers, slice thin, and refrigerate in a bowl of salted water; drain thoroughly and dry in a towel before serving. Separate the leaves from the central stems of the endive and refrigerate in a damp towel and plastic bag. Place the mustard, lemon juice, and oil in a screw-topped jar, season with salt and pepper, shake to blend, taste, and correct seasoning.

At serving time, toss each ingredient separately in a little of the dressing (well shaken first), correct seasoning for each, and make your arrangement. One I like is to place the endives first, like the spokes of a wheel, then make a bed of cress, and a topping of cucumber slices. (You may also like a sprinkling of fresh minced dill or parsley tossed with your cucumbers, and a few halved cherry tomatoes placed around for color.)

Fresh Pear Sherbet

For about 1 quart

5 or 6 fine ripe pears, to make about 2 cups (½ L) purée

2 lemons

¾ cup (1¾ dL) sugar—instant superfine, if possible (for fast dissolving)

1 egg white

3 to 4 Tb best-quality white pear liqueur, such as Eau-de-Vie de Poire Williams (optional but highly recommended)

Equipment

A dasher-type ice-cream freezer; crushed ice; coarse salt; a vegetable mill or food processor for puréeing pears

Note: I have tried this sherbet in machines other than the old-fashioned dasher type, and have not been pleased with the results, which are not as smooth. The non-dasher ice-tray method is unsatisfactory, since the sherbet needs beating. I am sure the one-unit freezer-dasher luxury priced electric machine would do a beautiful job.

Wash the pears and lemons. Grate the rind of 1 lemon into a large mixing bowl, and strain the juice of both (or 4 tablespoons) into the bowl. Quarter, peel, and core the pears, and cut into chunks; toss, as you do them, in the bowl with the lemon and a sprinkling of the sugar. (Lemon and sugar prevent the pears from darkening, and you want to keep them white.) Immediately the pears are prepared, purée them with the lemon juice, adding the rest of the sugar and puréeing until you are sure all sugar granules have dissolved completely. (Test by tasting.) If you used a food processor for puréeing, add the egg white to the container and purée a moment more. Otherwise, beat the egg white in a small bowl until it forms soft peaks and fold into the pear purée.

Prepare ice-cream freezer, using 1 part coarse salt to every 4 parts crushed ice. (The salt lowers the temperature of the ice. And it is important that the ice be finely crushed: if you use cubed or coarsely chipped ice, the salt slips down to the bottom and will have no freezing effect.) Pour pear purée into freezing container; if you are using it, stir in the pear liqueur only at the last moment, so that it hasn't time to darken the pears. Freeze the

sherbet, which will take about 25 minutes; then pack it in a sealed airtight container and store in the freezer for at least 4 hours to cure. (Sherbet does not develop its full flavor until it has cured.) Set in refrigerator for 20 to 30 minutes before serving to let it soften.

⏱ Sherbet may be made several days in advance, although it gradually loses its freshly made texture and develops crystals that make it less smooth—in that case you could let it soften, and freeze again in the ice-cream machine.

A pretty way to serve this sherbet is to spoon it into goblets and stick a chocolate heart in each helping.

To Make Chocolate Hearts:

Melt 4 ounces (115 g) semisweet and 1 ounce (30 g) unsweetened chocolate: break it up into a small saucepan, cover and set in a larger pan of boiling water, remove from heat and let sit 5 minutes or so, until soft; then stir up to make a smooth shining mass. Remove pan from heat and stir with a wooden spoon until bottom of pan is almost cold to your hand. Then spread an even 3/16-inch (¾-cm) layer on wax paper over a baking sheet and let cool until it clouds over and is almost set. Press heart designs into chocolate with a small cookie cutter (or outline hearts in the chocolate with the point of a small knife), and peel paper and surrounding chocolate from each heart. Store on wax paper in refrigerator or freezer, and handle with wooden or rubber-covered tongs.

⏱ Timing

Despite its elegant character, this is not a tricky meal. Just remember to put the sherbet in the refrigerator to soften before you sit down to lunch or before the salad course, depending on whether your guests are lingerers or gobblers. The Choulibiac will stay warm for almost half an hour in the turned-off oven, though it does exude juice. (Incidentally, if it does, add the juices to your sauce.) Ideally, you'd start baking it when you fix the salad, about 15 minutes before your guests come. You can assemble it first thing in the morning and refrigerate it until time to bake. Also during the morning, make its sauce, chill your wine, and prepare your salad ingredients.

You can make the sherbet several days beforehand; you can make and freeze the crêpe, the fish mousse, the *duxelles,* and the chocolate hearts any time; and the *choux* pastry will keep 2 or 3 days in the refrigerator —but remember to reheat it just to tepid, beating it over hot water, so that it will be soft enough for easy spreading.

Menu Variations

Choulibiac: You can omit the *choux*-paste envelope and the giant pancake, and simply pile and bake fish fillets, layered with fish mousse, on a bed of *duxelles.* The dish is done when the fillets begin to shrink and exude juice (which you drain off—it's easy with a bulb baster; you rapidly reduce the juices and add them to your sauce). Or you can roll the fillets around the mousse, poach them in wine and fish stock on the bed of *duxelles,* reduce this liquid, and turn it into a sauce. *Mastering I* and

J.C.'s Kitchen both contain classic dishes of fillets of sole with mushrooms; there are fish-and-mushroom soufflés; and the combination is excellent in a *vol-au-vent* case. Or—but this is really an alternative, not a variation—you could return to the Choulibiac's Russian ancestor and make a *coulibiac;* there is a home-style version of that in *The French Chef Cookbook.*

Pear sherbet: If you can't obtain first-rate pears at their peak of flavor, pick another fruit for this recipe, like fresh peaches or pineapple, or canned apricots. Or try the non-cranking sherbet recipes in *Mastering II* and *J.C.'s Kitchen.*

Leftovers

You can keep opened *Champagne* in its original bottle. Just look around for a patent metal Champagne cork that clamps on the top of the bottle and keeps in the fizz; store the bottle in the refrigerator.

The Choulibiac can be reheated in foil, but be sure to serve it with sauce, either the Vin Blanc or a hollandaise. You could serve leftovers as a cold first course or as another luncheon dish if you scrape off the *choux*-paste covering and the crêpe bottom; mask the fish attractively with a sour cream sauce or homemade mayonnaise lightened with sour cream or minced cucumbers. Or you could chop or purée the remains and stir them into a cream of

fish soup, a cream of celery soup, or a leek and potato soup, adding more cream or sour cream as need be.

Fish sauce can be frozen and mixed into a new sauce, or stirred into a fish soup as a special enrichment.

Leftover salad is leftover salad, to my mind, and has little charm for me except possibly at breakfast the next day, or washed off immediately and chopped up for addition to a vegetable soup of the minestrone type.

The sherbet can be refrozen. See notes about this at the end of the recipe.

Postscript: On playing with your food

Some children like to make castles out of their rice pudding, or faces with raisins for eyes. It is forbidden—so sternly that, when they grow up, they take a horrid revenge by dying meringues pale blue or baking birthday cakes in the form of horseshoes or lyres or whatnot. That is not playing with food, that is trifling.

"Play" to me means freedom and delight, as in the phrase "play of imagination." If cooks did not enjoy speculating about new possibilities in every method and each raw material, their art would stagnate and they would become rote performers, not creators. True cooks love to set one flavor against another in the imagination, to experiment with the great wealth of fresh produce in the supermarkets, to bake what previously they braised, to try new devices. We all have flops, of course, but we learn from them; and, when an invention or a variation works out at last, it is an enormous pleasure to propose it to our fellows.

Let's all play with our food, I say, and, in so doing, let us advance the state of the art together.

A gorgeous spread for people you really want to see; and a revolutionary method to make puff pastry an everyday staple.

Cocktail Party

Cocktail parties aren't what they used to be, and that's all right with me. Goodbye to boozing and starving and crowding and screaming, to five-to-seven and six-to-eight, to the sudden exodus, to the ruined parlor; and goodbye, above all, to that day-after-Christmas feeling, when you realize you never had a minute with the people you most wanted to see. And welcome, with three loud cheers, to easy evenings of good wine and good food and good friends.

We like to give our guests a *spread.* I hate it when people get hungry after a couple of drinks and charge out somewhere to supper before I even get to see them. So Paul and I set out plates and forks and napkins as a hint to stay; and I serve a great big puffy something I baked specially, and something fishy and fresh, and lots of good hearty treats on the side: chicken wings and oysters and clams and stuffed eggs, and meatballs and rabbit food. And peanuts too. Of course we serve the usual drinks—including at least one of Paul's special inventions—but our friends mostly prefer wine for a long evening, so we have plenty of that.

In line with the good new custom of more cheer for fewer people, we give our parties in the kitchen, right in the heart of the house. People can't come into a kitchen and not relax. And we've gotten bored anyway with "Queen Anne in front and Mary Anne behind": the parlor gussied up with coasters and teeny napkins while frenzy reigns out back. Yes, there's some mess. Puff pastry means crumbs and shellfish mean shells. We just line a couple of wastebins with plastic bags which we replace as they fill up and hoist out the back door.

Paul had the thought of making a big wood frame lined with heavy plastic (with a drain for drips) for the cold things. We heap it with ice and set it right on the stove top, where it looks bounteous. We flank it with hot dishes on an electric tray, and use cutting boards to serve a couple of ham Pithiviers tarts, high as hassocks and light as clouds. They're not much work, if you make your puff pastry in advance and do it the fast new way. Puff pastry can be your best friend too, and if you've not yet mastered it, bear in mind three great truths. Don't be afraid of it. Keep it cold. And finally, don't fight it: rest it often, just as you would a fussy baby.

That big slab of fish on the ice mound is *gravlaks,* salmon rubbed with salt, bedded on dill (and spruce twigs if you have them), anointed with Cognac, weighted down, and macerated in the refrigerator for three or four days at least. It's an exquisite preparation, fresher and more delicate than smoked salmon but not raw-tasting (for the salt "cooks" it). I first sampled *gravlaks* in Oslo when Paul was Cultural Attaché at the American Embassy. The salmon was served with scrambled eggs and creamed potatoes as a main course. Delicious! But I also like it for cocktails served with buttered pumpernickel.

Spicy things are nice with cocktails, too, and I always like something hot, so we make minimeatballs of ground beef mixed with a bit of pork sausage for richness, as well as a delightful, vaguely Oriental preparation of chicken wings. Radish roses with little top-knots of sweet butter, stuffed eggs flavored with lemon and anchovy and topped with enormous capers the size of fat peas, and peanuts, of course. Without peanuts, it isn't a cocktail party.

Preparations

Recommended Equipment:
You'll want plenty of beer can openers, oyster knives, and paring knives for the shellfish, and something you can make a bed of ice in: a giant bowl, a washtub, or a deep tray. Or, if you have two sinks, use one for the purpose, as we do our vegetable sink.

A proper rolling pin is essential for puff pastry, one at least 16 inches (40 cm) long. If yours is too short, you're better off with a broomstick. (See the recipe for details and illustrations.) A pastry marble, cut to fit your refrigerator shelf, is most desirable if you are going in for any serious pastry making. (Look in the Yellow Pages under Marble or Tombstones; the seller will cut one to size for you.) A heavy-duty electric mixer is the way to lightning-fast puff pastry; but, if you do it by hand, don't use a pastry blender for the new method. It cuts the butter too fine. Pleasant but nonessential aids are a roller-pricker and a large ravioli cutting wheel.

A pastry bag with two cannelated (toothed) tubes, one medium sized for the eggs, one tiny for the radishes, will prettify them.

An electric warming tray and a couple of portable cutting boards are a great help in serving, as are two or three wastebins with plastic trash bag liners for the debris.

Marketing and Storage:
Staples to have on hand

Salt
Peppercorns
Granulated sugar
Orange bitters
Bottled sweetened lime juice
Hot pepper sauce, soy sauce, Worcestershire sauce
Capers
Orange marmalade
Oregano or thyme
Italian seasoning (an herb blend)
Mustard, the strong Dijon type (see page 6)
Tomato purée or sauce, canned

Olive oil or fresh new peanut oil (see page 52)
Garlic; shallots or scallions
Beef stock or bouillon, frozen or canned
Fresh bread crumbs (in the freezer; see page 6)
Wines and liqueurs: dry white French vermouth, Cognac, orange liqueur

Specific ingredients for this menu

Boiled ham (6 ounces or 180 g per Pithiviers)
Center-cut fresh salmon and/or other fresh fish (5 pounds or 2½ kg per recipe *gravlaks*) ▼
Fresh pork sausage meat (4 ounces or 115 g per recipe meatballs)
Lean ground beef (1 pound or 450 g per recipe meatballs)
Chicken wings (24 per recipe)
Small amounts (optional): fermented dry black Chinese beans; dark sesame oil; dried Chinese mushrooms; fresh or pickled ginger—for chicken wings ▼
Mayonnaise, anchovy paste, curry powder, and/or other items for stuffing hard-boiled eggs
Pumpernickel bread
Peanuts and/or various nuts, to serve with drinks
Heavy cream (4 Tb per Pithiviers)

Eggs (3 per Pithiviers, 1 for the meatballs, plus however many you wish for stuffed egg recipe)
Cheese for grating—Cheddar, Swiss, Parmesan or a combination of all three (1 pound or 450 g at least; to be used for cheese appetizers and 6 ounces or 180 g per Pithiviers) ▼
Unsalted butter (2½ pounds or 1125 g for puff pastry, plus butter for pumpernickel bread, radishes, and other purposes)
Cake flour, plain bleached (1 cup or 140 g per puff pastry recipe)
All-purpose flour, unbleached (3 cups or 420 g per puff pastry recipe) ▼
Lemons (4 per chicken wing recipe, plus those needed for serving oysters and clams, drinks, etc.)
Limes, for drinks
Oranges (1 per apéritif recipe for 6 people)
Parsley and/or watercress, for decoration
Fresh or fragrant dried dill weed and, if available, spruce branches for *gravlaks* ▼
Radishes
Oysters and clams ▼
Ice cubes for drinks, and crushed ice for shellfish
Red wines, white wines, and dark Jamaica rum
Other drinks for your usual bar set-up

▶ *Remarks:*

Fresh fish: be sure to buy the fish for your *gravlaks* well enough ahead—see recipe for details. *Fermented dry black Chinese beans and dark sesame oil:* obtainable in Chinese and Japanese grocery stores and many fancy food stores; good items to know because they add a very special flavor to all kinds of dishes, not only chicken, but shrimp, fish, and so forth. No reason to confine them to Oriental cooking. *Dried Chinese mushrooms:* you need only 2 or 3 of these pungent mushrooms to give a fine mushroom flavor to many a dish; soak them in warm water until they have softened, and if the stems remain tough, cut them off and discard them. Then slice or chop the mushrooms and use like fresh mushrooms. *Ginger:* fresh gingerroot is to be had in many supermarkets these days. You can freeze it and grate or slice it—still frozen—into whatever you are cooking, using just what you need and storing the rest in the freezer. Pickled ginger, put up in brine and usually vinegar, keeps for months in the refrigerator; you can normally find it in Japanese and Chinese grocery stores. *Cheese for grating:* I find it a very good idea to grate up leftover hard cheeses like Cheddar, Swiss, and Parmesan and to package them together in a plastic bag or container in my freezer; I always have cheese on hand, then, and none is wasted. *Unbleached all-purpose flour:* essential, in my experience, for puff pastry, since bleached flour makes a tough pastry and is also hard to roll out; if your market doesn't carry unbleached flour, look for it in health food stores. *Dill weed:* fresh dill is always preferable to dried when you can find it, and you can store it in your freezer: stem it, wash and dry it thoroughly, then chop it fine and pack it in small parcels for freezing. This works with chives too. The secret is to exclude all moisture and air before freezing. Sometimes you can find fragrant dried bottled dill weed; smell it before using to be sure it is full of flavor and aroma. *Oysters and clams:* see "Fish Talk," page 111, for details, including a clever way to open oysters.

A Preamble to French Puff Pastry — made a new fast way

The most marvelous of all doughs, to my mind, is French puff pastry, the pastry of a thousand leaves that puffs up in the oven as it bakes because it is made of many many layers of paper thin dough interspersed with many many layers of butter. It is light as air, flaky, tender, buttery, and so good to eat just of itself that it hardly needs an accompaniment. It not only makes *vol-au-vent* pastry cases and patty shells, but all manner of tarts and cookies, cheese and ham concoctions, dessert cakes, and so forth. For a cocktail party it is practically a must, and, since you can prepare it months and months ahead, you could even consider it a staple ingredient to have on hand in your freezer. Once made, it can quickly be turned into a spectacular, like the ham Pithiviers to serve at this party—shown below just out of the oven.

I must admit to having spent years and years on puff pastry, starting out in Paris way back in the early 1950s. I learned to make it in the classical way, where you start with a flour-water dough that you spread out into a thick pancake and fold around an almost equal amount of butter. Next, you roll that out into

a long rectangle and the butter follows along inside the dough. Then you fold that into three, like a business letter, and roll it out again. All the time the butter is extending itself in layers inside the dough, and every time you fold it those layers triple in number until by the sixth roll-and-fold you have 729 layers of butter between 730 layers of dough.

All this manipulation gives the dough a heavy workout, which is fine when you have flour with a low gluten content, like French flour. But when you are working with regular American all-purpose flour, which has a relatively high gluten content, the dough becomes rubbery, refuses to be rolled out, and you have to let it rest and relax until you can continue. My French colleague Simone Beck and I almost gave up on *pâte feuilletée with* American flour until I happened to be doing a television show on entertaining at the White House, and their then pastry chef, Ferdinand Louvat, produced some splendid *vol-au-vent* structures. He used all-purpose flour, he told me, but for every 3 parts all-purpose flour he put in 1 part cake flour; the cake flour lowered the gluten content and made the dough easy to handle.

That was our first breakthrough, and the recipe for classic puff pastry using that formula is in Volume II of *Mastering.* The second breakthrough is an entirely new way of making the pastry, suggested by a reading of *La Cuisine de Denis* (ed. Robert Laffont, Paris, 1975). Instead of forming the dough into a package encasing a mass of butter, you break the butter up into large pieces the size of lima beans and mix them with the flour, salt, and water; then you form this messy-looking mass into a long rectangle, patting and rolling it out. You fold it into three, roll it out, fold it again, and it begins to look like dough. After 2 additional turns it is smooth and fine; you then rest it 40 minutes and it is ready for its final 2 rolls and folds and its forming and baking. Now puff pastry can be made in an hour, rather than the 3 or 4 hours usually necessary for the classical method using all-purpose flour.

Because the butter is in large lumps, they form themselves into the required layers as you proceed to roll and fold the dough. You can see from the illustrations that the puff pastry rises dramatically as it should—just as much if not more so than the classical puff pastry. In fact, since experimenting with this new system I've not gone back to the old method at all.

Puff pastry proportions
Proportions for the new fast puff pastry are 5 parts butter to 4 parts flour—the large amount of butter necessary because you have to flour the dough more as you roll it than in the old method. These amounts easily translate into metrics as 125 grams butter for every 100 grams flour. In cups and spoons they approximate:

1 cup (5 ounces or 140 g) flour as follows: ¾ cup (3½ ounces or 105 g) unbleached all-purpose flour, and   ¼ cup (1¼ ounces or 35 g) plain bleached cake flour
1½ sticks plus 1 Tb (6½ ounces or 185 g) chilled unsalted butter
Scant ½ tsp salt
¼ cup (½ dL) iced water

Hand versus machine
I like to make my pastry in a heavy-duty electric mixer with flat beater, using 4 cups of flour and ending up with a goodly amount of dough. It does not work well in a food processor, because the butter becomes too much broken up and the pastry does not puff dramatically. Mixing by hand works out nicely, but be sure not to soften the butter too much; cut it into ½-inch dice, then rub it with the flour between the balls of your fingers until it is broken into thickish disks, like fat cornflakes. The water goes in after the butter and flour have been mixed together, making a very rough, barely cohesive mass.

Fast French Puff Pastry

Pâte Feuilletée Exprès

For one 9-inch Pithiviers and 36 or more cheese appetizers; or for a rectangle of dough some 36 by 12 by ¼ inches (90 x 30 x ¾ cm)

Note: Measure flour by dipping dry-measure cups into container, then sweeping off excess even with lip of cup; no sifting necessary.

3 cups (420 g) unbleached all-purpose flour
1 cup (140 g) plain bleached cake flour
6½ sticks (26 ounces or 735 g) chilled unsalted butter
1½ tsp salt
1 cup (¼ L) iced water
Equipment
A heavy-duty electric mixer with flat beater (useful); a 1½-by-2-foot (45-x-60-cm) work surface, preferably of marble; a rolling pin at least 16 inches (40 cm) long; a pastry sheet (for lifting and turning dough) about 10 inches (25 cm) wide; a pastry scraper or wide spatula; plastic wrap

Mixing the dough

Place the flour in your mixing bowl. Rapidly cut the sticks of chilled butter into lengthwise quarters, then into ½-inch (1½-cm) dice; * add to the flour—if you have taken too long to cut the butter and if it has softened, refrigerate bowl to chill butter before proceeding. Add the salt. Blend flour and butter together rapidly, if by hand to make large flakes about an inch in size. By machine the butter should be roughly broken up but stay in lumps the size of large lima beans. Blend in the water, mixing just enough so that dough masses roughly together but butter pieces remain about the same size.

The first 4 turns

Turn dough out onto a lightly floured work surface, as illustrated in the first picture on the right. Rapidly push and pat and roll it out into a rectangle in front of you—12 to 14 inches for 2 cups of flour, about 18 for 4 cups (30 to 35 cm and 40 to 45 cm). It will look an awful mess! Lightly flour top of dough and, with pastry sheet to help you, flip bottom of rectangle up over the middle, and then flip the top down to cover it, as though folding a business letter. Lift dough off work surface with pastry sheet; scrape work surface clean, flour the surface lightly, and return dough to it, settling it down in front of you so that the top flap is at your right. Lightly flour top of dough, and pat, push, and roll it out again into a rectangle; it will look a little less messy. Fold again into three as before—each of these roll-and-fold operations is called a "turn." Roll out and fold 2 more times, making 4 turns in all, and by the last one the pastry should actually look like dough. You should see large flakes of butter scattered under the surface of the dough, which is just as it should be. With the balls of your fingers (not your fingernails) make 4

*If you have bought the kind of butter that seems soft and sweats water when you cut it, that means it is inferior quality and will not make this puff pastry rise as it should. In this case you eliminate the extra moisture by first kneading it in ice water and then squeezing in a damp towel to remove excess water. Then chill.

depressions in the dough to indicate the 4 turns, as I've done in the final picture below—just in case you go off and forget what you've done.

Finishing the dough—the 2 final turns
Wrap the dough in plastic, place in a plastic bag, and refrigerate for 40 minutes (or longer) to firm the butter and relax the gluten in the dough. Give the dough 2 more turns, beating it back and forth and up and down first if chilled and hard. Let dough rest another 30 minutes if it seems rubbery and hard to roll; then it is ready for forming and baking.

● Dough may be frozen after the first 4 turns, although it is easier to complete the 6 of them before freezing. It will keep, wrapped airtight, for months. Defrost overnight in the refrigerator, or at room temperature.

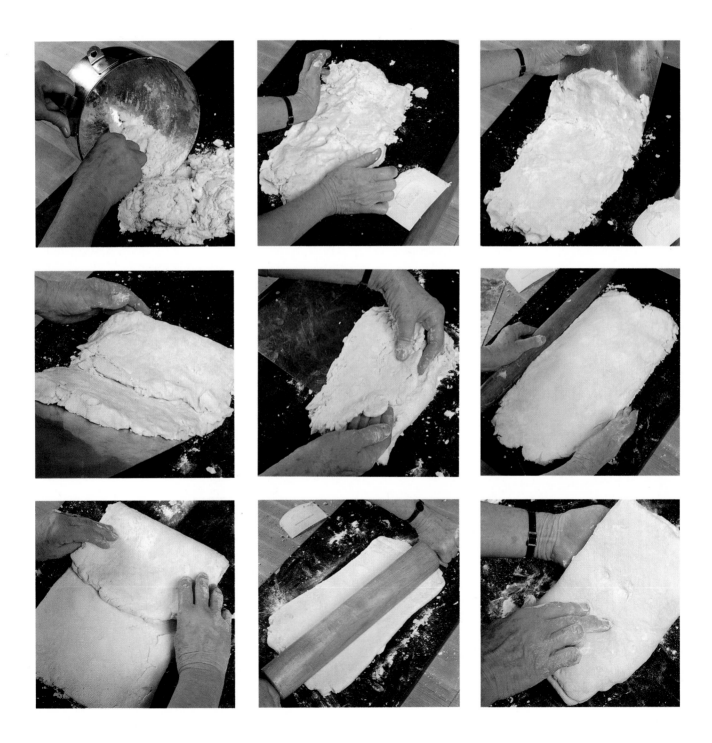

Ham Pithiviers

Puff pastry tart with ham filling

For a 9½-inch (24 cm) tart serving 8 to 10 generously, or 20 cocktail bites

⅔ previous puff pastry (cut after rolling out, as described in this recipe)

6 ounces (180 g) best-quality boiled ham

2 Tb butter

2 Tb minced shallots or scallions

2 egg yolks

¼ cup (½ dL) heavy cream

Drops of Worcestershire sauce

Drops of hot pepper sauce

Freshly ground pepper

6 Tb freshly grated Parmesan, Swiss, and/or Cheddar cheese

Egg glaze (1 egg beaten with 1 tsp water)

Equipment

(In addition to items suggested for puff pastry recipe above): a baking sheet, round nonstick pizza tray recommended; a roller-pricker, or two table forks; a pastry brush

The ham filling

Cut the ham into thin irregular slices about 1 by 1 by ⅛ inches (2½ x 2½ x ½ cm) and sauté briefly in the butter with the shallots or scallions, just to warm through thoroughly. Remove from heat. In a small bowl, beat the egg yolks with the cream; stir this mixture into the ham along with drops of Worcestershire and pepper sauce and freshly ground pepper to taste. Warm over low heat, folding the ham into the sauce, until it thickens but does not boil. Set aside to cool and thicken even more. It should be cold when it goes into the Pithiviers.

🕐   Filling may be prepared in advance and refrigerated.

Forming the dough

Roll the dough (the whole of the recipe) out into a rectangle about 18 by 9 inches (45 x 20 cm) and cut into thirds crosswise; refrigerate 2 pieces, wrapping and storing one of them for another use. Roll remaining piece, which will be the bottom of the tart, into a square 12 inches (30 cm) to a side; using a pie plate or cake pan to guide you, cut a 9½-inch (24-cm) disk out of the center of the dough. Remove surrounding dough and set on a bake sheet for reconstituting later. Lightly fold disk in half

and set upside down on dampened baking surface. Roll out second piece of dough to a thickness of slightly more than ¼ inch (¾ cm)—it must be this thickness to puff dramatically—and cut it into a disk the same size as the first. Refrigerate it along with the surrounding dough pieces from both disks.

🕐 Dough disks may be formed and stored in the freezer.

Assembling the Pithiviers

With the balls of your fingers, push and pat bottom disk of dough out onto its baking surface to make an even circle slightly larger than your cutting guide. With a roller-pricker or two forks, prick dough all over at ½-inch (1½-cm) intervals, going down through dough to pastry sheet to keep this bottom layer from rising too much. Form the ham into a round cake, about 4½ to 5 inches (12 to 13 cm) across—layers of ham interspersed with

sprinklings of cheese— and place in the center of the dough. It is important to leave a 2-inch (5-cm) border of clear dough all around the ham to prevent leakage of filling during baking. Paint border of dough with cold water, and immediately center top layer in place, stretching gently as necessary. With a sharp-pointed knife, make a little hole ⅛ inch (½ cm) wide in the center of the dough, going down into the filling, to allow for escaping steam during baking. Then, with the ball of your first three fingers, firmly press the two pieces of dough in place all around. (Dough should probably be chilled at this point, but if it is still firm, proceed to the scalloped edging described in next step, then chill it.)

🕐 May be wrapped airtight and frozen at this point, or after its scalloped edging. May then be decorated and baked, still in its frozen state.

Decorating the Pithiviers

Preheat oven to 450° F/230°C, and set rack in lower-middle level. Make a scalloped edging around the Pithiviers as follows: set an upturned bowl slightly smaller than the Pithiviers over it, and use it as a guide in cutting 2-inch-wide (5-cm) scallops all around the circumference; decorate their edges all around by pressing upright lines against them with the back of a knife. Just before putting it in the oven, and after making sure top of dough is chilled and firm, paint the top with a film of egg glaze; then wait a moment and paint with a second film of glaze. Finally, with the point of a small knife, cut decorative lines 1/16 inch (¼ cm) deep in the top of the dough. A typical pattern is curving lines from center to edge, like the spokes of a wheel; or trace 4 long ovals from center to edge with straight line down the center and shallow crosshatch marks in between.

Baking, holding, serving

Baking time: 45 to 60 minutes

Immediately set the Pithiviers in the preheated oven and bake for about 20 minutes, until it has puffed and is beginning to brown nicely—it should rise dramatically, to a height of at least 2 inches (5 cm). Turn oven down to 400°F/200°C and bake 20 to 30 minutes more, watching it does not brown too much—cover loosely with foil if it does, and turn thermostat a little lower if you think it necessary. Baking takes longer than you might think, since all the pastry layers should cook and crisp. The Pithiviers should be done when the sides feel quite firm; to be sure, turn oven off and leave the Pithiviers in for another 10 to 15 minutes. You may keep it in a warming oven or on an electric hot tray for an hour or more, but the sooner you serve it the more tenderly flaky and delicious it will be. To serve, with a serrated knife simply cut into wedges like a pie.

Puffed Cheese Appetizers

Reconstituted leftover puff pastry dough
You can easily turn the fresh leftovers of your unused dough back into first-class puff pastry as follows: keep the bits and pieces all in one flat layer and glue them together by wetting the edge of one piece with cold water, laying the edge of another piece on top, and so on until you have made a patchwork mat of dough. Roll it with your pin, and give it 2 turns (rollings and foldings into three). If you want to use it plain, give it 2 more turns, but to transform it into cheese appetizers, roll it out into a rectangle, and for a piece 12 by 14 inches (30 x 35 cm), spread about 4 tablespoons grated cheese across the middle. Flip bottom of dough over to cover it, spread more cheese on that upturned portion, and flip the top third of the dough over to cover it. Repeat with another roll-out and cheese fold-up, then roll out the dough into a rectangle slightly thicker than ¼ inch (¾ cm). Cut into strips 2 inches (5 cm) wide—if too narrow the appetizers will topple over as they rise in the oven. Then cut into lengths 3 inches (8 cm) long and set on a bake sheet.

🕐 May be wrapped and frozen at this point.

Just before baking, preheat oven to 450°F/230°C, paint tops of pieces with egg glaze, and sprinkle on a layer of grated cheese. Bake about 15 minutes, until appetizers have puffed and browned. Best kept warm until serving time, but they can be frozen and reheated, still frozen.

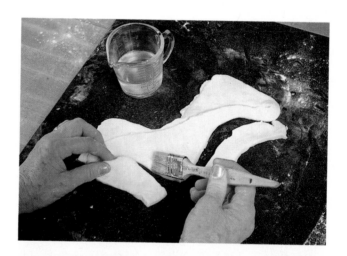

Gravlaks

Dilled fresh salmon (or sea bass)

For a 5-pound center cut of fish, boned (thus in two large halves or fillets), with skin intact

Spruce branches (if available)

2½ Tb salt and 1¼ Tb sugar mixed in a small bowl

Large bunch fresh dill weed, or 1½ Tb fragrant dried dill weed

4 to 5 Tb Cognac

Equipment

A porcelain, enamel, or glass dish, just large enough to hold fish comfortably; wax paper or plastic wrap; a plate or board that will just fit inside dish; a 5-pound (2-kg) weight

Rub fingers over the flesh to locate any bones that may still remain; salmon fillets often have small bones running slantwise from top to bottom of the thick side of the flesh. Remove with pliers.

If you have fresh spruce, cut enough twigs to cover the bottom of the dish and arrange a layer of fresh dill on top. Lay one fillet of fish skin side down in the dish and the other skin side down on your work surface. Rub the flesh sides of each fillet with the salt-and-sugar mixture and the dried dill if you are not using fresh. Sprinkle on the Cognac. (If you are using fresh dill, arrange a layer over the fish in the dish.) Place second fillet over first, flesh to flesh, but reversing its direction so that the thick or backbone part of the second fillet is resting against the thin or belly part of the first. Cover with more fresh dill and spruce twigs if you have them. Spread paper or plastic over the fish and the plate or board, and weight. Refrigerate for 2 days, basting with liquid in dish two or three times. After 2 days, taste by slicing a bit of fish off; add a teaspoon or so more salt if you feel it is not salty enough, and perhaps a sprinkling of Cognac. Reverse the fish so bottom fillet will be on top and return to refrigerator with board and weight for another 2 to 3 days, making 4 to 5 days in all. Taste carefully; the fish should now be ready to eat.

To serve

Set a fillet skin side down on a board and with a very sharp, long knife, start 4 to 5 inches (10 to 13 cm) from larger end of fillet and make paper-thin slices toward the tail, with your knife almost parallel to the board.

Remarks:

For a quicker cure, 3 to 4 days at most, you may slice your fish before curing and arrange in slightly overlapping layers, lightly salted and dilled, until the dish is full. Cover, weight, and refrigerate as before.

🕐 Dilled fish will keep for 10 days to 2 weeks under refrigeration.

Minimeatballs

*For 40 to 50 meatballs about 1 inch
(2½ cm) in diameter*

½ cup (4 ounces or 115 g) pork sausage meat

2 cups (1 pound or 450 g) lean ground beef

1 egg

⅔ cup (1½ dL) fresh nonsweet white bread
crumbs soaked in 5 Tb dry white French
vermouth

2 cloves garlic, puréed

8 drops hot pepper sauce

2 tsp soy sauce

1 tsp salt

8 grinds black pepper

½ tsp oregano or thyme

Flour (for dredging)

Serving sauce

1 cup (¼ L) beef stock or bouillon

1 tsp soy sauce

2 Tb Dijon-type strong prepared mustard
beaten to blend with ½ cup (1 dL) dry white
French vermouth

Salt, pepper, and oregano or thyme

2 Tb tomato purée or sauce (optional)

Beat meat, egg, crumbs and seasonings
together, using a food processor if you want a
very smooth mixture. Roll gobs into balls 1
inch (2½ cm) in diameter; roll lightly in flour,
and arrange in one layer in a lightly oiled baking dish or jelly roll pan. Bake in a preheated
450°F/230°C oven in upper-middle level, 7 to
8 minutes, turning once or twice, to brown
nicely and just to stiffen. Drain in a sieve or a
colander. Boil down the ingredients for the
sauce until lightly thickened, carefully correct
seasoning, and fold in the minimeatballs.

At serving time, reheat and place in a
casserole on an electric warming device, or in
an electric frying pan on lowest heat. Have a
jar of toothpicks close by.

Peking Wings

Sautéed chicken wings with Oriental overtones

24 chicken wings, folded akimbo
4 lemons
4 thin slices fresh or pickled ginger (optional)
2 Tb soy sauce
½ cup (½ dL) olive oil or fresh peanut oil
1 tsp dark sesame oil (optional)
1 tsp thyme or Italian seasoning
4 large cloves fresh garlic, puréed
½ tsp cracked peppercorns
Salt and pepper
Fresh minced parsley (optional)
Optional Oriental touches, to be added to pan after chicken has browned
2 Tb fermented dry black Chinese beans
Handful of dried Chinese mushrooms, softened in warm water, stemmed, and sliced

Marinating the chicken

Dry off the chicken in paper towels and place in a stainless steel bowl. Zest 2 lemons (remove yellow part of peel with a vegetable peeler), and cut zest into julienne (matchstick) strips along with the optional ginger. Add both to the chicken as well as strained juice of 2 lemons, the soy sauce, 4 tablespoons oil, the optional sesame oil, the thyme or Italian seasoning, the garlic, and the peppercorns. Turn and baste the chicken. Marinate for 2 hours or longer in the refrigerator, turning and basting several times. Just before cooking, scrape marinade off chicken and back into bowl. Pat chicken dry in paper towels.

Cooking the chicken

(The wings are first browned, then simmered in their marinade liquid.) Film a large frying pan with oil and heat to very hot but not smoking; then brown on all sides as many chicken wings as will fit easily in one layer, remove, and brown the rest. When all chicken wings are browned, lower heat and return them to pan with the marinade ingredients and optional black beans and mushrooms; cover, and simmer. Meanwhile slice remaining lemons thin; carefully remove seeds. After 10 minutes, turn the chicken and baste with the accumulated juices; spread the lemon slices over the chicken.

🕐 You may complete the recipe to this point, uncover the chicken, and set aside until 10 minutes or so before you wish to serve.

Continue cooking the chicken slowly 8 to 10 minutes longer, or until tender when pierced with a small knife; baste several times during this final cooking. Correct seasoning; if you wish, sprinkle parsley over the chicken, and the wings are ready to serve. Transfer to an electric heating device (or an electric frying pan) along with the cooking juices and keep over low heat.

Oysters and Clams:

See illustrated directions for opening them, as well as directions for buying and storing them, in "Fish Talk," page 111.

Stuffed Eggs:

Directions for hard-boiling and painless peeling are on page 34. For a party like this I like a quite simple filling made of sieved yolks flavored with salt, pepper, homemade mayonnaise, and a little anchovy paste, lemon, capers, or curry powder, and no recipe is needed for this. However, I do think eggs look most attractive and professional when filled with a pastry bag and cannelated tube.

Buttered Radishes:

Combining the bland and peppery flavors of butter and radishes is very French. A pretty way is to cut radish roses, let them spread out overnight in a bowl of iced water, hollow the white tops a bit with a knife point, and pipe in a little squirt of beaten unsalted butter. Chill again in iced water and serve in plenty of crushed ice to keep the topknots stiff.

A la Recherche de l'Orange Perdue

Paul Child's rum and orange cocktail
For 6 cocktail-size drinks, using jigger measurement of 1 ½ ounces

2 jiggers (6 Tb) dark Jamaica rum

½ jigger (2 tsp) bottled sweetened lime juice

Juice of 1 lime

½ jigger (2 tsp) orange liqueur

1 Tb orange marmalade

3 jiggers (9 Tb) dry white French vermouth

1 whole orange, quartered

5 shakes orange bitters

6 ice cubes

Place all ingredients in jar of electric blender and blend 20 seconds. Strain through a sieve into a pitcher. Cover and refrigerate until serving time. Stir before serving, and pour into chilled cocktail glasses.

⏱ *Timing*

There are no last-minute jobs for this party, since you open the oysters and clams as you serve them. We find, too, that people enjoy doing their own, by the surefire method described on pages 112-4.

Cook the chicken wings that afternoon for best flavor; but if you do want to do it earlier, peel off as much skin as you can right after cooking—that's where the reheated flavor seems to lodge. It's so difficult to keep the stuffed eggs from darkening and drying that I usually pipe in the stuffing (prepared earlier and covered closely) just before the party; but you could do it that morning and sprinkle the tops with finely minced chives, parsley, or ham.

Puff pastry is at its glorious best served fresh from the oven, but you can make, shape, and freeze the dough months in advance, make and refrigerate the ham filling a day early, and assemble the pastries in the morning. Keep chilled until you bake them.

Cut the radish roses the night before, refrigerate them in iced water, stuff them in the morning, and put them back in more iced water.

Oysters and clams keep very well properly packed and refrigerated; buy them a day or two beforehand and store unopened.

Gravlaks, if you're doing it in two pieces, must be started almost a week beforehand and tasted after two days to see how it's doing. If you slice it before salting, three or four days should suffice.

Menu Variations

Puff pastry: The possibilities are limitless—see *Mastering II* and *J.C.'s Kitchen* for many good ideas.

Gravlaks: Salmon is always very expensive and sometimes unobtainable, and (though *laks* means salmon) I find the method for *gravlaks* works beautifully for sea bass and bluefish, and often, as in this menu, I like to serve two kinds. A warning: sole (perhaps because it is so lean) is, I think, less successful in taste and texture.

Peking wings: Using the same general cooking techniques, you could substitute small drumsticks for chicken wings, or pieces of boned chicken breast served on toothpicks.

Oysters and clams: If you don't like your shellfish raw, you can make a noble presentation by boiling a monster lobster, cooling it, and serving the meat, cut in chunks, in the shell. It is simply an old wives' tale that large lobsters are tough. They're delicious.

These are Cotuit oysters from Cape Cod.

Leftovers

Puff pastry: The Pithiviers and the cheese appetizers can be frozen and reheated. Although they will never have quite their glorious original taste, they will still make very good eating.

Gravlaks: Will keep for ten days or so under refrigeration. As to using it hot, I find it very salty if baked or broiled—a good illustration that you oversalt cold dishes slightly, and should exercise restraint with hot ones. However, I have used it in a creamy fish soup, as part of a quiche mixture, with creamed potatoes, and as part of a fish stuffing, since in these cases the surrounding ingredients draw the salt out of the salmon. One has to be careful, of course, not to salt anything else because of the salmon's salt.

Minimeatballs: These can be reheated, or served cold with sliced onions, tomatoes, cucumbers, and so forth. Or you can chop them and add to a hearty soup.

Peking wings: These are delicious cold, but if you want to reheat them, skin them first. The meat is good in a salad, sandwich, or soup.

Oysters and clams: These will keep unopened in the refrigerator for a week or more. They are delicious broiled on the half shell, or in a stew or chowder.

Postscript

I can't leave this cocktail party without again extolling the virtues of French puff pastry. It is now, with this fast method, so easy to make and is so infinitely versatile that I always have a hefty package of it on hand in my freezer. After one television bout some years ago, I kept several batches of it for two years! It thawed, rolled out, and baked just as beautifully as anyone could wish when I finally exhumed it. If you enjoy pastry making, this is a very satisfying dough, all neat and squared when you get the turns going, and it lends elegance to any menu. It even sounds nice when you break or bite into it—something between a crackle, a crunch, and a rustle, like a fire as it kindles.

Essay

An assortment of New England fish and shellfish.

Fish Talk

The average American consumes only eleven pounds of fish a year, which argues that he doesn't like it much…"it" meaning not the whole marvelous universe of fish, but the frozen packaged fillets which are his staple purchase. Habit, I think, is why many of us buy fish that way, habit and caution. Freezing *seems* a safeguard when everybody knows that fish deteriorates from the moment it leaves the sea (unlike meat, which has to be hung for an interval to become tender). And it's true that a good fish which is gutted, filleted, and flash-frozen (in immaculate conditions, and as soon as caught) and which arrives on your stove in no more than three months—having been maintained throughout that time at a temperature of $-5\,°F/-20.5\,°C$—is very fine eating indeed. You will not often find such fish, and only rarely from mass packagers: remember, the majority of them get most of their fish from abroad and cannot control shipboard conditions. I think it's safer to find a dealer you can trust, a specialist in fish who knows his suppliers.

Anyway, if you do buy frozen packaged fillets (and I'd certainly rather have them than no fish at all), open the package in the store and inspect it with a jaundiced eye and alert nostrils. Complain to the manager (who will pass it on and maybe improve his stock) *if:* the cut edges look dry; or the flesh has whitish patches; or there is any discoloration, especially a yellowish or even rusty streak down the center of the fillet's darker side. The same goes for frozen fillets bought by the piece. Frozen whole fish should be completely encased in a glaze of ice, and shrimp should be frozen in their shells in a solid block. Thawed fish should be treated like fresh: bedded on ice in the dealer's case.

If you buy any thawed or fresh fish, remember that fish has no odor when just caught; in the store it should have at most a mild, faint, fresh scent, which I find very appetizing. Insist on the sniff test; and check the thermometer in the freezer compartment: $1\,°F$, no higher—and preferably lower.

Away from the coast, you really can't expect to find the very perishable shellfish, like shrimp and scallops, sold fresh; twenty years ago, any fresh seafood—and all but local freshwater fish, like the beautiful Idaho trout and upper Great Lakes whitefish—was hard to find anywhere inland. But nowadays, with our airfreight network so well developed, with the Bureau of Fisheries' careful policing, and with modern techniques of aquaculture, we could, if we insisted on it, have fresh-caught fish available daily all over the country, at least in cities and towns. Once one has tasted it, little else will do; it's like a sunny day compared to a smoggy one.

It is not difficult to identify fresh-caught fish. The skin color is intense and bright, the gills are bright red inside, the eyes are bright and bulging. After two days, the eyes begin to flatten; don't buy a fish whose eyes are flush with its skin. Another test, especially if you are buying fresh fish by the piece, is to press the flesh with a fingertip; the imprint should quickly disappear. You can soon become expert; but you still need a good dealer. The Japanese Americans, who use only the most

perfect fish in raw dishes like sushi and sashimi, are the people to follow. If you are lucky, like me, in having a local Japanese-American population, find out where they buy fish.

Fresh fish will stay fresh longest when it is kept at a temperature of 30.5°F/−1°C, which you achieve by packing in ice. Incidentally, fish does not freeze at this temperature—water does. The best way to keep fish when you get home is to unwrap it, place it in a plastic bag, and set it in the refrigerator in a bowl of ice sprinkled with a little coarse salt; pour off the water as it accumulates and renew the ice twice a day. Very fresh fish will keep even two or three days when handled this way.

Shellfish must be alive until eaten or cooked. When you buy bivalves (oysters, clams, mussels, scallops, etc.), they should be tightly closed. If the shells are slightly ajar, rap them sharply; they should close at once. If any bivalve feels unduly light, it means the occupant is dead. If unduly heavy (especially in the case of clams or mussels), the shell may be full of seabed sand or mud. Don't use any with chipped or broken shells.

The general rule for storing bivalves is to take them home promptly, scrub the shells thoroughly with a stiff brush, and refrigerate. Cover oysters with dampened paper towels and foil, and be sure to store them with the larger, more convex side down so the oyster may bathe, and live, in its juices.

Now that the sturgeon are returning to a few of our refreshed rivers, it may not be long before we're all preparing a cheap and nutritious household staple: our own caviar. Meanwhile, since we have relearned the 2000-year-old art of oyster culture, oyster prices are on the decline. Where I live, a dozen great succulent Cotuits, so fresh they twitch under a squirt of lemon juice, cost less than a good delicatessen sandwich. I hope they (or another good variety) are available where you live; and there's no reason they shouldn't be. Refrigerated properly, they keep an amazing four weeks after harvesting; certainly you are safe in storing them at least a week after buying

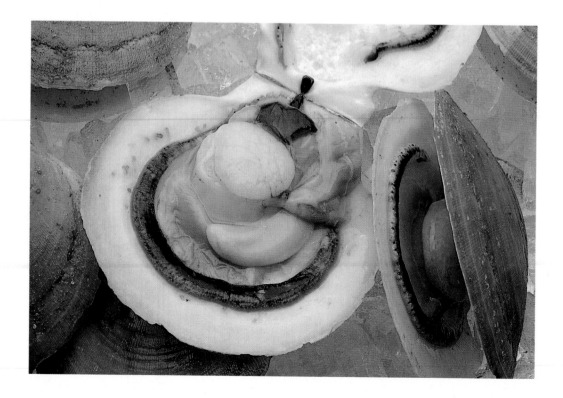

them. In the 1880s, my own grandmother in rural Illinois would have oysters shipped from the East during the winter months and always kept a barrel of them in her cellar.

Always open oysters *as,* not before, you eat them; savor the flesh and every drop of the liquor, and you will have tasted the very essence of the living, fertile sea. In our family we eat them with spoons rather than the conventional forks, and drink the liquor from the shell.

Except—perhaps—at breakfast (a fine time for them), oysters are best accompanied by quartered lemons, a pepper grinder, buttered dark bread, and a dry white wine. They aren't that hard to open—after all, some Stone Age peoples managed—but since, unlike those of the other bivalves, oysters' shells seal tightly shut and, moreover, overlap, it's difficult to find the seal itself. Oysters can be obdurate, and I am afraid many of us give up and buy them already shucked by a professional. His method is to use a strong, long-bladed knife, both for levering the shells apart and for scraping the inside of each shell in order to detach the firm adductor muscle which binds shell to flesh. I've learned something new since I described this method in detail (in *J.C.'s Kit-*

chen). The oyster's hinge is not as strong as its muscle, and you can lever the shells apart by using an ordinary beer can opener: place the oyster curved side down, hinge toward you; poke around the hinge for an opening into which you can plunge the point of the opener— its curved side down—thrust it in, pry open the hinge, and you'll hear it pop. Once the shells part slightly, use an oyster knife, or even a paring knife, to sever the muscle under the top shell, northeast-by-east side. Protect the oyster-holding hand with a pot holder, and don't jab or shove.

For the occasional diehard, try the conventional method of opening at the side, using an oyster knife. If that doesn't work, the fol-

lowing two methods are inelegant but sure-fire. You can "bill" oysters by knocking off a bit of the lip with a hammer, producing a crevice for your knife tip. Or you can heat them quickly in a 450°F/230°C oven or over a burner, just till the shells part. The flesh will still be cold.

Other bivalves aren't so firmly sealed, which makes them easier to open and harder to keep. Unlike oysters, they should be stored uncovered in circulating air; and, if you ice them, be sure to pour off the melt frequently. The illustration below shows a clam-opening procedure.

To open scallops, the easiest of the lot, just feel with your knife for a vulnerable spot in the seam between the shells, starting about one-third of the way outward from the hinge, and simply lever open. Actually, it's most unlikely you'll be able to buy scallops in their beautiful fluted shells (since these take too much room in the scallop boats' holds). But if you do get some, don't throw away the delicious red or golden tongue-shaped roe, which constitutes one-third of the scallop. Eat it raw or in a *seviche* (see "Chafing-Dish Dinner," page 183), or cooked—just as you would the white portion, which is the scallop's muscle and the only part you can usually buy in fish stores. And when you buy them, keep them iced and eat them soon; they don't keep longer than a day or so.

Crustaceans are arthropods, meaning creatures with jointed feet: shrimp, lobsters, various kinds of crab, and crayfish. The best way to buy shrimp, since only one percent of the catch is sold fresh, is frozen: in their shells, in a solid block. (See Remarks in "Lo-Cal Banquet," page 40, for details.) Incidentally, when you see the word "scampi" on a restaurant menu, it undoubtedly means shrimp, since *scampi* is Italian for the rare "Dublin Bay" prawns or langoustine, small lobsterlike sea creatures.

The best-known crabs of the Atlantic are the blue crabs, which when molting are known as soft-shell crabs and are cooked and eaten almost whole; when their shells are hard, you boil them, as you do all other kinds of crab. Unless you live in Alaska, you are not likely to acquire a king crab fresh, and if you did, you might find it an alarming guest: one enormous leg can make a couple of servings. Generally,

These are Eastern bay scallops, the female has an orange roe, the male gray roe. The fluted shell belongs to the European scallop. (Below) Pulling out the black intestinal vein from a shrimp.

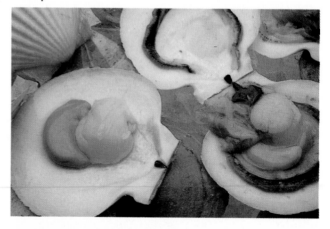

To open clams, insert knife one-third of the way down from the hinge; press, using the fingers of your other hand for leverage; and pry open.

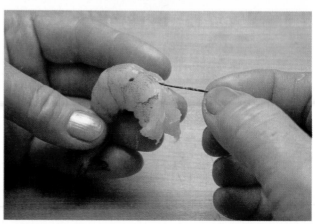

king crabs are sold boiled and frozen in the shell, in segments. Two other well-known varieties are the large delicious Dungeness crab of the Pacific and the stone crab of Florida.

The thing to remember about frozen crabmeat, which is what most of us buy—or really about any frozen flesh—is to thaw it slowly, in the refrigerator, so that lingering ice crystals don't pierce the thawing flesh, making it mushy. An excellent alternative to frozen crabmeat is canned pasteurized crab, which will keep for months in the refrigerator.

There's not space here—or anywhere!— to say all I want to about fish and shellfish: their thousands of fascinating species, their variety of life cycles, their value and their vulnerability, their beauty and their excellence. Though overfishing, careless fishing, and pollution have badly depleted our supply, we can take heart—provided we and our elected representatives remain vigilant. New regulations and treaties, and new techniques of water management and of sea farming (as well as pond and river farming) are gradually changing all that. Thank goodness, for fish is a good source of protein and trace minerals, has about one-quarter the calories of meat, is more easily digested, cooks many times faster (saving energy), and uses Earth's resources better. An acre of sea can produce 23 tons of oyster meat, for example—150 times the weight of beef produced by an acre of pasture.

The best specific information you can get, and the most up to date (for their research is unending), is from the U.S. Bureau of Fisheries. Its devoted, diligent, and cooperative public servants will share their expertise and enthusiasm with you for the price of a telephone call. For the moment I have to content myself with summarizing my advice in four maxims whose initials—with a wrench or two—spell FISH. Buy fish and shellfish *fresh* whenever you can; buy from an *immaculately* clean place; *store* it on ice; and eat it in a *hurry*.

These lovely crabs are (clockwise from left) the Alaskan king crab, stone crab claws, Dungeness, blue crabs (female with roe), and soft shell crabs.

An impressive dinner for guests who like their food conservative and luxurious; and a dissertation on choosing, trimming, and roasting fine beef.

Dinner for the Boss

Menu

Consommé Brunoise
Melba Toast

Standing Rib Roast of Beef
Timbale of Fresh Corn
Brussels Sprouts Tossed in Butter

Macédoine of Fruits in Champagne
Bourbon-soaked Chocolate Truffles

Suggested wines:
A fine full-bodied Burgundy or Pinot Noir;
Champagne with dessert

What I mean at the moment by "boss," you might mean by the Queen of England or the Chairman of the Membership Committee: a formidable personage (a) whom you want to impress and (b) whose taste in food runs to the conservative, the expensive, and the simple. For somebody like that, I think automatically of roast beef. Like the "Blue Danube," it may be square, but it's wonderful and everybody loves it. Before spending all that money, though, we ought to know a few things about the choosing and roasting of beef. However, roast beef isn't the only possible choice for the boss, so in case it is too expensive for you, I have listed a number of other ideas in Menu Variations, farther on.

Speaking of menus, I all but fell into an elementary planning error myself when I did this meal. I wanted to end it with a knockout blow, like a soufflé, and was mooning over the extravagances of Escoffier: Soufflé à la Régence? à la Reine? Rothschild? Sans-Souci? Vésuvienne? But, running an imaginary tongue over the succession of dishes, I tasted an over-richness, an imbalance... anyway, something wrong. The soufflé on top of the timbale was the trouble, I realized: eggs twice. It wrecks a menu to repeat ingredients, so I eliminated the soufflé.

As for the timbale, I never even used to consider recipes that called for grated fresh corn. It was just too much work to run a knife point down every single row on the ear and then to scrape out the milk and pulp with the back of the blade. Then my brother-in-law gave me a wooden corn scraper one Christmas, and, mad to use it, I discovered that fresh corn was available almost all year round. I confess I had never looked at it before—dismissing it as inedible out of the summer season. But I found it delicious when scraped off the cob with my new grater and turned into cream-style dishes. I also discovered that there are a number of scraper gadgets on the market, mostly available through mail-order catalogues for country-store type places.

Then, given the warm colors and flavors of the beef and the corn, I wanted a strong-tasting, unstarchy green vegetable with some crunch—so, Brussels sprouts. Green, I say; and crunchy, I insist. Overcooking has given the cabbage family a bad odor and a bad name. Apropos, I remember a story about my old *maître,* Chef Max Bugnard, who did one stage of his classic apprenticeship at a station hotel in London where, he related, cabbage was boiled for several hours, drained, piled into a round platter, and formed into a solid cake by jamming it hard against the kitchen wall. Then this cabbage cake was placed in a steamer and sliced into wedges on demand. Chef said it was years before he could bear boiled cabbage again, or any member of the cabbage family,

for that matter. I thought of him in our TV studio when our director wanted a boiling pot on the stove; we didn't think to change the water after lifting out our Brussels sprouts, and pretty soon a dismal reek, familiar from bad old days and bad old hotels, began to overwhelm the fresh aromas of corn and beef. The smell bore no relation to the briefly boiled emerald green sprouts awaiting their final toss in hot butter; it simply proved once again that overboiling the cabbage family produces nauseating results.

Green, red, and gold on the plate, the sprouts, beef, and corn demand a pretty dessert. Something cool and delicate, too, not puddingy after the timbale, but something inviting to the tooth. So, I thought, fruit—with a splash of Champagne for tingle. The sparkling macédoine's name, incidentally, means any kind of a combination of fruits—or vegetables—from Alexander of Macedon, whose vast empire included so many disparate populations.

The consommé, though it comes first, was my last decision. Something light before beef, something classic to please the boss, something hot and savory to kindle a good appetite. The brunoise garnish of minced vegetables looks like a scattering of jewels and adds a fresh flavor to the strong winy broth. A pleasantly crisp accompaniment when you don't want anything buttery like cheese straws is homemade Melba toast. The only difficulty with that, however, is finding a loaf of plain nonsweet white sandwich bread that is unsliced. The last time I traipsed all over town to find unsliced bread, I realized I would have saved myself time and energy had I made my own!

The truffles (so called because they look vaguely like the rare underground fungus sniffed out by special dogs—sometimes pigs—in the oak groves of Périgord and sold like diamonds to bosses and their ilk) were not a decision but a fantasy. They are fun to make and unctuous to the tongue: a luxurious final touch.

Preparations

Recommended Equipment:
A corn scraper, as previously mentioned, is virtually essential for the timbale recipe.

Marketing and Storage:
Staples to have on hand

Salt
Peppercorns
Hot pepper sauce or Cayenne pepper
Grated cheese (in the freezer; see page 6)
Fresh bread crumbs (in the freezer; see page 6)
Unsalted butter (½ pound or 225 g)
Eggs (6)
Heavy cream (½ pint or ¼ L)
Onions (6)
Carrots (6)
Garlic
Fresh parsley and/or other fresh herbs
Bay leaves
Dried thyme
Wines and liqueurs: Port, Madeira, or sherry;
	dry white wine or dry white French vermouth; bourbon whiskey or dark
	Jamaica rum

Specific ingredients for this menu

Prime roast of beef, fully trimmed (3 to 5 ribs)
Consommé (2 quarts or liters)
Unsliced nonsweet white sandwich bread, 1
	day old (1 loaf)
Gingersnaps, best-quality (6 ounces or 180 g)
Semisweet baking chocolate (7 ounces or 200 g)
Unsweetened baking chocolate (1 ounce or 30 g)
Unsweetened cocoa powder (½ cup or
	2 ounces, or 60 g)
Instant coffee (¼ cup or 1 ounce, or 30 g)
Celery (2 stalks)
Leeks (2)
White turnips (2)
Fresh green beans (¼ pound or 115 g)
Fresh corn (12 to 14 ears)
Fresh fine Brussels sprouts (two to three 10-
	ounce or 285-g packages)
Fruits for the dessert (see recipe)
Ripe tomatoes (1)
Champagne for dessert (2 bottles)

How to Buy and Trim a Rib Roast of Beef

A rib roast comes from one side of the steer's back and includes the ribs from the primal (wholesaler's) "rib" cut only. As you can see from the drawing, the ribs are cut off at two-thirds their length from the backbone (or chine, pronounced "shine").

The primal cut looks like this (opposite, left) when it comes from the wholesaler to your butcher. Nothing has been removed but the hide.

On the fat, notice the purple U.S. Department of Agriculture grade stamp. This particular cut is stamped Prime, or top quality, which means that the beef has firm, pale fat and that the lean is bright red and well marbled. Marbling refers to the white web of fat diffused in three dimensions throughout the lean. The meat has a tender, close-grained, glossy texture. Not all butchers carry top-quality, Prime beef since it is in great demand by hotels and restaurants. (Incidentally, the term "prime rib roast of beef" refers to the beef quality, not to the ribs themselves.) The next grade of beef is labeled Choice and is very good, too, although not as heavy and not as marbled. Frankly, I would not buy a beef roast at all if it were not at least Choice in grade; I would pick another cut or kind of meat.

Under the thick outer layer of fat lie two thinnish pieces, called "cap meat," which though sometimes left on should really be removed since they are for pot-roasting.

The short rib ends should be sawed off close to the end of the rib-eye meat. The ends nearest the shoulder are trimmed of excess fat and may be braised; the others, with less meat, are scraped clean and the meat is used for hamburger. The backbone or chine should be sawed off and all vestiges of it removed for ease in carving. There is also a tough nerve running along the top outside edge, which should be cut out.

Here is a cross section of a rib roast showing the differences between the small or loin end, with its solid eye of meat, and the large or shoulder end. Note that the meat from the shoulder end shows separations and that the eye of the roast is smaller. Note also the cap of meat under the top layer of fat; you are paying roast beef prices for stew meat here.

In other words, the choice end of the roast is the small end; you should know what you are asking for and call it by the right name. If you say you want "the first four ribs," you have made a meaningless and confusing request since ribs are officially numbered from the neck or shoulder end. Ribs numbers 1 through 5 are part of the shoulder. Ribs numbers 6 through 12 are part of the rib roast, and the ribs nearest the loin are the ones you want: numbers 12, 11, 10, 9, and 8—if you want a 5-rib roast. You can also request "a roast from the small end," but you are safer specifying both "small end" and rib numbers.

This is a 5-rib roast from the small end, ribs 8 through 12, trimmed and ready for the

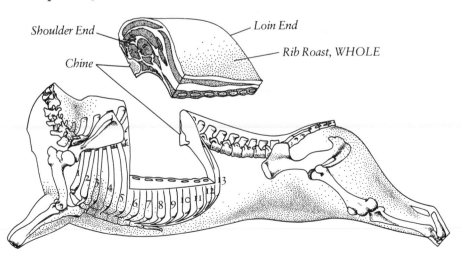

Shoulder End

Chine

Loin End

Rib Roast, WHOLE

oven. It is a Prime roast, weighs 11½ pounds (5¼ kg), and takes 2½ hours in a 325°F/170°C oven—or some 13 minutes per pound—for the internal temperature at the small (loin) end to reach 120°F/49°C, meaning that the loin half will be pinky-red rare, and the large end red rare. It will serve 14 to 16 people. So why buy such a large roast for 6 people when a 3-rib roast would do? Well, if I am going to have a roast of beef at all, I like a big one, since I can use it twice for guests, once hot and once cold. And any leftovers will provide a plush family meal, sliced and carefully reheated in foil.

Meat Temperatures:

We like rare beef in our family, and I find that 120°F/49°C at the small end is just right for us. That means the temperature before the beef is removed from the oven, since it gradually goes up when you take the roast out and soon reaches 130°F/54°C because the hot juices at the outside layer of meat recirculate into the interior, raising the temperature accordingly. Please note, however, that a temperature of 140°F/60°C before the roast is taken out of the oven—meaning 5 minutes or so longer per pound or half kilo, and a pinky-gray color—is the official safe temperature for cooked meats, where salmonella and other sick-making bacteria are surely killed off. Thus we rare-meat lovers eat red beef at our own peril and should be sure of our butchers, restaurateurs, and other purveyors of raw and/or rare beef.

Speaking of temperatures, I do think an accurate meat thermometer is essential for the home cook, and the instant or microwave oven thermometer illustrated here is available in most good cookware shops; put it in the meat and leave 30 seconds to give it time to register, then take it out—it does not roast with the meat. The advantage here, besides accuracy, is that you can test several areas of the meat, since all do not register the same; this is particularly true of legs of lamb, where the circumference varies from one part to another.

Roasting Methods and Roasting Times:

There is certainly more than one way to roast beef. Some cooks swear by the slow roasting method, where the meat goes in a preheated 200°F/95°C oven for 1 hour per pound—per-

Short rib ends and backbone, sawed off

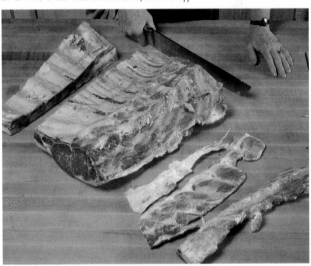

Primal cut

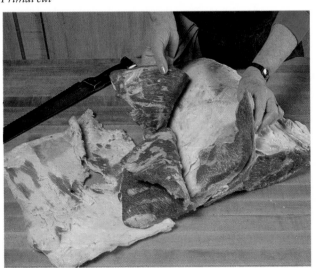

Loin end (above) and shoulder end (below)

fect meat, no loss of weight, and so forth, say they. Other cooks are equally enthusiastic about the Anne Seranne/Craig Claiborne system, whereby you have your ready-to-roast ribs of beef at room temperature and place the meat in a preheated 500°F/260°C oven for exactly 15 minutes per rib; you then turn off the oven and never open its door for 2 hours or even 3 or 4 hours—crunchy brown outside and beautifully rare inside.

As for myself, I like to feel in complete control of my roast of beef, and find that an even 325°F/170°C works well for me with large roasts of three ribs or more. For smaller pieces, which might not brown sufficiently in their shorter roasting times, I sear them first at 450°F/230°C for 15 minutes, then reduce the thermostat to 325°F/170°C for the rest of the roasting, periodically checking the internal temperature with a meat thermometer well before the end of the estimated time. As soon as the instrument registers 105°F/41°C, I check every 5 minutes or so since the temperature can go up rapidly from then on. Here is the meat roasting chart that I use:

Chart for Roast Ribs of Beef

Choice graded roasts will usually be a little lighter in weight and take a little less time per pound to roast than Prime ribs. In addition, the particular way your market trims its roast determines its total weight, such as how much or little fat is left on, how close to the eye—the main muscle of meat—the ribs have been sawed off, how much of the backbone has been removed, and how much of the cap meat remains on the roast. I calculate 13 minutes per pound (or 450 grams) for rare-roasted, fully trimmed Prime ribs, and about 12 for Choice. The following chart gives rib counts and the weights and time estimates I have figured out for roasts of beef, but timing—if your roast weighs less than the rib count shown here—should be based on weight. Any chart, however, is only a guide, and you must rely on your accurate meat thermometer, starting to take temperatures half an hour before the end of the estimated roasting time. As for number of servings, it is safe to count on 2 people per rib of roast beef, which gives generous helpings and perhaps some leftovers.

Rib Count	Approximate Weight	Oven Temperature*	Total Estimated Time	Meat Thermometer Reading (Rare)†
2 ribs	4–5 lb (1¾–2¼ kg)	450–325°F** (230–170°C)	60–70 minutes	120°F/49°C
3 ribs	7–8½ lb (3–3¼ kg)	325°F/170°C	1½–1¾ hours	120°F/49°C
4 ribs	9–10½ lb (4–5 kg)	325°F/170°C	1¾–2¼ hours	120°F/49°C
5 ribs	11–13½ lb (5–6 kg)	325°F/170°C	2¼–2¾ hours	120°F/49°C
6 ribs††	14–16 lb (6¼–7¼ kg)	325°F/170°C	3–3¼ hours	120°F/49°C
7 ribs††	16–18½ lb (7¼–8½ kg)	325°F/170°C	3¼–4 hours	120°F/49°C

*   Be sure your oven thermostat is correct, or your timing will be way off.

**   Sear a 2-rib roast for 15 minutes at the higher temperature, then turn to the lower temperature for the rest of the cooking.

††   I do think you are better off with two 3- or 4-rib roasts than a single 6- or 7-rib one simply because those last 2 ribs at the large end are the least desirable; however, there is no denying the grandeur of that one magnificent spread of meat.

†   Add 2 to 3 minutes more per pound for less-rare beef (125°F/52°C), and medium-rare (130°F/54°C), and 5 to 6 minutes per pound more for medium (140°F/60°C).

Consommé Brunoise

Consommé garnished with very finely chopped fresh vegetables

Homemade consommé is a wonderful treat, and I shan't go into the making of it since it is in both *Mastering I* and *J.C.'s Kitchen*. When I haven't had the time to make my own, however, I have used some excellent canned consommés, one of which is a duck bouillon. Browse among the shelves of your fancy food store, try out several brands, then stock up on your favorites for emergencies. (There is no reason to be a food snob about canned consommés, say I, since one can simmer them with a little wine or dry white vermouth, some chopped onions, carrots, celery, and herbs, and come up with a very respectable brew for the following recipe.)

For 6 people

The garnish

1/3 cup (¾ dL) each of the following vegetables, very finely and neatly diced into 1/16-inch (¼-cm) pieces: carrots, onions, celery, white of leek, white turnips, fresh green beans

2 Tb butter

Salt and pepper

About 2 quarts (2 L) excellently flavored consommé

Several Tb dry Port, Madeira, or sherry

Several Tb minced fresh chervil, parsley, and/or chives

Reserve the beans. In a covered saucepan, cook the other vegetables slowly in the butter until nicely tender but not browned, then season to taste and simmer several minutes in a cup or so of the consommé. Blanch the beans in a quart of lightly salted boiling water just until barely tender, drain, and refresh in cold water.

🕐 May be completed well in advance to this point.

Shortly before serving, pour the remaining consommé into the simmered vegetables and bring to the simmer; add the blanched beans and taste very carefully for seasoning. Off heat, stir in driblets of wine to taste. Pour either into a tureen or into individual soup cups and decorate with the chopped herbs.

Remarks:

You can simmer rice, tiny pasta, or tapioca in the soup to give it more body. You can also finish it off with a poaching of finely diced fresh tomato pulp, which adds a pretty blush of color. You are aiming for delicious flavor as well as colorful effect, and should feel free to let your fancy roam—and that can include diced truffles and mushrooms, too.

Melba Toast

Melba toast couldn't be simpler to make if you can just find the right kind of unsliced bread. The best is a nonsweet sandwich loaf, close grained and a day old—a recipe for just such a loaf is in both *Mastering II* and *J.C.'s Kitchen*. Cut the bread into very very thin slices 1/16 inch (¼ cm) thick; either leave slices whole or cut diagonally into triangles. Arrange, in one layer preferably, on one or two pastry sheets and bake slowly in the upper and lower-middle levels of a preheated 275°F/140°C oven for about 20 minutes, or until the bread has dried out and is starting to color lightly. Cool on a rack.

🕐   May be done well in advance, and recrisped in the oven before serving. May be refrigerated or frozen.

Standing Rib Roast of Beef

A 5-rib fully trimmed Prime or Choice roast of beef (or a 3- or 4-rib roast, timed according to roasting chart earlier in this chapter)
2 Tb soft butter
2 medium-size carrots, roughly chopped
2 medium-size onions, roughly chopped
2 cups (½ L) excellent beef broth (see directions at end of recipe)
Equipment
A reliable meat thermometer; a low-sided roasting pan (2½ inches or 6½ cm deep); a rack to fit the pan

For accurate timing, particularly if you are doing a 3-rib roast, leave the meat out at room temperature an hour before it is to go into the oven. And, since I always like plenty of leeway, I start my roasting half an hour to an hour ahead of schedule; in other words, I estimate that a 5-rib roast will take 2½ hours, so I start it 3 to 3½ hours before I plan to serve. It is easy to keep it warm, as you will see at the end of the recipe, and I want to be sure I get it done on time.

Therefore, 3 to 3½ hours before serving, have oven preheated to 325°F/170°C and rack placed in lower level. Smear cut ends of beef with the butter and place it fat side up (ribs down) on the rack in the roasting pan. Set in oven, and there is nothing more to do than rapidly baste the cut ends with accumulated fat from the roasting pan every half hour and, about an hour before the end of the roasting time, strew the chopped vegetables into the pan. Then, half an hour later (in this case, after 2 hours of roasting), start checking temperature. When the thermometer reaches 105°F/41°C, watch closely and check every 7 minutes or so, until desired temperature is reached—about 2½ hours in all. The small end will register the highest temperature, and if you want some meat pinky-red rare and the rest very rare, roast to 120°F/49°C. On the other hand, if you want the small end medium rare and the large end pinky red, roast a few minutes more, to 125°F/52°C, and so forth for more doneness. As soon as the temperature has been reached remove the roast from the oven.

🕐 Keeping the roast warm until serving time: If you know your oven is absolutely accurate and that you can keep it at around 115°F/46°C, turn it off, remove roast, leave door open to cool oven for 15 minutes, then set thermostat at 115°F/46°C and return roast to oven. You can safely keep it in the oven for an hour or two, even longer; the meat and its juices, communing together, make for even more delicious eating. Otherwise let the roast cool out of the oven for 15 minutes, then set it over a large kettle of hot but not simmering water; place the top of a covered roaster or a large pan over the beef to keep it warm. Leave meat thermometer in place and check every 15 minutes or so to be sure everything is under control. The temperature will rise some 10°F/5°C at first, then gradually subside; 100°F/38°C is plenty warm enough for serving.

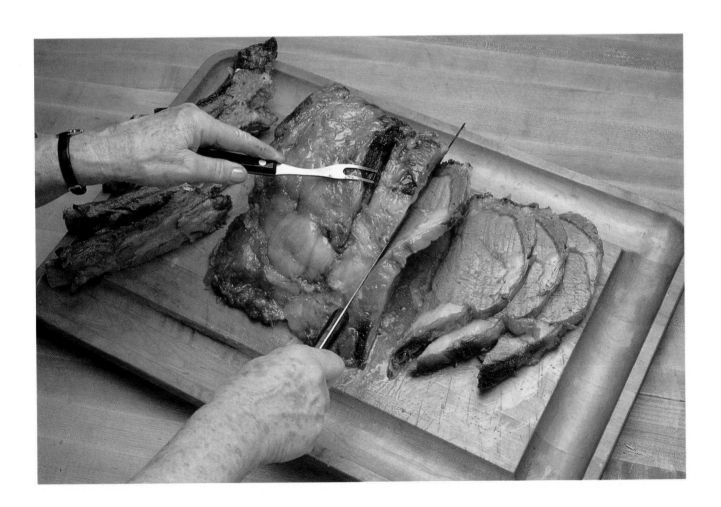

For the sauce or "jus"

Remove beef from roasting pan, pour out accumulated fat, pour in the beef stock, and swish about to dislodge any coagulated roasting juices (there will be little of these if you have roasted to very rare). Pour the liquid and roasting vegetables from the pan into a saucepan and simmer, mashing the vegetables into the liquid. Season carefully to taste, and skim off surface fat. Just before serving, strain into a hot sauce bowl, adding also any juices accumulated from the waiting roast. You should have a tablespoon or so per serving.

To serve

You may wish to bring the roast to the table just as it is, perhaps garnishing the platter with watercress or sprigs of parsley. However, I like to remove the rib bones in the kitchen (another reason for getting the roast done ahead of time); I turn it upside down and cut close against the line of bones, then cut the bones apart. To serve, I set the roast right side up on a big carving board, place the bones at one end, and if there is no enthusiastic carver at the table, I slice a first helping of meat and arrange that at the cut end of the roast. This makes for easy serving, plus the promise of big bones on the plates of those who love them.

Beef Stock:

Brown a pound or more of chopped meaty raw beef bones in a little cooking oil with a chopped onion and carrot, then add a medium-size chopped but unpeeled tomato, 1 cup (¼ L) dry white wine or vermouth, water to cover ingredients by 2 inches (5 cm), and the following, tied in washed cheesecloth: 1 bay leaf, ½ teaspoon thyme, 6 parsley sprigs, and 2 cloves unpeeled garlic. Simmer partially covered for 3 to 4 hours, adding more water if liquid evaporates below level of ingredients. Strain, degrease, and refrigerate or freeze until needed. You will want 1 cup (¼ L) for 6 people; double the amount for 12 to 14.

Timbale of Fresh Corn

*For an 8-cup baking dish, serving
8 people*

12 or more ears fresh corn (to make about 3
cups or ¾ L cream-style grated corn)

6 eggs

2 to 3 Tb grated onion

1 tsp salt

4 to 5 Tb fresh minced parsley

⅔ cup (1½ dL) lightly pressed down crumbs
from crustless nonsweet white bread

⅔ cup (1½ dL) lightly pressed down grated
cheese (such as a mixture of Swiss and/or
Cheddar or mozzarella)

⅔ cup (1½ dL) heavy cream

6 drops hot pepper sauce (or ⅛ tsp Cayenne
pepper)

8 to 10 grinds fresh pepper

Equipment

A corn scraper or grater; a straight-sided 8-cup
(2-L) baking dish, such as a charlotte mold 5 to
6 inches (13 to 15 cm) deep, and a larger baking dish in which to set it

Scrape or grate the corn and turn into a measure to be sure you have about 3 cups or ¾
liter. Beat the eggs in a mixing bowl to blend;
then add all the rest of the ingredients listed,
including the corn.

🕐 Recipe may be completed even a day in
advance to this point; cover and refrigerate.

Preheat oven to 350°F/180°C. About 2
hours before serving, butter the 8-cup (2-L)
baking dish and line bottom with a round of
buttered wax paper. Stir up the corn mixture
to blend thoroughly and pour into the dish. Set
corn dish in larger dish and pour boiling water
around to come two-thirds up the sides of the
corn-filled dish. Bake in lower-middle level of
oven for half an hour, then turn thermostat
down to 325°F/170°C. Baking time is around
1¼ to 1½ hours, and water surrounding timbale should almost but never quite bubble; too
high heat can make a custard (which this is)
grainy. Timbale is done when it has risen
almost to fill the mold, the top has cracked
open, and a skewer plunged down through the
center comes out clean. Let rest 10 minutes or
more in turned-off oven, door ajar, before
unmolding.

🕐 May be baked an hour or so before serving; the timbale will sink down as it cools, but
who would ever know how high it might have
been, once it is unmolded?

Brussels Sprouts Tossed in Butter

Here is one method for serving Brussels sprouts that are fresh and bright green. Blanch them until just cooked through, drain and cool them, halve or cut them into thirds, and set aside until just before serving. Then toss them in a big frying pan in hot butter and seasonings, just to heat them through, and serve them forth. A marvelous vegetable when done this way.

For 6 people

Two to three 10-ounce (285-g) packages fine fresh green hard-headed Brussels sprouts

Salt

4 or more Tb butter

Pepper

Equipment

A kettle large enough to hold at least 6 quarts or liters water

Preparing sprouts for cooking
One by one, pull any small or withered leaves off root end of sprouts, shave root close to base of remaining leaves (but not so close that leaves will come loose); with a small knife,

pierce a cross ⅜ inch (1 cm) deep in root ends —to make for fast and even cooking. Throw out any wilted or soft-headed sprouts.

🕐   May be prepared in advance even a day before cooking; cover and refrigerate.

Preliminary cooking—blanching
Fill a large kettle with at least 6 quarts or liters of water, adding 1½ teaspoons salt per quart or liter. Cover and bring to the rapid boil. Meanwhile wash the sprouts under cold running water. (Old recipes call for soaking sprouts in salted water, presumably to make them disgorge bugs, weevils, ants, and whatnot. I have never found any such fauna in any of my Brussels sprouts, and have therefore never done more than simply wash them rapidly.) When water is boiling, plunge in the sprouts, cover kettle, and as soon as water boils again uncover and boil slowly for 4 or 5 minutes. Sprouts are done when just cooked through but still slightly crunchy and bright green—taste one or two, to verify the cooking. Drain them at once, by holding a colander in the kettle and pouring off the water. Then, with colander still in place, run cold water into the kettle to refresh the sprouts, to set the green color, and to preserve the fresh texture. Drain in a moment or two, then halve the sprouts lengthwise, or cut into thirds, to make them all the same size.

🕐   May be prepared several hours in advance to this point; arrange in a bowl, cover, and refrigerate.

Final cooking
Between courses, and just before serving, melt as much butter as you think sensible and/or decent in a large frying pan, add the sprouts, and toss and turn (shaking and twirling pan by its handle rather than stirring with a spoon). Season to taste with salt and pepper, and sample a sprout or two to be sure they are thoroughly heated through.

Serving
Either turn the sprouts into a hot vegetable dish or surround the preceding unmolded timbale of fresh corn.

Macédoine of Fruits in Champagne

Plan as attractive a mixture of cut-up fruits as you can muster, considering the season of the year. Summer is ideal, of course, with fresh apricots, peaches, cherries, berries, and all the bounties the warm months can offer. December is more of a problem. However, one can still have fresh oranges and grapefruit cut into skinless segments, an occasional strawberry or melon, pineapple, bananas, and grapes to peel and seed. And there are nuts to sliver or chop, and shavings of ginger (either candied or fresh). And, of course, the canned and frozen fruits that can marry with the fresh. Among canned fruits I do like figs in syrup, dark purple plums, and sometimes mandarin or tangerine segments, as well as the exotic fragrance of a few kumquats, sliced thin and seeded. Frozen blueberries have the charm of deep purple for color, and sometimes whole strawberries are successful. I shall not offer a combination since it is too personal and seasonal a dish, but I do suggest a careful design plan for the arrangement, squeezings of lemon, and sprinklings of kirsch, white rum, or Cognac, if you like such additions. Let the fruits macerate together in their covered serving bowl in the refrigerator for several hours, and taste frequently in case more lemon, or even orange juice, or liqueurs are needed—and you may want to drain off some of the juices before serving. Then, at the table, and just before ladling out, pour some Champagne from the bottle either into the serving bowl or into each dish—that fizzling sudden sparkle of foam transforms a simple collection of cut-up fruits into a dressy *macédoine au Champagne*. Then pour out a glass of the same Champagne for each guest, to accompany the fruit.

Bourbon-soaked Chocolate Truffles

For 12 to 18 pieces

7 ounces (200 g) semisweet baking chocolate

1 ounce (30 g) unsweetened baking chocolate

4 Tb bourbon whiskey or dark Jamaica rum

2 Tb strong coffee

1 stick (4 ounces or 115 g) unsalted butter, cut into 1-inch (2-cm) pieces

6 ounces (180 g) best-quality gingersnaps (to make ¾ cup or 1¾ dL pulverized)

½ cup (1 dL) unsweetened cocoa powder

¼ cup (½ dL) powdered instant coffee

Equipment

Paper or foil candy cups

The mixture

Break up the two chocolates and place in a small saucepan with the bourbon or rum and the liquid coffee. Cover, set chocolate pan in a larger pan of boiling water, and turn off the heat under it. When chocolate is melted and smooth, in 5 minutes or so, beat in the butter piece by piece (a portable electric mixer is useful here), then the pulverized gingersnaps. Chill for several hours.

Forming the truffles

Mix the cocoa powder with the powdered coffee and spread on a plate. With a soup spoon or teaspoon, depending on the size you wish, dig out gobs of the chocolate mixture and form into rough, roundish, rocklike, trufflelike shapes. Roll in the cocoa and coffee powder, and place in candy or cookie cups. Refrigerate in a covered container until serving time.

🕐   Truffles may be kept under refrigeration for several weeks or frozen.

🕐 *Timing*

Since this menu calls for two dishes that need oven cooking, the beef and the corn timbale, can you manage with only one oven? If it's big enough you can put the corn in with the beef. Since you can roast the beef and keep it warm over hot water, as described in the recipe, you can bake the corn after you remove the beef. But with only one oven, you may wish to substitute another vegetable for the corn timbale, attractive as it is; suggestions for other vegetables are in the following section.

In any case, you have few last-minute jobs. The Brussels sprouts, which have been lightly precooked, are tossed in hot butter between courses while you arrange the beef for serving. The timbale stays warm in its baking dish and is unmolded just before serving, and then you can surround it with the hot sprouts. All you do before dinner is check on your beef, remove its ribs if you wish to do so, and reheat the consommé.

An hour before your guests arrive, the timbale goes into the oven and, if you can control oven temperatures, your roast is done and cooling, to be kept safely at 115° to 120°F (45° to 50°C) until you are ready to serve it.

Two hours before dinner, chill the Champagne, stir the final flavorings into your macédoine of fruits, and let it continue macerating in the refrigerator.

Three to three and a half hours before serving, put the roast in the oven. You have set it out at room temperature an hour beforehand, and the oven has been preheated.

In the morning, prepare the vegetables for the soup, blanch the beans (also for the soup), trim and blanch the sprouts, prepare the timbale, and compose the fruits for the dessert.

If you are making your own consommé, you can do so days in advance—it freezes nicely, as do the chocolate truffles and the simple beef stock for the roasting sauce.

Menu Variations, of a Conservative Sort

The soup: Consommé variations are infinite, as a quick trot through Escoffier or even *J.C.'s Kitchen* will show you. You could change from consommé to clams or oysters, or cold lobster or crab as an appetizer. I'm always partial to fish soup, but that might offend a conservative meat-and-potato palate. Better stick to consommé or shellfish.

The roast: Substitute a rib eye of beef (meaning the roast is boned); a sirloin strip—a fine boneless roast this is, less dramatic than the rib but easy to carve; a well-aged Prime rump roast; or a tenderloin. Try a roast leg of veal, if you can get a large, Prime, pale, and perfect piece—not easy. Or roast leg of lamb, if you have an expert carver to handle it. Saddle of lamb is elegant but needs carving expertise, too. Though a roast loin of pork and fresh ham are delicious, they are never considered as dressy for this kind of occasion, unless you know the tastes of your principal guests.

The vegetables: Instead of fresh corn for the timbale, you could use spinach, broccoli, or cauliflower—but these alternative vegetables should be blanched, chopped, and turned in butter first; grated zucchini should be squeezed dry and sautéed in butter. Cauliflower or zucchini timbale surrounded by fresh peas would be lovely. Sautéed mushrooms could surround a timbale of spinach or broccoli. Rather than using a high molded structure for the timbale, you could bake it in a ring mold and pile the other vegetables in the middle for serving. You could get away from the timbale idea entirely and serve braised lettuce or endive and cleverly cut sautéed potatoes or scalloped potatoes, with something colorful and red, like tomatoes Provençal or baked cherry tomatoes.

The dessert: Serve a homemade sherbet of strawberries or grapefruit, or the delectable Fresh Pear Sherbet on page 89. Or fresh fruits, like a fine ripe pineapple, or melon with grapes, or freshly poached fresh peaches sauced with raspberry purée. With fresh fruit, homemade cookies, like almond tuiles, walnut wafers, or madeleines, would be attractive, and you could omit the bourbon and chocolate truffles.

Leftovers

The consommé: Eat it cold or reheated; use for stock; or freeze. The *brunoise garnish,* if not overcooked, makes a nice hot or cold *macédoine* to garnish a platter.

Roast beef: One advantage of a conservative menu with simple (as opposed to composite) dishes is the fine array of possibilities for leftovers. Perhaps you planned in any case to arrange a beautiful cold beef platter for another party; it could be accompanied by a salad or made into one with potatoes, cherry tomatoes, and hard-boiled eggs on lettuce—a Salade de Boeuf à la Parisienne.

I'd save any well-done roast beef, or the coarser parts surrounding the eye, to dice for a hearty roast beef hash, to grind for shepherd's pie, or to grind and combine with sausage meat in patties.

To reheat slices as is, layer them on a platter, cover with foil, and set in the oven at

375°F/190°C; watch carefully and remove when just warmed through. To reheat in a sauce, try adding mustard and cream to your gravy or to some beef broth, or fresh tomato pulp with garlic and fresh basil or dried thyme; if you add red wine, then season it with tomato paste, bay leaf, and thyme, and reduce it by half, you have a great sauce which, if you add poached beef marrow, becomes à la Bordelaise. Or finish your gravy with savory *pistou* or *pipérade.* (For these two preparations, see *Mastering II.* Detailed descriptions of the previous dishes are in *J.C.'s Kitchen.*)

If you have enough of the fine lean eye section, still very rare, you could slice and combine it with mushrooms, onions, and sour cream for beef Stroganoff, or spread it with mushroom *duxelles* and bake in a pastry case for beef Wellington. Or, to serve cold, try it with drinks, in spiffy canapés (on buttered toast, for instance, with a corner spread with caviar); cut in chunks, with a spicy hot or cold dip; or sliced thin and spread with a horse-radish and cream cheese mixture, rolled, and sliced across. Or line cornet molds with small perfect slices, stuff with a piquant mousse or *macédoine,* coat with aspic, and chill till firm —to decorate a cold main dish.

Brussels sprouts: Even if they have been buttered and heated, they should still be green and crisp. You can simply reheat them, or add them to soup, or, if you have lots, make a timbale by the method in this chapter (allowing more milk) or as suggested in *Mastering I.*

If the sprouts have been blanched but not buttered, you have accomplished the first step in a choice of classic dishes. One group, described in *Mastering I,* includes sprouts braised in butter, with cream, or with chestnuts, or gratinéed à la Mornay, or coated with cheese and browned.

Or have the blanched sprouts cold in salad or with drinks. To be posh, you could hollow them out and pipe in a squirt of ham mousse or some savory mixture.

Corn: Any timbale leftovers can be sliced and eaten cold, or easily turned into a hot soup.

As the ears vary so in yield, you may have extra pulp and milk on hand. If so, try corn chowder (see "New England Potluck Supper"), or make skillet corn dowdy, corn flan, or corn crêpes (for directions, see "From Julia Child's Kitchen" in the September 1977 *McCall's*). Or have corn fritters for breakfast; or combine the pulp with other crunchy bits of vegetables, in puffy eggs fu yung.

The dessert: Any fruit which has been champagne'd should be eaten right up. But if you kept some fruit in reserve, the possibilities (according to the combination you chose) are endless. To keep cut fruit, pack it close in careful layers in a glass bowl, pour over orange juice to cover, shake to make sure there are no unfilled crannies or airholes, cover well, and refrigerate; it keeps 2 or 3 days. Serve as is or drained, in a melon case or ripe papaya cases. Or make a fruit salad, or mold the fruit in aspic (but omit fresh pineapple as it's anti-jelling). Or try a hot fruit curry on steamed rice.

There are lovely compotes, hot or cold, with the fruit juices reduced with wine and cinnamon or flavored ad lib with liqueurs or pure vanilla or almond extract; you can present them baked deep-dish fashion under a meringue or pastry lid. Or make a fruit tart in a rich pastry case. A mixed-fruit sherbet is easy (see "VIP Lunch" for a basic method); or fruit can be liquefied for a refreshing punch. And if a few fine sections or specimens remain, glaze them in their own well-reduced syrup to garnish an elegant platter.

Postscript

About beef there is always so much more to learn. Since meat is such a big budget item, the whole subject is well worth study, and here are some books you may find useful. All of them were written not as texts but for the consumer.

Barbara Bloch, with the National Live Stock and Meat Board, *The Meat Board Meat Book*. New York: McGraw-Hill Book Company, 1977.

Merle Ellis, *Cutting-Up in the Kitchen: The Butcher's Guide to Saving Money on Meat and Poultry.* San Francisco: Chronicle Books, 1975.

Travis Moncure Evans and David Greene, *The Meat Book: A Consumer's Guide to Selecting, Buying, Cutting, Storing, Freezing and Carving the Various Cuts.* New York: Charles Scribner's Sons, 1973.

Leon and Stanley Lobel, *All About Meat,* edited by Inez M. Krech. New York: Harcourt Brace Jovanovich, 1975.

Phyllis C. Reynolds, *The Complete Book of Meat.* New York: M. Barrows & Company, 1963.

For families who like to cook and eat together, this homey, savory menu starts from the ground up with jobs for all ages.

Sunday Night Supper

Menu

Ivan's Apéritif

*Corned Beef and Pork Boiled Dinner with
Steamed Vegetables
Cream of Garlic Sauce with Horseradish
Fresh Tomato Fondue—Diced tomatoes
simmered in herbs and oil*

Homemade Noodles

Sherbet with Strawberries en Chemise

*Suggested wines:
Red Beaujolais or Zinfandel, beer, cider, milk*

Take 1 cup (140 g) flour, add enough salt to render it unappetizing, and blend in vegetable dye by droplets, kneading with enough water to form a stiff, elastic dough. Yield: 2 good fistfuls, depending on age. Keeps well in a wide-mouthed screw-top jar. Some cookbook this is; but I mention play dough, the toddler's joy, to remind you of the deep satisfaction we all, even babies, derive from kneading and manipulating dough. In the Child clan, we like to save Sunday night for a do-it-yourself family cooking bee; and anyone old enough to stay up is welcome. The most popular project with all ages is noodle-making-and-eating; all the more so since Paul and I acquired a thrifty, efficient little hand-cranked machine which makes lumps into sheets and then into ribbons— wavy, pale gold strips a yard long which are briefly dried over a broomstick suspended between two chairs. At table the younger members learn, by practicing it, the small, gratifying art of eating noodles deftly: the fork, held vertically to the plate, engages a few strands with the tines and rotates against the inside of a spoon, making a neat parcel. Decorum reigns, unless Paul elects to demonstrate noodle eating as we learned it in China during World War II. I am sorry to say that his deafening inhalations are widely copied.

However you eat them, noodles are not only amusing but delicious—and almost universal, as you discover in any wheat-growing corner of the world. Just how delicious, you won't discover until you make your own. The machine does practically all the kneading and all the rolling and cutting. It's a pleasure to use, and we all take turns cranking it and catching the ribbons as they fall from the cutters. Homemade noodles have a lovely nutty flavor and a tender texture. They cook in half the time of store-bought noodles and cost precisely half as much. We reckoned it out that the compact, well-built machine had paid for itself after 76 two-egg batches ... rather soon, in other words, since people borrow it constantly.

Noodles are good with almost anything, but once or twice a year Paul and I start well in advance and corn our own meat for a Sunday party. I suppose this sounds like reinventing the wheel! Meat used to be corned (salted and spiced) in order to preserve it, which in these days of refrigeration is unnecessary; and, if you do like corned beef, you can buy it anywhere. But we like corned pork sometimes (which you can't often buy); we prefer short-fibered cuts to the usual brisket; and, finally, we fancy our own combinations of spices and

the appetizing light brown color of meat corned without nitrates (potassium salts) to turn it commercial red. Before refrigerators, the process was cumbersome: you needed a big stone crock with a lid fitting inside it like a piston in a cylinder; weights for the lid; and, most important, a cold room or outbuilding where the temperature stayed at 37°F/3°C. But this is usual refrigerator temperature, and a plastic bag works just as well as a crock—provided you remember to massage the package daily for a minute or two. (Using a crock, you didn't have to do that, since the meat was surrounded with brine; in a bag, the salt and meat juices create a brine, but you have to be sure it cures the meat on all sides.)

While the meat is cooking and the noodles are being kneaded, extruded, draped, and dried, other pairs of hands are preparing a bouquet of beautifully trimmed vegetables for the steamer. And the smallest hands are at work on a decoration for our dessert of store-bought strawberry sherbet or ice cream, a soft fresh flavor to round off a savory dinner. The makings are a tray of plump strawberries with a bowl of quickly prepared royal icing to dip them in; it clothes each berry in a little white velvet shirt—hence the name *en chemise*. A few strawberries always seem to disappear at this stage—which is only fair, since we elders are sipping away as we putter. There are fresh tomatoes to be peeled, seeded, juiced, and chopped, and a pot to be watched as the pale, subtle cream of garlic sauce is reduced and a touch of horseradish added.

Since we are, after all, busy accomplishing something, our drink is a mild one, something I first tasted in California. With its mixed vermouths and the light filming of gin (not for kick, but for flavor and satiny flow), it's finely, richly aromatic. And lovely to behold. Properly served in a big goblet of ice, with a goldfish-sized curve of orange zest, it looks so full and glowing that I wonder if my brother-in-law, who invented it, was inspired by the California sunset. Anyway, the family has named it Ivan's Apéritif for him, and we always like to have it together on the night that rounds off the week.

Preparations

Recommended Equipment:

For corning the meats, you'll need sturdy plastic bags with fasteners, a large bowl with a plate or pan that fits inside it, and a 10-pound (5-kg) weight to set on it.

For making noodles, a hand-cranked pasta machine (which also makes lasagne and thin noodles) is desirable. The electric models are at least five times the price and are supposed to be good, but I've never tried one.

To cook dinner, you'll need three big pots, at least two of them with well-fitting lids, and a metal colander which fits one of the pots (or else—and preferably—use the steaming rack illustrated in "Lo-Cal Banquet," page 44).

Marketing and Storage:

If you are going to do the corned meats for this menu, you'll need to start two weeks in advance, so I have marked the items for corned meat making with an asterisk on the list.

Staples to have on hand

Table salt
*Coarse or kosher salt
*Black and white peppercorns
*Powdered spices and herbs: allspice, thyme, sage, paprika, bay leaf
*Optional: juniper berries
 Whole cloves
 Whole imported bay leaves
 Prepared horseradish
 Olive oil
*Granulated sugar
 Confectioners sugar
 Cornstarch
 Flour
 Eggs (about 6 "large")
 Butter
 Heavy cream (1 cup or ¼ L)
*Garlic (2 heads)
 Parsley
 Optional: chives
 Shallots and/or scallions
 Lemons (2)
 Oranges (2)
 Cognac

Specific ingredients for this menu

*Beef and/or pork, braising cut (see recipe)
*Carrots
 White turnips (at least 3 or 4)
*Rutabaga (1 large)
*Onions and/or leeks
 Celery
 Optional: green beans (1 pound or 450 g)
 Tomatoes (8 to 10; see "Tomato Talk," page 159)
 Strawberries (24 large)
 Strawberry sherbet or ice cream (2 quarts or liters)
 Sweet white French or Italian vermouth
 Dry white French vermouth
 Optional: milk, cider, apple juice

Ivan's Apéritif

Mixed vermouth with orange

Ingredients per drink

1 jigger dry white French vermouth (Noilly Prat, Martini & Rossi, or Boissière)

1 jigger sweet white vermouth (Cinzano, Gancia, Lillet, or white Dubonnet)

1 Tb gin

1 fresh zest of orange (a 2½-inch or 6-cm strip of the orange part of the peel)

Equipment

A large, clear, stemmed wineglass; ice cubes

Fill the wineglass with ice cubes, stir in the vermouths, float the gin on top but do not stir in, squeeze the zest over the glass, then rub the rim of the glass with it and drop the zest into the glass.

A Junior Version:

For the vermouths and the gin, substitute apple juice or cider. The orange zest, the big glass, and the ice are the important parts.

Corned Beef and Pork

Potted, salted, and/or spiced meat—home cured in plastic bags rather than in a crock or pot

Salt and Spice Mixture:
For 10 to 12 pounds or 4½ to 5½ kg meat

1⅓ cups (3¼ dL) coarse or kosher salt

3 Tb granulated sugar

1 Tb cracked peppercorns

2 tsp each powdered allspice and thyme

1 tsp each powdered sage, paprika, and bay leaf

Special Optional Aromatic Vegetable Mixture for Beef:
For 4 to 5 pounds or 2 to 2½ kg meat

½ cup (1 dL) each: minced rutabaga, onion, and carrot

2 large cloves garlic, minced

Special Optional Addition for Pork:
For 4 to 5 pounds or 2 to 2½ kg meat

2 Tb crushed juniper berries

The Meat—One Kind or Cut, or a Mixture:

Beef: brisket, chuck, eye round roast, bottom round

Brisket.

Pork: shoulder arm picnic or blade (butt); loin, blade end (bone-in or boneless for either shoulder or loin)

Equipment
Sturdy plastic bags, one for each piece of meat; secure fastenings for bags; a large bowl or other receptacle to hold meat; a plate or pan to cover meat; a 10-pound (5-kg) weight to set in plate or pan; washed cheesecloth

Curing the meat
Trim meat of excess fat (and bone it, if you wish, but do not tie it until the curing is finished). Blend the salt and spice mixture in a bowl, set the meat on a tray, and rub mixture into all sides of meat and down into crevices. Set each piece into a bag, divide remaining salt and spice mixture among the bags (including all that has dropped onto the tray). Add optional ingredients. Close bags, squeezing out as much air as possible, and pack into bowl, cover with plate or pan, and weight. Set in the bottom of the refrigerator, where temperature should remain between 37° and 38°F/3° and 4°C. Within a few hours juices will begin to seep into bag, showing that the curing process is taking place. Turn bags and massage meat daily to be sure salt is penetrating all sides. Curing takes a minimum of 2 weeks, but you may let meat cure for a month. (If you leave it longer or if bags leak or break, repackage the meat, returning all juices and half again as much new salt to the new bags.)

Preliminary soaking before cooking
Wash off meat in cold water, and soak in a large bowl of cold water, changing it several times—I soak mine for 24 hours to be sure excess salt is out. As the salt leaves the meat, the meat softens and will feel almost like its original self. (Tie with white butcher's twine if you think meat might fall apart during cooking.)

Remarks:
You will note that there is no saltpeter, nitrite, or nitrate in the curing pickle here; thus the cooked meat will be turning a brownish, rather than the store-bought reddish, color.

Clockwise: boneless chuck, top round, and fresh pork shoulder

Corned Beef or Pork Boiled Dinner

For 4 to 5 pounds or 2 to 2½ kg meat

1 onion stuck with 4 cloves

1 large carrot

2 celery stalks

A large herb bouquet (8 parsley sprigs, 3 bay leaves, 1 tsp thyme, 3 cloves unpeeled garlic, tied in washed cheesecloth)

Set the meat in a kettle with cold water to cover by 2 inches (5 cm); add the onion, carrot, celery and herb bouquet. Bring to the simmer, skim off any scum for several minutes, set over it a cover slightly askew for air circulation, and simmer slowly—usually for 3 to 3½ hours, or until meat is tender when pierced with a fork. (Add boiling water if liquid evaporates below level of ingredients; after 2 hours taste meat and add salt to water if needed.)

🕐   May be cooked an hour or more in advance and left, partially covered, in its cooking bouillon; reheat slowly before serving.

Serving suggestions

Carve the meat into serving pieces and arrange on a hot platter with, if there is room, the steamed vegetables in the following recipe. Garnish with sprigs of parsley. Moisten with a ladleful of degreased cooking bouillon and pass a pitcher of bouillon, along with the garlic and tomato sauces, for the meat and noodles.

Remarks:

Solid pieces of meat can be carved more attractively than pieces with muscle separations—like those in the beef chuck and in the pork shoulder and the blade end of the pork loin. This is probably why the beef brisket, even though rather stringy in texture, is always popular—it slices evenly; but do note that if you get an edge cut (or double) brisket, you should separate it before carving since you have two muscle layers, each going in a different direction.

A Mixture of Steamed Vegetables

To accompany a boiled dinner and noodles

For 8 people

6 carrots

1 large rutabaga

3 or 4 (or more) white turnips

8 leeks and/or white onions

Enough boiled-dinner bouillon to fill steaming-kettle by an inch or so

Fresh parsley

Equipment

A steamer rack (see illustration, page 44) or metal colander; a kettle to hold whichever you use; a close-fitting cover

Preliminaries

Since these vegetables all take about the same time to cook, you can arrange them together on the steamer or in the colander; or cook them separately. The number and variety is up to you and the appetites of your guests. To prepare the vegetables, peel the carrots, cut into quarters, and cut the quarters in half. Peel the rutabaga and cut into pieces about the size of the carrots, and do the same with the turnips. Cut the roots off the leeks and cut leeks into 3-inch (8-cm) lengths (saving tender green part of tops for soup); if the leeks show any sign of sand or dirt, split into quarters lengthwise down to within 1 inch (2½ cm) of the root end and wash thoroughly under running water. Drop onions into boiling water, boil 1 minute, then shave off the two ends and slip off the peel; for even, nonburst cooking, pierce a cross ¼ inch (¾ cm) deep in root ends.

🕐   Vegetables may be prepared several hours in advance; cover with dampened paper towels and refrigerate in a plastic bag.

Steaming

About half an hour before serving, arrange the vegetables in separate piles on the steamer or in the colander, pour the bouillon into the kettle, and cover closely—if need be, arrange foil over the steamer or colander to make a close seal. Bring to the boil on top of the stove and steam slowly until vegetables are tender; do not overcook—vegetables should just be done.

🕐 If done somewhat ahead, it is best to undercook; set aside partially covered and reheat just before serving.

Serving

Arrange the vegetables either on the platter with the meat or on a separate hot platter; ladle a little of the steaming-liquid over them and decorate with parsley sprigs. Add the rest of the savory vegetable steaming liquid to the bouillon you pass with the meat.

Fresh Green Beans Simply Boiled

The fresh green beans here are mostly for color and need no formal recipe since they are so easy to do the French way. Choose crisp snappy ones, rapidly pull off one end, drawing it down the bean to remove any lurking string, and do the same with the other end. Wash in cold water, drain, and, if you are not cooking them soon, wrap in paper towels and refrigerate in a plastic bag. When ready to cook them—which you can do several hours in advance—have a large kettle with 6 quarts or liters rapidly boiling salted water at the ready (for 1 to 2 pounds or ½ to 1 kg beans; you will need the smaller amount for this dinner), drop in the beans, cover the kettle until the beans come back to the boil, then uncover and let beans boil rapidly for 5 minutes or so. Test by eating one or two, and as soon as just cooked through, set a metal colander curved side down in the kettle and tip to drain the beans. Then, with colander still in, refresh the beans for several minutes in cold water—you can even add ice cubes to the water to speed the cooling. This sets the fresh green color and the texture.

🕐 If boiled in advance, drain thoroughly and refrigerate in a clean towel.

Shortly before serving, toss in a large frying pan for a moment to evaporate excess moisture, then toss with butter, drops of lemon juice, and salt and pepper to taste. Or, drop for a minute or so in a kettle of boiling salted water, drain, and serve at once. (Or serve cold, with oil and lemon dressing, a sprinkling of minced shallots or scallions, and parsley.)

Cream of Garlic Sauce with Horseradish

To serve with boiled dinners, boiled fish or chicken, boiled potatoes

For about 2 cups or ½ liter

1 large head garlic
2 Tb butter
½ cup (1 dL) dry white French vermouth
1 Tb cornstarch
2 cups (½ L) bouillon from the boiled dinner, or from another source
1 or more Tb white prepared horseradish
1 egg yolk
4 Tb heavy cream (a little more if you wish)
Salt and white pepper
2 Tb fresh minced herbs, such as parsley and chives

To peel the garlic cloves, separate them from the head and drop into boiling water for 1 minute; the skins will slip off easily. Then simmer with the butter in a small saucepan for 5 minutes without browning; add the vermouth, cover, and simmer 10 to 15 minutes more or until very tender and liquid has evaporated completely. Purée by rubbing through a sieve with a wooden spoon, then scrape garlic off sieve back into saucepan. Blend in the cornstarch, gradually beat in the bouillon, and bring to the simmer, stirring. Simmer 2 minutes and remove from heat. In a small bowl, blend 1 tablespoon horseradish, the egg yolk, and 4 tablespoons cream; by dribbles beat in half of the hot sauce, then by dribbles beat this mixture back into the pan with the rest of the sauce. Bring again to the simmer, stirring, and taste carefully for seasoning, adding salt and pepper and more horseradish and cream if you wish.

◑   May be prepared in advance. Set aside off heat, and float a spoonful of cream over surface of sauce to prevent a skin from forming.

Reheat just before serving, stir in the herbs, and pour into a warm sauce bowl.

Fresh Tomato Fondue

A sauce to serve with boiled meats—or with fish, eggs, soufflés, and so forth

For about 2 cups or ½ liter

8 to 10 firm ripe red tomatoes—plus some drained and strained Italian plum tomatoes for added taste and color if you feel them needed

2 Tb olive oil

2 Tb minced shallots or scallions

1 clove minced garlic (optional)

¼ tsp thyme

1 bay leaf

Salt and pepper

Peel, seed, and juice the tomatoes (see "Tomato Talk," page 159), and dice them into pieces of about ⅜ inch (1 cm). Heat the oil in a medium-size saucepan, stir in the shallots or scallions and optional garlic, simmer a moment, then add the tomato (and strained canned tomato if you are using it). Add the thyme and bay and simmer several minutes, tossing and folding, until tomatoes have rendered their excess juice and have formed a fairly thick sauce. Season carefully with salt and pepper. Serve hot, warm, or cold—without the bay leaf.

🕐 May be cooked in advance.

Homemade Noodles

Kneaded and cut in a noodle machine

For about 24 ounces (675 g) noodles, or the equivalent of 2 standard boxes of commercial egg noodles, serving 8 people generously

The Noodle Dough:

1 ¾ cups (4 dL) all-purpose flour

2 "large" eggs

2 to 4 Tb cold water

Equipment

A mixing bowl, wooden spoon, and rubber spatula, or a food processor; a noodle machine (either hand-crank or electric); 1 or 2 clean broom handles to be suspended (for instance, between 2 chairs)

Forming the noodle dough by hand
Place the flour in a mixing bowl, make a well in the center, and break in the 2 eggs; blend them with 2 tablespoons of the water, and gradually mix in the surrounding flour with a wooden spoon or a spatula. Blend vigorously to make a stiff dough; turn out onto a work surface and knead vigorously with the heel of your hand, adding droplets more water to unblended bits. Dough should just form into a mass—the machine will do the rest.

For the food processor

Add all ingredients to the machine, using 2 tablespoons water, and process (using metal cutting blade); in about a minute, if you have enough water for the temper of the day, the dough will usually form itself into a ball on top of the blade. Sometimes the dough will not form a mass but seem to be made up of granular particles; however, as long as you can squeeze it into a coherent mass when removed from the food processor, all is well. In any case, experience will be your judge as to whether or not to add droplets more water. Turn dough out onto work surface and knead together to blend. Dough should be firm; if soft and/or sticky, knead in a sprinkling of flour.

Remarks:

A little too much water, in my book, is no disaster, since you can always knead in more flour to make the requisitely stiff dough. Again, your own experience will guide you, eventually, but don't be afraid of the dough. Not much can go wrong as long as it is stiff enough and dry enough to pass through the kneading and cutting rollers of your machine. Tenderness and exquisiteness of texture can come later, and will be part of your own particular secret genius with the noodle.

🕐 Dough may be formed half an hour or so in advance, and some practitioners prefer to let the dough rest before forming it; in this case, wrap it airtight in plastic to keep it from crusting over. (I have found, by the way, that dough made with unbleached flour turns a grayish yellow when refrigerated overnight; however,

it kneads and cooks up satisfactorily when cooked the next day.) Freshly made dough may be frozen.

Finishing the dough and forming noodles

Cut the dough in half and cover one piece with plastic while forming the other. Flatten this piece of dough into a cake the size of your palm, and pinch one edge so it will fit into the machine. Set smooth rollers to their widest opening—number 8 on most machines. Crank the dough through. Fold dough in half, end to end, and crank through several times until dough is smooth and fairly evenly rectangular; as necessary, brush dough with flour before passing through rollers, since it will stick to the machine if it is too damp.

When dough is smooth, reset rollers to the next lower setting and crank it through, then to the next lower, and the next—which is usually number 5. By this time your strip of dough will be so long you will probably want to cut it in two; now pass the first and then the second half through number 4, the setting that gives, I think, the right thinness for noodles and lasagne. Hang each strip as it is finished on a broom handle to dry out briefly (but not to stiffen—4 to 5 minutes are usually enough). Repeat the process with the reserved piece of dough, then crank the dried strips through the noodle roller, set at number 4, and hang noodles on broom handles as you cut them.

🕐 Noodles may be formed and cooked at once, or formed in advance and cooked later. For instance, you may let them hang on the broom handles until they have dried thoroughly, and then package them. Or you

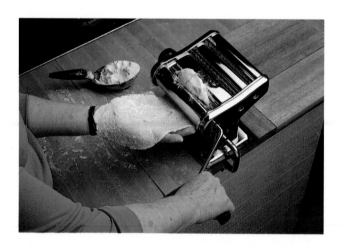

may like to preserve them in a semifresh state. In this case, arrange a layer of noodles on a tray, sprinkle corn flour over lightly (if you can't find corn flour, pulverize cornmeal in your blender), cover with wax paper, and continue with successive layers of noodles, ending with wax paper; set in the refrigerator overnight, or until dry, then package in their laid-out state, and freeze. (If you freeze noodles when they are damp they will stick together, and it is almost impossible to separate the strands while they cook.)

Cooking Noodles:
A large kettle filled with at least 8 quarts or liters rapidly boiling water
2 tsp salt per quart of water
A large colander (for draining)
Butter and olive oil (or your choice of dressing)
A hot platter and 2 large forks for tossing and serving
Salt and pepper

About 5 minutes before serving, plunge the noodles into the rapidly boiling water and cover until boil is reached. Then boil uncovered, frequently testing the noodle cooking by eating a strand or two—fresh soft noodles take but a minute of cooking, while semifresh and dry noodles take a minute or two longer. Do not overcook or the noodles will be mushy—better slightly under- than slightly overcooked.

Once they are done, drain in a colander, shaking vigorously to remove excess water. Spread a little butter and oil (or dressing) in the platter, turn into it the steaming noodles, and toss with the forks, adding salt and pepper, more butter and oil (or dressing), and tasting to be sure all is perfectly seasoned. Work rapidly and rush them to the table, still steaming.

Strawberries en Chemise

Icing-coated strawberries, to decorate desserts and ice cream

For 24 large strawberries
1 cup sifted confectioners sugar (a little more if needed)
1 tsp raw egg white (a little more if needed)
¼ tsp fresh lemon juice
Drops of Cognac or more lemon juice (as needed)
Fresh strawberries, washed rapidly and laid on a rack
Equipment
A portable electric mixer or a wire whip

Place the sugar, egg white, and lemon juice in a smallish high-sided mixing bowl and beat a minute or more with electric mixer or wire whip until sugar forms a quite stiff mass that "forms the beak"—makes stiff points when a bit is lifted in the blades of the beater. Thin out with a droplet or two of Cognac or more lemon juice—icing should be thick enough to enrobe strawberries. Holding a berry by its topknot, swirl it in the frosting to cover two-thirds the way up its sides, and replace on rack.

🕐 May be done an hour in advance.

Arrange over strawberry sherbet or ice cream just before bringing to the table.

⏱ *Timing*

Boiling and draining the noodles is *the* last-minute job for this dinner. They must be eaten the moment they're done, and homemade ones take only minutes to cook. About 20 minutes before putting on the water for the noodles, start the vegetables steaming. *N.B.:* If you plan to add the optional green beans to the vegetable bouquet, blanch them and refrigerate that afternoon, and toss in butter right after you've put the noodles into the pot.

The two sauces are quick to make, and the strawberries, to dip. But remember to put the sherbet or ice cream in the refrigerator to soften at about the time you sit down to dinner.

You should start cooking the corned meat about 3½ hours before you eat it, and it must be soaked for 24 hours before that. Salt and spice it at least 2 weeks in advance, though it can stay in its brine for 2 months. And don't forget to massage and turn it every day during that 2-week period.

One nice thing about shopping for this dinner is that every ingredient except the strawberries (and, if you're having them, the green beans) can be bought days in advance.

Pasta primavera—cooked noodles have been tossed in slivered garlic and oil, then simmered in heavy cream (or béchamel); now blanched, diced, buttered fresh vegetables are added; and finally cheese is sprinkled over all.

Menu Variations

The main course: Rather than cured meat, you may like fresh meat with noodles, or a boiled fowl; if you do either, I'd suggest adding a cooking sausage, such as chorizo or Polish kielbasy. Salted goose or duck would be elegant and is made in exactly the same way as corned meat. Both are simple cousins of the French preserve, or *confit.*

Noodles are delicious tossed in olive oil in which you have sautéed a clove of garlic; they are then simmered in cream and tossed with cheese. You could elaborate on this, especially in summer, by adding a bouquet of bright diced and cooked vegetables and tossing again for a Pasta alla Primavera. Going further, you could add diced ham.

The pasta machine Paul and I have makes either thin or medium-width noodles; and, as you know, noodle dough tastes quite different in its many forms. A lasagna made with uncut homemade noodle dough is an experience (for a nice recipe, see the French-Italian one in *J.C.'s Kitchen*). Most general cookbooks—and most ethnic ones, for that matter—have useful suggestions for other, myriad uses of this dough.

The dessert: I do think something light and fruit flavored will taste best to you after noodles and cured meat: a homemade sherbet, perhaps (see "VIP Lunch," page 89), or a fruit compote (see "Dinner for the Boss," page 129). Or you could offer a basket of fresh fruit. The children will enjoy arranging a lovely still life and maybe learn to eat even such difficult delights as ripe figs in the French manner, with knife and fork.

Leftovers

You can rinse leftover cooked *pasta* by a quick plunge in boiling water; then drain well and serve hot with any of an enormous variety of accompaniments. Or use it, rinsed in cold water after draining and drained again, in a composed salad. Leftover raw pasta can be frozen.

Cured meat can be reheated, even several times. Sliced, it makes splendid sandwiches, or can be served as a salad platter, close cousin to Salade de Boeuf à la Parisienne (see "Dinner for the Boss," page 131). Ground and mixed with chard, cheese, and egg (see *Mastering II*), it makes a fine hamburger. I'd add sausage meat if I planned a meat loaf or patties. You can make a vegetable-and-meat loaf, to serve with tomato sauce, as follows: run leftover vegetables, along with noodles, through the food processor; then process twice as much meat. Combine these ingredients, then add 1 egg for each 2 cups (½ L) of the mixture, add a bit of sausage meat for richness, mix, and bake. To make that delicious classic, corned beef hash—or for that matter, corned pork hash—see page 172. Also, if you have boned your own pork loin for corning, you'll find you have enough pork meat clinging to the bone to make scrapple, page 174.

The bouillon is delicious; why not add to it some of the leftover noodles, some of the meat, and some of the vegetables for a splendid soup? A bit of the *garlic sauce* would be excellent with either this soup or the meat loaf.

Postscript: On cooking with children

Influenced, perhaps, by my early experience at a Montessori school, and surely by living in a clan full of carvers, painters, carpenters, and cooks of all ages, I am all for encouraging children to work productively with their hands. They learn to handle and care for equipment with respect. It is good to give them knives, for instance, as early as you dare. A knife is a tool, not a toy. A sharp, clean knife is safer to use than a dull, rusty one—easier too: a four-year-old will discover that for himself as you teach him to slice a hard-boiled egg neatly and then to fillet a fish. Talk to children as you plan menus. Let their small, sensitive noses sniff the fish as you shop. Work together at the counter and let your children arrange platters. Nothing gives them more pleasure than setting things in rows and rosettes.

The small rituals, like the clean hands and clean apron before setting to work; the precision of gesture, like leveling off a cupful of flour; the charm of improvisation and making something new; the pride of mastery; and the gratification of offering something one has made—these have such value to a child. And where are they so easily to be obtained as in cooking? The patience and good humor demanded of you by cooking with a child are a good investment.

Do taste everything together, at every stage, and serve to children what you eat yourself. Once they have enough teeth to cope with any food, children, with their unjaded palates, are a keen, responsive audience for an enthusiastic cook.

Advance preparation, easy service, and a charming main dish adapted from a classic of the haute cuisine; *special treats for a big crowd.*

Buffet for 19

Menu

Oysters on the Half Shell

*Turkey Orloff—turkey breast scallopini
gratinéed with mushrooms, onions, rice,
and cheese*
*Fresh Green Beans with Watercress and
Tomatoes, Oil and Lemon Dressing*
French Bread

Jamaican Ice Cream Goblet

Suggested wines:
*Chablis, Muscadet, or Riesling with the
oysters; red Bordeaux or Cabernet
Sauvignon with the turkey*

Supper for a crowd nowadays means buffet service. I ask of a good buffet main dish that it be easy to serve, hold heat well, be reasonably compact to save oven and table space, that it be neither expensive nor pretentious, and that it may be prepared largely in advance. At once I add: the dish must be delicious, handsome, and a little unusual. Just because the guests have been invited en masse, they mustn't be let think that their dinner has been indifferently chosen or perfunctorily prepared.

Except for our kitchen Cocktail Party, none of the menus in this book requires a special setting or unusual kitchen facilities. But a meal for a big crowd puts special demands on almost any house, host, and hostess. I am not mad about buffet dining, but when it is unavoidable I like guests to help themselves to the main course, then be served more wine and second helpings. I like their plates to be cleared and the dessert to be passed to them.

In this menu, the oyster bar makes for fun and informality, but it does need a special place of its own. After serving them, arrange with a good friend, or your helper if you have one, to dismantle the remains of the once splendid set-up while the guests are moving on to the main course. At home, Paul and I have enough room so we can enjoy our oysters in one place and then grandly waft everyone off to another for the sit-down part of dinner. We generally arrange platters at either end of our long table, so that people can help themselves quickly and find a place to sit down.

In any crowd, there are invariably a few people who simply cannot face oysters, so we offer them a simple alternative like cheese or thinly sliced salami. We allow three oysters per person, which seems to average out for those who can leave them and those who so love them that they will eat four or five or even more. Now that we have learned to open them easily, we do so as we serve them, which is always advisable anyway. Once our guests get the knack of prying up the shells with a beer can opener, or, as college wags used to put it, a church key, we find that most of them find it great fun doing their own. We set out plates and napkins, oyster forks for the conventionally minded, and spoons for those who eat oysters, as we do, in one voluptuous slurp. We add lemons and a pepper grinder—but no cocktail sauce!—and buttered dark bread.

The Turkey Orloff is a modern, streamlined cousin of an elaborate dish, Veal Prince Orloff, named for a notable Russian gourmet of the nineteenth century by some forgotten Paris chef. It is a saddle of veal that is roasted, sliced, then re-formed with a stuffing of mushrooms and *soubise* (rice braised with onions) and gratinéed with a rich creamy sauce. It is a noble dish; but its price is almost prohibitive since you must use a very choice cut of veal, and it is almost fiendishly fattening. The turkey variant is much less expensive, less rich—and less work. But it is a recipe designed for the food processor, where you can make light of slicing 15 cups of onions and mincing quarts of mushrooms. If fresh sliced turkey breast is not available at the supermarket, frozen breasts always are. The finished dish, whose layers of white turkey meat are interleaved with a rice, onion, and mushroom stuffing and finished off with a golden gratin, has a deep, subtle flavor and an agreeable, fork-tender texture.

When you're planning a vegetable here, you have to think about the number of people you're serving, and about your kitchen facilities. A great platter of hot broccoli, fresh peas, or beans would be lovely. But for 19 people? That's much too difficult, I think. I'd rather have something cold, but not the usual green salad. Instead, I have chosen a beautiful platter of fresh green beans, cooked, chilled, and lightly dressed with oil, lemon and mustard, and brightened up with red onion rings and tomatoes.

Dessert for a crowd. You want it dressy, delectable, original, but easy to handle. The idea here is simple indeed: store-bought vanilla ice cream, each serving topped with a spoonful or two of dark rum, then dusted with powdered coffee. It's a surprise dessert with a sophisticated air—and there's something wonderfully sensuous about spooning up this ambrosial combination from a big opulent goblet that a pedestrian old bowl simply doesn't supply.

Preparations

Recommended Equipment:

For your oyster bar, you will need a space about the size of two card tables, a big tub and plenty of chopped ice for the oysters, some kind of receptacle for their shells, a pepper mill or two, and several beer can openers. (Or see the set-up described in "Cocktail Party," pages 93-4). Have paring knives for separating the muscles from the shells and a conventional oyster knife or two for recalcitrant cases.

For every multiple of the turkey recipe (which is given for 8 persons), you'll want a baking-and-serving dish 2 inches (5 cm) deep. As I've said, the turkey recipe is designed for the food processor; if you don't have one, see suggestions for other main courses in Menu Variations.

Marketing and Storage:

A note on quantities: the recipes, and therefore the lists below, are for 8 "average" appetites. Multiply by 2½ if the dinner is for 19—or even 20—people.

Staples to have on hand

Salt
Peppercorns
Mustard (the strong Dijon type; see Remarks, page 6)
Herbs: dried tarragon, thyme or sage, imported bay leaves
Flour
Celery, onions, and carrots (small quantities for making stock)

Garlic
Powdered instant coffee (for the dessert topping)

Specific ingredients for this menu

Turkey breast (either 2½ pounds or 1¼ kg fresh slices or half a frozen 9-pound or 4-kg bone-in breast) ▼
Fresh oysters in the shell (24 to 30)
Salami (16 thin slices)
Cheese (if you wish it, as an alternative to oysters)
Cocktail sausages (16)
Olive oil or salad oil (4 ounces or 1 dL)
Plain raw white rice (2 ounces or 60 g or ¼ cup)
Thin-sliced dark bread (20 slices), pumpernickel or rye
French bread, 2 loaves
Butter (½ pound or 225 g or 2 sticks)
Eggs (3)
Low-fat cottage cheese (4 ounces or 115 g)
Mozzarella cheese (4 ounces or 115 g), coarsely grated
Fresh mushrooms (½ pound or 225 g)
Yellow onions (1 pound or 450 g, or 5 or 6 medium-size)
Red onions (2 medium-size) or scallions (1 bunch)
Cherry tomatoes (1 quart or 1 L) or ripe red regular tomatoes (3 or 4)
Watercress (2 or 3 bunches) or romaine (1 head)
Fresh green beans (2½ pounds or 1¼ kg)
Fresh parsley
Lemons (5)
Vanilla ice cream (1½ quarts or 1½ L), best quality
Dark Jamaica rum (8 ounces or ½ L)
Crushed ice for the oysters and ice cubes for drinks

▶ *Remarks:*

In providing for non-oyster-eaters with cheese, salami slices, and hot cocktail sausages, I allow about 2 ounces of each per person, since some oyster eaters will consume both. I also count on 2 or 3 slices of dark bread per person, and 2 tablespoons softened butter to spread on each 10 to 12 pieces. *Turkey breast:* Fresh ready-sliced turkey breast meat is available in many markets: look in the poultry section, where it is usually attractively packaged in flat see-through trays. If you are buying frozen breasts, the best size, I think, is around 9 pounds (4 kg); have the breast sawed in half lengthwise if you are doing the turkey recipe for only 8 people, and you can store the other half in your freezer. It is always best to defrost frozen turkey slowly in the refrigerator, since you will then have juicier and firmer meat.

Turkey Talk:

You can begin with sliced raw fresh turkey breast meat, or with half a 9-pound (4-kg) frozen turkey breast. Once a turkey breast has thawed, peel off and discard the skin, remove the breast meat in one piece from the bone, and cut it into 12 or more serving slices about ⅜ inch (1 cm) thick with a very sharp knife.

The Stock:

Chop up the carcass and simmer it and any turkey meat scraps for 2 hours in lightly salted water to cover, with a chopped carrot and onion, 2 celery ribs, and an herb bouquet (8 parsley sprigs, 1 large imported bay leaf, and ½ teaspoon thyme or sage tied in washed cheesecloth); strain, degrease, and refrigerate until needed.

If you've no homemade stock, use canned chicken broth but flavor it as follows: for each 2 cups (½ L), simmer for 30 minutes with 3 tablespoons each sliced onions, carrots, and celery, ½ cup (1 dL) dry white wine *or* ⅓ cup (¾ dL) dry white French vermouth; then strain.

Turkey Orloff

Turkey breast scallopini gratinéed with mushrooms, onions, rice, and cheese

For 8 people

¼ cup (½ dL) plain raw white rice

Salt

1 pound (450 g or 5 to 6 medium-size onions

1½ sticks (6 ounces or 180 g) butter

1 egg plus 2 egg yolks

½ pound (225 g or 3 to 3½ cups) fresh mushrooms

A handful fresh parsley sprigs (to make 3 Tb minced)

½ tsp fragrant dried tarragon

Pepper

12 or more turkey breast slices (see notes preceding recipe)

5 Tb flour for sauce, plus extra for turkey sauté

1 Tb vegetable oil

3 cups (¾ L) hot turkey stock (or chicken stock—see notes preceding recipe)

½ cup (1 dL) low-fat cottage cheese

1 cup (¼ L or 4 ounces) lightly pressed down coarsely grated mozzarella cheese

Rice and onion soubise

Preheat oven to 325°F/170°C. Drop the rice into a saucepan with 2 quarts (2 L) rapidly boiling salted water and boil uncovered for exactly 5 minutes; drain immediately and

reserve. Meanwhile peel and then chop the onions in a food processor; (it needs no washing until after its last operation). To do onions, prechop roughly by hand into 1-inch (2½-cm) chunks and process them 1½ cups (3½ dL) at a time, using metal blade and switching machine on and off 3 or 4 times at 1-second intervals to chop onions into ⅜-inch (1-cm) morsels. Melt 4 tablespoons of the butter in a flameproof 6- to 8-cup (1½- to 2-L) baking dish, stir in the chopped onions, the drained rice, and ¼ teaspoon salt, mixing well to coat with the butter; cover the dish and bake in middle level of oven for about 1 hour, stirring up once or twice, until rice is completely tender and beginning to turn a golden yellow. When the rice is done and still warm, beat in the egg; taste carefully and correct seasoning.

🕐 May be done a day or two in advance.

Mushroom duxelles

While rice and onion *soubise* is cooking, trim and wash the mushrooms. For the food processor, first chop roughly by hand into 1-inch (2½-cm) chunks, then process into ⅛-inch (½-cm) pieces, using the 1-second on-off technique. Mince the parsley in the machine afterward. By handfuls, either twist mushrooms hard in the corner of a towel or squeeze through a potato ricer to extract as much of their juices as possible. Sauté the mushrooms in 2 tablespoons of the butter in a medium-size frying pan over moderately high heat, stirring and tossing until mushroom pieces begin to separate from each other—5 to 6 minutes. Stir in the tarragon and parsley; season to taste with salt and pepper. Stir half of the mixture into the cooked rice and onion *soubise;* reserve the rest.

🕐 Mushroom *duxelles* may be cooked in advance and may be frozen.

Preparing the turkey scallopini

Pound the slices between 2 sheets of wax paper, with a rubber hammer, a rolling pin, or the side of a bottle, to expand them about double and to thin them down by half. These are your turkey scallopini; cover and refrigerate them until you are ready to sauté them.

Sautéing the turkey scallopini

Salt and pepper the turkey slices lightly, dredge in flour and shake off excess, sauté for about a minute on each side in 1 tablespoon of the oil and 2 tablespoons of the butter (more if needed)—just to stiffen them and barely cook through. Set slices aside on a plate as you finish them.

The gratinéing sauce

Make a turkey *velouté* sauce as follows. Melt 4 tablespoons of the butter over moderate heat in a heavy-bottomed 2-quart (2-L) saucepan, blend in the flour, and cook, stirring with a wooden spoon until flour and butter foam and froth together for 2 minutes without turning more than a golden yellow. Remove from heat and, when this *roux* has stopped bubbling, pour in 2 cups (½ L) of the hot turkey or chicken stock and blend vigorously with a wire whip. Return to heat, stirring slowly with wire whip to reach all over bottom, corner, and side of pan, and boil slowly for 2 minutes. Taste and correct seasoning. Sauce should be thick enough to coat a wooden spoon nicely, mean-

ing it will coat the turkey. Beat in more stock by droplets if sauce is too thick. In the food processor or an electric blender, purée the egg yolks with the cottage cheese (or push through a fine sieve and beat in a bowl with a wire whip); by dribbles, beat the hot sauce into the egg yolk and cheese mixture.

Assembling the dish

Choose a baking-and-serving dish about 10 by 14 by 2 inches (25 x 35 x 5 cm); butter the inside, and spread a thin layer of sauce in bottom of dish. Make a neat, slightly overlapping pattern of the turkey slices down the center of the dish, spreading each, as you go, with the *soubise*. Spoon remaining mushroom *duxelles* down the sides. Spoon remaining sauce over the turkey and spread the mozzarella cheese on top.

🕐   Recipe may be prepared a day in advance to this point; when cool, cover and refrigerate. If, before proceeding, you note that the sauce does not cover some parts of the meat, spread more mozzarella on these areas.

Final baking and serving

Turkey will take about 25 minutes to heat and for the top to brown; it should be served fairly promptly since the meat will be juicier if it does not have to wait around. Set uncovered in upper third of a preheated 400°F/200°C oven until contents are bubbling hot and sauce has browned nicely.

Fresh Green Beans with Watercress and Tomatoes, Oil and Lemon Dressing

For 8 people

2½ pounds (1¼ kg) fresh green beans, trimmed and blanched (see page 40)
Salt and pepper
2 or 3 bunches watercress, or 1 head romaine
For the dressing
1 lemon
1 small clove garlic (optional)
1 tsp prepared mustard, Dijon type
6 or more Tb olive oil or salad oil
2 medium-size mild red onions, or 1 bunch scallions
1 quart (1 L) cherry tomatoes, or 3 or 4 ripe red regular tomatoes

Prepare the beans in the morning, wrap in a clean towel and then in a plastic bag, and refrigerate. Also remove tough stems from watercress, wash the cress, and fold in a clean towel and plastic; refrigerate (or if using romaine, wash, separating leaves, wrap like the cress, and refrigerate).

An hour or so before serving, prepare the dressing as follows. Cut the zest (yellow part of

peel) off half the lemon and mince very fine. Place in a small mortar or heavy bowl with the salt; purée in the optional garlic. Pound into a fine paste with a pestle or the end of a wooden spoon, then beat in the mustard, a tablespoon of juice from the lemon, and the oil. Carefully correct seasoning—dressing should not be too acid, only mildly so because of the wine you will be serving with the dinner.

Peel the red onions and slice into thin rings; toss in a bowl with the dressing (or mix chopped scallions with the dressing); cover and refrigerate. Halve the cherry tomatoes, place cut side up in a dish, and salt lightly (or peel, slice, and lightly salt regular tomatoes); cover and refrigerate. If you are using romaine rather than cress, gather leaves by handfuls and slice crosswise into ⅜-inch (1-cm) julienne strips; refrigerate in a plastic bag.

Shortly before guests are to arrive, arrange the watercress or romaine in the bottom of a wide salad bowl or platter and toss with a sprinkling of salt. Toss the blanched beans in a bowl with the onions or scallions and dressing, taste carefully for seasoning, and arrange attractively over the cress or romaine, with the tomatoes around the edges. Baste tomatoes and beans with dressing left in bean bowl. Cover and keep cool until serving time.

Jamaican Ice Cream Goblet

This dessert needs no actual recipe since it consists only of a healthy helping of the best vanilla ice cream in a big goblet (if possible! or a pretty bowl or a dessert plate), a spoonful or two of dark Jamaica rum, and a sprinkling of powdered instant coffee (if you have only the freeze-dried granular type, pulverize it in a blender). It couldn't be simpler, but the rum and coffee blending into that vanilla cream combine into a marvelous medley of tastes. I usually assemble this in the kitchen, with a friend or two to help pass it around. But with not too big a crowd, it's rather fun to pass the goblets of ice cream and let guests help themselves to the rum, in a pitcher with ladle, and to the coffee, in a bowl with teaspoon.

P.S. Bourbon whiskey can substitute for rum—but in that case it must be called a Bourbon rather than a Jamaican goblet.

🕐 Timing

Midway through your menu, perhaps when you move on from the oysters to the turkey, remember to take your ice cream out of the freezer and put it into the refrigerator to soften.

Just before the guests arrive, assemble the salad platters while you heat the cocktail sausages or crisp the French bread.

Since Turkey Orloff shouldn't sit around too much after its 25- to 30-minute baking, when you put it in depends on your party-giving style.

An hour or so before the guests are to arrive, slice the onions, tomatoes, and other green bean fixings. Set up the oyster bar.

In the morning, blanch and chill the beans, wash and pick over the cress or wash the romaine. Butter the brown bread for the oysters, etc.; stack the slices on a tray between sheets of wax paper and chill, ready to be arranged on a board or platter when you set up the oyster bar. Buy the ice.

You can assemble the Turkey Orloff in the morning or the day before, and as you'll see from the recipe, parts of it may be made days in advance.

A day or even two or three before the party, buy the oysters, clean them, and stack them.

Buy the wines and other drinkables well ahead, so that those needing remedial rest will have their due.

Menu Variations

Oysters: You could also include clams and cooked shrimp. For a quite different dish—but similar in also being something raw, not too highly flavored, and obviously very special—serve Steak Tartare. Grind it yourself from beef tenderloin butts or tails, season lightly with salt and pepper, beat in raw egg yolks (one per half pound), and serve the trimmings separately: more salt, a pepper grinder or two, capers, anchovy fillets, finely minced onion, and chopped fresh herbs like parsley and chives. Guests pile their own on buttered dark bread and mix in the trimmings of their choice.

Turkey Orloff: For other dishes comprising poultry with an elegant stuffing, you might consider a boned stuffed turkey *ballottine* (as described in *The French Chef Cookbook*), or the Chicken Melon (see page 20) served hot, or boned ducks or chickens in pastry crusts. You could make your Orloff dish with chicken, veal, or thinly sliced loin of pork.

Vegetable or salad: Delicious, in season, would be fresh asparagus vinaigrette, or artichoke hearts with a few halved cherry tomatoes for decorations. A platter of sliced cucumbers with a light dressing and a wreath of watercress is another green idea, or that always amenable standby, fresh broccoli vinaigrette. Finally, just have fine big bowls of fresh mixed salad greens.

Dessert: You could make peach Melba, or serve your ice cream with poached pears and chocolate sauce (*poires belle Hélène*), or garnish the ice cream with canned peaches simmered in their own syrup that has been boiled down with wine and cinnamon. And there are a thousand ways of using liqueurs, of freezing store ice cream into a bombe, and of serving it with meringues. Or change from ice cream to fruit and have the macédoine suggested on page 129, or one of its variations; and with it you could serve cake or cookies.

Leftovers

Oysters: See the Leftovers section in "Cocktail Party," page 109.

Turkey Orloff: You can reassemble, sprinkle on more cheese, and regratiné the dish; it will not have quite its original glory, but it will still make very good eating. You can chop the turkey bits, mix everything together, and use for stuffing crêpes; or make an elegant turkey hash. Or grind everything up in a food processor, add a little fresh sausage meat, and 1 egg per cup of mixture, and turn it into a meatloaf. Or chop or grind up everything and simmer with a chicken stock to make a rich and hearty soup.

Green beans: I would prefer not to have leftovers in this category since the beauty of the fresh bean is fleeting. Serve them again the very next day as a salad would be my suggestion. However, you could try dropping the whole mixture briefly in boiling water to wash off the dressing, draining, and boiling up in a soup.

Postscript

Luxury and quantity, like the lion and the lamb, don't often consort; and it is not easy to serve a really fine meal to great numbers, especially without expert household help. I won't bore you with admonitions about counting silver, shifting furniture, and all those preparatory chores; but it is very certain that planning is the essence of a successful party, and I do think too many hosts skimp on menu planning, though this is the most important thing of all. My own practice is to choose a simple workable menu and to do as much as possible in advance, such as freezing what can be frozen of the menu's elements, like the *duxelles*, precooking the stock and *soubise* for the turkey, and saving a bit of that valuable last-minute time for some truly special touch. Nothing gives a party so much personal warmth as the guests' sense that you wanted to give them a particular treat. One remarkable dish has twice the effect of several run-of-the-mill ones.

Steak Tartare with trimmings.

Essay

A *basketful of common varieties of tomatoes, green and ripe,*
with Italian plum cooking tomatoes and small cherry
tomatoes beside them.

Tomato Talk

Tomatoes come in all sizes; cherry tomatoes are the smallest sold, but "currant" types exist. Except for the rare yellow varieties, the skin and flesh of fine tomatoes are intensely, evenly red. The perfect tomato is plump, heavy, smooth, and unblemished, though "cat faces," or scars around the blossom end, are harmless; and the locules, the interior chambers containing jelly and seeds, should be few. Our gardening friends tell us that the plants are thrifty, bounteous, and easy to cultivate. For home consumption, they grow the thin-skinned, deep-flavored varieties, and pick them at their peak of ripeness—at which point a day's chilling in the fridge will do no harm, if you can wait that long to bite into these summer miracles of sun and light sweet soil, and gentle handling.

How to choose them

Varieties like these are too fragile for commercial cultivation and shipping; nor, except in rare instances, can you expect to buy market tomatoes which were picked at full ripeness. At their best, typical market tomatoes will have been picked fairly near ripeness and are then termed "greenhouse" or "hothouse." The calyx, the little star of leaves at the stem end, will be fresh and bright green; and, if a bit of stem is left on, the tomato will keep better— but stems are a packer's bane, for they puncture the tomato's neighbors in the crate. Next best is the "vine-ripe" tomato, which was harvested when merely pink. Third best is "mature-green," which you won't see often, since the wholesaler usually holds it until it has reddened in his ripening room.

Perfect or not, the market tomato is an indispensable item. It has lots of Vitamin C and some A, its appearance is pretty, its texture and flavor are unique, it is a basic and versatile element in most Occidental cuisines, and it is available all year round. When you consider what treatment it undergoes before you ever see it, you may think its reliable presence a commercial miracle. Typically the poor thing is picked, packed in field crates, shipped to the packing house, unloaded, weighed, checked, washed, dried, waxed, sorted, graded, sized, packed for transport, loaded and shipped, unpacked for federal and/or state inspection, repacked, shipped again, unloaded, sorted (several operations here), repacked, trucked to the ripening room, unpacked, shelved till it's pink or red, repacked, trucked to the market, trucked to the retailer, probably unpacked and repacked again in trays, marked with an appalling price, and set out at last to wait for you. Not only can it be bruised or punctured at any of these stages, it is extremely vulnerable to chill from cold weather or imperfect storage. The effect of cold below 55°F/13°C on a tomato is to inhibit, even prevent, its ripening; and the effect is cumulative. A cold snap in the field, plus a day in a gelid refrigerator car, plus a few more on a sidetrack in winter can cause imperceptible damage which dooms the fruit (that's what it is, botanically: a berry, in fact—so's a banana) to die unripened.

The tomato hides its griefs. Internal damage is hard to spot, but beware of flattened or indented sides, skin discolorations, and skin cracks which invite bacteria. A few yellowish spots near the stem end are common, though not desirable. If when you cut it a tomato turns out to be puffy—watery flesh plus empty pockets in the locules—it's a total dud. Complain to your market.

Well. Suppose you have bought a presentable tomato, *do not chill it.* Don't leave it in sunlight, either, or at a temperature above 80°F/27°C. Unless you got it from the garden or a local stand, it needs to ripen for a few days, at room temperature and preferably in a container which will trap the ethylene gas all fruit exudes as it ripens. When the tomato's color has deepened and its scent intensified, it's ready.

How to use them

I like to eat a fine summer tomato just as it comes, or sliced and sprinkled with minced herbs and a *vinaigrette* dressing; and I love the thin tomato sandwiches which are so popular at English summer tea parties: the trick is to spread the butter thinly but carefully, to seal the bread against sogginess. If you slice tomatoes vertically, the jelly won't ooze out.

In cooking it's best to use the pulp only, since the jelly juice has little flavor, and the seeds harden as they heat. To skin a tomato, drop it in boiling water to cover, count off ten seconds exactly (slowly intoning, "one thousand, two thousand" up to ten), then cut out the stem and pull off the skin. To empty the locules of seeds and jelly, cut the tomato in half crosswise, and squeeze each half gently; or cut off the top and ream out each pocket with your fingertip. To extract more juice, you may salt the cavities lightly and set the tomato upside down. Juice will gradually exude.

The chopped, sliced, or diced pulp is a basic kitchen ingredient. If you judge it weak in flavor, add canned pear-shaped tomatoes, drained and sieved; for even more intense savor and color, blend in canned tomato paste.

Start cautiously, since the sugary, herbal flavor of tomato paste can overpower a dish: try one tablespoon per cupful of fresh tomato pulp, and taste before adding more.

On cooking tomatoes whole or halved: leave the skins on, so they'll keep their shape, but seed and squeeze them; and cook them at the last minute. Since they blacken so quickly, instead of broiling them, I bake them for about ten minutes at 400°F/200°C. For a fine full Provencal flavor, try a classic French stuffing: mix fresh (not dry) white bread crumbs with a good sprinkling of fresh minced herbs and garlic; flavor to taste with dried herbs, salt, and pepper; fill the tomatoes and drizzle on a little olive oil. About a cupful of stuffing should suffice for 6 good-size tomatoes. Or give them an American accent by tossing the bread crumbs in melted butter with a little brown sugar, salt, and several generous grindings of fresh black pepper.

As a garnish, cherry tomatoes, raw or quickly baked, are a familiar pleasure. Less well known but delicious is tomato fondue, tomato pulp cut in neat strips or diced and cooked briefly in oil with minced shallots or scallions, to lend piquant flavor and pretty color to a soup or a dish of vegetables—cauliflower, for example, or puréed spinach.

However you use them—and there are hundreds of ways—do have the patience and take the pains to buy tomatoes beforehand, store them right, and wait, to taste them at their best.

Your own sausage and scrapple, and a home-made muffin worthy of eggs Benedict, a noble dish whose true tale now stands revealed. And other contributions to Joy in the Morning!

Breakfast Party

Menu

*Eggs Benedict, with Homemade English
Muffins and Three Ways of Poaching Eggs*

❧

Corned Beef Hash

❧

Sautéed Chicken Livers

❧

Sour Cream and Bread Crumb Flapjacks

❧

Scrapple

❧

Homemade Sausage Cakes

❧

Fresh Fruit

❧

Milk, Fruit Juices, and Bloody Marys

There are reasons, and then there are excuses. The excuses for being festive at breakfast time (whatever that is at your house) can be anything—a football game to follow, perhaps. For me the best of all reasons is that it's an occasion to serve that beloved combination, eggs Benedict: an easy dish to mass-produce, yet one that everyone considers a special treat. It's an American dish, quite different from the French *oeufs à la Bénédictine* (a tartlet lined with *brandade de morue*—a garlicky purée of salt cod—which is surmounted by a poached egg and napped with a creamy sauce). I had understood that it was originated at the New York Yacht Club by Commodore E. C. Benedict. However, a recent check with the club's librarian, Sohei Hohri, and with Mrs. Allan Butler of Vineyard Haven, Massachusetts, has set the record straight. It seems it wasn't Mr. Benedict (who wasn't commodore at the N.Y.Y.C., but somewhere else), but his cousin Mrs. LeGrand Benedict, Mrs. Butler's great-aunt, who invented the dish; and the place wasn't the N.Y.Y.C. but Delmonico's, an elegant place to lunch at the turn of the century. Mrs. Benedict, bored with the luncheon menu, asked the maître d'hôtel to suggest something new; he asked her if she had any ideas…and, just like that, she said, "What if you put a slice of ham on half an English muffin, and a poached egg on the ham, and hollandaise sauce on the egg, and truffles on top?" And lo, a star was born.

Honor, then, to our benefactress Mrs. Benedict; and honor, too, to the butter-loving British. The object of the English muffin is to be a butter mop, and that's why it is so honeycombed with little holes, or butter wells. The recipe I use is for something between a muffin and a crumpet—cruffin? mumpet?; it is baked in rings on a griddle and made of a very spongy yeast batter, not a dough. Since I am not about to get up at 3 a.m. to cook breakfast, I make my muffins days or weeks in advance. And, when I do make them, I mix the batter the night before and let it rise once, then stir it down and often give it a second rising in the refrigerator, where it can await my pleasure. Coming down next morning, I find a swollen, adhesive, bubbly mass that looks uncannily alive. And the little yeast plants are alive, of course, and lively, because they have been gorging on starch all night. As soon as one scoops up this mass and drops it into the baking rings, set on their hot griddle, the batter becomes excited by the heat. Bubbles form at the bottom, rise upward, and seem to wink as they burst on the surface, leaving behind them little vertical wells. So graphic is this illustration of the vigor of yeast that it might give pause to believers in the transmigration of souls, the "Don't swat that fly, it might be Grandma" people.

It's nice to have the poached eggs already cooked, ready to be reheated in warm water, so famished guests can fall to at once; but what if they want seconds? Let those who want to poach them make their own. Why not? And if you have a flameproof glass saucepan, let them try the old-fashioned whirlpool method, so that they can crouch down to observe the process: the yolk twirling in its veil of white, trapped in the cone-shaped vortex. Some might want their second eggs with different underpinnings, so have some scrapple or fresh pork sausage waiting, and/or some crusty corned beef hash or sausage cakes, and a bowl of fresh tomato sauce or warm chili sauce or ketchup to splosh on top. Or perhaps they'd enjoy eggs Henriette, so have some sautéed chicken livers ready too. And stacks of pancakes, with hot butter and maybe syrup or honey to slather on.

If you have room in your kitchen, it's a great place to give this kind of party. We like to eat right there, at the big table where the morning sun falls brightest, so we set out our cold offerings on the counter tops: pitchers of milk

and of orange and tomato juice—with the Bloody Mary pitcher clearly distinguished so that guests who feel fragile in the morning won't get any untoward surprise—and a great bowl of the loveliest fresh fruit we can find. From the warming drawer we bring forth platters of homemade doughnuts and coffee cake or Danish pastry. And the stove, or part of it, becomes our hot table. The bowls of chicken livers and of warm sauce are set in water-filled shallow roasting pans over low heat; platters sit on cake tins, also full of water to keep them warm; and that still leaves us a burner or two for poached egg experiments.

Right on the table we set two cozy little warming lamps, over which go two fat pots, one of strong fresh coffee and one of our favorite China tea. Made our way—we carefully measure out both boiling water and tea, and brew it in a stainless-steel pan, then strain it through a very clean stainless-steel sieve into our teapot—it keeps perfectly for hours. And it will have to. Guests at this comfortable meal will eat to bursting and then stay around to chat drowsily cuddling their warm mugs, until it's practically sunset. Don't say I didn't warn you!

Preparations

Recommended Equipment:
For homemade English muffins, you will need muffin rings, crumpet rings, or shallow tin cans with the tops and bottoms removed, and a griddle or heavy frying pan. See recipe for details.

For the other dishes, all kinds of makeshifts will work. Be sure to check out the recipe for poached eggs in advance, as various methods depend on various gadgets.

Marketing and Storage:
Staples to have on hand

Salt
Peppercorns
Herbs and spices: dried sage, oregano, thyme, tarragon; paprika, mace, and allspice

Double-acting baking powder
White vinegar or cider vinegar
Olive oil or cooking oil
Chicken bouillon and/or meat bouillon (see recipes for Corned Beef Hash, Sautéed Chicken Livers, and Scrapple for kinds and quantities)
Flour, butter, and eggs (see recipes for quantities needed)
Milk
Parsley
Fruit juices to your taste
Coffee and/or tea to your taste

Specific ingredients for this menu
All ingredients calculated for 6 people unless otherwise indicated in recipes

For Homemade English Muffins:
Dry active yeast (1 Tb)
Instant mashed potatoes (2 Tb) or raw potatoes (1)

For Eggs Benedict:
    Sliced boiled ham (about
    ½ pound or 225 g)
    English muffins (6) ▼
    Lemons (1)
For Corned Beef Hash:
    Cooked corned beef (4 cups or 2 pounds
    or 1 kg), preferably homemade
    (see page 138)
    "Boiling" or all-purpose potatoes (6 to 8)
    Onions (3 or 4)
    (Optional: heavy cream (½ cup or 1 dL)
    Fresh tomato sauce (see page 143) or chili
    sauce or ketchup
For Sautéed Chicken Livers:
    Chicken livers (1 pound or 450 g)
    Optional: fresh mushrooms (½ pound
    or 225 g)
    Port, Madeira, or dry white French ver-
    mouth
For Sour Cream and Bread Crumb Flapjacks:
    Nonsweet white bread (to make 1 cup or
    ¼ L crumbs)
    Wondra or instant-blending flour (½ cup
    or 70 g)
    Sour cream (½ cup or 1 dL)
    Syrup, honey, or whatever you fancy
For Scrapple:
    Sausage meat (4 cups or 1 L),
    preferably homemade (see page 175)
    Yellow cornmeal (1 cup or ¼ L),
    preferably stone ground
    Fragrant leaf sage
For Fresh Sausage Meat:
    Fresh ground pork (8 cups or 2 L)
    Dry white wine or vermouth
Fresh fruits in season
Optional: Assorted coffee cakes, doughnuts,
    and/or Danish pastry

▶ *Remarks:*

English muffins: Let's not be muffin snobs;
store-bought are excellent. Homemade are,
simply, something else.

Homemade English Muffins

For 10 to 12 muffins

1 Tb dry active yeast dissolved in ¼ cup
(½ dL) tepid water

2 Tb instant mashed potatoes softened in ½
cup (1 dL) boiling water (or ¼ cup or ½ dL
grated raw potato simmered until tender in 1
cup or ¼ L water)

½ cup (1 dL) cold water (or cold milk if using
raw potato)

2½ cups (6 dL) all-purpose flour in a 3-quart
(3-L) mixing bowl

To be added after first rise: 1½ tsp salt dissolved in 3 Tb tepid water

2 to 3 Tb butter, softened

Equipment

A heavy griddle or large frying pan, or a nonstick electric skillet; muffin or crumpet rings or
cat-food or tunafish cans about 3 inches (8 cm)
in diameter with tops and bottoms removed; a
4- to 5-Tb ladle or long-handled cup; spatulas
(both rubber and metal); and, perhaps, pliers

*Pikelets (top left). Oven-baked muffins (top right).
Crumpet-muffins (bottom).*

The dough

While yeast is dissolving, assemble the other ingredients. Then into the instant potatoes beat the cold milk, and stir it along with the water and dissolved yeast into the flour. (Or, if using raw potato, stir the cold milk into the potato pan, then stir both into the flour, adding dissolved yeast only after mixture has cooled to tepid.) Beat vigorously for a minute or so with a wooden spoon to make a smooth loose thick batter, heavier than the usual pancake batter but not at all like the conventional dough. Cover with plastic wrap and let rise, preferably at around 80°F/27°C, until batter has risen and large bubbles have appeared in the surface (usually about 1½ hours—it must be bubbly, however long it takes).

Stir the batter down, then beat in the salt and water, beating vigorously for a minute. Cover and let rise until bubbles again appear in the surface—about an hour at 80°F/27°C. The batter is now ready to become English muffins.

🕐 Batter may sit for an hour or more after its second rise, or you may use one of the delaying tactics suggested at the end of the recipe.

Preliminaries to cooking the muffins

When you are ready to cook the muffins, brush insides of rings or tins fairly generously with butter; butter surface of griddle or frying pan lightly and set over moderate heat. When just hot enough, so that drops of water begin to dance on it, the heat is about right. Scoop your ladle or cup into the batter and dislodge the batter into a ring or tin with rubber spatula; batter should be about ⅜ inch (1 cm) thick to make a raised muffin twice that. (Batter should be heavy, sticky, sluggish, but not runny, having just enough looseness to be spread out into the ring—if you think it is too thick, beat in tepid water by driblets.)

Cooking the muffins

The muffins are to cook slowly on one side until bubbles, which form near the bottom of the muffin, pierce through the top surface, and until almost the entire top changes from a wet ivory white to a dryish gray color; this will take 6 to 8 minutes or more, depending on the heat. (Regulate heat so that bottoms of muffins do not color more than a medium or pale brown.) Now the muffins are to be turned over for a brief cooking on the other side, and at

Batter on left has risen.

this point you can probably lift the rings off them; if not, turn them over and dislodge rings with the point of a knife, cutting and poking around the edge of rings if necessary. Cans are sometimes more difficult to remove; you may find it useful to have a pair of pliers for lifting, as well as a small knife for poking. Less than a minute is usually enough for cooking the second side, which needs only a token browning and drying out. Cool the muffins on a rack.

🕐   Fresh but cold muffins freeze beautifully and keep freshest when stored frozen, although they will stay fresh enough wrapped airtight in a plastic bag for a day or two in the refrigerator.

To serve English muffins
The muffins must be split (not cut) in half horizontally, since the inside texture should be slightly rough and full of holes (the bottoms are always solid, however). To split them, you can use a table fork, pushing the tines into the muffin all around the circumference, then gently tearing the two halves apart. Or use a serrated knife, cutting a slit in one side, then tearing the muffin apart all around and inside,

using short slashes made with the point and top ½ inch (1½ cm) of the knife.

An electric toaster is not at all suitable for homemade English muffins: since the muffins are damp in texture they must be toasted very slowly under a broiler; the slow browning dries out the interior while crusting the surface. Toast the uncut side a minute or so, then turn and toast the cut side for 2 to 3 minutes, until lightly browned. Butter the cut side and return under the broiler for a moment to let the butter bubble up and sink in. Serve as soon as possible.

Remarks:
Delaying tactics and sourdough: Not much can happen to ruin this dough, as long as you have achieved the necessary bubbles. You may let it wait at room temperature for an hour or more before baking; or you may even refrigerate it overnight. If it seems to have lost its bubble, you can bring it back to life by beating in another cup of flour blended with enough tepid water to make a batter; this will give the yeast something more to feed on and in an hour or so it will rise and bubble again as it gobbles its new food.

You can even turn this batter into a sourdough. Simply let it sit at room temperature for a day or two until it has soured, then bottle and refrigerate it. You can now use it in any sourdough recipe, or you can make sourdough English muffins: blend ½ cup of it with 1 cup flour and enough water to make a batter, add 1 tablespoon dissolved yeast, and let it rise; then beat in more flour and water, or milk, and add salt (proportions make no difference as long as you get your bubbles); let it rise and bubble again; and cook your muffins. Replenish the sourdough starter by mixing it with more flour and water or milk blended into a batter, and let sit at room temperature until it has bubbled up and subsided; refrigerate as before.

To Poach an Egg

Here are three ways to poach eggs in water—and I am not talking about the electric poacher, which is really a steamer. If you are lucky enough to have very fresh eggs very recently out of the hen, you will have no trouble whatsoever; you simply break the egg into a pan of barely simmering water and in a few minutes you have the most beautiful neat perfect oval of a poached egg, the yolk cozily masked by the white all over. It is when you have store-bought eggs of uncertain date that you can at times run into exposed yolks, wispy whites, and quite unpresentable results that can be served only under a thick disguise.

However, when your eggs are reasonably fresh you can do very well as follows:
The 10-second firm-up: First prick the large end of each egg with a pin or an egg pricker, going down ¼ inch (¾ cm) into the egg; this will let the air from the pocket in the large end escape in the hot water, and prevent a burst of white from coming out of any crack in the shell. Then lower the eggs, using a slotted spoon, into a pan of boiling water, boil exactly

10 seconds, and remove at once; this gives just a little cohesion to the white, but not enough to stick it to its covering membrane or shell.

The vinegar coagulant: Vinegar coagulates the surface of the white as soon as they come in contact with each other, and although vinegar does very slightly toughen the outermost surface of the white, you are wise to use it when your eggs are not newly laid. For every quart or liter of water, pour in 2½ tablespoons of white or cider vinegar.

Timing poached eggs: The perfectly poached egg, besides being attractive, has a tender white that is just set all the way through, and a yolk that is still liquid. I find that 4 minutes in barely simmering water is just right for "large" and "extra large" eggs.

I. The whirlpool poach. Choose a rather high saucepan, 6 to 7 inches (15 to 18 cm) in both diameter and depth, add water to come ⅔ the way up, bring to the boil, and pour in 2½ tablespoons vinegar per quart or liter. Prick the eggs and boil 10 seconds in the shell. Then stir the water with a wooden spoon or spatula, going round and round the edge of the pan to create a whirlpool; quickly break an egg into the center or vortex and the swirling water

should form the egg neatly. Leave at the barest simmer for 4 minutes, then remove with a slotted spoon to a bowl of cold water.

II. *The free-form free-floating egg.* This is a neat trick when it works, and makes the cook feel clever. Fill a wide shallow saucepan with 1½ inches (4 cm) of water, adding the required 2½ tablespoons vinegar per quart or liter. Then, with water at the barest simmer, crack an egg and, holding it very close to the water, your fingers all but in it, swing the shell open and let the egg drop in. If you are lucky, it will form into a quite neat oval, but you can often help it, if help it needs, by rapidly rolling it over and over with a wooden spoon before it has coagulated. Set timer for 4 minutes and continue with the rest of the eggs, adding 4 to 6 in all, depending on the size of your pan; for accurate timing, start the first egg at the handle side of the pan, and move around clockwise, taking out the first egg as the timer goes off, then the second, and so forth, dropping each as it is done into a bowl of cold water.

III. *The oval egg holder triumph.* A most satisfactory solution to egg poaching and one which produces a handsomely shaped egg is the oval metal egg poacher with perforated bottom. (Before each poaching session, be sure to wash and wipe carefully to remove any rust or dirt in the holes.) Place the poachers in 2 inches (5 cm) of water, and proceed exactly as in the preceding directions, dropping the eggs one by one into the poachers. When your 4 minutes are up, remove the poachers one by one and very gently scoop the egg out with a dessert spoon into a bowl of cold water.

Storing poached eggs. Refrigerate poached eggs in a bowl with enough cold water to submerge them completely, but do not cover the bowl. They will keep perfectly for 2 or 3 days.

To reheat cold poached eggs. Drop into a pan of barely simmering salted water and leave for 2 minutes, then remove with a slotted spoon, and roll against a folded towel to dry them.

Eggs Benedict

For 12 eggs, 2 per serving

12 toasted and buttered English muffin halves (recipe on page 166)

12 rounds of boiled ham, lightly sautéed in butter

12 beautifully poached eggs (the preceding recipe)

About 1½ cups (½ L) hollandaise sauce (the following recipe)

Optional topping: <u>Either</u> slices of truffle <u>or</u> 1 hard-boiled egg, chopped, tossed with 3 Tb minced fresh parsley, 2 Tb minced cooked ham, and salt and pepper

Just before serving, place 2 hot toasted muffin halves on each plate and top each with a piece of ham. Heat the eggs as described in their recipe and rapidly remove from hot water with a slotted spoon, rolling each against a folded towel as you do so. Set an egg on each ham-topped muffin, spoon over a good dollop of hollandaise, and lay a slice or sprinkle on a big pinch of the optional topping. Serve at once.

A Light Hollandaise Sauce

For about 1 ½ cups

3 Tb fresh lemon juice and 3 Tb water in a small saucepan

½ tsp salt

1 whole egg and 2 yolks in a smallish stainless-steel saucepan

6 to 8 ounces (180–225 g) warm but not bubbling-hot butter in a small saucepan

Salt, pepper, and more lemon juice to taste

Shortly before serving, bring the lemon juice and water to the simmer, adding the salt. Meanwhile, vigorously beat the egg and yolks in their pan with a wire whip for a minute or so until they are pale and thick. Then set the yolk mixture over moderately low heat and whisk in the hot lemon juice by driblets. Continue whisking, not too fast but reaching all over bottom and corners of pan, until you have a foamy warm mass; remove from heat just as you see a wisp of steam rising. (Do not overheat or you will coagulate the egg yolks.) Immediately start beating in the warm butter by driblets, to make a thick, creamy, light yellow sauce. Taste carefully for seasoning, adding salt, pepper, and more lemon juice to taste.

🕐 This is such an easy sauce to make that I think it best done at the last moment. Otherwise I would suggest a regular hollandaise, and if it must wait and stay warm for any length of time, beat into it 2 tablespoons of *béchamel* (white) sauce for every 2 cups or ½ liter of hollandaise; this will help to hold it. However, any egg yolk and butter sauce can be kept only warm, not hot, or it will curdle; and remember that sauces with egg yolks are prime breeding grounds for sick-making bacteria. I would therefore not hold such a sauce longer than an hour, and would prefer to make fresh sauces as often as needed rather than risk the slightest chance of food poisoning.

Corned Beef Hash

To serve 6 to 8 people

Timing note: A good hash takes at least 40 minutes to make since it must have time to crust on the bottom, and that crust is stirred into the hash several times before the final crust is formed.

2½ cups (6 dL) minced onions

2 Tb or more butter

2 Tb or more olive oil or cooking oil

3 Tb flour

¾ cup (1¾ dL) or more bouillon (cooking liquid) from the corned beef, or chicken or beef broth

4 cups or more diced boiled potatoes (I like "boiling" or all-purpose potatoes because they keep their shape during cooking)

4 cups or more chopped or roughly ground cooked corned beef

½ tsp or so minced herbs such as sage, oregano, thyme, or a mixture

5 to 6 Tb or so minced fresh parsley

Salt and pepper

½ cup (1 dL) or so heavy cream (optional)

Equipment

A heavy frying pan or electric skillet with cover, 12 inches (30 cm) top diameter, and if you plan to unmold the hash it should be of well-seasoned iron or have a nonstick surface; an oiled pizza pan also, if you plan to unmold

The hash mixture

Sauté the onions slowly in 2 Tb each butter and oil for 6 to 8 minutes, stirring frequently, until tender, then raise heat slightly and let them brown a bit. Lower heat again; blend in the flour and a little more butter or oil if needed to make a paste; stir and cook slowly for 2 minutes. Blend in ¾ cup (1¾ dL) bouil-

lon or broth, let boil a moment, then mix in the potatoes, corned beef, herbs, and parsley. Taste carefully for seasoning, and if hash seems dry blend in tablespoons of optional cream or more bouillon.

Cooking the hash

Rather firmly, press the hash down all over with the flat of a spatula, set a cover over the pan, and cook slowly for about 15 minutes or until the hash has crusted on the bottom. Stir it up to mix some of the crust into the body of the hash, and repeat the process being careful not to overcook and dry it out (or it will not be cohesive enough to unmold properly). Taste and correct seasoning.

❶   Hash may be cooked in advance to this point; set aside off heat, and you may cover and refrigerate it when cold. Reheat slowly, covered, then proceed.

Some 10 to 15 minutes before serving, uncover the hash, press it down all over with a spatula, and let it form its final crust over moderate heat.

Serving

You may serve the hash as is, turning each serving upside down on the plate to present a crusted surface. Or you may wish to unmold it in a half-moon shape onto a platter: to do so, start sliding the large cake of hash onto a hot platter but stop at the halfway mark, then, holding pan by its handle, your thumb underneath, quickly flip pan upside down to turn other half of hash neatly over the first, crusted bottom in full view. (This can often be a tricky business, but it does help to have the first half of the hash thinner than the other half and a small pan is far easier to control than the large one described here.) A second unmolding system is to slide the whole cake of hash out onto an oiled pizza tray; then turn the frying pan or a round platter upside down over it and reverse the two, leaving the hash crusted side up. In either case, cracks and musses can be hidden under a sprinkling of chopped parsley.

Accompaniments

Serve each helping of hash with a fried or poached egg on top, and a dollop of fresh tomato sauce or of warm ketchup or chili sauce.

Sautéed Chicken Livers

For 6 to 8 small servings

1 pound (450 g) chicken livers

Salt, pepper, and flour

2 Tb butter and 1 of oil (more if needed)

About ½ cup (1 dL) chicken stock or broth (more if needed)

4 Tb Port, Madeira, or dry white French vermouth

A sprinkling of tarragon (optional)

½ pound (225 g) fresh mushrooms, quartered and sautéed separately in butter (optional)

1 Tb or more butter as final enrichment (optional)

2 to 3 Tb fresh minced parsley

To prepare the livers for cooking, look them over to be sure no black or greenish bile spots are on the surface. If so, shave them off since they are bitter; although this is a rare occurrence, it is well to watch for it. Just before sautéing, dry the livers in paper towels; then place on wax paper and toss with a sprinkling of salt and pepper, and then of flour, to give them a light dusting. Immediately, then, get to the sautéing: set a heavy 10-inch (25-cm) frying pan over high heat, add to it enough butter to film the bottom, plus ½ that amount of oil. When the butter foam begins to subside, toss in as many livers as will fit in one layer. Turn and toss for 2 to 3 minutes until, when you press them, the livers have changed from squashy raw to just resistant to your finger. Pour in the stock and wine, the optional tarragon and mushrooms, and boil rapidly, tossing and turning the livers for a moment or two until liquid thickens lightly. Taste and correct seasoning.

🕐 May be cooked in advance; set aside uncovered.

Just before serving toss over moderately high heat, adding more liquid if you feel it necessary, a tablespoon or so of butter if you wish, and the parsley.

Sour Cream and Bread Crumb Flapjacks

Tender pancakes
For about 10 pancakes 4 inches in diameter

1 cup (¼ L) toasted fresh, nonsweet white bread crumbs

4 Tb melted butter

1 egg

½ cup (1 dL) Wondra or instant-blending flour

½ cup (1 dL) sour cream

½ cup (1 dL) or more milk

½ tsp double-acting baking powder

Salt and pepper

To make toasted bread crumbs, crumb fresh bread in a blender or processor, then spread out in a roasting pan in a preheated 350°F/180°C oven, and toss until lightly browned—15 to 20 minutes. Toss in a frying pan with the melted butter over moderate heat.

Blend egg, flour, sour cream, ½ cup (1 dL) milk, and baking powder in a 4-cup (1-L) measure; fold in the buttered crumbs and salt and pepper to taste. Stir in driblets more milk if you think it necessary (but can you tell until you have tried a pancake?).

Drop batter onto a buttered hot skillet and cook pancakes, turning when bubbles appear on the surface.

Serve with melted butter and maple syrup or honey.

Scrapple

For an 8-cup loaf pan, serving 12 or more

4 cups (1 L) sausage meat, preferably homemade (see recipe following)

4 cups (1 L) pork stock or other flavorful meat stock in a 3-quart (3-L) saucepan with heavy bottom

1 Tb or more fragrant leaf sage

1 cup (225 g) yellow cornmeal, stone ground preferred

½ cup (1 dL) cold water

3 eggs

Salt and pepper

Equipment

An 8-cup (2-L) loaf pan or baking dish, and a board or plate that will fit into it for weighting down scrapple after baking

Sauté sausage meat in a large frying pan until it turns from pink to gray, breaking it up with a fork as you do so—5 minutes or more. Drain in a sieve set over a bowl, and reserve fat—which may be used for sautéing finished scrapple later.

Meanwhile, bring the stock to the boil, adding sage to taste. Mix the cornmeal with the cold water in a bowl, then whisk in a cupful of the hot stock. Return cornmeal to stock, bring to the boil whisking slowly, and cook for 5 minutes or more until mixture is thick, like cornmeal mush. Cover pan, set in a larger pan of simmering water, and cook for 30 minutes. Remove from pan of hot water and boil over moderately high heat, stirring with a wooden spoon, until cornmeal is thick and heavy and holds its shape in a spoon—the thicker the better, so that it will unmold and slice easily later.

Beat the cooked and drained sausage meat into the cornmeal, breaking it up so that it will blend nicely, and boil, stirring and beating, for 3 to 4 minutes. Beat in the eggs. Taste carefully for seasoning: scrapple is traditionally fragrant with sage and highly seasoned.

Butter an 8-cup (2-L) loaf pan, line bottom of pan with wax paper, and turn the cornmeal mixture into it. Cover with wax paper and aluminum foil and bake for an hour or more in a preheated 350°F/180°C oven, until mixture has swelled and is bubbling hot.

Remove from oven, place a board on top of the scrapple (over the wax paper and foil) and a 5-pound (2¼-kg) weight (canned goods, meat grinder, etc.), and let cool. When cold, remove weight and board, cover airtight, and chill.

🕐 Once baked in its pan, scrapple will keep for at least 2 to 3 weeks in the refrigerator. It can be frozen; however, pork products tend to lose texture and savor after 2 months or so in the freezer.

To serve, run a knife around inside of mold, then set mold on top of stove to heat and loosen bottom; unmold onto a cutting board. Slice into serving pieces about ⅜ inch (1 cm) thick. Dredge lightly in cornmeal, and brown on both sides in rendered sausage fat or butter.

Serve for breakfast with fried or poached eggs, or fried apple slices; or use as a dinner meat, accompanying the scrapple with green vegetables such as broccoli or cabbage, or a green salad, or cole slaw.

Remarks:

Traditional farm scrapple is made, literally, from pork scraps and bones that are boiled up together for 2 hours or so with herbs and aromatic vegetables—carrots, onions, celery. The meat adhering to the bones is then scraped off and chopped, along with the other pork meat scraps. The cooking broth is strained and boiled up with the cornmeal, then the two are combined, and that is the scrapple. If you have cured your own pork, as in the recipe on page 000, you can use the same system whether you decide to bone your pork before or after salting (and soaking) it. Once you have chopped the boiled meat, you can substitute it for the sausage in the preceding recipe. Simply stir it into the saucepan of cooked cornmeal, which has been boiled up with your pork-cooking liquid, and continue with the recipe.

Fresh Sausage Meat

For about 8 cups, or 4 pounds

8 cups (2 L) fresh ground pork—including 2 to 3 cups (½ – ¾ L) fresh pork fat or blanched salt pork fat—from shoulder, rib, or loin

1 Tb salt

1 Tb sage

1 tsp mace

½ tsp cracked pepper

1 tsp paprika

4 to 5 Tb white wine or vermouth

Optional other herbs: thyme, allspice

Grind pork not too fine in meat grinder or processor, beating in seasonings and wine or vermouth (to lighten the mixture). Sauté a spoonful and taste, then correct seasoning as you feel necessary.

🕐 Best made a day ahead, so that flavoring will have time to blend with meat.

To be used in the preceding scrapple, or to sauté in cakes, as breakfast sausage.

Scrapple made from fresh cornmeal and fresh sausage meat surrounding a platter of scrambled eggs.

🕐 Timing

Because breakfast is such a personal meal, this chapter offers you a choice of dishes from which you might like to compose your own menu. Supposing, however, that you want to take on the whole shooting match, the work could be divided up as follows:

During the party, cook pancakes and assemble eggs Benedict to order. This means having on hand a pitcher of pancake batter, a bowl of warm water (to reheat the eggs), hot toasted and buttered muffins, hot sautéed ham slices, and warm hollandaise sauce. You can prepare all of these half an hour in advance.

Scrapple, too, is fried to order, or fried just beforehand and kept warm; and the same goes for the sausage cakes.

Corned beef hash takes about 45 minutes (with some attention from you) to form a good crust; it may be kept warm over hot water. You could cook it till not quite done the night before, cool and refrigerate, and finish the crust 10 minutes before the party.

Eggs may be poached up to 2 or 3 days in advance and kept refrigerated, uncovered, in a bowl of water.

Muffins freeze perfectly; you can wait until that morning to thaw, split, toast, butter, and toast again.

Coffee and tea must be made that morning, but will keep over low heat if you don't let them get cold—or scalded—at any time.

Corned beef keeps almost indefinitely; sausage meat and scrapple can stay in the freezer for up to 2 months.

Menu Variations

English muffins: See the Postscript to this chapter for other kinds of yeast batter griddle cakes. And I need not remind you that the English muffin, known in my youth as the Garbo, can get away with almost anything, including peanut butter. Peanut Garbos! Divine.

Eggs Benedict: You can substitute Canadian bacon for the ham, and toast or little pastry cases for the muffins. Keeping only the poached egg, you can switch everything else around: with chicken livers, it's an egg Henriette; with spinach, an egg Florentine; you can sit it on a sliced grilled tomato; you can use cheese sauce (eggs à la Mornay), or tomato sauce, or a *soubise*.... Escoffier has some 19 recipes, all with resounding names.

Corned beef hash: See page 138 for how to corn pork, and try hashing that. Or add beets for red flannel hash. Or cook it in little cakes; it doesn't have to be a big pillow. Or hash leftover chicken or turkey, going a bit lighter on the seasoning and adding cream. Or hash lamb, perhaps adding cooked rice or kasha instead of potatoes.

Chicken livers: You could broil them on skewers instead of sautéing them, or use duck or other poultry livers if you like a stronger flavor. Chopped fine, combined with mushroom *duxelles,* quickly sautéed and moistened with a little leftover gravy flavored with Port or Madeira, they make a luxurious spread for hot buttered toast. Thinly sliced sautéed calf's liver is also nice with eggs for a hearty breakfast.

Pancakes: These are fairly close cousins to the muffin variants in the Postscript—to pikelets in particular. You can bake almost any batter on a griddle (buckwheat, rye, oat, barley, corn, etc.), and don't forget the charm of grated potato pancakes blobbed with sour cream, or mashed-potato pancakes (see page 191). Or lovely yeasty blini, nice with smoked fish as well as with caviar—nice with butter and honey, for that matter. Or Swedish pancakes, maybe with lingonberries. Or French crêpes, rolled around a creamed mixture and sauced, or, especially for children, rolled around a spoonful of jam and dusted with confectioners sugar. Or palatschinken, or tortillas, or...well, every nation has its pancakes.

Scrapple: You can eat it with fried tomato or apple slices; you can use pork liver and other scraps in the recipe; you can use oatmeal instead of cornmeal (in which case it's called "goetta")—but I can't really think of any variations in cooking it.

Sausage meat: For other sausage makings, check out *Mastering II* and *J.C.'s Kitchen.* And sometime try baking homemade sausage in a pastry crust.

Grated potato pancakes and sausages waiting for their blob of sour cream.

Leftovers

Poached eggs: If you have extra ones, even rewarmed, congratulations. Coat them with aspic for eggs *en gelée*—an exquisite cold appetizer. Warm them, then sauce and bed them with and on practically anything. Tuck them into a soufflé, bedded on about ⅓ of the mixture, then covered with the rest. *Ham:* I don't need to suggest what to do with extra sliced ham. *Muffins:* If you have some unsplit, they freeze (or refreeze) perfectly. *Hollandaise sauce:* If it has sat around long, I don't think it's safe to keep. If it hasn't, you can refrigerate and rewarm cautiously to tepid.

Hash and *scrapple:* Chill or refreeze any uncooked leftovers. And do likewise with uncooked *sausage meat,* although this you can combine with other meats, in meatballs (see page 105), in hamburgers, and in terrines and *pâtés.*

Chicken livers: Once they're cooked, I'd make them into a simple *pâté*—you can just run them through a processor or blender with a little cream and beat into softened butter, then chill.

Pancakes: Leftover cooked pancakes will freeze but, because it contains baking powder, the batter won't keep. However, if it's still fairly lively you could stir in enough flour to make a light dough, and bake in muffin tins.

Postscript: More on muffins

Remember the schoolbook story of how King Alfred let the poor cottager's cakes burn as he sat by the hearth worrying about the Danish invaders? Even back in the 800s, those "cakes" were probably muffins and probably made with yeast, which has been known since the dawn of history.

Most home cooks in France, where I got my culinary education, never learn bread making at all, so I came late to its ancient mysteries, which still give me a sense of awe—a sense shared, and poetically expressed, by Elizabeth David. If you too are fascinated, I refer you to her masterly account of British baking, *English Bread and Yeast Cookery* (London: Penguin Books, 1978).

Apropos muffins and crumpets, Mrs. David says, in a whole chapter devoted to them, that the distinction is rather foggy and the batter similar; but the crumpet is only half as thick and holds more butter because you don't split it. The same combination of yeast batter and griddle cooking (using all kinds of flours) gives you the pikelet (baked without a ring, flat and free-form), the girdle cake, the bannock, and the scone of Scotland. The latter two may be baked in the oven, as is the plump Scottish bap. Mrs. David says that many country kitchens in the British Isles still keep their ancient bake stones and baking irons, used right in the hearth. King Alfred would feel right at home.

At this intimate dinner you can cook right at the table and not miss a word of the conversation. And for chocolate lovers, there is a treat in store.

Chafing-Dish Dinner

What to do about conversations you can't bear to miss? Cook at the table, of course, says Paul, adding sagely that we'd better practice first. How right he is. Chafing-dish jokes, featuring splashes and scorches, were a staple in our parents' day, when the kitchen belonged exclusively to the cook but the family tried to play too. People nowadays do seem to use chafing dishes on buffet tables, as food warmers, but are apt to ignore their usefulness as small, real stoves, not to mention their dramatic possibilities.

Flambé dishes are fun but a bit too obviously showy. So we settle on Steak Diane, to make a party chic as well as intimate. Why Diane? Nobody remembers. Why a French name, since it's not related to the French Sauce Diane, a creamed-up version of the classic gamy *poivrade?* Anne Willan, in her Grand Diplôme series, suggests that the dish originated in Australia. Anyway, that touch of Worcestershire sauce would indicate the New World—but if the dish resembles its namesake, the mysterious Diane must have been quite a girl: good-looking, classy, brisk, and modish but not faddy. The sauce has a tangy, refreshing taste, not too overpowering before a rich dessert. The meat is pounded to make it thinner for swift searing; and for this you need a very strong heat source (see Recommended Equipment for details). We have experimented with various fuels and have found that liquid denatured alcohol is an absolute essential because of its hot, clear, odorless flame. For Steak Diane we practice such flourishes as pouring oil from on high, and turning the meat with a deft flick of the wrist—two wrists I mean, one for each fork. Great fun.

If you have friends who are chocolate addicts, do something special to indulge their passion. For instance, there used to be a chocolate cake in New York in the thirties, legendary among connoisseurs. It was made by a smart little bakery whose dour proprietress has never revealed her secret recipe. This much-discussed cake, which I unfortunately never tasted in those halcyon days, was baked in a loaf shape and had a fat and unctuous texture and intense chocolate flavor; it sank in the middle, and this trough was, accordingly, mounded with curled shaved chocolate. Fanciers were all agreed that the cake must have involved a lot of butter, egg whites and yolks beaten separately, and practically no flour (one very skillful cook, it was said, evolved a near replica using only one tablespoonful). But what effect, I wonder, would so little flour have, anyway? I made a number of serious tries, but then sailed off on a different tack. What finally came out of endless experiments was a cake I have proudly named Le Gâteau Victoire au Chocolat, Mousseline. Its components sound like custard makings, its airiness suggests a mousse, and yet, it is a cake: a cake with no butter, no flour at all, a simple

method, and an incredibly sparse list of ingredients. Sparse but sumptuous: it includes one whole pound of chocolate.

I happen to love the old-fashioned combination of peas and mashed potatoes—plain but exquisite if you have good fresh peas and Idaho potatoes, and wonderful with steak. You might think this would involve long minutes away from the table. But mashed potatoes can, in fact, be done ahead and kept warm: the trick is to cover them only partially, to give them air. (By that same token, a baked potato also acquires a dank, stifled flavor if you let it sit unopened. Slash it and give it a squeeze.) By doctoring them with cheese and whatnot, busy people can make do pretty well with dehydrated or otherwise pre-prepared potatoes; but these are not for plain mashing. You must use the real thing. Why not recoup peeling time by shelling the peas mechanically? I have found an ingenious device, something like an old-fashioned laundry mangle in miniature, which you can crank by hand or else attach to an ordinary electric beater (see page 186). You feed the pea pods into it and, with efficient little zips, it gobbles up the pods and spews them out one side while the peas—quite unharmed—bounce briskly out the other. This chapter's section on Menu Variations does not include vegetables, since almost all vegetables are good with steak; but my recommendation, if the menu seems too starchy to you, would be to substitute tomatoes, baked or *à la provençale* (with garlic, olive oil, and bread crumbs), and string beans or broccoli for the peas and mashed potatoes.

Anyway, the goloptiousness, as Winnie-the-Pooh would have said, of this menu decided us on a light first course—rather reminiscent of the *nouvelle cuisine*—which has a good deal of subtle charm. Sea scallops are sliced into a lime juice marinade which "cooks" them briefly—something to do with enzymes, I understand. Then they are arranged with sliced fresh artichoke bottoms, tomatoes, and watercress or romaine; the delicate sauce *vinaigrette* is given a little body by the addition of an egg white.

With its easy, uninterrupted flow, this kind of little dinner is usually a happy one. My own enthusiasm is divided about equally among the nimble pea sheller, the efficient, energy-saving little stove, and that super chocolate cake.

Preparations

Recommended Equipment:
For the potatoes and the peas, you'll need a potato ricer and two heavy pots. For the cake, a 10-cup (2½-L) cake pan, which must be at least 2 inches (5 cm) deep. I usually measure a new pan's capacity by pouring it full of water and measuring the amount; then I scratch "10 c" or whatever on the back of the pan. A nonstick surface is strongly recommended. You need a larger pan, also, to serve as a bain-marie (water bath) for the cake pan.

For your dinner table: see the Steak Diane recipe for the sauce set-up, which should be conveniently arranged on a tray. You'll need an electric warming tray, or trays, with room

enough for dinner plates, a small serving dish for the steaks, and a serving dish or dishes for the vegetables. The heat source should sit on a metal tray. You can use an electric skillet or a camp stove in place of a chafing dish; all you need for tabletop sautéing is strong heat and a wide pan. About chafing dishes: many pretty ones of open, leggy design, while fine for scrambling eggs or other slow-heat cookery, don't work for sautéing. This is because you need a focused flame, which you can't get unless it is enclosed at the sides with just enough air circulation to keep it burning. You could surround a leggy chafing dish with a collar of sheet metal with a few holes cut in near the top. Denatured alcohol gel won't give you enough heat; you must have liquid denatured alcohol.

And play safe: if you have to replenish the fuel (though the usual-sized container will hold enough for hours), douse the flame and let the lamp cool a bit before adding more alcohol. And in the—very unlikely—case of fire, have baking soda handy and remember that the quickest way to extinguish any blazing pan is to clap a well-fitting lid on it.

For serving your cake you will need a platter or board with flat surface large enough to hold the unmolded cake.

Marketing and Storage:
Staples to have on hand

Salt
Black and white peppercorns
Optional: bottled green peppercorns ▼
Mustard (the strong Dijon type; see Remarks, page 6)
Soy sauce
Worcestershire sauce
Olive oil
Optional: peanut oil
Flour
Cornstarch
Unsweetened baking chocolate (2 ounces or 60 g)
Semisweet baking chocolate (14 ounces or 400 g)
Sugar (about ½ cup or 1 dL)
Optional: confectioners sugar
Pure vanilla extract
Eggs (7 "large")
Butter
Heavy or whipping cream (at least 2 cups or ½ L)
Milk
"Baking" potatoes (3 or 4 large) ▼
Parsley
Shallots or scallions
Limes (1)
Lemons (3 or 4)
Beef bouillon (1 cup or ¼ L)
Instant coffee
Cognac
Port or Madeira
Dark Jamaica rum

Specific ingredients for this menu

Steaks (4; see recipe)
Fresh sea scallops (8 to 10 large)
Artichokes (2 or 3 large fine)
Fresh green peas (about 2 pounds or 1 kg) ▼
Watercress or romaine
Tomatoes (2 or 3) or cherry tomatoes

▶ *Remarks:*
Staples

Green peppercorns: buy them "au naturel," meaning they are packed in lightly salted water. They will keep several weeks in the refrigerator; for longer storage freeze them.
Potatoes for mashing: you want floury potatoes so that they mash fluffily; you don't want new potatoes or waxy potatoes, which mash lumpily, and even glue-ily.

Ingredients for this menu

Store-bought fresh *peas* can be perfectly good, although not always as fresh and as young as you would like. But properly cooked, they're so much better than frozen or canned. Be sure the pods are fresh and crisp and neither too full (meaning the peas are large and old) nor too flat (meaning the peas have not formed). If in doubt, discreetly tear open the package a little bit and taste—right there in the supermarket.

Seviche of Sea Scallops with Fresh Artichokes

Sea scallops have a lovely freshness of taste and texture when sliced thin and marinated raw in lime juice, salt, parsley, and minced shallots or scallions—the lime juice cooks them, as it were. For a light first course you need only 2 or 3 per serving, and half a large artichoke bottom plus a little fresh tomato and watercress or romaine for decoration.

For 4 servings

8 to 10 large fresh sea scallops
1 fresh lime
Salt and white pepper
½ Tb minced shallots or scallions
2 Tb minced fresh parsley
2 Tb flour
2 or 3 lemons
2 or 3 large fine artichokes
1 tsp Dijon-type mustard
1 Tb raw egg white
4 to 5 Tb light olive oil
For decoration: watercress or shredded romaine, sliced tomatoes or cherry tomatoes

The scallops

Wash and drain the scallops to remove possible sand. Dipping a sharp knife in cold water for each cut, slice them crosswise (across the grain) into pieces 3/16 inch (¾ cm) thick.

Toss in a bowl with the juice of the lime, a sprinkling of salt and pepper, the shallots or scallions, and the parsley. Cover and marinate (let sit) in the refrigerator for half an hour, or until serving time.

The artichokes

To make a *blanc* or cooking liquid that will keep the artichokes white, place the flour in a medium-size saucepan, gradually beat in 1 cup (¼ L) cold water, stir in 2 more cups (½ L) water, a tablespoon of lemon juice, and 1½ teaspoons salt; bring to the boil, stirring, then remove from heat. One by one, break stems off artichokes and bend leaves back upon themselves all around to snap them off the base until you come to the bulge at the top of the artichoke bottom; cut off crown of leaves at this point, and trim base all around to remove greenish parts—rubbing frequently with cut lemon to prevent darkening. Drop each as done into the cooking water. Simmer 30 to 40 minutes, until tender when pierced with a knife, and leave in cooking water until ready to serve.

🕐 Will keep 2 to 3 days under refrigeration.

Wash under cold water, scoop out chokes with a teaspoon, and cut into 3/16-inch (¾ cm) slices going from top to bottom. Fold gently in a bowl with the following dressing.

Vinaigrette Liée:

(lightly thickened French dressing)
For about ⅓ cup dressing, beat ½ teaspoon salt with 1½ tablespoons lemon juice and the teaspoon of mustard, beat in the egg white, and then, by dribbles, the oil. Taste carefully for seasoning, adding pepper to taste—dressing should not be too strong or it will mask the taste of the artichokes.

Assembling

Line individual small plates or shells with watercress or shredded romaine. Then arrange slices of artichoke interspersed with tomato, for instance, around the edges of the dishes and a rosette of scallop slices in the middle, with a central dot of tomato for accent. Cover with plastic wrap and refrigerate until serving time.

🕐 May be prepared up to an hour ahead.

Steak Diane

For 4 people

4 steaks (about ½ pound or 225 g trimmed) cut ½ inch (1½ cm) thick from the top loin strip (or tenderloin, or Delmonico, or rib-eye steaks)

1½ Tb green peppercorns packed in water, or freshly ground pepper

Drops of soy sauce

Olive oil or peanut oil

The Sauce Set-up for the Dining Room:

A small pitcher of oil and a plate with a stick of butter

¼ cup (½ dL) each minced shallots or scallions and fresh parsley, in small bowls

A pitcher or bowl containing 1 Tb cornstarch blended with 1 Tb Dijon mustard and 1 cup fragrant beef bouillon

Worcestershire sauce

A lemon cut in half

Cognac and Port or Madeira

Equipment

A heavy frying pan about 12 inches (30 cm) top diameter for tabletop sautéing; a strong heat source; 2 large forks for turning and rolling up steaks; 2 dessert spoons, 1 for stirring and 1 for tasting; a butter knife; matches; 4 hot dinner plates

Preliminaries

Trim steaks of all fat and gristle—especially the piece of gristle at large end of loin under fat. One at a time, pound steaks between pieces of wax paper to enlarge them and reduce them to an even ¼-inch (¾-cm) thickness; use a wooden mallet, metal pounder, rubber hammer, rolling pin, bottle, or other handy object. Crush drained green peppercorns with the back of a spoon and spread a little on one side of each steak (or rub into steaks a grind or two of regular pepper) along with a few drops soy sauce and oil. Roll up each steak like a rug from one of the small ends and arrange on a platter; cover and refrigerate until serving time.

Prepare ingredients for the sauce set-up.
🕐 May be done several hours in advance. Cover shallots or scallions and parsley with dampened paper towels and plastic wrap and refrigerate; refrigerate the bouillon mixture.

Sautéing Steaks Diane at the table
Preheat frying pan in the kitchen to a reasonably hot temperature and bring it and the steaks with you to the table. The sauce set-up should be already in place near the chafing-dish burner.

The steaks are sautéed two at a time as follows: Pour 1 tablespoon oil into the pan as it heats on the flame and add 2 tablespoons butter. Butter will foam up, gradually foam will subside, and just as butter begins to brown, unroll one steak and immediately a second in the pan. Sauté 30 to 40 seconds on one side, turn with forks, and sauté on the other side—steaks will barely color and will just become lightly springy to the touch—for rare. Rapidly roll them up with your forks and replace on the platter. Sauté the other two steaks in the same manner, and roll up beside the first.

Add another spoonful or two butter, and when foaming stir in a big spoonful of shallots or scallions and parsley, let cook for a moment, then stir in the pitcher or bowl of bouillon mixture. Stir about for a moment, then add a few drops of Worcestershire and the juice of half a lemon (pierce lemon with fork, picking out seeds first, and squeeze with flourish). Add droplets of Cognac and Port or Madeira, taste, and add droplets more—again with flourish. Finally with forks and fanfare, and one by one, unroll each steak and bathe in the sauce, turning and dipping with your two forks, before placing it on a hot dinner plate.

When the other steaks are sauced and in place, spoon the rest of the sauce over them and serve.

Fresh Green Peas

(the store-bought kind)

For 4 people

3 cups (¾ L) shelled fresh peas (about 2 pounds or 1 kg large fresh peas in the shell)

Salt

2 or more Tb butter

1 or more tsp sugar

Pepper

2 Tb minced scallions (optional)

Drop the peas into a large saucepan containing at least 3 quarts (3 liters) rapidly boiling salted water and boil slowly, uncovered, for 5 minutes or more, until just cooked through—taste several to make sure. Immediately drain and refresh for several minutes in cold water to set the green color and preserve the fresh texture.

🕐 May be precooked several hours in advance; cover and refrigerate.

Half an hour or so before serving, smear a heavy saucepan with butter, pour in the peas, and toss with 1 teaspoon sugar. Several minutes before serving, toss with salt, pepper, and the optional scallions and add several tablespoons water. Cover and bring to the rapid boil, tossing, to warm through. Taste carefully for seasoning—you may wish a little more sugar, just enough to give the illusion of fresh-picked sweetness. Toss with more butter if you like, turn into a hot dish, and serve immediately.

The mechanical pea-sheller.

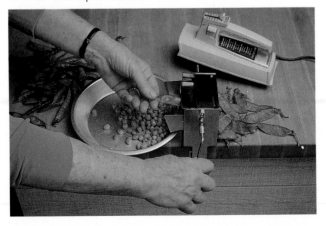

Real Mashed Potatoes

For 4 people

3 or 4 large "baking" potatoes

Salt

Milk and/or cream

Butter

White pepper

   Equipment

A potato ricer

Wash and peel the potatoes, cut into lengthwise quarters, and set in a saucepan with lightly salted water to cover. Boil for 15 minutes or so, until potatoes are tender when pierced with a knife—cut a piece in half and taste to be sure. Immediately drain and put through ricer into a heavy-bottomed saucepan. Stir with a wooden spoon over moderate heat for a minute or more until potatoes begin to film bottom of pan, indicating excess moisture has been evaporated. Beat in several tablespoons milk and/or cream to lighten them slightly, then a tablespoon butter, and salt and white pepper to taste. If you are serving immediately, beat in milk and/or cream until the potatoes are the consistency you wish, and more butter if you like, then turn into a hot dish and serve at once.

🕐 You may cook them an hour or so ahead. In this case, add only a minimum of milk and/or cream and butter and set pan of potatoes in another and larger pan of hot but not simmering water. Cover the potato pan only partially—hot potatoes must not be covered airtight or they develop an off taste. At serving time, uncover, raise heat, and beat the potatoes with a wooden spoon, beating in more milk and/or cream and butter to taste.

Le Gâteau Victoire au Chocolat, Mousseline

Chocolate mousse dessert cake

Here is a very tender, moist, and delicate, and very chocolaty, dessert confection that is more like a cheesecake or custard than a cake, yet it is a cake—almost. However, it is cooked in a bain-marie—a pan of barely simmering water —in the oven, and it contains no flour or starch and no baking powder, only chocolate, a little sugar, eggs, and whipped cream. It is best served tepid, or at least at room temperature.

For a 10-cup (2½-L) cake pan, such as a square one 9 by 9 by 2 inches (23 x 23 x 5 cm), serving 8 to 10 or more

1 Tb instant coffee
4 Tb hot water
4 Tb dark Jamaica rum
14 ounces (400 g) semisweet baking chocolate
2 ounces (60 g) unsweetened baking chocolate
6 "large" eggs
½ cup (100 g) sugar
1 cup (¼ L) heavy or whipping cream, chilled
1 Tb pure vanilla extract
Confectioners sugar
Equipment
A 10-cup (2½-L) cake pan, preferably with nonstick lining, buttered, bottom lined with buttered wax paper, and floured; an electric mixer with round-bottomed bowl or a hand-held mixer or a large whisk and a metal bowl of the same type

Preliminaries

Preheat oven to 350°F/180°C and place rack in lower-third level. Prepare cake pan. Choose a roasting pan large enough to hold cake pan easily, fill with enough hot water to come half-way up cake pan, and set in oven. Assemble all ingredients and equipment.

The chocolate

Swirl the coffee and hot water in a medium-size saucepan, add the rum, and break up the chocolate into the pan. Bring 2 inches (5 cm) of water to the boil in a larger pan, remove from heat, and set chocolate pan in it; cover and let the chocolate melt while you continue with the recipe.

The egg and sugar mixture

Break the eggs into the beating bowl, add the sugar, and stir over hot water for several minutes until eggs are slightly warm to your finger—this makes beating faster and increases volume. Then beat for 5 minutes or more, until mixture has at least tripled in volume and forms a thick ribbon when a bit is lifted and falls from the beater; the eggs should be the consistency of lightly whipped cream. (You must have beating equipment that will keep the whole mass of egg moving at once, meaning a narrow rounded bowl and a beater that circulates about it continually.)

The whipped cream

Pour cream into a metal mixing bowl. Empty a tray of ice cubes into a larger bowl, cover them with cold water, then set the cream bowl into the larger ice-filled bowl. Beat with a hand-held mixer or large balloon whisk, using an up-and-down circular motion to whip in as much air as possible, until cream has doubled in volume and holds its shape softly. Whip in the vanilla.

Assembling and baking

Beat up the melted chocolate with a whisk; it should be smooth and silky. Scrape it into the egg-sugar mixture, blending rapidly with a rubber spatula, and when partially incorporated, fold in the whipped cream, deflating cream and eggs as little as possible. Turn batter into prepared cake pan, which will be about two-thirds filled. Set it at once in the pan of hot water in the preheated oven. Cake will rise

some ⅛ inch (½ cm) above edge of pan, and is done when a skewer or straw comes out clean—after about 1 hour of baking. Then turn off oven, leave oven door ajar, and let cake sit for 30 minutes in its pan of water, so that it will sink evenly. Remove from oven, still in its pan of water, and let sit for another 30 minutes so that it will firm up before unmolding and serving. Cake will sink down as it cools to about its original volume.

◑   This cake is at its most tender and delicious when eaten slightly warm; however, you may cook it even a day or two in advance, leave it in its pan (covered when cool, and refrigerated), then set it in a 200°F/95°C oven for 20 minutes to warm gently.

Serving suggestions

Unmold the cake and decorate with a sprinkling of confectioners sugar, or with pipings of whipped cream, or with a soft chocolate icing (semisweet chocolate melted and beaten with a little soft butter). You may wish to pass a custard sauce or sweetened and vanilla-flavored whipped cream with the cake.

Remarks:

Since this is a most delicate confection with only enough body to hold itself together, it does not always cut neatly like a regular cake. Furthermore, once unmolded it cannot be lifted and transferred from one serving platter to another unless you reverse it again into its pan.

◑ *Timing*

Coming into the dining room, your guests should feel like first nighters at a magic show. There, carefully disposed, are the props: dinner plates on their warming tray and an array of condiments and implements. Under the chafing dish, the alcohol lamp is ready for flaming: what next? But first, the appetizer. When this is eaten, there is a pause.

After removing the used plates to the kitchen, you start heating the steak pan on the stove, to speed things up in the dining room. You toss the blanched peas in their buttered pot and give a quick stir to the potatoes. In moments, you return with the vegetables to the dining room, set them on the warming tray, fetch the steaks and the hot pan, set it on the chafing dish, and begin. The actual job of making Steak Diane is a matter of 2 minutes in all for searing the steaks, which you do two at a time—it goes fast on such a hot, wide cooking surface—and then 2 minutes more for combining and reducing the sauce, and 1 minute for bathing the steaks in it. However, with your warming tray at hand, you have no reason to rush, and a suave performer never looks hurried.

In a second brief pause, you remove the dinner and serving dishes, and decorate the cake with the whipped cream you have standing ready (in the refrigerator in a sieve lined with cheesecloth, so it won't get watery while standing).

The cake can be made in the morning, or even the day before, but don't unmold it. Half an hour before dinner, warm it (if you wish) to tepid (see recipe), and unmold it just before you call in your guests.

In principle, the potatoes should be done as late as possible, but you'd be surprised how long they keep their goodness, partly uncovered over hot water.

All the appetizer elements can be prepared in the morning, for assembly not more than an hour before serving. You can blanch, drain, and chill the peas in the morning, and, that afternoon, set them in their buttered pot. During the day, pound the steaks and refrigerate till just before serving.

Well in advance and at leisure, carefully arrange your dinner table. For chafing-dish meals, I even make a check list, for an omission is almost as ignominious as forgetting the salt on a picnic!

Menu Variations

The appetizer: Before a hearty, tangy main course and a rich dessert, you want something light, like oysters or a variant of the little shell-fish salad (see "Lo-Cal Banquet," page 40, or "Birthday Dinner," page 6), or a piquant consommé (see "Dinner for the Boss," page 123). *Gravlaks* (see kitchen "Cocktail Party," page 104) would be appropriate in flavor and texture, but perhaps too simple-looking. Before dishes like steak and cake, it's nice to have something "composed."

The main course: See "Menu Alternatives," page 460, for chafing-dish food that is cooked slowly. The parameters, or ground rules, here are: something sautéed, with or without deglazing sauce; something not so redolent as to argue with dessert, and some-

thing handsomely and quickly done. Many kinds of scallopini are practical; pounded steaks are a kind of scallopini anyway. Veal, chicken, turkey, pork tenderloin? And you can do these with the same Diane sauce. High heat is for delicate things. You could blanch and slice brains or sweetbreads beforehand, dredge with flour, and finish them at table with browned butter and capers; or dredge thinly sliced calf's liver and sauté, adding thin onion slices halfway through; or do chicken livers with sliced mushrooms. Shad roe is a chafing-dish classic, as are veal kidneys.

The vegetables: As noted earlier, anything goes with steak. What's good today in the market?

The dessert: I hate to commend any other cake to you until you have tried the Victoire. But if you want a chocolaty one with no last-minute worries, you might consider the almond-rich Reine de Saba ("Queen of Sheba") or Le Marquis, a chocolate sponge cake, both in *Mastering I,* or the all-chocolate layer cake, Le Glorieux, in *Mastering II,* where you will also find a chocolate-filled cake, La Charlotte Africaine, made with slices of yellow or white leftover cake. In *J.C.'s Kitchen,* there is a section on working with chocolate, and one remarkably light though buttery chocolate cake called L'Eminence Brune. This particular name is a small joke: on *l'éminence grise,* the "gray eminence," as Père Joseph du Tremblay, Cardinal Richelieu's secret counselor, was nicknamed in the seventeenth century—and also on the name of a certain beautiful, green-eyed Persian pussycat. Christening a cake in the fanciful French style is almost as much fun as creating it.

And then, of course, you might want to save your performance at the chafing dish for dessert. One thinks automatically of cherries jubilee (or ice cream with other hot, liqueur-flavored sauces, some of which are flamed), and of crêpes Suzette, or the many other dessert pancakes in *Mastering I* and in *J.C.'s Kitchen;* or you can make sweet omelets, stack them on a warm side dish, and create a sauce in the pan.

Crêpes Suzette being bathed in orange butter and folded into a triangle before being flamed in Cognac and orange liqueur.

Leftovers

The smaller your party, the more precisely you can plan quantities; so, unless a guest can't make it at the last minute, you won't have much left over. If you should have one raw *steak,* for some such reason, you can put it to good use (and stretch it to feed two) in beef Stroganoff or in one of those pleasant Oriental dishes like sukiyaki or beef with pea pods. Or split it between the two of you next morning, in a good old steak-and-eggs.

Mashed potatoes, though, are worth making in an overlarge quantity for the sake of two nice by-products. In the proportion of 2 cups mashed potatoes to 3 egg yolks, beat the mixture smoothly to make *pommes duchesse,* which, piped through a large rosette tube, makes a handsome border for a platter or for ramekins. Or beat 1 egg yolk into 1 cup *warmed* mashed potatoes, beat in 1 table-spoonful each parsley and chives, and fold in 1 beaten egg white to make an excellent mixture for mashed-potato pancakes. If you have just a small amount of mashed potatoes left, use them to thicken a soup or add to a bread dough.

You could rewarm the *cake* to tepid (back in its mold, of course), or eat it cold and call it a mousse or a super-rich brownie.

Postscript: Cooking in public

Preparation is everything, as the length of this chapter's Timing section suggests. At our TV studio, we have a backstage kitchen, where we prepare our stand-in dishes and those which must emerge in finished form seconds after the star has been prepared before the cameras. Careful charts are made of the cooktop and working surfaces so that every implement and ingredient is on hand and in place. Bottle tops are unscrewed beforehand, wastebins—out of camera range--are strategically placed (everybody asks me, "When you fling scraps over your shoulder like that, where do they land?"), and shallots, scallions, tomatoes, etc., are chopped and measured beforehand. What I do for the cameras looks easy because it *is* easy, with all the dirty work out of the way. At home, it's not a cinch for anyone; and then the telephone rings just as the aspic jells or the soufflé gasps and sinks.

In private or public cooking, broad, firm gestures are the most efficient. Wallop your steaks! Whoosh up your egg whites! And, behind your chafing dish and before your guests, act with assurance and decisiveness. Let every move accomplish something, and don't twiddle. As brevity is the soul of wit, spareness or "line" is the basis of bravura. And "line" is a matter of practice and preparation, which really is not dirty work for those who love to cook.

Let it rain! This no-fuss, no-muss barbecue can be given indoors just as well.

Indoor Outdoor Barbecue

We love to eat out on a flowery terrace above a fragrant garden with a little breeze keeping everything astir; an occasional zesty whiff from the grill doesn't at all interfere with the roses and heliotrope. But in our part of the world there's an old saying, "If you don't like the weather, wait a minute," and, unfortunately, it works the other way too. Just as we have the coals ready, just as we take our grand big hunk of meat from its marinade, dark clouds herd up and cover the sun, a sudden evil wind flips the leaves inside out . . . and blam: here it comes, and in we go.

But all those good smells and sizzles, so appetizing in the open air, can be just a bit much inside with the windows shut against a downpour. By using a leg of lamb boned and flattened out, which can be grilled out of doors or roasted indoors with only a final browning under the broiler, we have solved the problem to our great satisfaction. And this method solves three other problems as well. Boning makes it possible to cook this big cut, whose flavor adapts so beautifully to marinating and grilling, over coals in a reasonable time, getting it cooked through without charring and without searing its odd shape unevenly. It makes carving a matter of seconds. And it produces glorious leftovers—which can't be said for shish kebab.

The heavy, complicated structure of tail, hip, and shank—almost half the weight of a lamb leg—is hard to carve around but easy to extract before cooking. If you've never boned meat before, a lamb leg would be ideal as a practice victim; nothing much can go wrong. Calling it a butterfly, as butchers do, is a joke like naming your bloodhound Fifi. Far from being fluttery or ethereal, the lamb is hearty, richly flavored from its marinade, and something like a beef *filet* in texture. The meat firms up as it cooks into a thick juicy slab. We like it rare, firm and dark-brown outside and an even bright peony-pink within and we cut it in thick slices. It's an American technique to butterfly and grill a lamb leg and one which delights and surprises our French guests, who don't even recognize their old friend the *gigot.*

A perfect accompaniment to grilled lamb, and a convenient one since it's good hot or cold, is a dish of topinambours, a vegetable which gardeners tell me grows like a weed and which markets have begun to offer regularly. The word is French, adapted from the Portuguese, which is in turn an alteration of *tupinamba*—short for *batata tupinamba* or tupinamba potato, according to the big Webster's. And according to a French source, the Tupinamba are a small native tribe in Brazil who presumably nourished themselves on the vegetable that bears their name. The vegetable is related to the sunflower family, and since sunflower in French is *girasol,* it is probable that the nickname "Jerusalem artichoke" is a corruption of what was originally *"girasol artichaut."* But the topinambour vegetable is neither potato, nor is it artichoke. "Sunchoke," as the topinambour is sometimes called, is a modern publicity-stunt name invented to intrigue the buyer and only adds to general confusion. When this delightful vegetable is not available for a barbecue menu, I cook artichokes in a particularly flavorful way (since they too can be served hot or cold and suit lamb very well); see the bonus recipe in the Menu Variations section.

Speaking of names, the Zabaione Batardo Veneziano, which sounds like Iago badmouthing Otello, *basso profondo,* is called "Venetian" because it is based on a lovely concoction we first ate at a hotel in Venice; "Zabaione" because it involves egg yolks beaten with Marsala; and "Batardo" because it is bastardized by being stabilized with gelatin and served cold. Real *zabaione* is just egg yolks, wine, and sugar and is served still warm in a wineglass the moment it's made.

We don't have too leafy a salad, since so many guests enjoy stuffing theirs into a pita pocket: a mixture of bite-sized vegetables with just enough foliage for texture seems to work best. We always did like store-bought pita; but then we tried making our own and got addicted. Homemade pita, which you can attend to unhurriedly, permitting two rises and a rest before baking, has a fuller flavor than the store kind and a pleasing tender chewiness—even though it looks like the makings of a snow-

boot, suede-smooth outside and fleecy inside. If you and your guests have had to move indoors, and especially if some of them are teenagers, do take a few unbaked pita disks and some grated cheese from your freezer, add some herbs and some Italian tomato sauce (the store-bought kind can be very good), and give them homemade pita pizzas as an effortless extra. Or, if you have a glass-fronted oven or can borrow one of the portable electric ones, you might feature pita baking as a rainy-day double feature. About one minute after the inert white disks go into the oven, at highest heat, they begin to stir mysteriously, swelling and heaving from side to side. At full inflation, the edges lift right off the baking surface and the pita stand on tiptoe as if aspiring to flight. The moment is brief, the striving too strenuous, and they sink back, but only a little: still unbowed, I like to think.

In a similarly poetic mood, my husband one day christened a beautiful and potent emerald-green cocktail of his own invention. Remember the doggerel ballad by one J. Milton Hayes about the dashing young subaltern in Inscrutable India, who stole "The Green Eye of the Yellow God" to gratify the whim of his love, the Colonel's daughter? Alas for impetuous youth! In the rhythm of "Polly-Wolly-Doodle," the verses trot to a melancholy conclusion, for the god took his revenge.

There's a one-eyed yellow idol to the north of Khatmandu,
There's a little marble cross below the town;
There's a broken-hearted woman tends the grave of Mad Carew,
And the Yellow God forever gazes down.
Paul's delicious creation is luckily not so malevolent as its namesake; but be warned. It's every bit as powerful.

Preparations

Recommended Equipment:
If you don't own a charcoal grill, or if you plan to improvise one, I suggest you take a look at the detailed and practical section on outdoor cooking in *Joy of Cooking*, a book that surely needs no introduction. The only equipment specifically needed for doing butterflied lamb over coals is a hinged two-sided rack with a long handle for easy turning. See the pita recipe for a discussion of alternative baking methods.

For the cocktail, the wine, and the dessert, note that you will need 18 goblets.

Marketing and Storage:
Quantities for 6 people
Staples to have on hand

Salt
Peppercorns
Hot pepper sauce
Dry mustard
Rosemary
Cream of tartar
Pure vanilla extract
Soy sauce
Red wine vinegar
Cooking oil
Olive oil for optional marinade and for salad (or use another fine salad oil)
Plain unflavored gelatin (1 package)
Granulated sugar
All-purpose flour (2¾ cups or 390 g), unbleached recommended
Plain bleached cake flour (¾ cup or 105 g)
Recommended: Wondra or instant-blending flour (⅓ cup or 50 g)
Dry active yeast (1 Tb or 1 package)
Butter (1 stick)
Heavy cream (1 cup or ¼ L, plus more if using for dessert decoration)

Eggs (4)
Lemons (2)
Garlic (2 heads)
Parsley and/or chives
Shallots and/or scallions

Specific ingredients for this menu

Leg of lamb (note that a big, 7-pound or 3½-kilo leg will serve 12 to 14 when butterflied)

For optional lamb stock: 1 carrot, 1 onion, 2 or more celery ribs, 1 leek, and an herb bouquet

Topinambours (Jerusalem artichokes or sunchokes), 14 to 18

Romaine (1 medium-size head)

Watercress (1 or 2 bunches)
Red onions (1 medium-size)
Green and/or red sweet peppers (2)
Cherry tomatoes (12 to 18)
Fresh herbs (if possible): tarragon, chervil, basil
Feta cheese (½ pound or 225 g)
For *zabaione* decoration: cocoa or grated chocolate, or home-candied orange peel
Sweetened bottled lime juice (Rose's recommended)
Green crème de menthe (mint liqueur)
Gin
Marsala wine (best quality), ⅛ bottle
Peanuts, to serve with the cocktail

Buddha's Eye

A gin and lime cocktail with green crème de menthe

A strong clean drink to be served in small upstanding stemmed glasses

5 parts gin

2 parts sweetened lime juice (Rose's recommended)

2 parts green crème de menthe (mint liqueur)

Stir all ingredients together in a pitcher with ice cubes and, as soon as well chilled, pour into the glasses.

Butterflied Leg of Lamb

For barbecuing or roasting

To butterfly a leg of lamb means to bone it so that the meat may be spread out in one large piece. You can then barbecue it or roast it, and not only does it cook in half the time of an unbutterflied leg, but carving is wonderfully easy.

Fat removal and bone location

To prepare the lamb, first cut off as much outside fat as you can from all sides of the meat, then shave off the fell (membrane on top side of leg), and it is ready for boning. The whole leg of lamb contains the hipbone and tail assembly at the large end, the main leg bone that slants crosswise from the socket of the hipbone to the knee, and the shank bone from the knee to the ankle at the small end. All the boning takes place on the underside of the leg, not on the top or fell side.

Hipbone

The first and the worst bone to tackle is the hipbone-tail assembly, a complicated and convoluted structure if there ever was one. Lay lamb so its large end faces away from you and plunge fearlessly in with a very sharp, rather short knife; and by always cutting against the bone rather than against the flesh in any boning operation you are doing the right thing. Start at the exposed cut end of the hip that sticks out in the upper middle of the underside at the large end. Cut around under it (the side of the bone facing you, and the small end of the leg), branching out both right and left as well as down, and you will find that it attaches itself at about its middle to the main leg bone: you will gradually uncover the round ball end of the leg bone that fits into the socket of the hip. By cutting around the ball end you will detach its tendons from the hip socket, and then as you follow on down the hip and cut around under it, you can quite easily detach it from the meat.

Leg bones

With the hip out of the way, do the shank bone next, at the small end of the lamb, starting again on the underside. Cut the meat from the sides of the bone and under it, and proceed up to the knee joint but do not cut around it yet. Now you will make a frank cut in the meat, still from the underside of the lamb, going from the knee joint in a direct line to the ball joint where you removed the hip. Cut around the main leg bone thus exposed and the knee, being careful not to pierce the flesh on the top side of the meat (although there is no great harm done if you do), and you will free the leg and shank bones in one piece. Cut out the white cartilaginous disk that is the kneecap, as well as all chunks of interior fat.

Final rites

Lay the meat out, boned surface up, on your work surface, and you will note that it forms two large lobes. (If you have a large leg and are serving only 6 people, you may wish to cut off one of the lobes and freeze it for another roast or for shish kebabs.) For even cooking, I always slash the lobes in 2 or 3 places, making long cuts about 1½ inches (4 cm) deep; otherwise these thick pieces of meat will take longer to cook than the rest. Then, to keep the roast in shape, I like to push long skewers through the wide sides of the meat, one through the top third, and the other through the bottom third.

🕐 Lamb may be boned and prepared for roasting a day in advance; wrap in plastic and refrigerate.

Optional Marinade:		
3 to 4 Tb olive oil		
2 Tb soy sauce		
The juice of ½ lemon, plus the grated peel if you wish		
½ tsp or so rosemary		
1 or 2 cloves garlic, puréed (optional)		

Rub the unboned side of the lamb with a tablespoon of olive oil and place, oiled side down, in a baking pan. Rub the rest of the oil and the soy, lemon juice and optional peel, rosemary, and optional garlic into the top side. Cover with plastic wrap and marinate until you are ready to cook the lamb—an hour or more, if possible.

Lamb leg (underside) before trimming and after. Note the ball of the leg bone and the socket of the hip.

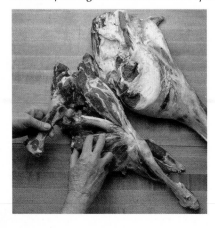

To barbecue the lamb

When the coals are just right, place the lamb in an oiled, hinged (double-sided) rack and barbecue, turning every 5 minutes or so and brushing with oil, for 45 minutes to an hour, depending on the heat of your coals and the way you like your lamb. If you want it rosy red, it is done when it begins to take on resistance to your finger, in contrast to its soft raw state. A meat thermometer reading would be 125°F/51°C. Remove the lamb to a carving board and let it sit for 8 to 10 minutes, allowing juices to retreat back into the meat before carving. To carve, start at either of the small ends and, to make attractively largish slices, begin somewhat back from the edge, angling your knife as though carving a flank steak (or even a smoked salmon).

To roast in the oven

I prefer to roast the lamb and then finish it off under the broiler. To do so, place the marinated lamb flat, boned side up, in a roasting pan in the upper middle of a preheated 375°F/190°C oven and roast for 20 to 25 minutes, or to a meat thermometer reading of 120°F/49°C. (I do not turn the lamb on its other side.) Then baste with oil and set for 2 to 3 minutes under a preheated broiler to brown lightly. Always let it sit for 8 to 10 minutes outside the oven before carving and carve as suggested in the preceding paragraph.

Save All Bones for Soup or Sauce:

You can make a wonderfully hearty broth out of lamb bones and meaty scraps. Whack the bones into convenient pieces with your cleaver, then brown bones and scraps in a 450°F/230°C oven in a roasting pan with a quartered onion and carrot. Drain off accumulated fat and dump contents of pan into a large saucepan with water to cover. Then deglaze the roasting pan: set it over heat with a cup of water, scrape up coagulated juices, and pour them into the saucepan. Simmer, skim, add a couple of celery ribs, a little salt, an herb bouquet, a leek if you have one, and a clove or two of garlic. Cover partially and simmer 3 hours or so, then strain, degrease, and that's all there is to it. Recipes for sauces are in *Mastering I,* and for soup see *J.C.'s Kitchen.*

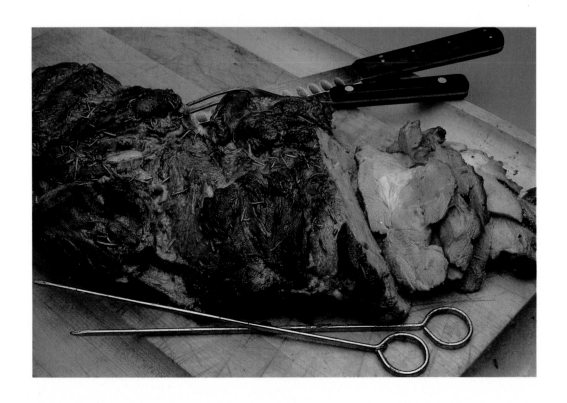

Pita Bread

Armenian, Syrian, or Israeli flat bread
Pita bread, the flat pale bread-dough Near Eastern pancakes that you can separate into two layers, is easy indeed to make when you have constructed yourself a simulated baker's oven. That means you have quarry tiles or a stoneware griddle to set on your oven rack, onto which you slide the dough to bake. Although you can cook pita on top of the stove, the complete puff is not always achieved, and the bottom layer remains thicker than the top layer. And although you can also bake pita on cookie sheets in the oven, it is not as satisfactory as the griddle. Griddles, by the way, are available via many country store catalogues. They are often sold as pizza sets and include a wooden sliding board or baker's peel; the rectangular griddle is the one to order since it is a more useful shape than the round one for breads, rolls, and pita, as well as for pizza. Pita dough makes wonderful pizza, too.

Like homemade English muffins, your own-made pita cost you less than half the price of store-bought ones, in addition to being fun and dramatic to make.

For 12 pita 6 inches in diameter

1 Tb (1 package) yeast dissolved in ½ cup (1 dL) tepid water

About 1 pound (450 g) of flour as follows:
  2¾ cups (390 g) all-purpose flour, unbleached recommended
  ¾ cup (105 g) plain bleached cake flour

2 tsp salt

1 Tb olive oil or tasteless salad or cooking oil

1 cup (¼ L) tepid water; droplets more as necessary

  Equipment

Best, a tile or stoneware baking surface to fit your oven rack; second best, an aluminum baking sheet. A wooden sliding board, shingle, or peel. A long-handled pancake turner. A cake rack or racks for cooling baked pita. A rolling pin

Making the dough

When yeast is thoroughly dissolved, combine it with the ingredients listed, kneading in enough of the water to make a moderately firm dough. When well blended, let rest for 2 minutes, then knead vigorously until dough is smooth and elastic and does not stick to your hands—5 minutes or more. Place in a clean, fairly straight-sided 4-quart (4-L) bowl, cover, and let rise at 75°F to 80°F (24°C–27°C) until slightly more than doubled in bulk—2 hours or so. Deflate by pulling dough inward from sides of bowl, cover, and let rise again to slightly more than double—about 1½ hours.

🕐 Second rise may be completed in the refrigerator, and when risen, you may punch down dough, cover with a weight to keep it down, and leave for 24 hours—or you may freeze it.

Forming the pita

Turn dough out onto a floured work surface and lengthen it by rolling it back and forth under the palms of your hands, forming a thick sausage shape about 16 inches (40 cm) long. Cut even portions all the same size by halving the dough crosswise, halving the 2 halves, then cutting each of these 4 pieces into thirds. Then, to make the pancake shape more even, first form a cushion out of each piece of dough by bringing the 4 corners together and pinching to seal them, then turn seal side down and roll under the palm of one hand to make a ball; set each aside, as you form it, on a floured corner of your work surface, and cover with a lightly floured sheet of plastic.

These balls of dough are now to be rolled into pancake-size disks which are to rest either on a floured wooden surface or on floured towels for 20 minutes or so while the oven heats. Proceed as follows: one at a time, with a rolling pin on a quite heavily floured surface, roll each ball into a disk ¼ inch (¾ cm) thick

and 6 inches (15 cm) across. Place disk on prepared resting surface, cover with floured plastic, and continue with the rest.

Baking the pita

Set quarry tiles, griddle, or bake sheet in lower middle level of oven, and preheat to 500°F–550°F (260°–270°C)–highest heat! When oven is ready, lightly flour the sliding board, place on it 2 or 3 pita, and slide then onto the hot baking surface. In about 1 minute, large bubbles will appear on surface of the pita and they will then quickly and dramatically puff up like pillows, reach their maximum, and subside slightly. Leave for a moment (baking should take about 2 minutes in all) and remove with a pancake turner before they have time to color or harden. Continue with remaining pita. Let cool completely; they will gradually collapse.

🕑 Leave on rack for an hour or two, then stack together, pressing out air, and store in a plastic bag; refrigerate for 2 to 3 days, or freeze.

Manufacturing Notes:

You may find, as I did, that although pita are easy to make, it does take a session or two to perfect your techniques. It seems important to watch that the dough is fairly firm, since if it is too soft the disks are sticky to roll and limp to handle. They must be smooth, unwrinkled, and at least ¼ inch (¾ cm) thick, too, or the pita may not puff up into the proper pillow shape.

Pizza:

Roll the pita dough to any size you wish, but the 6-inch (15-cm) pita shape is just right for individual servings. When oven is ready, place 3 or 4 dough disks on lightly floured sliding board, rapidly garnish with the pizza topping of your choice, and slide onto hot baking surface in oven, exactly as though you were baking pita. Topping will prevent dough from puffing, and when bottom is lightly browned, in about 5 minutes, the pizza is done.

Notes on Freezing:

You can roll out the dough into disks, flour the disks, stack each between sheets of plastic wrap, and freeze in a bunch. You can then take them singly from freezer to oven; although they will bake into pita, they do not puff quite as much as when fresh—and whether you bake a pita solidly frozen or thawed seems to make little difference. I find the frozen disks just fine for pizza, however, either frozen or thawed before baking.

Serving Suggestions:

Pita pocket sandwiches. Cut the baked pita in half crosswise, gently pull the two halves apart, and fill with any kind of sandwich mixture, such as a salad, hamburger and trimmings, scrambled eggs, a cooked eggplant and tomato mixture, and so forth. Or make your filling and bake it in the pita pocket.

Toasted pita triangles. Split the pita breads—it is often easiest to cut all around the circumference with scissors to make an even split—and cut into triangles of whatever size you wish. Brush with melted butter and, if you wish, a sprinkling of mixed dried herbs and/or grated Parmesan cheese. Arrange buttered side up on a baking sheet and place for a few minutes in a preheated 350°F/180°C oven to crisp and brown lightly. Serve with soups, salads, cheese, or with drinks.

Topinambours

Also called Jerusalem artichokes or sunchokes

These little knobby roots grow underground like potatoes and do remind one in taste of artichokes, yet they are crisp like water chestnuts when raw, and have a very special and mildly pungent taste of their own when cooked. Hot, buttered, and tossed with parsley or chives, they go nicely indeed with roast lamb—or with roast pork, turkey, or beef, for that matter. Cooked and cold, they make an attractive salad vegetable. Since they discolor rapidly, they should be cooked in a *blanc* (a thin solution of flour and water with salt and lemon), the same way you would boil artichoke bottoms or salsify.

For 6 people as a vegetable course

⅓ cup (¾ dL) flour, preferably the instant-blending kind
6 cups (1½ L) cold water; more if necessary
3 Tb lemon juice
2 tsp salt
14 to 18 topinambours
If serving hot—3 Tb or more butter, salt, pepper, and minced parsley and/or chives If serving cold—minced shallots, salad or olive oil, fresh lemon juice, salt, pepper, and parsley and/or chives

To make the *blanc* liquid, place the flour in a saucepan and beat in the water gradually, to prevent flour from lumping. Add the lemon juice and salt and bring to the simmer. Set the pan by your work surface, and peel the topinambours one by one (using a small knife and simply removing the little knobs along with the peel). Cut the topinambours into ¼-inch (¾-cm) slices and drop the slices into the *blanc* liquid as you proceed. When all are sliced, bring to the boil and simmer 15 to 20 minutes or until just tender when pierced with a knife. (You will notice a remarkable change in taste, from crisp and raw with no pronounced flavor to cooked and with a definite yet subtle taste that is reminiscent of artichoke, yet utterly and uniquely topinambourish.)

🕐 May be cooked in advance. Leave them in their liquid until you are ready to proceed.

To serve hot

Drain (reserving the cooking liquid for a soup base) and toss gently in a sieve under cold running water. Then melt the butter in a saucepan, add the topinambours, and toss gently to coat with the butter and to heat through. Taste carefully for seasoning, then toss with the herbs and serve.

To serve cold

Drain and wash as described in preceding paragraph, then toss with minced shallots, oil, lemon, salt, pepper, and herbs.

Seasonal Salad

Of romaine, watercress, red onion rings, green and/or red peppers, cherry tomatoes, and feta cheese

This is a salad of the season and needs no formal recipe. One suggestion is to tear the romaine into bite-size pieces, stem the watercress, wrap them together in a damp towel, and place in the refrigerator in a plastic bag several hours before serving. Also some hours before serving, slice the red onions and, to minimize their sting, place the slices in a sieve and run boiling water then cold water over them; drain thoroughly and toss in a bowl with a spoonful or two of your salad dressing. Halve, seed, and slice the peppers; refrigerate in a covered bowl. Cut the feta cheese into ½-inch (1½-cm) dice and taste; if salty, soak 10 minutes or so in a bowl of cold water and drain. Toss with freshly ground pepper, thyme, oregano, or a mixture of herbs, and a tablespoon or two of olive oil; let macerate for several hours, tossing once or twice. Shortly before serving, wash, stem, and halve cherry tomatoes; sprinkle lightly with salt. At serving time, toss all ingredients except the cheese together in a big salad bowl with your dressing (see next recipe and index for suggestions) and with fresh herbs if you have them. Taste, correct seasoning, then fold in ¾ of the cheese cubes, strewing the remainder on top.

Vinaigrette Salad Dressing

I have found the following a useful base for salad dressing made in quantity for a large gathering. Use the best and freshest of everything for success!

For 30 people or more, 3 ½ cups (1 scant liter) dressing

4 Tb minced shallots or scallions

2 Tb dry mustard

5 to 6 shakes hot pepper sauce

Grinds of fresh pepper to taste

1 tsp salt, or to your taste

5 Tb red wine vinegar; more as needed

2 Tb or more fresh lemon juice

3 cups best-quality olive oil, new fresh peanut oil, or other oil of impeccable quality

Fresh herbs of your choice, such as tarragon, chervil, or basil

Beat all ingredients together in an electric mixer or shake in a large screw-topped jar. Taste carefully, and correct seasoning. After you dress your salad, taste a leaf or two and toss in more salt and pepper if needed.

The following proportions would be about right for 6 to 8 people. Simply reduce accordingly for a smaller number.

2–3 tsp minced shallots or scallions

½ tsp dry mustard

Grinds of fresh pepper to taste

¼ tsp salt, or to your taste

1 Tb red wine vinegar

1 Tb fresh lemon juice

½ cup best-quality olive (or other) oil as above, plus fresh herbs

Beat together with a whisk or shake in a screw-top jar. Correct seasoning to your taste both before and after dressing your salad.

🕐   May be made somewhat in advance, but it is never a good idea to let salad dressing sit around for more than a day or two; it loses its freshly made quality.

Zabaione Batardo Veneziano

Mock zabaione

This turns out to be, actually, a Marsala-flavored Bavarian cream. One friendly warning is to watch out when you combine the Marsala custard with the whipped cream at the end: if the custard is warm it will deflate the cream, yet if it is too cold the chilled cream will cause the gelatin in it to set and get lumpy before you complete the folding process.

For about 6 cups, serving 6 to 8

⅓ cup (¾ dL) plus 1 Tb sugar

¾ cup (1 ¾ dL) best-quality sweet Marsala wine in a 6-cup (1 ½-L) saucepan

1 ½ level tsp plain unflavored gelatin

4 egg yolks in a 2-quart or -liter stainless-steel saucepan

1 Tb pure vanilla extract

2 egg whites in a clean dry beating bowl

A pinch of salt and ⅛ tsp cream of tartar

1 cup (¼ L) heavy cream for whipping in a 2-quart or -liter stainless-steel bowl

A large bowl with a tray of ice cubes and water to cover them

Decoration

Whipped cream and/or cocoa or grated chocolate, or home-candied orange peel

Combining
Marsala custard ingredients

Stir ⅓ cup (¾ dL) sugar into the Marsala, sprinkle the gelatin on top, and set aside to soften while you assemble the rest of the ingredients listed. Then, with a wire whip, vigorously beat the egg yolks in their saucepan for a minute or two until they are thickened slightly and pale yellow. Now set the

Marsala over moderate heat (but do not bring it to the boil) and stir to dissolve both gelatin and sugar completely, looking carefully to be sure there are no unmelted granules of either in the liquid. Finally, beating the egg yolks with your whip, slowly dribble in the hot Marsala.

Heating the Marsala mixture

The Marsala and egg yolk mixture is now to be thickened over heat like a custard. To do so, set it over a moderately low (but not too low) burner, and beat with your wire whip as it slowly warms. As you beat and heat it the mixture will start to foam, and in a few minutes it will be entirely foamy throughout—keep testing with your impeccably clean finger. When it is too hot for that finger you should almost at the same time see the first wisp of steam rising from the surface, and the custard is done. Remove from heat, and beat vigorously for a minute or two to stop the cooking; beat in the vanilla, and set aside.

Beating egg whites and whipping cream

Beat the egg whites slowly until they begin to foam, then beat in the salt and cream of tartar; gradually increase speed to fast and continue until they form shining peaks, then sprinkle on the tablespoon of sugar and beat vigorously to stiffen them more. Delicately fold them into the warm Marsala custard.

Then whip the cream, setting it in the ice cubes and water, until it has doubled in volume, beater leaves light traces on its surface, and cream holds its shape softly—this is now *crème Chantilly,* or lightly whipped cream.

Combining the elements

Set custard pan in the ice cubes and fold custard delicately (so as not to deflate it) with a rubber spatula, testing continually with your finger just until custard is cool but not cold or chilled. Immediately remove pan from ice and at once fold in the whipped cream to make a beautifully smooth, creamy pale yellow ambrosia. Turn it either into a serving bowl or into individual goblets, cover, and chill for 2 hours or more.

🕐   May be completed a day or two in advance.

To serve

Decorate with swirls of whipped cream and/or cocoa or grated chocolate—or with a julienne of home-candied orange peel.

⏱ *Timing*

This meal could hardly be easier to plan for. Just before serving time, dress and toss the salad, whip the cream, if you're using it, for the dessert decoration, and reheat the topinambours if you're having them hot. Remember to give the lamb a 10-minute sit after it's cooked; and, if you're cooking indoors, it needs watching during its 3 minutes in the broiler. Oven roasting, with an occasional baste, takes 20 to 25 minutes.

If you're outside, allow an hour, with frequent basting and turning, for the lamb to grill. At least an hour before cooking, set the lamb in its marinade. At that stage start your fire. Any time during the day, wash, dry, and trim the salad makings, prepare the dressing, and cook the topinambours.

You can bone the lamb the day before. The *zabaione* can be made one or two days before, and the pita, two or three. (Or you can freeze the pita dough, made long before; but they don't puff quite so high.)

Menu Variations

The barbecued meat: Other large cuts of meat to marinate and grill would include beef, both steak and roasting cuts, not more than 2 inches (5 cm) thick. You can of course grill chops, and there is always chicken; but, if you are forced indoors, they will have to be done under the broiler and given close attention.

The salad: There are several salad recipes in this book; with full-flavored meat and wine, have something rather assertive and oniony.

The zabaione: See the Menu Variations in "Informal Dinner" for other custardy desserts you can make ahead of time.

The topinambours: The only other vegetable that remotely resembles topinambours in flavor is the artichoke. See the recipe for preparing artichoke bottoms on page 183. Or forget that flavor altogether and do one of the eggplant recipes in *Mastering II*. Lamb and eggplant go beautifully together.

Sauté of Fresh Artichoke Hearts with Onions and Garlic

Onions and garlic and a whisper of wine vinegar give a special taste to this sauté of artichokes. Serve it hot with roast or barbecued meats, cold as an hors d'oeuvre, or with sausages, or with hard-boiled eggs and sliced tomatoes.

For 6 people as a vegetable accompaniment

6 to 8 fine fresh artichokes
1 lemon
4 Tb or so olive oil
1 head garlic
4 large onions
Salt and pepper
Thyme or mixed dried herbs
2 Tb or so butter
1 to 2 Tb wine vinegar
Minced fresh parsley
Equipment
A heavy deep frying pan or an electric skillet

Preparing the artichokes

Artichoke hearts include the artichoke bottom and the tender part of the inner cone of leaves. When artichokes are very young and fresh, you can use the whole cone without removing the choke; however, it is rare indeed to find such quality outside the artichoke-growing regions. I prepare the usual store-bought artichokes as follows, one at a time. Cut the stem off an artichoke, close to the base. Then bend the leaves at right angles to the base until they snap close to their large end; pull down toward the base to snap the leaf off, leaving the tender part of its base attached to the artichoke bottom; continue rapidly until you reach the pale creamy cone of leaves covering the choke. Shave the tough green from around the base of the artichoke, using a small knife at first, then a vegetable peeler. Frequently rub cut portions of artichoke base with half a lemon as you go to prevent discoloration. After trimming you will usually have to cut off the top part of the cone, down to where you judge the tender part begins. Cut the heart in half lengthwise and, if large, in quarters. Scoop out the choke (hairy portion covering bottom) with a small knife, and rub the quarters again with lemon. As soon as one heart is prepared, drop it into your frying pan with the olive oil and set over low heat, tossing to cover with the oil. Continue rapidly with the rest of the artichokes.

The sauté

With the artichokes still over low heat and being tossed now and then (toss by swirling and shaking pan by its handle), separate the cloves of garlic and drop them into a pan of boiling water for a moment to loosen the skins. Peel the cloves, halve or quarter them lengthwise if large, and add to the artichokes. Peel, halve, and slice the onions lengthwise; toss them into the pan with the artichokes and garlic. Season with salt, pepper, and herbs; add 2 tablespoons butter and toss to melt it. Cover the pan and cook slowly until artichokes are just tender when pierced with a knife—20 minutes or so—and toss once or twice. Pour in the vinegar, toss, cover, and cook 5 minutes more. Correct seasoning.

🕐   May be cooked in advance; set aside uncovered and reheat, tossing and adding a little more oil or butter if you wish.

To serve hot

Toss with minced parsley.

To serve cold

Let cool after their initial sauté and, if you wish, chill. Before serving, toss with a little lemon juice, a little olive oil, salt and pepper to taste, and fresh minced parsley.

Leftovers

The barbecued lamb: This is as good cold as it was hot, in slices or sandwiches. If you have only scraps, think of curry, shepherd's pie, hash, or add to a hearty soup based on lamb stock made from the bones (see recipe).

There's little to be said about the other elements in this meal, except to warn you not to keep any eggy mixture, like the *zabaione,* for more than four days unless you freeze it.

Postscript: On eating

In planning meals for company, we all think carefully about our resources of money, kitchen equipment, serving possibilities, and, especially, time. And at the shopping stage we are careful about quality and flexible (if what we wanted isn't there) about varying our menus. Feasible preparation, graceful service, good food: can one ask any more than that?

Yes. One ought, in planning menus, to ponder the act of eating as much as the food itself. One of the nice things about this barbecue, for instance, is the agreeable option for guests of stuffing a pita pocket with salad, mingling moist and dry, crunchy and chewy, sharp and bland for that first alligator-size bite. Instruments and gestures matter: the light supple grasp of chopsticks, for instance, affords a sensation different from the stab and leverage of a fork: which one suits your menu? What happens to a mouthful? A cannelated tube doesn't merely make a purée prettier; the tongue delights in smoothing the little corduroy ridges to velvet.

Eating wasn't done with the fingers when I was young, except with bread, corn on the cob, and, in some parts of the country, asparagus. I have come to wonder if all the *do*'s and *don't*'s about eating, rather than the anxiously cramming mothers the shrinks love to belabor, weren't the reason why so many children had "feeding problems" then. How *could* anybody not love to eat, unless it had always been made a penance?

I agree, of course, that table manners are important. Dribblers, twiddlers, spillers, garglers, smokers at meals, and panters are unwelcome company. And such legerdemain as filleting a sautéed trout or carving a squab (a bird I really prefer, however, to eat in gluttonous solitude) is as pleasant to watch as to perform. During one stay in Rome, Paul and I went daily to the same little trattoria expressly to watch one of their regular client's beautifully deft way with the peeling of whole oranges and pears, and the neat dismemberment of small spit-roasted birds; his awareness of our admiration seemed to stimulate him to heights of virtuosity.

But it would have been a pointless performance if the old gentleman hadn't eaten with such relish. Food like love is a deeply emotional matter. Intrusive or assertive displays aside, do you really mind, do you find indecent, the sight of intense bliss, of a child's pointed pink tongue molding the ice cream in a cone, of a friend's half-closed eyes and expanded nostrils as he inhales the scent of your good brandy? Isn't there joy in the sound of a fork's first break into a puff pastry, and a doomsday note in the expiring gurgle of a chocolate soda's last drop on its way up the straw?

I like to watch my guests eat and to imagine their pleasure in the lobster's clawlets as they suck, or in something so simple as the smoothness, form, and heft of a hard-boiled egg. I think of Muriel Spark's loving glimpse in *Memento Mori* of a grandmother feeding a baby, her mouth moving in unconscious sympathy as he eats. Nominally about death, that novel is about the preciousness of life, and so, however modestly, is every honest cookbook.

Bon appétit, then…and *vive la compagnie!*

*A meal you'd cook for (and maybe with) other
cooks. Plus talk of mussels*

UFOs in Wine

Menu
For 6 people

Moules Marinière —Steamed mussels
Hot French Bread

Rock Cornish Hens Broil-roasted with
* Garlic, Cheese, and Wine*
Giant Straw Potato Galette
Cherry Tomatoes Tossed in Butter and Herbs

Fresh Orange Blueberry Bowl

Suggested wines:
A Chablis, Pouilly-Fuissé, Pouilly-Fumé,
Sancerre, or dry riesling with the mussels; a
red Bordeaux or cabernet with the birds; and
there would be nothing wrong in serving a
Champagne or sparkling wine with the dessert

Eating this meal demands fingers, and cooking it demands loving, last-minute attention. The right people to ask to this dinner party are knowing, sensuous eaters whom you welcome backstage because they understand and enjoy what's going on there. Dine in the kitchen, if you have room, so your friends can breathe in that first waft of perfumed steam when you uncover the mussel pot. Let them await in suspense that soul-satisfying plop when the big potato pancake is flipped in sizzling butter. And don't feel rushed arranging the main course stylishly; it only takes a moment, and is served all on one platter except perhaps for the cherry tomatoes. (Big tomatoes wouldn't, I feel, be in the right scale for these small birds on their neat round nest.)

A *paillasson,* or straw mat, is what the birds' nest looked like to Fernand Point when he used to serve the straw potato *galette* at his legendary restaurant, La Pyramide, in southern France. According to Point's former apprentice, chef Joe E. Hyde, in his engaging cookbook *Love, Time, and Butter* (New York: Richard W. Baron, 1971), Point's version was cooked first on the stove, and then the frying pan was moved to the oven. But that was before the blessed advent of nonstick cooking utensils.

As to the Flying Objects, they truly are Unidentified, as this recipe works well for many kinds of small birds. But since squab pigeons, partridge, quail, etc., are rather hard to come by, and the season for game birds is short anyway, I chose Rock Cornish hens. Just for fun, I looked up their origin in the *Encyclopaedia Britannica,* and discovered that in the late eighteenth century cocks were imported here from Cornwall and mated with our Plymouth

Rock hens. So it's an old breed, though we didn't hear much about it until the middle of this century. I think the first person to have raised Rock Cornish commercially was the humorist-cum-pianist Victor Borge, at his farm in Connecticut. For some years you could buy them only frozen, but growing demand has made fresh Rock Cornish hens more and more available. At about a pound, a hen serves one jumbo or two standard-sized guests. Mussels, though not a bit fattening, are so filling that I figure, for the next course, half a hen is better than one.

These elegant birds have a slightly more pronounced flavor than does chicken, but it's still mild; so I step it up with a marinade (which you wouldn't need with a squab or a wild bird) and intensify it by cooking them under a light blanket of shredded Swiss cheese.

UFOs—in this case fresh Cornish hens—being arranged on their straw potato galette

That might sound odd, but you don't taste the cheese as such—you just taste the bird more, and of course it browns beautifully. I use a good nutty Gruyère, sometimes mixed with mozzarella, almost as freely as butter—not so much for its own very unassertive flavor as for the way it enhances others. (See the crêpe-and-vegetable gâteau on page 340, for instance, where the custard binding is fortified and enriched with cheese, and the stuffing for the stewing hen on page 305.) The marinade is quickly turned into a savory little sauce, and the mushrooms and garlic are strewn over all. Don't worry about the garlic: blanching and roasting tame it down.

Fresh fruit is a perfect follow-up to such richly flavored first and second courses, and it should be something not too sweet, with the tang of citrus and a soft plumpness for contrast. Above all, after such an artful, even whimsical dish as the birds on their nest, the dessert should be pretty but matter-of-fact. Even something like the charming *vacherins* on page 240 would look a bit much this time. There are lots of possibilities, but we finally elected to layer sliced fresh oranges and blueberries strewn with glossy amber shreds of home-candied orange peel. And you can see how attractive it is in the giant crystal goblet that shows it off properly.

Our friend Rosie said delightedly, "This is such a *foody* meal!" and it is, if you see what we mean. The precise word for it, though, occurs only in French—*raffiné,* meaning 1 part refined, 2 parts canny, 3 parts subtle, plus 1 dash amusing: a nice cocktail of an adjective.

Preparations and Marketing

Recommended Equipment:

To steam the mussels, use an 8-quart (8-L) soup kettle with a lid; enamel or stainless steel is preferable to aluminum, which turns wine gray. You'll need something to dip the mussels out with.

For the potato *galette,* a nonstick frying pan 11 or 12 inches (28 to 30 cm) in top diameter, with some kind of cover, and a long-handled pancake turner. Be sure the well of your serving platter matches or exceeds the frying pan in size.

The tomatoes should have a sauté pan just big enough to hold them in one layer.

Before clarifying butter, don't forget to check your cheesecloth supply.

Staples to Have on Hand:

Salt
Peppercorns
Sugar
Optional: fragrant dried tarragon
Imported bay leaves
Flour
Optional: olive oil

Corn syrup
Chicken stock or broth ▼
Shallots or scallions
Butter
Clarified butter ▼
Carrots (1)
Onions (4 or 5)
Celery (1 small stalk with leaves)
Parsley
Port or Madeira wine
Dry white French vermouth or dry white wine
Orange liqueur

Specific Ingredients for This Menu:

Mussels (5 to 6 pounds; about 4 quarts or
4 L) ▼
Rock Cornish hens (3), fresh preferred
Swiss (Gruyère) cheese mixed with mozzarella
(1 cup or ¼ L, grated; about ½ pound
or 225 g)
Garlic (2 or more heads)
Mushrooms (1 pound or 450 g)
Potatoes (6 medium), "baking" type preferred
Ripe cherry tomatoes (36 to 48) ▼
Fresh green herbs, such as parsley, chives,
tarragon, or chervil
Seedless oranges (5 or 6 large "navel" type)
Blueberries (1 pint or ½ L), fresh or frozen

▶ **Remarks:**
Staples to have on hand
Chicken stock or broth: the recipe for making it is in this chapter; you can, however, use canned broth. *Clarified butter:* the recipe for it is on page 463. We treat it as a staple because it's so good to have on hand all the time, and it keeps for months refrigerated.
Specific ingredients for this menu
Mussels: moules marinière begins with fresh, live mussels in their shells. Before you buy them, please read the note preceding the recipe; a few hints on gathering your own mussels are given in the Postscript to this chapter. *Cherry tomatoes:* since you can rarely buy them perfectly ripe, allow a few days' lead time. For tips on tomatoes generally, see page 337.

De-bearding a mussel

Mussels:

Quantity note: for the average-sized mussels commercially sold, you can figure that 1 quart equals 1½ pounds (675 g) equals 25 mussels in the shell equals 1 cup (¼ L) mussel meat. This rule of thumb comes from Sarah Hurlburt.

Preparing mussels for cooking

Mussels are perishable, and you should plan to cook them as soon as possible after buying or gathering them. The latter will need more cleaning than cultivated mussels. First, wash the mussels. Then, with a short, stout knife, scrape off any seaweed, barnacles, etc. Pull off their wispy beards as illustrated. Discard any mussels that do not quickly close when tapped, any mussels with cracked or broken shells, any that feel unduly light (they may be empty), or any that feel unusually heavy (they may be full of sand).

Soak the mussels (whether cultivated or gathered) in a bowl of cold water, swishing and knocking them about with your hands for a few seconds, and let them sit for 5 minutes. Lift them out, and if there is any sand at the bottom of the bowl, rinse out and repeat the process, doing so several times if need be. Since there is nothing worse than sandy mussels, I also take a final step: I put 4 or 5 tablespoons of flour in the bottom of a bowl, blend it with cold water, then fill the bowl with 4 quarts or so (4 L) cold water, add the mussels, swish about again, and let them sit for 15 to 20 minutes—the theory being that they eat the flour and while doing so disgorge the rest of their sand. (I am sorry to report that despite all you can do, you will once in a while run into a batch of mussels that are gritty—Sarah Hurlburt, author of *The Mussel Cookbook* (Cambridge: Harvard University Press, 1977), tells me this is caused, strangely enough, by eider duck droppings in the sea water near mussel beds. Some kind of a chemical reaction then irritates the mussels, and they produce calcium granules in their flesh, like tiny oysters. Too bad, if this happens; but you can steam them open, as in the following recipe, and use their juices, and perhaps even purée and strain the meat.)

Swish and jostle the mussels in clear, then floury, water so they will disgorge their sand.

Moules Marinière

Mussels steamed in wine, minced onions, and parsley

For 6 people as a first course

5 to 6 pounds (about 4 quarts or 4 L) mussels, prepared as in the preceding directions

3 to 4 Tb butter

1 cup (¼ L) minced onion

3 to 4 Tb minced shallots (optional)

1 or 2 cloves garlic, minced (optional)

A large handful of fresh chopped parsley

About 2 cups (½ L) dry white wine or dry white French vermouth

Equipment:

An 8-quart (8-L) stainless-steel or enamel (not aluminum) soup kettle with lid, and a perforated scoop

Prepare the mussels as described. A few minutes before serving time, melt the butter in the kettle, stir in the onion and optional shallots and garlic, and cook slowly for 4 or 5 minutes, until wilted. Then add the parsley and the mussels; cover kettle and shake to mix mussels with the rest of the ingredients. Pour in the wine or vermouth, and shake again. Turn heat to high, cover kettle tightly, and let steam for 3 to 4 minutes (do not shake again or you may toss sand into the mussels), until the mussels are open. As soon as they open, they are done.

Dip the mussels, shells and all, into a big serving bowl or into individual soup bowls. Let liquid settle for a minute in kettle, then pour liquid, and spoon onion and parsley, over mussels, being careful not to add any sand that may be in the bottom of the kettle.

To eat the mussels

To eat the mussels, use your fingers, plucking the mussels out of their shells. Or, for slightly more elegance, after eating one with your fingers, use the shells from that mussel as pincers to pick the meat out of the rest. Either pile the shells neatly interlaced at the edge of your bowl or have a shell dish at your side, then spoon up their delicious juices, like a soup.

🕐 Mussels should be served as soon as they are cooked; they will toughen and dry out if you attempt to keep them warm. However, this recipe is a starting point for many other delicious preparations, including the mussel soup and the mussels in mayonnaise on the half shell described later in the chapter.

Rock Cornish Hens Broil-roasted in Wine

This is a fine recipe for any small young birds—like pigeon, quail, partridge—and is particularly good with fresh Rock Cornish game hens.

For 6 people

3 Rock Cornish hens (1 pound or 450 g each)

Ingredients for Brown Poultry Stock and Sauce:

1 medium carrot and onion, chopped

1½ cups (3½ dL) chicken stock or broth

½ cup (1 dL) dry white wine or dry white French vermouth

1 imported bay leaf

1 small stalk celery with leaves

Ingredients for Optional Marinade:

Salt and pepper

1½ tsp fragrant dried tarragon

2 Tb finely minced shallots or scallions

About ½ cup (1 dL) dry white wine or dry white French vermouth

3 to 4 Tb light olive oil (optional)

Other Ingredients:

Salt and pepper

Melted butter, or clarified butter

1 or more heads garlic

About 1 cup (¼ L) coarsely grated Swiss cheese

½ cup (1 dL) or so Port or Madeira wine, or dry white French vermouth

1 pound (450 g) fresh mushrooms, trimmed, washed, and quartered

2 Tb or more butter for sauce enrichment (optional)

Preparing the hens

(The birds are to be split down the back and spread out, browned under the broiler on both sides, then sprinkled with cheese, surrounded with wine and garlic cloves, and baked until done. The mushrooms are added during the last minutes of cooking.) With

Cornish hens nesting on their straw potato galette

shears or a sharp knife, cut down each side of the backbone from neck to tail, and remove backbone. (Chop the backbone into 2 or 3 pieces and reserve for stock, later.) Turn the birds flesh side up and pound breast flat with your fist. To tuck drumsticks into slits in lower breast skin as shown, first bend knees and push up to shoulders, then tuck ends in. Fold wings akimbo behind backbone each side.

Brown Poultry Stock for Sauce:

For about 1½ cups (3½ dL)

Brown the reserved backbones, necks, and giblets (if any) and the chopped carrot and onion in a frying pan with a little oil or clarified butter (page 463). Scrape into a saucepan, discard browning oil, and rinse frying pan with the stock or broth to dislodge all flavorsome browning particles; pour liquid into saucepan. Add the wine or vermouth, ingredients from the optional marinade, bay leaf, and celery. Bring to the simmer, skim off surface scum for a few minutes, then cover pan loosely and simmer slowly for 1 to 1½ hours. Strain, skim off surface fat, and stock is ready to use.

🕐   May be prepared ahead; refrigerate in a covered jar when cold, or freeze.

Plain Poultry Stock — Chicken Stock:

To make a plain stock simply omit the browning of the ingredients. You may even omit the vegetables altogether, and simmer the carcass bones and scraps, raw or cooked, in lightly salted water.

Optional Marinade:

A simple wine marinade will give the usually mild Cornish hens more flavor. Salt and pepper them on both sides and sprinkle with tarragon. Arrange in a bowl, sprinkling each with shallots or scallions, wine, and optional olive oil (oil distributes the flavors of the marinade). Cover and, if kitchen is warm, refrigerate. Marinate for 3 to 4 hours (or longer), turning and basting the birds with the marinade several times. When you are ready to proceed, scrape off marinade and reserve in bowl; dry the birds with paper towels.

Browning under the broiler

Having dried the birds (salt and pepper them lightly if you did not marinate them), brush with melted butter and arrange in one layer skin side down in a broiling or roasting pan. Preheat broiler and set pan so surface of meat is about 3 inches (8 cm) from heat source; brown, basting several times with melted butter, for about 5 minutes on the flesh side; turn, and brown nicely on skin side.

🕐   Recipe may be completed several hours in advance to this point. Although you can refrigerate them, it is best to leave the hens at room temperature if wait is not too long and kitchen not too warm.

Put legs through slits in lower edge of breast skin to make a neat shape.

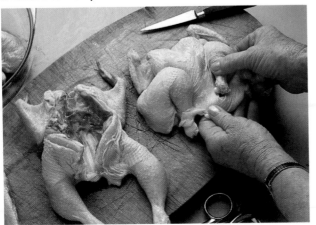

After initial browning, sprinkle hens with grated cheese.

Other activities before roasting

Separate garlic cloves and drop into a saucepan of boiling water; simmer 3 or 4 minutes to soften slightly, then slip off the skins and reserve garlic in a small bowl. Grate the cheese, set out the wine, and prepare the mushrooms.

Roasting

About ½ hour at 400°F/205°C

Preheat oven in time for roasting, and plan to roast 30 to 40 minutes before serving. Salt and pepper the skin side of the birds lightly, divide the cheese over them, and strew the garlic around them. Pour in enough wine to film pan by about ¼ inch (¾ cm). Place pan in upper middle level of oven. Baste every 6 minutes or so with the liquids in the pan as the birds slowly brown on top. After about 20 minutes, strew the mushrooms around the birds, basting with liquids in pan. Continue until birds are tender when thighs are pierced with a sharp-pointed fork; juices should run clear yellow with no trace of rosy color.

Finishing the sauce

(I didn't have time for this on our television show, but here is how I would have liked to have done it.) Remove the birds to their platter, arrange around them the mushrooms and half the garlic, scooped out with a slotted spoon. Keep warm for a few minutes in turned-off oven, door ajar, while you complete the sauce. Pour the brown poultry stock into the roasting pan and set over high heat to dislodge any roasting juices, scraping them up with a wooden spoon. Strain them into a small saucepan, leaving garlic in sieve. Skim surface fat off liquid, and rub garlic through sieve with wooden spoon, scraping it off bottom of sieve into the liquid—garlic purée will thicken the liquid as you rapidly boil it down for a moment to concentrate its flavor. When lightly thickened, taste sauce carefully for seasoning. Off heat, if you wish, beat in the enrichment butter by spoonfuls.

Serving

For this menu, the birds are arranged on a giant potato *galette* (following recipe), with the mushrooms and garlic. Either spoon the sauce over the hens, or pass in a warm bowl.

Giant Straw Potato Galette

An enormous pancake of matchstick-sized potato pieces

Potatoes cut into matchstick-sized pieces and pressed into a layer in a large frying pan with hot butter, cooked to a fine walnut brown on each side—what a beautiful bed for our little birds, or for many another morsel, like chops, tournedos, or even fried eggs.

Manufacturing Note:

Potatoes are odd creatures indeed, and one of their peculiarities is that some turn brownish or reddish almost while you are cutting them. Although a sojourn in cold water usually brings them back to white again, the water soaks out the starch—which

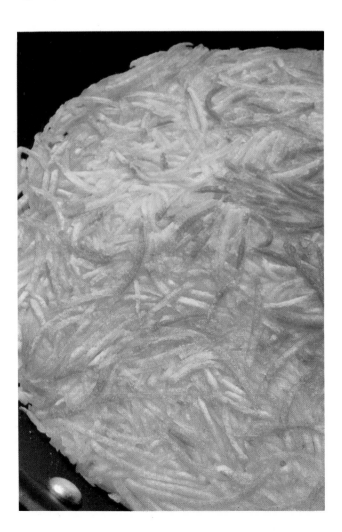

you need for this recipe because you want the potatoes to stick together and form a mat as they cook; no starch and they tend to separate. Thus potato cutting must be a last-minute affair. The cooking of the *galette* is, too; if it sits around, its tender inner core begins to discolor, and the whole *galette* slowly loses its buttery freshly cooked potato taste. Finally, clarified butter is really a must here, since ordinary butter, with its milky residue, can make the potatoes stick to the pan, which spells certain disaster. An excellent way to clarify butter is described on page 463.

For a 9- to 10-inch (23- to 25-cm)
galette serving 6 people

About 6 medium potatoes, preferably "baking"
6 Tb or more clarified butter (page 463)
Salt and pepper

Equipment:

A nonstick frying pan 11 to 12 inches (28 to 30 cm) top diameter; a cover of some sort for the pan; a long-handled pancake turner; a round serving platter to hold the galette

Just before you are to cook the *galette,* peel the potatoes, drop into a bowl of cold water, and then cut them into matchstick-sized pieces: either use a big knife, slicing them first, and cutting the slices into sticks; or use the coarse side of a hand grater; or use the grating attachment of a food processor. Do not wash the potatoes once cut; simply dry them in a kitchen towel.

As soon as the potatoes are cut and dried, film the frying pan with a 1/16-inch (1/4-cm) layer of clarified butter, and heat to very hot but not browning. Turn in the potatoes, making a layer about 3/8 inch (1 cm) thick. Sprinkle with salt and pepper, and 2 or 3 spoonfuls more butter, then press them down firmly all over with the spatula so they will mat together as they cook. Frequently press them down while they slowly brown on the bottom, and shake pan gently by its handle to be sure potatoes are not sticking to the pan.

When browned, in 2 to 3 minutes, cover the pan and lower heat to moderate. Cook for 6 to 8 minutes, or until the potatoes are tender on top, but watch they do not burn on the bottom. Press them down again, and the *galette* is ready to brown on its other side.

To turn it: either slide it out onto an oiled baking sheet, turn the frying pan upside down over it, and reverse the two so the *galette* drops into the pan, browned side up; or flip the *galette* in its pan, which, of course, is much more fun and faster—just have the courage to do it! Raise heat slightly, and brown lightly on the other side (which will never show, but browning crisps it). Slide the *galette* onto its platter, and plan to serve it as soon as possible.

🕐   May be kept warm, uncovered, but the sooner you serve it, the better.

Cherry Tomatoes Tossed in Butter and Herbs

Cherry tomatoes, for this delicious recipe, are peeled and then tossed gently in butter, salt, pepper, and herbs just to warm through but not to burst, before serving. A labor indeed it is, but well worth it for beloved family and special friends.

For 6 people — 6 to 8 tomatoes apiece

36 to 48 ripe red firm cherry tomatoes

2 Tb or more butter

3 to 4 Tb fresh green herbs, such as parsley, chives, tarragon, and chervil — alone or mixed

Salt and pepper

Equipment:

A nonstick stainless-steel or enamel frying pan just large enough to hold tomatoes in one layer

A handful at a time, drop tomatoes into a saucepan of boiling water and boil 3 or 4 seconds, just enough to loosen the skins. With a small sharp-pointed knife, cut around each stem to remove it, and slip off the skin.
🕐 May be done several hours in advance; place tomatoes in one layer in a glass or enamel plate, cover, and refrigerate.

Just before serving, heat the butter to bubbling in the frying pan, turn in the tomatoes, and roll over heat (shaking and twirling pan by its handle) with the herbs and seasonings just until warmed through. Turn into a hot vegetable dish (or spoon around your meat or vegetable platter); serve at once.

Orange Blueberry Bowl

For 6 people

5 or 6 large fine bright firm ripe seedless "navel" oranges

Sugar syrup: 1 cup (¼ L) sugar, 5 Tb water, and 1 Tb corn syrup

1 pint (½ L) blueberries, fresh or frozen

Sugar, as needed

2 Tb or more orange liqueur

Candied Orange Peel — for Decoration: With a vegetable peeler, remove in strips the orange part of the peel of 3 (or all) of the oranges, and scrape off any white residue from underside of peel. Cut the peel into very fine julienne strips — as fine as possible.

Drop into 1 quart (1 L) simmering water and simmer 10 to 15 minutes, or until tender. Drain, and rinse in cold water; pat dry in paper towels.

Meanwhile, bring the 1 cup (¼ L) sugar, water, and corn syrup to the boil in another saucepan (doubling syrup ingredients if you have used all the orange peel), twirling pan by its handle until sugar has dissolved completely and liquid is perfectly clear. Then cover pan and boil over high heat for a few minutes until syrup has reached the soft-ball stage, 238°F/115°C (bubbles are big and thick, and droplets of syrup form soft balls in cold water). Drop the peel into the syrup and boil slowly for several minutes, until syrup has thickened again. Set aside until ready to use.

🕐 May be done weeks in advance, and stored in a covered jar in the refrigerator.

Preparing the oranges and blueberries
Not more than a few hours before serving, neatly trim off the white part of the peel from the oranges to expose the orange flesh. Cut the oranges into neat crosswise slices, and, if you are not serving for more than an hour, place slices in a bowl, cover, and re-frigerate. Defrost the blueberries if necessary; if they need sugar, toss in a bowl with several tablespoons of sugar and let macerate, covered, in the refrigerator.

Assembling the dessert
Not more than an hour before serving, drain the candied peel, reserving the syrup. Choose an attractive glass serving bowl or individual coupes, and arrange a layer or 2 of orange slices in the bottom, spoon over them a little of the orange peel syrup, and add a few drops of orange liqueur. Drain the blueberries and sprinkle a layer on top of the oranges. Continue to build up the dessert in layers, ending with a handful or 2 of candied orange peel strewn on top. Cover and refrigerate until serving time.

🕐 If the dessert is assembled too soon, the blueberries exude purple coloring down into the oranges—in case that bothers you! And sliced oranges lose their fresh taste as they sit about.

Scrape away all the white from the peel to make the zest.

Before slicing, cut away all peel to expose the juicy flesh of the oranges.

⏱ *Timing*

This is not at all an ahead-of-time meal, and that is certainly one of its charms. Your guests will be getting the finest kind of food freshly cooked and served at once. That means there will be last-minute work for the cook before every course except the dessert. If you have a big family-style kitchen/dining room, you can finish practically all the main cooking right there with your guests, doing only the preliminaries before they come—such as the marination of the birds, the cleaning of the mussels, the peeling of garlic, and the candying of the orange peel. But if you haven't that kind of a kitchen, you'll need to do some planning, as follows.

Last-minute items are the mussels, but they take only 5 minutes or so to steam, plus 4 to 5 minutes to wilt the onions, and while you are cooking them you can finish the sauce for the birds and give the potato *galette* its final flip.

The roasted birds can wait, so they can be finished just before the guests arrive; keep them warm in a turned-off oven, its door ajar, reheating them briefly if need be just before serving. The potatoes could be started at this time, too. And the tomatoes could be given a preliminary toss, but set aside off heat—to be finished just before you serve them.

You'd start roasting the birds half an hour before the guests are to arrive, and preheat the oven 15 minutes before that. Since you need to be around to baste the birds frequently, you could be arranging the dessert at that time, and getting out anything else that you will need.

Scrub the mussels and start their soaking in mid-afternoon. Peel and slice the oranges at this time, too.

This brings us up close to dinnertime again. Backtracking to midday or even morning, you can give the birds their preliminary browning (or marinate them at this point and brown them later), prepare the garlic and mushrooms, peel the cherry tomatoes, and defrost the blueberries, if you're using frozen ones.

The day before, you can buy fresh Rock Cornish hens, prepare them for their cooking, and marinate them. Also, you could simmer their backbones, necks, and giblets for stock; otherwise, make it any time and freeze. If you can buy only frozen birds, be sure to allow 2 days for defrosting in the refrigerator—always the best way. The orange syrup can be prepared now, or even weeks before, from the skins of oranges you may be using for other things.

Even though the cooking of each dish is done at the last, this is not a tricky meal. There are no surprises, and it's unusually delicious as well as being special.

Menu Variations

Moules marinière: there's a variant recipe, thickened with bread crumbs, in *Mastering I,* which has several other classic mussel recipes. That book was intended to explain the dishes and methods my co-authors and I thought most important in traditional French cooking, where mussels count for a lot. But I didn't do anything more about mussels until the frabjous day when they became generally available in this country. Now, joyously making up for the lean years, I have tucked in two more mussel recipes at the end of this section. However, if your fish dealer is still in a rut and you can't get these wonderful shellfish but like the *marinière* idea, you might try clams, as the Italians do: use steamers. I do think a hot, fairly substantial shellfish dish makes an exciting opener for the

Cherry tomatoes tossed in butter and herbs

little birds, but I wouldn't come on too strong. Bouillabaisse, for instance, would be just too much garlic at one meal, but a small serving of Mediterranean fish soup, scallop soup, broiled oysters or a small oyster stew, or a little crab or lobster in mayonnaise would be fine.

Game hens: for a classic dish, *coquelets sur canapés,* roast the birds and serve them with a deglazing sauce on sautéed bread *canapés* (sofas, literally), spread with a pâté made of their livers. Substitute other birds, as the recipe explains, or you can use Rock Cornish hens in many chicken recipes. They're nice served cold, with liver stuffing and Cumberland sauce.

Potato galette: with small birds, crisp potatoes are classic. Homemade potato chips are exquisite, as are waffled potatoes (you need a special cutter), or sautéed potatoes or *pommes soufflées,* for which you can do most of the work beforehand; the final frying in very hot fat goes fast.

Cherry tomatoes: I love the trim look of each guest's plate at this party; but any other lively-tasting, lively-looking vegetable would be nice with the birds.

Fruit desserts: surely you'd want something cold and fresh after *moules marinière* and roast birds with garlic; it's just a matter of the season. Fresh pineapple (see "Cassoulet for a Crowd" on how to buy, cut up, etc.) might be lovely; or a basket of perfect ripe fruit, such as pears, peaches, apricots—it's about the most voluptuous dessert you can offer, yet has a country air like the birds on their nest. Or a bowl of cherries layered with ice to make their skins snap when you bite.

Leftovers

You won't have much in the way of leftovers in this meal. Mussels can go in a salad or soup, as described in the next section.

Bird bones and tomatoes, mushrooms and garlic are also candidates for soup. The potatoes have no future but—oranges and blueberries for breakfast? And now for more mussels!

Soupe aux Moules

Mussel soup

Moules marinière can turn themselves into a perfectly delicious soup, delicate, fragrant with a variety of thinly cut vegetables, and tasting subtly of wine and cream with a tiny spark of curry for the *je ne sais quoi* chic a good soup should have.

For about 2 quarts (2 L)

2 large carrots
2 medium onions
1 or 2 leeks (optional)
2 or 3 celery stalks
6 Tb butter, more if desired
2 cucumbers
Salt and pepper
The recipe for mussels steamed in wine, mussels removed from shells, and cooking liquid with onion and parsley warmed (without sand!)
2 tsp curry powder
4 Tb flour
2 cups (½ L) or more milk, or as needed
2 egg yolks
5 Tb or more heavy cream
Minced fresh parsley

The vegetables

Cut the carrots into julienne matchsticks, and the onions into slices about the same size. Discard roots and tough green parts of leeks, slit leeks lengthwise halfway from root end, turn and slit again; wash, spreading leaves under cold running water, and cut into julienne; cut the celery likewise. Simmer these vegetables slowly in a heavy-bottomed saucepan with 2 tablespoons butter, until wilted but not browned. Meanwhile, peel the cucumbers, cut in half lengthwise, scoop out seeds with a teaspoon, and cut cucumbers into julienne. When other vegetables are almost done, stir in the cucumbers, and salt lightly to taste. Continue cooking for 3 to 4 minutes, then stir in a cupful of mussel-cooking juice and simmer 5 minutes to blend flavors.

The soup base

In a 3- to 4-quart (3- to 4-L) heavy-bottomed stainless-steel saucepan, melt the rest of the butter, blend in the curry and flour, and stir over moderately low heat until butter and flour foam and froth together for 2 minutes without coloring. Remove from heat, and when the *roux* has stopped bubbling, pour in a ladleful of warm mussel liquid; blend vigorously with a wire whip. When smooth, beat in the rest of the liquid, adding enough milk to make about 2 quarts (2 L). Bring to the simmer, stirring slowly with wire whip, and simmer 2 minutes. Fold in the cooked vegetables, simmer several minutes; taste and carefully correct seasoning.

Blend the egg yolks in a medium-sized bowl with 5 tablespoons cream. By dribbles beat in a ladleful of hot soup, then pour the mixture back into the soup. Bring just to the simmer, stirring, so that the yolks may cook and thicken in the soup. Fold the mussels into the soup.

🕐 May be completed to this point. Film top with a spoonful or 2 of milk or cream to prevent a skin from forming. When cool, cover and refrigerate.

To serve

Bring just to the simmer. Correct seasoning again, thin out with milk or cream if necessary, and, if you wish, stir in a little more cream and/or butter. Ladle into soup bowls or a big tureen, and decorate bowls or tureen with a sprinkling of parsley.

Variations:

This soup is very good in itself, even without mussels, using chicken stock or clam juice. Or you could add oysters and fish stock, or diced raw sole or trout fillets that cook for a few minutes in the soup. Or poach scallops in wine and shallots, dice them, and add with their cooking juices to the soup.

Creamy wine-flavored mussel soup with its julienne of vegetables

Moules Farcies

Mussels on the half shell with herbed mayonnaise

For 54 mussels, serving 6 people as a first course

| About 3½ pounds (2½ quarts or 2½ L) mussels steamed in wine (about ½ the recipe given earlier in the chapter) |
| 1½ cups (3½ dL) homemade mayonnaise (page 466) |
| ½ cup (1 dL) sour cream |
| 2 Tb finely minced shallots or scallions |
| 1 tsp curry powder (optional) |
| 2 Tb very finely minced parsley |
| 1 Tb very finely minced fresh dill (or a big pinch dried dill weed) |
| Salt and pepper |
| Drops of hot pepper sauce |

Remove the cooked mussels from their shells but save one of the shells from each mussel. (Save mussel liquid for soup or sauce, or freeze it.) Blend the mayonnaise in a mixing bowl with the sour cream and other ingredients, and taste very carefully for seasoning, adding what else you think would enhance the mayonnaise without masking the delicate taste of the mus-sels. Place mussels in another bowl, and fold in as much mayonnaise as needed to enrobe them.

🕐 May be prepared in advance several hours before serving; cover and refrigerate.

Shortly before serving time (so mayonnaise topping will not crust over), spoon a sauced mussel into each shell and arrange on special shellfish plates, or on plates lined with shredded lettuce.

🕐 *Ahead-of-Time Note:* Because of the mayonnaise crusting problem, you often find, on buffet setups, that the mussels are prepared with the mayonnaise and then coated with a film of aspic, which seals them. Another solution is to spread finely chopped hard-boiled eggs and parsley over each, on a rack set over a tray, then to arrange the mussels on their dish or dishes.

Variations:

Instead of serving the mussels in their shells, heap them into serving shells and decorate with watercress, or with whatever else you wish. Or mound them into tomato shells, or serve them in a dish as part of a cold platter. Or spoon them around a cold poached fish, or make them part of the cold fish platter. Or fold them into cold cooked rice or pasta. And so forth . . .

Postscript: More on mussels

This chapter's so long I'll try telegraphese. Mussel is: *Mytilus edulis,* edible bivalve, familiar foodstuff worldwide. Consumed in U.S. by coastal Indians, witness prehistoric shell middens; appreciated by Pilgrims, early settlers. Seemingly forgotten, eighteenth to mid-twentieth centuries. Rediscovered, now sold quick-frozen, canned, pickled.

Why? Many virtues. Mussel is: (1) *Delicious!* and adaptable; (2) Not an acquired taste—liked even by shellfish neophytes; (3) Satisfying. Dieters note: 25 mussels (1 quart or 1 ½ pounds in shell) = 235 calories meat, feels like big meal; (4) Profuse. Cultivated by Spanish method (ropes hung from rafts), 1 acre sea gives *1,000* times as much meat as 1 acre pasture gives beef. Diet of future Americans need not be algae, bean sprouts. Absurd neglect of great resource.

Mussel life-style: efficient. Low on food chain, all bivalves filter seawater; mussels especially "good doers," since filter more. Plankton, other nutrients, unwastefully converted into flesh. Unfussy mussel tolerates high or low salinity; has freshwater, riverbed cousin, also edible but used chiefly for mother-of-pearl shell lining; all mussels also make pearls, not valuable.

Natural beds often several acres, containing millions; occur on Atlantic coast south to Cape Hatteras, on Pacific, south to Mexico. U.S. should cultivate on large scale, like Spain, France, Holland. To harvest own mussels: plumpest to be found below low-tide mark, where submerged, hence eating, all day. Seek on rocks, sandbanks, pilings; mussels cling to them, or to other mussels, by "byssus threads" or "beards," extruded steel wool–type filaments, very tough. Gather in cleanest, purest water only. Avoid "red tides," common on West Coast in summer, less common East: sudden proliferations of reddish dinoflagellates, microorganisms making mussels fat, people sick. Red tides monitored by U.S. Coast Guard, U.S. Fish and Wildlife Service. Check.

Check locally. Unposted areas not necessarily safe. Inquire town shellfish warden, if any, re sewage outlets, etc. If license to gather is required, try town hall. Then help self. Recommended equipment: screwdriver or chisel, gloves if sea cold, carrying bag, rinsing bucket. Best harvest only for immediate use. For storage—2 days at most—refrigerate clumps as is in plastic bag; don't separate or disturb.

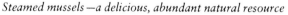

Steamed mussels—a delicious, abundant natural resource

*A savory pie, fresh garden truck: an eclectic
menu for good sound appetites*

Country Dinner

Menu
For 6 people

*Mediterranean Hors d'Oeuvre Platter —
Sliced Green and Red Peppers in Oil
and Garlic, Anchovies, HB Eggs,
Olives, Syrian String Cheese
French Bread, or a Braided Loaf*

*Leek and Rabbit Pie with Buttermilk-
Herb Biscuit Topping
Snow Peas Tossed in Butter*

*Petits Vacherins — Individual Meringue Cases
Filled with Ice Cream and Topped with
Sauced Fruits*

*Suggested wines:
A strong dry white with the hors d'oeuvre,
such as a Mâcon, Châteauneuf, or pinot
blanc; a rather mellow red with the rabbit —
Beaujolais, Châteauneuf, Bordeaux, or
cabernet; Champagne, a sparkling wine, or a
Sauternes with the dessert*

The marketing list for this meal looks terribly jumbled, for the menu draws on the very different cuisines of the Mediterranean and the Orient, on down-home American cooking, and on the classical French tradition. Nevertheless, the piquant red-green-gold-black appetizer, the cozy, fragrant rabbit pie, the fresh snow peas, and the delicate dessert make a lovely harmony. Nothing very fancy about it, but it's hard to think of a restaurant where you could order all of these dishes. Restaurants tend to specialize. And most restaurants seem needlessly conservative, lagging far behind the supermarkets' resources, which increase constantly in bounty and variety. The supermarkets, in turn, lag behind seedsmen and gardeners, who prove every day that all sorts of "exotics" can flourish almost anywhere.

Though a good market can, in fact, furnish you with all these ingredients, this menu is designed especially to honor the gardeners who grow their own, sometimes on lots half the size of a tennis court. For very little money, they can eat heavenly food like this all summer long. In all but the hottest weather, they can harvest snow peas for months, by making successive plantings; since they pick their snow peas — ordinary peas too — in the dewy morning and refrigerate them at once, the quality is superlative. (If peas are harvested too old, or if they sit even a few hours in the heat after picking, they taste flat. Either way, their natural sugar has been converted into starch.) As for leeks, while you certainly can buy fine ones, the price is shocking except in the fall. That's when the crop is mature, and commercial growers harvest and sell it all at once. The rest of the year, markets must import their leeks from wherever they're mature at the moment.

But leeks are good at any age, and home gardeners pick them when they please. Peppers are expensive because they don't store well, and since they become more fragile as they ripen, the red or fully ripe ones are relatively scarce.

Like most of the Victorian houses where we live, ours sits on a lot big enough to feed us—if we would only cut down all the big old trees, that is. On our one sunny spot, the top front doorstep, we grow pot herbs, but otherwise our crops are restricted to shade-loving things like lily of the valley and a wisteria vine that reaches out to the sun. So it's a great treat for us to dine out with our gardening friends and enjoy their exquisitely fresh vegetables and fruit. Amazing what ingenuity can do in a city backyard! To save ground space, our friends grow strawberries and cucumbers and tomatoes on trellises, and espalier fruit trees on sunny southern walls. Their ripening melons, groaning with juice, hang heavily in little net hammocks suspended from fence posts. Peppers, so beautiful and bountiful, are grown as ornamental plants on patios. And grapevines flourish on pergolas built over heat-reflecting concrete driveways.

And livestock! A very elderly resident, who grew up across the Common from us, on so-called Tory Row, says that at the turn of the century would-be ten-o'clock scholars like himself were roused daily at dawn by cackles and squawks and cock-a-doodle-doos. No such rustic racket around here nowadays; maybe too many sleepyheads took their troubles to city hall. But we do see an occasional rabbit hutch, and their numbers are growing. Few cities have ordinances prohibiting rabbits, since they have zero nuisance value: no smell, clean habits, no diseases in most climates, and no noise at all.

Living all over the world, wherever the State Department sent us, we got used to rabbit as a staple and a delight. The meat is delicate and fine-textured, pearly pink when raw but all white when cooked, with a flavor something like chicken, but richer and meatier. You can use it in any recipe designed for chicken. It's high in protein, low in fat, and, according to the U.S. Department of Agriculture, no other meat is as nutritious. When we first returned to this country, rabbit was hard to find in markets, but now most of them carry it, usually cut-up and frozen.

It's nice to see city people raising their own for home consumption, as country people always have. In these days of scarcity and high prices, it's worthwhile pondering the fact that "one doe, in one hutch, can produce 70 to 95 lbs. of dressed, edible meat in one year," and that a hutch can be less than a yard square. By the age of 2 to 3 months, a "fryer" rabbit weighs 4 to 5 pounds, more than half that when dressed; by 7 to 9 months, a "roaster" rabbit gives you over 4 pounds of meat. Fryers are more easily found but twice as expensive; it's a mystery to me why market rabbits should cost so much anyway, since they're incredibly cheap and easy to raise. We got these inspiring facts from the American Rabbit Breeders Association, which estimates that about half its members are backyard farmers, raising rabbits for the pot. If you're inspired too, you can write to the association at 1925 South Main Street, Box 426, Bloomington, Illinois 61701, and ask for their free *Beginners Booklet,* enclosing 50 cents for postage, or you can purchase their *Official Guide to Raising Better Rabbits.* And should you wish to go commercial, be advised that Pel-Freez Rabbit Meat, Inc., of Rogers, Arkansas, will set you up in business if you ask for a franchise.

Except, perhaps, for the eggs for our meringue dessert, this really could be called a Backyard, rather than a Country Dinner. Wonderful what you can do right in town, I mused, as I cooked this lovely food. My imagination blazing with possibilities, I wandered out into my own yard seeking what might be devoured. Any stuff is potential foodstuff to a cook. (My friend Chef Cazalis of the fine Restaurant Henri IV in Chartres, hearing once of an elephant that would have to be destroyed, acquired and cooked the trunk . . . 250 servings, he says; delicious too.) Wisteria? I thought; lily of the valley? But my gardening neighbor stayed my hand. "Are you mad?" he inquired. "They're both poisonous."

Preparations and Marketing

Recommended Equipment:

You need a large platter on which to display the hors d'oeuvre.

To brown the rabbit, a large frying pan; to simmer it, a 4-quart (4-L) covered pot or flameproof casserole; to bake the pie, the same pot or a big baking-and-serving dish. Obviously, the wider the baking dish, the more crust. The one we used on TV is of American-made earthenware, with a smoky-blue glaze inside; I think it's a beauty.

For the peas, a wok is nice, but you could use your rabbit-browning frying pan.

For the *vacherins,* you need a pastry bag fitted with a cannelated (toothed) tube whose opening is ⅛ inch (½ cm) in diameter. It's very important to have the right kind of pastry bag; it makes things so much easier. The best one I have run into is of lightweight, waterproof, flexible vinyl, as yet not manufactured here but imported from France. Also 2 or 3 large pastry sheets, preferably nonstick, and a 3-inch (8-cm) circular something for marking them.

Staples to Have on Hand:

Salt

Peppercorns

Sugar, preferably superfine granulated

Flour (3½ cups or ⁴/₅ L; 1 pound or 450 g)

Optional: dried rosemary leaves

Optional: fennel seeds

Optional: imported bay leaves

Pure vanilla extract

Optional: soy sauce

Olive oil

Optional: cooking oil

Vegetable shortening

Chicken stock, or chicken and beef bouillon
     (3 cups or ¾ L)

Small black olives ▼

Double-acting baking powder

Baking soda

Cream of tartar

Butter

Chives

Parsley

Onion (1 large)

Garlic (1 head)

Optional: lemon (1 large)

Specific Ingredients for This Menu:

Rabbit (4½ to 5 pounds or 2 to 2¼ kg), cut
     up ▼

Chunk of bacon (8 ounces or 225 g)

Red or yellow bell peppers (2 or 3) ▼

Green bell peppers (2 or 3) ▼

Anchovies (1 can)

Fresh snow peas (1½ to 2 pounds or ¾ to
     1 kg) ▼

Leeks (5 to 6 pounds or 2¼ to 2¾ kg) ▼

Celery (1 pound or 450 g) ▼

Syrian or Armenian string cheese (one third to
     one half of a 1-pound or 450-g package)

Buttermilk (1½ cups or 3½ dL)

Eggs (6 "large" plus 4 whites)

Fillings and toppings for *vacherins* (see recipe,
     pages 241 and 242)

Dry white wine or dry white French vermouth
     (2 cups or ½ L)

▶ **Remarks:**

Staples to have on hand

Small black olives: I like the "Nice" type of olive packed in brine, or the small Italian olives, also in brine, both of which are full of flavor. You might also try the imported, dry, oil-packed ones. Taste one, and if it seems too salty, simmer them in water for 10 minutes or so.

Specific ingredients for this menu

Rabbit: for your pie, use the "roaster" size, about 4½ pounds (2 kg) dressed weight, if you can find one. The small "fryer" rabbit is twice as expensive and is really too young and tender for stewing; but it can be used if that's all you can buy. If you have frozen rabbit, which comes already cut up, it's best if you allow 2 or 3 days' thawing time, in the refrigerator. Do not soak it. Rabbit meat can absorb up to 25 percent of its own weight of water. *Bell peppers:* the green or immature ones keep better than the red, mature peppers, but in any case I'd use bell peppers within 3 or 4 days of buying or harvesting, because they soften and spot quite rapidly. Refrigerate them, wrapped in plastic. *Leeks:* buy them fresh-looking, with firm green leaves. They keep well for a number of days when stored in a plastic bag in the refrigerator.

Mediterranean Hors d'Oeuvre Platter

Peeled sliced green and red peppers in oil and garlic, anchovies, HB eggs, olives, Syrian string cheese

For 6 people

2 or 3 green bell peppers

2 or 3 red bell peppers (and/or yellow peppers)

Salt and freshly ground pepper

2 or 3 cloves garlic

Olive oil

Syrian (or Armenian) string cheese

3 hard-boiled eggs

1 can anchovies packed in olive oil

A handful or so of small black olives

The peppers

Place the peppers on a piece of foil in a broiling pan and set them so their surface is 2 inches (5 cm) from a red-hot broiler element. When skins have puffed and darkened on one exposed side—in 2 to 3 minutes—turn with tongs onto another side, and continue until peppers have puffed and darkened all over. At once, while still warm, cut 1 of the peppers in half and drain its juice into a bowl. Scrape seeds from insides, and cut the pepper into finger-width strips—for easier peeling. Pull off the skin—which should come off easily enough if really puffed and darkened. Cut the strips in half, and place in the bowl with the juice. Rapidly continue with the rest of the peppers.

Note: The preceding system works well for me, but there are other pepper peeling methods listed on page 244 that you might try if you are having difficulties.

Peeled red and green peppers make a colorful beginning when cleverly arranged with eggs, olives, anchovies, and string cheese.

Oil and garlic sauce

Place ½ teaspoon or so of salt in a small mortar or bowl, and purée into it the garlic. Mash with a pestle or the end of a wooden spoon to make a perfectly smooth paste, then whisk in several tablespoons of oil. If the pepper slices are swimming in too much of their juice, pour some of it out, then fold the peppers with the garlic and oil.

🕐   Peppers may be sauced several days in advance of serving; cover and refrigerate, but let come to room temperature (to decoagulate the oil) before serving.

The string cheese

The cheese comes in a tightly twisted 1-pound/450-gram hank, as you can see in the photograph. Untwist it, as shown, and cut as many pieces of it as you think you will need into 8-inch (20-cm) lengths—one third to one half the package. Pull strands of cheese down the length of each piece—picky work but worth it. Taste several strands, and if cheese seems too salty, rinse in a sieve under cold run-

ning water, drain well, and toss in paper towels to dry. Before serving, you may wish to toss the cheese in a bowl with olive oil and freshly ground pepper.

🕐   Cheese may be strung, but not sauced, in advance; wrap loosely in slightly dampened paper towels, and refrigerate in a plastic bag. Will keep nicely for a day or 2 at least.

Assembling the platter

One idea for assembling the platter is shown on page 233 in the photograph, with one side for red peppers and the other for green; wedges of egg at the two ends, anchovies over peppers, cheese in the middle, and olives (rolled in olive oil) at the sides.

🕐   Platter may be assembled several hours in advance except for the anchovies, which go off in taste if opened more than a few minutes before serving—at least that is so in my experience. Cover platter closely with plastic wrap, and refrigerate, but let come to room temperature before serving so that olive oil will liquefy.

Peppers must be really broiled black for the skin to loosen easily.

Threading string cheese is a labor of love.

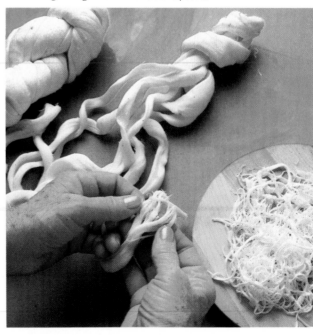

Leek and Rabbit Pie

Serving 6 to 8 people

About 5 pounds (2 ¼ kg) rabbit, cut up

Optional Marinade:

6 Tb light olive oil, or other fresh fine cooking oil

4 cloves garlic, finely minced

1 tsp dried rosemary leaves

2 Tb soy sauce

The strained juice and the zest (yellow part of peel) of 1 large lemon

½ tsp fennel seeds

2 imported bay leaves

Other Ingredients:

An 8-ounce (225-g) chunk of bacon

1 large onion, sliced

Olive oil or cooking oil

5 to 6 pounds (2 ¼ to 2 ¾ kg) leeks, to make 6 to 8 cups (1 ½ to 2 L), julienned

About 1 pound (450 g) celery, to make 2 cups (½ L), julienned

Salt and pepper

Flour

If rabbit was not marinated, add the garlic, rosemary, fennel, and bay as indicated in those directions

2 cups (½ L) dry white wine or dry white French vermouth

About 3 cups (¾ L) brown chicken stock (or chicken and beef bouillon)

Beurre manié (4 Tb soft butter blended to a paste with 4 Tb flour)

Biscuit Crust:

3 cups (430 g) all-purpose flour (measure by dipping dry-measure cup into flour container and sweeping off excess)

2 tsp salt

4 tsp double-acting baking powder

1 tsp baking soda

8 Tb (½ cup or 1 dL) chilled vegetable shortening

4 Tb fresh minced chives, or 2 Tb freeze-dried

Hiding under this savory biscuit topping is a leek and rabbit stew.

4 Tb fresh minced parsley

2 eggs

1 ½ cups (3 ½ dL) buttermilk, plus drops more if needed

Egg glaze (1 egg beaten with 1 tsp water and a pinch of salt)

Equipment:

A stainless-steel or glass bowl large enough to hold cut-up rabbit if you are to marinate it; 1 or 2 large frying pans (nonstick recommended), for browning the rabbit; a 4-quart (4-L) flameproof casserole or covered pot for simmering the rabbit; the same casserole or another for final baking; a pastry brush

Optional marinade
6 to 24 hours

If you wish to marinate the rabbit, which will give it a more interesting flavor, beat the listed ingredients together in a bowl large enough to hold the rabbit pieces. Turn the rabbit in the marinade; cover and refrigerate, turning and basting the rabbit several times with the marinade. Before using, scrape marinade off rabbit pieces back into bowl, and reserve.

Preliminaries

Remove and discard the rind, and cut the bacon into *lardons* (sticks 1 ½ by ¼ inches, or 4 by ¾ cm) and blanch them (drop into a saucepan containing 2 quarts or 2 L water, simmer 5 to 7 minutes, drain, rinse in cold water, and dry). Set aside.

Cook the onion slowly in a small saucepan with 1 tablespoon oil until tender, then raise heat slightly and cook, stirring frequently, until a light mahogany brown—this is to color and flavor your cooking liquid, later. Set aside.

Trim and wash the leeks—cut off and discard root ends, and cut off the green part a finger width or so from where the white begins, where the green is still tender. Slit lengthwise 2 or 3 finger widths from root, give a ½ turn and slit again, as shown. Spread leaves apart as you wash the leeks under cold running water. Cut into 2-inch (5-cm) lengths, and then into julienne (strips ⅛ inch or ½ cm wide). Trim, wash, and cut the celery also into julienne.

🕐   All of these preliminaries may be done even a day in advance; cover and refrigerate.

Browning and simmering the rabbit— Rabbit stew

Cook the blanched bacon slowly in a large frying pan filmed with oil, browning it lightly and rendering out its fat; remove bacon to a side dish, leaving fat in pan. Meanwhile, dry the rabbit pieces in paper towels, season lightly with salt and pepper, dredge in flour,

Quarter the leek lengthwise to get at the sand.

Flour the rabbit on a tray to avoid mess.

and shake off excess. Brown the rabbit pieces on all sides (as many as will fit comfortably in one layer) in the bacon fat, and place in the cooking casserole as each is done (add oil to pan if you need it during browning, and regulate heat so fat is always hot but not burning or smoking). Stir the leeks and celery into the frying pan. Toss and turn to blend ingredients; cover and cook slowly 5 to 7 minutes, stirring up once or twice, until softened. Spread them over and around the rabbit pieces, with the browned onions and bacon, and ingredients from the marinade. (If you did not marinate the rabbit, stir in the garlic, rosemary, fennel, and bay.)

Pour in the wine, and enough chicken stock or bouillon barely to cover the rabbit. Bring to the simmer, cover, and simmer slowly until rabbit is tender when several pieces are pierced with the sharp prongs of a kitchen fork. (Older and heavier rabbits may take as much as 1 or even 1½ hours of simmering to cook tender; young ones as little as 30 minutes.)

Arrange the rabbit pieces in a cooking-and-serving casserole. Skim any accumulated fat off surface of cooking liquid, and taste liquid very carefully for seasoning, adding more salt and pepper if needed, more herbs, etc., etc. You should have about 3 cups or ¾ L. Off heat, beat the *beurre manié* into the liquid, and bring to the simmer, stirring with a wire whip. Sauce should be lightly thickened. Pour it (with its vegetables, but without bay leaves) over the rabbit.

🕐 Recipe may be completed to this point even 2 days in advance (and may be served as is—a rabbit stew). If you are not serving or proceeding, let cool, then cover and refrigerate—heat to the simmer before final baking.

Biscuit dough for crust
Place the flour, salt, baking powder, and baking soda in a mixing bowl and cut in the chilled shortening—using 2 knives or a pastry blender—continuing rapidly until fat is broken up into pieces the size of coarse (kosher) salt.

🕐 May be done to this point several hours in advance; cover and refrigerate—liquid is added only the moment before using, because the baking powder starts its action immediately.

Stir the herbs into the flour mixture. Blend the eggs in a large measure, beat in the buttermilk, and mix rapidly into the flour with a rubber spatula, turning and pressing the ingredients together to form a dough. Scoop out onto a lightly floured work surface, and with the floured heels of your hands rapidly knead the dough to give it enough body so that you can pat or roll it out—the less you work it the more tender it will be, but it must have enough body to hold its shape softly.

Food Processor Note: To make the dough in a processor, first blend dry ingredients and chilled shortening briefly with on-off spurts, then, with the processor going, pour in the mixed liquids and blend again in spurts just until dough has massed. Turn out and knead briefly as described.

🕐 Dough must now be used immediately.
Final baking
About 20 minutes at 400°F/205°C
About half an hour before you plan to serve, have the oven preheated and set rack in lower middle level. Then, with the contents of your casserole well heated, place the dough on a lightly floured work surface. Either pat it or roll it rapidly out to a thickness of about ½

Layering the browned rabbit pieces with the cooked leeks

inch (1 ½ cm), and cut it into the size and shape of your casserole top. Flour dough lightly, fold in half, then unfold over the rabbit, pressing dough lightly against the sides of casserole. (Brush off any excess flour from top of dough.) Paint dough with a coating of egg glaze, and set in oven. Bake for about 20 minutes, or until topping has risen nicely and browned on top.

🕐   May be kept warm for half an hour or so, as long as casserole contents are kept below the simmer so rabbit doesn't overcook.

Serving

Serve right from the casserole, cutting down through the biscuit crust and including a nice piece of it at the side of each serving; baste the rabbit with a good spoonful or 2 of the sauce—and extra sauce and biscuits are nice to have on hand, too, as in the following suggestions.

Use any handy object the same size as the top of your casserole for cutting the dough.

For extra sauce

Either simmer the rabbit in a larger amount of liquid than you need, or make a separate sauce with the same flavorings—chicken stock enriched with a little beef bouillon, and simmered for half an hour with leeks, rosemary, fennel, wine, and garlic; then strain it if you wish, and thicken with *beurre manié* (about 1 ½ tablespoons each flour and butter per 1 cup or ¼ L liquid). Serve in a gravy bowl.

Buttermilk-Herb Baking Powder Biscuits:

For about 36 biscuits 2 inches (5 cm) in diameter

The same dough you used for the crust makes very nice biscuits, too—although if you are only making biscuits you may wish to cut the recipe in half.

Preheat oven to 450°F/230°C, and set racks in upper and lower middle levels. Make the dough as described in the crust recipe, and after its brief kneading on a floured surface, roll it out ½ inch (1 ½ cm) thick; use a 2-inch (5-cm) cutter to form the biscuits. Place them on lightly floured pastry sheets, leaving about 1 inch (2 ½ cm) between the biscuits. Gently knead dough into a ball after each series of cuttings, roll out again, and continue thus until all dough is used.

Bake at once in preheated oven for about 10 to 15 minutes, or until biscuits are nicely puffed and lightly browned on top. Serve as soon as possible, while they are hot and fresh.

🕐   Biscuits may be kept warm, and leftovers may be frozen and reheated, but nothing has quite the taste of biscuits freshly baked.

Plain Buttermilk Baking Powder Biscuits—for Shortcakes:

This same formula, without the herbs, also makes a very fine biscuit, and is particularly recommended for strawberry shortcakes. In this case, you might want to add a tablespoon or so of sugar to the dry ingredients before the buttermilk goes in.

Snow Peas Tossed in Butter

For 6 servings

1 ½ to 2 pounds (¾ to 1 kg) fresh snow peas

About 4 Tb butter

Salt and pepper

Equipment:

A wok is especially useful here, but a large frying pan, preferably nonstick, will do; a long-handled spoon and fork for cooking

To prepare the snow peas for cooking, pull the tips off and down each side to remove strings. Wash rapidly in cold water.

🕐 May be prepared hours ahead of cooking; wrap in slightly dampened paper towels and refrigerate in a plastic bag.

Since snow peas cook so rapidly, it is best to do them really at the moment of serving so they will retain their fresh taste, texture, and bright green color. Melt 2 tablespoons butter in your wok (or frying pan) over high heat; when bubbling, toss in the snow peas. Toss and turn with spoon and fork constantly for several minutes, until the peas turn a bright green. Taste one as a test for doneness—it should be crisply tender. Sprinkle on salt and pepper, toss with another spoonful or so of butter, and turn out onto a warm serving platter.

String snow peas before cooking

Petits Vacherins

Individual meringue cases

For 10 cases, the 4-piece assembled kind

4 "large" egg whites (½ cup, or 1 dL plus)

¼ tsp cream of tartar

Pinch of salt

⅔ cup (1½ dL) sugar, preferably superfine granulated—to be beaten in

1½ tsp pure vanilla extract

⅓ cup (¾ dL) sugar—to be folded in

Equipment:

Very clean and dry egg-white beating equipment (see page 465 for illustrated details); a 12-inch (30-cm) pastry bag with toothed tube opening ⅛ inch (½ cm) in diameter; 2 or 3 large pastry sheets, preferably nonstick, buttered and floured; a 3-inch (8-cm) cutter or any circular marker

The meringues will take about 2 hours to bake, in all, or you can start them in the evening for 1 hour, turn off the oven, and leave them there overnight to finish baking.

Oven Note: Gas ovens are more tricky for meringues than electric ovens—perhaps, I suppose, because the gas surges on and off, coloring the meringues if you are not careful. You may find that 200°F/95°C is best in a gas oven, but that 225°F/110°C is right for an electric one. But you will judge that for yourself after a meringue session or 2— ideally meringues should hardly color at all; at most they should be only a light ivory when baked. They are, actually, not baking; they are only drying out in the oven.

Preliminaries

Prepare the egg-white beating equipment, pastry bag, and pastry sheets. With the cutter, mark circles on the sheets to guide you in forming the meringues. Preheat oven to 200°F/ 95°C—if you have 2 ovens, so much the better.

The egg whites and meringue mixture

Pour the egg whites into the bowl of your electric mixer (or into a stainless-steel or copper beating bowl). If egg whites are chilled, stir

Fill the meringue cases with fruits, sherbets, or ice cream, and sauce them to suit your fancy.

over hot water until barely tepid—they will not mount properly if too cold. Start beating slowly for a minute or so until they are foaming throughout, then beat in the cream of tartar (not needed if you are using copper) and salt. Gradually increase speed to fast and beat until egg whites form soft peaks. Continue beating while sprinkling in the sugar, and keep beating for a minute or more until egg whites are stiff and shining—a spatula drawn through them will leave a distinct path, which remains. Beat in the vanilla, then remove bowl from stand and fold in the remaining sugar by large sprinkles.

🕐 Meringue should be used at once.

Forming the vacherins

You may form the *vacherins* all in 1 piece, as shown, or in 4 pieces—a bottom and 3 rings that are baked then glued together with leftover meringue and baked briefly again to set. This latter method produces a so much better-looking meringue in every way that I shall describe it alone—and it takes about the same total time to bake as the 1-piece model.

Form 10 bottom disks in the circle outlines on the baking sheets as shown, then form 30 rings; meringue should be about the thickness of your little finger or less. (Reserve 3 tablespoons meringue for gluing, later.)

Baking

About 1 hour plus 30 to 40 minutes

Set at once in oven or ovens, switching baking sheets from lower to upper racks several times, and watching that the meringues do not color more than a light ivory. Raise or lower oven heat if you think it necessary. Meringues are not done until you can gently push them loose—they will loosen when they have dried out and are ready to come off.

To assemble the cases, spread a thin coating of reserved meringue on the bottom of 1 ring, and set it on a bottom disk; continue with 2 more rings. Assemble all in the same way, and return to oven for another 30 to 40 minutes, until the meringue has dried and glued the pieces of the case together.

🕐 Baked meringues may be kept in a warming oven for a day or 2 to prevent them from getting soggy, but the safest place for long storage is the freezer. You may take them directly from the freezer for filling and serving. If meringues are left out on a damp day they will soften and even collapse.

Fillings for Vacherins:

You may fill *vacherins* with fruits or berries; with whipped cream and a topping; with Bavarian cream mixture, which can then be chilled and set; or with ice cream and various fruit toppings as shown here. You can use either vanilla ice cream or a sherbet, and the *vacherins* can go back into the freezer until serving time—the meringue softens after a day or so, but is equally delicious either soft or crisp, at least that is what I think.

A pastry bag makes the neatest forms.

Peach topping

Use fresh peaches, or canned clingstones (more flavorful than freestone). For fresh peaches, slice them and sprinkle with a little sugar and lemon juice and let stand 10 minutes or so, until their juices have rendered out; drain the juices and simmer with a little arrowroot or cornstarch to thicken lightly. Taste carefully for seasoning, adding a few droplets of rum or Cognac if you wish, and fold in the peaches. Use the same system for canned peaches, although they will probably need no sugar—only lemon juice, thickening, and perhaps a few drops of liqueur.

Berry topping

Use the same system described for peaches.

Glue the rings to the base with leftover meringue.

⏱ Timing

You do have some last-minute work for this menu, but not too much. Just before serving the main course, cook the snow peas—a matter of only 2 or 3 minutes. At this time too, if you filled and froze the *vacherins*, put them in the refrigerator so the ice cream will soften a little. If your ice cream is in bulk, however, it may need a good half hour in the refrigerator to soften—unless it is the nonhardening type.

Open the anchovies just before serving the Mediterranean platter.

Set the rabbit pie in the oven when you expect your guests to come; it can wait safely if need be. Baking time is 20 minutes or so, and you must mix and roll the dough right before it goes in the oven; but the dry ingredients can be mixed long beforehand.

Several hours before dinner, you can assemble the hors d'oeuvre platter, and wash, trim, and refrigerate the fresh snow peas. Now's the time to sauce the cheese, if you wish to, and to make the fruit sauces for the *vacherins*.

A day or 2 before the party, you can string the cheese (but not sauce it)—a longish job, so allow for that. At this time, you can make the rabbit stew. If you want to marinate the rabbit pieces, start from 6 to 24 hours earlier.

Several days beforehand, you can peel and sauce the peppers.

The meringues can be made anytime and frozen. Or you can keep them for several days in a very dry place; damp weather collapses them.

Menu Variations

Hors d'oeuvre platter: for other ways to use peppers, see pages 244, 245. Instead of bread, serve the platter with pita pockets, so guests can make their own sandwiches (a recipe for homemade pita is on page 200). If Syrian string cheese is hard to find, try julienned pieces of mozzarella or crumbled feta. Or you could use celeriac instead (see page 251). A somewhat similar hors d'oeuvre is a platter (or several small dishes) of cold, cooked vegetables in a vinaigrette dressing or *à la grecque,* page 432: ideal for the gardener-cook who might, in late summer, prefer to offer a leaf-lined basket of home-grown sliced melon.

The main course: cassoulet (see page 289), the farmer's joy and catchall, would be a hearty substitute for the rabbit pie. You can make this same dish with chicken, or with the garlicky duck ragout on page 15. Or leave the crust off and serve your rabbit stew over rice, or make a different rabbit stew, like the one with lemon in *J.C.'s Kitchen.* Or make a puff pastry crust by the new fast method on page 98, or use the pâté crust here on page 372; see also the suggestions in the Q & A section, page 464. No other vegetable is quite like snow peas, except the recently developed sugar snap pea with edible pods and full-sized occupants; but green peas or broccoli flowerettes would be nice with the rabbit.

The dessert: instead of topping your ice cream-filled *vacherins* with fresh or canned peaches or berries (see the recipe), you could use chocolate sauce (see page 464), or shaved chocolate. Or caramel sauce (see page 360), or simply use frozen raspberries or strawberries puréed in a blender or processor and, in the case of raspberries, strained. Stewed fresh rhubarb is another idea, as is a nut brittle that you have pulverized, or even our old favorite—a spoonful of rum or bourbon poured over the ice cream followed by a generous sprinkle of powdered instant coffee. For a supremely festive look and a delicious prickle on the tongue, you could swathe each little case with spun caramel, or cover each with a caramel cage, as in *J.C.'s Kitchen.* Or set a poached pear or peach (see page 356) in each *vacherin,* and top off with caramel, chocolate, or raspberry sauce. Or make the classic Mont Blanc, and fill each case with a sweetened purée of chestnuts forced through a ricer and surmounted by whipped cream. And so on, and so forth…

Leftovers (and Bumper Crops)

Hors d'oeuvre platter: though the anchovies are through for the day, all the other ingredients will keep for several days, well covered, in the refrigerator. For ways to use peppers, see page 244. If unsauced, already-strung string cheese keeps well when properly wrapped (see recipe), and is delightful used like feta (the soft, snowy Greek cheese) in salads and on other vegetable platters. Spare hard-boiled eggs, or egg pieces, can be sieved to top hot vegetables or salads (see the mimosa salad on pages 244, 245). Or you can stuff cherry tomatoes with egg salad.

The main course: rabbit quickly becomes stringy if overcooked, so if you want to reheat the stew, keep it below the simmer. The stew can be frozen, or used as a soup (bone and mince the rabbit pieces; add stock). And what about too many rabbits, the classic bumper crop? Australia solved the problem by importing mongooses, which prey on rabbits. More economical would be to find a butcher who rents freezer lockers. *Baked biscuits* can be frozen and reheated, though with some loss of texture. Raw biscuit dough doesn't keep; but see the recipe for ways to use it. *Leeks:* if you bought and cooked extra leeks, use them in a quiche (see *Mastering I*), or a leek-and-potato soup (*Mastering I, J.C.'s Kitchen*), which you can turn into vichyssoise, or vary with watercress or celery; or serve your vichyssoise *à la russe,* with beets, as in *The French Chef Cookbook.* Extra raw leeks would be delicious braised, and you can serve them sauced and gratinéed (*Mastering I*). Any soup stock is improved by tossing in a leek. And they are delicious cold, *à la grecque* (page 432). *Snow peas:* reheated cooked ones lose their crispness; but extra raw ones will keep a few days wrapped in paper towels and refrigerated in a plastic bag, or invest in Irene Kuo's *The Key to Chinese Cooking* (New York: Alfred A. Knopf, 1977), for all the delicious Chinese ways of cooking them. Or adapt them to a soup designed for ordinary pea pods, in *Mastering II.*

The dessert: extra raw meringue must be used up promptly, and you could change to a large star or rosette tube and make one-squirt meringue kisses, to bake along with the *vacherin* cases. Once it's baked, meringue freezes well. You can even fill cases with ice cream (see recipe) and freeze them that way. But don't let baked meringue stand around in damp weather. Any fresh fruit toppings should be used quickly; they don't freeze well.

Postscript: Pecks of peppers

Why peel peppers, when they're so good with the skins on? They're lovely and crisp raw, in salads; unpeeled, they can be seeded, sliced, and sautéed with onions, or cooked with tomatoes, onions, and bits of ham for a *pipérade,* page 268, so delicious with eggs, hot or cold. You can cook and marinate them *à la grecque,* for a cold hors d'oeuvre, or serve a casserole of peppers and eggplant, with plenty of garlic and fresh basil in season. They can help to stuff beef rolls, or zucchini, and with leeks they make a fine soup. Even after publishing pepper recipes in all my previous books, I'm still exploring.

But a peeled pepper is another matter. You have to heat it to get the peel off, so the flesh is slightly cooked; but it has a flavor completely different from what you taste in, say, a baked stuffed pepper. It's very subtle and tender, with an exquisite texture, and the color remains very bright.

Peeling is worthwhile, but it's quite a job. Years after my peeling experiments for *Mastering II,* I did another series which brought me back to my original conclusion, that the broiling method (see the recipe) works best. To get others' views, though, in November 1978 I asked the helpful readers of my *McCall's* column for further suggestions. They offered several. 1) Dip the peppers in boiling water, then pop them into a paper bag for a few minutes. 2) Freeze, then peel. 3) Freeze, then put the frozen peppers in boiling water for 20 to 30

Whatever method you use, skins must really be puffed (left) before you can peel that peck of peppers.

minutes, take off heat, leave for another 5 minutes, and wash with cold water before peeling. 4) Sauté them in a nonstick pan, with or without oil, for 10 to 20 minutes over a very low flame, covered; shake often to prevent sticking. 5) Drop the peppers into hot fat, then into cold water as soon as the skins change color. 6) Use a potato peeler on an untampered-with pepper, cutting it into strips first to make the job easier. 7) Hold a pepper over a gas burner with tongs, turning it to char evenly, then put it in a covered pan.

Covering the peppers after heating them was suggested by several readers, for varying lengths of time, anything from 10 minutes to several hours. I have not myself found it necessary to cover the peppers, since when properly broiled the skin comes off easily.

One suggestion has worked well with the red, mature peppers but less so with the green ones. That is to use a pressure cooker: wait till you see steam, then put on the gauge, bring just to full pressure, and turn off the heat, waiting till the cooker is cool before removing the peppers.

Peppers do vary a great deal, however. Though the broiler method has worked best for me, your peppers may be different; I hope you'll find that one of my correspondents' ideas will help. Just don't give up!

For those who didn't give up, and now find themselves with lovely peeled, sauced, peppers, here are a couple of good ideas for their use, and a recipe for a third. With pasta: either leave the pepper strips whole or chop them into dice, then toss them with hot cooked spaghetti or noodles, adding oil or butter, a good sprinkling of freshly grated Parmesan cheese, and salt and pepper to taste. With cooked leftover rice: make a delicious salad sauced with oil and garlic, and shallots; when you add the peppers, also add some minced parsley, chopped black olives, pine nuts, and what seasonings you fancy after tasting. And here is an excellent sauce to serve with hard-boiled eggs, or boiled fish, potatoes, beef, or chicken, or to use as a dip with cocktail snacks.

Pepper and Anchovy Sauce

For about 1 cup or ¼ L

About ½ cup (1 dL) sauced green or red peppers, page 233

4 to 6 anchovy fillets

1 or more tsp capers

1 or more cloves garlic, puréed

5 Tb or so fragrant olive oil

Salt and pepper

Optional: fresh or dried herbs such as parsley, thyme, oregano, basil

This is easy to make in a blender or processor. Put the peppers in the container of the machine and, if anchovies are packed in oil, add them as is along with some of their oil. If they are salted anchovies, wash them off, split and bone them, and you will probably need no more salt for the sauce. Add the capers and garlic, and purée for several seconds or until smooth. Then begin adding the oil by dribbles until the sauce is the consistency you wish it to be—I like mine quite thick. Taste carefully for seasoning, adding aromatic herbs if you wish them, and parsley for a greenish tinge, if such is your desire.
❶ Will keep several days, refrigerated in a covered jar.

Pork can be stylish too.

Butterflied Pork for a Party

Menu
For 6 people

Celery Root Rémoulade
French Bread

Butterflied Loin of Pork
Butternut Squash in Ginger and Garlic
Collards, Kale, or Turnip Greens

Gâteau Mont-Saint-Michel —
A mound of French crêpes layered
with apples and burnt-almond cream

Suggested wines:
A dry white wine on the light side —Sancerre
or dry riesling —with the first course; a light
red like a Beaujolais or zinfandel with the
pork, or a rosé, or even a sturdy white
Burgundy or chardonnay; a sweet wine with
the dessert, such as Sauternes, or a sparkling
wine

Since fresh pork was "only served at family and bourgeois meals," Escoffier wrote in 1903, in his guide for professional cooks, he "would, therefore, give only a few recipes." Twenty years later, Edouard de Pomiane lamented that "pork is considered to be undistinguished, and at grand dinners one never sees a crisp-skinned pork roast or a fragrant *andouille*" (a hearty pork tripe sausage). Poor piggy, when he's so delicious. The tradition is as old as it is foolish; even the Old Testament, in Leviticus and Deuteronomy, calls him unclean and forbids us to eat him. Pigs do wallow in mud to get cool, but they love a fresh bath and they can be housebroken. (I knew of a very polite pet one, named Ointment.) Thoroughly nice, clean, well-conducted, respectable animals, and I side with open-minded de Pomiane, for whom even the humblest of pork dishes, grilled pigs' feet, was *un plat royal.* Quite right; it is.

Snobberies and shibboleths had no place in the happy world of this great teacher of cooking. Unlike Escoffier, de Pomiane was not a professional chef but a nutritionist, who published the book from which I quote, *Le Code de la Bonne Chère,* under the sponsorship of the Scientific Society of Alimentary Hygiene. It is prefaced with an apology to the great chefs. "Indeed," he says, "unlike them I have not catered to thousands of gourmets. For thirty years I have simply been preparing dinner for myself and my family, experiencing in my kitchen the same scientific and artistic delight I feel in my physiology laboratory, before my painting easel, or at my music stand when we play string quartets." Warmly pro-feminist, he found that the newly liberated, well-educated young women of France scorned cooking as too simple-minded, a hodgepodge of unrelated commonplaces to be learned by rote. Therefore, he taught cooking in a structured, theoretical way, in order to interest minds trained in logic. Yet his books are full of poetic descriptions. Vital, enthusiastic, imaginative, de Pomiane called gastronomy "the complete art" because it appeals to all the senses.

I wish I'd known him, and could ask him over to enjoy this party meal at our table. He would consider this dish to be unusual and distinguished, as indeed it is. In fact, it seems to me altogether appropriate for a state banquet. The only reason de Pomiane could find for the unposhness of pork was that it could be so filling as to blunt the diners' appetites for the courses to follow; but on a present-day menu, this argument doesn't apply at all. Certainly butterflying, roasting, and a final quick broil give this pork a sumptuous quality. The lean, even slices have a close grain like velvet, and carving takes only seconds. The herbal marinade accents a certain undertone in the flavor of fine pork, a subtle taste that is often lost if you accompany pork with applesauce or sauerkraut. And butterflied, it cooks in half the

time of a bone-in roast. People are mistaken, by the way, if they think pork has to be cooked to bath-towel consistency in order to be safe. *Trichinae*—rarely found nowadays—are destroyed at 137°F/58°C, when the meat is rare. At 160°F/71°C, the meat has lost its pinkness and is an appetizing ivory color, and still full of juices.

The roast is prefaced by an hors d'oeuvre that is commonplace in Europe but less known here. Celery root—alias celeriac, knob celery, turnip-rooted celery, and in French *céleri-rave*—is simply a variety of celery that is grown for its great bulbous bottom rather than for its stalks. It's said to be easy to grow, and it keeps well through the winter after harvesting in fall. You can braise it in meat stock or chicken stock, or shred it and sauté it slowly in butter, or boil it and mash it with potatoes, or use it in soup for its intense celery flavor, but I think it is at its finest raw, cut into fine strands, and served up in a mustard dressing. (Most restaurants call it a *rémoulade* sauce, so I do; but a real *rémoulade,* a mustardy mayonnaise with capers and chopped pickles, would be too heavy and oily in this case.)

The squash and greens are for beauty as well as flavor. I'm fond of the sturdy greens, with a taste slightly more bitter than spinach, to offset the pork's suavity, and ginger seems to give winter squash more character, besides complementing the pork.

We'll have our apples after, not with, the pork; if the freezer is stocked with crêpes, a plumply layered gâteau is quick to make: a charming dessert, flavored with burnt-almond cream. To caramelize the exterior, I use my nephews' favorite kitchen implement, my indispensable blowtorch. De Pomiane, who learned to cook on a Bunsen burner, would have loved to play too.

Preparations and Marketing

Recommended Equipment:

To julienne the celery root, you really need a machine of some kind because it must be cut very thin. Some processors have disks with holes just the right size to produce strips the thickness of a rawhide shoelace. I find my little French rotary cutter, which comes with several disks, does a perfect job (see illustration, page 251).

Check that you have a broiling pan, or shallow roasting pan, large enough to hold your big flat cut of pork. And if you haven't one already, I urge you to buy an instant, or microwave-type, meat thermometer—you'll have lots of use for it.

A nonstick frying pan with an 8-inch (20-cm) bottom diameter is needed for the crêpes; and be sure the inner surface of your baking-and-serving dish is that size or larger.

Staples to Have on Hand:

Table salt
Coarse or kosher salt
White peppercorns
Dried rosemary leaves
Dried thyme
Powdered allspice
Dijon-type prepared mustard
Pure almond extract
Pure vanilla extract
Olive oil
Optional: salad oil
Flour (preferably Wondra or instant-blending
    type)
Milk
Optional: light cream
Butter (3 sticks; 12 ounces or 340 g)
Eggs (5 "large")
Fresh parsley and/or chives
Lemons (1 or 2)
Dark Jamaica rum
Orange liqueur or Cognac
Sugar

Specific Ingredients for This Menu:

Sirloin half of a pork loin (about 7 pounds or
    3¼ kg), bone in ▼
Sour cream
Blanched, toasted, ground almonds (1⅓ cups
    or 3¼ dL) ▼
Celery root (1 with a 3-inch or 8-cm
    diameter) ▼
Optional accompaniment for celery root:
    green beans, or see Serving Suggestions
    following the recipe for Celery Root
    Rémoulade
Collards, kale, or turnip greens (about 3
    pounds or 1350 g) ▼
Yellow butternut squash (about 2 pounds or
    less than 1 kg)
Large apples (12) ▼
Garlic (about 7 large cloves)
1 small fresh ginger root

▶ **Remarks:**

Pork loin: see the recipe later in the chapter for a picture and a detailed description of the cut you want. You may have to show it to your butcher. With lamb, a "butterfly" means the boned leg, so remind him you don't want leg, you want loin in one piece— the sirloin half of the loin, including the loin strip and tenderloin, the twelfth and thirteenth ribs, and the end of the hipbone. *Almonds:* for blanching, toasting, and grinding, see directions on page 463. Nuts stay freshest when kept in the freezer. *Celery root:* see the picture and information about choosing and storing in the recipe that follows. I'm not talking about the root of ordinary celery, though the taste is similar. *Greens:* collards, kale, turnip greens, mustard greens, and beet greens—any of which will do—are usually more abundant during cool rather than hot weather. When buying any of them, look for firm, fresh, crisp, tender leaves; take a bite out of a few, to be sure the greens are quite tender and sweet, not old, tough, and bitter. Like spinach, they wilt down as they cook, and you will be using only the leafy parts, not the stems. So if they're leggy, you'll need more. *Apples:* buy Golden Delicious, or another variety that keeps its shape during cooking.

The boneless butterflied loin of pork cooks fast and carves easily.

Celery Root Rémoulade

Finely shredded celery root in mustard and sour cream dressing

For 6 people as part of a cold hors d'oeuvre selection

2 to 3 Tb or more Dijon-type prepared mustard

2 to 3 Tb olive oil or salad oil (optional)

4 to 6 Tb or more sour cream

Droplets of milk or thin cream if necessary

Salt and white pepper

1 fine firm celery root about 3 inches (8 cm) in diameter

Equipment:

A medium-sized mixing bowl; a wire whip; a julienne cutter of some sort is really essential

This inexpensive julienne cutter also has slicing and grating blades.

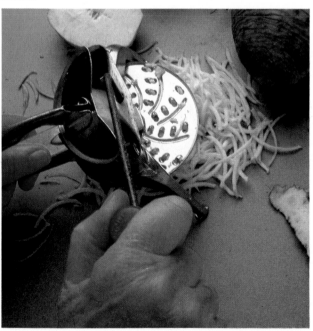

A Note on Choosing and Storing Celery Root: Pick celery roots that are firm and hard all over; big ones are just as tasty as small ones as long as they look and feel whole and healthy. The ideal storage place is a cool dark root cellar, where they will keep throughout the winter and early spring. Those of us without such conveniences should wrap each celery root in a dry paper towel and store the celery roots in a perforated plastic bag (for air circulation) in the refrigerator, where they will keep nicely for a week or more.

When peeled, the flesh of a healthy fresh celery root has a strong and vigorous celery aroma; it is crisp and hard. Its color is creamy white with faint wandering lines of pale tan. As it becomes stale, the flesh darkens and softens.

The Sour Cream and Mustard Dressing: Place 2 tablespoons of mustard in the mixing bowl, then beat in the optional oil and the sour cream; mixture should be quite thick and creamy. If stiff, thin out with droplets of milk or cream. Season well with salt and pepper; sauce should be quite strongly flavored with mustard, since it is the mustard that seems to penetrate and tenderize the celery.

Peeling and shredding the celery root (Because the celery can discolor, you shred it the moment before saucing it.) Peel the celery root, using a short stout sharp knife and cutting just down into the white flesh all around. When you come to the creased portions at the root, slit down into the celery to remove them. At once cut the root into very fine julienne, and toss in the prepared sauce. (If you are doing several celeries, shred and sauce each as you go along, to prevent discoloration.)

🕐 Sauced celery root will keep for 2 to 3 days refrigerated in a covered container.

Serving Suggestions— Celery Rémoulade Garni:

You can, of course, serve the sauced celery root as it is, or simply garnished with lettuce leaves or watercress. But I like to dress it up, as we have in this menu, with lightly cooked fresh green beans and sliced tomatoes, seasoned sparingly with oil, lemon, salt, and pepper. However, depending on your menu, you could add quartered hard-boiled eggs and black olives, or even sliced salami or chunks of tuna fish or sardines to make a quite copious first course or main-course luncheon dish.

Julienne of celery root in mustard sauce, garnished with green beans and tomatoes

Pork Talk

Spiced Roast Pork Shoulder:

When I decided to do a menu around pork roast, I thought of a whole shoulder, which I prepared by removing the rind that it came with and slicing off all but a thin layer of fat. Then I put the shoulder in a dry spice marinade for 3 days. It weighed 5½ pounds (2½ kg), so I used 2 tablespoons salt and 1½ teaspoons of my mixed spices (described on page 468), rubbing salt and spices into the pork all over and packing it pretty airtight in a plastic bag. After its marinade I washed and dried it. Then I roasted it to 160°F/71°C in a 425°F/220°C preheated oven for 15 minutes to brown, and I finished it off at 350°F/180°C, which took some 2 hours in all. It was delicious, juicy, and tender. But that marinade was too reminiscent of our preserved goose, and I wanted a change—though I highly recommend it to you for pork chops as well as roasts; it gives pork a particularly succulent character.

Stuffed Pork Loin:

Then I said to myself, why not stuff a loin of pork, thinking it would have flaps like veal or lamb that could enclose a stuffing once the loin had been boned; but it doesn't have that kind of folding flap. Instead I cut crosswise slices from the top almost to the bottom of my boned loin so that each slice would be a serving. I made a delicious mixture of liver pâté, sausage meat, shallots, garlic, thyme, and Cognac, spread it over each slice, tied up the roast, set it in a pan with a sliced carrot and onion, and roasted it 1½ hours to the peak of perfection, as they say in the advertisements. But it didn't taste like pork anymore—it was good, but not porky. And it was tough! Why?

About Pork Quality:

I asked my butcher why my pork was tough, and all he could say was that sometimes pork is tough. It's got to be young enough, he told me, and the color should be pale, almost like veal. Several people I talked to said they'd run into a tough pork chop now and then. So our chief researcher, Marilyn Ambrose, got on the telephone to various authorities, including the National Live Stock and Meat Board people in Chicago. David Stroud, president of the board, writes that the single most important factor in getting tender pork is the age of the animal—it should be under eight to ten months old; their ideal is to have all pork for the retail trade six months old. The second most crucial factor is the psychological state of the pig at the moment of slaughter: if it is worn out from traveling, or shocked, or scared, its endocrine glands begin working furiously and that alters the texture of the flesh. Now, if you have ever wondered why your pork chop was tough, you can tell for sure it came from an old and/or scared pig. But who knows if you can observe these signs at the meat counter?

After clarifying the toughness question somewhat, I got back to the idea of stuffing a loin, and back to the boning of one. It's easy to bone the sirloin half that contains both the tenderloin and the loin and a bit of the hip. Looking at that fine big boneless flat piece of meat, I said to myself, why even stuff it—why not cook it just like that? All spread out, butterflied, and slathered with a bit of a marinade—garlic, rosemary, and oil. We'd done butterflied lamb, so why not pork? And a great idea it is, we found; it cooks in a little over an hour, roasted at first, on the inside side, then turned and browned under the broiler on the fat side. And carving is a breeze: you slice off the tenderloin strip, then slice up the tenderloin and the loin strip, giving you chunks for the tenderloin and neat large slices for the loin. As to flavor, it's some of the best pork I've ever eaten.

Temperature control

As noted, there is no excuse at all for overcooking pork, since *trichinae* are eliminated when the meat is still almost rare. I personally like my pork to be done at around 160°F/71°C, when it is possibly the faintest bit pink but more on the ivory side, and the meat has not lost its juice. The Meat Board recommends 170°F/77°C, as do some other sources. I think it is a question of personal taste, and you should try out various temperatures (over 140°F/60°C!) and make the decision yourself.

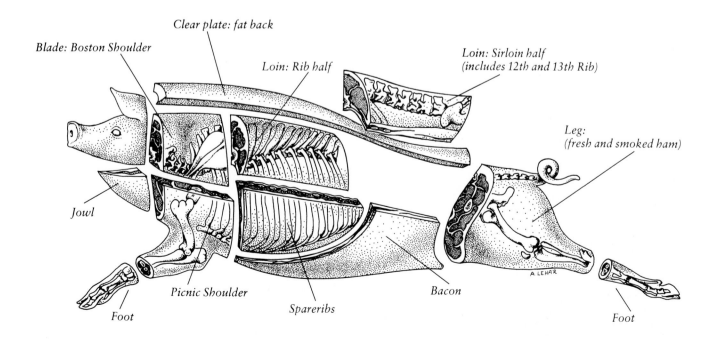

Clear plate: fat back

Blade: Boston Shoulder

Loin: Rib half

Loin: Sirloin half (includes 12th and 13th Rib)

Leg: (fresh and smoked ham)

Jowl

Picnic Shoulder

Spareribs

Bacon

Foot

Foot

Butterflied Loin of Pork

Roasted with an herb and garlic marinade

For 6 to 8 people, with leftovers

The sirloin half of a pork loin (about 7 pounds or 3¼ kg, bone in)

1 or more tsp coarse salt

For the Marinade:

2 or 3 large cloves garlic

2 tsp salt

½ tsp each dried rosemary leaves and thyme

⅛ tsp powdered allspice

About 3 Tb olive oil

Equipment

3 skewers about 9 inches (23 cm) long (useful); a roasting or broiling pan large enough to hold meat easily and, if you wish, the bones too; an instant meat thermometer (recommended)

Butterflying the pork loin

The full sirloin half of the pork loin includes the twelfth and thirteenth ribs at the small end, the end of the hipbone at the large end, the loin strip (the large eye of meat on one side of the central bone) and the pork tenderloin, the long conical strip that is small at the rib end and large at the hip end of the loin (illustrated on page 253). To bone, cut down the length of the backbone on the tenderloin side, starting at the small end, scraping always against the bone and not against the flesh. The bone is shaped like a T; the flat top is the fusion of vertebrae that form the backbone, and their fat prongs go down into the flesh, separating the tenderloin from the loin strip.

When you come to the large end, you will have to cut around the hipbone (the only slightly complicated part of the job); then cut around the fat prongs, going up under the T and around it, to separate bone from flesh. Spread out the meat, flesh side up, and cut out any interior fat. Turn it over, and slice off all but a ¼-inch (¾-cm) layer of fat—or more, if you wish, but the fat, which will be slashed and salted near the end of cooking, makes a decorative top.

Cut down length of backbone on the tenderloin side.

Cutting around the hipbone

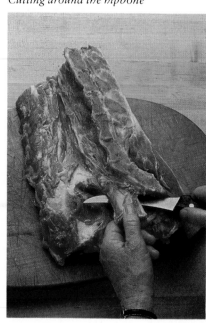

Cut around the prongs and up, to release backbone.

Marinating the pork

30 minutes to 24 hours

Peel the garlic cloves and purée with the salt (page 466). Grind the rosemary leaves, using a small mortar and pestle or small bowl and the handle end of a wooden spoon; add the thyme, allspice, and puréed garlic, then stir in the oil.

Spread out the pork, fat side down, and paint the flesh side with the marinade. Skewer the meat flat, if you wish, and place the pork, fat side down, in an oiled roasting pan.

🕐 Pork may be prepared to this point a day in advance; wrap and refrigerate.

Preliminary roasting

About 1 hour at 375°F/190°C

Preheat oven in time for roasting, then set meat in upper third level. Roast the pork (and the bones too, if you wish), basting with accumulated juices in pan, for about an hour, or to a meat thermometer reading of 140°F/60°C. Remove from oven. (Bones will need 15 to 20 minutes more.)

🕐 Preliminary roasting may be completed an hour before serving; set at room temperature, and cover with an upside-down bowl.

Final browning

About 10 minutes if done immediately

Pork is now to be turned over and browned on its fat side; either place it on another pan or scrape juices out of roasting pan into a saucepan. Turn pork fat side up.

Preheat broiler to very hot. Meanwhile, with a sharp knife cut crosswise slashes ¼ inch (¾ cm) apart down the length of the pork, and sprinkle with a thin layer of coarse salt. Place meat so its surface is 3 inches (8 cm) from heat source, to let it brown nicely and finish cooking. Meat is done (to my taste, at least) at an internal temperature of 160°F/71°C—when it is still juicy. It is a shame to overcook pork! (See notes on that subject earlier in the chapter.)

🕐 The pork may be kept warm for half an hour or more in a warming oven at 120°F/49°C.

Carving and serving

To carve, cut off the tenderloin strip, going the length of the loin. Carve it into as many crosswise nuggets as you have guests, and pile at one end of your platter. Then cut the loin strip into crosswise slices. Skim fat off roasting juices, and spoon a little over the meat; pour the rest into a hot sauce bowl and moisten each serving with a spoonful. (The bones make nice finger food for tomorrow's lunch.)

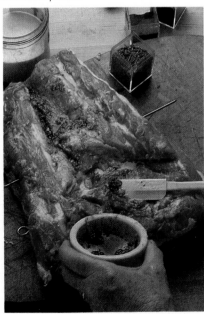

Herb and garlic marinade enhances flavor.

Score the fat side before final broiling.

Separate the tenderloin (left) from loin before carving.

Butternut Squash in Ginger and Garlic

For 6 to 8 servings

A yellow butternut squash (or other winter squash) of about 2 pounds (under 1 kg)

½ tsp salt

2 to 3 Tb butter (optional)

4 or more Tb meat juices (optional)

2 Tb each finely minced fresh ginger and garlic

More salt, and pepper

2 to 3 Tb fresh minced parsley and/or chives

Equipment:

A good vegetable peeler; a stout soup spoon; a vegetable steamer (optional)

Butternut squash

Preparing the squash

Cut the squash in half lengthwise; scrape out the seeds and strings, digging in hard and close to the flesh. Remove outer skin with a vegetable peeler, going over the squash several times to expose the deep-yellow flesh. Cut the squash into strips, and the strips into thumbnail-sized dice. You will have about 5 cups (1¼ L).

🕐 May be prepared ahead; cover and refrigerate.

Cooking the squash

You may steam the squash, if you wish, simply by putting it into a vegetable steamer set in a covered saucepan over an inch or so (3 to 4 cm) boiling water. Or you may boil it in a covered saucepan—my preferred method—as follows. Pour in enough water almost to cover the squash, add the salt and, if you wish, 1 tablespoon butter; cover and boil slowly for about 10 minutes, or until squash is just tender—do not overcook.

Whether you have steamed or boiled the squash, drain the cooking water into another saucepan and boil it down rapidly with the optional meat juices and, if you wish, 2 more tablespoons butter, plus the finely minced ginger and minced garlic. When well reduced and liquid is almost syrupy, pour it over the squash. Toss with the liquid and correct seasoning.

🕐 May be cooked in advance. Reheat the squash (or set over a pan of boiling water to reheat or keep hot). Just before serving, shake and swirl pan by its handle to toss the squash with the herbs.

Variations with Rutabaga and Turnips: Use the same method with rutabaga or white turnips, which also go beautifully with pork.

Collards, Kale, and Turnip Greens

As well as mustard greens and beet greens—whichever you decide to serve, they all cook the same way

How much to buy?

You'll have to judge by eye, remembering that greens, like spinach, wilt down considerably as they cook, and you will be using only the leafy parts, not the stems. A 10-ounce (285-g) bunch or package of trimmed greens should serve 2 people, but if they are leggy or long stemmed—?

Trimming the greens

So that the greens will cook quickly and retain their bright green color, you should remove all parts of the stems, going up into the leaves, where stems may be tough and woody. Discard any tough or withered leaves. Wash in several changes of cold water, drain in a colander, and if leaves are large, cut into chiffonade (thin strips).

Cooking

Heat a tablespoon or 2 of butter or oil in a large stainless-steel or nonstick frying pan or wok. Put in as many greens as will fit; turn and toss with a long-handled spoon and fork over moderately high heat until the greens begin to wilt (remove and add a second batch if you couldn't fit them all in the first time, then combine to finish cooking). Season lightly with salt and pepper and, if you are using it, toss in a clove of finely minced garlic (for this menu I would dispense with it because we have enough garlic elsewhere). Continue tossing and turning for several minutes until the greens are as tender as you wish them to be—you may have to add a few tablespoons of water, cover the pan, and steam them for a few minutes to complete the cooking; then uncover the pan and let the liquid evaporate. You may wish to toss them with a tablespoon or 2 of butter just before serving.

🕐 Greens may be cooked somewhat in advance; set aside uncovered. Toss for a moment over moderately high heat before serving.

Collards, kale, and mustard greens

Tear green leaves off tough stems.

Gâteau Mont-Saint-Michel

A mound of French crêpes layered with apples and burnt-almond cream

Here is a delicious, dramatic, and very easily assembled dessert, once you have your crêpes—which can be waiting for you in your freezer. And you can make a gâteau of as many crêpe layers as you wish. The one suggested here will easily serve 8 people, perhaps more, depending on waistlines and appetites. It calls for a burnt-almond cream. And why is it called *burnt* almond? Nobody knows. Why is black butter sauce called black when it is only brown?

Gâteau Mont-Saint-Michel

For 8 people

Batter for 8 eight-inch (20-cm) dessert crêpes:

¾ cup (1 ¾ dL) each milk and water

1 "large" egg

2 egg yolks

1 Tb sugar

⅛ tsp salt

3 Tb orange liqueur, rum, or Cognac

1 cup (¼ L) flour, preferably Wondra or instant-blending (measure by dipping dry-measure cup into flour container and sweeping off excess)

5 Tb melted butter

The Burnt-Almond Cream:

⅔ cup (1 ½ dL) sugar

1 stick (115 g) unsalted butter, preferably at room temperature

2 "large" eggs

1 ⅓ cups (3 ¼ dL) ground blanched and toasted almonds (directions on page 234)

½ tsp pure almond extract

½ tsp pure vanilla extract

3 Tb dark Jamaica rum

Pinch of salt

The Apples:

About 12 large fine apples that will keep their shape while cooking, such as Golden Delicious

Juice of 1 or 2 lemons

Sugar, as needed

Melted butter, as needed

Equipment:

A nonstick frying pan with an 8-inch (20-cm) bottom diameter, approximately (for the crêpes); a baking-and-serving platter of a size to hold the crêpes when mounded; a jelly-roll pan or roasting pan for the apples

The crêpes

Turn to page 132 for illustrated directions on how to cook, stack, and store or freeze crêpes. You will need at least 4, probably 6.

The burnt-almond cream

Beat all ingredients together in a bowl with a whip or beater, or in a food processor. If made ahead, stir over warm water to loosen, for easy spreading, before mounding the crêpes.

The apples

Quarter, core, and peel the apples, and spread in a buttered jelly-roll or roasting pan, tossing with as much lemon juice, sugar, and melted butter as you think appropriate. Bake for 30 minutes or so in a 400°F/205°C oven, tossing up several times, until tender.

🕐 Crêpes may be made weeks in advance and stored in the freezer, as may the burnt-almond cream; the apples may be baked a day or 2 in advance, cooled, covered, and stored in the refrigerator.

Assembling the gâteau

Brush the inside of the baking-and-serving platter with a film of butter and lay a crêpe, best side up, in the center. Cover with a layer of apples, then several spoonfuls of almond cream, then a crêpe, pressing down on its center to spread apples out to the edge and to prevent the whole structure from humping in the middle as layers build up. Continue in layers until you have used all but a layer's worth of apples; end with the apples. Sprinkle lightly with melted butter and sugar.

🕐 May be assembled even a day in advance; cover and refrigerate.

Build up layers of crêpes, apples, and burnt-almond cream.

Baking and serving
About 30 minutes at 375°F/190°C

Bake in middle level of preheated oven until bubbling hot and apple topping has browned nicely. If it has not browned, set it under a moderately hot broiler for a moment, or use the professional pastry chef's blowtorch technique illustrated on page 40. Serve hot, warm, or tepid.

🕐 May be kept warm for an hour or so covered on an electric hot tray, or in a warming oven.

Variation—
Giant Flip-Flop Apple Crêpe:

When you have only 2 or 3 people to serve, make them a giant flip-flop crêpe, which you can flame at the table, if you wish. Make the crêpe batter with just 1 egg, no extra yolks, and half the rest of the ingredients. Dice 2 or 3 apples that you have quartered, peeled, and cored, and sauté with butter, sugar, and a spoonful or 2 of rum or bourbon and perhaps a sprinkling of cinnamon—letting the apples caramelize a little in the pan. Choose a large nonstick pan, brush with butter, and set over high heat. When very hot, pour in a thin layer of batter, let it settle for a moment, then spread on the apples; spoon a layer of batter over the top, and cover the pan. When top of batter has set, in 2 to 3 minutes, it is time to brown it. Either turn by flipping it over in the pan and browning over high heat; or sprinkle lightly with melted butter and sugar, and set pan under the broiler, watching constantly, until crêpe browns lightly, in a minute or 2.

Slide it out onto a hot platter, and if you wish to flame the crêpe at the table, sprinkle with a little more sugar, pour over it several spoonfuls of hot Cognac or bourbon or rum, and ignite with a lighted match. Then spoon the flaming liquid over the crêpe for a few seconds while the flames die down. Serve in wedges.

🕐 The cooked crêpe can wait, but it all goes so quickly that I think it best done at the last moment.

⏱ *Timing*

This is what I'd call a mother-in-law dinner: impressive, fresh-tasting, sophisticated food with no last-minute fluster.

In less than 5 minutes, between courses, you can toss the two vegetables in their buttered pots, defat the meat juices, and slice the pork.

Since the pork and the gâteau can safely sit in a warming oven, your only job after the guests arrive is to take the previously arranged hors d'oeuvre platter from refrigerator to table.

Half an hour before serving, brown the pork under the broiler. If you don't have a separate broiler, it's safe to remove the baked gâteau from the oven while the meat browns; it'll keep warm under an inverted bowl. Give the greens a preliminary cooking.

An hour before serving, set the gâteau in the 375°F/190°C oven, along with the pork, which has already been cooking for half an hour. (This gâteau doesn't mind sharing an oven, though a cake or a soufflé would.)

Several hours before dinner, cook the squash, for rewarming later. Do the squash first, and let its juices reduce while washing and trimming the greens. If you're having green beans and sliced tomatoes with the celery root, blanch the former and peel and slice the latter now, arrange your hors d'oeuvre platter, and refrigerate, covered with plastic wrap. Don't put the celery root on the platter till serving time, since the other vegetables would soak up some of its sauce, and you want contrast.

The day before your party, bone the pork and refrigerate in its marinade. You can assemble the gâteau now, and refrigerate till baking time. The apples can be baked a day before this, and refrigerated.

Two days ahead, you can shred and sauce the celery root, which actually improves by keeping.

Any time at all, you can make and freeze the crêpes and the burnt-almond cream.

Menu Variations

Celery root: it's unique, and can only be had in the fall or winter months. What would be nice before the pork? Nothing rich like a pâté or quiche. What about the cold beet and cucumber soup, on page 267? Gazpacho, on page 367? A hot consommé sparked with a dash of Port wine, page 284?

Butterflied pork: this, too, is unique. Pork cooked by traditional methods (lots of recipes in *Mastering I*) tastes nothing like it. Butterflied lamb, which we did on page 197, is delicious, but, again, quite different, and I think I'd want other vegetables with it.

Winter squash: you could use root vegetables as a substitute, like rutabagas or turnips or salsify (oyster plant). Or new potatoes.

Greens: you could use young beet or mustard greens, or chard (save the delicious chard stems for another dish), or spinach, broccoli, or Brussels sprouts.

Gâteau: like King Solomon when he was sick of love, I comfort me with apples all the time; all my books have apple desserts. I wonder how this gâteau would be with pears?

Leftovers

Celery root: since it keeps very well in its mustard sauce, do make extra, and see the recipe for suggested garnishes.

Butterflied pork: it's excellent cold. Rewarmed, I think it's best in a sauce, either diced or ground, or perhaps sliced, but in any case heated *with* the sauce. If you just have scraps, they can be hashed or dropped into a soup (wonderful in a hearty bean or split pea soup).

Vegetables: Fine added to soup.

Gâteau: you can reheat it, or you can serve it cold. If you made extra crêpes, freeze them, and the same for almond cream, which you can use like hard sauce on hot desserts, as stuffing for a *pithiviers*, or in your own improvisations. It's a versatile kitchen staple.

Postscript: Learning to cook

As a penniless student at the Sorbonne, Edouard de Pomiane used to cook his own lunch in the laboratory, presumably over a Bunsen burner. Eventually he was caught in the act by his mentor and professor, who, instead of reprimanding him, appeared the next day with two chops and "a superb *gâteau feuilleté*" and asked de Pomiane to cook for two. De Pomiane describes the event:

"Where did you learn cooking?" he asked me.

"In your physiology course," I replied.

It was the truth. From his lucid teaching, I had learned what meat is. . . . I had heard him speak of the coagulation of albuminoids and the caramelization of sugars. . . .

"Why then," Dastre told me, "Brillat-Savarin was wrong in saying that 'one may become a cook but one has to be born a *rôtisseur*.' Anyone will know how to grill meat if he takes the trouble to think about what's going on during the grilling.' "

Think what you're doing is indeed a golden rule. Think not just about the why but about the how, for you can save a great deal of time by mastering routine processes. I was surprised the other day to find that one of the *J.C. & Co.* team, who has cooked for twenty years, had never really learned to chop parsley. She was holding the knife wrong, and, though the parsley did get chopped, it took ten minutes.

On the other hand, I didn't know until she told me that chopped parsley freezes perfectly. I'd just assumed it didn't, or just hadn't

tried it . . . like the butterflied pork in this chapter. Butterflying is for leg of lamb, I thought, and thought no more. *Don't take things for granted.* Keep searching for better techniques, new applications, new ways of combining flavors. *Try things out.* One's imagination can play one false: the only real test is to taste.

Try things twice, and yet once more. "It has worked this way for me" is a valid judgment; you have to trust yourself and your experience. But be willing to test again and again—you may have done something just a shade differently the other time, and a little change in measurements or techniques can sometimes make a real difference. De Pomiane, in his classes, taught cooking as an exact and orderly science, but as an experimental science, too. In a laboratory, in theory if not always in practice, the constant factors can be controlled, so you can get a fair look at the variable; but that's not always true in a kitchen. As an example, it took me 29 trials to solve the mystery of a fresh strawberry soufflé. It worked fine that time, but it was far too fragile. The strawberries too often sank to the bottom of the baking dish, and finally I had to abandon the original recipe altogether and develop a quite different technique for keeping the strawberries suspended where they belonged.

Time yourself. Find out not only how long it takes you to accomplish a whole recipe, but also how much time you need to slice a pound of mushrooms or peel six tomatoes. The result of such self-awareness is order, efficiency, and composure. Some menus, especially those with several last-minute jobs (UFOs in Wine, for instance, on page 211), demand it of you.

Eat out. Drink good wine. It doesn't have to be often, but your palate becomes dulled, if you go too long without stimulus or without quality. That's when an otherwise excellent cook will begin to overseason.

Respect your work. Noncooks think it's silly to invest two hours' work in two minutes' enjoyment; but if cooking is evanescent, well, so is the ballet. As de Pomiane put it, "Gastronomy is an art, because in addressing our senses it refines them, and because it evolves, in turn, as a consequence of their refinement."

A fresh light colorful meal —quick to prepare and easy on the budget

A Fast Fish Dinner

Menu
For 6 people

Cold Beet and Cucumber Soup
Fingers of Buttered Pumpernickel Bread

Monkfish Tails en Pipérade —Green and red
peppers, onions, herbs, and garlic
Fresh Tomato Fondue (optional)
Sauté of Zucchini & Co.
French Bread

Cream Cheese and Lemon Flan
Cherries, Grapes, Tangerines, or Berries in
Season

Suggested wines:
A strong dry white wine with the fish:
Burgundy, Côtes du Rhône, chardonnay.
You might also serve a sparkling wine or
a gewürztraminer with the dessert.

When a commercial fisherman hauls in his vast nets, all sorts of finny creatures tumble out; of these, many are edible and some, delicious. But only a few kinds ever turn up on ice at the fish store, and it's a shame. Among the missing until fairly recently was monkfish, also called anglerfish, goosefish, allmouth, molligut, and fishing frog; in French it's *lotte* or *baudroie;* in Italian, *rana* or *coda di rospo* (toad's tail); and its Latin name is *Lophius americanus,* for the American species, and *L. piscatorius,* for the European. European cooks consider it a delicacy; because of the great demand, it's expensive there, with much of it imported from our waters. Monkfish is a good resource in these days of inflation and scarcity. What you buy is thick, firm, snowy-white fillets, chunky things you halve or cut into steaks. Monkfish is a cook's delight because it is so adaptable; its firm texture suits it to dishes like bouillabaisse, and its mild flavor can be stepped up with sauces and marinades.

Quickly cooked fish is a shrewd choice for party hosts who will have to be out all day. For this light, attractive meal we chose a cold beet and cucumber soup and a cream cheese and lemon flan, parts of which can be made in advance, and the monkfish is accompanied with a beautiful platter of sliced and quickly sautéed vegetables. The fish is cooked with a *pipérade,* that classic combination of peppers, onions, and garlic; the juices are reduced and added to a fresh tomato sauce (recipe on page 468), making a pretty dish full of flavor. In Europe, monkfish is often mixed with lobster meat, whose flavor and perfume it absorbs, for an effect of vast opulence.

When we decided to cook monkfish for television, we asked our favorite fish purveyor to supply us with a whole one, not an easy trick since fishermen routinely cut off the edible tail (about one fifth of the total weight) and throw the rest of the fish overboard. But if anyone could procure a whole monkfish it would be he, one of the sons of a whole family of fish dealers. My request made him shout with laughter. But he found us the 25-pounder you see here.

Even in France, these fish are considered so terrifying to behold that dealers never display them. He was half right. Nobody in the studio fainted, but everybody screamed when the incredible monster was wheeled in on a cart. Imagine a tadpole almost the size and shape of a baby grand piano, with strangely elbowlike jointed fins on either side,

In this ferocious-looking 25-pound monkfish, only the tail is edible and prized.

no scales, and skin as loose as a puppy's. Where the piano has keys, the fish has spiny teeth angled inward to form a giant bear trap, and more teeth in patches farther back, and still more under its upward-glaring eyes. The fleshy tongue is as big as your hand; the domed roof of the mouth is as hard as steel plating. Three little wands protrude from the top of the head; the tip of the foremost bears a tiny flap of flesh, the "bait," so called because so used. According to Alan Davidson in *Mediterranean Seafood* (Harmondsworth, England: Penguin Books, 1972), the monkfish's "habit is to excavate and settle into a shallow depression on the bottom. By the time sand particles disturbed by this process have drifted down over the angler it is almost invisible. . . ." It waits, motionless except for the "bait" fluttering in the ripples, just above the gaping maw. Any passing fish or diving bird might well think it was a tidbit floating there. Picture the awful scene!

In the stomach of one monkfish, observers found 21 flounders and 1 dogfish, all eaten at one sitting; in another, 7 wild ducks; in another, a sea turtle. Monkfish apparently don't attack swimming humans, but otherwise, as another fish book reports, "nothing edible that strays within reach comes amiss" to this Sidney Greenstreet of the ocean. The enormous mouth makes it possible for the creature to prey on fish almost its own size; one young 26-incher was found to enclose a 23-inch codling.

The book that provides the above riveting facts is a sober-looking, scholarly volume called *Fishes of the Gulf of Maine,* by Henry B. Bigelow and William C. Schroeder (Washington: U.S. Government Printing Office, 1st revision, 1953). My edition is now out of print, but the book has been republished by Harvard University (Cambridge: Harvard Museum of Comparative Zoology, special publication, 1972). My sources at the museum say there's lots of demand for it. Nothing could be a better sign for American cooks than an increased public interest in fish; it points toward an increased variety at the fishmarket.

Preparations and Marketing

Recommended Equipment:

You can chop the soup vegetables finely by hand, or in a vegetable mill, but a blender or food processor makes it a breeze.

For the fish and its *pipérade,* you need 2 large nonstick frying pans (or 1, if you make the *pipérade* early), and 1 cover of some sort. Another large frying pan, or a wok, is right for the zucchini dish, and a hand-held slicer or *mandoline*—or a very clever knife.

For the flan, I use a flan ring, foil, a baking stone, and a baker's peel or paddle, or a baking sheet, for sliding; but it can be cooked on a baking sheet or even in a pie pan in the usual manner.

Staples to Have on Hand:

Salt
White peppercorns
Sugar
Nutmeg
Italian or Provençal herb mixture
Pure vanilla extract
Horseradish, bottled or grated fresh
Wine vinegar
Olive oil
Chicken broth (1 cup or ¼ L; recipe for homemade on page 10)
Fish broth (1 cup or ¼ L), or more chicken broth

Note "bait" on wand protruding from monkfish head.

Butter
Eggs (4 "large")
Flour
Garlic
Shallots and scallions
Fresh herbs, such as dill, chives, parsley, chervil, basil
Yellow onion (1 large)
Carrots (2 or 3 large)
Lemons (2 or more)
Dry white wine or dry white French vermouth

Specific Ingredients for This Menu:

Monkfish fillets (3 ½ pounds or 1 ½ kg)
Heavy cream (½ cup or 1 dL)
Sour cream (1 cup or ¼ L, or more)
Cream cheese (8 ounces or 225 g) ▼
Young white turnips (2 or more)
Parsnips (2 or 3)
Zucchini (2 or 3)
Cucumbers (1)
Red bell peppers (2 large) ▼
Green bell peppers (2 large)
Beets (a 1-pound or 453-g can, or 5 large fresh) ▼
Beet juice or bottled borscht (1 cup or ¼ L, or more)
Chopped walnuts (4 to 5 Tb)
Optional: ingredients for Fresh Tomato Fondue (pages 143, 468)

▶   Remarks:

Cream cheese: try to get the fresh kind, with no additives to glue it up, but plan to use it within a few days because it contains no preservatives. However, it freezes successfully, and the thawed cheese is fine for cooking. *Red bell peppers:* if you can't find them fresh, use canned or bottled pimiento, or tomatoes. *Beets:* if you plan to use fresh ones, please look at the Post-Postscript of this chapter for hints on their preparation.

Cold Beet and Cucumber Soup

With sour cream and dill, and buttered black bread

This is on the idea of a borscht because it is a beet soup. Otherwise it follows no traditions except the taste of its maker. I love fresh beets in season, but am delighted that canned beets have such good flavor and color; I find them excellent here.

For about 6 cups (1 ½ L)

3 or 4 scallions, or 1 or 2 shallots

1 cucumber, peeled and seeded

A 1-pound (453-g) can of beets, whole, sliced, or julienned, or 2 cups (½ L) cooked fresh beets, including some juice

1 cup (¼ L) or more beet juice or bottled borscht

1 cup (¼ L) or more chicken broth, fresh (see recipe on page 10) or canned

1 tsp or more horseradish, bottled or grated fresh

1 Tb or so wine vinegar

Salt and pepper to taste

For garnish: 1 cup (¼ L) or more sour cream and a handful of fresh dill sprigs (or chives or parsley)

Equipment:

An electric blender or food processor, or vegetable mill, or wooden bowl and chopper

With an electric blender or food processor, first chop the scallions, then all the rest of the solid ingredients with just enough of the liquids to blend—do not purée too fine; thin out to desired consistency with beet juice and broth; season to taste. Or, if using a vegetable mill, purée solids into a bowl with enough liquid for their passage (by hand, chop solids fine); blend in liquids and flavorings.

Chill several hours. Carefully taste and correct seasoning again, since it may need more after chilling. Serve in individual bowls, and top each portion with a spoonful of sour cream and a sprinkling of dill, chives, or parsley.

🕐 May be made 2 or 3 days in advance of serving; store in a covered container in the refrigerator.

Buttered fingers of pumpernickel bread accompany cool beet and cucumber soup.

Monkfish Tails en Pipérade

Fish steaks simmered in herbs, wine, and red and green peppers

The firm, close-textured lean flesh of the monkfish needs a little extra cooking time to make it tender, and it wants to simmer with flavorful ingredients because it has no pronounced taste of its own. The hearty Basque combination here does the work it should, besides being wonderfully colorful to look at. Incidentally, this also makes a delicious cold fish dish, as noted at the end of the recipe.

For 6 people

The Pipérade Mixture:

2 large green bell peppers

2 large red bell peppers (if you have none, use tomatoes or pimientos as noted in recipe)

1 large yellow onion

2 Tb or so olive oil

2 or 3 cloves garlic, puréed

1 tsp or so mixed herbs, like Italian or Provençal seasoning

¼ tsp or so salt

Freshly ground pepper

The Fish and Other Ingredients:

3½ pounds (1½ kg) trimmed monkfish fillets

Salt, pepper, and flour

2 Tb or so olive oil

About 1 cup (¼ L) each dry white wine or French vermouth, and fish or chicken broth

Fresh tomato fondue (pages 143, 468), optional

Equipment:

1 or 2 large frying pans, nonstick recommended

Preliminary cooking of the pipérade vegetables

Wash, halve, stem, and seed the peppers, and cut into very fine long thin slices. (If you have no red peppers, you may use peeled seeded tomatoes, cut into slices and added when the green peppers go over the fish; or use slices of canned red pimiento.) Peel the onion, halve through the root, and cut into thin lengthwise slices. Film a large frying pan with the oil, add the sliced vegetables, and cook over moderate heat for 4 to 5 minutes while you add the garlic, herbs, and seasonings. Vegetables should be partially cooked; they will finish with the fish.

🕐 May be done in advance to this point; let cool uncovered, then transfer to a bowl, cover, and refrigerate.

Preliminary sautéing of the fish

Cut the fish into serving chunks. Just before you are to sauté it, season all sides with a sprinkling of salt and pepper, dredge lightly in

In the unlikely event you catch your own monkfish, here is how to clean it.

Monkfish tail: loose skin cuts and pulls off easily.

Cut closely against each side of single central bone to fillet the fish.

Note firm white flesh of monkfish fillet.

flour, and shake off excess. Into a second frying pan (or in the same one, if you have done the vegetables ahead), pour in enough oil to film it and set over moderately high heat. When very hot but not smoking, add the fish in one layer. Sauté for 2 minutes, then turn and sauté for 2 minutes on the other side—not to brown, merely to stiffen slightly. Spread the cooked vegetables over the fish.

🕐 May be done several hours in advance to this point; let cool uncovered, then cover and refrigerate.

Final cooking

10 minutes or so

Pour in the wine and broth—enough to come halfway up the fish. Cover and simmer about 10 minutes. Fish is done when it has turned from springy to gently soft—it needs a little more cooking than other fish, but must not overcook and fall apart. Arrange fish and vegetables on a hot platter and cover. Rapidly boil down the juices in frying pan until almost syrupy, then spoon them over the fish, and serve, surrounded by the optional tomato fondue.

🕐 Fish can wait, unsauced, 15 minutes or so on its platter; cover and set over a pan of hot water. Boil down the juices separately, drain juices from waiting fish and add to sauce, then spoon sauce over fish just before serving.

Variations on the Sauce—with Cream, or with Aïoli:

Because this menu ends with a cream cheese flan, I did not enrich the cooking juices. Two luscious alternatives, especially if you wish to accompany the fish with plain boiled rice—which goes nicely—are the following:

Cream. When you have boiled down the fish cooking juices until they are almost syrupy, dribble them into a small mixing bowl containing ½ cup (1 dL) heavy cream blended with an egg yolk. Return sauce to the pan and stir over low heat just until thickened lightly but well below the simmer. Pour over the fish and serve.

Aïoli. Another suggestion is to have a mixing bowl ready with 1 cup (¼ L) *aïoli*—thick garlic mayonnaise (page 466). Beat the boiled-down juices by dribbles into the *aïoli*, return to the pan to heat gently for a moment without coming near the simmer, then spoon over the fish and serve.

Monkfish en Pipérade Cold:

This recipe is also very good served cold, but you will need to strengthen the flavors. If you are planning to serve it cold, boil down the juices as described; season them highly with lemon juice, more garlic, salt, pepper, and herbs. Spoon sauce over the warm fish, and then let it cool. Serve with lemon wedges and black olives.

Or beat the juices into an *aïoli* garlic mayonnaise, as described in the preceding variation.

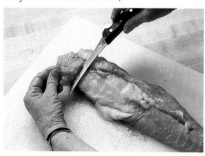

Be sure to cut and peel off grayish membrane covering outer side of fillet, and fish is ready to cook (some markets may not have done this).

After its preliminary sauté, monkfish simmers with wine and pipérade.

Monkfish ready to serve after basting with its concentrated juices

Sauté of Zucchini & Co.

A fast sauté of thinly sliced carrots, turnips, parsnips —and zucchini

Here is a lovely fresh vegetable combination, but while the vegetables may be cut in advance, they can be cooked only at the last moment or they wilt. However, the cooking is a matter of minutes only.

For 6 to 8 people

2 or 3 zucchini

Salt

2 or 3 large carrots

2 or more fine young white turnips

2 or 3 parsnips

2 Tb or more butter

Pepper

Minced fresh green herbs, such as chives, basil, chervil, parsley (optional)

Equipment:

A hand-held vegetable slicer is useful here— a food processor can't do the work neatly enough; a large frying pan or wok

Cut the tips off each end of the zucchini, and scrub but don't peel them; slice very thin crosswise—⅛ inch (½ cm). Toss in a bowl with a good sprinkling of salt, and let drain while preparing the other vegetables. Peel and cut all of them into equally thin rounds.

🕐 Vegetables may be prepared several hours in advance; cover and refrigerate.

Just before serving, heat the butter in a frying pan or wok and add the carrots, turnips, and parsnips, tossing them almost continually over high heat. Meanwhile, drain the zucchini and dry in paper towels; when the other vegetables are becoming tender, add the zucchini. Toss for 2 or 3 minutes. Vegetables should retain a lightly crunchy texture. Season to taste, toss with a little fresh butter if you wish, and the optional green herbs. Serve at once.

This vegetable sauté is a quick last-minute affair.

Forming Tart Shells in a Flan Ring

An open-faced tart or flan encased in just its shell is always chic. The dough is formed in a bottomless ring that sits upon a baking sheet or, in this case, upon a thin sheet of foil placed upon a baker's peel, or rimless cookie sheet, or anything from which you can slide the flan ring and foil onto an oven baking stone.

Always be sure the dough is well rested and chilled, and work as rapidly as possible so that it will not soften and be difficult to handle. If it does soften, refrigerate everything— dough, flan, baking sheet—let chill for 20 minutes, and then take up where you left off.

Butter the inside of the ring and the foil or baking sheet. Roll out the dough to a thickness of 3/16 inch (scant ¾ cm), and 2 inches (5 cm) larger all around than your flan ring.

Here is how to form the dough (formulas are on page 464):

1) Fold the dough in half, and the half in quarters. Set buttered flan ring on buttered foil or baking sheet, and position point of dough in center of ring.

2) Unfold dough and press it lightly against foil or baking sheet, and rest it against edge of ring. Then gently ease and push almost ½ inch (1½ cm) of it down side of ring all around, to make its wall thicker.

3) Fold dough outward from side of ring, and roll pin over top of ring to cut off the excess dough.

4) Gently push the dough lining up from the edge all around ring, to make it stand about ⅜ inch (1 cm) above rim.

5) Press a decorative pattern all around top rim of dough with the back of a knife.

6) Prick bottom of dough, going just down through to foil or baking sheet, with a sharp-pronged fork to make tiny holes that will prevent pastry from rising during baking.

Cream Cheese and Lemon Flan

A cheesecake tart

This combination has more texture than a plain custard, and is moister than most cheesecakes I have known. I like it served slightly warm, or at room temperature, although it is good cold, too.

Manufacturing Note:

There is no requirement that you bake the flan on a pizza stone, as illustrated here. Form and bake it in a ring set on a pastry sheet, or in a pie tin, or use a frozen pie shell, or no pastry shell at all—just a baking dish. I developed the pizza stone system because I use one for baking French bread, pizzas, and pita breads; its hot surface gives a crisp brown crust without your having to prebake the shell before you fill it. No soggy bottom!

For a 10-inch (25-cm) flan, serving 10

A 10-inch (25-cm) dough-lined flan ring set on buttered foil (see manufacturing note above, alternatives at end of recipe, and dough formulas on page 464)

The Cream Cheese and Lemon Filling:
About 2 ½ cups (6 dL)

4 "large" eggs

¼ tsp salt

½ cup (1 dL) heavy cream

The grated rind of 1 lemon

4 Tb fresh lemon juice (or more if you like a very lemony flavor)

8 ounces (225 g) cream cheese, preferably fresh

4 Tb sugar

A pinch of nutmeg

1 tsp pure vanilla extract

For Top Decoration During Baking:

4 to 5 Tb each sugar and chopped walnuts

Equipment:

A pizza stone or oven griddle and baker's peel or a baking sheet; an electric blender or food processor is useful for the filling, or a vegetable mill or sieve and wire whip

Prepare the pastry dough in the flan ring and chill for 20 minutes. Meanwhile, either whisk up all the filling ingredients in a blender or food processor, or purée the cream cheese through a vegetable mill or sieve, and beat in the rest of the items with a wire whip.

❶   Both dough-lined ring and filling may be prepared hours in advance; cover each and refrigerate.

Either Baking on an Oven Stone:

30 to 35 minutes at 425–350°F/ 220–180°C

Set pizza stone or oven griddle on a rack in the middle level of the oven and preheat oven for 15 to 20 minutes to be sure stone is really hot. Then slide out oven rack, slide flan and foil onto stone (1), and pour in the filling to within ⅛ inch (½ cm) of rim (2). (Do not overfill or you risk spillage during baking.)

Bake for 10 minutes, or just until filling has set a little; spread the sugar and walnut mixture over the surface (3). Bake another 10 minutes, then lower oven temperature to 350°F/180°C. Flan is done when it has puffed and browned lightly, and when bottom of crust has browned—30 to 35 minutes in all.

Serving

Remove flan from oven, let settle 5 minutes, then with flan ring still in place, slide off foil onto a rack. Let cool to tepid before serving. Or serve it cold.

❶   Flan is at its best when freshly cooked, but you may cover and refrigerate the leftovers, and serve flan cold or rewarmed the next day.

Or Baking in the Conventional Way:

I do think that if you are cooking a tart, quiche, or flan in a pie tin or in a ring set on a baking sheet, you are wise to precook the pastry before filling it. This will prevent the crust from being uncooked or partially cooked on the bottom. To do so, simply line the pricked raw dough-filled form with lightweight buttered foil, fill with dried beans or rice (which you keep on hand for this purpose), and bake at 400°F/205°C for 10 minutes, or until when you lift the foil you see the pastry has set. Then remove foil and beans, prick lightly again, and continue baking for 5 minutes or more until dough is just beginning to color and just starting to shrink from sides of mold. Then pour in the filling, and proceed to bake as in the preceding recipe.

❶   Partially baked pastry shells may be frozen.

⏱ *Timing*

You'll need to be at the stove for about 7 to 8 minutes to cook the sautéed vegetables. If you don't want to spend that much time between courses, leave the root vegetables a bit underdone off heat, while you're having your soup; then add the zucchini and give the mixture a careful 2 to 3 minutes' sauté before serving it. Final cooking of the monkfish takes only 10 minutes, and can be done along with the vegetables or a few minutes earlier, since this dish can wait a little.

Otherwise, you have no problems at all. The soup, the *pipérade*, tomato sauce, and the pastry dough and filling for the flan can be made the day before your party; then you assemble and bake the flan late in the afternoon on the "day of." At that time you would cut the vegetables, while the flan bakes. Or you could make and freeze the *pipérade* and the flan dough far in advance.

In short, if you possess a food processor, this very festive meal can be executed in less than an hour's working time, comfortably broken into short bouts.

Menu Variations

Other cold *soup* recipes are discussed in "Picnic," page 378. There are many possible versions for beet soup and borscht.

Other firm lean white *fish* that can be cut into steaks are conger eel, cusk, and halibut. See also skate wings in black butter and caper sauce, in the Postscript. Tuna (or swordfish, which I much prefer) is good in *pipérade* or braised with lettuce, herbs, and wine (in *J.C.'s Kitchen*), or you could use bluefish. For other ways of cooking monkfish, see farther on.

This would make a wonderful summer meal, but you'd need to suit your *vegetables* to the season—zucchini, carrots, and cucumbers, for instance. The wok sauté of spinach and zucchini on page 56 is a summery thought.

A lemon *dessert* is a natural for a fish dinner. There are other lemon tarts (or flans) in *Mastering I* and *J.C.'s Kitchen;* if you want to make this light meal still lighter, what about a sherbet? Or, in between, a lemon soufflé?

And now for more monkfish!

Lotte à l'Américaine

Monkfish steaks with wine and tomato sauce

This is a splendid combination, and one that though usually associated with lobsters is also traditional in France with monkfish. Start out in exactly the same way as in the original recipe, seasoning, flouring, and sautéing the fish steaks in oil. When the time is up you may, if you feel flush, pour in ¼ cup (½ dL) Cognac, let it bubble, then ignite it with a lighted match. Flame it away a few seconds, then douse it with the white wine or vermouth. Add the sautéed onion, and garlic, but instead of peppers use tomatoes—spread on and around the fish 2 cups (½ L) fresh tomato pulp and 2 tablespoons tomato paste. Use ½ teaspoon tarragon instead of mixed herbs. Cover and simmer 10 minutes, then remove the fish to a platter, boil down the sauce to thicken it, taste carefully for seasoning, spoon over the fish, decorate with parsley, and serve.

Broiled Monkfish

Since monkfish has no distinctive flavor of its own, I find it needs assistance when it is baked or broiled. I've had good success slicing a large fillet in half horizontally, so it will not be more than about ¾ inch (2 cm) thick. Then I paint it with a mixture of puréed garlic, salt, lemon juice, oil, and thyme, rosemary, oregano, or an herb mixture, and let it marinate for an hour or more before cooking it. I then like to sprinkle the top with a little paprika, broil it close to the heating element for 5 minutes or so, and bake at 400°F/ 205°C for another 10 minutes, basting it with a little white wine or vermouth.

Leftovers

The *soup,* since it keeps for several days refrigerated, is a good recipe to double. I think it loses a bit of its keen flavor if heated, but you might prefer it that way.

The *fish* dish is just as good cold as hot. If you bought extra monkfish, the recipe has variants, and there are two more in Menu Variations. As for *pipérade,* it is a splendid kitchen staple. Here in our recipe it is not fully cooked when it goes over the fish, but while you are at it you could double the amount of vegetables in the pan initially, use half for the fish, and continue cooking the rest until the vegetables are just tender. Then you can bottle and refrigerate or freeze it, and use it, for instance, to garnish an open-faced omelet, or bake it in the egg-and-cheese mixture for a quiche, or serve it as an accompaniment to pasta, hamburgers, steak, broiled fish, or chicken. It's wonderful to have a quick ready-made garnish on hand to dress up otherwise simple dishes.

The *vegetable* sauté is not reheatable, but it's fine in a soup.

Refrigerate the delicious *flan,* which is nice cold, and will keep for several days.

Postscript: Another odd fish

It's odd enough that a squash should behave like spaghetti, but how about a fish? When you eat skate, you don't just cut down through it; you draw your knife horizontally over the flesh, which promptly separates into long juicy white strands, slightly gelatinous and of the most delicate flavor. In Europe, it's tremendously popular, and savvy fish cooks here have always served it, but it should be more widely known. Especially so since skate are profuse in our waters—hideous creatures, cousins to the devilfish and the manta ray. The barn-door skate's flat diamond-shaped body is often 5 feet (1½ meters) long, but you'll rarely see a whole one. Only the wings, or side fins, of skate are eaten, and those generally sold weigh from 1½ pounds (675 g) each untrimmed. Several varieties, all very similar, are marketed here.

A story which keeps turning up in cookbooks is that skate wings are often cut into rounds and sold as scallops, or "mock scallops." It seemed unlikely to me, since scallop flesh is grained vertically, and skate horizontally—moreover, skate meat separates so readily when cooked. But I checked with two experts. George Berkowitz said that in his 30 years' experience in the fish business, he'd never seen it done. Bob Learson, of the National Marine Fisheries laboratory in Gloucester, Massachusetts, pointed out that the way cartilage is distributed in a skate wing would make the process impractical on a commercial scale. Both men dismiss the scallop story as an old wives' tale.

If you go fishing for skate, you'll have fun. They'll bite at any bait and fight like fury.

Having caught a skate or bought a piece of one, you give it special treatment. The skin is covered with a gluey wet film that should smell very fresh, not at all ammoniac, and you remove this by washing the wing in several waters. It should then be refrigerated overnight in water. My favorite way of cooking skate is to be found in a French classic, *La Cuisine de*

Madame Saint-Ange (Paris: Larousse, 1958; now out of print, but there is a Swiss edition). Cook the wings of all skate the same way and for the same length of time, as their thickness doesn't vary with their breadth. Cut off the thin, finny, outer-fringe part of the wing with scissors, discard it, and lay the remainder in a high-sided pan like a chicken fryer, cover by at least ½ inch (1½ cm) with cold water, adding 5 tablespoons wine vinegar per quart (or liter), with 1 tablespoon salt, a small onion sliced thin, an imported bay leaf, a pinch of thyme, and 8 to 10 parsley stems. Bring just to the boil, turn down heat, cover, and let poach below the simmer for exactly 25 minutes. Carefully scrape the skin from each piece (it comes off easily), and return to the poaching water until you are ready to serve. I like it best with black butter sauce. For black butter, heat butter until it begins to turn medium brown; remove it from the heat and toss in a spoonful of capers. Sprinkle chopped fresh parsley over the skate, and watch it bubble as you pour over it the hot butter sauce. A wonderful dish.

Post-Postscript: Fresh beets

Fresh beets, with their dusty ruby-purple bulbs and dark green leaves that are ribbed in red, are available every month of the year but appear abundantly in most markets only between May and October. I must admit to quite a passion for fresh beets, with their full-bodied taste and hearty color. I feel I am eating something really worthwhile in the vegetable line, and indeed I am because beets are full of vitamins and minerals as well as flavor. As a matter of fact, plain cooked fresh beets are great food for dieters just because they are so nourishing, and they can be eaten as is, with no butter or oil or cream to fatten your calorie count. Thumbing through my handful of vegetarian cookbooks, by the way, I find among them no interest in beets.

Why, when beets have so much going for them in every way?

Anyone who has lived in France remembers the large cooked beets at the vegetable stalls in the markets. You peel them, slice them into a vinaigrette with minced shallots, and surround them with watercress or *mâche* (corn salad, or lamb's lettuce, or *Valerianella olitoria*, which grows wild in this country but is cultivated as a salad plant in Europe). The beets you buy in France have been cooked in an oven, and they are much larger and probably older than ours because they presumably bake for 6 to 8 hours. In an old French book I consulted, I read that one should put the beets on a bed of wet straw, cover them with an upside-down earthenware bowl, and bake them until the skins are shriveled and even charred. The straw and the charring must give French beets their very special taste. (My book doesn't tell me what size of beet, nor what temperature of oven, but I have heard they used to be cooked in baker's big ovens, after the bread for the day was done. It must, then, have been in a slow oven.)

Fresh beets can be boiled, baked, steamed, or pressure cooked. I like boiling the least because you lose color and, I think, a bit of flavor. Baking takes too long—2½ to 3 hours in a slow oven. Steaming works well, and the beets are done in about 40 to 45 minutes. Pressure cooking is my choice because it takes but 20 minutes, there is little loss of color, and the flavor is fine. I did not, by the way, find that baked beets had better flavor than steamed or pressure-cooked beets, but I had them in a covered casserole at 275°F/135°C along with a sample batch of individual beets wrapped in foil—had no straw on hand!

To prepare beets for cooking
Cut off the stems about 1½ inches (4 cm) above the tops of the beets, snip off their tails about ¼ inch (¾ cm) below the bottoms, and be sure the bulbs of the beets are whole and unblemished—a bit of stem and a tight skin will prevent the vivid color and vital juices from escaping too much during cooking. Brush the beets clean under cold water.

Steamed Fresh Beets:

For young beets about 2 inches (5 cm) in diameter

Place prepared beets in a vegetable steamer or on a rack in a saucepan with 1 inch (2½ cm) or so of water, cover tightly, and steam 40 minutes, or until beets feel tender when pierced with a small knife, and peel loosens easily.

Pressure-cooked Beets:

For 2-inch (5-cm) beets

Place beets on rack in pressure cooker with ½ inch (1½ cm) water, and bring to full pressure. Cook for 20 minutes, then release pressure. (Somewhat smaller and somewhat larger beets will take the same amount of time, and slight overcooking seems to do little harm.)

Some Ideas for Hot Fresh Beets:

Slice off the stem ends, peel the beets, and they are ready to serve in any way you choose. The simplest and one of the best ways is that of quartering or slicing them, then tossing in butter, salt, pepper, and perhaps a sprinkling of minced shallots or scallions, and parsley or chives. Serve them with chops, steaks, hamburgers, broiled fish, or broiled chicken.

Beets Gratinéed with Cheese:

Here is certainly one of the most delicious ways to serve hot beets, and especially recommended if you are having a meatless meal because beets and cheese make a full and almost meaty combination. The only drawback is looks—purply red plus the brown-yellow of the baked cheese—and I don't know how you get around that except to revel in the flavor.

Warm the cooked sliced or quartered beets in butter, salt, pepper, and a sprinkling of minced shallots or scallions, then simmer for 5 minutes or so with spoonfuls of heavy cream (a spoonful per beet would be ample). Arrange in layers in a shallow baking dish with a good sprinkling of cheese, either Parmesan alone or a mixture, and spread grated cheese over the top. Shortly before serving, set under a moderately hot broiler to let slowly heat through until bubbling, and the cheese has browned lightly on top.

These would go nicely with eggs, or broiled meats, fish, or chicken, or could be a separate course.

Some Ideas for Cold Fresh Cooked Beets:

Slice off the stem ends, peel the beets, and slice, quarter, dice, or julienne them. Simply toss them in a vinaigrette dressing (examples are on page 468), decorate with minced parsley and/or chives, and serve them alone, or with watercress or other greens, or with cold string beans, or with potato salad—but do not mix them with other ingredients until the last minute unless you want everything to be stained purple beet color. Serve as a first course, or with hard-boiled eggs, cold fish, or cold cuts.

Or serve them with a sour cream or yogurt dressing—blend into either one prepared mustard and horseradish to taste, season with salt and pepper, and spoon into a serving dish; arrange the beets on top, and decorate with parsley. Serve as a salad course or first course, or to accompany broiled or boiled fish or chicken.

Beet Greens—Beet Leaves:

The fresh leaves from a bunch of young beets make a fine green vegetable. Remove leaves from stems, cut leaves into chiffonade, very thin strips, and sauté in a frying pan or wok, as described on page 257—like kale or collards or turnip greens. I tried blanching beet greens, and found that the green color held up beautifully but the flavor was far less interesting than the plain sauté.

To Get Beet Juice Off Your Hands, Etc.:

Rinse your hands in cold water, then rub table salt over them; wash in cold soap and water, then in warm soap and water. (Salt helps to remove the red color—just as salt on a red wine spill will speed the washing.) Fingernails are another matter—I scrub them, then use cuticle remover solution, and scrub again. Use household bleach on your work surfaces for stubborn beet stains.

*For centuries of thrifty peasants, for eminent
gastronomes —and for your own hungry horde*

Cassoulet for a Crowd

Menu
For 10 to 12 people

Consommé au Porto
Toasted Armenian Cracker Bread

Cassoulet—Beans baked with goose, lamb,
*   and sausages*
Pickled Red Cabbage Slaw
Hot French Bread

Sliced Fresh Pineapple—En Boat

Suggested wines:
A hearty red with the cassoulet—Burgundy,
Côtes du Rhône, pinot noir, zinfandel

Cassoulet, that best of bean feasts, is everyday fare for a peasant but ambrosia for a gastronome, though its ideal consumer is a 300-pound blocking back who has been splitting firewood nonstop for the last twelve hours on a subzero day in Manitoba. It feeds a lot of people and can be made a day or even two days in advance, with much preparation done even before that, so, when the Child household is expecting a horde of peasants, gastronomes, and blocking backs, cassoulet is what they'll get. Sunrise smiles break out as they come through our door, for the whole house is filled with a full-bodied, earthy fragrance. In every heart the joyous resolution forms: "I am now going to eat myself silly."

It's a mighty dish, with its fragments of rich meats, its golden-brown juice thick with starch from the beans, its top crunchy and flecked with green (and with bits of pork rind, if you decide to use it). But the great thing is the wonderful taste of the beans, which absorb and blend the complex savors of the well-seasoned meats. And there is a mysterious charm in how, by long cooking, a stony little white bean becomes pale amber, redolent, swollen, velvety. Eating one bean at a time, crushing it against the palate, you could make a career of, and some cassoulet buffs apparently do.

Many of us have been privileged to witness the uproarious kangaroo court that all bystanders rush to join whenever one French motorist so much as nudges another.

If you can imagine this in full cry for two centuries, you will know what is implied by the Great, Ancient, Passionate, 98 Percent Fact-Free Cassoulet Controversy that still rages unabated. Three neighboring hill towns north of the Pyrenees in Languedoc define this small battleground, but the hullabaloo is audible all over the world. The January 1979 issue of the *International Review of Food and Wine* neatly summarized and simplified the conflicts of the past as follows: "In Castelnaudary, the legend goes, the dish was invented, and therefore a 'pure' version is served. The haricots are cooked with chunks of fresh pork, pork knuckle, ham, pork sausage, and fresh pork rind. In Toulouse the cooks add Toulouse sausage and either *confit d'oie* or *confit de canard* (preserved goose or duck), while in Carcassonne chunks of mutton are added to the Castelnaudary formula, and, during the hunting season, an occasional partridge too." Clear enough, but in the course of their research the authors of this article, William Bayer and Paula Wolfert, soon found that "these regional distinctions are now completely blurred, and that cassoulet, like life itself, is not so simple as it seems."

Mr. Bayer and Ms. Wolfert had traveled to the battlefront for a restaurant tour, with the sensible object of reporting not on the "original" cassoulet or the "definitive" one, both mythical anyway, but simply on the versions they liked best. Their favorite turned out to be a radical-revisionist one using *fresh* beans, favas. I recommend their article to admirers of sound, felicitous food writing as well as to cassoulet fanatics, who will enjoy pondering both the unusual fava formula and another Toulousain type that turned out, after much sampling, to be the authors' favorite of the traditional recipes.

My own current version, the fourth I've developed, is a selection and synthesis of traditional methods and components, but in fact you can use almost anything you have handy in making cassoulet, and I'm sure the cooks of Languedoc have always done likewise. So why such a fuss? Partly, I think, because the instruments so inspire the imagination that any creative cook is periodically compelled to reorchestrate them. And partly because a fuss is a very French way to have fun.

My efforts have tended toward a progressively lighter and leaner dish, as I see looking back at the recipes in *Mastering I*, *The French Chef Cookbook*, and *J.C.'s Kitchen*, which has a quickie version using lentils. Even so, this cassoulet remains hearty indeed. What to eat with it is no problem, since its full flavors need no rounding out or complement. You just want something assertive for contrast and, given the main dish's rather stolid quality, something very light. Nothing sharpens appetites like a perfect, crystalline consommé, and with that I like the crackly crunch of storebought Armenian flatbread, crisped in the oven. For a juicy crunch, and for an offset to stodge, suavity,

Cassoulet country centers around Toulouse, Carcassonne, and Castelnaudary.

and succulence, the cassoulet is accompanied here by pickled red cabbage and hot French bread. Fresh pineapple, honey-sweet but with that haunting acid tang, is an ideal dessert if you can find fruit that were harvested when perfectly ripe. (For clues, and a bit of debunking, see Remarks later in this chapter.)

Some cooks say they serve cassoulet only to joggers and only at midday, so they can run it off before bedtime. I like it any time at all, but especially on the eve of that movable and dire feast (joke) which opens the Season of Nemesis. Hail, Cassoulet! We who are about to diet salute you.

A Note on Beans and Intestinal Motility:

Intestinal motility is polite gobbledegook for flatulence, which in turn means gas. What about that problem and beans? It seems, according to scientists at the Western Regional Center in Albany, California, that beans contain the difficult-to-digest sugars, stachyose and raffinose. The human body does not have the enzymes to break them down, and when these culprits reach the lower intestine of some diners, their resident bacteria react violently, producing gas or, in a word, motility.

The good news, however, is that these same scientists have discovered you can boil 1 cup (¼ L) beans in 10 cups (2½ L) water for 3 minutes, soak them for 10 hours or overnight in the same water, drain and rinse them, and set them to cook in fresh water. This, they assure us, eliminates 80 percent of the trouble.

P.S.: This account came from a newspaper report, but in later correspondence with Alfred Olson, leader of the U.S.D.A.'s bean study group, he writes that he has changed the word "motility"—although he likes the sound of it, he is not sure of its accuracy in this connection, and has regretfully substituted the more prosaic but possibly more safely descriptive "trouble."

Preparations and Marketing

Recommended Equipment:

For clarifying the consommé, you need sieving equipment—cheesecloth for lining an 8- to 10-inch (20- to 25-cm) sieve, a colander to rest the sieve over, and a bowl into which the consommé can drip freely.

For the cassoulet you need a 6-quart (6-L) flameproof baking-serving dish or casserole, illustrated on page 289. You will want an 8-quart (7- to 8-L) pot in which to boil the beans before they go into the casserole.

For preserving the goose you'll need a big bowl or crock in which the cut-up goose pieces may sit during their salting, and something the size of a preserving kettle or stockpot for rendering the fat and then for cooking the goose. If you plan to put the goose down for storage in its own fat, you will want a crock or bowl large enough to hold the cooked goose pieces, and to fit into your refrigerator, plus a rack that will fit in the bottom. A deep-fat-frying thermometer is useful here.

To shred the red cabbage very fine indeed, a shredding or sauerkraut cutter is useful, or a very sharp knife and a practiced hand. The knife is also needed for the pineapples.

Marketing Note: If you are to preserve your own goose for this menu, you will be starting from twenty-four hours to several weeks in advance, so I have marked the items for goose preservation with an asterisk on the lists.

Staples to Have on Hand:

Salt
*Optional: coarse or kosher salt or sea salt
Black peppercorns
*Special spice mixture (page 468) or ground allspice and thyme

Mustard seeds
Juniper berries
Imported bay leaves
Optional: dried tarragon
Tomato sauce (page 468) or tomato paste
Beef stock or bouillon (at least 3 cups or ¾ L)
Meat or poultry stock, or a mixture of canned chicken broth and canned consommé (2 quarts or 2 L)
Optional: more stock or consommé (1 cup or ¼ L)
Butter or cooking oil
Yellow onions (3 large)
Dry white wine or dry white French vermouth

Optional: white rum, kirsch, or savarin syrup (page 409)
Port wine
Red wine vinegar

Specific Ingredients for This Menu:

* Optional: saltpeter (from a pharmacy)
* "Roaster" goose (10 to 12 pounds or 4½ to 5½ kg) or preserved goose (3 pounds or 1350 g) ▼
Cooking sausage, like kielbasy, chorizo, or sausage meat (1½ to 2 pounds or 675 to 900 g)
Bone-in lamb shoulder (about 4 pounds or 2 kg), sawed into stewing chunks

Optional: salt pork, fat-and-lean type, with
rind (1 pound or 450 g)
* Fresh pork fat and/or lard (about 1 pound or
450 g)
Dried white beans (2 pounds or 900 g) ▼
Red onion (1 large)
Parsley (1 large bunch)
Optional: fresh mint
Garlic (1 large head)
Red cabbage (1 head fresh; about 1 ½ pounds
or 675 g)
Optional: sweet red bell pepper (1 large)
Optional: small quantities of aromatic
vegetables like celery, onion, leek, carrot
Tart apples (4)
Pineapples (2 to 4), depending on size ▼
Canned beet juice, or borscht (½ cup or 1 dL)
Egg whites (5)
Nonsweet white French or Italian bread
(½ loaf)

▶   **Remarks:**

Preserved goose (*confit d'oie*), if you don't
want to make your own, may be bought in
cans at the fancier "gourmet" shops. If you
can't get it, don't give up having cassoulet, as
several substitutions are possible (see Menu
Variations). *The goose:* you will probably
have to buy it frozen, and geese freeze well
when kept properly, at a constant temperature below −5°F/−20°C for no more than
six months. Defrost it either for several days
in the refrigerator (in its plastic package), or
in a tub of cold water (in its package), where
it will take 4 to 5 hours. Plan to use it within
a day of its defrosting. *Dry white beans:* I
use the medium bean, Great Northern, but
small white pea beans will do nicely, too.
Pineapples: I have learned so much myself,
since our encounter with them preparing this
dinner, that I think they deserve a special
place here. Now, praises be, thanks to modern refrigeration and fast transportation, it is
possible to buy field-ripened fresh sweet pineapple anywhere in this country. As a matter of fact, if it was not picked ripe in the
first place, it will not ripen at all because of
the way the pineapple is built: the fruit gets

its nourishment from the stump of the plant
on which it grows, and when the starch in
the stump turns to sugar, the sugar moves up
into the fruit and that is what ripens and
sweetens the pineapple. Once it is cut off
from its stump, its sugar supply ceases, and it
cannot, physically, get any sweeter. It will
lose some of its acidity if you keep it for a
few days at room temperature, but its sweetness—or lack of it—was predetermined the
moment it was picked. Obviously, then, we
need good pickers in those pineapple fields,
and we want to buy from shippers who
know their pickers, and from merchants who
are well aware of the whole pineapple syn-
drome. As usual, it is up to us, the buying
public, to heckle our markets into providing
us with the fine, ripe, large, sweet pineapples
that they can procure for us—and they can,
we know it.

A ripe pineapple has a sweet pineapple aroma.

But how to tell, when buying a pineapple in a strange place, that it is sweet and ripe? First, you'll have your best luck in full pineapple season, when they are at their peak, from April through June. Color is no indication of ripeness, because a fine sweet specimen can vary from green to greenish yellow to yellow. Pulling a green leaf out of the crown doesn't mean a thing, nor does the sound of the thumping thumb. Probably the best test is the nose test—does it smell sweetly like a nice ripe pineapple? Aroma can be difficult to pick up if the pineapple has been chilled, but a faint perfume should exude even so.

Choose the largest fruits you can find—the bigger they are, the more flesh. The whole fruit should look fresh and healthy, with no leaking juices, bleary eyes, or soft spots. The crown of leaves should be freshly green and smartly upstanding. If the pineapple does not seem quite as ripe as it could be, keep it in a shady spot at normal room temperature for a few days, which should help it lose some of its acidity. Then, when it smells ripe (but do not let it soften and spoil), refrigerate it in a plastic bag, and plan to eat it as soon as you can.

By the way, when you have sliced up your pineapple but left the crown intact, you can plant the crown and grow yourself a pineapple plant like the one in the photograph. Slice off the top ½ inch (1½ cm) with the crown of leaves, says our gardening expert Jim Crockett, and scrape out the flesh. Let the crown dry in the sun for 2 weeks, then plant it in potting soil 2 inches (5 cm) deep and leave in a warm sunny place. Keep it barely moist and it will grow and produce a baby pineapple—presumably even if you have a black rather than a green thumb. (I have never grown one myself, but the one pictured here was grown indoors during the coldest January and February known in Massachusetts for almost 50 years—so there's living proof it can be done.)

Clear Consommé au Porto

The term "a clear consommé" means a perfectly clear, see-through sparkling dark amber liquid. It is a rare meat stock, bouillon, or canned consommé that can meet these requirements, and if you want them you will have to clarify a soup yourself. It's a quite magical process anyway and a most useful one to know when you need not only a perfect consommé, but aspic to coat a cold fish or a chicken or a poached egg.

For about 2 quarts (2 L)

2 quarts (2 L) meat or poultry stock, or canned chicken broth and canned consommé
Salt and pepper as needed
5 egg whites
Optional for added flavor: 4 Tb each minced celery, onion, leek if available, carrot, parsley stems, and ½ tsp dried tarragon
1 cup (¼ L) dry white wine or dry white French vermouth, or another cup of stock
4 Tb or more Port wine

Equipment:
A large sieve lined with 5 thicknesses of washed cheesecloth, set over a colander set over a bowl (colander must be large enough so its bottom will not rest in the consommé to come); a ladle

Before you begin, be sure that your meat stock, homemade or canned, is thoroughly free of fat or grease, and the same for all of your equipment—otherwise your clarification may not succeed.

Bring all but 1 cup of the stock to the simmer in a large saucepan; correct seasoning. Meanwhile, whip the egg whites lightly in a bowl and mix thoroughly with the 1 cup stock, optional flavoring ingredients, and wine. When stock is simmering, dribble 2 cups (½ L) of it slowly into the egg whites, beating all the while. Then beat the egg white mixture into the pan of hot stock. Set over moderate heat and, stirring slowly but reaching everywhere throughout the liquid with a wire whip, bring just to the simmer. Do not stir again. (Stock is constantly stirred so that egg whites will be thoroughly distributed and will draw to themselves all the cloudy particles in the stock, until simmer is reached.) Set saucepan at side of heat and let it almost simmer at one point for 5 minutes; rotate the pan ⅓ turn and let almost simmer another 5 minutes; rotate again, and repeat the process. (This coagulates the egg whites so that they will have enough body to hold themselves back when stock is strained.)

Gently and carefully ladle stock and egg whites into the lined sieve, letting the clear liquid drip through undisturbed. When dripping has ceased, remove straining contraption to another bowl and gently squeeze cheese-cloth to extract a little more. If it is perfectly clear, pour it into the rest. Continue, stopping when the slightest suggestion of cloudiness appears.

Pour the Port wine into the clear soup by spoonfuls to taste, and the consommé is ready to serve or to reheat.

🕐 May be prepared in advance. When cool, cover and refrigerate or freeze.

Jellied Consommé:

For each 3 cups (¾ L) of consommé desired, soften 1 envelope (1 Tb) plain unflavored gelatin in ¼ cup (½ dL) cold soup or white wine or vermouth. Then heat it with ½ cup (1 dL) or so consommé until completely dissolved; stir into the rest of the consommé. Chill until set, then spoon into chilled consommé cups.

Aspic:

Use the same system as above for making aspics, but with the following proportions. However, always test your aspic consistency before using: pour 1 tablespoon aspic into a saucer, chill until set, then fork up and leave for 10 minutes at normal room temperature to see how it holds. These few minutes of caution may save you from disaster.

For simple aspics
1 envelope (1 Tb) gelatin for each 2 cups (½ L) consommé
For lining a mold
1 envelope (1 Tb) gelatin for each 1½ cups (3½ dL) consommé

Preserved Goose

Confit d'oie

In the old days before anyone had heard of refrigerators and freezers, and even before the invention of canning, you had to preserve meats in some manner to last you through the lean months. For meats, a typical method was first to salt them, then to cook them slowly in fat, and finally to put them down in fat. In French that process was known (and still is) as a *confit,* which comes from the Latin *conficere,* to digest— and that, in a way, is what salt does to meats and sugar to fruits; the fat holds the cooked food in hermetically sealed suspension. A *confit* is a primitive form of canning.

Why bother doing it nowadays, then, when we have modern preserving methods?

Clockwise from upper left: gizzard and carcass bits for broth, fat for rendering, liver and heart for pâtés (page 414); skin cracklings; cut-up goose pieces ready for confit; broth; the whole goose; the finished confit

Well, it has a special character all its own, just as corned beef and sausages have their own special tastes. And, if you don't want to cook a whole goose, you can turn part of it into a ragout, and preserve the rest in a *confit.* Then, for people who love to cook it's fun and interesting to do, and a wonderful resource to have in one's refrigerator, since it is ever ready to furnish forth an unusually fine emergency meal.

Fat Note: This type of preserving sounds as though it would result in very fatty meat, but the contrary is true because the fat renders out of the goose skin as it cooks, and the goose meat, which is lean anyway, does not absorb the rendering fat. You can skin the goose after cooking, and dip each piece into hot broth or even hot water to dissolve and remove all of the clinging preserving fat. Goose fat, however, is a delicious commodity for use in frying potatoes, flavoring vegetables, basting meats, and it keeps for months in your refrigerator— or may be used again and again for preserving more geese, ducks, pork, and so forth and so on.

For Salting the Goose—24 hours:

A 10- to 12-pound (4½- to 5½-kg) "roaster" goose

4 to 5 Tb coarse or kosher salt, sea salt, or regular salt

⅛ tsp saltpeter (from a pharmacy; optional)

½ tsp special spice mixture (page 468) or the following: ⅛ tsp pepper and a big pinch each juniper berries, allspice, thyme, and bay leaf, all finely ground

---
For Rendering Fat and Cooking Goose:

6 to 8 cups (1½ to 2 L) fat—goose fat and fatty skin, plus fresh pork fat and/or lard (more if needed)

1 cup (¼ L) water

Equipment:

A large crock or heavy plastic bag to hold the goose pieces and something to weight them down during maceration; a large kettle or saucepan for rendering fat and cooking goose; frying thermometer for testing fat useful; a crock or bowl fitted with a rack for storing goose

---

Cutting up and salting goose
(24 hours)

Remove wings at elbows, and cut goose into drumstick, thigh, wing–lower breast, and breast-with-bone pieces; chop breast into three crosswise pieces. Chop up carcass, neck, and wings, and save for a stock (see page 288) or soup; heart and peeled gizzard can go into the

Weigh down the goose pieces after salting.

confit, or into a stew (gizzard peel into soup); liver can be used like chicken liver.

Mix the salt, optional saltpeter (for preserving rosy color), and spices in a bowl; rub into all sides of goose. Pack goose pieces into crock and weight down with a plate and canned goods or other heavy objects; or pack into a bag, squeeze out air, and tie closed, then weight down in a bowl. Leave for 24 hours.

🕐 You may leave it a day or 2 longer—but if you want to keep it for several weeks, triple the salt and spices, and remember to soak the goose pieces overnight in cold water to remove excess salt before using.

Rendering the fat
About 1 hour

Meanwhile, cut fat and fatty skin pieces into rough slices and place in kettle over moderate heat; add the water and cover the kettle to let the fat liquefy and render out slowly—20 to 25 minutes. When it has rendered, skin pieces will begin to brown; watch fat temperature from now on. Fat must remain a clear yellow; temperature should not go over 325°F/165°C. When skin pieces are a light golden brown the fat has rendered; dip them out with a slotted spoon or sieve, and drain fat drippings back into kettle. (Save pieces and turn into cracklings; see end of recipe.)

🕐 Fat may be rendered in advance. When cool, cover and refrigerate.

Cooking the goose
About 1½ hours

When you are ready to cook the goose, rub off the salt with paper towels, and liquefy fat if it has cooled and congealed. Place goose in kettle

When skin pieces are lightly browned, fat has rendered.

with fat; goose pieces will swell slightly as they cook, and skin will render more fat, but the pieces should be covered by liquid fat at all times. Add lard, if necessary. Start timing when fat begins to bubble, and maintain temperature at 200 to 205°F/95 to 96°C. Goose is done when meat is tender if pierced with a sharp-pronged fork.

To preserve the goose
The goose is delicious, hot and just cooked, as is, or allowed to cool and eaten cold. To preserve, remove goose pieces from fat and arrange them in a crock, wide-mouthed jar, or bowl that has been fitted with a rack—goose pieces should not rest on the bottom because you want liquid fat to surround and protect them. (Dry twigs, bark removed, work perfectly well here instead of a rack.) Bring the cooking fat to the simmer and let cook until it stops spluttering—5 minutes or so—indicating any liquids have evaporated. Pour it through a strainer, lined with several thicknesses of cheesecloth, over the goose pieces. Shake crock gently to allow grease to flow throughout, and when goose is completely covered, let cool and congeal. Pour on more fat if any pieces protrude. Cover with plastic wrap and refrigerate.

🕐   The goose will keep at around 37°F/3°C for 3 to 4 months or longer.

Removing pieces of goose
To remove goose pieces, set container in a bowl of hot water until fat has softened, then remove as many pieces as you wish. Cover the rest completely with the fat, and store as before.

Meat shrinks from drumstick during cooking. You can remove bone if you wish.

Goose Fat:
Goose fat, as previously noted but it bears repeating, will keep for months in a covered jar in the refrigerator. Use it for sautéing potatoes, for basting roasts, for cooking such earthy items as cabbage, dried beans, turnips, or for cooking more *confit*.

Cracklings—Residue from the Rendering of Fat:
You may toss the bits of browned skin, left from fat rendering, in a sprinkling of salt, pepper, and either allspice or special spice mixture (page 468), and serve either as a cocktail snack or along with the cassoulet. Or chop them fine, warm briefly in a frying pan with the seasonings, pack into a jar, and cover with a thin layer of hot goose fat; seal top with plastic wrap and refrigerate—for use as a cocktail cracker spread (known in French as *frittons* or *grattons*).

Goose Stock:
To make a stock out of the chopped-up carcass, wings, neck, and gizzard peelings, place in a large saucepan with a peeled and quartered onion, a carrot, a small leek if you have one, and a celery stalk with leaves. Pour on cold water to cover ingredients by 2 inches (5 cm), salt lightly, and add an herb bouquet (6 parsley sprigs, 1 bay leaf, 1 garlic clove, 4 allspice berries, and ½ tsp thyme). Bring to the simmer, skim off gray scum, which will continue to rise for several minutes, then cover loosely and simmer 2½ hours, adding more water if liquid evaporates below level of ingredients. Strain, let cool, then refrigerate; remove congealed fat from surface when chilled. Use for soups and sauces, or combine with other stock for the consommé earlier in this chapter.

🕐   Will keep several days under refrigeration; may be frozen for several months.

Preserved Duck, Turkey, Pork, and Small Game Such as Squirrel and Rabbit:
Treat any of the above as you would goose, cutting the meat into serving pieces before salting it and simmering it in rendered pork fat or lard.

Cassoulet

Beans baked with lamb, goose, and sausages

For a 6-quart (3-L) casserole, serving 10 to 12 people

For the Beans:
To make 3 ½ quarts or 3 ¼ L cooked beans

5 cups (2 pounds or 900 g) dry white beans—Great Northern or small white

4½ quarts (4 L) water

1 pound (450 g) fat-and-lean salt pork with rind (optional)

1 large yellow onion, peeled and sliced

1 large herb bouquet (8 parsley sprigs, 4 cloves garlic, ½ tsp thyme, and 2 imported bay leaves, all tied in washed cheesecloth)

Salt as needed

For the Lamb:

About 4 pounds (2 kg) bone-in lamb shoulder, sawed into stewing chunks

Rendered goose fat, or cooking oil

2 large onions, sliced

4 or 5 large cloves garlic, minced

½ cup (1 dL) tomato sauce (page 468), or 4 or 5 Tb tomato paste

½ tsp thyme

2 imported bay leaves

2 cups (½ L) dry white wine or dry white French vermouth

3 cups (¾ L) or more beef stock or bouillon

Salt and pepper

Other Ingredients:

About ½ the preserved goose in the preceding recipe, and the cracklings

1 ½ to 2 pounds (675 to 900 g) cooking sausage such as kielbasy or chorizo, or sausage meat formed into cakes

3 Tb or more rendered goose fat or melted butter

2 cups (½ L) moderately pressed down, fresh white crumbs from crustless nonsweet French or Italian bread

½ cup (1 dL) moderately pressed down minced fresh parsley

Equipment:

An 8-quart (7- to 8-L) kettle or pressure cooker for the beans; a medium-sized casserole or chicken fryer for the lamb; a 6-quart (6-L) flameproof casserole for baking the cassoulet

The beans

Pick over the beans to be sure there are no stones or other debris among them, wash and drain them, and place in a large kettle or in the bottom of a large pressure cooker. Add the water, cover, and bring to the boil. Boil uncovered for exactly 2 minutes. Cover and let sit for exactly 1 hour. (This takes the place of the old-fashioned overnight soak.) Meanwhile, if you are using salt pork, remove the rind, and cut the pork into slices ½ inch (1½ cm) thick; simmer rind and pork in 3 quarts (3 L) water for 15 minutes to remove excess salt; rinse in cold water, drain, and set aside.

As soon as the beans have had their soak, bring to the simmer again, adding the optional pork and rind, the onion, the herb package, and 1 tablespoon salt if you have not used salt pork—½ tablespoon if you have. Either simmer slowly, partially covered, for about 1½ hours or until the beans are just tender (add boiling water if needed, to keep beans covered at all times, and salt to taste near end of cooking). Or pressure cook as follows: cover and bring to full pressure for exactly 2 minutes; remove from heat and let pressure go down by itself for 15 minutes, then remove pressure knob; taste, and add salt as necessary.

🕐   The beans may be cooked 2 or 3 days in advance; when cool, cover and refrigerate. Bring just to the simmer before proceeding with the cassoulet.

The lamb—braised shoulder of lamb

Dry the lamb pieces. Film casserole or chicken fryer with fat or oil, heat to very hot but not smoking, and brown the lamb pieces, a few at a time, removing those that are browned to a side dish. Pour out excess fat, and brown the onions lightly. Then return all lamb to casserole, add the garlic, tomato, herbs, and wine or vermouth, and enough stock or bouillon just to cover the lamb. Salt lightly to taste, cover, and simmer slowly for about 1½ hours, or until lamb is tender. Carefully correct seasoning; when cool, remove and discard bones from lamb.

🕐   May be cooked several days in advance; when cold, cover and refrigerate the lamb in its cooking liquid. Discard congealed surface fat before using.

The braised lamb shoulder (a good dish just as is)

Assembling the cassoulet

Remove bones from preserved goose and, if you wish, the skin; cut goose into serving chunks about the same size as your lamb pieces. If you are using salt pork, cut it into thin slices. If you are using sausage such as kielbasy, cut in half lengthwise, then into chunks, and brown lightly in a frying pan with goose fat or oil. If you are using sausage meat, form into cakes about 1 ½ inches (4 cm) across, and brown in fat or oil.

With a slotted spoon, dip beans from their liquid (be sure to save it) and arrange about ⅓ of them in the bottom of the casserole you have chosen for the cassoulet. Cover with a layer of lamb, goose, sausage, a handful of goose cracklings and, if you are using it, half the salt pork. Repeat with a layer of beans and of meat; end with a layer of beans, coming to within about ¼ inch (¾ cm) of the rim of the casserole. Ladle on the lamb-cooking liquid plus as much bean-cooking liquid as needed just to cover the beans. Spread bread crumbs and parsley over the top.

🕐 May be assembled a day or even 2 days in advance, but if the beans and lamb have not been freshly cooked, be sure to bring them to the simmer for several minutes before assembling, to prevent any possibility of spoilage. When cool, cover and refrigerate.

1) Cutting the sausages before browning

2) A layer of beans goes in.

3) Spooning liquid over top

4) Breaking the crust into the beans

Warning on refrigerated cassoulets

The assembled cassoulet needs a good hour of baking so that all elements can combine deliciously together, thus the contents of the casserole must be decongealed and simmering before the actual baking effect can begin. Heating on top of the stove can be risky because you may scorch the bottom of the beans. I suggest, then, that the casserole be covered and set in a 325°F/165°C oven for an hour or so until its contents are bubbling; test center with a thermometer if you have any doubts—it should read 212°F/100°C. Then proceed with the baking in the next step. (I have had my troubles in this category, thinking that, because things were bubbling in the oven, the cassoulet was baking properly when it was just cooking around the edges but had not really heated through.)

Baking

About 1 hour

Preheat oven to 400°F/205°C. Bring casserole to simmer on top of the stove (or see preceding paragraph if casserole has been refrigerated), then set in oven. Bake for 20 to 30 minutes, until bread crumb topping has crusted and browned lightly; break the crust into the beans with the back of a spoon, and return the casserole to the oven. Lower thermostat to 350°F/180°C, and continue baking for another 15 minutes or so, until a second crust has formed itself on top. Break it, in turn, into the beans, and if cooking liquid seems too thick or the beans dry, add a spoonful or so of bean-cooking liquid from your pot. When the crust forms again, leave it as is; the beans are ready to serve.

🕐 The beans will stay warm in a turned-off oven, door ajar, for a good half hour, or you may keep them warm on an electric hot tray. They will gradually dry out if kept too warm for too long a time.

Pickled Red Cabbage Slaw

You can't treat red cabbage like green cabbage, I have found, at least if you want to serve it raw. It needs to be very finely shredded and wants a maceration of a day or 2 in a solution of salt and vinegar to tenderize it; being a red vegetable, it must have some acid with it anyway to keep its color. The following is, I think, a refreshing way to serve it, being neither too sharp nor too picklelike, and a fine accompaniment to the likes of a cassoulet.

For about 2 quarts (2 L)

A good fresh red cabbage weighing about 1½ pounds (675 g)

A large red onion

A large sweet red bell pepper (optional)

2 to 3 cloves garlic, minced

4 imported bay leaves

1 tsp mustard seeds

½ tsp juniper berries

½ cup (1 dL) canned beet juice, or borscht

1 cup (¼ L) red wine vinegar (more if needed)

The sweet-and-sour charm of pickled red cabbage slaw

2 cups (½ L) water (more if needed)

2 Tb salt (more if needed)

1 Tb sugar

4 tart apples

4 handfuls minced fresh parsley

Equipment:

A cabbage shredder, such as a mail-order sauerkraut cutter, or other device, or an expert person with a very sharp stainless-steel knife (carbon steel can turn the cabbage blue)

Discard wilted outer leaves, halve and quarter the cabbage, and cut out the core. Cut cabbage into shreds as thin and fine as possible—^{1}/16 inch (¼ cm); do the same with the onion and optional pepper. The finer and thinner you cut the vegetables, the more efficiently the flavors can penetrate and tenderize the cabbage and the more successful your relish. Toss in a bowl with the garlic, bay, mustard, juniper, and beet juice or borscht. Bring the vinegar and water to the simmer with the salt and sugar, pour over the cabbage, and toss to mix well. Pack into a 2-quart (2-L) jar. Liquid should just cover ingredients by a finger width—add more vinegar and water in the proportions of 1 part vinegar to 2 parts water if necessary. Cover and refrigerate, turning jar upside down several times for the first 2 days; taste, and add a little more salt if you feel it necessary. The relish should marinate for 2 days at least.

When ready to serve, dip out as much of the relish as you think you will need, and for every 2 cups (½ L), blend in 1 minced apple and a handful of parsley.

⏱ The cabbage will keep for at least several weeks under refrigeration, and the pickling juice may be used over and over again—just add more seasoning if you think it is needed.

Sliced Fresh Pineapple— En Boat

In its shell

For 10 to 12 people

2 of the largest, ripest, sweetest, and finest pineapples available (or 3 or even 4 smaller pineapples; see Remarks, page 283)

Sprigs of fresh mint, if available

White rum or kirsch, or savarin syrup, page 409 (optional)

Equipment:

A very sharp, long heavy knife for slicing the whole pineapple; a smaller very sharp flexible knife for other cutting; a platter upon which to serve the pineapple

Cutting and Slicing Note:
While trying things out for the television show depicting this dinner, all of us cooks had a hand in cutting pineapples. We used the coring gadget. We tried a long knife. We shaved off the peel all around and spiraled the eyes out of a pineapple. And we even butchered another pineapple trying a half-remembered system of somebody's grandmother, who, it was said, cut diamond wedges around each eye, slanting into the pineapple so each wedge could be pulled out individually—the pineapple collapsed halfway through. We all preferred the following.

Cut the pineapple in half, being very careful when you come to the crown to keep it attached to the fruit—for decoration later. Then cut the halves into lengthwise halves or thirds. Cut out the hard core at the top of each wedge; with a sharp flexible knife, cut close against the skin to free the wedge of flesh. Then, if the wedge seems a bit wide, cut it in half lengthwise before cutting it crosswise into wedge-shaped slices. Replace the slices on the skin—or boat—and arrange attractively on a platter with, if you wish, sprigs of fresh mint.

🕐   If not to be served promptly, cover closely with plastic wrap and refrigerate.

As you serve the pineapple at the table, and particularly if it is not as sweet as you could wish, you might drizzle a few drops of rum or kirsch, or savarin liqueur-flavored syrup, over each wedge.

Cut against skin to release pineapple wedges; at the table drizzle on rum or kirsch.

🕐 *Timing*

Last-minute planning won't work for a cassoulet party, obviously, but the nice thing is that there are practically no last-minute *jobs* with this menu.

Half an hour before sitting down, put the cracker bread in the oven to crisp for 5 minutes (careful it doesn't scorch), set the consommé on the stove ready to heat, and check the cassoulet. If it is done, turn off the oven.

Whether it should be 1½ hours or 3 hours before you intend to serve the cassoulet that you put it in the oven depends on whether or not it was made ahead and refrigerated. Since how long it simmers is crucial to its final flavor, please see the discussion of that important matter in the recipe itself, page 292.

Sometime in the afternoon, or even that morning, cut and refrigerate the pineapple, closely covered with plastic wrap.

The day before your party, or even the day before that, assemble the cassoulet. That same day, buy the pineapples, and maybe some parsley to garnish the red cabbage.

The day before *that*, in other words up to three days before your party, cook the lamb and the beans, and make and cook the sausage if you're doing your own. (There's a good recipe for homemade sausage meat on page 175.) You could preserve the goose now, if you had thought to buy and defrost your bird 2 or 3 days beforehand; then you could cook the *confit* while you were braising the lamb—the goose needs a 24-hour salting before it cooks, however. But you can cook a *confit* months ahead and "put it down"—that's the point of it anyway, to have something marvelous and waiting.

As much as 2 weeks beforehand, you can pickle the red cabbage, but it does need its jar tipped once or twice for the first 2 days.

Clarify the consommé any time at all, and keep it in the freezer.

Menu Variations

If you weren't having a fruit dessert, you could move your pineapples up front and, rather than consommé, serve them sliced with prosciutto, or use some other fruit for your *first course*. I love a plain chilled half grapefruit or melon—a perfect specimen. Just be sure you have something light before cassoulet; shellfish seem to me too bland and too meaty, somehow. You want piquancy.

The *cassoulet* can be infinitely varied. Bearing in mind that the dish was not conceived in a fancy restaurant with bought-to-order ingredients, do experiment with whatever you have on hand. Some of your combinations will, of course, be better than others, and some you may decide never to try again. You can use sausages only, or roast or braised pork instead of lamb, or duck or turkey instead of (or along with) goose, or ham hocks or veal shanks, or such small game as squirrel or rabbit. You can use other kinds of dry beans, or lentils, or even fresh beans. I've never tried limas or Kentucky Wonders, but you might. One item you must have, however, is a good cooking stock of some sort to pour over the beans and give them real flavor during their final baking. As for a vegetarian cassoulet, how about lots and lots of garlic, onions, tomatoes, herbs, and perhaps the sautéed eggplant on page 338?

Not too many accompaniments occur to me as good substitutes for the *pickled red cabbage*. Sauerkraut is a possibility, or coleslaw, or you might like a chiffonade salad—lettuce with sliced cooked (preferably pickled) beets and a light sieving of hard-boiled egg, for that sweet-sour taste. Or you could try sliced cucumbers, lightly wilted with salt, then drained well, tossed in a little lemon juice with a few grains of sugar and some finely chopped red onion, and sprinkled with parsley.

For *dessert*, pineapple does seem ideal to me; but you could serve ice-cold very ripe persimmons, Persian or honeydew melon, or sliced oranges, plain or with blueberries, as on page 221, or perhaps glazed, as in *Mastering I*, or perhaps a sherbet. If you had a first course of fruit, a coffee granita (the large-crystal sherbet) might be nice. Here's a last-minute trick we tried and liked after one cassoulet dinner: if you have a food processor, use the steel blade and dump in frozen sliced peaches cut in chunks plus ⅓ their volume of Champagne and drops of lemon juice; process, sugar to taste, and process again. The whole thing takes two minutes and gives you a sherbet of perfect ready-to-eat consistency.

Leftovers

A fully cooked *cassoulet* can be reheated and is very good, but usually not quite as good as after its first baking. Be sure it is moist enough; add a little stock if it's not. Or you can turn the remains into a soup: mince the meats (slicing the sausage) and add them to the beans, puréed in stock.

When you have made your own *preserved goose*, you have a splendid kitchen staple on hand, in fact several. The *fat* can be re-used many times, if you don't overheat it, and is delicious for preserving other meats, or for frying. The *goose stock*, like any stock, can become a consommé or can go into soups, sauces, and stews, and can of course be frozen. If you have *cracklings* to spare, you can treat them as suggested earlier in the chapter and use as a cocktail cracker spread. The preserved meat is delicious cold: dip the pieces in boiling stock or even boiling water to remove fat, and you may also wish to discard the skin. Season lightly and roll in a mixture of finely chopped parsley and shallots. Serve with potato salad, watercress, or curly endive with a garlic and bacon dressing, or with a hearty mixed vegetable salad. If you're having a pot of beans, lentils, sauerkraut, braised cabbage, or the like, you can bury the goose pieces in the beans or cabbage and let them warm up for 8 to 10 minutes before serving. Or you can add pieces of preserved goose to a boiled dinner or *pot-au-feu*, giving them 4 to 5 minutes to simmer with the meats, just before serving. (They do get stringy if overcooked, so be careful.) Or you can roll the goose pieces in seasoned bread crumbs, baste with droplets of goose fat, and let warm under a slow broiler for 4 to 5 minutes on each side, or until hot through and tender. Serve with a purée of turnips, potatoes, parsnips, dried beans or lentils, or braised onions, celery, or leeks, or with sauerkraut or braised cabbage, or with Brussels sprouts or broccoli.

The *pickled cabbage* will keep for weeks in the refrigerator, and may be used hot as well as cold; wouldn't it be nice in a sizzling Reuben sandwich? And you can re-use the pickling juice when you run out of cabbage.

Pineapple doesn't keep long. You can serve leftover bits the next day with other cut-up fruit (strawberries especially), or use it instead of crackers with cream cheese and guava jelly or Bar-le-Duc preserve. With slices of prosciutto, it makes a sublime first course, and dieters, as we all know, mix it with their penitential low-fat cottage cheese. But don't try freezing it or putting it in an aspic: no go.

Postscript: They're funny that way

Cassoulet de Castelnaudary, Cassoulet de Toulouse, Cassoulet de Carcassonne . . . they're all good, and so's the cassoulet I've just described. So too are any number of variants. For most of us, which cassoulet we make or concoct depends on what looks good in the market. For the peasant cooks who probably thought up the dish in the first place, it most certainly depended on what was available. Fresh meat would have been used if an animal had just been slaughtered; otherwise, before the invention of refrigeration, every Mrs. French Peasant had to rely on what she had preserved. If she raised geese for a cash crop of *foie gras*, using only the livers, then *confit d'oie* would take care of the liverless gaggle. At hog-killing time, salting and the making of "summer" (keeping) sausage would preserve any meat not eaten fresh. From *confit d'oie*, she could progress to *confit de canard* if she raised ducks. Dry beans keep and they, like other legumes good for cassoulet, can be grown almost anywhere.

Certainly cassoulet's earthy simplicity, its lack of expensive or exotic ingredients, its nourishing heartiness suggest a peasant origin. Because an oven was something of a luxury in the poorer farmhouses of France, country women always used to carry their pots to the village baker, to be placed in his still-hot oven when the morning's last batch of bread was done.

Only history locates cassoulet in Languedoc, since the ingredients are easily produced almost anywhere in France. But that doesn't prevent French gastronomes from endlessly rehashing often unsubstantiated legends about the veritable cassoulet, and quarreling fervently over which of three towns—all quite close by— produced the truest and best, the one and only, cassoulet.

And yet I wonder: why *are* the French so passionate, not just about food itself or about naming dishes for their authentic region of origin (like potatoes *à la dauphinoise*, or our New England baked beans)—but for naming them after tiny, insignificant localities? We Americans have a few dishes named for big cities, and the English have a few named for counties (Devonshire cream, Cornish pasties, Yorkshire pudding, etc.), but nothing like this intense particularity. Doesn't the brouhaha over names and attributions arise from an almost amorous sense of place, a lover's appreciation of the special character of every corner of the land? For it's not just cassoulet the French are geographically potty about, it's bouillabaisse and pâté and all kinds of things to eat. Why they and not other great cooks like the Chinese?

There is, though, another nation of great cooks, the Italians, who are similarly inclined, with their myriad dishes *alla* somewhere-*ese*. The scholar Mario Pei has said that's because Italy was broken up until so recently into tiny city-states, each with its own cuisine. Not so true of France.

But almost every little place in both France and Italy makes its own particular wine, and it is part of wine's magic to speak with eloquence and precision of the very earth it came from. Grow the same grapes by similar methods in vineyards yards apart, and you often get unlike wines. How natural, then, for the children of wine-making cultures to be so sensitive to the special personality of every field and hill. How natural for them to name a garnish of peas for Clamart, an otherwise dull place that grows fine peas, or one of spinach for little Viroflay, or to name variants, as with cassoulet, for the places where they are supposed to have been invented.

For a Frenchman, a mental map of France must look like a vast hexagonal buffet. Even for me, some dishes powerfully evoke a beloved region. When I taste an apple tart *à la normande,* all fresh and creamy, my mind's eye dwells on the drowsy cattle and the scented orchards Paul and I drove past en route to Paris from the war-shattered docks of Cherbourg, on my first day in France thirty-odd years ago. And where is my mind's eye now, as I taste this excellent cassoulet? Why, on the busy kitchen behind the *J.C. & Co.* set, where we of the cooking team developed our own version. Above us looms not the sunny sky of fabled Languedoc, but a frightful mess of pipes and lights and rubber-covered cables. Nevertheless, this too is a beloved place. Ought we, perhaps, to name our dish in the classic fashion *Cassoulet des Coulisses de J.C. et Cie.,* or J.C. & Co.'s Backstage Cassoulet?

An elderly hen, if you treat her right, becomes lady bountiful.

Old-fashioned Chicken Dinner

Menu
For 6 people

*Long Fresh Asparagus Spears, with Oil and
    Lemon*
French Bread

*Hen Bonne Femme—A sprightly stuffed fowl
    poached whole, and served with onions,
    mushrooms, and Sauce Ivoire*
Steamed Rice

Tossed Green Salad
Melba Toast or French Bread

*Bombe aux Trois Chocolats—A chocolate
    mousse hidden under a mold of
    chocolate fudge cake, topped with
    chocolate sauce and a sprinkling of
    walnuts*

Suggested wines:
*Although some worthy wine wallahs abstain
from wine with asparagus, I like a light dry
riesling or Sancerre; a full dry white would go
with the chicken, like a Burgundy or
chardonnay, or you could present a light red
Bordeaux or cabernet; sweet Champagne or a
sweet but still wine would go with the
chocolate dessert—a Sauternes, Vouvray, or
gewürztraminer.*

When a hen's too old to lay, she still is useful for something—good eating! Her great egg-producing days are over, and it doesn't pay the poultry man to keep on feeding her. So we feed *on* her, and well, for the great thing about this beldame is her wonderful flavor. Mass produced (battery raised, as some call it), with no exercise and standardized rations, young chickens today don't have the rich taste they used to when they ran around snacking on anything they fancied in the hen yard; but with age and, I presume, experience, they acquire flavor as people do character. Matronly hens taste the way all chicken used to and ought to.

My market says there's not much demand for stewing chickens nowadays, because a lot of customers don't know how to cook them. They treat them like roasters, end up with rubber chicken, and come back to the store mad. But, though you may have to special-order your stewing chicken (or fowl, to be technical), it is available. The demand comes from commercial food processors, and from hotels and restaurants, which use fowl by preference for salads and sandwiches. It's not just because of the fowl's rich taste: hens, not *old* but of a certain age, have an excellent, tender texture when cooked right. The key is long simmering—but not too long, for just after the point of perfection is reached, utter disintegration sets in and the meat falls flaccidly from the bone. It's curious: the fowl stays obdurately tough for the longest time, then its consistency changes quite quickly; you really have to keep testing.

A "boiled fowl" (gross phrase!) is so useful a resource to have on hand that more households—particularly where everybody goes out to work—should make it a staple.

The next step is so quick and easy, whether you opt for chicken stew, pie, salad, or sandwiches, and the golden broth makes sauce or soup. But don't use a capon or a young chicken or a middle-aged roaster for the purpose. They don't have enough flavor, and long cooking practically dissolves them. (Best moist-cooking method for roasters, in my experience, is the casserole poach, where there is little liquid and the bird steams in a covered pot in the oven, as described in *Mastering I* and *The French Chef Cookbook*.) With a fine fowl (see page 302 for standards of quality), I use a stuffing to bring out the grand flavor, and the broth for sauce (the rest for soup later), and carve before serving. For the price of 3 lamb chops, one can serve from 6 to 8 people, or get at least 3 well-varied dinners for a couple.

Practicality, of course, is something a party should possess but certainly not proclaim! Don't think there is anything humdrum about our "elegant fowl" (as the Owl was addressed by the Pussycat). This is the finest of party food. The full, super-chickeny taste marries so well with a good wine, and the platter looks handsome: smooth-grained meat, ivory satin sauce, and a pretty array of vegetables.

Sauced chicken flanks the stuffing, while mushrooms and onions garnish the platter.

It's an easy dish to serve. And to eat, which can be a consideration. (I remember a very young niece, returning from her first dinner dance in pink tulle—and red wrath. "I'm starved!" she howled. "All the kids are! It was *squab!*" If you have young guests all gussied up in their first party clothes, do feed them something manageable.)

The choice of a first course before chicken is no problem at any time, but in joyful springtime asparagus, for me, is the ideal thing. Is there anything it doesn't complement? (Scallops, maybe—too much too sweet—or a very spicy "made dish" like lasagne . . .) Anyway, the clear fresh green of it and the soft flavor—sweet in the stalk and subtle, vaguely mushroomy, in the tip—are bliss before the sturdy yet delicate chicken. Why before and not with? With is fine, I concede, but consider the sumptuousness, the sheer all-outness, of a whole plateful of nothing but asparagus!—peeled, of course, so the pure green is streaked with ivory. And perfectly drained, and cooked just to the pivot-point between crunchy and soft, and very, very cold—or very, very hot. Rapture . . .

With a bread crumb stuffing and a rich dessert, you don't need bread or rice for starch; but for texture they are nice—fresh French loaf for contrast, the rice (recipe on page 467) for a sauce sopper-up. The salad, with a vinaigrette dressing, is just a hyphen, a refresher.

The dessert on this menu is called Bombe aux Trois Chocolats because it looks like a floating mine and the threat is triple: chocolate mousse encased in chocolate cake, and then, forsooth, coated with more chocolate. (But a little lightly whipped cream, passed separately, softens the chocolate onslaught.) Anybody who comes to this dinner will gaze upon the dark and lustrous dome and know he's at— A Party.

Preparations and Marketing

Recommended Equipment:
Start with one big pot. It's essential that the one for your chicken be deep enough so that the liquid level can be 4 inches (10 cm) above the chicken; stainless steel or enamel is best for cooking with wine, and the pot has to be covered. For asparagus, a large oval casserole or roaster is ideal. For lots of asparagus, a rack fitting the pot (as in a fish steamer) is a nice convenience for lifting out and draining. To truss the chicken, you need plenty of soft white string.

A covered, heavy-bottomed saucepan is a help with rice, and you need 2, preferably 3, more saucepans for sauce, onions, and mushrooms. Onions can, if you like, be precooked and reheated with the mushrooms when you do them.

For the dessert, you need a jelly-roll pan to bake the fudge cake, and a homemade paper pattern or template (which you can file and reuse) as a guide to cutting it. To form the bombe, use a 6-cup (1½-L) bowl, or smooth-sided mold, or even a flowerpot.

Staples to Have on Hand:

Salt
White peppercorns
Granulated sugar
Confectioners sugar
Dried sage
Imported bay leaves
Dried thyme
Whole cloves
Pure vanilla extract
Optional: chicken stock
Gelatin
Butter (3 sticks; 12 ounces or 340 g)
Swiss cheese (2 ounces or 60 g)
Day-old nonsweet white French- or Italian-type
    bread (½ loaf)
Flour
Garlic (2 or more cloves)
Optional: leeks (1 or 2)
Celery (3 stalks)
Carrots (2 medium)
Lemons (1)
Cognac, dark Jamaica rum, or bourbon
    whiskey

Specific Ingredients for This Menu:

Stewing chicken (5 to 6 pounds or 2¼ to
    2¾ kg) ▼
Best-quality semisweet chocolate (16 ounces or
    450 g)
Unsweetened chocolate (6 ounces or 180 g)
Walnuts (2 Tb, chopped)
Heavy cream (3¼ cups or 7 dL)
Eggs (7 "large" plus 2 whites)
Parsley (1 good-sized bunch)
Yellow onions (4 or 5 large)
Small white onions (18 to 24)
Mushrooms (1 quart or 1 L), preferably small
Asparagus (36 to 48 spears) ▼
Optional: dry white wine (1 bottle)
Optional: dry white French vermouth (2 cups
    or ½ L), or use more dry white wine

▶   **Remarks:**

Chicken: a good stewing chicken, or fowl, or stewing hen, is just on the shady side of middle age. An "old hen" is great for soup, but too tough to eat. What you want is a bird from 14 to 16 months old, weighing between 4 and 6½ pounds (1¾ and 3 kg), in general—but buy one on the big side to feed 6 amply. She should be plump and chunky-looking; her skin should be white—not yellow; her breast is reasonably full, and her breastbone, if you feel it down to the tip, is not cartilage but solid bone—that shows she's at least a year old. See the introduction to this chapter for more details on this somewhat-neglected—but highly meritorious—type of bird. Since you may have to special-order your fowl, it's worth knowing what to ask for and what you can expect. *Asparagus:* fresh asparagus is sold nowadays from February to June. For information about buying, storing, and preparing, see the following.

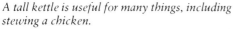

A tall kettle is useful for many things, including stewing a chicken.

Fresh Asparagus

Buying

Fat asparagus is just as tender, in my opinion, as thin asparagus, but I do think you should choose spears all of the same diameter to be sure of even cooking. Pick them spear by spear if you can, choosing firm stalks with closely clinging leaves at the bud ends; the peel from end to end should be tight, bright, and fresh with no creased or withered areas. The butt ends should look moist, and if your grocery store is really serious about asparagus, they will have it standing upright in a tray with an inch of water. Asparagus spears are like flowers: they wilt without moisture.

Storing

When you bring your asparagus home, unwrap it at once, cut a finger width off the butts to reach the moist ends, and it is a good idea to let the asparagus lie for half an hour in warm water, which will refresh it. Then stand the spears upright in a bowl, their butts in 2 inches (5 cm) of cold water, cover loosely with plastic wrap or a plastic bag, and store in the refrigerator. Treated this way, fresh asparagus will stay fresh for 2 or 3 days.

Peeling

There is no doubt at all in anyone's mind who has compared peeled asparagus with unpeeled asparagus—they are two different vegetables. Peeled asparagus cooks evenly from tip to butt in half the time, remains greener, and has a far better texture than unpeeled asparagus. (The same is true of peeled versus unpeeled broccoli.) To peel the spears, you want to take the tough outer skin from the butt end up to near the tip, where the skin is tender. I use a small knife, and lop off a finger width of the butt—or if necessary, I make the cut where the green begins. Then, starting at the butt end, and holding the spear butt up, I start the peel, cutting down to the tender flesh and making the cut more shallow as I reach the tender area near the tip. Using a knife, you can direct the depth of the peel, and it is also good practice in control of the knife. However, you can use a vegetable peeler: hold the spear on your work surface, its butt away from you, and go round and round until you get down to the tender flesh—but be careful holding and turning it, so as not to break the spear.

If you bend an asparagus spear to where it breaks, you are losing a lot of asparagus, whereas a properly peeled spear can be eaten from butt to tip.

Store asparagus with the butts in water; peel just before cooking.

Plain Boiled Asparagus

For 6 people, with 6 to 8 spears per person

36 to 48 fine fresh asparagus spears all the same diameter, peeled

4 to 5 quarts or liters rapidly boiling water

1 ½ tsp salt per quart or liter water

Equipment:

A large oval casserole or roaster; 2 wide spatulas for lifting asparagus out of water; a tray, or rack over tray, lined with a clean towel if asparagus is to be served cold; a platter lined with a double-damask or linen napkin if asparagus is to be served hot

With a small amount of asparagus, there is no need to tie it in bundles for cooking if you have an oval casserole or roaster that will hold it comfortably so that it does not tumble about as it boils.

Bring the water to the rapid boil with the salt, lay in the asparagus, and cover the casserole just until the water begins to boil again—the sooner it reaches the boil, the greener the asparagus; but the casserole must be uncovered while the asparagus is actually boiling—again to keep it green.

Boil slowly, uncovered, for 4 to 5 minutes, or just until asparagus spears start to bend a little when lifted. Remove a spear; cut and eat a piece from the butt end to make sure. Asparagus should be just cooked through, with a slight crunch. Immediately remove the asparagus from the water.

To serve cold

Arrange in one layer on the towel-lined tray or rack, and cool near an open window if possible. Serve with lemon wedges and a pitcher of good olive oil, or with vinaigrette or one of its variations, or with mayonnaise —recipes for which are on page 466.

To serve hot

Arrange on napkin-lined platter and pass lemon wedges and melted butter, or lemon butter, or hollandaise, page 406, or one of the butter sauces on page 464. Another method, which I always remember delighting in at my grandmother's house, was to arrange the hot asparagus on a rather deep rectangular platter, season it with salt and pepper, pour lots of melted butter over it, and stand small triangles of white toast all around the edge of the platter.

Asparagus is cooked when the spears bend just a little bit.

Whole Stuffed and Poached Stewing Chicken

"Boiled Fowl"

For 6 to 8 people

Herb and Bread Crumb Stuffing:

1 cup (¼ L) minced onions

3 Tb butter

The gizzard, heart, and liver of the chicken (optional)

2 or more cloves garlic, minced

1 celery stalk, minced

1 "large" egg

2½ cups (6 dL) lightly pressed down crumbs from crustless day-old French- or Italian-type nonsweet white bread

½ cup (1 dL), lightly pressed down, fresh minced parsley

½ tsp dried sage

Salt and pepper

½ cup (1 dL) coarsely grated Swiss cheese

For Stewing the Chicken:

A 5- to 6-pound (2¼- to 2¾-kg) fine plump white-skinned stewing chicken, ready to cook

About 6 quarts (6 L) liquid: 1 bottle dry white wine, plus half-and-half water and chicken stock; or chicken stock and water; or water only

Salt to taste (1 tsp per quart or liter if using only water)

2 large celery stalks

2 medium carrots

1 large peeled onion stuck with 2 cloves

1 or 2 washed leeks, or another large onion

1 large herb bouquet (8 parsley sprigs, 2 imported bay leaves, and 1 tsp dried thyme, tied together in washed cheesecloth)

Equipment:

Either a trussing needle and white string, or a lacing pin (for neck skin) and 4 feet (120 cm) of soft white string (butcher's corned-beef twine recommended); a stew pot just tall enough to hold the chicken submerged plus 4 inches (10 cm) of extra room (make it stainless steel or enamel if you are cooking with wine; aluminum can discolor both the wine and the chicken)

Herb and bread crumb stuffing

Cook the onions slowly in the butter until tender and translucent. Meanwhile, peel and mince the gizzard, and add to the onions; then mince the heart, and add to the onions; and finally, when onions are almost tender, mince the liver. Stir it in and cook a minute or 2, just to stiffen. Scrape into a mixing bowl, stir in the rest of the ingredients, and season carefully to taste.

Preparing and stuffing the chicken

Pull any clinging fat out from the chicken's cavity, and make sure the cavity is free of other extraneous bits. For easier carving, re-move the wishbone: open skin flap at neck and feel the fork of the bone with your fin-ger, running from top of breast down each side; cut around the 2 tines of the fork and the top, then cut down to detach fork ends at each side. Cut off wing nubbins at el-bows. If you wish an automatic basting sys-tem and there is enough chicken fat to do so, place fat between 2 sheets of wax paper and pound to a thickness of about ⅛ inch (½ cm). Slip your fingers between skin and

flesh over the breast on both sides, to detach skin, and slide in the fat over the breast meat. Secure the neck skin (below) against the back of the chicken and fold wings akimbo.

Just before cooking it, salt the cavity of the chicken lightly, spoon in the stuffing (picture 1, below), and truss the chicken.

Trussing a Chicken with String:

Sew or skewer the neck skin against the neck end of the backbone, to hold it in place. Provide yourself with a piece of soft white string (butcher's corned-beef twine recommended) 4 feet (120 cm) long and proceed as follows:

2) Set chicken on its back, its tail toward you. Fold the string in half, and place its center under the chicken's tail piece.

3) Cross the string over the top of the tail piece.

4) Bring one end of the string from its side of the tail piece *under* the end of its opposite drumstick, then up over it, and down toward the side of the tail piece from which it came. Repeat the same movement from the other side.

5) To close the vent and bring the drumstick ends together, pull the 2 ends of string away from the sides of the chicken.

Turn the chicken on its side.

6) Fold the wings akimbo, wing ends tucked against the back of the neck. Bring the end of string nearest you along the side of the chicken and on top of the folded wing on the same side, then under the wing, coming out at the back again from under the armpit. Repeat with the string on the other side—along side of chicken, over top of wing, under it, and back again under armpit.

7) Pull both string ends tight across back to hold the chicken in form, and by doing so you will make the wings stand out akimbo to brace the chicken when you turn it breast up. Tie the string ends together at one side of the backbone.

Note: You may have to sew or skewer the vent opening closed if you have a loose stuffing, but the string truss is often sufficient to hold everything in place.

1

2

3

4

5

6

7

Chicken should be stuffed only just before cooking, since stuffing may start to spoil (especially because it contains bread crumbs), and that will spoil the whole chicken, resulting in a nasty case of food poisoning for all who dine upon it.

Poaching the chicken
2½ to 3 hours

Place the chicken in the pot and pour on enough liquid to cover it by 3 inches (8 cm). Add the specified amount of salt, cover loosely, and bring rapidly to the simmer. Skim off gray scum that will continue to rise for 5 minutes or more, then add the vegetables and herb bouquet. Maintain at the slow simmer, partially covered, for 2 hours. (A hard simmer or boil will break the flesh apart.) Add water if liquid evaporates to expose ingredients.

Chicken is not done until a sharp-pronged fork will pierce the large end of the drumstick easily. For 2 hours or more, flesh will be rubbery; then, suddenly, it will become tender, and it should be tested frequently, at 7-minute intervals, when the time might be close. Drumstick meat will just begin to fall from bone when chicken is done; white breast meat will hold, but be tender. Do not overcook.

Chicken will stay warm in its pot for 2 hours or more, partially covered, and may be gently reheated if it cools too much. Chicken should stay in its poaching liquid until serving time; the meat dries out otherwise.

Warning about Covered Pots: Always allow for air circulation, especially when the chicken is not simmering. Cooking liquid and chicken can easily spoil in a nonsimmering covered pot, due to some chemical or bacterial relation between closed containers and warm chicken.

Serving suggestions

The chicken is now ready to be eaten. To serve it cold, let it cool in its cooking liquid and it is ready for salads and sandwiches.

Here is one way to serve it hot:

Hen Bonne Femme

Poached stewing chicken with onions, mushrooms, and white-wine sauce

For 6 to 8 people

The preceding poached stuffed chicken
18 to 24 small white onions
1 quart (1 L) small fresh mushrooms
1½ tsp fresh lemon juice

For White-Wine Velouté Sauce (sauce suprême—sauce ivoire): *4 cups (1 L)*
About 6 cups (1½ L) degreased chicken cooking stock
2 cups (½ L) dry white French vermouth or dry white wine
5 Tb butter
6 Tb flour
½ cup (1 dL) heavy cream
Salt and white pepper
Drops of fresh lemon juice as needed

Braised White Onions:

Drop the onions into a saucepan of boiling water, boil 1 minute to loosen skins, and drain. Shave tops and bottoms off onions, peel them, and stab a cross in their root ends to discourage bursting during cooking. Place in one layer in a covered saucepan with an

Stab roots of onions to prevent bursting.

inch or so of cooking stock, cover, and simmer slowly for 20 to 30 minutes, or until tender when pierced with a knife. They should keep their shape. Set aside, reserving cooking liquid. Reheat before serving.

🕐   May be cooked in advance.

Stewed Mushrooms:

Trim ends off mushrooms. If they seem dirty, drop into a bowl of cold water, swish about, and immediately lift out into a colander. Or wipe them off with a towel. Place in a stainless-steel or enamel saucepan with several spoonfuls of chicken cooking liquid and 1½ teaspoons lemon juice. Toss mushrooms with the liquid. Cover pan and simmer 3 to 4 minutes, until just tender. Set aside, reserving cooking liquid. Reheat just before serving.

🕐   Best not cooked much more than half an hour in advance so the mushrooms will not darken, although you may prepare them for cooking several hours before and refrigerate in dry paper towels and a plastic bag.

The White-Wine Velouté Sauce:

Boil the chicken stock and wine slowly in a stainless-steel or enamel saucepan until reduced to about 4 cups or 1 liter. Melt the butter in a separate enamel or stainless-steel saucepan, blend in the flour, and stir over moderately low heat until butter and flour foam and froth together for 2 minutes without turning more than a buttery yellow. Remove from heat, and when this *roux* has stopped bubbling, pour in a ladleful of the hot chicken stock and vigorously beat to blend liquid and *roux;* blend in another ladleful, and when smooth pour in all but a ladleful. Beat in all but a spoonful or so of the onion and mushroom cooking liquids. Bring sauce to the simmer, stirring, over moderately high heat and simmer 2 to 3 minutes—if you have time, let sauce simmer half an hour or so, stirring frequently; longer cooking will only improve its flavor. Stir in the heavy cream and simmer a few minutes longer; carefully correct seasoning with salt and pepper, adding lemon juice to taste. (Sauce should be just thick enough to coat a wooden spoon nicely, meaning it will just coat the chicken; thin out with chicken stock or cream if necessary. To thicken, boil slowly, stirring, to concentrate it.)

🕐   May be made an hour or so in advance—add the mushroom juices before serving in this case. To prevent a skin from forming on the surface, lay plastic wrap right on top of the sauce, leaving air space at 2 or 3 places around the edge of the pan.

Serving the chicken

At serving time, remove the chicken from the pot to a carving board with a curved edge—to catch juices. Cut off trussing string, and remove the leg-thigh assembly from one side—it should fall off easily. Peel off and discard the skin and remove the meat—which will be so tender you can probably use a spoon and fork—and arrange on a hot

If your mushrooms are large, quarter them.

To serve the chicken, first remove leg-thigh sections; after peeling the skin off the breast, carve the meat.

serving platter. Peel skin off breast, and slice breast meat off the now legless side—breast meat may also be so tender it will come off with a fork and spoon. Arrange breast meat at the other side of the platter, and repeat on the second side of the chicken. Spoon out the stuffing and arrange down the middle of the platter, as shown. Arrange the onions and mushrooms around the meat, and spoon some of the sauce over the meat. Serve rest of sauce separately, in a warmed bowl.

🕐 Chicken should be sauced and served as soon as it is arranged on the platter, to prevent meat from drying out.

The Cooking Stock:
You will still have a good amount of fine chicken stock to use in soups and sauces. Simmer the chicken carcass and scraps in it for half an hour or so, strain and degrease it. Store in the refrigerator in a covered container when it is cold, and boil it up every several days, or freeze it.

Variations on the Sauce:
You can have no sauce at all, if you are counting calories: instead, boil down a good quantity of the degreased cooking liquid until its flavor is full and fine, and spoon some of that over the chicken and vegetables, ending with a generous sprinkling of parsley over the chicken itself; pass the rest of the liquid in a warm sauceboat. Or you can be far richer and creamier with your sauce: boil

Assembled platter; the chicken waiting for its sauce

down 4 cups (1 L) degreased cooking liquid with half that amount of dry white wine or dry French vermouth until reduced by half or less, and then boil down with 2 to 3 cups (½ to ¾ L) heavy cream until sauce has thickened lightly; season to taste, adding lemon juice if needed; pour some over the chicken and pass the rest in a warm bowl.

Variations on the Vegetables:
Rather than onions and mushrooms, you might use the kind of vegetables you'd have with the usual boiled dinner—carrots, turnips, cabbage wedges, onions, and potatoes —all boiled or steamed separately in some of the chicken cooking liquid.

Variations on the Chicken Cooking Method:
Rather than poaching the chicken whole, cut it into serving pieces and place the carcass remains, gizzard, and neck in the bottom of a casserole, topped by the dark meat, and ending with the breast and wings; add the same vegetables to the casserole, and enough liquid to cover the ingredients; cooking time may be a little shorter. By the way, I tried out the oven-steaming method in a covered casserole with a stuffed stewing hen, liquid coming up to mid thigh, wax paper on, and an oven heat of 275–300°F/135–150°C; the breast, wings, and thighs were fine, but the drumsticks dry and strange; the chicken took about 3¾ hours to cook tender. Perhaps the whole bird needed draping in a sheet of pork fat? I have not yet gone into the pressure cooker or slow cooker—they will have to wait for another hen party.

Chicken Pot Pie:
Using the chicken and its sauce and vegetables, turn them into a chicken pie: arrange in a pie dish or casserole, cover with the buttermilk and herb biscuit dough described for the rabbit pie (page 235), and bake in the same way. Or use the pâté dough (page 372). Baking time is about 30 minutes in a 400°F/205°C oven.

Bombe aux Trois Chocolats

A chocolate mousse hidden under a chocolate-covered fudge cake dome

This is a dessert for true chocolate lovers, and one that's beautiful to look at and fun as well—though not difficult to make. It consists of a chocolate fudge cake, a kind of brownie mixture, that bakes in a jelly-roll pan. When that is cool, you cut it so that it will line a bowl—or a soufflé mold, if you wish—you fill the lined bowl with chocolate mousse and chill it for 6 hours or overnight. Then unmold (it unmolds easily because first you have lined your bowl with plastic wrap), spoon a little melted chocolate on top, sprinkle on a pinch of chopped nuts for decoration, and you have an incomparable combination of three chocolates: the taste of brittle chocolate topping, the crunch of fudge cake, and the smooth velvet of the mousse.

Our cooking team worked on this for weeks. I had for some time been developing a rich dark mousse, trying to duplicate one I had found remarkable at André Surmain's restaurant in Mougins, in the south of France. But we all thought the mousse cake idea was what we were after, so we set our two chefs, Marian and Sara, to work on developing the perfect combination of cake, mousse, and molding technique. They made more than a dozen, which we solemnly tasted, one by one, and voted upon, narrowing the field to 3. Ultimately, this one really took the cake—and it was the cake indeed that made all the difference, because we wanted the contrast in texture vis-à-vis mousse that the solid fudge cake gave us.

Manufacturing and Timing Note:

I find it best to make the mousse first, so it can set a little bit, yet be soft enough to spoon into the lined mold. While the fudge cake is baking and cooling, you can cut out the template, or pattern, that will guide you in lining your bowl or mold with the cake. (Once I got my first template made, I kept it on file so I wouldn't have to go through that fussy fitting of things again.) The recipe here is for a 6-cup (1½-L) bowl of about 8 inches (20 cm) top diameter, which fortunately just works out for the standard rectangular jelly-roll pan that is about 11 by 17 inches (28 by 43 cm). A charlotte mold or even a flowerpot could be used, of course, and either is fine because they are both tall enough for drama.

For the Mousse—Chocolate Mougins

For 4 ½ cups, serving 8 people

12 ounces (340 g) best-quality semisweet chocolate
1 ½ ounces (45 g) unsweetened chocolate
2 ½ tsp plain unflavored gelatin
3 Tb dark Jamaica rum, Cognac, or bourbon whiskey
3 "large" eggs
2 egg whites (4 Tb)
1 ½ cups (3 ½ dL) heavy cream
1 ½ Tb pure vanilla extract
Large pinch of salt
3 Tb sugar

Equipment:

A small covered saucepan for melting the chocolate and a larger pan with water to set it in; a 2-quart (2-L) stainless-steel saucepan for the custard sauce; a very clean bowl and beater for egg whites, which can also serve for chilling the mousse

Flavor Note: This is a very strong, rich, dark, very chocolaty mousse, on the bittersweet side. It consists only of melted chocolate that is folded into a rich custard sauce, and is lightened by beaten egg whites, yet given body with a little gelatin.

Melting the chocolate

Break up the two chocolates and set in the small covered saucepan. Bring 2 inches (5 cm) of water to boil in a larger pan; remove from heat. Cover chocolate pan and set in the hot water. Chocolate will melt while you proceed with the rest of the recipe. Renew hot water if necessary; chocolate should be smoothly melted and darkly glistening.

The gelatin

Measure gelatin into a bowl or cup, pour on the rum or other liquid, and let soften.

Custard Sauce—Crème Anglaise:

Separate the eggs, dropping the whites, plus the extra whites, into the beating bowl, and the yolks into the stainless-steel saucepan. Set whites aside for later. Beat the yolks for a minute with a wire whip, or until thick and sticky; then blend in the cream. Stir rather slowly over low heat with a wooden spatula or spoon, reaching all over bottom of pan, as liquid slowly heats. (Watch it carefully, and do not let it come to the simmer.) Bubbles will begin to appear on the surface, and in a few minutes the bubbles will start to subside. Then watch for a whiff of steam rising—this indicates that the sauce is thickening. Continue for a few seconds until the sauce clings in a light layer to the back of your spatula or spoon. Immediately remove from heat, and stir for a minute or so to stop cooking.

Combining custard, gelatin, and chocolate

At once stir the softened gelatin mixture into the hot custard, stirring until the gelatin has dissolved completely. Stir in the vanilla, then the melted chocolate.

Finishing the dessert

Set the egg white beating bowl over the hot water that melted the chocolate, and stir for a moment to take off the chill (egg whites mount faster and more voluminously when slightly warmed). Beat at slow speed until they are foamy, beat in the salt, and then gradually increase speed to fast until egg whites form soft peaks. Sprinkle in the sugar, and beat until egg whites form stiff shining peaks. Fold them into the chocolate, then return the whole mixture to the egg white bowl, cover, and chill. Mousse should be somewhat set, not runny, when it goes into the cake-lined mold.

❶ If made and chilled in advance, leave out at room temperature until it has softened. Mousse will keep several days under refrigeration or may be frozen.

Note: This makes a delicious chocolate mousse just as it is. Turn the mousse into an attractive dish or individual pots, and serve with bowls of chocolate sauce (page 235) and of whipped cream.

Kate's Great Chocolate Fudge Cake

Note: This recipe was developed by our Chef Marian's daughter, Kate Morash, when she was only twelve years old, and makes a most superior brownie as well as perfect cake to surround a mousse—it is crunchy-chewy, yet soft enough to bend to the contours of a bowl.

For a jelly-roll pan about 11 by 17 inches (28 by 43 cm)

| Butter and flour for baking pan |
| 1 stick (4 ounces or 115 g) unsalted butter |
| 4 ounces (115 g) unsweetened chocolate |
| 1 more stick (4 ounces or 115 g) unsalted butter, cut into 8 pieces |
| 2 cups (380 to 400 g) sugar |
| 3 "large" eggs |
| 1 tsp pure vanilla extract |
| ½ tsp salt |
| 1 cup (140 g) all-purpose flour (measure by scooping dry-measure cup into flour container and sweeping off excess) |

Equipment:

A jelly-roll pan and wax paper; a saucepan for melting chocolate and butter, and another saucepan in which to set the first; an electric mixer, or a food processor; a flour sifter; a cake rack

Preliminaries

Preheat oven to 350°F/180°C. Butter the jelly-roll pan (so the paper will stick to it), cut a sheet of wax paper to fit it with 2 inches (5 cm) of overhang at each end, and press into pan. Butter and flour the paper, knocking out excess flour. Measure out all your ingredients.

Melting the chocolate

Set the first stick of butter and the chocolate in their melting pan, and place in the other pan with 2 to 3 inches of water; bring near the simmer and let the chocolate and butter melt together while you continue with the next step.

Hand-made or mixer-made batter

Cream second stick of butter with the sugar until light and fluffy. Beat in the eggs one by one, and the vanilla and salt. Stir in the warm melted chocolate mixture, then gradually sift and fold in the flour. Spread the batter evenly into the pan, and bake at once in middle level of preheated oven, setting timer for 25 minutes.

Food-processor-made batter

Or—cream butter and sugar in processor fitted with steel blade; add eggs one by one, then vanilla, salt, and chocolate. Pour in flour by thirds, blending with 2 or 3 on-off flicks. Spread evenly into pan, and set in middle level of preheated oven.

Baking and cooling

Bake about 25 minutes, until set but top is still spongy. A toothpick inserted into the cake should come out with a few specks of chocolate on it. It should be chewy when cool, and you want it to bend a little so that you can mold it into the bowl; do not let it overcook.

Remove from oven and let cool in pan for 10 minutes. Then turn pan upside down over a cake rack and unmold the cake, gently pulling off wax paper. Cool 10 minutes more.
* May be baked in advance. When cool, cover with wax paper, reverse back into baking pan, and cover airtight; store in the refrigerator for a day or 2, or freeze.

Brownies

When cool, cut the cake into 3- by 1½-inch (8- by 4-cm) rectangles. Serve as is, or you may glaze them with the chocolate and nuts suggested at the end of the bombe recipe.

Spread the batter with a rubber spatula.

Assembling the Bombe aux Trois Chocolats

The preceding recipes for chocolate mousse and chocolate fudge cake

4 ounces (115 g) best-quality semisweet chocolate

½ ounce (15 g) unsweetened chocolate

2 Tb chopped walnuts

A bowl of lightly whipped cream sweetened with confectioners sugar and flavored with vanilla (page 464)

Equipment:

A chilled serving platter and, if you wish, a paper doily

The template—or cut-out pattern

Whatever you have chosen as a container for molding the dessert, you will need a pattern of cut-outs to guide you in fitting the cake into the container. This is the system we use for our round bowl: a small cake circle for the bottom of the bowl; 7 wedges of cake to rest on the circle and touch the top of the bowl all around with a little space between each wedge, allowing the mousse to peek through its encircling walls of fudge cake. We also have a large circle to cap the mousse, and all scraps of fudge cake go into the center, giving the bombe a little extra sturdiness for its life out of the mold.

Molding the bombe

Before cutting the fudge cake, slice off a ½-inch (1½-cm) border all around the rectangle, since the edges tend to be brittle—these cut-offs make nice little cookie bits to serve another time. Then cut around the pattern.

Line the bowl with plastic wrap (for easy unmolding), and arrange the cake pieces in the bowl, pressing gently in place, best side out, as shown. Pile half the mousse into the bowl, cover with scraps of the cake (leftovers from cutting patterns). Fill with the remaining mousse and place the large circle on top, pressing it down to force the mousse into the bowl and around the cake. Cover and chill at least 6 hours or overnight.

🕐 Bombe may be refrigerated for several days. It may be frozen, and thawed before serving—several hours at room temperature, or a day or more in the refrigerator.

Unmolding

Loosen the bombe from the mold by pulling up on the plastic wrap, then fold wrap down the outside of the bowl. Center the serving platter (with doily if you are using one) over the top of the mold and reverse the two, unmolding the bombe onto the platter. Melt the chocolate over hot water, as described at the beginning of the mousse recipe, and pour over the top of the bombe, letting the chocolate drip lazily and unevenly down the sides. Top chocolate, while still warm, with a sprinkling of the chopped nuts.

Serving

Cut into wedges, like a round cake, and let each guest help himself to the whipped cream.

Keep your paper pattern for the next bombe.

A layer of cake scraps stabilizes the filling.

After the chocolate sauce, chopped nuts top it off.

⏱ *Timing*

This easy dinner allows you lots of flexibility. If guests are late or want to linger over their cocktails, no harm is done. Your first course of asparagus can be either hot or cold, and that is up to you. If cold, you have nothing to do at the last minute, your chicken and vegetables can wait, and you can go in to dinner whenever you wish. (I shall assume that you are serving cold asparagus in what follows.)

Just before the guests arrive, warm the chicken sauce, the onions and mushrooms together, and the rice—use the restaurant trick of having a roasting pan of simmering water on the stove, big enough to hold those three saucepans, each loosely covered. Have the salad in its bowl, covered and refrigerated, undressed but with dressing ready. Warm the bread if it needs freshening.

About an hour before that, test the chicken for doneness; once tender it can sit in its pot for 2 hours or more, just keeping itself warm. Ladle off the broth you'll need from the pot for cooking the mushrooms, onions, and sauce; if you expose the chicken, drape it in washed cheesecloth and baste with broth—cheesecloth should extend down into the broth on all sides and will draw it up like a wick, thus continuously basting the chicken. Make the sauce now, and you can cook both mushrooms and onions—although the onions could have been cooked in the morning. Whip the cream for the dessert.

Four and a half hours before you plan to serve, stuff and truss the chicken, and start it cooking—you could have made the stuffing in advance and have refrigerated it. Peel and cook the asparagus too, and make its vinaigrette sauce. Prepare the mushrooms for cooking now; wrap in dry paper towels and refrigerate in a plastic bag. You might also sauce the chocolate bombe and finish its final decoration, prepare the salad greens, and cook the rice (page 467).

The day before your party, take the dessert from the freezer, if you made it beforehand, and set it in the refrigerator to thaw. Or make the dessert now—or assemble it from its thawed, prefrozen components. Just be sure it has 6 hours or more to sit, in the refrigerator.

Menu Variations

Out of *asparagus* season, what would be a fitting preface for boiled fowl? Artichokes vinaigrette would be my choice, or a salad of sliced artichoke hearts with bits of crab or shrimp or lobster. Young string beans, tossed with butter, lemon, and parsley—another attractive idea, or a salad of cold fresh string beans dressed with onion rings and tomatoes. Still another suggestion, and a nicely old-fashioned one, is clear chicken broth made from your fine pot of chicken-cooking stock.

The chicken: rather than stewing it whole, see the suggestions at the end of the recipe. Or add other meats to simmer with it, like beef, pork, sausages, for a super boiled dinner. Or use turkey instead of chicken. Or serve the braised beef, on page 426.

The sauce: in some families melted butter with parsley and lemon is traditional for boiled chicken, as is hollandaise sauce, recipe, page 406. Some like tomato sauce, and some prefer sour cream with mustard and horseradish, much like the sour cream sauce served with the terrine in the "Picnic," page 371.

The vegetables: rather than onions and mushrooms, you could serve boiled or mashed potatoes, or braised topinambours, or something green like Brussels sprouts or broccoli or peas. You could arrange the chicken over a bed of buttered noodles, surrounding it with a green vegetable or with broiled tomatoes.

The *dessert:* the chocolate bombe is indeed a rich and now, because of the price of chocolate, an expensive dessert. You could have the pretty filled meringue cases, or *vacherins* (page 240), or the apple-filled burnt-almond-and-rum-layered gâteau of crêpes on page 258. Other chocolate cakes in other books are the Victoire on page 187, and the always popular Reine de Saba chocolate-almond cake in *Mastering I* and in *The French Chef Cookbook.*

Leftovers

Asparagus leftovers will be rare, if you have bought 6 to 8 spears per person; they can be used in a salad the next day, or in the vegetable and crêpe gâteau, on page 340.

Any leftover *chicken, mushrooms,* and *onions* can be arranged in a buttered baking dish along with leftover *sauce* and perhaps a sprinkling of cheese from your frozen and grated hoard; bake in a hot oven until bubbling and nicely browned on top, and you have another splendid meal. Or put them into a chicken pot pie, as suggested at the end of the recipe. Ground *chicken* can be added to a stuffing for braised cabbage or stuffed vegetables, or can go into the makings of a meat loaf. Salads and sandwiches are obvious choices for *chicken* — great club sandwich possibilities are there, and it's always handy to have a little chicken to garnish a chef's salad or as an inspiration to make the handsome Cobb Salad on page 326. The *mushrooms* and *onions* can be reheated in leftover sauce and served another day; or put them into a chicken soup.

There is never any problem with leftover *rice,* since it can be reheated (see page 467), or turned into a salad, or stirred into a soup.

Simmer all *chicken bones* and scraps in the cooking broth to enrich that already delicious brew, and plan to use it for chicken soup or as a general sauce base.

That good old hen is a good provider!

There will be leftovers of *cake,* thank heavens, because it is so rich you won't be serving it in great hunks. You might make more fudge cake, and then you could trim the leftover dessert cleverly, press decorative pieces of fudge cake onto it, and perhaps pass it off as a brand new *bombe.* It's worth a try, anyway, because it keeps nicely for several days in the refrigerator, or can be frozen.

Postscript: *De gustibus nil nisi bonum*

I translate this as: somebody likes it, so don't knock it.

Now and then our team throws itself a party, complete with spouses, paramours, and other affiliates; but the other night we threw a plebiscite. We wanted to hear the voice of the people, on the merits of our three competing recipes for a triple chocolate bombe. After butterflied lamb, scalloped potatoes, and a great vat of vegetable salad, the three candidates, each bearing a numbered banner, were paraded forth and tasted. Comment sheets were pinned up on which everyone wrote his or her opinion of each cake.

The cake that appears in this chapter was by far the popular choice. "Excellent," wrote Dick Graff, a visiting vintner, "good contrast in texture (brownielike cake), luscious chocolate." "Clearly, the only serious choice," proclaimed Russ Morash — unswayed, I feel sure, by the fact that his daughter Kate had developed the fudge cake recipe. Nevertheless, the two other candidates won a share of support, though it was of an ambiguous kind. The same cake Herb Pratt called "nice and wet" Dick Graff perceived as "light and spongy"; and the third seemed to me "a bit soft," though a noncook found it "robust," and added, "Grand bouquet, elegant nose." Wine-taster's terms, but the word "nose" does apply in a way. The nose anyone follows in designing a recipe is, ultimately, his own; it has to be. Follow a recipe precisely the first time is my advice. But then, if you don't quite like it, don't lump it. Change it, and suit yourself.

A French classic, with a great California salad

Soup for Supper

It could be said that the onion has done a lot more for France than Napoleon, and deserves its own Arch of Triumph, whose design might include bas-reliefs of grateful peasants holding soup tureens over their hearts, in salute to onion soup and the comfort and sense of luxury that it has brought over centuries to France's thrifty farmers. All it takes is onions from the kitchen garden, broth from Sunday's boiled dinner (maybe the week's only meat, so its juices provide a welcome memory), cheese and wine very likely made at home, and yesterday's hard bread: not a crumb wasted, and its staleness treated as a virtue. So far as I know, the French haven't built it a monument, but they do honor their national dish by calling it *soupe à l'oignon,* in the singular not the plural; otherwise they say *soupe aux pois, aux carottes,* etc.: not onions, in other words, but The Onion.

No other soup can compare in flavor with the rich, mahogany-colored brew of slowly caramelized onions simmered in a meaty broth; and it can be expanded into a hearty one-dish meal, La Gratinée Lyonnaise, by alternately layering the tureen with toasted rounds of French bread and cheese, right up to the top, pouring in soup to fill every cranny, and slowly baking to produce a fragrant onion and cheese pudding. This is described farther on as a variation of the classic recipe, along with other ways of using this excellent soup.

It's excellent at any time of day, too. In our youthful Paris years, we had it to top off a night on the town at one of the all-night cafés in Les Halles, the central market that no longer exists. At the same time, onion soup was eaten for breakfast by the farmers who'd just carted in their produce and by the *titis parisiens* and the *forts des Halles*, the blue-smocked workmen and porters, who took their soup with a *p'tit coup* of red wine and a *p'tit coup de fouet*, a whiplash of bitter coffee: guaranteed to grow hair on the chest—or depilate it, I suspect, if applied externally. On cold evenings nowadays when we come home in need of a quick restorative, we've even been known to heat up canned onion soup, pour a bit of wine into it, slice and toast some of the homemade French bread we frequently have on hand, and float it on the soup with plenty of grated cheese from the freezer. And it makes a fine lunch for unexpected guests: a meal in itself if you wind it up with a basket of crisp, chilled apples. We find both canned and dehydrated onion soup extremely good; homemade is just that much better, simply because it tastes homemade. (A warning, however: you don't gain anything by slicing and cooking your own onions if you then simmer them in canned broth—the result will taste as though all of it came out of a can.)

Homemade stock couldn't be easier. Plan to make it some day when you'll be at home, starting it after breakfast and letting it simmer practically unattended until dinnertime. Its presence in the freezer makes homemade onion soup an easy possibility when you're planning a company menu. For anything but a formal dinner, a hearty soup can certainly be the centerpiece of a meal, and you can't beat onion for popularity, especially when you dress it up with Cognac and top it with a beautiful gratin of mixed cheeses. Then, for more drama at the table, just before serving tweak up a corner of the puffy, bubbling, fragrant gratin and stir in egg yolks whisked with Port wine. It imparts a smooth texture, the flavor booms out like a gong, and there's something warm and hospitable about this final gesture. When our nieces and nephews were

little, we'd sometimes give them purses or wallets for Christmas, and Paul always slipped in a shiny dime before wrapping them; the feeling is a bit like that.

If it's an informal supper party, you might well prefer the statelier pace, and of course the variety, of a three-course menu, simple though it may be, with a pretty, light dessert and a fairly substantial salad. The one I am suggesting here was born in California, certainly the cradle of salads in this country. I am not, by the way, offering anything like the one I shall always remember at a ladies' luncheon (of non-Californians) some years ago; it was composed of chopped marshmallows and bottled mayonnaise molded with pineapple gelatin into the shape of a peeled banana and posed upright on one piece of pale iceberg lettuce far too small for the cleverest of diners to hide anything under. No. I am proposing a famous salad served for the first time at the Hollywood Brown Derby, not the original restaurant designed by Wilson Mizener in the shape of a hat on Wilshire Boulevard, but the Brown Derby at Hollywood and Vine.

It was invented there in 1936 by Robert Cobb, president of the restaurant group, who apparently improvised the dish from leftovers

The original Brown Derby Restaurant, Wilshire Boulevard, Los Angeles

in the refrigerator, just as any cook will serve a few savory scraps on lettuce and call it a chef's salad. But Cobb's leftovers included good Roquefort cheese, chicken, avocado, bacon, hard-boiled eggs, herbs, tomatoes, and a variety of salad greens; he diced them fine, the greens too, and tossed them all together. An epicure's inspiration. He was bragging about his invention one day when Syd Grauman came to the restaurant. Grauman wanted one, and he found it so good he told all his friends about Cobb's marvelous salad. Friends told friends, and so forth . . . And no wonder. Each mouthful rewards you with a whole spectrum of delicious flavors, and of textures ranging from rich and suave to downright crunchy.

You present Cobb Salad beautifully arranged in strips or segments, and then you have the fun of tossing it into confetti, a savage joy rather like jumbling up a completed jigsaw puzzle before passing it on to your little brother. A more sophisticated pleasure, if you enjoy tabletop cookery, is the concoction of Vesuvial Bananas in a chafing dish. It takes a good 5 minutes for the sauce to boil down to a syrup while the bananas cook through, and when I'm all alone on the stage or the TV screen, I have to have some trifle ready to fill the silence like "Life in California in the Golden Age of Cobb (or of Caesar, he of that other salad)" or even "Big Bananas I Have Known." But at home, you don't need talk or stunts. The bananas are spectacle enough, from the appetizing sizzles of their buttery beginning, through the expanding fragrances of their liquorous cooking, right on to the climactic fiery cloudlet of their final moment. Certainly, good points about this menu are its relative ease of preparation and its quite reasonable expense—take or leave a few dollops of wine and spirits along the way—and, except for a rapid change of plates between courses, you can be in the dining room with your guests the whole way through.

Preparations and Marketing

Recommended Equipment:

To serve the soup, you'll need either a 3-quart (3-L) ovenproof tureen, or else individual ovenproof bowls. For slicing onions, you can use (in order of expense and splendor): a sharp knife; an efficient small slicer, The Feemster, made by the M. E. Heuk Company, Cincinnati, Ohio 45223; a cabbage shredder often shown in country store catalogues; the chic and intricate *mandoline* manufactured in France by the Bron people (and maybe other companies); or a food processor.

To serve Cobb Salad, a wide bowl is desirable, so that you can present it, before tossing, with each colorful ingredient mounded separately on the greens.

Although you can do the Vesuvial Bananas in an electric skillet at the table, a chafing dish setup is far more attractive. You do not need the intense heat provided by the fluid-alcohol flame in our professional burner (page 328), but it must be strong enough to cook the orange syrup in a reasonable amount of time. In my numerous struggles with public flaming, I've found it perfectly satisfactory to take a can of Sterno and either remove the lid and use the can itself as a container, or scoop the material into a small metal bowl with a top diameter of about 4 inches (10 cm). What you need is a large burning surface that you can rig to fit your chafing dish contraption. I also find it a good idea to set the chafing dish apparatus on a tray to catch spills, hold utensils, etc.

Staples to Have on Hand:

Table salt
Optional: coarse or kosher salt
Peppercorns
Sugar
Imported bay leaves
Dried thyme
Whole cloves or allspice berries
Olive oil and/or fresh peanut oil
Flour
Eggs (3 to 5)
Unsalted butter (less than 2 sticks)
Garlic
Optional: Port or Madeira wine

Orange liqueur
White rum, dark Jamaica rum, or bourbon
    whiskey
Optional: Cognac

Specific Ingredients for This Menu:

Meaty soup bones (2 or more quarts, or 2 L;
    see recipe, plus suggestions for a boiled
    dinner in Manufacturing Note preceding
    recipe)
Boneless chicken breast halves (2)
Bacon (6 slices)

Roquefort or best-quality blue cheese (2 ounces
   or 60 g)
Firm Swiss cheese, of several kinds, if possible—
   such as Gruyère, Emmenthal, Fribourg,
   Sbrinz (9 ounces or 250 g)
Salad greens: 1 green crisp head iceberg lettuce;
   1 smallish head chicory; 1 smallish head
   romaine; 1 medium-to-large bunch
   watercress ▼
Parsley ▼
Shallots ▼, scallions, or chives
Celery (1 head)
Optional: 1 leek
Yellow onions (about 3½ pounds or 1½ kg)
Carrots (2 large)
Tomatoes (2; see recipe)
Avocado (1)
Lemons (2)
Oranges (2)
Bananas (6) ▼
An accompaniment for the bananas: fresh
   strawberries (2 pints or 900 g)
Dry white wine or dry white French vermouth
   (2½ cups or about ½ L)
Bread for French Onion Soup ▼

▶   **Remarks:**

Salad greens: surround with slightly dampened paper towels, and store in plastic bags
in the refrigerator. Wash watercress, shake or
spin fairly dry, wrap in paper towels, and
refrigerate in a plastic bag—cress is perishable and will keep only about 2 days before
beginning to turn yellow. *Parsley* is more
sturdy: prepare like watercress, but it will
keep several days longer. *Shallots:* shallots
will keep in a cool, dry place for a number
of weeks, but if you happen to have more
than you need, you can freeze them whole, in
a plastic bag or container. They soften up as
soon as they thaw, so peel and mince them
almost as soon as you take them from the

freezer; they are then fine for cooking,
though too limp for salads. *Bananas:* for
cooking, they should be just barely ripe—all
yellow, but without any soft spots. Store at
room temperature. *Bread for French onion
soup:* you want white bread with body here;
if it is soft and fluffy and squashy to begin
with, it will become a miserable disintegration of white slime when baked in the soup.
Ideally you would use old-fashioned French
bread, from the regular long loaf cut into
crosswise slices less than ½ inch (1 cm)
thick. But if your French bread is soft and
limp, you will be better off with a firm loaf
of nonsweet sliced sandwich bread, cut into
rounds about 3 inches (7 to 8 cm) in diameter.
If you have any doubts, toast a slice of bread
and simmer it to see what happens. Your
own homemade French bread would, of
course, be ideal.

The right kind—and the wrong kind—of French bread

French Onion Soup

Entirely homemade onion soup base

Manufacturing Note:

As long as you are making a beef stock, you may also want to include the ingredients for a boiled dinner, such as a piece of stewing beef or pork, or a chicken, or a fresh beef tongue. Tie it up and attach a long end of its string to the handle of your kettle; then you can pull it up for checking, and remove it when it's done. If you want vegetables with this boiled dinner, tie them in a piece of washed cheesecloth, and they are easy to remove, too, when their time is up.

**Plain Brown Beef Stock —
Fonds Brun Simple:**

*For about 2 quarts or 2 L,
serving 4 to 6 people*

For the Beef Stock:

2 or more quarts (2 L) sawed beef bones, including knuckles and some meaty scraps attached; plus veal and poultry bones, raw and/or cooked

2 large carrots, scrubbed and roughly sliced

3 large onions, peeled and roughly chopped

Sufficient cold water to cover all ingredients

1 large leek, washed (optional)

3 celery ribs with leaves, washed

1 Tb coarse or kosher salt (or table salt)

1 large herb bouquet tied in washed cheese-cloth (8 parsley sprigs, 1 large imported bay leaf, 1 tsp dried thyme, 4 whole cloves or allspice berries, 3 large cloves garlic, unpeeled)

Spread the bones and meat scraps (except for poultry) and the carrots and onions in a roomy enough roasting pan; set in the upper middle level of a 450°F/230°C oven and roast for 40 or more minutes, turning and basting ingredients several times with accumulated fat until nicely browned. Transfer to a large soup kettle, leaving fat in pan. Discard fat and de-glaze pan—pour in a cup or so (¼ L) of water and set over heat, scraping coagulated roasting juices into the liquid. Pour into the kettle, and add enough cold water to cover ingredients by 2 inches (5 cm). Bring to the simmer, skim off gray scum that will rise to the surface for several minutes, then add rest of ingredients. Cover partially and simmer slowly 4 to 5 hours at least, adding more water if needed to cover ingredients. Strain into a large bowl, chill, peel coagulated fat off surface, and your stock is finished.

Before and after—browned bones and vegetables at top

⏱ Stock may be refrigerated in a covered bowl, but needs boiling up every 2 or 3 days to prevent spoilage; or it may be frozen for several months. If your stock lacks savor, boil it down in a large kettle (after degreasing) to concentrate it.

Meat Glaze—Glace de Viande:

You can concentrate your stock even further, almost to the consistency of a bouillon cube, actually. Keep on boiling it down until the stock thickens into a syrup (be careful near the end since it burns easily); pour into a jar, and cover it. Meat glaze will keep for months in the refrigerator, ready at all times to enrich a soup or a sauce, or to become a bouillon. A real kitchen treasure to have on hand, and it doesn't take up much space, either.

For the Onion Soup:
3 Tb butter
1 Tb olive oil or cooking oil
6 cups (1½ L) quite thinly sliced yellow onions (about 1½ pounds or ¾ kg)
½ tsp sugar (which helps the onions to brown)
1 tsp salt

Six cups of onions cook down to less than one when really caramelized.

2 Tb flour
2 quarts (2 L) homemade stock, heated (the preceding recipe)
2 cups (½ L) dry white wine or dry white French vermouth
Salt and pepper as needed

Melt the butter with the oil in a heavy-bottomed 4-quart (3¾-L) pan; stir in the sliced onions. Cover the pan and cook slowly for 15 to 20 minutes (or cook them in a 350°F/180°C oven), stirring up occasionally, until onions are tender and translucent. Raise heat to moderately high, stir in the sugar and salt, and cook 20 to 30 minutes more, stirring frequently, until onions have turned a fine deep caramel brown.

Lower heat to moderate, blend in the flour, and cook, stirring, for 2 to 3 minutes. Remove from heat, and blend in 2 ladlefuls hot stock. Stir in the rest, and the wine. Season lightly to taste, bring to the boil, then simmer slowly, partially covered, for 30 minutes. Carefully correct seasoning.

⏱ May be cooked several days in advance. When cold, cover and refrigerate, or freeze.

Serve as is, with a bowl of grated cheese and toasted French bread, or make onion soup gratinée as follows:

French Onion Soup Gratinée — The Classic Version

There are a number of opinions on the very best recipe for gratinéed onion soup. My French colleague Simca has her excellent version in Volume I of *Mastering*, and I did it also for *The French Chef* black-and-white TV series: it has a little grated raw onion and some slivers of cheese in the soup before its toast and cheese topping go on, and it finishes with a *de luxe* enrichment of Worcestershire sauce, egg yolk, and Cognac that is slipped under the brown crust just before serving. A trip through other French sources confirms a spirited egg-yolk finish, and also reveals conflicting information on what can cut down on the length of the cheese strings that drip from the spoon as you consume your soup—although certainly to some enthusiasts those dangling ropes of cheese are a large part of the soup's authentic character.

Stringy cheese solutions
1) Rather than grating the cheese, either cut it into small dice or very thin slices. 2) Use two or three kinds of cheese rather than just one. 3) Beat egg yolks into the soup before gratinéing, and bake it in a pan of boiling water. 4) White wine can de-string cheese—as suggested by Jim Beard and confirmed by the French—and it does indeed work for a cheese sauce. Well, I've tried all but method number 3, and my soup-cheese does string somewhat, though not excessively. However, I think one should select pieces of cheese that are on the rather hard and dry side, and I do use a good bit of spirits.

For a 3-quart or 3-L ovenproof tureen or casserole, serving 4 to 6 people

A loaf or 2 of firm, full-textured French bread
2 Tb or more butter
3 ounces (85 g) firm Swiss cheese in a piece, cut into very thin slices
Freshly ground pepper—2 to 3 turns of the pepper mill
2 quarts (2 L) or so simmering onion soup
4 to 5 Tb Cognac (optional)
1 ¼ cups (3 dL) lightly packed, coarsely grated mixed Swiss cheeses
2 egg yolks, beaten with 4 to 5 Tb Port or Madeira wine (optional)

Equipment:

An ovenproof tureen or casserole; a serving spoon and fork for the crust; a ladle for serving the soup; and a platter on which to set the tureen. A small decorative pitcher for the optional egg yolk and wine mixture

Toasted French Bread Rounds:

Preheat oven to 425°F/220°C. Cut bread into slices less than ½ inch (1 cm) thick, place in one layer on a baking sheet or sheets, and dry out in upper third (or middle and upper third) level of oven, watching and turning frequently until bread is a fairly even lightly toasted brown. (You may want extra bread rounds to pass with the soup; do them now, too, and/or do extras, since they freeze nicely for several weeks.)

Filling and baking the tureen
About 45 minutes

Preheat oven to 425°F/220°C. Smear a tablespoon of butter in bottom of tureen and arrange over it a closely packed layer of toasted bread; spread over bread layer the sliced cheese, grind on pepper, ladle in the boiling soup, and pour in the optional Cognac. Float a closely packed layer of toast on the top of the soup, and spread over it the grated cheese with a few grinds of pepper; sprinkle over that a tablespoon or 2 melted butter. Set tureen in middle level of oven and bake for about half an hour, or until soup is bubbling hot and top has browned nicely.

🕐 Plan to serve the soup fairly soon, for fear the crust might sink down into it. Until then, keep it hot, almost at the simmer.

At the table, and just before serving, lift a side of the crust with a serving fork, pour into the soup the optional egg yolk–wine mixture, and stir gently under crust with your ladle. Serve, giving each guest some of the top crust along with the soup.

Individual Servings of French Onion Soup Gratinée:

Use the same system as that outlined above, but make individual servings in ovenproof earthenware bowls set on a sturdy baking sheet; they will take about 20 minutes in the oven.

Adding spirited finish to onion soup at the table

Preparing an individual bowl of onion soup

**Thick French Onion Soup—
La Gratinée Lyonnaise:**

Proceed in exactly the same way as in the
master recipe, but fill the tureen with layer
upon layer of toasted bread rounds, each
topped with a mixture of grated cheese and
sliced cheese. (You will need probably 1½
times more cheese and soup than the
amounts specified.) Pour the soup in to cover
the bread and bake for 30 minutes or until
soup is absorbed and cheese has browned on
top; then pour in more soup and bake another 5 to 10 minutes. Stir in the optional
egg yolk and wine mixture at the table. The
bread and soup will have combined and
transformed themselves into a richly flavored,
soft, melting cheese-and-onion dumpling in
your bowl—a very special Old World dish.

Cobb Salad

Ingredients for 6 to 8 people

½ head firm fine green iceberg lettuce

1 small head chicory (frizzy lettuce)

½ medium head romaine

1 medium bunch watercress—to make a cup
or so (¼ L) of leaves and tender stems

2 poached chicken breast halves (see
directions at end of this recipe)

Salt

Freshly ground pepper

1 lemon

Olive oil or fresh peanut oil

6 slices crisply cooked bacon

3 hard-boiled eggs

2 Tb minced fresh chives (or the white part
and some of the tender green of scallions, or
a mixture of shallots and fresh parsley)

2 ounces (60 g) real Roquefort cheese or
best-quality blue cheese

2 medium-sized ripe red firm tomatoes (out
of season, mix tomatoes with drained,
seeded, Italian plum tomatoes and/or canned
red pimiento)

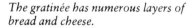
*The gratinée has numerous layers of
bread and cheese.*

About 1 cup (¼ L) plain vinaigrette dressing
(page 468)

1 fine ripe firm avocado

🕐 **Preliminaries**
(To be done several hours in advance if necessary)

Separate the leaves of the salad greens, discard tough or wilted parts, wash leaves and spin dry; wrap loosely and refrigerate in a clean towel. Pull off leaves and tender stems from watercress (discard tough bits); wash, wrap in a damp paper towel, and refrigerate in a plastic bag. Cut the chicken breasts into fine dice (by first cutting into thin slices, the slices into strips, and the strips laid lengthwise then cut crosswise into dice, as illustrated); toss in a small bowl with a sprinkling of salt and pepper, a few drops of lemon juice and of oil; cover and refrigerate. Mince the cooked bacon and set aside in another bowl; chop or sieve the eggs (or use the 3-way egg-slicer method illustrated), and toss in another small bowl with a sprinkling of salt and pepper. Mince the chives or scallions fine, and put them in the bowl with the eggs, and do the same with the Roquefort or blue cheese (dicing in the same fashion as

you did either the chicken or the eggs; you should have about ½ cup or 1 dL diced). Drop the tomatoes for exactly 10 seconds in boiling water, and set aside (to loosen their skins for later peeling). Prepare the vinaigrette.

🕐 **Half an hour or so before serving**
(Items that wilt if done too soon)

Choose a fine big salad bowl. With a large, very sharp knife, cut the salad greens into very fine dice, 3/16 inch or ½ cm. The easiest method, I think, is to lay 3 or 4 leaves flat, cut them into fine julienne shreds, pile the shreds together lengthwise, and cut across them—as for the chicken. The object here is to make clean nonbruising cuts. Place the greens in the bowl, mince the watercress also, and add to the greens. Peel, seed, and juice the tomatoes (cut out stem, peel, halve horizontally—not through stem— squeeze each half gently and poke out seeds, as illustrated); dice fine, and set aside on your chopping board with a sprinkling of salt and pepper. Halve the avocado (as illustrated); peel and dice it, and scoop into a sieve, then swish in a bowl of cold water for a moment and drain (water bath helps prevent avocado from discoloring); turn into a small bowl and

Chicken breasts are first cut into strips, then diced.

Egg slicer makes HB eggs easy to dice.

Blanching has loosened the tomato skin, for peeling.

A gentle squeeze ejects tomato seeds and juice.

Open the cut avocado with a twist of the wrist.

fold with a sprinkling of salt and a few drops of lemon juice and of oil.

🕐   **Just before serving**

Beat up the vinaigrette and toss about ⅓ of it with the minced greens, taste for seasoning, adding a little more dressing, salt, and pepper, etc., if necessary; arrange greens in a shallow mound. Arrange the rest of the ingredients attractively over the greens. Present at once to the table for general admiration, then toss the salad and serve it forth.

Note: If you wish to arrange the salad somewhat in advance, do not season the various ingredients, or they will lose their freshness; arrange the salad, cover with plastic and refrigerate, then toss with the dressing at the table.

Variations:

Arrange the salad in individual bowls, and each guest may then toss his own—or not— as he desires. You may substitute fresh mushrooms for chicken, or shrimp, crab, ham, or lobster; capers are also permitted when accompanying anchovies.

Poached Chicken Breasts:

Lay boned chicken breast halves in a lightly buttered saucepan just large enough to hold them in one layer. Pour in ½ cup (1 dL) dry white wine or dry white French vermouth, enough cold water just to cover the breasts, and add a bay leaf, a finely minced shallot or scallion, 3 parsley sprigs, 4 peppercorns, and ½ teaspoon of salt. Bring just to the simmer, cover, and cook at the barest simmer for 8 to 10 minutes, until the meat is springy to the touch. Let cool for 30 minutes in the cooking broth, then drain, let cool, wrap, and refrigerate. (Save cooking broth and add to your store of chicken stock, or use in soups and sauces.)

Vesuvial Bananas

Bananas simmered in orange butter and flamed in rum

Almost everyone loves bananas, and they make a most delectable flaming dessert when you want a chafing dish finish. Desserts done at the table demand the drama of flaming and, besides, that burning evaporates the alcohol— what we want with our bananas is the flavor of those spirits, not the kick! Although you may serve them just as they are, I think you'll find they most definitely need something to dress them up, such as a mound of sherbet or ice cream that they might surround, or a sprinkling of cinnamon or shaved chocolate. My solution is strawberries sliced and spread over

Professionals use this alcohol-fueled burner for tabletop cookery.

the banana midriffs and placed whole at their either ends, then a basting of all elements with the buttery cooking juices.

For 6 people

Note: Because of timing restrictions on our television program, I did only 4 bananas, but our dinner here is for 6 people and so is the following recipe.

2 oranges
½ cup (1 dL) sugar
¾ stick (3 ounces or 85 g) unsalted butter
5 Tb orange liqueur
5 Tb white rum, dark Jamaica rum, or bourbon whiskey
1 lemon
1 pint (½ L) fresh strawberries, halved or quartered lengthwise
1 pint (½ L) fresh strawberries, whole, stems removed
6 bananas

Equipment:
A chafing dish large enough to hold the bananas easily; a burner with a reasonably strong heat source (or an electric frying pan); a tray to set the cooking apparatus upon; a long-handled spoon and fork for the bananas; a table fork for the lemon; a platter and/or dessert plates

Preliminaries in the kitchen

Arrange the dining room accessories on the tray. Just before dinner, so it will not lose its freshness, grate the peel of 1 orange onto a decorative plate, with the sugar and butter. Squeeze the juice out of 1 ½ of the oranges and pour into a pitcher; refrigerate, along with the butter and sugar plate. Set out the bottles of orange liqueur and rum, and halve the lemon. Ready your strawberries and place in decorative bowls. Peel the bananas, removing any strings clinging to their flesh, only the moment before cooking, either in the kitchen or at the table.

The cooking

Set the chafing dish on the lighted burner and add the butter. Let it bubble up, then stir in the sugar and grated orange peel. Pour in the orange juice and, with drama, pierce the cut side of a lemon half with your fork as you squeeze in the juice from on high, repeating with the second lemon half. Pour in the orange liqueur—from the bottle, if you can judge the amount of approximately 5 tablespoons. Let the liquid bubble up, then arrange the bananas in the pan. Baste them with the liquid almost continuously as it cooks and bubbles and gradually turns into a thick syrup, almost a caramel. This will take some 5 minutes of basting and animated conversation. However, do not cook the bananas too much or they will be too limp to transfer from chafing dish to platter or plates.

The flaming finish, and serving

As soon as you conclude the bananas are done and the syrup is thick enough, pour in the rum or whiskey, let bubble up, then either tip the pan into the flame, or ignite with a lighted match. Spoon the flaming liquid over the bananas until the flames subside. Arrange them either on a platter and decorate with strawberries as illustrated, or serve onto individual plates. Baste bananas and strawberries with the syrup.

Baste bananas frequently with the syrup as they cook.

◑ Timing

Long before you ever thought of this party, you might—just as a matter of good kitchen routine—have stocked your freezer with home-grated cheese, hard-toasted French bread rounds, and good brown stock. Perhaps you've been fooling the family dog all along by freezing any leftover bones, though you'd want to add a couple of good fresh meaty ones before boiling up your hoard. It does take from 6 to 7 hours to make a meat stock, but you can set it to boil whenever you wish, and stop and start it at will. Homemade onion soup is never a last-minute decision, then, but since so much can be prepared beforehand, including the onions (several days), it's not a last-minute job either.

The day before you serve Cobb Salad, you can poach and chill the chicken breasts, then dice them, as well as cooking and dicing the bacon and the eggs. You can also wash, dry, and refrigerate the greens.

In the late afternoon, organize your chafing dish tray, but keep the butter, orange peel, and juice refrigerated. Peel the tomatoes, make the vinaigrette, and prepare the cheese for the onion soup.

An hour before your guests come, prepare the tureen or bowls for the onion soup, except for the topping. Finish the topping and slip the tureen into the oven 45 minutes (20 to 25 for individual bowls) before supper. Then dice your salad greens, tomatoes, and avocado.

Just before dinner, arrange the salad bowl and prepare the egg yolk and wine mixture for the tabletop finish of your gratin. Peel bananas just before you cook them.

Menu Variations

The recipe gives you three ways of serving *onion soup*, whether homemade or canned; and some other hearty soups are mentioned in the section on Menu Alternatives.

Cobb Salad, if you beef it up as suggested in the recipe, can be almost a supper in itself—a lunch, certainly. Other sturdy salads might well follow onion soup: a beef salad *à la parisienne;* a turkey salad; chicken salad; fish and shellfish salads; lentil and dried bean salads; *salade niçoise* with tuna, oil-cured black olives, egg, and anchovy. Other composed salads, like a *salade à la d'Argenson* of rice and beets, or a vegetable salad of the season, might need some additions, like fish, meat, poultry, cheese, or chick-peas. You might arrange a pretty Greek salad, with zucchini and porphyry-purple Calamata olives snowed with feta cheese. If you enjoy the speckled, sparkly look of Cobb Salad but want something lighter, try dicing colorful raw vegetables for an old-fashioned Calico Salad. An amusing variant, nice with cold ham, is blanched chopped carrots with blanched shredded red cabbage, cooled and marinated in a sweet-sour vinaigrette or sour cream dressing.

For other chafing dish *desserts*, there are always sweet omelets, and crêpes Suzette, and ice cream bathed in hot blazing fruits or flaming sauces, such as the mincemeat in rum on page 344.

Leftovers

French *onion soup* has as many cheerful consequences as saying "I do." That meat you might have removed when just tender from your possibly meaty soup bones could in itself become a small boiled dinner, or could make a fine hash. But beef stock aside, you can do a lot with leftover onion soup. You can add cooked rice or potatoes to it, with some cream, and process the whole lot for a soubise soup. If you strain out the onions, you have a delicious, freezable broth to add to other soups, or to sauces or stews (if not already oniony); and you might even clarify it and reduce it to make an aspic coating for the likes of chicken livers or duck. The beef broth, if you made extra, is of course a kitchen fundamental, as acknowledged in the French term *fonds de cuisine.* The toast rounds can be frozen or refrozen, as can the grated cheese; and the cooked cheese topping can be puréed, to be added as thickening to the same soup, or to another soup another day.

You can't keep a finished, tossed *Cobb Salad,* but you could simmer its remains in those of an onion soup for a sort of "Robert Cobb minestrone." If you diced but did not dress more ingredients than you needed after all, they can be put to excellent use. The lettuce and greens can be tossed into a *potage santé* or a vegetable broth (the French heal-all for a cold or an upset stomach). You dice a turnip, an onion, two carrots, a large potato, and very little parsley, add lettuce if you have it, and simmer in water for 20 minutes, then strain. It's pallid but pleasant, and it does stay down. Extra avocado can be run through the processor with a scallion or small onion, lemon juice, salt and red pepper to taste, and a little cream cheese, if you like, for thickening; this gives you a version of guacamole, or try the avocado *brandade* spread on page 422. It also stuffs cherry tomatoes, as does a mixture of minced hard-boiled egg, bacon, and chives, bound with mayonnaise. That same mixture, without the mayonnaise but with browned buttery crumbs, makes a nice garnish for cooked broccoli or spinach. Extra diced tomatoes can be simmered briefly in oil or butter and herbs for a delicious sauce.

If you have extra bananas and don't want to take them straight, you could process them with cream, lemon, rum, and sugar, then chill for a mousse or freeze for a sort of ice cream. Or use them in a fruit cup or, if they've ripened a bit, make banana bread. Finally, mine eyes have actually seen sandwiches of peanut butter and bananas—but this is more a dare than a suggestion!

Postscript: Una furtiva lagrima

Often before the piano, as French chefs call their stoves, I shed a furtive tear—not because I'm lovelorn like the poor tenor in *L'Elisir d'Amore,* but because I have onions to cut. So I took up the topic in my column in *McCall's* magazine, hoping my friendly correspondents would have some helpful ideas. I've learned a lot over the years from their letters. This time I got no fewer than 19 suggestions, every one guaranteed surefire. Space prevents my quoting them all, but here are a few.

Hold your breath while slicing, so that you don't breathe in the vapors. Slice by candlelight, and the vapors will be burned off by the flame. Hold a match between your teeth, flint end sticking out. Stand with a fan behind you and an open window in front of you. Keep your mouth open. Keep your mouth closed.

I've tried them all, to not much effect; but onions are worth a tear or two and, besides, one of these days I'll make my way to a sporting-goods store, to equip myself for a final experiment. One writer says she just puts on a diving mask or swimming goggles. "It looks funny," she says, "but it really works." I bet it does.

A delightful meal for epicures of almost any dietary persuasion

A Vegetarian Caper

Menu
For 6 people

Spaghetti Squash Tossed with Eggplant Persillade

Gâteau of Crêpes—Layered with vegetables and cheese

Mixed Green Salad
Hot French Bread

Ice Cream and a Rum and Meatless Mincemeat Sauce

Suggested wines:
A light red wine like a Bordeaux, Beaujolais, or merlot; or a rosé; or a dry riesling or Chablis

"That was *so* good!" a friend exclaimed the other day. "Maybe I'll change my ways, too!" It took me a minute to catch on: she thought Paul and I had become vegetarians because we'd just served a dinner without meat, fish, or fowl. (And why not? There's no law . . .) No, we're not about to change our ways, which are omnivorous; but our pace, certainly. Any time. And this was one of those mild late-winter days when melting snow trills in the gutters and you hear birds and smell the earth again. Suddenly we craved light food and fresh flavors, and this menu hit the spot.

We serve it to carnivores, but it was, I admit, designed originally for vegetarian friends who happen to be of the moderate, or ovo-lacto, persuasion, meaning that they use eggs and milk and cheese. On the whole, I think the soft full flavors of dairy items are the ideal enrichment for good fresh produce; indeed, this sort of cooking is a stimulus to me. I I would, though, find it a bit dull to work for long within the restrictions set by purist vegetarians.

Marcella Hazan, that queen of Italian cookery, presented me with my first spaghetti squash a few years ago, and it turns out that they are easily grown almost everywhere. We're seeing more and more of them in the markets, and a fine thing that is. You steam your great golden whopper whole, halve it and seed it, and then, heaven knows why, the flesh turns into spaghetti right under the spoon as you scoop it onto the platter: fine, long, bright gold strands with a crunchy juicy texture. Like spaghetti, its flavor is bland so that it takes beautifully to sauces and garnishes: all the exuberance of pasta without the concomitant calories! For this menu, and a hearty main dish to come, we use eggplant tossed with parsley and garlic (in itself a good dish); in the recipe I've suggested a nice variant as well, using sesame seeds. (If this meal weren't so strong in protein—I calculate that it affords one almost a full day's supply—sesame seeds would be a good way to boost it. Like mushrooms, they're prized by vegetarians for this reason. I like them simply because they are delicious.)

A stratum of practicality underlies the charm and the festive air of concerned hosts, and the same could be said of our main dish. Not only can it be largely prepared in advance,

but it's good hot or cold, and is so compact and easily served that we often take it along (in its mold, of course) on fork picnics. You can use any combination of vegetables to fill the crêpe-walled compartments. As for crêpes themselves, they're one of the most versatile elements in cookery, one of the first things a beginning cook should master. Only their name poses a problem.

For the tomato sauce recipe, don't look in this chapter but in the Q & A section in the back of this book, where I've grouped a few basics. This is a sauce I use to add piquant flavor and brilliant color to all kinds of dishes: it has accompanied a boiled dinner, lasagne, and a baked fish with equal success, which gives you an idea of its versatility; you might also like to try it with an omelet sometime, or with a soufflé. The gâteau doesn't need a sauce, having plenty of flavor on its own, but enhancement is the name of the game in cooking an all-veg meal, and I like the look of the stratified slice in a sparkling red puddle. (In general, I prefer the old-fashioned custom of saucing around, not over, food.)

One recipe I am sorry *not* to supply here is one for homemade French bread. I've given it twice before, in *Mastering II* and in *J.C.'s Kitchen,* and it just takes too much space. It's not that a long recipe means a long job; with practice, most cooks find it takes about 15 minutes' working time per batch. The quality is seraphic, and I hope you'll want to try it. As for green salad, look in Q & A again for a basic vinaigrette dressing, vary it to your taste, and choose the freshest greens in the grocery.

Marvelously inquisitive and resourceful, the really good cooks among my vegetarian friends have steered me toward many good things to eat. I have vast respect for their imagination and care in cooking, and for the way they seek out the ultimate in fresh, exquisite produce. And for their realism and, well, sense of proportion. In America we still eat needless, indeed preposterous, quantities of animal protein, but I think the time is coming when we'll have to join with the rest of the world.

Preparations and Marketing

Recommended Equipment:
If you don't have a big kettle or covered roaster, and a steaming rack, you can bake the spaghetti squash in the oven.

The gâteau recipe precisely fills a 2-quart (2-L) dish. I use the French charlotte mold 3½ inches (9 cm) deep, the one I like for soufflés, since it produces a dramatically tall Hadrian's Tomb–type cylinder; but any straight-sided, deep, ovenproof dish will do. When it's done, the gâteau will let you know by puffing up and becoming divinely fragrant, but you can make a more precise test by using an instant, microwave type of thermometer, a gadget you'll use for meats, poultry, and all kinds of other dishes as well.

For crêpes, while it's nice to have the classic French pan, a shallow iron one about 6 inches (15 cm) in diameter, with an angled handle for easy flipping will do; I also like an American-made one of thick cast aluminum with a nonstick lining. Because crêpe batter is very runny, you must have a pan the size you want your crêpe to be. That rules out pancake griddles and big frying pans, but not those amusing patented devices that make crêpes upside down or right side up.

Staples to Have on Hand:

Salt
Peppercorns
Nutmeg
Optional: fresh or fragrant dried dill weed
Optional: saffron threads
Optional: dried orange peel
Imported bay leaves
Italian or Provençal herb mixture
Olive oil ▼
Butter
Optional: fresh sesame or peanut oil
Flour: Wondra or instant-blending type
    preferred ▼
Milk
Optional: heavy cream (1 cup or ¼ L)
Garlic
Shallots or scallions
Lemons (1)
Optional: canned Italian plum tomatoes
Dark Jamaica rum or bourbon whiskey

Specific Ingredients for This Menu:

Swiss cheese (½ pound or 225 g)
Cream cheese (½ pound or 225 g) ▼
Eggs (9 "large")
Optional: Parmesan cheese (½ pound or 225 g)
Salad greens
Parsley
Onions (2 medium)
Broccoli (1 bunch) ▼
Carrots (1 pound or 450 g) ▼
Eggplant (1 large) ▼
Spaghetti squash (1 large) ▼
Tomatoes (9 or 10 large) ▼
Mushrooms (1 pound or 450 g) ▼
French bread
Vanilla ice cream (1½ quarts or 1½ L)
Meatless mincemeat (1 jar)

▶ **Remarks:**

Staples to have on hand

Olive oil: if you want the best quality and are willing to pay for it, see that it is labeled "virgin olive oil," which means that this was the first pressing of the olives and that they were pressed cold. Olives are pressed not once but several times, and in later batches, in order to extract more oil, they are usually warmed. Be sure in any case that the label reads "pure olive oil," since otherwise it may contain adulterants. On keeping olive oil, there are many and fervent controversies—whether to decant it, whether it should breathe, etc.—but I have never had any trouble keeping an opened half-gallon of olive oil, covered and stored in a cool dark closet. *Flour:* Wondra, or other instant-blending type, is good for crêpes, since it mixes smoothly and almost instantly in cold liquid, and you don't have to let your batter rest an hour or two before using it, as you would with regular flour.

Specific ingredients for this menu
(With special thanks to *Crockett's Victory Garden* and to *Wyman's Gardening Encyclopedia*)

Cream cheese: best of all is the fresh kind, without gluey additives and preservatives, but it will keep only 3 days or so in the refrigerator. *Broccoli:* it's passé if the florets have begun to open. Ideal stalk length, below where the stem branches, is from 4 to 6 inches (10 to 15 cm); if the base of the stem is hollow, cut that part off, since it will be tough. *Carrots:* buy firm crisp carrots, refrigerate them in a plastic bag, and use them soon. *Eggplant:* take pains; you can turn people off this lovely vegetable for life by serving a bad one. Buy shiny, firm, taut-skinned ones, use them within 2 or 3 days, and do not keep them too cold. Soft spots and the slightest sign of wrinkle or shrivel or flab are all bad news. Although they are picked when the seeds are still sparse, soft, and immature, eggplants vary greatly in shape and in size—from 6-inch (15-cm) midgets to foot-long monsters. Most of those in your market will be the deep purple variety, but ivory, green, and mottled purple types exist and are similarly cooked. *Mushrooms:* the cultivated ones are best when the caps are curled tight to the stem, so that you can't see the gills. Refrigerate in a plastic bag and use as soon as you can, before they darken or soften. For field mushrooms, pick none you can't positively identify as edible. Dr. Wyman recommends Alexander H. Smith's *The Mushroom Hunter's Field Guide* (Ann Arbor: University of Michigan Press, revised edition, 1969). A standard field guide used by many mycologists I know is *One Thousand American Fungi,* by Charles McIlvaine and Robert K. Macadam (New York: Dover Publications, 1973), and one of my favorites for recipes is Jane Grigson's *The Mushroom Feast* (New York: Alfred A. Knopf, 1975). *Spaghetti squash:* use the fingernail test to be sure the rind is soft; if hard, the squash was picked when too mature.

Eggplant and spaghetti squash

Here's a puzzle: the grower I consulted says its botanical name is *Cucurbita ficifolia,* and that it is a gourd of tropical origin. All the ones I've seen are bright gold, but a delightful old book by Cora, Rose, and Bob Brown, *The Vegetable Cook Book: From Trowel to Table* (Philadelphia: J. B. Lippincott, 1939), says it's cream-white like a honeydew melon. You can tell at a glance that it's a cucurbit, like cucumbers, squash, gourds, pumpkins, and some melons; but the great horticultural authority Dr. Wyman gives the name *C. ficifolia* to a white, *in*edible fruit (or vegetable) grown in the tropics and commonly called Malabar gourd. His encyclopedia doesn't describe anything like my big beauty. *Tomatoes:* the U.S. Department of Agriculture says so, county agents say so, any farmer who knows a hoe from a harrow says so, and I'm so sick of saying so that now I sing it instead. In my sleep. But the markets still plod along with their thumbs in their ears and their minds in neutral. What do we tomato lovers have to do, for pity's sake? Well, again: in the summertime, you can buy locally grown tomatoes that are ripe or that will ripen. However, no tomato at any season will ever ripen if it has been kept at a temperature of less than 40 °F/4.5 °C for any length of time; it may eventually turn red, but its flavor-developing facilities have been killed. In fact, any temperature less than 50 °F/10 °C is bad news for the tomato. Even a picked green tomato that is old enough to have developed the normal amount of seeds and jelly in its interstices will ripen in a few days at room temperature—in a week or so if kept around 60 °F/16 °C—if it was never abused by a low temperature. Tomatoes should never ever be refrigerated unless they are so ripe they will spoil! Any market that stores an unripened tomato in a refrigerated case has no sense of decency, no respect for tomatoes, and certainly no knowledge at all about them —or concern for us, the tomato-buying public. (End of tomato discussion—for this book, anyway.)

Spaghetti Squash Tossed with Eggplant Persillade

Serving 6 people

1 spaghetti squash about 10 by 7 inches (25 by 18 cm)

1 eggplant about 9 by 5 inches (23 by 13 cm)

Salt and pepper

4 or more Tb olive oil

2 or more large cloves garlic, minced

5 to 6 Tb minced fresh parsley (a small bunch)

2 to 3 Tb butter (optional)

1 cup (¼ L) freshly grated Parmesan cheese (optional)

Equipment:

A kettle large enough to hold the squash, and a vegetable steaming rack (or you may boil or bake the squash); 1 or 2 large frying pans, nonstick recommended; a long-handled spoon and fork for table tossing

Preliminary cooking of spaghetti squash
To cook the squash, you may bake it for 1½ hours in a 350 °F/180 °C oven, or boil it for 20 to 30 minutes, or steam it. I opt for steaming, as the easiest method. Place a rack or colander in the bottom of a large kettle or roaster with a tight-fitting lid, add 1½ inches (4 cm) water, lay in the squash, and bring to the boil. (Weight down the lid if necessary, so the steam can do its work.) Steam for 25 to 30 minutes, or just until the outside of the squash will cede to the pressure of your fingers. Cut the squash open lengthwise, and scrape out the thick yellowish threads and big seeds from the center, going crosswise with a big spoon—careful here or you will mix these nonspaghetti threads with the real meat of the squash. Then scrape down the squash lengthwise, and the meat will separate itself into strands.

🕐   May be cooked and scraped even a day in advance; cover the spaghetti and refrigerate.

The Eggplant Persillade—Eggplant with Garlic and Parsley:
Having chosen a fine, firm, shiny eggplant, cut off the green cap, and remove the skin with a vegetable peeler. Cut into ½-inch (1½-cm) slices, cut the slices into ½-inch strips, and the strips into ½-inch dice. Toss

in a colander with ½ teaspoon salt, and let drain for at least 20 minutes, then dry in a towel. Film a large frying pan (preferably a nonstick one) with ⅛ inch (½ cm) olive oil, and sauté the eggplant over moderately high heat for 4 to 5 minutes, tossing frequently, until tender—test by tasting a piece. Add the garlic and toss for a minute to cook it, then toss with the parsley only at the last moment. Incidently, this is a good dish all by itself, either hot or cold.

🕐   The eggplant may be cooked several hours in advance and set aside in a bowl, but do not add the parsley or reheat until the last moment.

Final assembly and serving

Heat several tablespoons of oil and/or butter in a large frying pan, add the spaghetti squash strands, tossing and turning over moderately high heat for several minutes to cook the squash a little more—or to your taste. Toss with salt and pepper, then turn out onto a hot platter. Spoon the hot eggplant in the center, and bring to the table. Then toss the spaghetti and eggplant together with, if you like, spoonfuls of cheese, and pass more cheese separately for those who wish it.

Variation:

Here is another squash and eggplant combination we like very much.

For the squash

Steam and shred the spaghetti squash as usual. Heat several tablespoons of oil in a large frying pan and swirl in 2 or 3 cloves of garlic, minced, cooking them gently for a minute or two. Then toss in the spaghetti squash and fold with the garlic, and salt and pepper to taste, adding more oil (or butter, if you wish) and cooking to the degree you prefer. Then toss with spoonfuls of Parmesan cheese, turn onto a hot platter, and garnish with the following eggplant. Serve the spaghetti squash with a piece or two of the eggplant—but do not toss them together.

Sesame baked eggplant

For one fine, firm, shiny eggplant about 9 inches long and 4 inches in diameter (23 by 10 cm). Cut the green top off the eggplant, and slice the eggplant into lengthwise quarters (or sixths), and each quarter (or sixth) into halves. Salt the flesh sides lightly and let stand 10 to 15 minutes, then pat dry with paper towels. Brush lightly on all sides with olive oil, and arrange skin side down in a shallow baking dish or jelly-roll pan. Bake in the upper third of a 425°F/220°C oven for about 15 minutes, or until the eggplant is soft. Meanwhile, toss ½ cup (1 dL) sesame seeds in a frying pan over moderate heat, shaking pan continuously until nicely toasted (they burn easily). Roll the cooked eggplant in the sesame seeds just before serving.

The squash turns into spaghetti as you scrape it out.

Gâteau of Crêpes

Molded mountain of crêpes layered with vegetables and cheese

Here is a handsome dish indeed, layers of fresh vegetables bound with a cheese custard, baked in a mold lined with crêpes—those multipurpose thin French pancakes. Serve it hot as a first course, a luncheon dish, or as the main course for a vegetarian meal, and any leftovers are good cold.

Serving 6 to 8 people

For the Crêpe Batter:

For 18 to 20 crêpes 5½ inches (14 cm) in diameter

1 cup (140 g) flour (Wondra or instant-blending preferred)

⅔ cup (1½ dL) each milk and water

3 "large" eggs

¼ tsp salt

3 Tb melted butter, or sesame or peanut oil

Vegetables and Cheese for Filling:

1 pound (450 g) carrots

6 to 8 Tb butter

Salt and pepper

½ tsp or so fresh or dried dill weed (optional)

1 pound (450 g) fresh mushrooms

4 Tb minced shallots or scallions

1 bunch (18 to 20 ounces or 500 to 550 g) fresh broccoli

2 cups (½ L) coarsely grated Swiss cheese

Custard Mixture for Filling:

1 cup (½ pound or 225 g) cream cheese

6 "large" eggs

1 cup (¼ L) milk and/or heavy cream

Salt and pepper

A pinch of nutmeg, to taste

Optional Sauce for the Gâteau:

2½ to 3 cups (about ¾ L) fresh tomato sauce (page 468; optional)

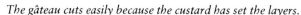

The gâteau cuts easily because the custard has set the layers.

Equipment:

A heavy cast-iron or cast-aluminum (nonstick recommended) frying pan with 5½-inch (14-cm) bottom diameter, for the crêpes; an 8-cup (2-L) baking dish, such as a metal charlotte mold, 4 inches (10 cm) deep; an instant (microwave) meat thermometer is recommended.

The crêpes—batter

Scoop dry-measure cup into flour container until cup is overflowing; sweep off excess with the straight edge of a knife, and pour flour into a pitcher or bowl. Blend the milk and water into the flour, beating with a whip until smooth (easy with Wondra or instant-blending flour), then beat in the eggs, salt, and butter or oil. Let rest for 10 minutes (an hour or 2 if you are using regular flour) so that flour granules can absorb the liquid—making a tender crêpe.

The crêpes—cooking

To cook the crêpes, heat frying pan or pans until drops of water sizzle on the surface. Brush lightly with a little butter (usually only necessary for the first crêpe), and pour 2 to 3 tablespoons or so of the batter into the center of the pan, turning the pan in all directions as you do so to spread the batter over the bottom surface. (If you have poured in too much, pour excess back into your batter bowl.) Cook for 30 seconds or so, until you see, when you lift an edge, that it is nicely browned. Turn and cook for 10 to 15 seconds more—this second

side never cooks evenly and is kept as the non-public or bottom side of the crêpe. Arrange crêpes, as they are made, on a cake rack so they will cool and dry off for 5 minutes or so. When dry (but not brittle!), stack together, wrap in foil, and place in a plastic bag.

🕐 Crêpes will keep for 2 to 3 days in the refrigerator. To freeze, it is best to package them in stacks of 6 or 8; either thaw at room temperature, or unpackage and heat in a covered dish in a moderate oven for 5 minutes or until they separate easily.

Note: I used to stack my cooked crêpes between sheets of wax paper or foil, but now that I have learned the cool-and-dry system, I have not found it necessary, even for freezing.

Preparing the vegetables

Trim and peel the carrots, and cut into julienne matchsticks. Sauté in 1½ tablespoons butter in a large frying pan, swirling and tossing frequently until carrots are nicely tender and being careful not to brown them. Season well with salt, pepper, and optional dill; set aside in a bowl.

Trim and wash the mushrooms, and cut into fine mince (a food processor is useful here); a handful at a time, twist the mushrooms in the corner of a clean towel to extract as much of their juice as possible. Sauté in the same large frying pan in 1½ tablespoons butter with the shallots or scallions, until the mushroom pieces begin to separate from each other. Season to taste with salt and pepper, and set aside in a separate bowl. This is now officially a mushroom *duxelles*.

Turning the crêpe to brown on the other side

Trim and wash the broccoli. Cut bud ends off stalks, to make them about 2 inches (5 cm) long. Starting at the cut ends, peel as much skin off as you easily can; peel skin off stalks, cutting down to expose tender whitish flesh, then cut into pieces half the length of your little finger—all this for quick and even cooking. Drop the peeled broccoli into 4 quarts (4 L) rapidly boiling salted water and boil uncovered for 3 to 5 minutes, or until just barely tender. Drain immediately; chop into pieces about ¼ inch (¾ cm) in size. Toss briefly in 2 tablespoons hot butter, and salt and pepper to taste. Set aside.

🕐 Carrots may be cooked a day ahead, and so may the broccoli; cover and refrigerate. Mushrooms may be cooked weeks ahead and stored in the freezer; be sure to defrost before using.

The custard mixture

To blend the cream cheese with the rest of the custard ingredients, either force it through a sieve with the eggs into a bowl and beat thoroughly, adding the rest of the ingredients, or mix everything together smoothly in a blender or food processor.

Assembling

Preheat oven to 350 °F/180 °C. Smear some butter over inside of baking dish and line bottom of dish with buttered wax paper. Fit 1 crêpe, good side down, in the bottom of the dish, and space 4 around the sides (the good sides against dish); cover with a second layer of 4 more overlapping crêpes, as shown.

Spread ¼ of the grated Swiss cheese in the bottom of the dish, cover with the carrots, pressing them well in place, and top with ⅓ of the remaining cheese. Ladle in enough custard mixture to come just to the level of the carrots and cheese. Arrange 1 crêpe on top, and spread over it the mushrooms and another ladleful of custard. Arrange 1 more crêpe over the mushrooms and spread on ½ of the remaining cheese, then the broccoli, and the final bit of cheese. Pour on the last of the custard mixture and fold the first layer of overhanging crêpes up over the filling; cover with a crêpe, fold the outside layer of overhang up over it, and cover with 1 or more crêpes (depending on their size and the top of your dish). Place a round of buttered wax paper over the dish, and cover with a sheet of foil.

1) Lining baking dish, brown side of crêpes against walls

2) Adding custard to first layer of carrots and cheese

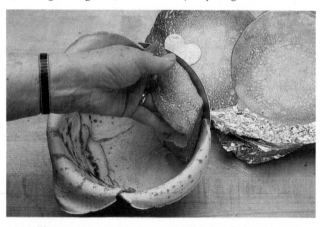

Peel broccoli for color and crispness.

⏱   I think it best to bake almost immediately, in case the custard leaks against the sides and bottom of the dish, sticking the crêpes to it and making a mess later when you attempt to unmold.

Baking

About 1 ¾ hours

Bake on lower middle rack in preheated oven, placing a pizza pan or something on the rack below to catch possible dribbles. In about 1 hour, when the gâteau has started to rise, turn oven up to 400°F/205°C. It will eventually rise an inch or more (2½ to 3 cm) and is done when a meat thermometer, its point at the center, reads 160°F/71°C. Remove from oven and let rest at room temperature for 10 to 15 minutes, allowing the custard to set and settle. Then run a thin-bladed knife carefully around inside of dish, and unmold onto a hot platter.

Surround the gâteau, if you wish, with fresh tomato sauce. To serve, cut into wedges, as though it were a cake, and spoon sauce around.

⏱   May be baked in advance; unmold the gâteau after its wait, and keep it warm in the turned-off oven, covered with an upside-down bowl. In any case, do not let the baked gâteau sit in its baking dish in a hot turned-off oven—as I did (but you did not see!) on our TV show. The cooking liquids leaked into the bottom of the baking dish, evidently, and the hot oven then glued the crêpes to the dish. Fortunately we had a standby gâteau safely loosened from its mold, which replaced my messy unmolding caper on the serving dish. There is indeed nothing like experience as a teacher!

To serve cold

This makes a delicious cold dish for a luncheon or to take on a picnic. Accompany with a tomato or cucumber salad and, if you wish, a sour cream dressing or the same tomato sauce, which also is good cold.

3) Centering crêpe over layer

4) Completing the final layers

Check doneness with an instant meat thermometer.

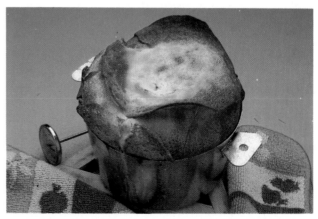

Ice Cream and a Rum and Meatless Mincemeat Sauce

Serving 6 people

Following the general line of quick and easy but good desserts, here is an idea for using a jar of mincemeat, which is so good it should be eaten more often than just on Thanksgiving. You need no recipe for this, only 1½ quarts (1½ L) or so best-quality vanilla ice cream and half a jar or so of good mincemeat. Place the ice cream in a serving bowl, and heat the mincemeat with several spoonfuls of dark Jamaica rum, or even bourbon whiskey, which is a fine substitute. Spoon the hot mincemeat sauce over each serving (you may wish to heat and flame it at the table), and you may also wish to pass some attractive sugar cookies along with the dessert.

To glamorize the mincemeat, heat it up with rum before serving it on vanilla ice cream.

⏱ Timing

You have little to do at the last minute to serve this meal, and more than half the work is already done if you make it a habit to freeze and stock such staple items as loaves of French bread, stacks of crêpes, grated Swiss cheese, mushroom duxelles, and fresh tomato sauce. Even if you must prepare these things specially for your party, you can do so 2 or 3 days beforehand, freeze the French bread, and store the other items in the refrigerator.

You can steam the spaghetti squash and prepare and cook the carrots and broccoli on the day before your party.

That morning, wash, dry, and refrigerate your salad greens, mix the vinaigrette dressing, compose (and refrigerate) the custard sauce for the gâteau, and cook the eggplant.

Two and a half hours before dinner, assemble the gâteau and start baking it.

Half an hour before serving it, test the gâteau for doneness. At this time you could start warming the mincemeat in a pan of water over low heat. Just before you sit down, unmold the gâteau, and move the ice cream from freezer to refrigerator, to soften, and reheat the eggplant and spaghetti squash and the tomato sauce. Toss your salad just before you serve it.

Menu Variations

All kinds of garnishes are nice with spaghetti squash—or you might use real spaghetti with the eggplant garnish for a main dish, instead of the gâteau. You can vary the gâteau itself by substituting other vegetables in the layers. Or you can make one of the filled crêpe recipes in *Mastering I*, assembling the entire dish in the morning and heating it just before dinner. The fillings can be infinitely varied—try cooked minced chicken sometime, for omnivores, or creamed shellfish—and the crêpes are served beautifully sauced in their baking dish. *J.C. & Co.* has other good toppings for storebought ice cream, and it's easy to think up your own.

J.C.'s Kitchen contains several good recipes for dried legumes, which make hearty main dishes for all vegetarians, including the strictest; if your guests, like ours, will eat eggs and cheese, that opens up a world of soufflés, omelets, and gratins. If, however, your guests are coming not just for a meal but for several days, you may want to look at a specialized vegetarian cookbook. Frances Moore Lappé's *Diet for a Small Planet* (New York: Ballantine Books, rev. ed. 1975) analyzes nonanimal proteins and shows how to boost protein values by combining complementary foods. It contains a lot of recipes, and even more may be found in its companion volume, *Recipes for a Small Planet,* by Ellen Buchman Ewald (New York: Ballantine Books, 1975). Martha Rose Shulman's *The Vegetarian Feast* (New York: Harper & Row, 1978) is concerned with fancier vegetarian cooking and helps out the amateur with a wide choice of menus. Finally, Anna Thomas's two volumes, *The Vegetarian Epicure* (New York: Alfred A. Knopf and Vintage Books, 1972 and 1978), have such delicious and well-considered dishes that they belong on the shelf of any blissfully greedy cook of any persuasion including Red Fang.

Leftovers

If you have last-minute no-shows, go ahead and cook all your eggplant, but put some aside before the addition of parsley and garlic. It's the foundation of several splendid dishes (see *Mastering II* and *J.C.'s Kitchen*), some of which you can eat cold. Two versions of eggplant caviar (a puréed spread or dip), one containing walnuts and the other sesame seed paste, are special treats for vegetarians.

With extra cooked vegetables, custard sauce, and cheese, you have the makings of a nice gratin or the filling for a quiche, and of course cooked or uncooked vegetable scraps are a natural for soup. I have no great suggestions for leftover salad. But extra French bread begs to be sliced and toasted for *croûtes* that you can store in the freezer until it's onion soup time again (see page 117); or blend or process them into crumbs—a jar of them, kept in the freezer, is a handy resource for any cook.

Leftover mincemeat, of course, makes splendid tarts, pies, and turnovers; since it keeps a long time in the refrigerator, once opened, you need be in no hurry to use it up.

Postscript: R&D in cooking

Certainly, one of the pleasures of cooking is thinking up new ways to present familiar ingredients. You will note that I have borrowed an engineering term rather than using the word "invent" because "invention," to me, means something like producing the very first mayonnaise, or puff pastry, or ice cream. Few cooks achieve such distinction, or have such happy accidents or discoveries. (Who could have known in advance that egg yolks would emulsify, or that flour and fat would separate in the oven into towering, airy layers?) But hardly any of us who cook has not put something together in an unusual, original, or different way, drawing from general knowledge, experience, and imagination.

I think our crêpe and vegetable gâteau could be called a creation, using the term loosely in its meaning of "investing something with a new form." Anyway, the recipe grew out of the combined activities of us cooks on the *J.C. & Co.* team, and we are very pleased with ourselves. I might mention that in our first experiments we baked the gâteau in a bain-marie (pan of water) in a 350°F/180°C oven; it came out beautifully—ideally, rather—but *3 hours* is a very long time, so for the recipe and for television we threw out the water and stepped up the heat. As noted, other cooks might like to fill the layers with other ingredients, keeping our R (Research) but continuing with their own D (Development). What we're offering you is an attractive idea, not a sacrosanct monument.

A splendid lunch for VIPs or favorite guests

Lobster Soufflé for Lunch

Even in the days when lobsters were common as pea gravel, they were prized like rubies by great chefs, who joyfully elaborated on their intense flavor and azalea coloring to create sophisticated dishes for the most elegant occasions. And family cooks loved to call out, "Have another, anybody?" over big red clattering piles of lobsters simply boiled in the shell. Recent experiments in commercial lobster farming give us hope that those days will return, but for the moment lobsters are mighty scarce. In natural conditions, only one in one thousand infant lobsters will survive the predators of its critical first three weeks, during which time it lives near the sea's surface and is frequently in molt; thereafter it takes six years (in northern waters) to attain a weight of one pound. So it will be a while before we can make up for a century of overfishing. Consequently, we think twice nowadays about serving lobster: *whether* to as well as *how* to. Luckily—as happens so often in cookery—the second question can be turned around karate-wise to resolve the first.

While it's expensive indeed to offer guests a lobster apiece, let alone seconds, you *can* offer a richly lobstery dish, affordably, elegantly, and without waste—though "stretching a lobster" sounds like the oddest, if not neatest, trick of the week. These crustaceans have more ——s (I'm in need of a word like "ergs" or "amps" here, for units of flavor) per milligram than almost any other foodstuff: the —— s are lodged in the shells themselves and in every cranny thereof. So take advantage of those shells, by chopping, then sautéing them until they yield their all to a lovely sauce (well, not quite all; after that the shells can still go into the stockpot and produce a fine lobster broth—that's how flavorful they are). Use every morsel but the small stomach sac (which enfolds the tiny, crowned, blue-robed "lady"); amplify the flavor with butter, aromatics, wine, spirits, and flame; enhance the rich texture with crisp croutons and a savory soufflé blanket, and you will find that the meat of two or three small lobsters, or one middle-sized, easily serves six.

The model for this idea is a classic dish, which was not devised in the first place for reasons of economy. It originated at the Plaza-Athénée Hotel in Paris, which in the old days was reputed to have the most exquisite cuisine-for-the-happy-few imaginable. Its base is the famous lobster *à l'américaine,* whose name is a pedant's delight. Chauvinists among French gastronomes say that nothing so delicious could possibly be American; the word, they claim, is a corruption of *armoricaine,* derived from *Armorique,* the romantic old name for Brittany, whose cold seas certainly do produce good lobster. Not so, retort the anti-*armoricaines,* the dish contains tomatoes and Brittany is not tomato country. It was surely invented in Paris, they affirm, probably by a tomato-loving chef with a Mediterranean background, and it was named for an American client, or for the Americas from which tomatoes came. The argument will continue, and we shall never know the truth. But back to those lobsters.

Mounding a soufflé over the lobster meat was the Plaza-Athénée's contribution to elegance. But why not bake it on a platter, rather than in a soufflé dish? It makes for a splendidly dramatic presentation, for easy serving, and for a rather sturdier party offering. While the soufflé doesn't rise as high as if baked in a dish, it doesn't have as far to fall. Though it takes a bit of doing, you can prepare most of it the day before. And, once you add this wonderful concoction to your repertoire, you have added the possibility of a grand array of easy variants.

The flavor is robust as well as subtle, and, especially at lunch, I like something simple and delicate to follow. Salade Mimosa, gold and pale green, soothes the excited palate; Melba toast makes an even crisper contrast if you do it with pumpernickel. A poached pear has a lovely cool suavity; you can dress it up and enhance its fragrance with a chocolate base—perhaps tucking in a wine-soaked macaroon as a buffer—and add a satiny caramel sauce at the last moment. Its smoothness, the pear's velvet grain, and the friable chocolate combine incomparably.

Chocolate cups may strike you as old hat, and, moreover, tricky to make. Well, I haven't seen one since the thirties. Is that old hat or is that classic? And in working out the recipe through many trials and experiments, our cooking team found that the cups are quite easy to form if you use chocolate bits, with their slight extra viscosity, and then chill them well before peeling off the paper cases that serve as molds. With its pretty serrated edge and finely fluted sides, the chocolate case looks as airy as a dry autumn leaf. But it's not riskily fragile. The pear squats on it with all the confidence of Queen Victoria, who never looked around for a chair but just lowered away, calmly relying on the alertness of her equerries. This royal reference is no accident, for here is a lunch befitting any palace.

Open the sand sack in the lobster's head—there is the "lady" enshrined. Her blue robe turns red when cooked.

Preparations and Marketing

Recommended Equipment:

To cook the lobsters, a casserole or kettle; to get at the meat, lobster shears, page 354, are useful; to bake and serve the soufflé, a large ovenproof platter, oval preferred, or a shallow baking dish.

Paper baking cups (cupcake size) are ideal molds for the chocolate cases; for added stability, they may be set in flat-bottomed custard cups, shells, small bowls, or large muffin tins. We flattened out our paper cups a trifle, to accommodate our fine big pears.

Macaroons are heavy work without a food processor.

Staples to Have on Hand:

Salt
White peppercorns
Hot pepper sauce
Dried tarragon
Optional: dried oregano, thyme, or herb mixture
Garlic
Cream of tartar
Stick cinnamon or powdered cinnamon
Prepared mustard
Pure almond extract
Tomato paste or tomato sauce
Olive oil or fresh peanut oil
Flour
Unsalted butter
Milk

Specific Ingredients for This Menu:

Lobster, boiled or steamed: one 2 to 2½ pounds (1 to 1¼ kg) or two or three 1-pounders (450 g) ▼
Lobster stock, fish stock, or chicken broth (1 cup or ¼ L)
Beef stock or bouillon (½ cup or 1 dL)

Swiss cheese (a 6-ounce or 180-g piece)
Parmesan or mixed hard cheeses (see recipe;
    2 ounces or 60 g)
Pumpernickel or rye bread, unsliced
Nonsweet homemade-type white bread
Eggs (9 or 10 "large")
Heavy cream (1 cup or ¼ L)
Chocolate bits or morsels (12 ounces or 340 g,
    or 2 cups or ½ L)
Almond paste (see recipe; 8 ounces or 225 g)
Sugar (3½ cups or 8 dL; 700 g)
Fresh green herbs: such as parsley, basil, chives,
    tarragon
Lettuce: Boston, butter, or romaine (1 or
    2 heads, depending on size)
Good-sized ripe unblemished pears: Anjou,
    Comice, or Bartlett (6)
Ripe red tomatoes (6 to 8 medium)
Carrots (1 medium)
Onions (1 medium)
Lemons (1)
Dry white wine or dry white French vermouth
    (4 cups or 1 L)
Optional: rum or bourbon whiskey
Cognac (⅓ cup or ¾ dL)

▶ **Remarks:**

Lobster: many fish markets carry ready-cooked lobsters. To boil or steam your own, which is usually more satisfactory, see recipe. Hen (female) lobsters are more desirable, since they contain coral (roe), to give your sauce extra red color. In buying live lobsters, choose the most active specimens; in buying ready-cooked ones, be sure that the tail is tightly curled and snaps back when pulled straight. Live lobsters can be kept for a day or 2 in the refrigerator, in paper bags pierced with a pencil for air.

Lobster Soufflé— on a Platter

A Plaza-Athénée-like soufflé accompanied by the famous lobster sauce à l'américaine

Manufacturing Note:

Although the classic recipe for lobster *à l'américaine* calls for it being cut up raw, sautéed, then simmered in its sauce, I have found that boiled lobster meat is a perfectly satisfactory alternative in this recipe, where the meat is seasoned with sauce made from the shells before the soufflé is mounded upon it. Boil the lobster, pick out its meat, make the sauce—all the day before—and you'll have only the actual soufflé mixture to complete before you pop the dish into the oven. Baking takes only 15 to 18 minutes, unsupervised.

Serving 6 people

The Lobster and Its Sauce Américaine:

Either one 2- to 2½-pound (1- to 1¼-kg) boiled lobster, or two or three 1-pound (450-g) lobsters (see directions at end of recipe)

4 Tb soft butter

2 to 3 Tb olive oil or fresh peanut oil

1 medium carrot, diced

1 medium onion, diced

⅓ cup (¾ dL) Cognac

1 cup (¼ L) lobster stock, fish stock, or chicken broth

½ cup (1 dL) beef stock or bouillon

1 cup (¼ L) dry white wine or dry white French vermouth

1½ cups (3½ dL) peeled, halved, and juiced tomatoes, chopped

2 to 4 Tb tomato paste or tomato sauce

1 tsp fragrant dried tarragon leaves

1 clove garlic, minced or puréed

Salt, pepper, and drops of hot pepper sauce

Beurre manié: 1½ Tb each flour and butter

Equipment:

A kettle, covered roaster, or steamer for cooking the lobsters; lobster shears are useful; a heavy large saucepan or casserole for simmering the shells

Because you will want the end section of the tail, the front part of the chest, and the claws for shell decoration, remove the lobster meat from the shells so as not to damage these parts (see illustrations, page 354). Discard sand sack and intestinal vein; scoop tomalley (green matter) and coral into a sieve set over a bowl. Rub through the sieve with the butter, scrape all residue off bottom of sieve into bowl, cover, and refrigerate, for enriching the finished sauce later. (Swish sieve into the sauce when it is boiling, to gather into the sauce all extra flavors.) Cut lobster meat into smallish pieces, the largest being about ½ inch (1½ cm); refrigerate until you are

ready to bake the soufflé. Chop the shells (after reserving those for final decoration).

Film a large saucepan with oil, set over high heat, and when very hot add the chopped lobster shells. Stir and toss for 2 to 3 minutes, then add the diced carrot and onion, tossing and stirring for 2 minutes more. Pour in the Cognac, ignite with a lighted match, and let flame for several seconds, shaking the pan; extinguish with the stock, bouillon, and wine. Stir in the tomatoes, tomato paste, tarragon, garlic, ¼ teaspoon salt, pepper, and drops of hot pepper sauce. Cover and simmer 30 minutes, stirring up once or twice. Turn into a large sieve set over another saucepan; stir and shake sieve to loosen vegetables from shells. Then remove shells and press juices out of vegetables in sieve. (Reserve shells and vegetable residue.)

You should have about 1½ cups (3½ dL) of rosy-colored wine-flavored lobster juices, which will need a light thickening with *beurre manié* as follows: Blend the butter and flour into a paste, and whip into the hot lobster juices. Simmer, stirring with wire whip, for 2 minutes, and correct seasoning. (Sieved tomalley-butter will go in just before serving.) Refrigerate until you are ready to assemble the soufflé.

(Simmer reserved shells and vegetables in lightly salted water to cover for 25 to 30 minutes. Strain, and you will have a good lobster stock to put in your freezer.)

A savory lobster stock made from shells and aromatic vegetables

The Soufflé:

3 ½ Tb butter
6 croutons (rounds of crustless white bread sautéed in clarified butter, see page 463)
The lobster meat, sauce, tomalley, and shells
3 Tb flour
1 cup (¼ L) hot milk
½ tsp salt
⅛ tsp white pepper
⅔ cup egg whites (5 "large" whites or 1 ½ dL)
A pinch of salt
¼ tsp cream of tartar
3 egg yolks
¾ cup (1 ¾ dL) lightly pressed down, coarsely grated Swiss cheese

Equipment:

A large ovenproof platter, such as a shallow oval about 16 inches (40 cm) long; a very clean dry bowl and beater for the egg whites (notes on beating them are on page 465)

Half an hour or so before you wish to bake the soufflé (which will take 15 to 18 minutes), you may prepare the platter: smear it with 1 tablespoon butter, arrange the croutons upon it, and divide the lobster meat over the croutons. Dribble ½ tablespoon of the lobster sauce over each portion of lobster. (Refrigerate the platter if you are not proceeding.)

Cheese Soufflé Base:

Preheat oven to 425°F/220°C. Prepare the rest of the ingredients listed. If egg whites are cold, pour into their beating bowl and set bottom of bowl in hot water, stirring the whites until they are just tepid to your finger—cold egg whites do not mount properly.

Heat 2½ tablespoons butter in a 2½-quart (2½-L) heavy-bottomed saucepan, and when melted stir in the flour; cook, stirring slowly until they foam and froth together for 2 minutes without coloring more than a buttery yellow. Remove from heat, and when this *roux* has stopped bubbling, vigorously beat in the hot milk with a wire whip and add the salt and pepper. Bring to the boil, stirring, for 1 minute. Remove from heat, clean sauce off sides of pan with a rubber spatula, and at once start in on the egg whites. Beat them at moderate speed until they start to foam, beat in the pinch of salt and cream of tartar; gradually increase speed to fast and continue beating until egg whites form stiff shining peaks when a bit is lifted up.

Immediately beat the 3 egg yolks into the hot sauce, then stir ¼ of the egg whites into the sauce (to lighten it). Scoop the rest of the egg whites onto the sauce and fold them together, alternating with sprinklings of cheese (but save 2 tablespoons for top of soufflé); operate deftly and rapidly so as to deflate the egg whites as little as possible.

Assembling and baking

Mound the soufflé over the lobster-topped croutons, topping each with a pinch of cheese. Bake immediately in the upper middle level of the preheated oven. Set timer for 15 minutes. Soufflé is done when nicely puffed and browned—it does not puff up like a soufflé in a dish, but rises at least 3 times its original volume. Tuck the shell and claws at one end of the platter, the tail at the other, and rush to the table.

While soufflé is baking, reheat sauce to the simmer, and correct seasoning; just before serving, remove from heat, whisk in the tomalley butter, and pour into a warm serving bowl. Surround each serving of soufflé with a ladleful of sauce.

Mounding the soufflé mixture over the lobster meat

A Remark on the Sauce:

Another trick for the sauce, after you have sautéed the shells and simmered them with wine and vegetables, is to remove the little legs, chop them and purée them in a blender with a cup of the sauce. Then rub this through a sieve and back into the sauce, thus catching a little puréed lobster meat in there, to act as a light thickening. (I felt the recipe was long enough without adding this to it!)

To Boil or Steam Live Lobsters:

Whether to boil or steam lobsters is, I think, a question of personal preference, number of lobsters, and equipment. If you are to boil them you need a large enough pot to hold them, and a strong heat source that will bring the water rapidly back to the boil when the lobsters go in.

To boil them, plunge them headfirst and upside down into enough rapidly boiling water to submerge them; cover the pot and weight it down if necessary. As soon as the water comes back to the boil remove cover, and boil slowly but steadily until the time (below) is up.

To steam lobsters, place a rack in a kettle or roaster, add 1½ inches (4 cm) water, and bring to the boil. Place lobsters on rack, cover closely—weighting down cover if necessary to make a tight seal—and when water starts steaming, set your timer according to the following chart:

1 to 1¼ pounds 450 to 565 g	10–12 minutes
1½ to 2 pounds 675 to 900 g	15–18 minutes
2½ to 5 pounds 1¼ to 2¼ kg	20–25 minutes

When is the lobster done?

It is done when the meat will just separate from the shells, and when the tomalley inside the lobster has coagulated. But how can you

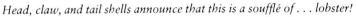

Head, claw, and tail shells announce that this is a soufflé of . . . lobster!

tell that without opening the lobster? I remove one of the little legs if I have any doubts; and if the leg meat is white and lobsterlike, I conclude the whole is cooked. Some experts can tell immediately by the look and feel of the underside of the tail section.

Removing the meat from a lobster

1) To separate the tail from chest, hold chest firmly with one hand and gently twist off tail with the other, drawing end of tail meat from chest.

2) Push tail meat out from the shell.

3) To remove intestinal vein or tube, cut a shallow slit down curve of tail meat, and pull it out—if you can see it.

4) Grab little legs, twist, and chest meat comes loose, along with legs, from chest shell.

5) Sand or stomach sac is inside chest cavity at the head; pull it out and discard it.

6) Delicious meat is in the chest interstices, but you have to dig it out bit by bit.

7) Bend the small claw down at right angles from the large claw and with it will come a large cartilage from the meat of the large claw. Then cut a window in the base of the large claw, and the meat can be removed in one piece. Dig the small sliver of meat out of the small claw.

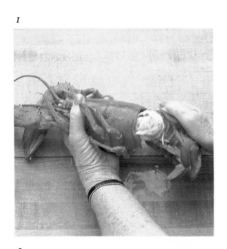

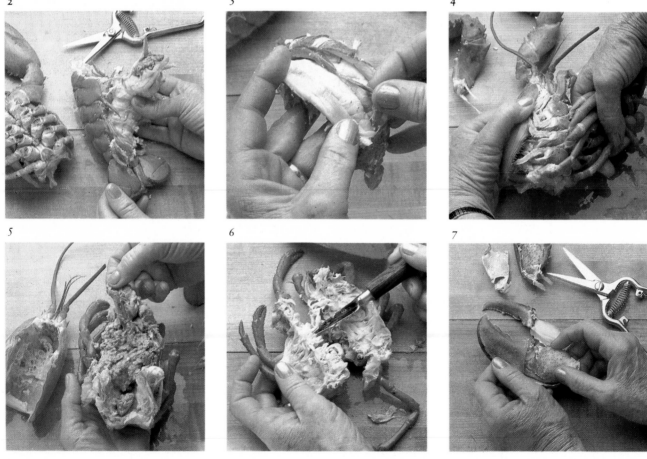

Salade Mimosa

Minced hard-boiled eggs and fresh green herbs tossed together do give a suggestion of flowering mimosa, that harbinger of spring along the Mediterranean. Sprinkle over a nicely seasoned tossed green salad and you have a very simple solution of how to dress it up for a party. Prepare the salad greens as usual—Boston lettuce or romaine seems best for this treatment. Mix the dressing (one of the vinaigrette choices on page 468). Hard boil 2 eggs and sieve or chop them (you might try the ingenious egg-slicer mincing technique on page 327) and mince enough fresh green herbs to make 2 to 3 tablespoons, using parsley, and chives, basil, or tarragon if you have them; toss herbs and eggs together in a small bowl with a sprinkling of salt and pepper. Just before serving, toss the salad with the dressing, taste, and correct seasoning; toss lightly with half the egg and herb mixture, and sprinkle the rest of it on top.

A sprinkling of chopped egg and parsley dresses up greens.

Pumpernickel Melba

Thin toasted cheese-topped pumpernickel, or rye

Southern California spawns many unusual and/or original edibles, from salads and avocado ice cream to this savory version of crisp, waferlike toast served in many a Beverly Hills restaurant—a dusky Melba of pumpernickel or rye bread, sprinkled with cheese and sometimes herbs as it crisps. The only actual problem, besides being capable of slicing it almost paper thin, is that of finding storebought unsliced bread if you've none homemade. That, as we found in the previous volume of *J.C. & Co.,* seems to be the ever-present Melba drawback.

For an unspecified amount

Stale unsliced pumpernickel or rye bread

Finely grated Parmesan cheese, or a mixture of hard cheeses like Cheddar, Swiss, etc.

Dried herbs, finely ground, such as oregano, thyme, or an herb mixture (optional)

Slice the bread as thin as possible, less than ⅛ inch (½ cm)—if it's not thin it will not curl as it bakes, the way Melba toast should. Lay the slices in one layer on a baking sheet or sheets, and place in a preheated 425 °F/ 220 °C oven. In 3 or 4 minutes, when bread has begun to crisp, sprinkle each slice with ½ teaspoon or so cheese and a pinch of the optional herbs. Continue baking a few minutes more, until crisp and, you hope, somewhat curled.

❶ Any leftovers may be packaged and frozen; warm again in the oven to crisp before serving.

Pears Poached in White Wine

Compote de poires au vin blanc

A compote of fresh fruit seems a far more European than American dessert, yet it is so simple to do and delicious to eat that we should think of it more often. Also, it solves the problem of how to cope with those pears and peaches that are ripe and ready to eat, and won't keep another moment without spoiling: once compoted, they will keep well a goodly number of days in the refrigerator, ready to be served up as is, or dressed in all manner of plain or fancy ways.

The Poaching Syrup for Raw Fruits:

The proportions of sugar to liquid for poaching raw fruits are 6 tablespoons per cup of liquid, which makes 1½ cups sugar per quart (6 Tb per ¼ L; 3½ dL per L).

For 6 pears of the Anjou, Bartlett, Comice size

3 cups (¾ L) dry white wine or dry white French vermouth
1 cup (¼ L) water
The zest (yellow part of peel) of 1 lemon, and 4 Tb of its juice
1 stick or ½ tsp powdered cinnamon
1½ cups (3½ dL) sugar
6 firm ripe unblemished pears

Pears have cooked in their fragrant syrup.

If you are to poach the pears whole, as for this recipe (rather than halved or quartered as in many other recipes), you may not have enough liquid for 6 large pears to be submerged; in that case, either poach them in 2 batches or make more poaching syrup according to the proportions noted.

Choose a saucepan that will be large enough to hold the pears submerged in the syrup, place the syrup ingredients in the pan, and bring to the simmer; simmer 5 minutes (to bring out the various flavors into the liquid), then remove from heat.

One by one, with an apple corer or grapefruit knife, core the pears from the bottom—however, you may leave them uncored if you wish. Peel the pear neatly and drop at once into the syrup to prevent discoloration. When all pears are done, bring just to the simmer and maintain liquid at the not-quite-simmer for 8 to 10 minutes, until pears are tender through when pierced with the sharp point of a small knife. (Careful not to boil them, since that can break them apart.) When done, cover pan and leave the pears to absorb the flavors of the syrup for 20 minutes, or until you are ready to use them.

🕐 May be done several days in advance; cover and refrigerate them.

Serving suggestions

Serve the pears in an attractive bowl, along with their poaching syrup; you may wish to accompany them with heavy cream, lightly whipped cream, fresh strawberry or raspberry sauce, chocolate sauce, custard sauce. Or you may drain them, set them on a round of sponge cake or a macaroon that has been sprinkled with some of the poaching syrup and a few drops of Cognac or rum, then spoon sauce over them. Or serve them on vanilla ice cream or sherbet, and top with a chocolate, custard, or fruit sauce. Or combine them with other fruits and serve in a savarin, as illustrated on page 409. Or serve them in chocolate cups, as described here.

A Pear and Chocolate Dessert

Les délices aux poires

Whenever you have pears poached in wine, macaroons, chocolate cups, and caramel sauce all at hand at one moment, this lovely dessert is a fast assembly job. However, because the chocolate cups can soften and collapse in a warm room, and the caramel topping will lose its sheen as it gradually slides off the pears, you cannot assemble all of it ahead of time. You can set the pears in their chocolate cups well ahead, however, if you have room in the refrigerator to store them on their dessert plates, but the sauce should either go on at the last minute in the kitchen, or be spooned over each pear as you present it at the table.

Note: Directions for the chocolate cups, macaroons, and sauce follow this recipe.
For 6 people

6 chocolate cups
6 macaroons (optional)
Droplets of pear poaching liquid
Droplets of rum, Cognac, or bourbon whiskey (optional)
6 pears poached in white wine (preceding recipe)
About 1 cup (¼ L) caramel sauce

An hour or so before serving, if you wish to ready things ahead, set the chocolate cups on individual dessert plates. Choose, or trim, macaroons, if you are using them, to fit the bottom of the cups, and place them in upside down. Dribble over each a few drops of pear liquid and the optional rum, Cognac, or bourbon. Trim bottoms of pears if necessary, so they will sit solidly, and set the pears on the macaroons.

❶   Must be refrigerated at this point if prepared in advance.

Just before serving, or at the table, spoon a tablespoon or 2 of the caramel sauce over each pear.

Wine-poached pear, macaroon cushion, and chocolate cup

Chocolate Cups

*To hold ice creams and sherbets,
Bavarian creams, poached fruits*

*About 12 ounces or 2 cups (340 g or
½ L) chocolate bits or morsels for 6
chocolate cups*

Choose fluted paper cupcake molds of any size you wish—the ones here have a 2¼-inch (5¾-cm) bottom, and were bought in a local supermarket. Because you want a wide cup to hold the fruit, press out the flutings between your thumb and forefinger. Provide yourself with several custard cups, shells, small bowls, or large muffin tins in which to set the chocolate-lined cups to congeal, later.

Then melt your chocolate—after numerous experiments we found chocolate bits more satisfactory than semisweet bars—bits, they say, have more viscosity, and that means spreading ability, which you need for this enterprise. To melt the chocolate, set it in a smallish saucepan; bring another and larger saucepan with about 2 inches (5 cm) water to the boil, remove from heat and let cool a moment, then cover the chocolate pan and set it in the hot water. In 4 to 5 minutes the chocolate bits will have melted; stir them up and they should form a shining liquid mass. (Be very careful not to use too much heat here, or the chocolate will harden into a lumpy or granular mess.)

Using the back of a teaspoon or a small palette knife, spread the chocolate up the sides of the cup, and in a layer on the bottom. Set each, as done, in a bowl or shell, and refrigerate until set—15 to 20 minutes. Carefully peel off the paper. Keep chilled until you are ready to fill and serve them.

Spread the melted chocolate up the sides of a fluted paper cookie cup.

Rosemary Manell's Almond Macaroons

Made in a food processor

My friend Rosie has conducted a good number of cooking classes featuring the food processor; this is the recipe for marvelous macaroons that she developed, and has kindly contributed. I've tried it in the blender without success; one could certainly adapt it to a large mortar and pestle in the time-honored hand-pounded way. But the processor is so quick and easy for macaroons that I've not gone into other methods seriously. By the way, Rosie prefers either Reese or "Red-E" almond paste, and brands of almond paste do vary in sweetness and consistency. Thus, if your first batch is too sweet, add less sugar the next time.

For 2 dozen macaroons 2 inches (5 cm) in diameter

8 ounces (225 g) almond paste
1 cup (¼ L) sugar
¼ tsp pure almond extract
A pinch of salt
¼ to ⅜ cup egg whites (2 to 3 whites; ½ to ¾ dL)

Equipment:
A food processor with steel blade; 2 baking sheets lined with brown paper (the shopping-bag kind); a pastry bag with ⅜-inch (1-cm) tube opening (optional)

Prepare cookie sheets, but do not grease them or grease the paper. Preheat oven to 325 °F/165 °C, and set racks in lower and upper middle levels.

Cut almond paste into ½-inch (1½-cm) pieces. Put into container of processor and cut up finely, turning motor on and off in 2-second spurts. When almond paste resembles coarse brown sugar, add the granulated sugar and process again in spurts, stopping several times to scrape down sides of container with a rubber spatula. Add the almond extract, salt, and ¼ cup (½ dL) egg whites, and process until no lumps of almond paste remain. The mixture should not be stiff, but should hold in a mass on a spatula. (If too stiff, add a little more egg white and process again.) This is the consistency for macaroons that are crunchy on the outside and chewy inside; if you like them softer and chewier, add more egg white by half teaspoons—after a batch or 2 you will arrive at the consistency you prefer.

Remove the mixture to a bowl and beat well with a wooden spoon, to be sure all is smooth and well blended. To form the macaroons, either drop mixture from a spoon, or use a pastry bag. If they are to fill chocolate cups, they should be small enough to fit inside easily: form ¾-inch (2-cm) blobs on the brown paper, spacing them 1½ inches (4 cm) apart because they spread a little as they bake. For larger macaroons, make the blobs 1½ inches (4 cm) across. Smooth tops of blobs with the back of a spoon dipped in cold water.

Bake in preheated oven for 25 to 30 minutes, switching sheets on the racks halfway through. The macaroons are done when lightly browned and crusty on top. Remove baking sheets from oven and let cool on cake racks. When cold, turn paper with macaroons attached upside down and dampen the back of the paper with a wet cloth or a brush; when macaroons loosen easily, peel away the paper. If they do not come off easily, dampen paper and wait a few minutes more. Set macaroons on cake racks for half an hour or so to dry.

🕐 Store in an airtight tin, or wrap airtight and freeze.

▶ **Remarks:**
We tried forming and baking the macaroons on floured and buttered nonstick pastry sheets. They came off all right, but the bottoms were concave, and they were very crisp. Silicone baking paper was also unsatisfactory.

Caramel Sauce

This is a rich and pure caramel sauce that you can serve either hot or cold—it thickens as it cools. You can also combine it with whipped cream or custard sauce, or use as a base for caramel ice cream.

For about 1 cup or ¼ L

1 cup (¼ L) granulated sugar
⅓ cup (¾ dL) water
An additional ⅓ to ½ cup (¾ to 1 dL) water
1 cup (¼ L) heavy cream

Boil the sugar and ⅓ cup (¾ dL) water in a small heavy saucepan, swirling pan by its handle until sugar has completely dissolved and liquid is perfectly clear. Put a lid on the pan and boil slowly until sugar bubbles thicken considerably. Then uncover, and boil undisturbed for a moment or so, until syrup begins to caramelize. Immediately swirl pan slowly by its handle until syrup has turned a nice walnut brown. Remove from heat, swirling (if pan is very heavy, set bottom in cold water to stop the cooking) until bubbling has ceased. Avert your face, pour in the additional water, and simmer, stirring frequently, until caramel has melted into the water; boil down until it is a light syrup. Add the cream, blend in thoroughly, and boil, stirring, for 2 to 3 minutes, to reduce the cream slightly. Serve cold, for the pears.

⏱   May be made several days in advance; can be frozen, but may need boiling up and/ or more cream before using.

⏱ *Timing*

The pumpernickel Melba, the chocolate cups, and the macaroons can be made any time and frozen.

Buy your pears several days ahead, since they usually aren't sold ripe; if you do have ripe ones, you may poach them several days in advance. At this time, make the caramel sauce, and you can sauté and freeze the croutons for the soufflé.

The day before your party, you can prepare your lobsters and their sauce. The chocolate cups may be peeled and rechilled.

In the morning, prepare your salad, and store the lettuce wrapped in damp towels in the refrigerator. Prepare the vinaigrette.

An hour or so before your guests come, prepare the soufflé platter with its croutons and mounds of lobster meat; cover and refrigerate it.

Half an hour before serving time, make the soufflé, which takes only 15 to 18 minutes to bake. Assemble the dessert, except for the sauce. Crisp the pumpernickel Melba in the oven if you have made it early and frozen it.

The salad is tossed just before you serve it. Same for saucing the dessert, so that the caramel keeps its sheen.

Pumpernickel Melba

Menu Variations

The soufflé: as long as you have your fine lobster sauce, you can mix some fin fish with your lobster, like monkfish or halibut—this is an old Norwegian trick I learned when we were living there. The flavor of lobster is so strong and fine that it pervades other fish, too. You may use the same sauce system for live crabs and for fresh or frozen shrimp in the shell. You must be very careful with frozen shrimp, however, to be sure they have not been adulterated with preserving chemicals—I've run into some loathsome examples that really exude a smell like that of floor-cleaning fluid. Read the label on the package! Rather than shellfish and sauce *à l'américaine,* you could use sole poached in white wine, to flake over the croutons, and turn the poaching liquid into a *sauce au vin blanc*—a hollandaise made with the reduced white-wine fish stock. Another idea is to place a cold poached egg on each crouton, and a piece of ham or a dollop of cooked spinach on the crouton first, if you wish. When the soufflé is cooked, the egg has miraculously just warmed through; serve the soufflé with a hollandaise sauce, and you have a beautiful dish. (A recipe for the fish soufflé is in *The French Chef Cookbook,* as is a conventional, rather than platter, one for poached eggs and spinach.)

The salad: to follow a subtle soufflé, I'd always choose a salad on the delicate side—perhaps Rosie's spectacularly arranged lettuce salad on page 28, or a salad of Belgian endive (if it's affordable) with watercress. Something like a *salade niçoise* would be too much, as would most vegetable combinations—tomatoes especially, since they'd repeat the sauce *à l'américaine.* You could certainly serve pita bread triangles, toasted and cheesed, instead of the *pumpernickel Melba.*

The dessert: apples, peaches, etc., could be poached in the same way as the pears and used instead. Rather than chocolate cups, you could use the vacherin meringue cases on page 240, or cookie cups. (A recipe for the latter is in *The French Chef Cookbook.*) Other fruit sauces are very easy to make: use frozen strawberries or raspberries and purée in a blender or processor, adding fresh lemon juice and more sugar as needed. For fresh berries, purée, beating in lemon juice and sugar to taste; raspberries need sieving, I think. See recipes for custard sauce (page 436), and for whipped cream Chantilly and chocolate sauce (page 464).

Leftovers

Little to say here! Any cook who would not promptly devour the last scrap of leftover lobster meat must be certifiably mad. Other uses for poached fruit and chocolate cases are in the recipes themselves. As for caramel sauce, who needs telling?

Postscript: Lunch or luncheon?

If you are requesting the pleasure of Mr. and Mrs. John Doe's company then you call it "luncheon." The added syllable gives extra employment to needy engravers, I guess, and anyway the word seems nicely old-fashioned to me. It does make one stop and think about menu planning for formal entertainment nowadays, when "tummy time," as Winston Churchill called his interior clock, has been reset by the press of our obligations.

Except on holidays, few of us can take our time at midday, whereas a dinner party can sprawl on into the wee hours. (Do we admit to sleeping off lunch?) If you and your guests are coring the heart out of a busy day, and devoting it to a meal that so many people are apt to skip or skimp, you are declaring an Occasion. A modern lunch*eon* menu should be light, and as compact and elegant as a sonnet. It is a good time to focus on one artful and unusual dish. And, since at midday people (a) come on time, and (b) don't want much to drink, you are secure in planning something that won't wait, like fish, or a grill, or a soufflé. No wonder so many enthusiastic cooks rise, like the sun, to their zenith at this hour.

Take it along in your Rolls, or your Volks;
the ritziest portable feast imaginable.

Picnic

Menu
For 8 or more people

Gazpacho Salad —Layers of colorful freshly cut vegetables with bread crumbs and garlic dressing in a cylindrical glass bowl

Fish Terrine, Straight Wharf Restaurant —A tri-color mousse of sole and scallops with watercress and salmon

Pâté en Croûte —Spiced and wine-flavored ground meats baked in a decorative pastry crust

A selection of accompaniments —Carrot sticks, cauliflowerettes, and olives, as well as rare mustards and pickles

A variety of fine fresh breads —French, sourdough rye both light and dark, and whole-grain loaves

A platter of cheeses, and bunches of grapes

Plantation Spice Cookies

Suggested drinks:
Chilled dry white wine (riesling, Muscadet, Chablis, or chardonnay), and a picnic red — Beaujolais or zinfandel; beer; iced tea; selected soft drinks; a large thermos of hot coffee

The best picnic I've ever read of was given during World War II by an Englishman of legendary courage, the Duke of Suffolk. This black-bearded daredevil had recruited and trained a squad of volunteers for the most blood chilling of all wartime duties, the defusing of live bombs. Having been called down to one of the Channel ports after a Nazi air raid, the duke and his men, tense and exhausted, were returning to London after a grisly day on the docks. Suddenly, on a muddy road in what must have seemed the middle of nowhere, Suffolk signaled the truck convoy to stop. He then blew a whistle and lo, out from behind a hedge purred his Rolls Royce, laden with hampers, crystal, silver, damask, and a butler who unpacked and served a noble feast. Unbeknownst to the men, their road home passed close to Suffolk's country seat.

It wouldn't have been possible, in those lean and rationed years, to offer the meal we're having today —although, goodness knows, no picnickers ever deserved it more than the bomb squad. But at any rate the party possessed the three characteristics I most enjoy at a good picnic: surprise, luxury, and plenty. It's not worthwhile eating too much —which you can't help doing outdoors —unless the food is marvelous. In our family, we all love hard-boiled eggs and tuna fish sandwiches. But that's not picnicking, that's brown bagging, something we all do once in a while when we're too busy to fix ourselves a fine lunch.

Paper plates and plastic forks have their place —in a brown bag. At a real picnic I like real cutlery, but don't of course insist on damask and porcelain. Our bright plastic plates travel nicely, as does every dish on the menu . . . the *pâté en croûte* snug in its mold, and the fish mousse in its thick-walled, chill-conserving terrine. For the gazpacho salad, we have used a straight-sided glass bowl, to show off the rainbow layers of vegetables. The whole works goes into insulated chests—how did we ever manage without?

Gazpacho in its primal state is a soup. But why not keep the gazpacho idea and serve it in a compact form? As a soup, gazpacho is an ancient dish, mentioned in both Old and New Testaments, and known in early Greece and Rome. Nowadays, however, most of us associate it with Spain, especially with the hot climate and searing summer sun of Andalusia, and in particular with the city of Seville. As with cassoulet and bouillabaisse, and even with our own Indian puddings and fish chowders, there are dozens of versions. Some thirty classic gazpachos exist, according to Barbara Norman in her *Spanish Cookbook* (New York: Atheneum, 1966). And there are variations on the thirty, she notes; a gazpacho can be thick or liquid, it can be served at any time during the meal, and rather than the traditional tomato red, it can even be white—when made with olive oil, garlic, and almonds. Alice B. Toklas, after the death of her friend Gertrude Stein, made a sort of gazpacho-quest of an Andalusian tour, and although she ate some marvelous examples, she could find no historical information on the subject in Spain itself. According to her lively account in *The Alice B. Toklas Cookbook* (New York: Harper, 1954), one clerk at a bookstore said to her, "Oh, gazpachos are only eaten in Spain by peasants and Americans." A final quote on the matter comes from M. F. K. Fisher, in *The Art of Eating* (New York: Vintage, 1976): "Above all it should be tantalizing, fresh, and faintly perverse as are all primitive dishes eaten by worldly people."

The word "gazpacho," it says in *The Cooking of Spain and Portugal* (New York: Time-Life Books, 1969), comes from the Arabic, and means soaked bread. And indeed bread appears in almost every version one runs into. Bread was much employed in the recipes of yore, not only as a thickener and nourisher, but simply so as not to waste a crumb. The recipe for the herb and bread crumb stuffing for chicken (page 305) is ancient too, as is the use of bread in onion soup, especially in its many-layered version on page 326.

Bread crumbs appear again in this meal, in the fish terrine—but I have no qualms about it because in the two dishes the taste and effect are so different that the crumbs become just another staple element, like salt. (Just be sure to get very good bread with body. Soft, squashy white bread will disintegrate.) A few years ago, the fish terrine would have been an unthinkable luxury at any but a princely picnic, because it took hours to purée the fish finely, pounding it in a mortar, sieving it, and finally adding cream, almost drop by drop. Even now, like the duke's crystal and silver in a brambly English lane, a fish mousse lends a note of slightly incongruous finesse, which I vastly enjoy, to an outdoor meal. It has a lovely texture; the flavor is unique, and suave to a degree, and the colors make one think of a subtle French painting—ivory-white, pearl-pink, and the green you sometimes see just after sunset. Celestial—and with a food processor, almost shockingly easy to do.

Equally luxurious, but in a quite opposite way—a portly burgher versus a court lady—is the hearty, handsome, porkily perfumed *pâté en croûte*. To call it a meat loaf baked in dough is true to the letter but not the spirit. Its rich meat laced with Port and brandy, spices, and herbs, its darkly gleaming aspic layer, and its greatcoat of heavy pastry, decorated fatly and fancifully—a traditional folk art—it is always the *pièce de résistance* on a table. Molds come in many shapes, but I find our corset-waisted one especially amusing. Set about with cheeses and big fresh country loaves, and grapes and bottles of wine, it looks almost pompously self-satisfied.

We wind up our feast with a delightful old-fashioned sort of cookie, a spice-ball variation containing peanuts, with the aroma of spices and dark molasses. Making these big savory cookies is easy, and children love to do it. The old meaning of the word "picnic" is a party to which everyone contributes, and I've purposely chosen every dish on our menu to be something one could easily carry to a friend's party as a welcome gift. If the children make the cookies, have them double the recipe, or they'll all disappear on the way.

Preparations and Marketing

Recommended Equipment:

A mincing meal indeed! Of course you can do it all by hand, but it's light work if you have a food processor for making bread crumbs and puréeing the fish for the terrine. A heavy-duty electric mixer with a flat beating blade is fine for both the crust and the filling of your *pâté en croûte*. Either a processor or a mixer will help with the cookie dough.

The gazpacho, however, demands good knife work: paring knives for trimming the vegetables and a very sharp French knife for mincing them and dicing them. You'll need 3 or 4 mixing bowls and 3 large sieves, and a 2-quart (2-L) cylindrical glass bowl is ideal for showing off your handiwork.

The mousse recipe was designed for a 5- to 6-cup (1¼- to 1½-L) terrine or loaf pan for baking and serving. (The mousse and its stripes could be adapted to a melon mold, however.)

A special spring-form mold, hinged and latched for easy removal, is ideal for baking *pâté en croûte;* the mold can be had at fancy cookware shops and comes in a variety of shapes. If you can't find one, don't be deterred; see recipe for other possibilities. You do need a pastry brush for glazing, and a bulb baster.

To chop peanuts for the cookies: blenders and processors won't work on the peanut shape. A nut chopper or grater is best, or a wooden bowl and an old-fashioned hand chopper. Have several baking sheets, since the recipe is for 24 cookies, and each sheet will take only 9.

Staples to Have on Hand:

Salt

White peppercorns

Sugar

Powdered cloves, cinnamon, nutmeg, allspice,
     and ginger

Ground imported bay leaves

Ground thyme

Fresh basil leaves, or dried oregano

Hot pepper sauce

Prepared Dijon-type mustard

Dark unsulphured molasses

Red wine vinegar

Prepared horseradish

Optional: capers, olives, anchovies

Baking soda

Gelatin (4 Tb or 4 packages)

Unsalted butter

Olive oil

Lard

French- or Italian-style bread (½ loaf)

Garlic

Lemons (2)

Scallions

Optional: shallots

Parsley; basil and chives if available

Specific Ingredients for This Menu:

Lox or smoked salmon (¼ pound or 115 g) ▼

Fillets of white fish (1½ pounds or 675 g) ▼

Scallops (½ pound or 225 g) ▼

Ground veal (1½ pounds or 675 g) ▼

Ground lean pork (1½ pounds or 675 g) ▼

Ground fresh pork fat (1 pound or 450 g) ▼

For optional pâté garnish: chicken livers, or
     boiled ham for dice or strips, or veal for
     strips, and/or truffles, or pistachio nuts,
     or your own choice (1 cup or ¼ L)

Optional: pig's caul (1 sheet) or strips of fresh
     pork fat ⅛ inch (½ cm) thick (about 1
     pound or 450 g) ▼

Best-quality clarified brown stock (page 76), or
     canned consommé (4 cups or 1 L)

Cucumbers (2 or 3)

Green bell peppers (2 or 3)

Red bell peppers (2 or 3), or red pimiento

Mild red onion (1 large)

Avocados (2 or 3), ripe and firm

Onions (4 to 6 medium)

Fresh tomato pulp (3 cups or ¾ L; 12
     tomatoes), and/or canned Italian
     tomatoes

Celery (2 or 3 stalks)

Watercress (1 large bunch)

Heavy cream (3½ cups, or 8 dL)

Sour cream (1 cup or ¼ L)

Unbleached all-purpose flour (7½ cups; 2
     pounds, 3 ounces, or 1 kg)

Eggs (1½ dozen "large")

Unsalted peanuts (1 cup or ¼ L)

Cognac or Armagnac; dry Port wine

Additional items as you wish: raw vegetable
     snacks, pickles, olives, mustards, grapes,
     cheeses, breads

▶   Remarks:

Fish fillets: you can choose among sole, flounder, conger eel, tilefish, petrale sole, monkfish, and halibut. For general remarks on buying and storing fish, see page 402. *Scallops:* even more perishable than fin fish, these should ideally be used the day you buy them. Sniff them in the market to be sure they're very fresh. *Fresh pork shoulder butt* has the correct proportion of fat to lean; buy a 2½-pound (1350-g) piece. *Pig's caul:* you don't have to have it, but if you want to use it, you may have to special-order this unless you live in a neighborhood that makes sausage cakes and caters to a European trade. It is the lining of the pig's visceral cavity, and every porker has one: a thin membrane streaked with cobwebby lines of fat that serves as an edible wrapping in sausage making, or for holding stuffing or flavoring around meat or poultry, or for lining pâté crusts. If more of us demanded pig's caul from our markets, we'd find it there. It freezes nicely, too. For pig's caul, substitute strips of *fresh pork fat:* this also may be hard to get. I generally trim mine from pork roasts, and freeze it. If the strips are too thick, cover them with wax paper and pound them with a rubber hammer, bottle, or whatever. If you can't get fresh pork fat, blanch bacon strips in a large pot of boiling water for 10 minutes.

Gazpacho Salad

Layers of diced peppers, onions, celery, cucumbers, avocados, and tomatoes interspersed with fresh bread crumbs and an herbal oil and garlic dressing

All the refreshing flavors of a gazpacho, but rather than being a soup it has become a mixed raw vegetable accompaniment to picnic food—a crudité combo in a pretty bowl. And it is equally delicious on any summer table with cold meats or fish, or with poached or scrambled eggs.

Manufacturing Note:

There is lots of dicing here—good practice—and it is far more attractive done evenly by hand than roughly by machine. Cut and flavor each item separately, and you want the tomatoes and cucumbers to drain well before they go into their final phase or they will exude so much water you will have soup rather than salad.

For 2 quarts (2 L), serving 8 or more

The Vegetables and Bread Crumbs:

3 cups (¾ L) tomato pulp—fresh in season or a combination of fresh and canned Italian plum tomatoes (see directions in recipe)

Salt and red wine vinegar as needed

2 or 3 cucumbers

¼ tsp sugar

2 or 3 each green bell peppers and red bell peppers (or, lacking red peppers, use a jar or so of canned red pimiento)

1 large mild red onion

2 or 3 celery stalks

About 2 cups (½ L) lightly pressed down, fresh crumbs from crustless nonsweet French- or Italian-style white bread (see directions in recipe)

The Herbal Oil and Garlic Dressing:

2 or 3 large cloves garlic

1 tsp salt, more if needed

Zest (yellow part of peel) of ½ lemon

Herbs: fresh basil leaves most desirable, otherwise fragrant dried oregano, or another of your choice

2 tsp prepared Dijon-type mustard

2 to 3 Tb lemon juice

½ cup (1 dL) or so good olive oil

Wine vinegar if needed

Freshly ground pepper and drops of hot pepper sauce

Other Ingredients:

2 or 3 ripe firm avocados

2 or 3 minced shallots or scallions

4 to 5 Tb fresh minced parsley

Capers, olives, anchovies for final decoration (optional)

Equipment:

3 sieves; 3 or 4 medium mixing bowls; a medium mortar and pestle, or heavy bowl and a masher of some sort (wooden spoon); a blender or food processor for making the bread crumbs; an attractive glass bowl of about 2 quarts (2 L) to hold the layered gazpacho

The tomatoes

Peel, seed, and juice the tomatoes (illustrated on page 327), and cut into neat dice about ¼-inch (¾-cm) size. Out of season, include a judicious amount of canned peeled Italian-style plum tomatoes—halve them, scoop out

Gazpacho salad

seeds with your fingers, and dice the flesh; they are usually rather soft, but they add color and flavor. Fold together in a bowl with about ½ teaspoon salt and 1 teaspoon or so of wine vinegar, let stand 5 minutes, then turn into a sieve set over a bowl to drain while you continue.

The cucumbers

Peel the cucumbers, cut in half lengthwise, and scoop out their seeds by drawing a teaspoon down their lengths. Cut into strips, then into dice about the same size as the tomatoes. Toss in a bowl with 1 tablespoon wine vinegar, ½ teaspoon salt, and ¼ teaspoon sugar. Let stand 5 minutes, then turn into a sieve set over a bowl to drain.

The peppers, onions, and celery

Halve the peppers, remove their seeds and stems, dice the flesh the same size as the tomatoes, and place in a bowl. Peel and dice the red onion (you should have about ⅔ cup or 1½ dL), drop for 15 seconds in a pan of boiling water to remove strong bite, drain, rinse in cold water, and drain again; add to the peppers. Dice the celery, add to the peppers, and then toss the three vegetables together with salt and drops of wine vinegar to taste. Set aside.

The bread crumbs

Cut off crusts, tear bread into smallish pieces, and crumb a handful at a time in a blender or food processor. (A good recipe for using the crusts is on page 463.)

The herbal oil and garlic dressing

Peel the garlic cloves, chop fine (or purée through a garlic press), and then pound in the mortar or bowl with 1 teaspoon salt until the consistency of a paste. Mince the lemon zest, add to the mortar, and pound until puréed, then add and pound the herb into the purée. Beat in the mustard with a small wire whip, then the lemon juice, and finally, by droplets, the oil—hoping for a homogenized sauce (but no matter if elements do not cream together: beat up before each use). Season well with more salt, drops of vinegar if needed, pepper, and hot pepper sauce to taste.

The avocados

Halve, seed, peel, and dice the avocados, page 327. Rinse in cold water to prevent discoloration, and set aside.

Arranging the gazpacho salad

4 to 6 hours before serving

Be sure the tomatoes are well drained; toss the cucumbers and the pepper-onion mixture in paper towels to dehumidify. The ingredients are to be spread in layers, to make an attractive design when you look through the glass; I shall specify 3 layers here.

Spread ¼ of the crumbs evenly in the bottom of the bowl, cover with ⅓ of the pepper-onion mixture, then ⅓ of the avocados, ⅓ the tomatoes, ⅓ of the cucumbers, then ¼ of the dressing. Continue with crumbs, pepper-onion mixture, avocados, tomatoes, cucumbers, dressing, and so on, ending with a layer of crumbs, then the remaining sauce. Toss the shallots and parsley together and spread over the top. Cover closely with plastic wrap and refrigerate. Just before serving, decorate with capers, olives, and anchovies, if you wish.

🕐 Once the vegetables are prepared, arrange the salad in its bowl so that the ingredients may commune together to make an interesting whole. Leftovers are still good the next day, or may be ground up in a blender or food processor (or stirred together) with tomato juice to make a gazpacho soup . . . in which you might include the preliminary vegetable drainings, which are full of flavor.

Neat knifework makes all the difference in the beauty and taste of a gazpacho salad.

Fish Terrine, Straight Wharf Restaurant— Terrine de Sole aux Trois Mousses

Mousse of sole and scallops layered with watercress and salmon

Here is a lovely terrine indeed, an ivory mousse of sole and scallops puréed together with cream and eggs, interlaced with strips of green watercress and of pink salmon. Serve it hot as a first course or for a luncheon dish, or take it cold, in its terrine or baking dish, on a picnic.

Note: A fish terrine—or pâté—is almost invariably a purée of raw fish that is bound together with eggs, and made light and, in fact, mousselike, with cream. Sometimes the fish mousse stands alone, having enough bodily gelatin and strength to need no other base. This always sounds stylish, but I like a panade (thick cream sauce or bread crumbs) in my mousses and I particularly like the use of fresh bread crumbs here; they absorb the fish juices that would otherwise exude in a sometimes distressing quantity.

Before deciding on this particular mousse, our cooking team tried out quite a number of others. I had myself worked on numerous versions of a scallop mousse and found that it was either rubbery when it had no panade, or it was lacking in scallop flavor when it did. Chef Sara and I tried a mousse of scallops and sole with cream and gelatin that had a delicious flavor—but the unappealing texture of fish gelatin pudding. Finally chef Marion suggested we try her fish terrine, the one she does in Nantucket, where she is summer chef at the Straight Wharf Restaurant. We all liked hers

immensely and this, with one or two jointly arrived-at modifications, is it.

Manufacturing Note—Molded Mousse: The recipe here is for a fish mousse served directly from its terrine or baking dish, since that is great for a picnic or a covered-dish party. If you want to serve it unmolded, however, just line the inside of the terrine with buttered wax paper, and the mousse will come out easily after it has baked.

For a 5-cup (1¼-L) terrine or bread pan, serving 8 to 10 people

The Garnish—Watercress and Salmon:

1 large bunch fresh watercress

4 or 5 scallions

2½ to 3 Tb butter

¼ pound (115 g) excellent lox or lightly smoked salmon

Fresh fish is essential for a fine terrine—let your nose be the judge.

For the Fish Mousse:

1 ½ pounds (675 g) of the finest, freshest-smelling fillets of sole or flounder (or other lean white fish such as conger eel, tilefish, petrale sole, monkfish, halibut)

½ pound (225 g) of the freshest-smelling scallops, washed rapidly and drained

2 "large" eggs

1 Tb (or a bit less) salt

2 cups (½ L) lightly pressed down crumbs from crustless nonsweet French- or Italian-style white bread (see gazpacho recipe for directions)

2 to 3 cups (½ to ¾ L) heavy cream

4 Tb fresh lemon juice

Freshly grated white pepper

A speck or so of nutmeg

Equipment:

A food processor; a 5- to 6-cup (1 ¼- to 1 ½-L) terrine or loaf pan; several rubber spatulas and soup spoons (useful); 2 or 3 medium mixing bowls; an instant (microwave) meat thermometer (useful)

Preliminaries

Preheat oven to 350° F/180° C and place a roasting pan half full of water in it, for baking the terrine. Cut a piece of wax paper a little larger all around than the terrine, and a piece of aluminum foil slightly larger than that. Butter one side of the wax paper.

Pull the tender leaves and top stems off the watercress (you may save the rest for watercress soup), and chop them into very fine mince with the white and tender green of the scallions; sauté slowly in 2 tablespoons butter for a minute or so, until limp. Set aside in a bowl. Look over the salmon to be sure there are no bones or other debris.

The fish mousse

(If you have a processor with a small container, divide the mousse ingredients in half and do in 2 parts, then beat together in a bowl to blend.)

Cut the fillets into 2-inch (5-cm) pieces and purée with the scallops, using the steel blade. Remove cover and add the eggs, salt, bread crumbs, 2 cups (½ L) cream, the lemon juice, 10 grinds of pepper, and nutmeg. Purée for 30 seconds or so. Remove cover; scrape and stir contents about, and purée longer if not smooth. When you spoon a little up, mousse should hold its shape softly—if you think it could take more cream, start the machine again, and add more in a thin stream, checking that you have not softened the purée too much. Remove cover, and taste carefully for seasoning—it should seem a little oversalted and overseasoned if you are to serve it cold, since the seasonings will become less strong once a mousse is cooked and cooled.

Assembling the terrine

(The mousse is arranged in layers in the terrine: plain mousse, green, plain mousse, salmon, ending with plain mousse. Some of the plain mousse is blended with the watercress and with the salmon; otherwise the layers would separate when the mousse is sliced.)

Spread a layer of plain mousse in the terrine, filling it by ¼. Smooth out with the back of a soup spoon dipped in cold water. Stir a dollop of mousse into the watercress (about twice the amount of mousse to cress) and spread into terrine, smoothing it also with a wet spoon. Spread on another layer of plain mousse, then remove all but a large dollop of mousse from the processor bowl. Place salmon in processor with the remaining mousse and purée for several seconds until smooth; spread the salmon in the terrine,

A layer of watercress gives its bright green color to the creamy layers of fish.

and top with a final layer of plain mousse, filling the terrine to the top. Cover with wax paper, buttered side down, then foil—paper and foil should not come too far down sides of mold, or water from baking pan may seep into mousse.

🕐 Assembled terrine should be baked promptly, since raw fish deteriorates rapidly even under refrigeration.

Baking

1 ¼ to 1 ½ hours

As soon as possible, set the terrine in the preheated oven in the pan of hot water. When mousse starts to rise above rim of terrine, after an hour or more, it is almost done—and not until then. At that point, also, you will begin to smell the delicious aromas of cooking fish. It is done at an interior temperature reading of 160° F/71° C—top will feel springy not squashy, and mousse can be gently pulled away from side of terrine.

To serve hot

Leave in pan of water in turned-off oven, door ajar, until serving time. Cut slices directly from the terrine and serve with the sour cream sauce described farther on, or with melted butter, white butter sauce (page 464), or hollandaise (page 406).

To serve cold

Remove mousse from oven and let cool. When tepid, drain off accumulated juices—there will be several tablespoons that you may use in your sauce. When cool, cover with plastic wrap and refrigerate.

Serve this beautiful tri-color mousse on top of—not under—its sour cream sauce.

To serve, cut slices directly from terrine, and accompany with the following sauce. (Spoon a dollop of it onto the plate, place the slice over the sauce, and decorate with a sprig of parsley or watercress.)

🕐 Baked terrine will keep for several days under refrigeration.

Sour Cream Sauce for Fish:

When you are serving a sauce with something as delicate as a fish mousse baked in a terrine, you want a sauce that will go nicely with it but not mask any of its subtle flavors. Go easy on the seasoning here, then, hoping to make it just right for that mousse.

For about 2 cups (½ L)

The mousse cooking juices
1 cup (¼ L) sour cream
2 egg yolks (optional, for color)
½ cup (1 dL) heavy cream
1 tsp, more or less, prepared horseradish
½ tsp, more or less, prepared Dijon-type mustard
Drops of lemon juice
Salt and white pepper

If you have more than about 4 tablespoons of cooking juices, boil them down until they have reduced to that amount. Then pour into a mixing bowl, beat in 2 or 3 tablespoons of sour cream, then the egg yolks if you are using them. Stir in the rest of the sour cream and the heavy cream, and season to your taste with the horseradish, mustard, lemon juice, salt, and pepper.

🕐 Store in a covered bowl in the refrigerator; will keep for several days.

Variation—Sour Cream Sauce with Herbs:

In some cases, minced green herbs would go well in the sauce, especially if you are serving it with plain boiled fish. Stir in minced chives, chervil, tarragon, parsley, basil—according to your particular fish and your own desires.

Pâté en Croûte

*Spiced and wine-flavored ground meats
baked in a pastry crust*

*For a 4- to 5-pound (1 ¾- to 2 ¼-kg)
pâté, serving 10 to 12 people or more*

Although you can form the crust on an upside-down bowl, as illustrated farther on,
and you can make it of any size or shape you
wish—a pâté baked in its own special spring-
form is particularly appealing because it
looks as if it came straight out of a French
charcuterie.

Manufacturing Notes:
Measuring capacity of mold

To determine the capacity of your mold, set it
on a large piece of newspaper or plastic wrap
on a tray, and measure into it beans or rice by
the cupful. The fluted one illustrated here
holds 10 cups (2½ L); the oval one, a little bit
less.

Dough talk

You need a dough that will stand up to 2
hours of baking, that will be strong enough
to hold up after baking, and yet that will be
reasonably good to eat—pâté doughs are not
epicurean delights anyway, but should be
palatable. Be sure you roll it thick enough, or
it will crack either during or after baking,
and will be very difficult to line with aspic.
(Note aspic layer between top of meat and
crust in the illustration: aspic is poured in
through holes made in top crust, after pâté has
baked and cooled.)

Fat content

A meat pâté is just not successful if you cut
down on the amount of pork fat needed to
make it tender and to give it the quality it
should have. A great deal of the fat renders
out during cooking, but if you are restricted
as to fats, pâtés are not the kind of food you
should even consider in your diet. Fat proportions in classic French recipes can be as
high as one to one, or at least 1 part fat to 3
parts meat; I am suggesting that ¼ of the
total amount be fat, which is as little as I
think one can use successfully.

Pig's caul—caul fat

In most recipes, a thin sheet of pork fat lines
the inside of the dough, before the meat mixture goes in. This not only bastes the outside
of the meat, but reinforces the crust. If your
crust is solid enough, you do not need that
extra fat, but I have included a pig's caul
lining—mostly because I like to use it, and
also to show you that it exists. (See notes,
page 366.)

Dough for Pâté:

*For an 8- to 10-cup (2- to 2½-L) spring-
form*

**5 ¼ cups (¾ kg) all-purpose flour, unbleached
preferred (measure by dipping dry-measure
cups into flour and sweeping off excess)**

1 Tb salt

**2 sticks (8 ounces or 225 g) chilled unsalted
butter**

8 Tb (4 ounces or 115 g) chilled lard

**1 ½ cups (3 ½ dL) cold liquid: 6 egg yolks
plus necessary ice water, plus droplets more
water if needed**

Equipment:

**A heavy-duty electric mixer with a flat beater
is useful here**

If you do not have a mixer of the right type,
rub flour, salt, and fats together with balls of
your fingers, rapidly, without softening fat,
until fat is broken into the size of small oatmeal
flakes; rapidly blend in the liquids, to make a
moderately firm dough. Knead into a rough
cake. Wrap in plastic and refrigerate.

  If you have a mixer, blend flour, salt,
and fats at slow speed until mixture looks
like coarse meal; blend in liquid, still at slow
speed, until dough masses on blade. Turn out
onto work surface, adding droplets more
water to any unmassed bits in bottom of
mixing bowl. Dough should be moderately
firm. Knead into a rough cake. Wrap in plastic and refrigerate.

  Dough should be chilled for at least 2
hours, to give flour particles time to absorb

the liquid, and to relax the dough after its mixing.

🕐 May be made in advance, but dough containing unbleached flour will turn gray after a day or so under refrigeration—it keeps perfectly in the freezer, however.

Veal and Pork Filling for Pâtés and Terrines:
For about 9 cups (2 ¼ L)

3 cups (1 ½ pounds or 675 g) ground veal

3 cups (1 ½ pounds or 675 g) lean pork ground with 2 cups (1 pound or 450 g) fresh pork fat*

4 "large" eggs

2 ½ to 3 Tb salt

4 large cloves garlic, puréed

1 ½ Tb thyme

½ tsp ground imported bay leaves

1 ½ tsp ground allspice

1 tsp freshly ground pepper

1 ½ cups (3 ½ dL) cooked minced onions (sautéed slowly in butter)

½ cup (1 dL) Cognac or Armagnac

⅓ cup (5 Tb) dry Port wine

Garnish for Interior of Pâté:

1 cup (¼ L) chicken livers sautéed briefly in butter, or diced boiled ham, or strips of ham alternating with strips of veal, and/or truffles, pistachio nuts, etc., etc., etc.

Equipment:

A heavy-duty mixer with flat beater is also useful here for filling (not garnish)

* *Note:* Fresh pork shoulder is ideal because it contains just about the right proportion of lean and fat.

Beat all filling ingredients together until very well mixed. To check seasoning, sauté a spoonful, turning on each side, for several minutes to cook through; taste very carefully —salt and seasonings should seem almost twice as strong as normal, since they become very much milder after the pâté has baked and

cooled. We found the listed proportions right for us, after a too mild pâté or two—but spices vary in their savor; measurements, as always, are only indications and suggestions from one cook to another.

Fitting the Dough into the Spring-form Mold:

The chilled and rested dough

Flour for rolling out, etc.

A little lard, for greasing mold

Equipment:

The spring-form mold; a heavy rolling pin; a cup of water and a pastry brush; an edged baking sheet or jelly-roll pan

Make a paper pattern to guide you in forming dough cover, later; grease inside of mold.

Pâté en croûte —its rich meat stuffing laced with Port and Cognac, spices, and herbs, all encased in a greatcoat of decorated pastry

The dough is to be formed into a pouch that will fit into the mold so there will not be extra folds of dough. Here is a clever system invented by some ancient and nameless *croûtiste*:

Place the chilled dough on a lightly floured work surface and roll rapidly out into a rectangle about 1 inch (2½ cm) thick, and several finger widths larger and longer than the top and side of the mold. (*1*) Paint short sides of dough with a strip of water, and spread a thin layer of flour on bottom half; (*2*) fold the dough in half and press dampened sides together to seal (flour prevents interior flaps of dough from sticking together).

To start forming the pouch, bend the two sides down toward you, as shown, then roll the dough away from you, gradually lengthening it into a pouch shape. Careful here not to thin out the dough too much—combined thickness of the 2 layers should be no less than ¾ inch (2 cm).

Lightly flour the baking sheet, and place the greased mold upon it when you have lengthened the pouch to the right size. (*3*) Lift the dough into the mold, and fit it gently onto the baking sheet and side of mold, being careful not to stretch or thin out the dough—which could cause leakage or cracks during baking.

Fold edges of dough down outside of mold, and trim off with scissors, leaving a 1-inch (2½-cm) overhang. If by any chance you feel dough is too thin in places, patch with strips of raw dough—painting surface lightly with cold water, and pressing new dough in place.

🕐 Mold may be lined an hour or more in advance; cover closely with plastic wrap and refrigerate.

Roll out the leftover dough to a thickness of about 3/16 inch (approximately ¾ cm). Cut 2 pieces the size of the paper pattern (for covers), and whatever decorative cut-outs you have decided to use. Place on a plate, cover with plastic wrap, and chill.

Filling the Dough-lined Mold, and Finishing the Pâté:

A sheet of pig's caul, or strips of fresh pork fat ⅛ inch (½ cm) thick, to line sides and bottom of mold (optional)
About 9 cups (2¼ L) meat filling—veal and pork, or other
A garniture, like sautéed chicken livers, or other (optional)
The dough-lined mold and decorative dough pieces
Egg glaze (1 egg beaten with a pinch of salt and 1 tsp water)

Equipment:
1 or 2 pastry brushes; aluminum foil or pastry-bag tubes (for funnels)

1

2

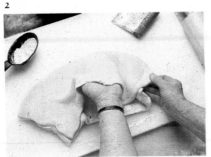

3

4

4) If you are using caul fat, drape it into the mold; or line bottom and sides with pork fat, if using.

5) Pack half the meat filling into the mold, press the optional garniture over it, and cover with the rest of the filling, reaching to the rim of the mold.

6) Press one of the cover pieces of dough over the filling, and fold the overhanging edges of the dough lining up over it. Paint with water, and press the second dough cover in place.

Paint top with water, and press decorations in place; press designs on top of the larger pieces with the back of a knife.

With a sharp-pointed knife, make 2 steam holes in top of dough cover, going right down into the meat. Wind 2 bits of aluminum foil around a pencil (or use metal tubes) to make funnels; butter them, and insert in the holes. (Needed to prevent crust from cracking as pâté steams and bubbles during baking.)

🕐 Pâté may be formed and decorated in advance, or may even be wrapped and frozen at this stage . . . thaw for a day in the refrigerator before baking.

7) Just before baking, paint with egg glaze, and make light crosshatchings in the glaze, over the dough, with the point of a knife.

Baking
Oven at 425°F/220°C and 350°F/180°C
Set in lower middle level of preheated oven and bake for about 20 minutes, or until pastry has started to brown lightly. Then turn the oven down and continue baking to an internal temperature of 155–160°F/67–71°C—which will usually take about 2 hours and 15 minutes for a 2-quart (2-L) mold of this general shape. Keep checking every 10 minutes after 1 3/4 hours, and if crust begins to brown too much, cover loosely with aluminum foil. Juices, bubbling up from pâté, should almost entirely lose their rosy color—being a faint pink at most, or a clear yellow. (Several times during baking, remove accumulated fat with a bulb baster or spoon from pan holding pâté mold.)

When done, remove from oven and let cool—2 hours or so are needed for the meat filling to consolidate itself, and for the crust to firm. After that time you may carefully remove the spring-form mold—or you may leave it on until pâté is cold. Then remove it.

Chill the pâté for 6 hours or longer, covered with plastic or foil. When thoroughly cold it is ready for its aspic lining—which fills the space between crust (where meat has shrunk during cooking) and meat.

🕐 A pâté (without aspic) will keep for 10 days under refrigeration. I do not think a cooked pâté freezes well, and do not recommend it—it has a damp quality when defrosted that cannot be disguised. However, I have not yet tried freezing, thawing, and reheating—it might help!

Filling the Spaces with Aspic:
4 cups (1 L) beautifully flavored aspic (see note next page)

The chilled pâté en croûte

Equipment:
A small-ended funnel or the metal tube from a pastry bag; a bulb baster

---

5

6

7

Note on Aspic: If you have no home-made beautiful clarified beef or brown poultry stock (pages 114, 218), use best-quality canned consommé: flavor it with dollops of Port or Madeira and Cognac to taste. Then dissolve 4 packages (4 Tb) plain unflavored gelatin in part of the cold liquid; when soft, heat it with the rest of the liquid, stirring, until gelatin is completely dissolved and there is not a trace of unmelted gelatin to be seen or felt. Very carefully correct seasonings, accentuating their strengths—remembering that flavors die down when foods are served cold. This is a stiff aspic, befitting an outdoor picnic pâté. Chill half of it, over ice, until cold but not set.

Aspic is now to be poured into the pâté, through the funnel holes; make sure they are not clogged, by poking down through them with a skewer to reveal the meat below. Place funnel or metal tube into one of the holes, and drop down through it dribbles of aspic, stopping now and then to tilt pâté in all directions. Continue until you see that aspic has come up to level of both holes. (Sometimes top of dough has not risen from top of meat, and you will not succeed in making the aspic enter—you may be sure crust has separated from meat in some places, however; you can only try your best to make it penetrate. If you do not succeed, pour the aspic into a pan, let it congeal in the refrigerator, then chop it up—crisscrossing with a knife in the pan—scoop the chopped aspic into a bowl, and serve along with the pâté, as a most pleasant accompaniment.)

To serve a pâté en croûte

How to cut up a *pâté en croûte*? You have to be daring when faced with fancy shapes like the fluted ogival—the one pictured. My system is to cut it in half crosswise with a serrated knife, then to cut the half lengthwise, and to cut each half of that into bias slices. Don't expect the slices to be neat and the crust to remain whole, especially with an edible crust such as this one. The crust may break, and the aspic may separate from the top, but you can arrange the slice neatly enough as you put it on the plate.

❶ A pâté baked in a crust with aspic filling will keep safely under refrigeration only for 3 or 4 days. If you wish to keep it longer, remove crust and aspic, and wrap meat filling securely in foil, where it will keep several days longer, and will always be welcome as a delicious plain ordinary marvelous pâté . . . or fancy French-type meat loaf.

Another Way to Make the Crust— Upside-down Molds:

If you don't have a spring-form hinged pâté mold, or want to make individual pâtés as illustrated here, a fine system is to form your dough on any kind of handy container that you turn upside down. Prick the dough all over, then set it in a preheated 400°F/205°C oven for 15 to 20 minutes to bake until set and barely browned. Unmold the crust, turn it right side up, fill it with pâté mixture, top it with a raw dough cover and decorations, and bake it as usual. Illustrated here are small pâtés that were baked about 45 minutes. The bottom crust is formed on an upside-down ovenproof jar. When filled, baked, and chilled, you may wish to pour in cold aspic, to fill empty spaces between meat and crust. Make pâtés this way in any shape and size you wish.

Single-serving pâtés

Plantation Spice Cookies

Sugar and molasses spice-ball cookies rolled in chopped peanuts

Variation on an old theme, this type of cookie is sometimes called a spice ball because it starts out round—though it ends up flat. They come in all sizes, but not many have these particular flavors. Easy to make and to bake, they are perfect for picnics or to serve with afternoon tea to sylphlike friends.

For 24 cookies 3 ½ inches (9 cm) in diameter

1 cup (4 ounces or 115 g) unsalted peanuts

1 ¼ cups (8 ½ ounces or 240 g) sugar

1 ½ sticks (6 ounces or 180 g) unsalted butter

1 "large" egg

⅓ cup (5 Tb) dark unsulphured molasses

2 cups (10 ounces or 285 g) all-purpose flour (measure by dipping dry-measure cup into flour container and sweeping off excess)

2 tsp baking soda

1 tsp powdered cinnamon

¾ tsp powdered cloves

½ tsp each powdered ginger and powdered nutmeg

¼ tsp salt

Equipment:

A nut chopper or grater (blenders and food processors do not work with peanuts); an electric mixer is useful; a flour sifter or a sieve; 2 or 3 large baking sheets, buttered

Grinding the nuts

Because of the peanut's shape and smoothness, it does not chop up evenly in a blender or food processor—you could chop the peanuts first in a bowl and finish in a processor, but that seems like double work. Buy them already chopped, or chop with one of the patent gadgets, or in an old-fashioned wooden bowl with a curve-bladed chopper. They should be in pieces of about 1/16 inch (¼ cm). Reserve half in a bowl with ¼ cup (50 g) of the sugar, for later.

Mixing the cookie dough

Place second half of peanuts in the mixer bowl with the rest of the sugar and the butter cut into pieces; cream together until light and fluffy. Beat in the egg, then the molasses.

Plantation spice cookies crusted with chopped peanuts and sugar

Put flour, soda, spices, and salt into sifter or sieve, and stir to blend; sift, then beat or stir into the cookie dough.

Forming the cookies
Oven preheated to 350°F/180°C
(The cookies are formed by rolling the dough into balls, rolling the balls in sugar and ground peanuts, then placing on baking sheets. If dough is too soft to form easily, chill for 20 minutes or until it has firmed up.)

Spread the reserved ground peanuts and sugar on a sheet of wax paper. With a tablespoon, take up a lump of dough and roll it into a Ping-Pong-sized ball. Roll ball in the sugar and chopped nuts, and place on a buttered baking sheet. (A 12-by-15-inch or 30-by-38-cm sheet will take 9 cookies—they spread as they bake.)

Baking
When one sheet is filled, place in middle (or lower or upper middle) level of preheated oven, fill the next sheet, and place in the oven, then the third. Cookies this large take about 15 minutes, and are done when set around the edges but still soft in the center—they swell as they bake, and the tops will crack. Take the cookies from the oven as done, and in 2 to 3 minutes they will crisp enough to be removed to a cake rack. Let cool.

To store the cookies, place in a cookie tin or airtight plastic bag, where they will keep nicely for several days. Or, for longer storage, freeze them.

Spice cookies flatten as they bake.

⏱ *Timing*

There are no last-minute or even last-hour jobs on this picnic, except to pack it, and that's easy if you have enough ice, or an insulated chest.

Your last job, which can be done 6 hours in advance, is to assemble the gazpacho salad. Allow at least half an hour for the trimmed vegetables to drain and to release some of their moisture. As you trim them, you can also trim and refrigerate the crudités.

The *pâté en croûte* can be baked as much as 3 days beforehand; the terrine, too. The cookies can be baked even a day or 2 earlier than that—or bake way ahead and freeze them.

The dough for the pâté crust can be mixed at any time, and so can the breads, if you are making them yourself. Both freeze well.

Menu Variations

Instead of having *gazpacho* in salad form, take gazpacho soup; among other good cold soups are cucumber, beet (page 267), mushroom, asparagus, peapod, spinach, green herb, celery, zucchini, turnip, tomato, watercress, and vichyssoise. If you're omitting the fish terrine, try cold scallop soup; cold white bean soup is delicious, too. Or, to return to salads, consider skewered vegetable salad, potato salad, or cold braised topinambours, or the cold artichoke hearts filled with shellfish or a vegetable mixture (page 384, or cold eggplant cases stuffed with mushrooms, or a cold ratatouille.

You can vary the fish terrine by coating it with aspic and serving it unmolded—though perhaps not on a very hot day! You can stuff it into edible sausage casings and serve "fish dogs," page 465. You can take along a whole poached fish, like salmon or striped bass, or poached fish steaks (page 405), or lobsters (page 353). Or if it's a boat picnic, take hook, line, and sinker, and good luck to you.

Pâté en croûte can be infinitely varied, or served crustless, as a terrine; most books, including my own, are full of recipes. And of course you can stuff a boned bird with a pâté mixture (such as the Chicken Melon on page 20). You can bake it with or without a crust, and/or coat it with aspic. The crust can be varied too, as in *Mastering II,* which has a pâté baked in brioche dough in a round pan (you cut it like a pie). Going a little further afield, you could serve a quiche, or a noble puff pastry Pithiviers stuffed with ham, or Cornish pasties, *chaussons,* and other meat turnovers.

As for the *cookies,* I do think it's nice to finish off with a crunch! The hazelnut wafers on page 392 are probably too fragile, but you could use the chocolate fudge cake recipe, page 312, in brownie form; the meringue-nut dough from the Los Gatos cake on page 11 makes a delicious crisp cookie; or, instead of forming meringue into *vacherins* (page 240), bake and serve it in cookie shapes. *Mastering I* and *II* both have *sablé,* or sugar, cookies (not sand cookies, as I've heard them called in English; they're named for Madame de Sablé, who invented them in the seventeenth century). *Mastering II* has cat's tongues, almond *tuiles* (fragile again), and two delightful puff pastry cookies; *J.C.'s Kitchen* has *tuiles* made with walnuts, cat's tongues, gingerbread, and two kinds of madeleines (really little sponge cakes— these would be delicious, though not crunchy).

Leftovers

The *gazpacho salad* will keep 3 to 4 days, but does lose a little of its charm. I think it might be nicer served as a soup, either hot or cold, with tomato juice added plus any other flavorful juices you saved when draining the trimmed vegetables.

The *fish terrine* keeps for several days; let's say 3 to play safe. If you have quite a bit, you might unmold it and serve it coated with aspic, as a beautiful first course for a fancy dinner, or turn the remains into a fish soup.

Once aspic'd, the *pâté en croûte* will not keep longer than a few days (see recipe).

On keeping *cheeses:* they vary, but remember to wrap them separately and they'll last much longer in the refrigerator. Cheese molds seem to turn each other on.

The *cookies* will keep for several days in a closed tin, or can be frozen.

Postscript: Picnic packing

Everybody has his own bag of tricks for this cheerful job; here are a few hints.

In case of damp or hard ground to sit on, take a rainproof poncho and a blanket. Our own green treasured blanket has accompanied us on picnics the world over, and is almost a talisman. Take extra water for drinking and hand washing, especially if the dog's coming along, and don't forget his favorite nibbles. We pack a roll of paper towels, extra—and extra-large—paper napkins, and we use insulated chests. If you like wicker hampers, line them with ant foilers (plastic dry-cleaner bags), so that if the basket is set on the ground, ants can't wriggle in through the crevices. I know families with children who pack light, compact amusements with every picnic, usually in a special box for just that purpose: a bat and ball, a kite, a Frisbee, horseshoes to pitch, cards, and a few books. Tied to one family's playbox, there is a whistle, for calling the children in. And speaking of tying, we've attached a bottle opener and a corkscrew permanently to our insulated chest, on long strings so they need never be detached—and lost. We always take rope or strong string when we plan to feast near an icy stream, so bottles can be suspended in the water—just as they can be lowered over the stern on a boat picnic.

Good gadgets to know about: one is a liquid, sold in metal containers; put them in the freezer, and they get ultracold and stay that way for an amazingly long time. We put a frozen one in the ice-cube chest, to delay melting. On chilling generally: since cold air moves downward, have flat-topped containers on which you can heap ice cubes.

Finally, as always: don't forget the salt!

For an intimate celebration —beauty, luxury, excellence, and ease

Rack of Lamb for a Very Special Occasion

Menu
For 6 people

Artichoke Scoops Garnished with Shellfish —
   A cold appetizer

Roast Rack of Lamb
Buttered New Carrots
Tomatoes Moussakaise —Baked tomatoes
   stuffed with lamb and eggplant
Gratin of Potatoes à la Savoyarde —Scalloped
   potatoes with onions and cheese

Fresh Strawberries and Hazelnut
   Cornucopias —Delicate rolled nut
   wafers filled with lightly whipped cream

Suggested wines:
Although some people avoid the combination
of wine and artichokes on the theory that
artichokes make wines taste sweet, I have
fortunately never found that to be the case
and would certainly serve a light dry white,
like a riesling. Bring out your very best red
Bordeaux —a Graves —or a well-aged
cabernet, for the lamb. A sparkling wine on
the sweet side, or a gewürztraminer,
Vouvray, or Sauternes, could go with the
dessert.

Before we go on to splurge on rack of lamb, that acme of expensive chic, please note that the back porch of this chapter, the Postscript, is comfortably occupied by two cozy, homey recipes for budget cuts of lamb. But tonight we're celebrating with all the stops out. Our guests are great travelers and restaurant connoisseurs, and in fact our first thought was to take them out for the kind of dinner they most appreciate. There are fine new restaurants around here, often run by young women chefs (our chefs Marian and Sara, for example), which have raised local standards to a much higher level of sophistication than we used to see. We *could* go out —but afterward, where would we install ourselves, as the French say, for the second half of the affectionate reunion that we all expect to go on until midnight?

And think of the price! Rack of lamb is not cheap at home, but it's half what it would be in a restaurant. And the nice thing is, it involves very little effort or last-minute preparation. (We've noticed about meat that the fancier the cut, the less trouble for the cook.)

So, home it is, and our easy menu gives us plenty of time to gussy up the place for that soigné look one enjoys in a top restaurant. Pat Pratt of the J. C. & Co. team folded our napkins into the fleur-de-lys shape she learned from her Danish grand-mother (see page 467 for her way of doing it). Tonight, we've tucked the crisp white flower-forms into big goblets— clear ones, not tinted.

so we can enjoy the color of the wine. When we choose things for the table, our first thought is whether they make the food look appetizing (as some magnificent china does not), and our second, whether they involve much fuss. The time we'd have to spend polishing silver we'd rather spend cooking.

At this dinner the food itself is so ornamental that it needs only the simplest setting. We left an inch of deliciously edible stem on the hollowed artichoke halves so that, heaped with the gold and pink of shrimp in an eggy vinaigrette, they'd have the air of bounteous little scoops. Interlaced like two Spanish combs, the racks of lamb are sculpturally elegant, yet the serving is not hindered at all. The crisp emerald green watercress sets off the perfect trim of the slim ribs, and the little golden carrots, gleaming with butter, provide a soft contrast in color and form. For the dessert, we found a bowl with a deeply scalloped rim to support the fragile cookie cornucopias around the rosy heap of strawberries; if one were lucky enough to own a Monteith, one of those punch bowls with crenelated sides that holds glasses, a truly splendorous effect could be achieved here.

The nicest food of all—I've said it before and will doubtless say again—gratifies all the senses at once, not just taste and scent, but sight, and even touch. All three of these courses tempt one to use fingers: the artichoke leaves, the last nibbly bits on the lamb ribs, the plump strawberries you take by the stem and dip into the cream-filled cornets. Whether the crisp dry crunch of these delicate cookies is more pleasant to feel or to hear, one can hardly say. . . .

"Our cat has a long tail tonight," once remarked Abraham Lincoln to dressy Mrs. Lincoln. Maybe it was Inauguration Night, for which that stout party wore enough purple velvet to drape a hearse, as you can see in the Smithsonian. Well, we're not that ambitious; but here we are with the house looking nice, an impeccable dinner well in train, a joyous reunion to come, and half an hour in hand. What about in a leisurely lemon verbena bath to honor *la vie en rose*?

Preparations and Marketing

Recommended Equipment:
To trim the lamb, you'll need a slicing knife, a paring knife, and possibly a small meat saw. To cook it, foil to protect the bare bones, and a roasting pan; to serve it with the racks interlaced and garnished, a wide platter.

A food processor is useful but not essential for grinding lamb to stuff tomatoes, for slicing onions and potatoes. For grinding nuts for the Plantation Cookies, you could use a knife or a nut chopper. You need a baking dish for the tomatoes, a baking-and-serving dish for the gratin, and a good-sized saucepan for the carrots.

To bake the cookies, you need a wide flexible spatula or a pancake turner. To form them, use metal cookie horns, or make your own out of brown paper (illustrated on page 393). Since baking is brief and precisely timed, a kitchen timer is a must.

I almost forgot cookie sheets. My oven repairman tells me that he often has calls from cookie cookers who complain that their oven thermostats are not working properly. It turns out that the cooks were apt to shove such large cookie sheets into their ovens that the heat could not circulate properly, and naturally the thermostats and the ovens themselves could not function as they should. He advises using a cookie sheet (or a baking sheet for any purpose) that will leave at least 1 inch (2½ cm) of air circulating all around its edges.

Staples to Have on Hand:

Salt
White peppercorns
Optional: hot pepper sauce
Granulated sugar
Confectioners sugar
Cream of tartar
Imported bay leaves
Dried thyme
Dried tarragon leaves
Optional: mixed herbs
Dijon-type prepared mustard
Pure vanilla extract
Wine vinegar
Light olive oil or best-quality salad oil
Optional: fresh peanut oil
All-purpose flour
Butter
Eggs (4 "large")
Heavy cream (1 pint or ½ L)
Fresh white nonsweet bread for crumbs
Garlic
Shallots or scallions
Parsley

Lemons (1)
Celery (1 stalk)
Dry white wine or dry white French vermouth
Dark Jamaica rum

Specific Ingredients for This Menu:

Cooked shellfish (see recipe); or use raw mushrooms (1½ cups; 12 ounces or 340 g) ▼
Racks of lamb (2, plus meat trimmings from them; see buying notes, page 385)
Artichokes (3 large fine)
Carrots (36 to 48 if 2 inches; 12 to 13 if large)
Eggplant (1 firm shiny, about 9 by 5 inches)
Tomatoes (3 large firm ripe)
"Boiling" potatoes (12 to 16 medium)
Onions (8 or 9 large)
Optional: watercress
Strawberries (about 2 quarts or 2 L)
Hazelnuts (¾ cup; 3 ounces or 85 g), shelled (also called filberts)
Grated Swiss cheese, or a mixture (1½ cups or 3½ dL)
Chicken stock (6 to 7 cups or 1½ to 1¾ L)

Some Mournful Remarks on Shellfish:
What filling to choose for the artichokes is a question of what is best and freshest-tasting in the market. I am sorry to report my growing disillusion with frozen shrimp, which, if I buy them peeled, have a pervasively chemical taste that seems slightly less pronounced in the frozen shrimp in shell that I find. Canned shrimp can be mushy, and fresh shrimp are rare indeed. The canned lobster I have sampled has been unthinkably bad in texture and taste, but I have tried some acceptable frozen lobster meat. Canned pasteurized refrigerated crabmeat, though terribly expensive, has been reliable in sauced dishes, but I have suffered some very poor examples of ordinary canned crab in the lower price ranges. Some frozen crabmeat has been excellent—when properly frozen and stored, and eaten soon—but frozen crab (and lobster too) must be thawed slowly in the refrigerator for a day or 2 to prevent it from becoming watery; I am told this has something to do with ice crystals that pierce the flesh if the thawing is too abrupt. If you cannot find good shrimp, crab, or lobster, switch to scallops, lightly poached in wine, or fresh raw mushrooms diced and tossed in the sauce.

Artichoke Scoops with Shellfish

Halved boiled artichokes and shellfish in egg yolk vinaigrette

For 6 people as a first course

Egg Yolk Vinaigrette:

½ Tb very finely minced shallots or scallions

½ tsp or more salt

¼ tsp dried tarragon leaves

1 raw egg yolk

1 tsp Dijon-type prepared mustard

1 Tb each lemon juice and wine vinegar

6 Tb light olive oil or best-quality salad oil

Freshly ground pepper

Drops of hot pepper sauce (optional)

Other Ingredients:

About 1½ cups (12 ounces or 340 g) cooked shellfish meat, or raw mushrooms

Artichoke scoops filled with shellfish

It is easy to scoop out the choke with a teaspoon.

Salt, pepper, oil, lemon juice—as needed

3 large fine boiled or steamed artichokes

The vinaigrette

Mash the shallots or scallions in a small bowl with the salt, then with the tarragon. Beat in the yolk and mustard, then the lemon juice and vinegar. In a small stream, beat in the oil. Season to taste with pepper, hot pepper sauce, and more salt if needed. Sauce should be a pale yellow cream with a light thickening so that it will film the shellfish but not mask it.

❋ Best made shortly before using. If it separates, shake in a screw-topped jar.

Assembling

Turn the shellfish (or mushrooms) into a bowl, and pick over to remove any possible debris. Fold in the dressing and let sit 10 minutes, folding several times. Taste, and add lemon, oil, and/or seasonings if you feel them necessary. Slice the artichokes in half lengthwise, and scoop out the central core of leaves and the chokes with a teaspoon. Shortly before serving, pile sauced filling into each cavity.

❋ It is best not to sauce the filling too far ahead for fear the sauce might separate. Instead, toss the shellfish with salt, pepper, and drops of lemon juice and oil; cover and refrigerate. Fold in the sauce and assemble 10 minutes before serving.

To Boil or Steam Artichokes the Simplest Way:

First hold each artichoke head under a stream of cold water, spreading the leaves gently apart to give a thorough washing. Slice off ½ inch (1½ cm) from the bottom of the stems, and pull off any small or withered leaves at the base. To boil, drop them into a large kettle of enough boiling salted water to submerge them completely, and boil slowly for 30 to 40 minutes, or until bases of artichokes are tender, and the bottom of a leaf is tender when you pull it through your teeth. To steam them, place in a vegetable rack in a covered kettle with 2 inches (5 cm) of water, and steam 30 to 40 minutes or until tender. Drain the artichokes bottom up, and serve them hot, warm, or tepid—or cold for the preceding recipe.

Buying and Trimming a Rack of Lamb

The rack of lamb is the whole rib chop section from one side of the lamb, going from the tip of the shoulder blade to the beginning of the loin, and comprising ribs number 6 through 12. (The official name for the rack is "lamb rib roast.") Although not as expensive as the saddle, which is the whole loin chop section from both sides of the lamb, the rack is a luxurious cut of exquisitely flavored tender meat. But there is not very much of it: 1 rack will serve only 2 to 3 people.

If you look closely at the photograph of our lamb here, which is indeed a fine specimen, you can see the purple grading stamp on the fat, U.S.D.A. Prime, which is the official federal classification for the very best grade of meat, more often reserved for restaurants than for the retail markets where most of us shop. Choice, the next grade, is very good too, but just not quite as perfect in every category and therefore not quite as expensive.

How to recognize quality in a rack of lamb

Look for the purple grade stamp, which should be left on the meat. The color of the meat should be fresh and deep bright red, with almost a silky sheen to it; the fat should be hard

Left to right: shoulder, rib section (or rack), loin (or saddle), the two legs (or baron). I'm holding a rack.

and creamy white; the eye of the meat—the large, most edible part of it—should be reasonably big and rounded. When you turn the rack over and look on the underside, the bones should be tinged with pink, and slightly rounded—they whiten and flatten with age. The best way to pick fine meat, for most of us, is to find a good meat market and make friends with the head butcher. Butchers are human, and most of them blossom into real friendliness when they find an interested customer who, too, is serious about meat.

To trim a rack of lamb

A rack of lamb is easy to trim, and it is not a bad idea to do it yourself—then you know it will be done right. Besides, you will get all the meat scraps to use, and the bone for making your sauce.

1)Removing backbone. The backbone should be very carefully detached from the tops of the ribs (on the underside or rib side of the rack), in such a way that the eye of the meat, lying right under the backbone, is not disturbed. If you don't have a saw, you can ask the butcher to do this for you, but ask him please to be very careful. When the tops of the ribs are loose, very neatly detach the meat from the under part of the backbone, then detach the backbone from the strip of fat covering the top side of the meat.

2)Trimming rack to expose lower ribs. Cut right down to the rib bones, about halfway from their tip ends to the eye of meat, as shown, cutting straight across, then slicing against ribs and down to rib ends.

3)Trimming excess fat and "cap" meat off the rack. One end of the rack is a little heavier than the other, because there are two layers of meat, with fat, covering the eye of the meat at that end. You want to remove all but a thin covering of fat. Start at the shoulder, or heavier, end.

*4)Note the eye of the meat. Lift, pull, and cut extra meat and fat layers off—they separate easily—leaving only a thin layer of fat over the whole eye area.

5)Frenching the bone ends. Cut the meat out from between the rib bones, then scrape the bones clean—this is picky work, but worth it if you want the rack to look its luxury price.

6)The trimmed rack. The fully trimmed rack illustrated here weighs less than 1½ pounds (¾ kg) with the fat, the cap meat, and the backbone removed. An untrimmed rack weighs 3½ pounds (1½ kg). However, you do have the backbone to use, and you can also recuperate a handful of usable meat between the fat layers you removed from the top and from between the ribs.

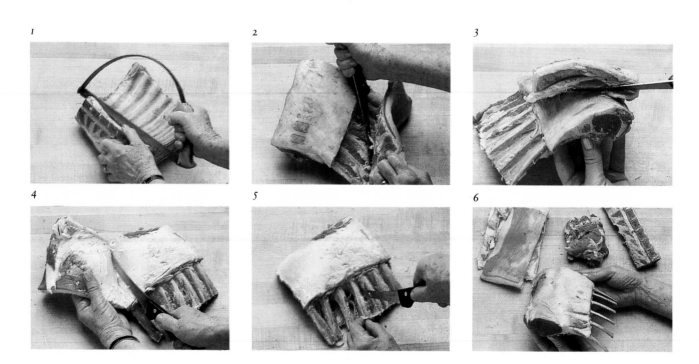

Roast Rack of Lamb

Carré d'agneau

Although the trimmed rack of lamb looks small, it does take about half an hour to roast in the oven. You can make the racks ready to roast well ahead; then, after their first searing, they need no more attention for 15 minutes—which could give you time for your first course. I have suggested a mustard and bread crumb coating here, which browns nicely and furnishes a gentle crunch.

For 6 people

2 racks of lamb, fully trimmed (see preceding directions)

For the Mustard Coating:

1 clove garlic

½ tsp salt

½ tsp dried thyme

2 to 3 Tb prepared Dijon-type mustard

3 to 4 Tb light olive oil or fresh peanut oil

Other Ingredients:

½ cup (1 dL) crumbs from fresh white nonsweet bread

3 to 4 Tb melted butter

A little sauce for the lamb (see directions following recipe)

Watercress leaves or parsley, for garnish

Equipment:

Aluminum foil to cover rib ends; a kitchen timer and an instant (microwave) meat thermometer are useful

Preparing the lamb for the oven

Score the tops of the racks lightly—making shallow crisscross knife slashes in the covering fat. Mash the garlic and salt together in a small bowl, mash in the thyme, then beat in the mustard and the oil. Paint mixture over tops and meaty ends of racks.

Set racks meat side up on an oiled roasting pan, and fold a strip of foil over the rib ends to keep them from scorching.

🕐 May be prepared several hours in advance; cover and refrigerate.

Roasting the racks of lamb

25 to 30 minutes

Preheat oven to 500°F/260°C and set oven rack in upper middle level. The first part of the roasting is to sear the lamb; when oven is ready, put the racks in and set timer for 10 minutes. When time is up, slide out oven rack and rapidly spread a coating of bread crumbs over the top of each rack, and baste with dribbles of melted butter. Turn thermostat down to 400°F/205°C, and roast for 15 minutes more, then begin checking. Lamb is done to a nice rosy rare at 125°F/52°C on an instant meat thermometer—or when the meat, if pressed with your finger, begins to show a slight resistance rather than being squashy like raw meat. (When you have a

After its mustard coating, cover rib ends with foil, and the lamb is ready for the oven.

special, expensive roast like this, it is better to err on the side of rareness, since it is a shame to serve it overdone unless, of course, your guests prefer their lamb that way.)

🕐   Although you are safer serving the lamb soon after it is done—giving it a few minutes before carving for the juices to retreat back into the meat—you can let it wait. Be sure, however, that you set it at a temperature not over 120°F/49°C so it cannot overcook—use a reliable warming oven, or let your roasting oven cool off with the door open and check with an oven thermometer before you put the racks back again. You can also do the preliminary searing, then set the lamb at room temperature and continue the final roasting in half an hour or so. The crucial consideration is that it not overcook. (I made the terrible mistake, once, of setting my beautiful, madly expensive, perfectly

Roast racks of lamb with their crisp mustard and bread crumb coating

roasted ribs of beef in the upper part of a double gas oven combination to wait for half an hour. The lower oven was on, and although the upper oven was off, that lower oven overheated my upper oven and the waiting roast came out well done. Tears of rage, but a lesson learned.)

Serving

The interlaced rib arrangement in the photograph here is attractive for 2 racks of lamb, and carving is easy. You cut down between the ribs on each side, and each guest gets 2 perfectly trimmed chops. Spoon a little sauce around the chops, garnish with watercress or parsley, and the buttered carrots.

A Little Sauce for the Lamb:
About 2 hours' simmering time

There will be little or no juice in the roasting pan because the lamb is cooked rare and no juices escape. But it is nice to have a little sauce to moisten the meat, and you can easily make one—but you will have to plan ahead for it—using the backbones you removed from the racks.

Whack the bones into convenient chunks and brown them in a medium-sized saucepan with 2 tablespoons oil, and a chopped onion and carrot. Sprinkle on 2 tablespoons flour and let brown for several minutes, stirring. Remove from heat and blend in ½ cup (1 dL) or so of dry white wine or vermouth, and 2 cups (½ L) chicken stock. Bring to the simmer, skim off scum for several minutes, then add a small celery stalk, a mashed garlic clove, ½ teaspoon dried thyme, and an imported bay leaf. Cover partially and simmer about 1½ hours, skimming occasionally and adding water if liquid evaporates below ingredients. Strain into another saucepan, degrease, and carefully correct seasoning. You should end up with a cup or so of delicious slightly thickened light brown sauce that tastes like lamb, and that will complement but not in any way overpower the delicate flavor of your roast.

Buttered Carrots

As a garnish

Your carrots must be delicious to eat, as well as providing color on the platter. Frozen or canned carrots simply will not do because they are, in my experience, mushy, and they certainly lack the flavor of fresh carrots. Baby fresh carrots, however, unless one has them fresh from a neighboring garden, can often be flavorless and textureless, too. Far better in many instances to trim mature fresh carrots, and have them taste as they should.

For 6 to 8 carrot pieces per person

Either 36 to 48 baby carrots about 2 inches (5 cm) long, or 12 or more mature carrots

Cold water

2 Tb butter for cooking, plus 2 to 3 Tb for final flavoring

1 Tb very finely minced shallots or scallions

½ tsp salt, more as needed

Freshly ground white pepper

1 tsp sugar

Trim and peel the carrots. If you are using mature carrots, halve or quarter them and pare to nice baby carrot shapes (save trimmings for salads or soup). Arrange in a roomy saucepan with enough water to come halfway up the carrots. Add the initial 2 tablespoons butter, the shallots or scallions, salt, pepper, and sugar. Cover the pan and boil for 5 minutes (or longer for mature carrots) until liquid has evaporated and carrots are just tender—careful at the end that carrots don't scorch. Correct seasoning.

🕐 May be cooked ahead. Set aside uncovered.

Shortly before serving, toss the carrots with the additional butter, so they are warmed through and glistening.

Tomatoes Moussakaise

Baked tomatoes stuffed with lamb and eggplant

I call these "moussakaise" because the stuffing is lamb and eggplant, and that's what makes a moussaka, a good accompaniment since there is not much meat on a rack of lamb. These stuffed tomatoes beef up the meal, so to speak.

For 6 tomato halves

1 firm shiny eggplant about 9 by 5 inches (23 by 13 cm)

Salt

A handful of parsley sprigs

1 or 2 cloves garlic, peeled

1 large onion, peeled and quartered

Olive oil or other cooking oil

The meat trimmings from the racks of lamb, or about 1½ cups (3½ dL; 12 ounces or 340 g) lean raw lamb stew meat

½ cup (1 dL) dry white wine or dry white French vermouth

1 cup (¼ L) chicken stock

½ tsp thyme (or rosemary, or mixed herbs, or tarragon)

3 large firm ripe tomatoes

Freshly ground pepper

Trimmings from racks of lamb make a delicious stuffing for accompanying tomatoes.

½ cup (1 dL) crumbs from crustless fresh white nonsweet bread

Equipment:

A food processor with steel blade makes quick work of the chopping.

Salting and draining the eggplant

Peel the eggplant and cut into dice ⅜ inch (1 cm) to a side; toss in a large sieve with 1 teaspoon salt and let drain.

Chopping onion and lamb

Meanwhile, if you have a food processor, start it running, and drop in the parsley, letting machine run for a few seconds until parsley is chopped; scrape parsley into a small bowl and reserve. (Do not bother to clean out processor too thoroughly.) Start running it again, and drop in the garlic; when minced, drop in the onion, turning machine on and off in several bursts until onion is chopped fairly fine. Film a medium-sized frying pan (nonstick preferred) with oil, turn the onion and garlic into it, and sauté slowly. Divide the lamb into 2 batches and grind 1 batch at a time with on-off spurts in the processor, adding each as done to the onion. (Otherwise, chop ingredients by hand, using a meat grinder, if you wish, for the lamb.)

Simmering the lamb

Sauté the lamb with the onion for a few minutes over moderately high heat, tossing and turning, until lamb has browned lightly and turned from red to gray; pour in the wine and stock, and stir in the herbs. Cover and simmer slowly for about half an hour, or until lamb is tender and liquid has evaporated. Turn lamb into a sieve set over a bowl, to drain out accumulated cooking fat.

The tomato shells

With a grapefruit knife, potato baller, or teaspoon, hollow out the tomatoes, leaving just the outer flesh. Salt lightly, and reverse on a rack to drain.

Finishing the stuffing

Dry the eggplant in paper towels; film the frying pan again with oil, and sauté the eggplant, tossing and turning, for several minutes until tender. Return the lamb to the pan with the eggplant and sauté a few minutes more, tossing and turning and letting the mixture brown very lightly. Toss with the minced parsley, and carefully correct seasoning.

🕐 Stuffing may be prepared a day in advance; refrigerate in a covered container.

Filling the tomatoes

Arrange the tomatoes hollow side up in an oiled baking dish. Fill them with the stuffing, spread on a spoonful of bread crumbs, and drizzle a little oil over the tops.

🕐 May be prepared several hours in advance. Cover and refrigerate.

Baking—or broiling

10 minutes or less

The tomatoes need just a thorough heating through, since the stuffing is all cooked and you don't want the shells to burst. Set them in the oven with the lamb, during its last bit of cooking. (Or bake 10 minutes or so in a 400°F/205°C oven, or set under a low broiler.)

🕐 Tomatoes should be cooked only at the last minute or they lose their shape.

Tomatoes with lamb and eggplant stuffing make a nice luncheon dish.

Gratin of Potatoes à la Savoyarde—or à la Lyonnaise

Scalloped potatoes baked in broth with onions and cheese

Some kind of potato dish is very good with lamb, and I like this one cooked in broth, rather than in milk like the famous potatoes dauphinoise, since it is less rich—although the cheese does add a certain heft. However, the lamb morsels are so small!

For 6 people

Several Tb soft butter
2 to 3 cups (½ to ¾ L) thinly sliced onions
12 to 16 medium "boiling" potatoes, peeled and thinly sliced
Salt and freshly ground pepper
1½ cups (3½ dL) coarsely grated Swiss cheese (or a mixture from your frozen hoard, page 235)
2 to 3 cups (½ to ¾ L) chicken stock

Equipment:

A food processor is useful for slicing onions and potatoes, or a hand slicer; a flameproof 2-quart (2-L) baking-and-serving dish, such as an oval one 9 by 12 by 2 inches (23 by 30 by 5 cm)

Assembling

Preheat oven to 425°F/220°C. Melt 2 tablespoons butter in a frying pan and sauté the onions slowly, stirring occasionally, while you peel and slice the potatoes. Smear the baking dish with butter and spread in a layer of potatoes, season lightly with salt and pepper, and spread in ⅓ of the onions (which need not be fully cooked), then ⅓ of the cheese. Continue with 2 more layers of potatoes, onions, and cheese, ending with the last of the cheese. Dot top with 2 tablespoons butter, and pour in enough chicken stock to come only halfway up the potatoes.

Baking

About 40 minutes

Set dish over moderately high heat on top of the stove, bring to the simmer, and place in lower middle level of preheated oven. Bake for 30 to 40 minutes. Ideally the liquid will have been almost entirely absorbed when the potatoes are tender; if not, remove baking dish from oven, tilt it, and draw out excess liquid with a bulb baster. Boil it down rapidly in a saucepan until thickened, pour it back into the dish, tilting in all directions, and return to oven for a few minutes to finish baking.

🕐 If potatoes are to stay warm for half an hour or so, remove from oven when they are tender but there is still a little unabsorbed liquid in the dish; keep warm, loosely (never tightly) covered, over a pan of simmering water, on an electric hot tray, or in a warming oven.

Thinly sliced potatoes cook quickly.

Hazelnut Cornucopias

Rolled cookies—cookie horns—tuiles aux avelines

This is the type of cookie that is soft and pliable when it has just come from the oven, giving you several seconds to roll or form it into a shape before it crisps. The formula makes a nicely delicate wafer, and the flavor of toasted hazelnuts is particularly delicious. If you cannot find fine fresh hazelnuts, however, substitute walnuts—which can be ground without toasting. (*Note:* All shelled or ground nuts keep freshest in the freezer.)

For about 16 cookies 4½ inches (11½ cm) in diameter

¾ cup (3 ounces or 85 g) shelled hazelnuts

½ cup (3½ ounces or 100 g) sugar

½ stick (2 ounces or 60 g) unsalted butter

⅛ tsp salt

2 Tb heavy cream

¼ cup (4 Tb or ½ dL) egg whites (about 2 whites)

4 level Tb (1¼ ounces or 35 g) all-purpose flour in a sifter

1 Tb dark Jamaica rum

A little soft butter

Equipment:

A blender or food processor (or nut chopper); 2 lightly buttered nonstick cookie sheets; a kitchen timer; a wide flexible spatula or a pancake turner; 3 or 4 metal cookie horns, or cornucopia shapes made from brown paper. Those illustrated here are 4½ inches long and 2 inches in diameter at the mouth (11½ by 5 cm); other sizes and shapes are illustrated at the end of the recipe.

Toasting and grinding the hazelnuts
(The hazelnuts are toasted to give additional flavor and also to loosen the outside skins; taste several to be sure they are not rancid.) Place them in a roasting pan and toast for 10 to 15 minutes in a preheated 350°F/180°C oven, stirring 2 or 3 times, until lightly browned. Rub by small handfuls in a towel to remove as much of their brown skins as you easily can. When cool, grind ⅓ of them roughly in a blender or food processor and set aside in a small bowl. Grind the rest of them with the sugar, and reserve for the following cookie mixture.

The cookie mixture
Preheat oven to 425°F/220°C, and set rack in middle level. Cream the butter in a mixing bowl (if chilled, cut into pieces and beat with a wooden spoon in a metal bowl over warm water; if it softens too much, then beat over cold water until a creamy mass). Blend in the sugar and hazelnut mixture, the salt, and the cream. Add the egg whites, stirring only enough to blend. Sift and fold in the flour by thirds, then fold in the rum. Mixture should look like a heavy batter.

🕐 Batter should be used promptly.

Forming, baking, and rolling the cookies
Before forming the cookies, be sure the oven is preheated, have your spatula and your metal or paper molds ready, and have your kitchen timer handy. Drop a 2-tablespoon blob of cookie mixture on a buttered cookie sheet, and spread it out, as illustrated, into a 4½-inch

There's room for only three cookies on this standard-sized nonstick baking sheet.

(11½-cm) circle with the back of a tablespoon, making sure that the edges are the same thickness as the rest of the shape, or about ¹/₁₆ inch (¼ cm). Form 1 or 2 more cookie shapes, leaving a good inch (2½ cm) between them. Sprinkle a pinch of chopped hazelnuts over each. Place in oven and set timer for 4 minutes, meanwhile forming another sheet of cookies.

Cookies are done when about ¼ inch (¾ cm) around edges is lightly browned (if they seem to be cooking too fast, lower oven thermostat slightly). Set cookie sheet on open oven door and let cool a few seconds. One at a time gently slither spatula or pancake turner under a cookie all around to loosen it, lift it off, turn it upside down on your work surface, and roll it around the metal or paper horn. Rapidly repeat with the other cookies—leaving them on the oven door keeps them pliable until you are ready to roll them.

Close oven door and wait for oven to come up to temperature again, then bake the other sheet, and form another batch. Meanwhile, in less than a minute, the rolled cookies will have crisped and you can gently dislodge the molds. Let cookies cool on a rack.

🕐 These cookies are fragile, and soften rapidly in damp weather. Bake them shortly before serving, or store in a warming oven at around 100°F/38°C, or freeze them.

Variations:

You can roll the cookies into other shapes, such as cylinders, using the end of a wooden spoon or a cylindrical cookie form. You can press the limp cookie over the outside of a small bowl or inside a teacup to make cookie cups. You can make the classic tile or *tuile* shape, when you drape the limp cookie over a rolling pin to crisp. Or, of course, you can serve them perfectly plain and flat—which makes them easier to store, and nice with tea or sherbets.

Work quickly while cookies are still warm and pliable. Use a metal form for rolling cookies or make one out of brown paper.

Variations on a cookie theme

Fresh Strawberries and Cream-filled Hazelnut Cornucopias

The reason for rolling the preceding hazelnut wafers into cornucopias is so that you can fill them with a light whipped cream and serve them with strawberries. You dip the berries by their stems into powdered sugar, and then into the cream—lovely finger food for all ages. However, plain whipped cream all by itself is, I think, so rich that I like it lightened with some beaten egg whites, which also serves to stabilize the cream.

For 6 people

About 2 quarts (2 L) beautiful fresh ripe strawberries

2 egg whites, a pinch of salt, and a pinch of cream of tartar

½ pint (¼ L) heavy cream, chilled

About 2 cups (½ L) confectioners sugar, sifted

Pure vanilla extract, or dark Jamaica rum, or kirsch

6 hazelnut cornucopias (preceding recipe), plus more, if you wish, to pass with the berries

2 Tb chopped toasted hazelnuts (preceding recipe)

Equipment:

A clean dry bowl for whipping egg whites, and a large wire whip or portable beater; a second bowl, of metal, for whipping cream, set into a larger bowl with a tray of ice cubes and water to cover them

The strawberries

If strawberries are sandy, drop them into a bowl of cold water, swish them gently, then lift out immediately and drain on a rack. Pick them over to be sure each is perfect, but do not stem them.

Whipped cream lightened with egg whites

Shortly before serving, beat the egg whites until they start foaming, then beat in the salt and cream of tartar, and continue beating until egg whites form stiff peaks. Set egg whites aside and immediately start whipping the cream, using the same beater—circulate it all around the bowl, incorporating as much air as possible, and whip until cream holds its shape nicely but is not too stiff. Fold in enough of the egg whites by dollops to lighten the cream, but it should hold its shape sufficiently to be spooned into the cornucopias. Fold in confectioners sugar to taste—2 to 3 tablespoons, and 1 teaspoon or so of vanilla, rum, or kirsch. (Complete information on egg whites, page 465; on cream, page 464.)

🕐 Strawberries may be prepared and left on their rack an hour or so in advance—refrigerate them on a hot day. If the cream is made somewhat ahead, turn it into a sieve lined with washed cheesecloth and set over a bowl; cover with plastic wrap and refrigerate—it will exude a little milky liquid.

Serving

The moment before serving, arrange the berries in a bowl or on plates. Fill the cornucopias with the cream, using a teaspoon or a pastry bag, and sprinkle a pinch of chopped nuts over the top of the cream; arrange the cornucopias in a bowl, as illustrated. Serve at once, passing separately bowls of powdered sugar and the remaining cream plus, if you wish, additional cornucopias or, better, the same cookie but in one of the other shapes illustrated on page 393.

🕐 *Timing*

You will need a few—a very few—extra minutes between each course of this dinner. Before dessert, you'd fill and arrange the cookies; take your time, they're fragile. Before the main course, first you'd take the lamb out of the oven. It will sit and re-absorb its juices while you change plates, toss the carrots in hot butter, garnish your warm platter, and bring forth the gratin. Surely you'll want to parade the stylish lamb platter around the table and then carve it right there, which takes seconds. Courses like these shouldn't follow like railroad cars anyway, jolt, jolt, jolt; they should be set apart by a tender moment of memory and anticipation.

If you have only one oven, do the potatoes ahead, and keep them warm while roasting the lamb. Or cook them partially and let them finish with the lamb. Ideally, the lamb should undergo its second stage of roasting, accompanied with the tomatoes, while you're enjoying the first course.

Just before dinner, then, set the crumbed and basted lamb back in the oven with the tomatoes. Just before that, sauce the shellfish and spoon into the artichoke halves, and arrange the strawberries in their bowl (strawberries can bruise each other so they're better fixed not too far ahead).

An hour before dinner (on the one-oven plan), the lamb gets seared; then the oven temperature is lowered and the potatoes are sliced and the gratin mixed and baked, while the lamb sits at room temperature. At this time you'd whip the cream and refrigerate it in a cheesecloth-lined sieve over a bowl, and make the sauce for your shellfish.

That morning, you would prepare the lamb for the oven and refrigerate it, cook the onions for the gratin, cook the carrots, and hollow, stuff, and refrigerate the tomatoes.

The day before, you trim the lamb, make sauce with the bones, and prepare the tomato stuffing. That day, or even the day before that, you can cook and refrigerate the artichokes.

The cookies can be made any time and frozen; just bear in mind that the batter should be baked right after mixing.

Menu Variations

See Mournful Remarks preceding the *artichoke scoops* recipe for artichoke-filling possibilities (and problems). Mayonnaise alone might be too rich, but you could simply spoon a little vinaigrette into the artichoke cavities. Or mound the scoops with highly seasoned egg or fish salad. An alternative would be asparagus, either hot or cold, or tucked into puff pastry rectangles as we did on the first series of the *Company* shows.

I can't think of any main dish so elegant as *rack of lamb*—and that's the point of this whole dinner.

As for *vegetables,* we chose the potato gratin for ideal flavor, and the others chiefly for their looks. You could stuff onions with the delectable lamb and eggplant mixture, and serve cherry tomatoes in butter with herbs (page 221). If they're small enough to be served one apiece, stuff your eggplant cases. I think you do want something tangy, so tomatoes in some form are good, and something hearty and rich; what about potatoes Anna or doing those "straw mat" potatoes (page 219), but in a square form, in an electric frying pan? Their tangly look would set off the sculptural symmetry of the lamb racks. The old-fashioned thing was to carve the racks and make a palisade, like a crown roast, around a heap of mashed potatoes, then put a paper frill on each rib end. Too thumby-looking for me.

The *cookie* recipe works perfectly with walnuts, if you can't get really fresh hazelnuts; and the cookies can be formed into several shapes, as suggested at the end of the recipe. If you made cookie cups, you might fill them with raspberries or blueberries, and pass whipped cream separately. Or you could make the *vacherins* on page 240, but very small ones, fill them with the cream, and surround each with strawberries. Various other cookies are suggested on page 379.

Leftovers

Cooked *artichokes* keep for 2 or 3 days. If you have spare ones, try slicing the bases and serving them in a thickened vinaigrette with scallops "cooked" in lime juice, as on page 183. Or mix artichoke bits into a salad. Extra shellfish can be minced and mixed with mayonnaise for a cocktail dip or spread.

Extra cooked *lamb ribs* are the cook's precious property. Bare your teeth and snarl, until lunch tomorrow.

Cooked *carrots* can be reheated, briefly. Or wash them off and dice them for a cold vegetable *macédoine,* or for a soup garnish. The *potato gratin* can be reheated, and so can the *tomatoes*—chop them and serve on toast.

As for the *dessert,* cookies freeze, and you can purée the strawberries, mix with extra cream, and freeze for a strawberry mousse.

Postscript: Two budget cuts of lamb

Flanks and Breast of Lamb:
Although a rack of lamb is costly indeed, the lamb flank, which is the continuation of the rack down the belly of the beast, sometimes comes free with the rack. If not, it costs $1/5$ as much, which is very reasonable. The breast of lamb corresponds to the brisket of beef; it is the flank and its continuation toward the front.

Separate fatty flank ribs from whole brisket, then loosen breastbone from ribs before cooking; remove it afterward.

Broiled or Barbecued Lamb Flanks

Epigrammes d'agneau

For 4 to 6 people—2 lamb flanks
Peel and cut fell (outside membrane) and fat from top of flanks; slit open and remove excess fat from inside. Cut the flanks into serving pieces, leaving riblets in the meat. Brown lightly in a frying pan in a little oil, with a chopped carrot and onion. Pour out browning fat, add half-and-half white wine or vermouth and chicken stock barely to cover the meat. Add a clove of garlic, an imported bay leaf, and a little dried thyme. Cover and simmer slowly for about an hour, or until lamb is tender. Remove to a platter, arrange in 1 layer, and set a pan and weight on top, to flatten the meat, which will have curled out of shape during its cooking. Leave for 20 to 30 minutes.

When ready to broil, cover 1 side of each piece with the mustard coating described for the racks of lamb, page 387, and spread on a layer of fresh bread crumbs and a drizzle of melted butter. When ready to cook, set for several minutes under a hot broiler until heated through and nicely browned.

You could boil down the braising liquid, after degreasing it, and serve it as a sauce; or keep it in the freezer for the next time you need a sauce for lamb.

Lamb flanks may also be barbecued.

Stuffed Braised Breast of Lamb

For 4 to 6 people
The breast of lamb contains the boat-shaped breastbone with a number of auxiliary bones attached, and some riblets. Leave the riblets in, but detach the breastbone from them; remove breastbone after cooking. Slice off the fell and fat from outside the meat. Cut a pocket the length of the meat going under the rib bones, removing any fat layers you can reach inside.

Use a rice and lamb or sausage stuffing, or bread crumb stuffing, or the lamb and eggplant stuffing suggested for the tomatoes on page 389. Sew or skewer the stuffing into the pocket left by the breastbone. Brown and braise the breast for about an hour, as described for the flanks in the preceding recipe— you may wish to add a peeled and chopped tomato or 2 along with the rest of the ingredients. Serve with a dish of fresh beets (page 276) or a salad, for a hearty informal meal.

Breast of lamb, stuffed and braised, makes its own savory sauce.

*Classic, delicate, and perfect for a fine day in
June . . . or November, for that matter*

Summer Dinner

Menu
For 6 people

A Platter of Chicken Livers Molded in Aspic

*Individual Fresh Salmon Steaks, Poached,
    and Served with Hollandaise Sauce*
New Potatoes
*Cucumber Triangles Sautéed in Butter
    and Dill*

*Savarin au Rhum et aux Fruits Exotiques —
    The giant ring-shaped cousin of rum
    baba, filled with a selection of tropical
    fruits*

Suggested wines:
*A light dry white with the first course, like a
riesling or muscadet. A fine full white with
the salmon, like a Meursault, Corton
Charlemagne, or well-aged chardonnay. A
sparkling wine with the dessert —semisweet
Champagne, Vouvray mousseux, Asti
spumante*

If we were serving this meal in cool weather, when it would certainly taste just as good, we might begin with hot consommé. But in warm weather, what could seem more piquant and inviting than these small oval aspics, clear as fine amber, set around a jackstraw pile of finely slivered crisp string beans? These fanciful trifles have a festive air, though their decoration is a simple matter, and the poached chicken livers, mysteriously brooding within, are delicately flavorful. Delicacy is, indeed, crucial, because salmon has so much character that it must dominate any menu on which it appears.

Since salmon has become increasingly expensive, we rarely buy a whole fish anymore; rather, we offer salmon steaks. In America, green peas from the garden are the classic accompaniment, especially on the Fourth of July, when salmon is traditionally eaten. Some prefer it with fresh asparagus; some like it cold, with mayonnaise and a cucumber salad. I like the cucumber idea, and agree with Scandinavian cooks that dill is the herb of choice with salmon. So we'll have our cukes cooked very lightly in dill and butter, dished up fragrant and crisp, with a golden hollandaise for pink fish and green vegetable. Cold salmon is delightful, but, now that this great fish is a rare luxury, we want it at its most glorious—in other words, hot. The platter looks particularly appetizing—appearance matters so much in summer meals! And you can't have boiled salmon without boiled potatoes, especially new ones cooked in their tender skins.

Our fish is a Pacific salmon, *Oncorhynchus*, 3 of whose species, the silver, sockeye, and pink, are most commonly found in fishmarkets. To acquire its Atlantic cousin, *Salmo salar*, you generally have to pack up your waders and head for Nova Scotia or Iceland. All salmon are rare these days, because for a century we failed to take into account their very special habits, and to preserve the complex environment they require. They're anadromous, meaning that they live and grow in the ocean but spawn in fresh water: always in the very water where they themselves were spawned. This may mean a tremendous journey upstream, leaping up falls or fish ladders built into dams. If the stream is obstructed or polluted, the salmon can't make it. Just lately, though, salmon have been found in rivers that had not known them for a century: children of spawn planted there by the U.S. Fish and Wildlife Service. Hope springs eternal!

Strawberries follow salmon on so many menus; though they'd be delicious with a savarin cake, we've opted this time for the doubly summery taste of tropical fruits, adding enormous black grapes to set off the green of kiwi fruit and the orange of mango and papaya. A few black grapes are saved, to be lightly frosted with sugar and set becomingly around the glazed, gleaming, rum-soaked cake. The traditional decoration is crystallized fruits, but I haven't found good ones here lately, and I wasn't foresighted enough to order replenishments from France. If you want the real thing, fruits big and brilliant as crown jewels and tasting intensely *like* fruit—not like rubber baby-buggy bumpers—you can write to Maiffret, Fabrique de Fruits Confits et Chocolats, 53, rue d'Antibes, 06400, Cannes, France, a house of master craftsmen that does a worldwide mail-order business.

As for the cake itself, it's made of the same simple batter as the more familiar small *babas au rhum*, a confection that is supposed to have been invented in the seventeenth century by the amiable king of Poland, Stanislas Lesczczynski, the French queen's father. Some say he named it for Ali Baba; but "baba" in Polish means "little granny," and I like the cozy thought. In the nineteenth century, a Parisian pastry cook baked the batter in a large ring mold and named it "savarin" in honor of the gastronome Brillat-Savarin. This too is a cozy thought: Savarin was a delightful man who named his favorite horse Joyous, who traveled in the American colonies and loved both us and our food. While here, in the woods near Hartford, he even shot a wild turkey, which he cooked and served to his American hosts. His book, *The Physiology of Taste*, translated by M. F. K. Fisher (New York: Alfred A. Knopf, 1971), is well worth any food lover's time some fragrant summer evening, made serene by a dinner like this one.

The best way to get at the mango (left) is to slice it in strips off its clinging flat oval seed. The kiwi (bottom) looks like a small potato; what a surprise to cut into it and find juicy-green flower-patterned flesh. The mild-mannered papaya (top right) is packed with peppery black seeds.

Preparations and Marketing

Recommended Equipment:

To jell small, manageable amounts of aspic, use a small saucepan you can quickly chill in a bowl of ice and water. To form the aspics, we used 6 oval molds, metal for easier unmolding, of ½-cup (1-dL-plus) capacity; you could use round molds, or large muffin tins. You'll need a tray to put the molds on.

To cook the salmon, use a pan big enough to hold all 6 steaks in 4 inches (10 cm) water, plus a kitchen timer, a skimmer, and a clean kitchen towel.

To make hollandaise, have 2 small stainless-steel saucepans and a wire whip.

For the cucumbers, a large frying pan, not of cast iron, and for the potatoes, a deep saucepan with lid.

The savarin recipe is for a 4-cup (1-L) mold. You don't need a special one; even a bumpy ring mold will do, or a cake pan or soufflé dish. The dough can be made by hand, but an electric mixer with a dough hook is helpful (dough is too soft and sticky for a food processor). To drench the cake with syrup, have a bulb baster; to glaze it, a pastry brush.

Staples to Have on Hand:

Salt
White peppercorns
Sugar
Dried tarragon
Optional: pure vanilla extract
Wine vinegar
Strong consommé or beef bouillon (1 cup or
    ¼ L, or more)
Butter (3 sticks; 12 ounces or 340 g)

Eggs (5 "large")
Dry-active yeast (1 package or 1 Tb)
All-purpose flour (1⅓ to 1½ cups or 190 to
    215 g)
Carrot (1 large)
Fresh dill or parsley
Lemons (1)
Port or Madeira wine (½ cup or 1 dL)
Dark Jamaica rum, kirsch, or bourbon whiskey

Specific Ingredients for This Menu:

Perfect whole chicken livers (6)
Salmon steaks (6, weighing 8 ounces or 225 g
    each, and ¾ inch or 2 cm thick) ▼
Wine-flavored aspic (recipe on page 285; 4 to
    6 cups or 1 to 1½ L)
Fresh green peas (1 cup or ¼ L podded)
Cucumbers (3 large)
New potatoes (18 to 24, 1½ inches or 4 cm in
    diameter)
Apricot jam (1½ cups or 3½ dL)
Fruits to fill savarin ▼
Optional: green beans (½ pound or 225 g)

Poached salmon with hollandaise sauce and dilled cucumbers

▶ **Remarks:**

Salmon: except for the color of skin and flesh, what follows applies to the buying and storing of any fresh fish. The scales should be shiny and fresh, and the skin color bright—bright silver for the lovely salmon. The eyes are bright and bulging—never buy fish when the eyes are flat or sunken—and the gills red . . . that is, if the head is on. The meat is red-orange—a deeper color if you can get the sublime King or Chinook Pacific salmon—and has a glossy sheen, and it feels firm and fresh to the touch, with a little give when pressed. A fish that is past its prime of freshness will begin to soften, its skin will lose its bright silvery color, the scales will be dry and dull, and the flesh will pale—an enzyme action is taking its toll on texture and flavor. Smell it; perfectly fresh fish has either no odor, or else a very mild, delicious one.

A good fishmarket doesn't stop at refrigerating its wares; the fish are bedded on ice. Do likewise. Rush it home (or have a plastic ice container with you), and place it in a plastic bag surrounded with ice, in a bowl, and refrigerate it. Drain out accumulated ice water, renew ice 2 or 3 times a day, and really fresh fish will keep well for 2 or 3 days; but, of course, the sooner you cook it the better.

Fruits to fill savarin: if you decide to use the tropical fruits shown here, be sure to buy them several days in advance. Kiwi fruit, mangoes, and papayas are all sold unripe; put them in a closed paper bag or a ripening container at room temperature, with a ripe apple or tomato for company if you want to hasten the process. You can judge the ripeness of mangoes, papayas, or kiwis by giving a gentle squeeze. They should feel like a ripe peach.

Chicken Livers in Aspic

Jellied anything, from consommé to eggs in aspic, is an inviting summer prospect, and these attractive chicken liver molds could serve as the main dish for a luncheon in any season, as well as being the first course for our summer dinner.

Timing: if you have never done this kind of thing before, it may look too difficult for any but a professional to tackle. However, it is purely an assembly job, the sole requirements being plenty of time, ice, room in the refrigerator, and quite a bit more aspic than you think you will need. You can take as little as an hour or as much as a day or 2 to complete the very simple steps here—5 in all—which consist of making layers of aspic and objects layered in aspic: each layer has to chill in the refrigerator until it sets—a matter of 10 to 15 minutes. Then the molds need an hour or more of overall setting time to be sure they are thoroughly jelled and can safely be unmolded. Aspic, by the way, is a liquid—consommé in this case—that has gone through a clarification process to render it clear and sparkling, and gelatin has been added to it so that it sets or jells as it chills.

Clear wine-flavored aspic holds poached chicken liver in gleaming display.

Ingredients Note: The better your aspic, the more delicious your final result. You can make it all yourself, or use canned chicken broth or canned consommé plus Port or Madeira wine, or a simmering of either with white wine and aromatic vegetables. What you use depends on your resources.

For 6 people

6 perfect whole chicken livers

1 cup (¼ L) strong fine consommé or beef bouillon

½ cup (1 dL) Port or Madeira wine (or consommé)

½ tsp dried tarragon

4 to 6 cups (1 to 1½ L) wine-flavored aspic (page 77)

Decorative suggestions (see others in Menu Variations): 1 large cooked carrot and 1 cup (¼ L) cooked green peas

Garnishing suggestions: ½ pound (225 g) green beans, blanched and finely julienned (optional)

Equipment:

6 oval or round molds or cups of about ½-cup (1-dL-plus) capacity, preferably of metal for easy unmolding—or you could use muffin tins; a small metal saucepan set in a bowl of ice and water

Poaching the chicken livers
To be done in advance

Pick over the chicken livers, removing any discolored spots and bits of fat. Place in a small saucepan with the consommé or bouillon, the wine, and the tarragon. Bring to the simmer, and cook at just below the simmer (water is shivering but not really bubbling) for 8 minutes. Cover loosely and let cool in the liquid—to pick up added flavor—for at least half an hour, or overnight. Drain, and chill. (This delicious liquid could be added to the rest, for clarification, as on page 285.)

The aspic

Prepare the aspic, and be sure to test it out—pour a little into a saucer, chill for 20 minutes, then fork it out onto a plate and leave 10 minutes or so at room temperature to be sure it will hold its own. On a warm day you may find you'll need a little more gelatin: 1 tablespoon for 1½ cups (3½ dL) liquid.

The decorations

I have chosen some very simple decorations here: the carrot slices go into the bottom of the mold over its aspic lining, and the peas go in at the end, so that when the aspic is unmolded all is reversed. Cut several gashes down the length of the carrot, so that when you then cut the carrot into thin rounds you'll get a decorative edging: if you wish, also make half moons out of other rounds. Place on a saucer. Slip the skins off the peas, and pick them in half—they separate easily; place in a small bowl. Chill both carrots and peas.

Assembling

Have your main supply of aspic liquefied in a pan or bowl; the reason for the small saucepan over ice is so that you can chill just what you need, until it is almost syrupy and about to set. When you have used that up, you pour a little more into the pan, chill, and continue. Otherwise you would be warming and then chilling such a large amount that your assembling would take hours to do.

Making chicken livers in aspic—the sequence of events from lower left to right and the ingredients above them

Set your molds on a tray, and pour a ¼-inch (¾-cm) layer of aspic into them. Make room in the refrigerator, and set tray on a perfectly level place; chill until set—10 to 15 minutes.

Pour a little aspic into the small saucepan, chill over ice until cold to your finger but not jelled. Spear a carrot round with the point of a small knife, dip into the cold aspic, and center into a mold, adding other carrot pieces if you wish. When all decorations are in place, set in the refrigerator for a few minutes until anchored.

Arrange the chilled livers in the molds, pour in ½ inch or so (1½ cm) cold aspic, and chill. (If you poured in tepid aspic, that could melt the bottom layer and the decorations would float up.)

When set, spoon in more cold aspic to cover the livers.

When that has set, in 10 to 15 minutes, spoon on a layer of peas, and fill the molds with cold aspic.

Chill for at least an hour, until thoroughly set.

🕐 May be assembled 2 or 3 days in advance of serving; cover with plastic wrap and keep chilled.

Serving

If you have allowed for enough aspic, you can use the remainder to decorate your plates or platter. Pour it into a pan to make a layer about ⅜ inch (1 cm) thick, and chill. Just before arranging the serving, cut the chilled aspic, still in its pan, into dice or diamonds or other shapes, or simply turn the whole sheet of aspic out onto your work surface and chop it with a knife. In the arrangement on page 398, the molds have been dipped, one by one, into hot water for 8 to 10 seconds, or just long enough to loosen the aspic, and they have then been unmolded onto the serving platter, with chopped aspic all around and a central spray of cooked shredded green beans.

Fresh Salmon Steaks, Poached

Plain poaching, or boiling as it is sometimes erroneously called, is certainly one of the easiest and most delicious ways to cook perfectly fresh fine salmon. Nothing disturbs its lovely natural flavors, and there are no pitfalls I can think of in its cooking.

For 6 people

6 salmon steaks 8 ounces (225 g) each and about ¾ inch (2 cm) thick (I prefer boneless steaks cut from the fillet, skin on)

2 tsp salt and 2 Tb wine vinegar per quart or liter cooking water

Sprigs of fresh dill or parsley

Ready accompaniments: the hollandaise sauce, boiled new potatoes, and sautéed cucumbers (following recipes)

Equipment:

Pliers or tweezers; a wide saucepan, chicken fryer, or roaster with about 4 inches (10 cm) boiling water; a kitchen timer; a large skimmer for removing the fish; a clean kitchen towel; a soup spoon and fork; a heated platter and something to cover it with

Preparing the salmon

Run your finger searchingly over tops and sides of fish, and if you feel any big or little bones, pull them out with pliers or tweezers. Otherwise there is nothing to do, since the fish will be skinned after poaching. Keep on ice until the moment of cooking.

Poaching the fish
8 to 10 minutes

About 15 minutes before you plan to serve, have the water at the boil, and pour in the salt and vinegar. Bring back to the boil, and lay in the salmon, piece by piece and skin side down. Set timer for 8 minutes. Regulate heat so water never comes near the boil again but stays at the shiver—no real bubbles, but a slight movement in the water to show it's cooking. When time is up, turn off the heat and let salmon rest for 2 minutes (or a few minutes longer if you are not ready to serve).

Peeling the salmon and placing it on the platter

With a folded towel in one hand, lift a piece of salmon out of the water with your skimmer; turn fish flesh side down on the towel. Place on your work surface, and lift off the skin with spoon and fork. Using the towel, reverse the steak right side up on the skimmer, and set on the hot serving dish. Cover and proceed rapidly with the rest of the salmon steaks. If your platter is large enough, you may wish to spoon a garland of cooked cucumbers around the fish, lay a ribbon of hollandaise down the center, and decorate that with wisps of fresh dill or parsley. Then pass the rest of the sauce, and the potatoes, separately.

❶ The cooked fish can safely wait in its cooking water for 15 minutes or so, but once peeled and plattered serve it immediately.

Salmon steaks take only eight minutes to cook.

Skin peels off easily after poaching.

Hollandaise Sauce

Although blenders and food processors do a quick and easy hollandaise, a good cook should be absolutely confident about whipping up a hollandaise by hand. It not only takes less than 5 minutes, but you are saved the time-consuming and messy task of scraping as much sauce as you can off prickly machine blades while getting it all over your fingers. With a handmade sauce all you need do is bang the whip on the side of the pan, scrape the sauce up in 2 or 3 scoops with a rubber spatula, and it's out in a neat matter of seconds. Counting everything from start to clean-up, I conclude it's faster by hand.

For about 1½ cups (3½ dL), serving 6

1½ to 2 sticks (6 to 8 ounces or 180 to 225 g) butter

3 egg yolks

The grated rind of 1 lemon (optional)

1 Tb fresh lemon juice; more if needed

1 Tb water or fish-poaching liquid

¼ tsp salt, or more as needed

Big pinch white pepper; more as needed

2 Tb additional butter

1 Tb or so fish-poaching liquid and/or cream (optional)

Preliminaries

Have all your ingredients and equipment at hand. Melt the 1½ to 2 sticks butter in a small saucepan, and you are ready to begin.

Thickening the egg yolks before heating

To prepare the egg yolks for their ordeal, place them in a stainless-steel pan and beat vigorously with a wire whip for a good minute, until they have thickened into a cream.

Adding the flavorings

Beat in the optional lemon rind, the lemon juice, and the water or fish-poaching liquid, along with the ¼ teaspoon salt and pinch of pepper. Add the 2 tablespoons additional butter as is; by melting slowly as you proceed in the next step, the butter will discourage the eggs from suffering heat shock, which might curdle them.

Thickening the yolks over heat

1 to 2 minutes

(Your object here will be to warm the yolks slowly enough so that they will thicken into a smooth creamy custard—too sudden or too prolonged heat will scramble them, and they cannot then absorb the melted butter to come. Remember you have complete control of your pan: you can lift it up from the heat, or set it aside, or even set the bottom of the pan in cold water to stop the cooking process at any time.)

Set pan over moderate heat and stir with your wire whip, reaching all over bottom of pan and taking about ½ second to complete each circuit. As the yolks slowly heat they will begin to foam—keep testing them with your finger, and when they feel hot, they are almost ready. Watch for a wisp of steam rising from the surface, which will also indicate their almost readiness. As soon as egg yolks have warmed, thickened, and creamed—which will happen suddenly—remove from heat and beat for a minute to cool them and stop the cooking.

Adding the butter

1 to 2 minutes

By droplets, beat the melted butter into the warm egg yolks, just as though you were making a mayonnaise—it is important to go slowly here, particularly at first, or the yolks cannot absorb the butter. Use as much butter as you wish, up to the maximum, to make a thick creamy sauce. Taste carefully for seasoning, adding more lemon juice, salt, and pepper as needed. To lighten the sauce, if you wish to, beat in droplets of warm fish-cooking liquid and/or cream.

Ahead-of-Time Notes: If you are doing the sauce in advance, beat in only 1 stick butter; then, just before serving, heat the remainder and beat it into the sauce. Less butter makes the sauce safer to hold, and the hot butter at the end will warm it nicely. To hold the sauce, leave at room temperature if the wait is but a few minutes, since hollandaise is served barely warm, never hot. Otherwise set it near a gas pilot light, or near a simmering pot, or in a pan of tepid (not hot) water. Remember that too much heat will gradually coagulate the egg yolks, they will release the butter from suspension, and the sauce will curdle. Remember also that it is dangerous to let a hollandaise sit around in the kitchen for more than an hour or so because egg yolks are fine breeding grounds for nasty bacteria.

Trouble Shooting:

If sauce refuses to thicken or if finished sauce thins out or curdles, sometimes the beating in of a tablespoon of cold water or an ice cube will bring it back. If not, beat a teaspoon of lemon juice and a tablespoon of the sauce in a small bowl until they cream and thicken, then drop by drop at first, beat in the rest of the sauce until you again have a creamy mass. However, if you have overheated the sauce and curdled the yolks, the best thing to do is to heat it more until they release most of their butter; strain it out, then start over using fresh egg yolks but the same butter.

Hollandaise sauce: beat in butter by dribbles at first, to make a thick cream.

Boiled New Potatoes

I like boiling rather than steaming for new potatoes because it seems to me that steaming can discolor them. In any case, they are easy indeed to cook and any leftovers can make a happy reappearance in a salad.

For 6 people

18 to 24 small new potatoes about 1½ inches (4 cm) in diameter

Salt

2 to 3 Tb butter

Equipment:

A saucepan large enough to hold potatoes comfortably, and with a lid; a larger saucepan to hold the first if potatoes must wait a bit

Wash the potatoes and pick them over, removing any blemishes with a knife. Arrange in saucepan and cover with cold water, adding 1½ teaspoons salt per quart or liter of water. About 35 minutes before you plan to serve them, cover and bring to a boil and maintain at a slow boil for about 25 minutes, or until potatoes are just tender when pierced with a sharp knife—eat one as a test if you are not sure. Drain out water, roll about gently over heat to dry them off, then roll with a little butter to glaze them.

These potatoes are at their best when served soon after cooking. If they must wait a bit, bring a little water to the simmer in the other pan, and set the potato pan in it, covering it loosely—potatoes must have air circulation or they will develop an off taste.

Cucumber Triangles Sautéed in Butter and Dill

The light fresh crunch of cucumbers and the flavor of dill seem always wedded to salmon. Here the cucumbers are cut, then tossed in butter and seasonings, with a sprinkling of dill. They still retain a bit of a crunch, and gain yet a different degree of cucumber flavor from being cooked.

For 6 people

| 3 large fine cucumbers |
| 2 Tb or more butter |
| Salt and white pepper |
| 2 to 3 Tb minced fresh dill, or a little dried dill weed and minced fresh parsley |

Equipment:

A large frying pan, not of cast iron

Peel the cucumbers, slice in half lengthwise, and scoop out the seeds. Cut each half in half lengthwise, and then into triangles, as shown.

🕐 May be prepared several hours in advance; refrigerate in a covered bowl.

Not more than 10 minutes before serving, melt the butter in the pan, add the cucumbers, and toss over moderately high heat, seasoning lightly with salt, until cucumbers are almost cooked through but still retain some crunch. Season to taste with more salt, pepper, and, if you wish, toss with a tablespoon or 2 more butter. Then toss with sprinklings of dill.

🕐 Cucumbers should be served promptly or they lose both their crunch and their freshly cooked look.

Peeled and seeded cucumbers are cut into triangles, which make attractive shapes around the salmon platter.

Savarin aux Fruits Exotiques

A large ring-shaped yeast cake drenched in rum syrup and filled with a mixture of tropical fruits

Timing and Manufacturing Notes:
The savarin is made of a simple yeast dough that when cooked makes a plain, dry cake that is strangely tasteless and coarse—purposely so, since its role is to be a sponge that will absorb an enormous amount of flavored syrup without collapsing. Given time to drink its fill, the savarin's every bite is deliciously moist, quite unlike anything else but the rum babas following this recipe.

Timing: you will need a minimum of 4½ hours: 1½ to 2 hours for the dough to rise in a bowl, 1 hour for it to rise in its mold, ½ hour for it to bake and cool, and a final hour for it to absorb its syrup and to drain before you can glaze and serve it. However, you can bake it ahead and freeze it; you can syrup and drain it in advance; you can glaze it ahead, as well.

Savarin dough can be baked and served in many ways: classic savarin with whipped cream and glacéed fruit (lower left), individual savarins and a rum baba (the cylindrical one), and our savarin with exotic fruits (top).

Avoiding dough troubles: be sure to dissolve your yeast in tepid water—hot water can kill it—and see that it is fully liquefied or it cannot do its work. Do not kill the yeast, either, by pouring hot butter on it. Give the dough time to rise; it may take longer than the amounts specified—it's the volume of the rise that you're looking for, not the time it takes to rise. Measure your flour correctly.

For 6 to 8 people

Dough for a 4-cup (1-L) Mold:
1 package (1 Tb) dry-active yeast
3 Tb tepid water (not over 110°F/43°C)
2 "large" eggs
2 Tb sugar
⅛ tsp salt
4 Tb tepid melted butter
1⅓ to 1½ cups (190 to 215 g) all-purpose flour—scoop dry-measure cups into flour and sweep off excess

The Rum Syrup:
2 cups (½ L) water
1 cup (¼ L; 7 ounces or 190 to 200 g) sugar
½ cup (1 dL) dark Jamaica rum, kirsch, or bourbon whiskey, or 2 to 3 Tb pure vanilla extract

Glazing and Filling:

1½ cups (3½ dL) apricot jam
4 Tb sugar
Mixed fruits such as 1 or 2 ripe mangoes, papayas, and kiwis, plus a small bunch of black grapes
Additional sugar as needed
Rum, kirsch, bourbon, or lemon juice to flavor the fruits (optional)
1 or 2 egg whites

Equipment:

A 2-quart (2-L) mixing bowl, or an electric mixer with dough hook; a 4-cup (1-L) savarin mold (illustrated), or other ring mold (or a cake pan or soufflé dish); a skewer; a bulb baster; a pastry brush

The Dough:
About 3 hours
Preliminaries

Stir the yeast into the tepid water and let dissolve completely while preparing the rest of the ingredients as follows. If eggs are chilled, warm them for 2 minutes in hot water, then break into mixing bowl. Blend in the sugar, salt, and butter. Measure the flour into the bowl, and stir in the completely liquefied yeast mixture.

Method for kneading by hand

Blend ingredients together with a rubber spatula or wooden spoon, and when too heavy to stir, begin kneading by hand: lift the dough with one hand, your fingers held together and curved like a spoon. Slap the dough against the side of the bowl, and vig-

orously repeat the process for a dozen sticky passes or more, until the dough begins to take on some body, and finally enough for it to be removed from the bowl. (This is supposed to be a soft and sticky dough, but if it is still too soft after vigorous kneading, work in a little more flour; if too stiff, knead in droplets of milk.) Remove dough to your work surface, and let rest 2 to 3 minutes while you wash and dry the bowl. Knead the dough again by slapping it against your work surface, pushing it out with the heel of your hand, and continuing vigorously for a minute or 2 until it begins to peel itself cleanly from your fingers—it should stick to them if you hold a pinch of it, however. It will have enough elasticity so that you can grab it in both hands, pull it out, and give it a full twist without its breaking.

Method for kneading by electric mixer
Knead at moderate speed for several minutes until dough has enough body to ball on the dough hook or beater. (If too soft or too stiff see preceding paragraph.) Remove from mixer, wash out bowl, and finish by hand, as described.

The initial rise
About 2 hours
Roll the dough into a ball and return it to the mixing bowl. Cover with plastic wrap and let rise at around 75°F/24°C until the dough has doubled in bulk and feels light, spongy—1½ to 2 hours, or longer if cooler.

🕐   If you are not ready to form the dough now, deflate it by pulling the sides toward the center, cover with buttered plastic, a plate, and a weight of some sort, and refrigerate. Push

Sticky dough gradually becomes elastic as kneaded.

It is ready when you can grab and twist it without its breaking.

For kneading by machine, dough is ready when it balls on hook.

down again if it starts to rise before it has chilled and its butter content has congealed. Will keep 12 hours or more.

Final rise in the mold
About 1 hour

Butter inside of mold. Form the dough into a rope 10 to 12 inches (25 to 30 cm) long, rolling it under the palms of your hands, and gradually separating them to extend the dough. Cut crosswise into half, cut each half into thirds, and then halve each third. Drop the pieces into the mold, and press together lightly with your fingers—no need to be too careful since dough pieces will come together as they rise. (Mold should be about half filled with dough.) Cover with plastic and let rise until dough has filled the mold—about 1 hour at 75°F/24°C. (Chilled dough will probably take an hour more.) Meanwhile, preheat oven to 375°F/190°C in time for baking.

🕐 You can delay the rising by refrigerating the mold; you can freeze it. Before baking, let chilled dough come to room temperature; thaw frozen dough and let warm to room temperature.

Baking
About 20 minutes at 375°F/190°C

Set mold in lower middle level of preheated oven. It is done when nicely puffed and browned, and when it comes easily out of the mold. If sides and bottom are not golden brown, return to mold and bake 4 to 5 minutes more. Unmold and let cool upside down on a rack.

🕐 When cool, you may wrap the savarin airtight in a plastic bag and refrigerate for a day or so; it will keep for weeks in the freezer.

The Savarin Imbibes the Syrup:
About 1 hour

Both the syrup and the savarin must be tepid for this step, since a cold savarin will not imbibe easily, and a hot one might disintegrate. If savarin is cold, then, set it in a warming oven or a 200°F/95°C oven for a few minutes. To make the syrup, pour half the water into a saucepan, stir in the sugar, and heat gently until sugar has completely dissolved, then pour in the rest of the water (to cool it); add the rum or liqueur or vanilla. Prick the savarin all over at 1-inch (2½-cm) intervals with a skewer, and set the savarin in a dish. Pour the syrup over it, and dribble the syrup over the top a number of times with a spoon or bulb baster. In several minutes, repeat the process. After about half an hour of frequent basting the savarin will have absorbed all of the syrup; it will look swollen and feel spongy. Transfer onto a rack set over a dish to drain for half an hour, and it is ready to glaze.

🕐 May be done several hours in advance; leave savarin in its dish, and cover with a bowl or with plastic, and refrigerate. Then drain on a rack; if it seems dry, make a little more syrup and baste it several times before glazing.

Apricot Glaze, and Glazing the Savarin:
Heat the apricot jam in a small saucepan with the sugar, stirring until sugar dissolves completely, then boil rapidly, stirring, until jam is quite thick and the last drops falling from your spoon are thick and sticky (the "thread stage," or 228°F/109°C). Push

Let dough (left) rise until it has doubled in volume; it will be light and spongy (right).

As they rise, dough pieces (left) merge to fill the mold (right).

The savarin swells like a sponge as it drinks up the liqueur syrup.

through a sieve to remove skin debris, and return the glaze to the pan.

🕐   If not to be used immediately, set pan in another pan of simmering water; it must be warm or it will not spread. Leftovers may be bottled, reheated, and used again.

Paint the glaze all over the surface of the savarin. Then set the savarin on its serving dish.

🕐   If the glaze has been properly cooked to the thread stage, it should set or jell on the savarin and act as a waterproofing seal; then the savarin can sit for several hours.

Finishing the Savarin:

Cut up the fruits (reserving some of the grapes), toss in a bowl with sugar and, if you wish, rum, liqueur, or lemon juice to taste. To frost grapes, beat the egg whites lightly with a fork to liquefy them, dip in the grapes one by one, roll them in granulated sugar, and let dry on a rack.

Just before serving, pile the fruits into the savarin, and decorate outside with the frosted grapes. To serve, cut wedges out of the savarin, and spoon a serving of fruit on the side. (You may wish to pass additional fruit with the savarin, and a bowl of lightly whipped and sweetened cream, on page 395.)

Variation: Babas au Rhum

Exactly the same dough makes babas, those individual rum-soaked yeast cakes. Use 12 well-buttered baba tins or muffin cups about 2 inches (5 cm) high and 2 inches across, and after the dough has risen in its bowl, form it into a rope, and cut it into 12 even pieces. Drop 1 piece into each cup, let dough rise just above the rims of the cups, and set on baking sheet. Bake about 15 minutes in the middle level of a preheated 375°F/190°C oven. They are done when they unmold easily, and are nicely browned. When tepid, imbibe with the same rum syrup, drain, glaze, and decorate if you wish. Serve as is, with whipped cream, or fruits flavored with the same liqueur.

🕐 *Timing*

This is an easy and relaxed dinner. Fill the center of the savarin with previously trimmed fruit just before you serve it. Before the main course, peel the salmon steaks (a matter of seconds if you chose the fillet, rather than cross-section, type), finish the cucumbers, give the potatoes a toss over heat in their butter, and arrange your platter.

Before sitting down, poach the salmon and leave it in its cooking water. Set the cucumbers in butter over heat, then set aside. Everything can wait off heat while you enjoy the first course. At this time, you can either make the hollandaise sauce (a 5-minute job once you've got the knack), or have it half made and beat in warm melted butter just before serving.

Half an hour before sitting down, start the potatoes boiling.

Several hours beforehand, prepare the fruit for the savarin, and dose the cake with syrup, then glaze it.

Two or 3 days before your party, make the aspics.

The savarin can be baked and frozen long beforehand, or baked the day before and kept in the refrigerator.

One last-minute job—serving the salmon

Menu Variations

Aspic does for any cold food what pearls do for any complexion. Instead of chicken livers, you could use poached eggs—a classic dish—or lobster claw meat poached in wine, or crab, or shrimp, or pieces of *foie gras* and truffle, or liver pâté. Or dress up a cold mousse in an aspic jacket. You might prefer one large mold to individual small ones—though perhaps not a ring mold if you're having the savarin. Decorations, of course, can be very varied; just bear in mind the color of the aspic. Instead of carrots and peas you could use crossed fresh tarragon leaves that have first been dipped in boiling water; or strips of boiled ham, pimiento, black or green or stuffed olives, blanched green pepper, the whites of hard-boiled eggs, and/or the yolks sieved with a little butter and pushed through a paper cone to form designs. Or don't decorate the molds at all; they're handsome as is.

Fish for poaching: if salmon seems too expensive or is unavailable, use some other firm solid fish that has good natural flavor. (Monkfish has the right texture but is altogether too bland.) Halibut and striped bass are delicious poached, as is swordfish. Large cod steaks can take to it but might be more successful in a court-bouillon (a mixture of water, wine, and seasonings simmered for half an hour with 1 or 2 finely sliced carrots, onions, celery, and herbs). Instead of *hollandaise sauce,* you could use melted butter with herbs, or lemon butter or white butter sauces (recipes are on page 464.) Dieters could use a decoration of dill sprigs and thinly sliced lemon, more fresh lemon on the side, and perhaps a bowl of sour cream or yogurt brightened with a little mustard, horseradish, fresh pepper, and minced herbs.

Cucumbers are the first thing I think of for salmon, but asparagus, peas, zucchini, or green beans would do very well.

New potatoes are ideal with poached fish, but can't always be had. You might substitute buttered and parslied potato balls, but I don't think any of the richer potato dishes (fried,

scalloped, mashed, etc.) would suit. In season, just-picked sweet corn might be nice.

Tradition being what it is, you cannot call anything a *savarin* unless you bake it in the traditional ring mold. But the same dough in another mold will taste the same, and you can call it a rum cake, or a strawberry shortcake if you split it, drench it with strawberry juice, decorate it with sliced berries, and serve it with whipped cream. It is also delicious with rhubarb, sliced peaches, wild berries, and raspberries—for which you might drench it with framboise, the delicious raspberry liqueur. Or have babas!

Leftovers

The *chicken liver aspic* will keep for 2 to 3 days. Or you might buy more chicken livers than you need, make a little extra aspic, and use it to coat a delicious pâté, for which a recipe is included in this section.

For leftover cooked *salmon,* I also include a recipe here, following the one for pâté. Cold poached salmon is delicious with cucumbers and sour cream or mayonnaise, but its beauty is fleeting. Eat it the next day; 2 days later, it'll be better in the nice old-fashioned gratin I've suggested. To stretch it, you can turn it into a sort of kedgeree by adding rice to the mixture.

Leftover *cucumbers* go into soup. But the *new potatoes* can be rinsed of their butter in boiling water, peeled, and used in salad. A slice of cold boiled new potato makes a better carrier than toast for some hors d'oeuvre—for instance, salmon roe with sour cream.

Hollandaise sauce must be discarded if it has sat at room temperature for an hour or more, since it is so vulnerable to bacterial action you can't detect. If it hasn't sat long, you can refrigerate it and reheat it cautiously.

A *savarin* loses its bloom rather quickly, but will still be good the next day. Or you can layer slices of it with custard, to make something resembling an English trifle.

Chicken Liver Pâté

For a 3-cup (¾-L) pâté

1 medium onion

2 Tb butter

2 cups (½ L) chicken livers

4 Tb Port or Madeira wine

½ cup (4 ounces or 115 g) plain or herbed cream cheese

6 Tb additional butter

½ cup (1 dL) aspic (page 285; or consommé and ½ Tb dissolved gelatin)

Salt and pepper

Herbs and spices: pinch of allspice or special spice mixture (page 468), and/or thyme or tarragon

Cognac or Armagnac in dribbles, if needed

Equipment:

A food processor makes quick work of this; or use a blender, or a sieve and wooden spoon.

Mince the onion and cook slowly in the butter until wilted. Meanwhile, pick over the livers, removing any discolored spots and fat. Stir them into onion and sauté several minutes just until stiffened. Pour in the wine and boil for a moment. Purée the livers with the cheese, additional butter, and aspic. Taste very carefully for seasoning to make a marvelous-tasting mixture, overseasoning a little since it will lose some of its flavor when it is cold. Pack into a mold or bowl, cover, and chill several hours.

* Will keep for about a week under refrigeration. May be frozen, but will lose something in texture when thawed.

Gratin of Poached Salmon

For 4 people

2 poached salmon steaks (or about 2 cups or ½ L salmon, cooked or canned)

4 hard-boiled eggs

1 large onion

4 Tb butter, more as needed

½ Tb curry powder

5 Tb flour

2 cups (½ L) milk, heated in a small pan

4 to 6 Tb dry white wine or dry white French vermouth

Salt and white pepper

1 tsp or so fresh minced dill weed, or big pinches of dried dill

About ⅔ cup (1½ dL) grated Swiss or mixed cheese (page 464)

Equipment:

A buttered 6-cup (1½-L) baking dish 2 inches (5 cm) deep

Flake the salmon, and slice or quarter the eggs. Mince the onion and cook slowly in the butter in a 2-quart (2-L) saucepan; when limp, stir in the curry powder and the flour, adding a little more butter if flour is not absorbed. Cook, stirring, for 2 to 3 minutes. Remove from heat, and let cool a moment, then blend in the hot milk with a wire whip. Return to heat and simmer, stirring, for 2 minutes. Add the wine, and simmer several minutes more, stirring frequently. Season carefully to taste.

Fold the salmon into the sauce, fold in the dill, and taste very carefully again; it should be delicious. Spread half the salmon mixture in the bottom of the buttered baking dish, and spread half the cheese over it. Arrange the eggs over the cheese, and spread the rest of the salmon over them, covering with the remaining cheese.

🕐 Baking dish may be arranged several hours in advance. Cover and refrigerate.

About half an hour before serving, preheat oven to 400°F/205°C. Place dish in upper third level, and bake until contents are bubbling and cheese topping has browned lightly. Do not overcook, or salmon will dry out and eggs will toughen.

Postscript: Hot-weather food

When you think of the foods native to hot climates, like our own gumbos and barbecues and chili, or the curries of India, or the rijstafel of Malaysia, or the tomatoey, garlicky soups and sauces of the Mediterranean, what they seem to have in common is their high, piquant seasoning. It strikes me that hot-weather food should be light but rarely bland; if the appetite

A cool aspic is the perfect start for a summer meal.

is excited, its satisfaction is more intense, and one can do with less. To think that cold food equals light food, however, seems to me an illusion. One double-dip ice cream cone is just as hearty as one steak.

What's called for, I think, is contrast and stimulus: hot and cold, sharp and bland, crunchy and creamy. Before a chicken salad, try a winy consommé, but piping hot, not jellied. And aim for variety. So often, all the dishes on a fancy cold buffet taste mostly of mayonnaise, vinaigrette, cream, and sour cream. One wearies of the ubiquitous lemon: sometime, instead of filling an avocado hollow with oil and lemon, try fresh orange juice spiked with hot pepper sauce. Try horseradish instead of mustard. Try a change of oil: fresh walnut oil, for example, is exquisite.

Our salmon dinner, though it would be nice in any season, seems to me to have a summery air, but temperately so. Of the menus in this book, "Fast Fish Dinner," with its cold beet and cucumber soup and the lively sauce over hot monkfish, would be ideal for a really sultry evening, though one might prefer a lighter dessert—fresh pear sherbet? In *Mastering I,* we devoted a chapter to the classical French cold buffet, and among good cookbooks, all with "summer" in their titles, are Judith Olney's (Atheneum), Molly Finn's (Simon & Schuster), and Elizabeth David's (Penguin).

In extreme hot weather, one can save jobs like baking and simmering for the cool of the evening, or use a hibachi set outside the kitchen door to avoid lighting the broiler. And one's eating as well as one's cooking patterns can be adapted: more for breakfast, and have it earlier, less for lunch, dinner after sundown.

In general, the best rule of thumb is that for dieters' food: in summer, meals should be exciting as well as delicious. Never forget, there was a record heat wave in Fall River, Massachusetts, on that fell morning when Lizzie Borden fetched her axe, and never forget what she had had for breakfast: overripe bananas, too-long-leftover cold mutton, and cookies. No wonder she couldn't keep her cool.

A lavish menu for a big crowd —but the single cook can swing it.

Buffet Dinner

An Expandable Menu
For 20 to 30 people or more

Sweet-and-Sour Sausage Nuggets
*Tarama Brandade—Carp roe with hints of
garlic, olive oil, and Provençal mysteries*
*Pissaladière Gargantua—Giant onion and
anchovy pizza*
*Toasted Pita Triangles; Raw Vegetable
Nibbles; Nuts and Crackers*

*Braised Pot Roast of Beef—Bottom round of
beef in red wine*
*Potato Gnocchi—Cheese and potato
dumplings browned in the oven*
Old-fashioned Country Ham
*A Cauldron of Home-cooked White Beans
with Herbs*
*Fresh Vegetables à la Grecque—Cold in
aromatic liquid*
Tossed Green Salad
Hot French Bread

*Orange Bavarian Torte—Dressed in whipped
cream and glazed orange peel*
Sliced Strawberries with Orange Liqueur

Suggested wines:
*White wine—French colombard or Chablis;
red wine—a Beaujolais, zinfandel, or cabernet.
Champagne or sparkling wine for the dessert*

A big bounteous party is fun for the cook the way a herbaceous border is fun for the gardener: you start with a gorgeous vision, make precise plans, execute them leisurely (smugly checking off item by item)—and lo! there it all is, right on time and a sight to behold. You really brought it off. Even for 30 people, this grand spread is entirely feasible for 1 cook—but if you want to vary it, there's a list of big-party dishes on page 461, all rated for their practicality. On this menu, the braised beef and the torte each serve 15, and the other recipes are for 10; so, for say 30 guests, braise 2 rounds, make 2 cakes, and otherwise multiply by 3.

Here's how I set party priorities:

1) *The End Result. Flavor*—will the meal be delicious, with each dish at its best? (This eliminates many pastas and hot fish things, which should be eaten soon after their preparation. At a very large buffet, plan on dishes that can sit around a bit.) *Appearance*—will everything look handsome and stay that way? By this token, do your own carving and slicing at table, or else appoint a friend to take it on; otherwise you'll have Devastated Areas. *Space*—if you haven't much, serve compact dishes, pots not platters. If you have lots, use several locations: one for appetizers, one for the main course, one for dessert. This keeps people moving and mingling, for one thing. *Temperature*—have you enough warming devices, and enough electric outlets to serve them? You can't use 2 on the same line, unless one is a low-voltage slow cooker. However, thick-walled casseroles stay warm a long time, and there are always chafing dishes and candle-heated stands. Have plenty of ice around for cooling wines and filling insulated chests, etc.

2) *Space* — not just for serving, but for storing dishes prepared in advance, and, before that, their components. Most refrigerators need a periodic clear out, and now's a good time. Anyway, we could all use our refrigerators more efficiently. Cake layers can be stacked with racks or strong cardboard in between. Square containers are more efficient than round ones. Flexible containers, such as plastic bags, fit anywhere. (A tip: having dried your salad makings, tear the greens and assemble the whole salad in 1 bag.) In winter, the back porch makes a good refrigerator annex; in summer, an insulated chest; perhaps your friends have space you can borrow.

3) *Equipment* — friends and space both count here. To my mind, it's pointless to have more than one rarely used, expensive, or space-consuming item per neighborhood. So why not a community duck press, lobster pot, fish steamer, *pâté en croûte* mold, spring-form pan? A portable tabletop oven is another very useful community item, as are slow cookers and electric hot trays. For the ham on this menu, as for, say, *gravlaks,* you need a fine slicing knife — expensive and not used every day — so share it! If you have only 1 oven, plan on dishes that can co-occupy it (cakes and soufflés can't), and that require the same temperature setting.

On ordinary staple equipment, my advice is not to stint yourself. Have plenty of bowls, strainers, spatulas, paring knives, and kitchen towels, so you don't have to waste time on petty calculations, or stop to wash single items.

4) *Rhythm and Timing.* It's very helpful to start a cooking bout by "doing your prep," as restaurant cooks say: squeezing lemon juice (keep refrigerated), chopping parsley, washing and drying salad greens, putting a kettle on to boil, starting a new batch of ice cubes. White wine can be chilled all day; red wine can be brought to room temperature early. Time savers: large flour, sugar, and salt containers, each with its own rarely washed set of measuring cups or spoons — otherwise, every time you open a package, you have to mop up spilled grains; a big pan of soapy water where used implements can soak; a portable pastry slab you can chill. Always read a recipe through beforehand, and assemble all the items and equipment before starting. Measure the capacity of molds and baking pans, and mark them.

Make and freeze "standard parts" like doughs, crêpes, and stock beforehand, and plan jobs for the time when something can simmer or bake unattended. (I know lots of cooks who budget their time but not their energy.) A job that takes 10 minutes when you're fresh can take 20 when you're not; you'll wind up livelier if you alternate sitting jobs with standing ones, chopping with paring, etc. Clutter is fatiguing; for me, frequent cleanups are more restful than one final bout.

5) *Cost Effectiveness* — really, Effort Effectiveness. Now, with a big party, is not the time to put in 100 percent more work for 5 percent more effect. Take this simple but sound braised beef. Old-fashioned recipes call for larding, marination, and a sauce slowly reduced to almost nothing, then reconstituted with wine. This is all very well if you've nothing else to do; but basically what gives a braise flavor and tenderness is cooking and keeping meat and liquid together. Reheating this dish is not merely a convenience but an improvement.

On the other hand, put your effort where it does count. Whipped cream, for instance, is much better made by hand, over ice, than with a mixer; a custard sauce can't be beaten mechanically — so much foam builds up that you can't see what you're doing. You could use machines, in this menu, for making pastry, cutting onions, mixing the *brandade* and the gnocchi, and whipping egg whites, but it's not really a menu planned for machines. For buffet dishes that are, see the Postscript.

6) *Resources,* and Your Own Resourcefulness. There's usually more than one way to skin a rabbit; the Timing section of this chapter gives you only one. However you go at it, you can do this meal alone, and so well in advance that at the time of your party, your kitchen can be sparkling, uncluttered, and all ready for a glorious evening.

Preparations and Marketing

Recommended Equipment:

Serving: let's suppose you're planning for 20 or 30 people, and for the full menu. You have first to decide whether to carve the beef and the ham at table, and if you do, that means 1 or 2 large carving boards, and, for the ham, a first-rate, razor-sharp slicing knife. The ham is served cold or cool; the beef is best hot but is still good at room temperature. The sausage nuggets and the beans will stay warm in slow cookers, or you can use warming devices; 1 big electric tray would hold them, plus the gnocchi. Freshly baked *pissaladière* will probably be eaten before it cools off! Allow space for your big salad bowl, your platter of cold vegetables, and your smaller bowls of *brandade*, raw vegetables, nuts, crackers, and pita triangles—plus more space for dessert, sauce, dessert plates, your bar setup, and your coffee tray. Remember that carvers need elbow room, and consider the number and location of electric outlets for warmers. At one efficient buffet served in a roomy kitchen, I remember hot dishes were served from the counter tops, and cold ones were bedded on ice in the sink; used dishes and silver were slid—gently and unobtrusively—into trash barrels filled with soapy water, to soak. A cooled-off oven also makes a discreet repository for such items, as does your dishwashing or laundry machine.

Be sure your knife is really sharp before you start slicing the beef.

Cooking: if you did each job in succession, using a minimum of pans, you'd need 1 skillet (preferably nonstick) for sausages and the pizza onions, and 1 large, heavy, stainless-steel saucepan to sauce sausages, simmer black olives, poach gnocchi, cook vegetables, and make custard sauce (the reason why it has to be stainless). For baking gnocchi and *pissaladière,* you need 2 jelly-roll pans (1 of which browned the beef), or 1, plus a baking sheet. A large, deep roaster, preferably with cover, will cook first the ham, then the beef. A food processor or mixer will help with several jobs. You need a casserole for the beans and a deep pan for the torte (10- by 3-inch, or 25- by 8-cm, spring-form preferred).

Be sure to check your supply of aluminum foil, plastic wrap, plastic bags, white kitchen string, and cheesecloth. Small implements needed: meat thermometer, pastry bag with large star tube, skimmer or slotted spoon, giant spatula and flexible-blade spatula.

Obviously, the more saucepans, bowls, sieves, colanders, and paring knives you have, the faster you can go.

Staples to Have on Hand:

Salt
White peppercorns
Granulated sugar
Eggs (17 "large")
Butter (1½ pounds or 675 g)
Confectioners sugar (½ cup or 70 g)
Dried herbs: oregano, thyme, allspice berries, imported bay leaves, whole cloves, mustard seeds, coriander, saffron threads, and fennel seeds; mixed herbs (optional)
Grated nutmeg
Pure vanilla extract
Olive oil
Cooking oil, or rendered beef or pork fat
Wine vinegar
Soy sauce
Hot pepper sauce
Dijon-type prepared mustard
Cream of tartar
Arrowroot, or rice flour, or potato flour, or cornstarch

All-purpose flour
Milk (2¼ cups or 5½ dL)
Butter, clarified (about ½ cup or 1 dL)
Grated Gruyère, Parmesan, or Swiss cheese
    (1¼ cups; 5 ounces or 140 g)
Beef stock or bouillon (5 cups or 1¼ L)
White nonsweet bread for crumbs (½ loaf)
Lemons (3)
Carrots (1 bunch)
Celery (1 bunch)
Garlic (1 head)
Parsley (1 large bunch)
Red wine (1 bottle; see beef recipe)
Orange liqueur (3 Tb; plus 7 to 8 Tb, optional)
Optional: concentrated frozen orange juice

Specific Ingredients for This Menu:

Excellent sausage meat (1 pound or 450 g) ▼
Bottom round of beef (1 whole trimmed, 10 to
    12 pounds or 4½ to 5½ kg)
Country ham (1 whole; see recipe)
Chilled pastry dough (1½ pounds or 675 g) ▼
Gelatin (6 Tb or 6 envelopes)
Flat anchovy fillets, packed in olive oil (two 2-
    ounce or 60-g cans) ▼
Black Mediterranean-type or Niçoise olives
    (about 24) ▼
Dry white beans (1 pound or 450 g)
Optional: fresh basil (1 bunch)
Apricot jam or chutney (4 Tb)
Tarama (salt carp roe) (½ cup or 115 g) ▼
Heavy cream (5 half-pints, or 1¼ L plus)

Orange juice (1⅓ cups or 3¼ dL)

Oranges (3)

Optional: candied orange peel (see page 13)

Cakes: *génoise*, yellow, or sponge (can be
storebought; 2 round, about 10 by 1
inches or 25 by 2.5 cm, see page 435)

Vegetables for cold platter (see recipe)

Vegetables for raw nibbles

Greens for salad

Potatoes (about 6½ pounds or 3 kg; or can be
instant—see recipe)

Yellow onions (about 3 pounds or 1350 g)

Ingredients for dessert sauce (see recipe)

Nuts, crackers, pita bread, etc. (ad-lib)

Plenty of ice cubes for cooling wine, etc.

Remarks:

Sausage meat: a quick easy recipe for making
your own is on page 175. *Pie crust dough:*
double the proportions for the pie and quiche
dough on page 464. *Olives:* the salt-and-oil-
cured Mediterranean type need blanching before you use them, to remove excess salt—simmer in 1 quart (1 L) water 5 to 10 minutes
(depending on how salty they are), drain, and
rinse. If you don't like to serve olives with pits,
you'll either have to pit them or switch to the
relatively tasteless pitted black olives you can
buy in any market. *Anchovy fillets:* don't use if
decorating *pissaladière* in advance; use more
olives. Always open anchovy cans at the last
minute. *Tarama:* this is a salty orange-pink
paste, often imported from Greece, that is sold
in Middle Eastern markets and delicatessens.

Onion pizza will be decorated with olives and anchovies.

Sweet-and-Sour Sausage Nuggets

You will note the perhaps odd addition of aspic to the sausage mixture here, a suggestion
from chef Joe E. Hyde, whose straw potato
pancake is described on page 219. His disciple,
our own chef Marian, says *he* says the aspic
makes the meatballs lighter, and indeed it
does, since these have a delightfully unheavy
texture.

For about 24 nuggets

The Sausage Mixture:

1 pound (450 g) best-quality well-seasoned
prepared sausage meat

1 "large" egg

5 Tb crumbs from fresh white nonsweet bread
with body

4 Tb strong liquefied aspic (a scant teaspoon
plain unflavored gelatin, softened and then
heated to dissolve in 4 Tb consommé)

The Sweet-and-Sour Sauce:

¾ cup (1 ¾ dL) well-flavored beef stock or
broth

1 Tb wine vinegar

4 Tb strained apricot jam or chutney

1 Tb arrowroot, rice flour, potato flour, or
cornstarch dissolved in 5 Tb orange juice

1 Tb soy sauce

1 Tb butter

1 Tb Dijon-type prepared mustard

6 drops hot pepper sauce

Salt and freshly ground pepper

Beat the sausage meat, egg, crumbs, and aspic
together in a bowl. If too soft to form, chill for
half an hour or so, or beat over ice. Using 1 ½
tablespoons of meat at a time, form into balls.
Chill for 30 minutes. Brown slowly in a large,
preferably nonstick skillet, and drain on paper
towels.

Meanwhile, blend the sauce ingredients together in a large, heavy stainless-steel saucepan; simmer 3 to 4 minutes, and correct seasoning, adding salt and pepper to taste, and drops more of the listed ingredients if you think them necessary. Fold the sausage into the sauce.

🕐 May be done a day or so in advance.

To serve

Reheat to the simmer for a minute or 2, then place in a decorative bowl or pan and set on an electric warmer, or in a pan of water over a chafing dish flame. Have a container of toothpicks at hand, for spearing.

Sweet-and-sour sausage nuggets stay warm over a water bath set on a chafing dish burner.

Tarama Brandade

A spread or dip —salted carp roe puréed with potato, garlic, olive oil, cream, and seasonings

The most famous *brandade* (it literally means "stirred vigorously") is a purée of salt cod, garlic, and olive oil, a marvelous concoction that originated in Provence, and there is every reason to put that brilliant concept to good use with other ingredients. The pink and salty carp roe, the kind you find in jars in Middle Eastern groceries, is a fine example. It is usually whipped up with soaked bread crumbs, but mashed potato makes an even smoother and more delicious mixture.

For about 1 quart (1 L)

2½ cups (6 dL) **warm cooked potatoes (baked, preferably, or boiled, or stiff instant mashed)**

½ cup (115 g) **tarama (salt carp roe)**

1 or more cloves garlic, puréed

½ cup (1 dL) **fruity olive oil**

½ cup (1 dL) **heavy cream**

Fresh lemon juice to taste

Freshly ground white pepper

Drops of hot pepper sauce

Equipment:

A food processor makes quick work here; or use an electric mixer; or a potato ricer or vegetable mill, mixing bowl, and wooden spoon.

If you are using a processor, purée the potatoes, using the steel blade, then add the *tarama* and puréed garlic and continue processing while you add olive oil alternating with cream to make a heavy creamy paste that holds its shape lightly when lifted in a spoon. Season to taste with lemon juice, pepper, and hot pepper sauce plus a little more oil, cream and/or garlic if you think them needed. (Otherwise, purée the potatoes and whip in the *tarama* and garlic, then the oil alternating with the cream, and finally the seasonings.) Pack into a serving bowl, or chill and mound on a serving dish as shown here.

🕐   May be made several days in advance; cover and refrigerate.

Variations:

Brandade de morue—purée with salt cod
Substitute 1 pound (450 g) cooked salt cod for the *tarama*, warming it first in a saucepan over moderate heat with 4 tablespoons olive oil, and beating with a large fork to shred it. Then purée with 1½ cups (3½ dL) cooked potato and 2 or more cloves garlic, puréed, adding alternate dollops of olive oil and cream, and seasoning with salt, pepper, and lemon juice. A marvelous mixture.

Avocado brandade
Use equal amounts of warm cooked potato and ripe avocado, puréeing them together with a small clove of garlic, puréed, and adding spoonfuls of heavy cream and olive oil. Season with salt, white pepper, and lemon juice. Makes a beautiful pale green creamy dip that keeps nicely in a covered jar in the refrigerator for a day or 2. I have added anchovies, chives, and capers to it, but I think the simpler version is more successful.

A rubber spatula makes decorative swirls on a mounded surface of tarama brandade.

Pissaladière Gargantua

A party-sized onion and anchovy pizza

I always like to have a pastry something for large gatherings, and the pizza idea in rectangular form is a good one because it is not too rich—no eggs, just pie crust dough, cooked onions, anchovies, black olives, and a sprinkling of cheese for the top. Another plus is that you can assemble and freeze it, all except for the anchovy topping. Furthermore, 1 large sheet of it will give you 20 generous portions, or 40 small ones.

For 20 appetizer-sized servings

4 cups (1 L) sliced yellow onions

4 to 6 Tb olive oil

Chilled pie crust dough (proportions for 3½ cups, 1 pound, or 454 g flour; double the recipe on page 464)

Salt and pepper

1 tsp or so dried oregano or thyme, or mixed dried herbs

Two 2-ounce (60-g) cans flat anchovy fillets, packed in olive oil

About 24 black olives (the dried Mediterranean type or other salty imported smallish black olives)

About ½ cup (1 dL) grated Parmesan cheese, or mixed cheeses from your frozen collection (page 464)

Equipment:

A jelly-roll pan, nonstick preferred, about 11 by 17 inches (28 by 43 cm)

Cook the onions slowly in 4 tablespoons of olive oil in a roomy covered frying pan or saucepan, stirring frequently, until they are soft and thoroughly tender, but not browned —20 minutes or more.

🕐   May be cooked ahead; cool, cover, and refrigerate for several days, or freeze.

Meanwhile, butter the bottom (not the sides) of the jelly-roll pan. Rapidly roll out the chilled dough into a rectangle ⅛ inch (½ cm) thick, and larger and wider than the pan. Fit it into the pan, and neatly trim off the overhanging edges. Fold edges of dough down against bottom all around; press a decorative border into them with the tines of a table fork. Prick inside surface of dough all over with 2 forks, as shown—to keep it from rising up during baking.

● Cover and refrigerate (or freeze) until you are ready to continue.

When onions are tender, season carefully with salt and pepper, and either let them cool or stir over cold water until cool. Spread them over the inside surface of the dough.

● Cover and refrigerate (or freeze) until you are ready to continue.

Baking

25 to 30 minutes at 425°F/220°C

While the oven is preheating, arrange a design of anchovies, such as the diagonal pattern illustrated, over the onions, with black olives at strategic intervals. Sprinkle the cheese over the onions and the design, and dribble on a tablespoon of olive oil (oil from the anchovy can, if you wish). Bake in lower third level of oven (where pastry will crisp better) until pastry has browned and is beginning to shrink from the sides of the pan.

Serving

Slide onto a serving board or work surface, and either let guests cut their own, or cut into serving pieces and arrange on a plate. Five strips across the *pissaladière* and 4 the length of it give you 20 pieces.

Assembling the anchovy and onion pizza

❶ I prefer not to arrange the anchovies more than 30 minutes or so before baking because I think they develop an off taste if they sit around out of their hermetically sealed can. And although it can be baked ahead, the *pissaladière* is at its most delicious served fresh and warm, rather than cold.

Variations:
Pizza
Use a regular pizza topping of tomato sauce, herbs, and cheese, plus, if you wish, diced cooked mushrooms, sausages, ham, and so forth. An interesting pizza additive is diced sautéed eggplant (use the recipe, on page 338, the garnish for our spaghetti squash).

Quiche
If you want a cheese and cream combination, which can be very good too, you will either have to make a prebaked crust with edging to hold the liquid quiche mixture or do as follows. Spread the surface of the dough with shaved or coarsely grated Swiss cheese, using about 2 cups (½ L). Beat 1 egg and 2 yolks in a bowl with ⅔ cup (1 ½ dL) heavy cream, season well with pepper, drops of Worcestershire, and a little sage or thyme. Just before baking, spread the egg and cream mixture over the cheese—it is to be a thick coating only; if you need more liquid, spread on a little more cream. Bake as described for the *pissaladière*. This makes attractively brown and cheesy mouthfuls.

Cocktail Miscellany

You will want the usual crackers and nuts, and something like potato chips or toasted pita triangles (there is a recipe for homemade ones on page 203), plus some raw vegetable nibbles for those who are well-disciplined dieters. Since every household has its favorites, I shall not go into details.

Notes on the Braising of Beef

Beef cuts for braising
I like the bottom round for braising—the long outside muscle of the leg; it is a solid piece with no separations, and it cuts into neat pieces. Other braising parts, like chuck, top round, and tip (or face), break into separate muscles, and that makes for messy carving. The brisket is a possibility, but not my favorite for this dish, and I have never cared for the stringy quality of the usually overpriced eye of the round.

If you are braising more than one
You will need either 2 covered roasting pans unless you have a mammoth one that will hold 2 beef bottoms. Or you can braise the roasts 1 at a time, and cool 1 while you are cooking the other—or others. You can braise the meat on top of the stove if you are careful with the heat, and turn the meat every 45 minutes or so, but an oven is more even—2 ovens are ideal.

The red wine sauce for the beef
Any meat that needs long simmering, as in a braise or a stew, wants some kind of a sauce. The meat is no longer moist after cooking because its juices have gone into the braising liquid: both meat and liquid take from and give to each other, which is one of the principal reasons that braised meat has such fine flavor. In this recipe the braising liquid is lightly thickened; when the beef is done the sauce is made.

Bottom round of beef

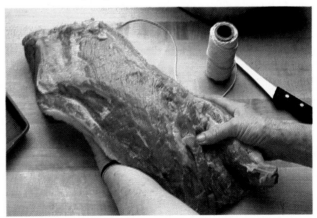

Braised Pot Roast of Beef

*Daube de boeuf—Boeuf à la mode
Whole bottom round of beef braised in
red wine*

A fine large pot roast of beef is ideal for a group because you can cook it 1 or 2 days before serving. In fact, it is better that you do so because the meat not only will pick up additional flavor from sitting in its braising juices but will also slice more neatly, since the meat fibers will have compacted themselves as they cool, and will hold together nicely when reheated. Furthermore, braised beef is easy to cook, and it stands up well during the leisurely pace of most buffets.

*For a 10- to 12-pound (4½- to 5½-kg)
roast, serving 15 to 20 people*

A whole trimmed bottom round of beef (10 to 12 pounds or 4½ to 5½ kg)
Rendered beef or pork fat, or cooking oil
6 Tb all-purpose flour
About 4 cups (1 L) beef stock (page 322), or best-quality canned beef bouillon
Salt
2 carrots, roughly chopped
2 large onions, roughly chopped
1 large celery stalk, roughly chopped
4 cloves garlic, not peeled
1 large herb bouquet (10 parsley sprigs, 3 or 4 imported bay leaves, 1 tsp thyme, 6 allspice berries, all tied in washed cheesecloth)
1 bottle healthy young red wine, like zinfandel, Chianti, or other of like quality

Equipment:
White string for tying the beef; a jelly-roll pan for browning it; a medium-sized heavy-bottomed saucepan, for starting the sauce base; a covered roaster, or a large roasting pan with sides 3 to 4 inches (8 to 10 cm) high and heavy aluminum foil

Browning the beef

Wind white string around the beef down its length, to hold the meat in place firmly during its cooking. Paint on all sides with fat or oil, set in the jelly-roll pan, and brown slowly on all sides under the broiler, being careful not to let the meat burn. This is a process that needs close watching, but it is the easiest way to brown such a large piece.

🕐   May be browned well in advance, if need be, and especially if you are doing more than 1 roast.

Preliminaries for the sauce base

Meanwhile, but keeping your eye on the beef as well, blend 5 tablespoons fat or oil in the heavy saucepan with the flour (if you are doing more than 1 bottom, double or triple this amount), and stir almost continuously, but rather slowly, with a wooden spoon over moderate heat as the flour gradually turns a quite dark nutty brown. Making a brown *roux* takes time and care—you don't want the flour to burn, just to darken slowly so it will not have a bitter taste. Time: about 10 minutes. Remove from heat and let cool several minutes, then blend in the beef stock and set aside.

Braising the beef
2½ to 3 hours

Preheat oven to 350°F/180°C. Salt the meat on all sides, using about 2 teaspoons, and set it in the roaster fat side up. Arrange the vegetables and garlic around the meat, add the herb bouquet, and pour in the wine and the beef stock—*roux*, plus a little more stock if neces-

Use a good healthy young red wine for your beef.

sary, to come almost halfway up the meat. Bring to the simmer on top of the stove; cover and set in lower third of oven. When contents are bubbling quietly, in about half an hour, baste the meat with the sauce and turn thermostat down to 325°F/165°C. Liquid should simmer quietly throughout the cooking; regulate oven accordingly. Baste and check on the cooking every half hour until 2 hours are up, then begin testing. The meat is done when a sharp-pronged fork can penetrate through the middle section with comparative ease. If you have any doubts, cut a piece off the large end and eat it: the meat should be somewhat firm, but not tough. Time of cooking will depend on quality of meat—a Prime well-aged piece will take a shorter cooking time, while a fresh Choice cut may take up to an hour longer.

🕐 Meat may be carved and served after a rest of half an hour or so, but is really better cooked several hours or a day in advance.

Finishing Meat and Sauce:

Let the beef cool for half an hour, basting it every 10 minutes or so with the sauce, and turning it several times. Then remove it and drain contents of roaster through a colander or sieve into a large saucepan, pressing juices out of braising vegetables into pan. Bring liquid to the simmer, skimming fat off surface as you do so; continue to skim for several minutes as fat rises to the surface while sauce very slowly bubbles. You can serve it now, but the sauce will really taste best if you have time to keep simmering and skimming it for half an hour as it slowly reduces. Taste carefully for seasoning and strength, and boil down slowly until the sauce coats a spoon just enough so you know it will coat the meat. (If by any chance sauce is strong and fine but not thick enough, soften 2 or more tablespoons of arrowroot, rice flour, potato flour, or cornstarch—or even all-purpose flour—in several spoons of wine or stock; remove sauce from heat, beat in starch mixture, then simmer for 2 to 3 minutes. On the other hand, if sauce is too thick, thin out with more stock.)

Pour the sauce around the meat, cover with foil or wax paper, and refrigerate.

Reheating and Serving:

You may reheat the beef whole, as is, or sliced and sauced. Here are the two alternatives.

To reheat the beef whole

Cover the beef closely and reheat either in the oven at around 300°F/150°C, or by simmering very slowly over low heat on top of the stove, turning the beef every 15 minutes. It will take 30 to 40 minutes to reheat, and the internal temperature need be no more than 120°F/49°C. It is important that you do not let the meat overheat and overcook, as it will fall apart when sliced. However, you may keep it warm once it is reheated. Just before serving, cut and discard the trussing strings.

Carving at the table. If you have reheated the beef whole and there is a willing carver available, it is always appealing to have meat sliced at the table. Set the beef on a handsome board, and have the carver start his work at the large end, as illustrated, making bias slices, since a straight cut across the meat would make too large a piece for 1 serving. When he gets near the tail end and notices any overt tendency to shredding, he cuts the meat into chunks. He should have a bowl of sauce on a hotplate at his side, and will ladle a spoonful or so over each serving.

Carved meat presented on a platter

Carve the meat in the kitchen and return it neatly to the roaster or a large baking pan; baste with the sauce. Let it warm through slowly, and keep it warm, then arrange it on a hot platter with sauce over each piece, renewing with meat and sauce as necessary.

Bottom round can be cut into neat bias slices.

Potato Gnocchi

Cheese and potato dumplings

Although the gnocchi is of Italian origin, when it came to France it turned into a dumpling, at least in this version, where it consists of mashed potatoes, cheese, and a *pâte à choux* (a heavy eggy white sauce that swells when baked). You give them a preliminary poaching in salted water, after which the gnocchi may be refrigerated or frozen; to serve, you brown them in the oven. For a starchy something to go with a party meal such as this, I think the gnocchi are a fine solution just because of their amenability. Besides, they make good eating with the braised beef and its red wine sauce.

For about 30 golfball-sized gnocchi

For the Pâte à Choux:
About 2 cups (½ L)

1 cup (¼ L) water

6 Tb (3 ounces or 85 g) butter

1 tsp salt

¾ cup (3½ ounces or 100 g) all-purpose flour (measure by dipping dry-measure cups into flour and sweeping off excess)

3 "large" eggs, plus ½ to 1 more egg if needed

Other Ingredients:

4 cups (1 L) firm warm mashed potatoes (see notes in recipe)

Gnocchi—browned, cheesy dumplings—garnish our platter of braised beef.

¾ cup (3 ounces or 85 g) finely grated Gruyère, Parmesan, or mixed cheese

A pinch of nutmeg

Salt and pepper

A little flour, for forming gnocchi

½ cup (1 dL) clarified butter (page 463), more if needed

Equipment:

A heavy 2-quart (2-L) saucepan; a wooden spatula or spoon; a hand-held electric mixer or a food processor is useful; 1 or 2 wide casseroles or saucepans, for poaching the gnocchi; a large bowl of cold water; a skimmer or slotted spoon; nonstick baking pans

The Pâte à Choux:

Measure out the ingredients listed. Bring the water to the boil in the 2-quart (2-L) saucepan, meanwhile cutting the butter in pieces and dropping it in, along with the salt. When water is boiling and butter has melted, remove pan from heat and immediately pour in all the flour at once, beating vigorously with wooden spatula to blend. Set over moderate heat, beating, until pastry cleans itself off sides and bottom of pan and begins to film the bottom of the pan. Beat for 2 minutes or so over moderately low heat to evaporate excess moisture. Remove from heat.

If you are continuing by hand or with a mixer, make a well in the center of the hot pastry with your spatula or mixer, break an egg into the well, and vigorously beat it in until absorbed. Continue with the next 2 eggs, one by one. Mixture should be quite stiff, but if too firm for easy beating, break remaining egg into a bowl, beat to blend, and beat driblets into the pastry to loosen it.

If you are using a processor, scrape the hot pastry into the container fitted with the steel blade. Turn on the machine and break the 3 eggs into it, one after the other. Stop the machine, test pastry for consistency, and add the fourth egg by driblets if pastry seems too stiff.

🕐 Pastry should be warm when you use it; set over warm but not hot water, and cover loosely. (If pastry is kept too warm the eggs will cook, and lose their puffing abilities.)

The potatoes

Either use plain mashed potatoes here, boiling, peeling, and putting them through a ricer. Or use instant mashed, which work perfectly well in this instance; when making them, use the amount of milk specified on the package, a little less of the water, and no butter. Potatoes should be quite stiff.

Combining, forming, and poaching the gnocchi

Bring 3 inches (8 cm) salted water to the simmer in the poaching pans. Beat the warm pastry and warm mashed potatoes together to blend; beat in the cheese, nutmeg, and salt and pepper to taste. Flour your hands, and with a light touch, rapidly roll gobs of the gnocchi mixture into balls 1¾ to 2 inches (4½ to 5 cm) in diameter, and drop into the water. (A sticky business!) Maintain water almost but not quite at the simmer (not bubbling) throughout the cooking—an actual simmer or boil can disintegrate the gnocchi. Gnocchi are done in about 15 minutes, when they have risen to the surface and roll over very easily. Transfer them with the skimmer to the bowl of cold water, and in a minute or so they will sink to the bottom—the cold water firms them and sets the cooking. Remove and drain on a towel.

🕐 The gnocchi may be prepared in advance to this point. Let them dry for half an hour, then chill for an hour. When thoroughly cold, arrange in a roasting pan between layers of plastic wrap; they will keep in the refrigerator 2 to 3 days, or may be frozen.

To serve gnocchi

20 to 30 minutes at 350°F/180°C

(The gnocchi need a final baking in the oven, and the conventional system is to arrange them in a buttered baking-and-serving dish with a covering of grated cheese and butter, or cheese sauce. Here, however, since they are to take the place of potatoes, they are rolled in butter and baked on a nonstick aluminum jelly-roll pan or pastry sheet so that they can be lifted off and placed on the meat platter for easy serving.)

Preheat oven, and heat the clarified butter to liquefy it; pour the butter into a dish or pie plate. Roll the gnocchi, a few at a time, in the butter, draining off excess with a slotted spoon. Arrange them ½ inch (1½ cm) apart on the pans and brown lightly in upper and middle third levels of the preheated oven, switching pans from one level to another for even cooking. The gnocchi are done when they have swelled gently, and they usually crack open a little bit; if they do not brown lightly on top, set for a few minutes under a moderate broiler, watching carefully that they do not brown too much.

🕐 May be kept warm for 20 minutes or more, but do not cover them . . . warm potatoes need air circulation.

Transfer poached gnocchi (bottom) to a bowl of cold water to firm them.

Old-fashioned Country Ham

Old Virginia Hams and Smithfield Hams:

These are very special hams, slow cured in the old-fashioned way and with a much drier, saltier, and more intense flavor than ordinary storebought hams. They are usually served cold, sliced paper thin, and make a delicious accompaniment to other dishes on a buffet table. I am particularly partial to a fine old ham served along with the remains of the Thanksgiving turkey, but here, on our buffet, the ham can take the place of a second helping of beef, to eat with the beans, or with bread and cheese.

Country Hams versus Virginia and Smithfield Hams:

What is the difference? Smithfield is easy: by law it can only be called a Smithfield ham if it has been processed in Smithfield, Virginia, by the Smithfield method—a dry salt cure followed by a coating of pepper, a long slow hickory smoking, and a final aging of up to a year or more. And the Smithfield hams have a different look than other hams because Smithfield hogs are of a special breed that produces longer and thinner hams. In addition, if the hogs are fed in the approved manner, they have a unique flavor because of the acorns and hickory nuts, among other delicacies, that make up their diet. A number of Virginia processors outside Smithfield produce the same kind of hams using the same type of hogs, feed, and methods; however, they must content themselves with the name "old Virginia" or "Smithfield type."

"The name Country Ham covers a multitude of sins," writes Colonel Bill Newsom of Kentucky, and he goes on to say that the Kentuckian's definition of a real country ham is one that is dry cured using salt and sugar, then smoked with hickory wood, and aged for 6 months or more. Todd's of Richmond, however, do not age their country hams, since in their opinion an aged ham does not lend itself to slicing thick and frying. In other words, you have to know your country hams because they differ widely in their manner of cure and in their aging. In general, though, I think it is true to say that the Virginias and Smithfields are older, drier, and saltier, as well as thinner and longer, than the country hams, and are really in a category by themselves.

Cooking Procedures:

An aged ham is not difficult to cook—a bit long and cumbersome perhaps, but not a tricky business. First you scrub it with a stiff brush under warm running water to remove any of the harmless mold that has collected on it due to its aging, and with it any pepper and other curing elements embedded in the surface. Then you soak it for a number of hours, depending on its type, to remove some of its salt. It is now ready to cook, either by simmering, or baking, or by a combination of both. When cooked, you slice off the rind and excess fat and, if you wish, you can bone it. Finally, to dress it up, you glaze it in a very hot oven either just as it is, or coated with bread crumbs, or brown sugar, or cloves, etc. A cooked dry-cured aged ham will keep nicely in the refrigerator for several weeks at least.

The exact details of its cooking are, of course, a matter of pride, family tradition, and very definite opinions among southern cooks, and I have no intention of pontificating on the subject. I have, none the less, cooked a good 2 dozen of these hams through the years and have some observations to offer. In the first place, anyone tackling this type of ham will do well to follow the directions of the packer, at least the first time, but keep notes on your results because next time you may want to change things a little, as I have.

Soaking

Soaking softens an aged ham to some extent, and does indeed remove a certain amount of saltiness. Packers' directions vary from 4 to 6 hours for many country hams on up to 48 hours for Smithfield types. I frankly do not like too salty a ham; I soak Smithfields for 3 to 4 days, and aged country hams for 2.

Simmering versus baking

Simmering (or "boiling") a ham takes a large container and a lot of water, but it does remove excess saltiness to quite an extent, and does make a slightly softer ham of a well-aged one. The usual rule is to simmer the ham about 20 minutes per pound (450 g), or until the bones from the hock (small end) can be pulled out of the ham.

The on-again-off-again baking system. Not too long ago an alternate method to simmering was developed. You put your scrubbed and soaked ham, fat side up, in a covered roasting pan with 5 cups (1¼ L) water, or part water and part wine or cider vinegar. You seal the roaster as airtight as you can with a sheet of aluminum foil, cover it, and set it in the oven, bringing the temperature up to 500°F/260°C (some say to 400 or 450°F/205 or 230°C). When it has reached that temperature, you time it for exactly 20 minutes, then turn the oven off. Do not open the oven door! Leave for 3 hours. Repeat the heating again, for 20 minutes. Turn the oven off. Do not open the oven door! Leave for 6 to 8 hours or overnight.

I have done several Smithfield-type hams this way; it works, and it is certainly easier than simmering a ham in all that water. But I shall not do it again for a country ham because the heat was too intense or prolonged or inappropriate for one I did recently that had not been aged—it shredded a bit around the edges. My last aged country ham, a buxom chunky beauty from Kentucky, was, I thought, a little too salty and too firm after this cooking.

Combination simmer-bake. For my next aged country ham I shall try simmering it for 10 minutes per pound (450 g), or half the usual time, then baking it in a tightly closed roaster with half a bottle or so each Madeira wine and dry white French vermouth. I'll bake it slowly at 300–325°F/150–165°C for about 1½ hours or to a meat thermometer reading of 160°F/71°C. Sounds like just the right system, and I hope it is.

Tough Edges and Bottoms:

I have asked several ham authorities why some aged hams have such hard bottom and side surfaces (those not covered by fat or rind). The hardening of the "face," as these parts are called in the trade, is a characteristic of the hams, and comes from salting, drying, and just plain old age. You may wish to trim off these hard surfaces before soaking the ham, or after cooking it. A crusty surface makes carving difficult, certainly, and although it seems as though you are removing a lot of meat as you trim it off, you are saving yourself a good deal of trouble when you come to slice and serve. Save the trimmings for flavoring bean or split pea soups, and those that are not too crusty can be ground up with a little of the ham fat to make a tasty ham spread for sandwiches.

To Carve the Ham:

It is a help in carving to pull out the hip bone from underneath the ham before that meat has cooled. Some carvers prefer the cross-grain cut, going straight down at right angles from the surface of the ham to the bone, after having cut an opening wedge out of the hock (small) end. Or slice parallel to the bone and the surface of the meat; start with a wedge taken out of the hock, then slice on the right then on the left side of the main leg bone.

Aged ham should be cut into the thinnest possible slices. You need a long, sharp knife, and don't saw at the meat; try for long even strokes the length of the blade.

Mail-Order Hams: See page 439.

White Beans with Herbs

For almost 2 quarts (2 L), serving 10 to 15 people

1 pound (450 g) dry white beans
2 quarts (2 L) water
1 large onion stuck with 2 cloves
1 herb bouquet (6 parsley sprigs, 2 cloves garlic, ¼ tsp thyme, and 1 imported bay leaf tied together in washed cheesecloth)
2 tsp salt
1 stick (4 ounces or 115 g) butter (optional)
3 or 4 cloves garlic puréed with 1 tsp salt (page 466)
5 to 6 Tb minced fresh parsley and/or basil
Bean cooking juices as needed
Salt and pepper

Cook the beans with the water, onion, herb bouquet, and salt, as described on page 82 (halving the recipe and omitting the pork). Shortly before serving, rewarm them if necessary. Melt the butter in a large serving casserole, stir in the garlic and let warm a moment, then fold in the beans and fresh herbs plus a little of the bean cooking juices if you feel them needed. Season carefully to taste. (If you omit the butter, simmer the garlic for a few minutes in a little of the bean cooking juices.)

🕐   May be kept warm on an electric hotplate.

Doubling and Tripling the Recipe:

Since a large quantity is often difficult to handle and to season properly, you are probably better off finishing and flavoring the beans in batches about this size, then combining them.

Fresh Vegetables à la Grecque

A selection of vegetables cooked in an herbal marinade, served cold

Unless one has restaurant facilities and plenty of kitchen help, I think a hot green vegetable is very difficult to serve successfully to a large group. I will always opt, instead, for a copious vegetable salad or something like the platter of cold cooked and marinated vegetables suggested here. They look attractive, they taste good, and since there will also be a fresh green salad on the table, I don't think you need more than a piece or 2 of each vegetable per serving, plus a spoonful of mushrooms.

The idea here is to make a communal cooking bath of spiced liquid, and to cook each batch of vegetables separately in the bath, each for its allotted time. Finally you reduce the liquid to an essence, and baste the vegetables with the resulting sauce—with the exceptions of the bright green vegetables, which are treated differently, as you will see.

For 10 people

Spiced Cooking Liquid à la Grecque: *6 cups (1 ½ L)*
1 cup (¼ L) thinly sliced onions
⅓ cup (¾ dL) olive oil
6 cups (1 ½ L) water
The zest of 1 lemon (yellow part of peel removed with a vegetable peeler)
4 Tb fresh lemon juice
⅛ tsp each mustard seeds, coriander, and saffron threads
½ tsp fennel seeds
8 peppercorns
8 to 10 parsley stems (not the leaves)
2 cloves garlic, crushed with their peel
1 tsp salt

For the Vegetable Platter:

Your choice of vegetables

Lemon juice

Fresh olive oil

Salt and freshly ground pepper

Parsley

Equipment:

A wide stainless-steel or enamel saucepan, casserole, or chicken fryer for cooking the vegetables; a skimmer or slotted spoon; various containers, such as glass baking dishes, to hold the marinating vegetables; 1 or several large platters to hold the finished product

Preparing the cooking liquid

Simmer the sliced onions for 6 to 8 minutes in the olive oil until tender and translucent, then add the rest of the ingredients and simmer slowly, covered, for 20 minutes. Drain through a sieve into another saucepan, pressing juices out of ingredients.

🕐 May be cooked a day or 2 in advance.

Small White Onions:

20 to 30

For easy peeling, drop the onions in a pan of boiling water, bring to the boil again, and boil 1 minute. Drain, shave off tops and bottoms, and slip off the skins. Stab a cross ¼ inch (¾ cm) deep in the root ends with the point of a small knife—to minimize their bursting while cooking. Drop into the cooking liquid, cover, and simmer slowly 20 to 30 minutes or until just tender. Remove with a slotted spoon and spread in a dish.

🕐 May be cooked a day or 2 in advance.

Zucchini and Yellow Summer Squash:

3 or 4 of each

Slice off the 2 ends, scrub the vegetables, and cut into crosswise chunks of about 1 inch (2.5 cm). Toss with 1 teaspoon salt and let drain for 20 minutes to rid them of excess moisture. Bring cooking liquid to the boil and drop in the vegetables; bring rapidly back to the boil and cook about 2 minutes, until barely cooked— still slightly crunchy. Drain and spread in a dish. (Zucchini and other summer squash need attention—too much cooking and they wilt, too little and they do not absorb the sauce.)

🕐 Best cooked the day of the dinner.

A sunburst of fresh vegetables à la grecque ready for the buffet table

Mushrooms:

1 quart (1 L)

Trim stem ends off mushrooms, drop the mushrooms into a large bowl of cold water, swish about, and drain immediately. Quarter or halve them if large, leave whole if small. Bring cooking liquid to the boil, drop in the mushrooms, and boil slowly for about 1 minute until barely cooked. Drain; place in a bowl.

🕐   May be cooked a day in advance.

Cauliflower:

Cut the head into flowerettes and peel the stems; cook as in the directions for mushrooms.

🕐   May be cooked a day in advance.

Leeks and Celery:

These always taste better than they look under such circumstances. You would use just the white part of the leeks, splitting it as shown on page 28 to remove any sand, then quartering or halving it after cooking. Cut celery stalks into 3-inch (8-cm) lengths about ½ inch (1½ cm) wide. Leeks need about 15 minutes of simmering; celery, about 10.

🕐   May be cooked a day in advance.

Topinambours or Jerusalem Artichokes:

Scrub and simmer whole in the boiling liquid for about 30 minutes. Peel after cooking.

🕐   May be cooked a day in advance.

Carrots:

Particularly attractive for their color, carrots are successful candidates because they do not get mushy. Select really fresh and flavorful baby carrots, or trim mature carrots into attractive small-carrot shapes; peel them before cooking. Simmer about 10 minutes in the liquid, until just tender but still with texture.

🕐   May be cooked a day in advance.

Green Beans:

Green beans will discolor if cooked in the spiced liquid. Trim them, leave them whole, and cook in a large kettle of rapidly boiling salted water until barely tender. Drain, and refresh in cold water to stop the cooking and to set color and texture. Chill them, and toss in the reduced cooking liquid (below) 5 to 10 minutes before serving.

🕐   Best cooked the day of the dinner.

Broccoli:

The same treatment goes for broccoli. Cut into flowerettes and peel stems; blanch in a large kettle of rapidly boiling salted water for 3 to 4 minutes only; drain; spread out in 1 layer to cool. Chill, and dress just before serving.

🕐   Best cooked the day of the dinner.

Reducing the Cooking Liquid to a Sauce:

When all the vegetables are done, boil the cooking liquid down rapidly to about 1 cup (¼ L), and carefully correct seasoning.

Dressing the Vegetables:

Spoon a bit of the sauce over the onions, squash, and mushrooms, as well as the cauliflower, leeks, celery, topinambours, and carrots, if you are using them. Let marinate in the refrigerator for several hours. Dress the beans and broccoli shortly before serving. And just before serving, freshen all vegetables with drops of fresh lemon juice, olive oil, salt, freshly ground pepper, and sprigs or a mince of parsley where needed.

Tossed Green Salad

You may trim and wash the greens the day before, spin them dry, and store in plastic bags. Vinaigrette dressing suggestions are on page 468, including 1 for quantity occasions. Make the dressing in the morning, but dress the salad only at the last minute, eating samples to be sure there is enough dressing and that the seasoning is perfect. (Too often a party salad is not carefully tasted by the cook, and the result is disappointing.)

Orange Bavarian Torte

Molded liqueur-soaked cake layered with Bavarian cream; whipped cream and glazed orange peel topping

For a large party you certainly want a delicious as well as spectacular dessert that needs no last-minute fussing—something like a molded concoction or a cake. The torte described here is a handsome example, with its snowy mountain of whipped cream and pretty strands of glazed orange.

Although the recipe looks long, it consists only of cake that is split into horizontal layers, each of which is flavored with orange syrup, spread with Bavarian cream, and molded in a spring-form pan (or soufflé mold). Bavarian cream is simply a custard sauce made light with beaten egg whites, enriched with a modest amount of whipped cream, and given staying power with gelatin. The torte can be assembled several days before your party, or you can even make it and freeze it; you complete the final decoration the morning of the party.

Manufacturing Notes:

A *spring-form mold* is what I've suggested here because it is convenient to use in this type of recipe. But if you don't have one you can adapt the system to the bowl-molding technique in the chocolate bombe recipe on page 313, or to a soufflé mold, or even to a casserole lined with wax paper.

The cake layers. The easiest way to form the torte is to have a cake or cakes the diameter of your mold, and slice horizontally into layers as illustrated, next page. On the other hand, you can cut and patch any size of cake to make layers; your surgery will never show because all is covered by frosting when the torte is served.

When I bake my own, I double the proportions for a 3-egg yellow cake, such as the one for *génoise* on page 487 of *Mastering II*,

which fills my spring-form pan by about a third. I have to bake 2 cakes this way to have enough for the Bavarian torte. (Once I tried tripling the recipe instead, to save myself baking 2 cakes, but though the triple-recipe cake looked fine as it emerged from the oven, when sliced horizontally, the center core hadn't cooked through—it was a wet mass of batter.)

How much filling to make. I believe in having more rather than less, and the proportions for the Bavarian cream here will give you about 12 cups (3 quarts or 2¾ L), which will probably be more than you need since the spring-form has a capacity of 4 quarts (3¾ L). However, you can always make the torte higher by pinning a collar of foil around the rim of the pan. Or you can make yourself a little molded dessert out of the excess; store it in the freezer and you'll have something nice on hand for unexpected guests.

Strawberry sauce adds its tart fresh taste to this gorgeous torte.

The Cake:
10- by 3-inch (25- by 8-cm), serving 12 to 16 people

2 round cakes about 10 by 1 inches or 25 by 2.5 cm (see preceding notes)

The Orange Bavarian Cream:
12 cups or 3 quarts (2¾ L)

The grated rind of 3 oranges

1 cup (¼ L) strained fresh orange juice

4½ Tb (4½ envelopes) plain unflavored gelatin

12 egg yolks

1½ cups (9½ ounces or 275 g) sugar

2¼ cups (5½ dL) milk, heated in a small saucepan

1 Tb pure vanilla extract (optional)

8 egg whites (1 cup or ¼ L)

½ tsp cream of tartar and ⅛ tsp salt

3 Tb additional sugar

¾ cup (1¾ dL) heavy cream

3 Tb orange liqueur (or concentrated frozen orange juice, defrosted)

The Orange Liqueur Syrup:

1 cup (¼ L) water

½ cup (100 g) sugar

4 to 5 Tb orange liqueur (or concentrated frozen orange juice)

The Whipped Cream Frosting and Accompanying Sauce:

3 cups (¾ L) heavy cream

About ½ cup (70 g) sifted confectioners sugar

1 Tb pure vanilla extract

3 Tb orange liqueur

Decorative suggestions: candied orange peel (page 13), or storebought kumquats in syrup cut into strips or designs

Sauce suggestions: sliced fresh strawberries flavored with sugar and a little orange liqueur, or a purée of sieved raspberries, or the sliced oranges (without blueberries) on page 14

Equipment:

A 10-by-3-inch (25-by-8-cm) spring-form pan (or other choices as noted earlier); wax paper; a stainless-steel 2-quart (2-L) saucepan for the custard; beating equipment for the egg whites; a giant-sized rubber spatula for easy folding; a bowl of ice cubes; a large metal bowl for whipping the cream; a round platter or board for serving the torte; a flexible-blade spatula and pastry bag with star tube for decorating

Preliminaries

Dot inside of spring-form mold with butter; cut a round of wax paper to fit the bottom and a strip to fit around the inside wall, and press them in place (butter will hold them there). Split the cakes, or cut to fit mold; you should have 3 or 4 layers; wrap in plastic to keep them from drying out. Grate the orange rind into a small saucepan, pour in the orange juice, and sprinkle the gelatin on top to soften. Make the orange sugar syrup: heat the water and sugar in another small pan; when sugar has completely dissolved, remove from heat and stir in the liqueur; cover and set aside.

Custard Sauce—Crème Anglaise:

Place the egg yolks in the stainless-steel saucepan. Using a wire whip, beat in the sugar by 2-tablespoon dollops with 3 to 4 seconds of beating between additions; continue beating for 2 to 3 minutes until mixture has thickened slightly. With a wire whip beat in the warm milk by driblets. Set over moderate heat and

Slice each cake in half horizontally to make four layers.

stir not too fast with a wooden spoon, reaching all over bottom of pan as custard slowly heats through. Watch carefully that you are not heating the sauce too fast or the yolks will turn granular; keep testing with your finger. When sauce is almost too hot, it is almost ready. Also watch surface of sauce: at first small foamy bubbles collect there, and as they begin to subside the sauce is almost ready. Finally, keep your eye alert for a wisp of steamy vapor rising from the pan—this, again, is an indication that the sauce is almost thickened. Keep on cooking slowly and stirring until the sauce is thick enough to coat the surface of the spoon as illustrated—if you overheat it, the egg yolks will curdle, but you must heat it enough to thicken. (Time: 5 to 8 minutes in all.)

Immediately remove from heat and continue stirring for a minute to stop the cooking. Stir in the vanilla, if you are using it.

🕑 May be cooked a day in advance, and needs no reheating before you continue.

Completing the Bavarian Cream:
(Once the Bavarian cream with its gelatin is completed you must go on to finish the torte or the cream will congeal.)

The gelatin. Set pan with orange and gelatin over moderate heat for a moment, stirring, to dissolve the gelatin completely: look closely to be sure there are no unmelted granules. By dribbles stir the gelatin into the custard.

The egg whites. Set beating bowl with egg whites over hot water for a moment to take off their chill, then start beating at slow speed. When foaming, in a minute or 2, beat in the cream of tartar and salt, and gradually increase speed to fast. When egg whites form soft peaks, beat in the additional sugar by spoonfuls, and continue beating for a few seconds until egg whites form stiff shining peaks. Fold the custard (warm or cold) into the egg whites.

Preliminary chilling. Set the custard bowl in a bowl of ice cubes (with water to cover them), and fold with the giant spatula several times, repeating almost every minute and reaching all around edge of bowl to draw cold custard from outside into the center. When center tests cool (but not chilled) to your finger, remove from ice.

Whipping and folding in the cream. Pour the ¾ cup (1¾ dL) cream into the metal bowl and whip over ice until the cream holds its shape softly (page 235). Fold into the cool custard, ending with the 3 tablespoons orange liqueur. Plan to assemble the torte at once, before the Bavarian cream starts to set. (But if by chance that does happen, fold gently over warm water just until it loosens.)

Assembling the torte
Place a layer of cake, cut side up, in the form, and baste with several spoonfuls of syrup. Ladle on a layer of Bavarian cream and top with a cake layer, cut side up. Baste with syrup, ladle on more cream, and, if there is room, make another layer. (You may have more Bavarian cream than you need; see notes preceding recipe.) Turn the final cake layer cut side up on

Custard sauce is done when it coats the spoon.

Fold whipped cream into cool (not chilled) custard.

your work surface, baste with syrup, and place, cut side down, over the final layer of Bavarian cream. Cover with plastic wrap and refrigerate for at least 6 hours to be sure the Bavarian cream and the torte itself have firmly set.

🕐   May be arranged 2 or 3 days in advance; may be frozen.

Note: If you are making more than 1 torte, and you have only 1 spring-form, wait for several hours until torte has set, then you can release the form. Slide the torte onto its serving platter or board, but keep the wax paper strip around the side of the cake; cover with a sheet of plastic wrap.

Decorating and serving

Whip the 3 cups (¾ L) cream over ice until quite firm, and it holds in fairly stiff peaks. Sift on and fold in sugar to taste, and droplets of vanilla and orange liqueur—but do not loosen the cream too much. Slip wax paper strips under edge of torte (so as not to mess up serving dish), and spread cream over top and around side of cake with flexible-blade spatula, saving enough for decorative swirls, which you will make with your pastry bag and star tube. Decorate with strands of glazed orange peel, kumquat, or whatever you have chosen.

🕐   Cake may be decorated several hours before serving. Keep chilled.

Cut like a regular cake, and serve the sauce on the side, or pass it separately.

Spreading the luscious Bavarian cream over liqueur-soaked cake layer

🕐 *Timing*

It's probably a good idea to read this chapter through, noting anything you find useful, and make out your own shopping and cooking schedule, spreading it out over several days. Since some of the dishes can be prepared well in advance, you have a good deal of flexibility. All I can provide here are a few mileposts.

An hour before the party, arrange your vegetable platter; but refrigerate it until you present the green salad. If you have only 1 oven, bake the gnocchi now, since they keep warm better than the *pissaladière.* When they're done, raise the oven setting, wait till oven heat is up, and bake the *pissaladière,* first opening and distributing the anchovies. Just about now (an hour before) you can reheat the beef, in the oven if you have 2, otherwise on the stove top, and keep warm. It only takes moments to rewarm the sausages, and they keep well over mild heat, so do it when you like. This is also true of the white beans.

Note: If you own, or can borrow, a slow cooker to warm the beans, your only dirty dish so far is the beef roaster. Refrigerator containers are all small enough for the dishwasher—and, now that their space is vacated, you can put Champagne in the refrigerator in good time for dessert. Jug white wines, of course, take longer to chill: do them in your ice chest.

The morning of the party: if you have enough saucepans and stove top burners, you can do your preparations in an hour. Cook the zucchini and yellow squash, the green beans, and the broccoli, for the vegetable platter. While the beans and broccoli are cooking, prepare the marinade and baste all vegetables except beans and broccoli. Next make your salad dressing; whip the cream and decorate the torte, then refrigerate. Now's the time, if you hadn't freezer space, to buy bagged ice cubes and store in ice chests; it won't hurt jug white wine to sit there for the rest of the day.

Note: Even on a gusty, dusty summer day, with all the windows open, you can set out your table well beforehand. Just cover things; some favor plastic cleaners' bags, but I find they grab at stemmed glasses and cause breakage. On flower arrangements: do them the day before, but in hot weather set them in a cool corner, out of the light; a wine cellar is ideal.

The day before: cook the beef, and finish its sauce. Prepare the salad greens and most of the makings for the cold vegetable platter: the onions, the mushrooms, cauliflower, leeks, celery, and topinambours. Now's a good time to set tables, "tidy all 'round," and fix flowers.

The day before that brown the beef and cook it, and do the sausages and their sauce.

Two or 3 days before, make and refrigerate the *tarama brandade,* and cook the onions for the *pissaladière.*

Any time at all: make and freeze the dough for the *pissaladière,* the gnocchi, and the torte.

Vegetables may be trimmed and some even cooked the day before the party; beef may be browned the day before that.

Leftovers

If you had 10 guests, you're certain to have leftover beef, ham, and cake. Of the other dishes, all keep well except an already-baked *pissaladière* or browned *gnocchi*—tolerable re-warmed, both of them.

Sausage, beef, and *beans* are easily re-warmed: the sausage nuggets in their sauce, the beef ditto, the beans with added liquid if they seem dry. Puréed, the beans make a delicious soup—add broth. If serving cold, chill, then add cream, lemon, and herbs. A country *ham* will keep several weeks at least, well wrapped, in the refrigerator and is a wonderful resource—excellent in paper-thin slices as an hors d'oeuvre. Or grind scraps and add to sandwich spreads, stuffed eggs, etc. Save the bone for soup—split pea or bean preferred.

The raw *vegetables:* make salad, or cook and dice them for a *macédoine,* or mince them to garnish a consommé. *Vegetables à la grecque:* finish them off next day, no later.

The *torte,* refrigerated of course, will be delicious next day—or scrape off the whipped cream, and freeze the nude remains, then re-dress. Purée and freeze any leftover sauce to make a strawberry sherbet.

Mail-Order Hams:
I have used the following sources at one time or another:

Callaway Gardens, Pine Mountain, Georgia
    31822
Gwaltney of Smithfield, P.O. Box 489, Smith-
    field, Virginia 23430
Jordan's Old Virginia Smokehouse, P.O. Box
    324, Richmond, Virginia 23202
V. W. Joyner & Co., Smithfield, Virginia
    23430
Col. Bill Newsom's Kentucky Country Hams,
    Princeton, Kentucky 42445
Smithfield Packing Co., Inc., Smithfield, Vir-
    ginia 23430
E. M. Todd Co., Inc., P.O. Box 4167, Rich-
    mond, Virginia 23220

Essay

Cooking to Bring

Here are a few thoughts for those happy occasions when everybody brings something: a cake for, say, a bake sale; a festive aspic for a summer weekend; a wondrously convertible stew/salad/casserole for any friend who is faced with a big crowd; an elegant egg dish you can bring to a lunch party and reheat; and, finally, an unabashedly fancy fish assemblage that could be the *pièce de résistance* at a cooking-club get-together. Since it has an alluring relative, the golden, feathery brioche loaf, I've included the recipe for that, too.

Chocolate-Chip Spice and Pound Cake

When they know you're coming, bring them a cake! And this one with its nicely spiced flavor and generous sprinkling of chocolate bits will go with fruits, ice cream, or just coffee and tea.

Manufacturing Notes:
Whenever you put something like candied fruits or nuts into a cake batter, you want them to stay put and not fall down to the bottom of the pan. That goes for chocolate chips, too. It turns out that the best kind of cake batter for this purpose is the pound cake formula, which is moistly buttery yet solid enough to hold fruits or chocolate in place; and you also moisten and flour these items to encourage - their suspension.

This is a recipe that calls for whole eggs and sugar beaten until they are thick and heavy like a mayonnaise, so you must beat them in a rounded bowl, one so shaped that the whole mixture is in motion at once; if your machine is equipped with a large flat-bottomed bowl— and I don't know why anyone continues to design mixers that way—substitute another bowl. My old mixer, as an example, came with the wrong kind of bowl. It now works nicely with a stainless-steel bowl 4¾ inches deep that is 7¾ inches across the top and 3 at the bottom (or 12, 19, and 8 cm, respectively). Now, after that bit of mechanical lore, here is the recipe.

Proportions for a 6-cup (1½-L) loaf pan about 10 inches (25 cm) long, serving 10 to 12

4 "large" eggs

⅓ cup (¾ dL) packed-down, dark brown sugar

½ cup (1 dL) white granulated sugar

Pinch salt

1 tsp powdered mace

1½ sticks (6 ounces or 180 g) unsalted butter

1¼ cups (175 g) all-purpose flour (measure by dipping dry-measure cups into flour container and sweeping off excess with the straight edge of a knife)

1¼ tsp double-action baking powder

6 ounces (1 cup or 180 g) semisweet chocolate chips (bits, morsels), in a bowl

Drops of rum, whiskey, or coffee

1 Tb pure vanilla extract

Other items

Soft butter, flour, and wax paper to line a loaf pan; a metal bowl for beating butter; the right bowl for your mixer—see discussion preceding recipe

Preheat oven to 350°F/180°C and place rack in middle or lower-middle level.

Beating the eggs and sugar

Place the eggs, sugars, salt, and mace in bowl of mixer and stir over hot water for a minute or so to take off chill. Then set on stand and beat at high speed for 5 minutes or more, until eggs are doubled in volume, form the ribbon, and are the consistency of lightly whipped cream or of heavy mayonnaise.

Other preliminaries

Meanwhile, cut up the butter, if chilled, and stir over hot water to soften it; then beat until light and fluffy (setting in cold water if it has softened too much)—it must be the consistency of the egg-sugar mixture. Set aside and beat up again later, if necessary. Butter the loaf pan, line bottom with wax paper, butter that, then dust with flour, knocking out excess. Measure out the 1¼ cups flour into a sifter and set on a piece of wax paper, then stir the baking powder into the flour. Toss the chocolate bits with a few drops of rum, whiskey, or coffee, just to coat them (pour out excess), then toss with a tablespoon or two of the flour, again just enough to coat them. You are now ready to combine the elements of the cake batter.

Finishing the cake batter

Being sure that the eggs are a thick mayonnaise-like consistency and are at room temperature (beat over hot water if not, or they will congeal the butter), beat in the vanilla. Check also that the butter is soft and fluffy, then beat a dollop—⅓ cup (¾ dL) or so—of the eggs into the butter. By fourths, and with a rubber spatula, delicately and rapidly fold the flour into the eggs, deflating them as little as possible until last addition of flour is almost incorporated; then scoop the butter into the eggs. Rapidly spread it out and then fold it in with your spatula until almost incorporated; fold in the flour-covered chocolate bits. Immediately scoop batter into pan, which will be filled by about two-thirds.

Baking, cooling, serving, and storing

Set at once in preheated oven and bake for 50 to 60 minutes. Cake should rise to fill pan and will brown nicely on top; it is done when top feels springy, when you can gently pull cake from sides of pan, and when a skewer plunged into center comes out clean (except for traces of melted chocolate). Remove from oven, set pan right side up on a rack, and let cool for 10 minutes. Then unmold on rack, peel paper off bottom of cake, and carefully, with the aid of a long spatula, turn cake right side up. May be served warm or cool; but if wrapped and chilled after cooling, it is best served at room temperature to bring out the texture and flavor of both cake and chocolate.

◑ May be wrapped airtight when cold and refrigerated, or may be frozen.

Ring Mold of Eggs in Aspic

Les Oeufs en Gelée à la Carrousel

Rather than preparing jellied eggs individually, do them all together in a ring mold and bring them along as a first course or as the star main course for a summer luncheon. You can fill the center of the unmolded aspic ring with sprigs of watercress tossed in an oil and lemon dressing, or a mayonnaise of shellfish, or a salad of fresh mushrooms and asparagus tips. The whole dish may be assembled and refrigerated a day or even two days in advance of serving.

Luxury Note:

The following recipe calls for truffle and *foie gras* because this is a very special dish—and besides, I've not used them at all in this book. However, a decoration of shrimp, lobster, or crab, or nicely cut ham slices, or fancifully shaped cooked vegetables would be equally appropriate.

For 6 servings

A 1-ounce (30-g) canned truffle and its juices
4 Tb Port or Madeira
2 envelopes (2 Tb) plain unflavored gelatin
4 cups (1 L) excellent clarified meat stock or consommé, in a saucepan
6 slices *foie gras* ⅛ inch (½ cm) thick, and egg shaped, or about ½ cup (1 dL) excellent liver mousse
6 small or medium poached eggs (page 169), chilled
Filling or sauce for serving (optional), such as the suggestion in the introductory paragraph, or a bowl of homemade mayonnaise

Equipment

A 4-cup (1-L) ring mold; a bowl large enough to accommodate mold with 2 trays of ice cubes and water to cover them; a small saucepan for chilling aspic; a chilled round serving platter

Cut the truffle into 6 slices and return to the can with its juices and enough Port or Madeira to fill it; let macerate until needed.

To make the aspic, sprinkle the gelatin over the cold stock or consommé, let soften 2 to 3 minutes, then stir over gentle heat until gelatin has dissolved completely. Assemble the rest of the ingredients listed. (If you are using liver mousse rather than *foie gras,* taste carefully for seasoning: you may wish to beat in a few drops of truffle juice, some pepper, a little soft butter, and a pinch of allspice.) Pour the truffle juice and remaining wine into the aspic; chill the truffle slices.

Pour a ⅜-inch (1-cm) layer of liquid aspic into the ring mold and chill in the bowl of ice 10 to 15 minutes or until set. Pour a little liquid aspic into the saucepan, stir over ice to cool, remove from ice, and dip truffle slices into it to coat them; arrange over the aspic layer in the mold—each slice marks the place for each of the 6 eggs. Cover each truffle with a slice of *foie gras* (or a spoonful of liver paste).

Trim eggs evenly and lay upside down over the *foie gras.* Pour a cup of liquid aspic into saucepan, chill over ice until syrupy and almost set, then pour a ½-inch (1½-cm) layer into mold around the eggs; chill mold in ice to set the aspic and hold the eggs in place. Chill remaining aspic in saucepan; when syrupy, pour around the eggs to fill the mold. Cover the mold and chill at least an hour in the refrigerator.

To unmold, fill a large bowl with very hot water. Run a knife between the aspic and mold, both outside and inside edges. Dip into hot water for 6 to 8 seconds, remove, and turn the chilled serving dish upside down over mold. Reverse the two, giving mold a sharp downward jerk to dislodge aspic. Remove mold, cover aspic with inverted bowl, and refrigerate until serving time; then fill center with whatever you have chosen. You may wish to decorate outside with chopped aspic or aspic cutouts. Pass mayonnaise separately, if you wish.

The eggs in this photograph were jumbo, so that the aspic on the inside of the ring did not quite cover them. Use small or medium eggs and you will not have to hide them with parsley and greens as we did here.

Turkey Wine Stew— Turkey Salad— Turkey Casserole

If you are bringing a main dish to a party, try a turkey salad or a turkey casserole for a change, either of which you can make from a turkey wine stew—and that means simmering the turkey in pieces, whereby it cooks much faster than whole turkey and the meat is moist and tasty.

Turkey Wine Stew

Note:
If turkey is frozen, thaw in its original plastic wrapping either in the refrigerator for several days or in a sinkful of cold water for several hours.

For about 3 quarts (3 liters) of cooked turkey meat

A 12- to 14-pound (5½- to 6¼-kg) turkey

2 large onions, peeled and quartered

1 large carrot, scrubbed and roughly chopped

1 large celery stalk, washed and roughly sliced

1 large leek, quartered, washed, and sectioned (optional)

1 large herb bouquet (10 parsley sprigs, 2 bay leaves, 1 tsp thyme or sage, tied together in washed cheesecloth)

2 bottles dry white wine (Chablis, white table wine, or anything that tastes fresh, strong, and healthy)

Chicken broth or water, as needed

Breast meat marinade (optional)
Salt and white pepper, 2 Tb Cognac or lemon juice, 1 tsp minced shallot or scallion, 2 Tb olive oil or salad oil
1 Tb salt, or to taste

Cutting up the turkey

Disjoint the turkey as follows. Remove leg and thigh sections in one piece, along with the nuggets of dark meat at the small of the back and from thigh joint to tail; separate drumsticks from thighs. Cut off wings close to body. Remove each breast-meat half in one piece, scraping it from ridge of breastbone and down rib cage to backbone; remove the white tendon that runs almost the length of the underside of each breast—scrape down each side and then draw it out. Pull and cut the skin off the breast meat, drumsticks, thighs, and as much of it off the wings as you easily can—the rest can be removed from the wings after cooking. (I discard the skin.) Chop the carcass into pieces that will easily fit into your stew pot.

Assembling the turkey in the pot

Arrange the carcass pieces in the bottom of your pot with the turkey neck, gizzard, and heart (reserve the liver for another dish). Place the drumsticks, thighs, and wings over the carcass pieces, add the vegetables and the herb bouquet, and pour in the wine and enough chicken stock or water to cover ingredients by 2 inches (5 cm). Bring to the simmer over moderately high heat. Meanwhile, place the breast meat in a bowl and, if you wish, add marinade: sprinkle with salt and pepper, the Cognac or lemon juice, shallot or scallion, and oil; turn the meat about in the bowl to cover with the marinade, then cover the bowl and refrigerate until it is time to add the breast meat to the stew pot.

Stewing the turkey

2 to 2½ hours

Skim off the gray scum which will continue to rise from the simmering turkey for several minutes. Salt lightly to taste, then cover partially and let simmer slowly for 1 hour. Add the breast meat and its optional marinade and a little more stock or water, if needed, to cover the meat; simmer about 45 minutes more, until breast meat is tender and cooked through (slice one in half lengthwise to see, if you are not sure). Remove the breast meat when done and dip out other pieces, such as the wings and second joints, if they are tender before the drumsticks; place removed pieces in a bowl and cover with turkey cooking stock to keep moist. When all the turkey pieces are done, return everything to the pot and let cool, uncovered, for half an hour or more, so that the turkey meat will remain juicy and will pick up the flavor of the cooking liquid.

Finishing the turkey

Dip the turkey pieces from the pot and remove meat from bone. If you are serving the turkey in a salad or casserole, cut the large pieces of meat into big-bite-size pieces. Discard skin from wings and remove as much wing meat as possible. When cool, refrigerate the turkey meat in a covered bowl. Return bones to pot and simmer them in the cooking liquid another hour, then strain, degrease, and save the stock for soup or sauces.

Turkey Pot-au-Feu—Turkey Boiled Dinner

I can't leave turkey stew without remarking that this turkey meat, boned or not, makes a fine simple meal served with the usual boiled-dinner vegetables cooked or steamed with the turkey stock—carrots, onions, turnips, parsnips, potatoes—and you could even add a sausage or two to liven things up. (See the Corned Beef and Pork Boiled Dinner on page 138 for ideas.)

Turkey Salad

Serving 16 or more

The preceding 3 quarts (3 L) of cooked turkey meat

Salt and white pepper

1 cup (¼ L), more or less, finely minced mild onion

2 cups (½ L), more or less, finely diced celery

4 Tb, more or less, capers

½ cup (1 dL), more or less, fresh lemon juice

4 Tb, more or less, light olive oil or salad oil

½ cup (1 dL) lightly pressed down, minced fresh parsley

6 hard-boiled eggs, diced

2 cups (½ L), or more, homemade mayonnaise

Decorative suggestions

Hard-boiled eggs, green or red peppers sliced into rings, capers

Toss the turkey in a very large mixing bowl with salt and pepper to taste, then toss with the onion, celery, capers, lemon juice to taste, and several spoonfuls of oil. Let stand, tossing several times and checking on seasoning, for 20 to 30 minutes before folding in the parsley, hard-boiled eggs, and just enough mayonnaise to coat the turkey lightly. Pile into a serving bowl, mask the surface with a light coating of mayonnaise, and decorate the top with sliced or quartered hard-boiled eggs, peppers, capers, and/or whatever other good ideas you have. Cover with plastic wrap and refrigerate until serving time.

Turkey Casserole

Turkey gratinéed in white wine sauce with mushrooms and onions

This is the kind of old-fashioned recipe that always makes good eating and is useful indeed when you have a crowd to feed since you can assemble the whole thing the day before.

Serving 16 or more

The preceding 3 quarts (3 L) of cooked turkey meat

Salt and pepper

2 quarts (2 L) fresh mushrooms

4 Tb minced shallots or scallions

2 Tb fresh lemon juice, or more if needed

2 quarts (2 L), more or less, strained and degreased turkey cooking stock, heated in a saucepan

1½ quarts (1½ L) sliced onions

1½ sticks (6 ounces or 180 g) butter

½ cup (70 g) flour

3 egg yolks blended in a mixing bowl with 1 cup (¼ L) heavy cream

3 cups (¾ L) lightly packed, grated cheese (Swiss, Parmesan, mild Cheddar, or a mixture of all three)

Toss the turkey meat in a very large bowl with salt and pepper to taste. Trim the mushrooms, quarter or halve them, wash rapidly, and drain. Toss them in a large saucepan with the shallots or scallions, lemon juice, and a cup (¼ L) of the turkey stock; cover the pan, bring to the boil, and simmer, tossing once or twice, for 3 minutes. Drain thoroughly, reserving liquid, toss with a sprinkling of salt and pepper, and add the mushrooms to the turkey. Return cooking liquid to pan, fold in the onions, a sprinkling of salt and pepper, and add 4 tablespoons of butter; cover and cook slowly until the onions are very tender, about 20 minutes. Drain thoroughly, reserving juices, and add onions to turkey and mushrooms.

Meanwhile, prepare the White Wine Sauce.

White Wine Sauce:

For 5 to 6 cups or 1 ¼ to 1 ½ liters
First, make a *roux:* melt 1 stick of butter in a large heavy-bottomed saucepan, blend in the flour, and stir with a wooden spoon over moderate heat as the flour and butter cook and finally foam and froth together; cook, stirring, for 2 minutes, not letting the *roux* turn more than a buttery yellow color. Remove from heat and, when it has stopped bubbling, pour in about 4 cups (1 L) of hot turkey stock, beating vigorously with your wire whip to blend. Beat in any mushroom/onion cooking juices. Set sauce over moderately high heat, stirring slowly with your whip, and bring to the simmer, thinning out with additions of stock to make a quite thick sauce. Let simmer, stirring with a wooden spoon and reaching all over bottom and corners of pan, for 5 minutes.

Remove from heat and, beating the egg yolk and cream mixture with your whip, dribble in 2 to 3 cups (½ to ¾ L) of the hot sauce, then beat the egg yolk mixture back into the sauce. Set over moderately high heat and stir slowly with a wooden spoon until sauce comes back to the simmer; simmer 2 to 3 minutes, stirring. Remove from heat and taste very carefully for seasoning, adding salt, pepper, and drops of lemon juice if needed.

Assembling and baking
Fold the turkey meat with the onions, mushrooms, more salt and pepper to taste, two thirds of the grated cheese, and two thirds of the sauce. Butter a 5- to 6-quart (5-L) baking dish and turn the turkey mixture into it. Spread the remaining sauce and cheese over the surface.

🕐   May be prepared in advance to this point. When cool, cover and refrigerate.

About an hour before serving, set in upper middle level of a preheated 375°F/190°C oven and bake until contents are bubbling hot and surface has browned nicely. If you are not serving soon, keep warm on an electric hot plate or over simmering water—do not overheat or you will ruin the texture and quality of the turkey.

Eggs Interalliés

*Scrambled eggs and mushrooms
gratinéed with cheese*

I ran across this recipe way back in the early
1960s when doing an article for *House and
Garden* on renowned Washington hostesses
and their favorite recipes. Mme Hervé
Alphand contributed the idea for this dish,
which she served at diplomatic luncheons in
the French Embassy, and I have always loved
it. It is simple yet unusual, as well as easy to
make, and it can be reheated. It would make a
welcome contribution to a lunch or brunch or
breakfast.

For 8 servings

1 pound (450 g) fresh mushrooms

About 1½ sticks (6 ounces or 180 g) butter

2 Tb minced shallots or scallions

Salt and pepper

6 Tb flour

About 2 cups (½ L) milk, heated in a small pan

About 1 cup (¼ L) heavy cream

Drops of fresh lemon juice

12 to 16 eggs

½ cup (1 dL) grated Parmesan cheese, or a
mixture of Parmesan, Cheddar, and/or Swiss

Equipment

A 9-inch (23-cm) frying pan, preferably nonstick, for both mushrooms and eggs; a lightly
buttered fireproof baking and serving dish,
such as an oval 9 x 12 x 2 inches (23 x 30 x 5
cm)

The mushrooms

Trim the mushrooms, wash rapidly, dry, and
cut into quarters. Sauté in 3 tablespoons butter
over high heat for 5 to 6 minutes or until they
are barely beginning to brown. Then stir in the
shallots or scallions and toss over moderate
heat for 1 to 2 minutes. Season to taste with
salt and pepper, and set aside.

The sauce
For about 3 cups
Melt 5 tablespoons butter in a heavy-bottomed saucepan. Blend in the flour with a wooden spoon and stir over moderately low heat until butter and flour froth together for 2 minutes without coloring. Remove from heat and vigorously beat in the simmering milk with a wire whip to blend thoroughly. Beat in half the cream and salt and pepper to taste. Boil slowly, stirring, for 4 to 5 minutes. Then thin out the sauce with additional cream, beaten in by driblets. Sauce should coat a spoon nicely but not be too thick. Correct seasoning and beat in drops of lemon juice to taste. Clean off sides of pan with a rubber spatula, then float a tablespoon of cream on top of sauce to prevent a skin from forming.

Scrambling the eggs
Note that the eggs must be very soft and creamy, or slightly underdone; they will finish cooking under the broiler. Beat the eggs and seasonings in a bowl until just blended. Smear 3 tablespoons of butter in the skillet with a rubber spatula. Pour in the eggs and stir over moderately low heat. When eggs slowly begin to thicken, in 2 to 3 minutes, stir rapidly until they scramble into very soft curds. Immediately remove from heat and stir in, if you wish, a tablespoon or two of additional butter. Season to taste.

Assembling and serving
Spoon a thin layer of sauce into the bottom of the oval dish and sprinkle over it 2 tablespoons of cheese. Spread on half the eggs. Fold a cup (¼ L) of the sauce into the mushrooms and spoon over the eggs, sprinkling on 3 more tablespoons of cheese. Cover with the rest of the eggs, then the rest of the sauce. Sprinkle with the remaining cheese, and dot with butter.

❶ May be prepared an hour or so in advance; set aside at room temperature.

Shortly before serving, preheat broiler to very hot and place dish so surface is an inch (2½ cm) from heating element for a minute or so, until lightly browned. Serve at once.

Fish en Croûte

Loup en Croûte—Whole striped bass, salmon, or trout baked in a brioche crust

Fish in a crust was conceived in France by, I think, Paul Bocuse, but the first time I had it was with my French colleague Simone Beck, at Louis Outhier's restaurant, L'Oasis, in La Napoule, on the Mediterranean. The *loup* was a large sea bass, and this one came to us in a fish-shaped crust—enormous, brown, and glistening. The headwaiter cut around the edges of the crust, lifted it off, and there lay the fish—steaming, fragrant, and ready to serve, a really remarkable sight. With each serving of fish we received a portion of the crust, a big spoonful of creamy, buttery sauce, and another of fresh tomato nicely flavored with shallots and herbs. Fortunately, it is actually an easy way to cook a whole fish, and one in which the flesh retains its juices and delicate flavor.

This is the kind of dish to bring to a small informal party where everyone enjoys cooking and eating, and where you can have access to the kitchen, since you will have to assemble and bake it on the spot. I would suggest that you have everything ready at home, such as the fish all cleaned, oiled, iced, and the dough made and chilled. You bring fish and dough with you (as well as the tomato fondue, if you want to serve it), your rolling pin, baking pan, serving board, and other minor accessories. Assembly will take less than 10 minutes, and baking about 45. If you're making the butter sauce, it will take but a few minutes, and you can whip that up just before serving the fish.

For a 3-pound (1 ½-kg) fish, serving 8 as a first course

A 3-pound (1 ½-kg) fresh striped bass, salmon, or trout (weighed whole) cleaned, scaled (but with head on, if possible), and brushed with olive oil

Salt and pepper

6 to 8 fresh parsley sprigs

½ tsp fennel seed, or a handful of fresh fennel or dill

Brioche dough, risen and chilled (the following recipe)

Egg glaze (1 egg beaten in a cup with 1 tsp water)

Optional: white butter sauce (page 225) and fresh tomato fondue (page 143)

Equipment

Brown paper to make a fish template; a buttered jelly roll pan large enough to hold the fish diagonally; the metal tube from a pastry bag or scissors to make decorations; a platter or board to serve the fish on, plus a side dish for scraps and bones

An hour before you plan to serve, preheat oven to 400°F/205°C and set rack in middle or lower middle level. Wash and dry the fish, salt and pepper it inside, and tuck the parsley and fennel or dill in cavity. Cut a brown paper silhouette of the fish. Roll the dough into a rectangle and cut in half. Chill one piece. Roll the other out rapidly about ⅛ inch (½ cm) thick. Using template, cut into a fish shape (see page 222), roll up on pin, and unroll it in place on the jelly roll pan. Refrigerate dough scraps. Lay the fish on the dough. Rapidly roll out second piece of dough and cut ½ inch (1 ½ cm) larger all around than template; roll up on pin and unroll over fish; press the 2 layers together all around and tuck under fish. Working rapidly, roll out scraps of dough to form mouth, eyes, back fin, and tail decorations; paint those areas with egg glaze and affix the decorations. Paint fish with egg glaze; let dry a moment, and paint again. Using metal tube end or scissors, cut upstanding snips in surface of dough to simulate scales. Fish should now be baked immediately, before dough has a

chance to rise, so that it will remain thin and crusty.

Bake about 45 minutes. Fish is done at an internal thermometer reading of 160–165°F/71–74°C—or just when juices begin to escape into the pan. Crust will be brown and slightly puffed. Serve as soon as possible, accompanied, if you wish, with the white butter sauce and the tomato fondue.

To serve, cut all around outside edge of crust and lift it off. Peel skin off top of fish, and serve pieces of fish from topside of bone. Then remove bone, and serve bottom side of fish. Cut a strip or two of the top crust for each serving. (The soggy bottom crust is discarded.)

Remarks:

You could, if you wished, use the giant crêpe described for the Choulibiac, page 82, rather than brioche dough for the bottom crust. You would cut it into a fish shape, following the template, and tuck half an inch (1½ cm) or so of the top covering brioche dough under the crêpe.

The fish we got for this picture was too big to fit on the pan so we had to cut off its head.

Plain Brioche Dough

*Pâte à Brioche Commune—
Made in a mixer or processor*

This is the dough for fish *en croûte*, beef Wellington, *coulibiac*, or best-quality bread for sandwiches, toast, and canapés.

Brioche dough—rich, buttery, eggy, light in texture, and almost cakelike in taste—is fast and easy to produce in either a heavy-duty mixer or a food processor; but in both cases I think it needs a few minutes' rest after making, then a few minutes of hand work just to be sure it is kneaded enough. For best taste and texture, any yeast dough, in my opinion, benefits from two risings before it is formed; while the first and most important rise is long, slow, and supervised, the second may take place in the refrigerator. (By the way, the food processor recipe is my adaptation of James Beard's method, which appeared in the April 1978 issue of *Cooking*, the Cuisinart magazine.)

Note: The following proportions will make a little more dough than you need for a 3-pound (1½-kg) fish *en croûte*, but you can turn the extra amount into a loaf of bread. Start the dough the day before you plan to use it; or even several days in advance, and freeze it. (The whole recipe will make the equivalent of 4 loaves of bread baked in 4-cup or 1-liter pans.)

For about 8 cups (2 liters) of dough

2 packages (2 Tb) dry active yeast dissolved in ½ cup (1 dL) warm water (100°F/38°C)
2 sticks (½ pound or 225 g) butter
½ cup (1 dL) milk
2 pounds (7 cups or 900 g) all-purpose flour—measure by scooping flour into cup and sweeping it off level with lip of cup
1 Tb salt
3 Tb sugar
8 "large" eggs (1⅔ cups or 3¾–4 dL)

Making the dough in an electric mixer
(A large heavy-duty mixer is best for this; use the dough hook and put on the splatter shield, if your machine is equipped with one. For a smaller mixer, do the dough in 2 batches and then combine them for the final kneading.) Prepare the yeast; cut the butter into smallish pieces and melt in a small saucepan with the milk. Measure all but 2 cups of the flour into the mixer bowl, add the salt and sugar, the melted butter and milk, and the eggs. Mix to blend; the mixture, which the eggs will have cooled, should be just warm to the touch; if too hot, wait for several minutes before adding the yeast. Beat at moderate speed for 2 to 3 minutes, gradually adding the rest of the flour. Continue (lifting beater out of dough to unclog the blades as necessary, if you have no dough hook), mixing until dough is elastic enough to retract back into shape when a piece is pinched away from the mass. Turn dough out onto a lightly floured board, let rest 2 minutes, then knead vigorously by hand for a minute or two until dough is smooth. (It will be a soft dough.)

Making the dough in a food processor
(This goes very fast indeed, but you will have to make the dough in 2 or 3 batches, depending on the size of your processor container: for the 2-quart [2-L] size, make 3 batches; for the larger container, make 2 batches. As each batch is made, a matter of less than 2 minutes, turn it out onto your work surface, then combine for the final kneading.) Dissolve the yeast, stir it up, and divide it into 2 (or 3) portions. Cut the butter into smallish pieces and divide into 2 (or 3) portions. Measure 3½ cups (⁴/₅ L) flour, for 1 of 2 batches (2⅓ cups or 4 dL, for 1 of 3 batches) into the container of the processor and add ½ (or ⅓) of the salt and sugar. Break the eggs into a metal bowl, add the milk, and stir over hot water to take off the chill; pour into a quart or liter measure. Turn

on the processor and blend several seconds and then in spurts until butter is completely broken up into the flour—30 to 45 seconds. Pour in ½ (or ⅓) of the eggs; process several seconds and then in spurts until dough masses on the blades and revolves against the top of the container; continue processing for 30 seconds or so—this is the kneading action. Remove the dough to your work surface and, without cleaning out the processor, continue with the next 1 or 2 batches. Let rest 2 minutes, then mass the batches together and knead vigorously on a lightly floured surface until dough is smooth. (It will be a soft dough.)

The rising of the dough
Place dough in a clean, fairly straight-sided 8-quart (8 liter) bowl, or divide into 2 bowls. Cover with plastic wrap and a towel and let sit at 72–75°F/22–24°C. (In hot weather, let the rise start, then refrigerate dough from time to time to slow the rise.) When tripled, in 3 hours or more, the dough will feel spongy and springy; turn it out onto your work surface. Pat into a rectangle with the palms of your hands, and fold dough in 3; repeat and return to cleaned bowl—this redistributes yeast cells throughout the dough to make a finer grain. Cover and let rise again, this time to slightly more than double (1½ to 2 hour).

🕐   You may wish to complete this rise in the refrigerator overnight; but if dough has already started its rise, cover with a plate and a weight to prevent its over-rising.

When second rise is complete, if you are doing the fish recipe, turn dough out onto work surface, flatten with palms of hands, and place on a lightly floured tray; flour lightly, cover with plastic, a board, and a weight. It must be chilled before you proceed with the fish recipe—or for making similar dough-wrapped creations like beef Wellington or *coulibiac*.

🕐   To delay the rise you can always refrigerate the dough; for a long delay, weight it down when it has chilled. To stop the rise, freeze the dough—up to 10 days; to continue, either thaw overnight in the refrigerator or set in a warm place until thawed and the rise has started up again, then proceed where you left off.

Brioche Sandwich Bread

Pain Brioché

A fine loaf of bread is always a welcome gift, and the preceding brioche dough makes perfect sandwich bread or toast for *foie gras*, smoked salmon, and other such delicacies. Rather than baking it in an open pan, you can cover the pan so that your loaf will be contained in an even rectangular shape. Although you can sometimes find covered pans known as Pullman pans or *pain de mie* pans in professional stores and import shops, you can easily improvise your own, as illustrated.

For 1 brioche loaf baked in an 8-cup (2-liter) pan

⅓ the preceding brioche dough, fully risen

Equipment

A buttered 8-cup (2-L) bread pan, as straight-sided as possible, to make a rectangular shape; a sheet of very smooth aluminum foil, buttered on the shiny side (to cover bread pan); a baking sheet and a heavy heat-proof weight of some sort like a brick, a big stone, or an axe head

Flatten the dough into a rectangular shape slightly shorter than the bread pan, fold in half lengthwise and pinch the two edges together, then fit seam side down into the pan, pressing dough in place with your knuckles. Dough should fill pan by slightly less than half. Cover loosely and let dough rise to fill pan only by about three quarters; it will rise to fill pan later while baking. (Preheat oven to 450°F/230°C and set rack in middle level before dough has completed its rise of about an hour.) Cover the pan with the foil, buttered side down, and set in oven. Place baking sheet and weight on top, and bake 35 to 40 minutes—do not peek or remove baking sheet and weight for 30 minutes. Bread is done when nicely browned on top, when the loaf has shrunk very slightly from sides of pan, and when it unmolds easily.

Let cool on a rack. When thoroughly cold, in several hours, wrap airtight and refrigerate or freeze. For easy sandwich slicing, bread should be a day old.

White Butter Sauce with Herbs

Beurre Blanc aux Fines Herbes

This is a more classic version of the lemon butter sauce on page 53, and I like it lightened with a little cream and brightened with a sprinkling of herbs. Unless you are familiar with it and know the tricks of making it ahead and keeping it, you're wise to make the sauce only at the last minute, although there are directions for ahead-of-time preparation at the end of the recipe.

For 1½ to 1¾ cups (3½ to 4 deciliters)

4 Tb white wine vinegar
2 Tb lemon juice
4 Tb dry white vermouth
2 Tb finely minced shallots or scallions
Salt
White pepper
2½ sticks (10 ounces or 285 g) chilled butter, cut into ¼-inch (¾-cm) slices
4 to 8 Tb heavy cream
Minced parsley and/or dill

Simmer the vinegar, lemon juice, vermouth, shallots or scallions, ½ teaspoon salt, and ⅛ teaspoon pepper in a 6-cup (1½-L) enameled or stainless-steel saucepan until liquid has reduced to 1½ tablespoons. Remove saucepan from heat and immediately beat in 2 pieces of the chilled butter with a wire whip. As butter softens and creams, beat in another piece. Then set pan over very low heat and, beating constantly, continue adding more pieces of butter as each previous piece has almost been absorbed into the sauce. Sauce should become thick and ivory colored, the consistency of hollandaise sauce. Remove from heat, add more salt and pepper to taste, and beat in the cream by spoonfuls to lighten the sauce. Beat in the herbs, turn into a warm (not too hot) sauce bowl, and serve.

🕐 If you wish to make the sauce ahead, omit cream and herbs and set sauce near a gas pilot light, or near a warm burner, just to prevent butter from congealing; at serving time, heat the cream and beat by driblets into the sauce to warm it, then beat in the herbs.

Menu Alternatives

To give you a wider choice in planning menus than this book would otherwise afford, here is an addendum for each chapter, suggesting other food that will fit the same requirements. Where the situation is unique, as in "Holiday Lunch," I've given a list of possibilities; otherwise I have created a menu for 11 of the 13 occasions, drawing recipes out of each one of my books. Here, recipe titles are usually given in French because that's the way my earlier books were set up, but there is sufficient description of each recipe in English to tell you what the dish is all about.

A Birthday Dinner Menu from *Mastering the Art of French Cooking, Volume Two*

Bisque de Crabes, Crab Bisque, page 36

Gigot Farci, en Croûte, Boned Stuffed Lamb Baked in Pastry, page 189

Gratin d'Épinards aux Oignons, Spinach Braised with Onions, page 360

Le Succès; Le Progrès; La Dacquoise, three names for the same cake: a meringue-nut layer cake with butter-cream frosting and filling, page 497

Suggested wines: a red Bordeaux–Saint-Emilion or Cabernet Sauvignon with the lamb; Champagne with the cake

Ideas for a Holiday Lunch from *Mastering the Art of French Cooking, Volume Two*

Main-dish soups

Soupe Catalane aux Poivrons, Catalonian Pepper and Leek Soup, page 21

Soupe à la Victorine, Purée of White Bean Soup, eggplant and tomato garnish, page 22

Pâtés and terrines

Terrine de Foie de Porc, Pork-Liver *Pâté,* page 320

Pâté de Campagne, Pork and Liver *Pâté* with Veal or Chicken, page 321

Pâté de Foie et de Porc en Brioche, Pork and Pork-Liver *Pâté* baked in *brioche* dough, page 322

La Terrine Verte; Pâté sans Porc, A Porkless *Pâté,* page 324

Pâtés en Croûte, *Pâtés* Baked in Pastry Crust, page 326

Luncheon stews

Boeuf en Pipérade, Beef Stew with a Garnish of Peppers and Tomatoes, page 152

Tripes à la Niçoise, Tripe Baked with Onions, Tomatoes, Wine, and Provençal Seasonings, page 244 (Must be served very hot, but can be repeatedly reheated)

Cold meat

Langue de Boeuf, Bouillié ou Braisé, Beef Tongue, Boiled or Braised, in several fashions, pages 232–42

Poitrine de Veau, Farcie, Breast of Veal Stuffed and Braised, page 216 (May be served hot or cold)

Jambon Persillé, Mold of Parsleyed Ham in Aspic, page 310 (Best made with home-cured pork—see recipes in *Mastering II* and in this book)

One-dish main courses

Chou Farci, Stuffed Whole Cabbage, page 379

-or-

Feuilles de Chou Farcies, Stuffed Cabbage Leaves, page 384

Feuilletée au Fromage; Jalousie au Fromage, Cheese Tart of French puff pastry, page 140 (This one is made with slats or Venetian-blind effect on top.)

Vegetables

Tian de Courgettes au Riz, Gratin of Zucchini, Rice, and Onions with Cheese, page 371

Oignons Farcis au Riz, Onions Stuffed

with Rice, Cheese, and Herbs, page 376

Gratin de Potiron d'Arpajon, Purée of Pumpkin or Winter Squash and White Beans, page 404

Purée Freneuse, Purée of Rice and Turnips with Herbs and Garlic, page 405

Salade de Poivrons, Provençale, Peeled and Sliced Sweet Bell Peppers in Garlic and Oil, page 411

Garnish

Petits Oignons Aigre-Doux, Sweet-Sour Onions Braised with Raisins, page 410 (May be served hot or cold)

Desserts

Le Marly; La Riposte, Strawberry Shortcake Made with Rum-soaked *Brioche,* page 448

Pain d'Épices, Spice Cake, page 481

Mille-Feuilles, Napoleons, page 462 (Layers of puff pastry and pastry cream or whipped cream, iced on top)

Bourbon-soaked Chocolate Truffles (in this book)

Couques and *Palmiers,* Caramelized Cookies Made from Puff Pastry Dough, pages 477 and 478

Lo-Cal Banquet Suggestions from *The French Chef*

Clams *en Gelée,* Clams in Aspic on the half shell, page 222

Choice of

Poularde Demi-désossée (or Half-Boned Chicken) poached in wine, unstuffed, with aromatic vegetables, page 389,

-or-

Saumon Poché, Whole Poached Fish, page 350 (Use the recipe for poached salmon, substituting any fish. Salmon is rather high in calories.)

-or-

Potée Normande; Pot-au-Feu, French Boiled Dinner, page 61 (Use chicken only, if you wish.)

Boiled Asparagus (in this book)
Grilled Tomatoes (in this book)

An Informal Dinner Menu
From Julia Child's Kitchen

Soupe au Pistou Verte, Green Zucchini Soup with a Garlic and Basil Garnish, page 8

Filets de Sole Dugléré, Poached Filets of Sole with White Wine Sauce and Tomatoes, page 138

Steamed Rice (in this book)

Chopped Cooked Spinach, page 420, or Green Beans (in this book)

Broccoli Flowerettes (in this book), or Asparagus (in this book)

Crêpes, Flambées, Sainte Claire, French crêpes with apricot flavor, flamed, page 537

Suggested wines: white Burgundy or Chardonnay

A VIP Lunch Menu
from *Mastering the Art of French Cooking, Volume One*

Filets de Poisson en Soufflé, Fish Soufflé Baked on a Platter, page 170, with Hollandaise Sauce, page 79

Épinards Étuvés au beurre, Spinach Braised in Butter, page 470

Oranges Glacées, Glazed Oranges, served cold, page 629, with *Reine de Saba,* Chocolate and Almond Cake, page 677

Champagne throughout is suggested.

Ideas for a Cocktail Party
From Julia Child's Kitchen

Cheese appetizers

Croque Madame and *Croque Monsieur,* Ham and Cheese Sandwiches, the former baked, the latter sautéed, pages 42–44; *Petites Fondues Frites,* Cheese Croquettes, page 45; cheese tarts, tartlets, covered tarts, and turnovers large and small, made from pie dough, mock puff pastry, and regular puff pastry.

Quiches

Lorraine, with cream and bacon, page 59; *au Gruyère,* with Swiss cheese, page 61; *au fromage,* with mixed cheeses, page 61; or with smoked salmon, eggplant, broccoli or spinach, with various other vegetables, and with shellfish, pages 62–64.

Homemade pizza, topped with tomatoes, cheese, and mushrooms, page 483; or *à la Niçoise,* with onions, olives, anchovies, and cheese, page 486; and—not a pizza, but similar—*Socca,* a baked pancake of chick-pea flour, page 486. Eggplant "pizza," page 398, has pizza topping, but the base is eggplant slices instead of dough—to be eaten with a fork.

Pâtés, terrines, and homemade sausage

A *pâté* of pork and liver with veal or chicken, page 368; a *pâté pantin* (free-form *pâté en croûte,* baked in a crust), page 372; a terrine of duck, page 369; a terrine of pork and veal with sweetbreads, page 371; and homemade sausage baked in a crust, page 364.

Fish and shellfish

Pain de Poisson, Loaf-shaped Fish Mousse, page 159, served cold and eaten with a fork. A similar mousse made with shrimp, page 155. Shrimp in a quiche, or *à la Grecque* (simmered in aromatic broth), or sautéed with lemon, page 64, 163, or 164. Scallops grilled on skewers, page 122. Two ways of broiling oysters in the half shell, pages 168–69 (must be served very hot, to eat with fork). The humane way to boil lobsters, page 174; serve the meat on toothpicks, with homemade mayonnaise (in this book).

Brochettes

Beef tenderloin, chicken breasts and livers, lamb, or scallops on skewers, page 287, 211, 292, or 122. Or braised ham, cubed, on toothpicks.

Vegetables

Homemade Potato Chips, page 413; *Caviar d'Aubergine,* Eggplant Caviar, page 400, or Eggplant Pizza, page 398; Mushrooms or Onions *à la Grecque,* page 407 or 408.

Eggplant caviar is generally used as a dip or a spread. Others: *Tapénade,* a Provençal combination of olives, capers, and anchovies, page 86; or two *brandades* (garlicky purées)—one of salt cod *(de morue),* page 179, the other of white beans *(à la Soissonaise),* page 342.

These dips can be used to flavor stuffed hard-boiled eggs. Other ways: with puréed asparagus, artichokes, smoked salmon, and shrimp, pages 85–86.

Garnish

Try recipes for preparing and storing the imported salt-packed large capers and whole anchovies one can find here in Italian markets, pages 437–38 and 49–53. I warmly recommend them.

A Dinner for the Boss Menu from *Mastering the Art of French Cooking, Volume Two*

Potage aux Concombres, Cream of Cucumber Soup, page 17 (May be served hot or cold)

Melba toast (in this book), made from *Pain de Mie,* Homemade White Sandwich Bread, page 74

Filet de Boeuf en Croûte, Tenderloin of Beef in Pastry—Beef Wellington, page 181 (This version, with a *brioche* crust, uses pre-sliced beef, and the mushroom stuffing lies between the slices. Another, equally good, is in *The French Chef Cookbook,* with a prebaked bottom crust and a mock puff pastry topping. Beef Wellington is another splendid dish that has lost its once-fine reputation through sloppy cooking, but again, as with Veal Orloff, it can be just as marvelous to eat as it is exciting to look at…and interesting to prepare.)

Sliced Fresh Asparagus Spears Tossed in Butter (in this book). Cut the asparagus on a diagonal, with the knife blade at a 20° angle to the stalk, for elegantly elongated slices.

Fresh green peas (in this book) or broccoli flowerettes (in this book)

La Surprise de Vésuve, French Baked Alaska, Flamed, page 432

Suggested wines: a red Bordeaux-Médoc or Cabernet Sauvignon with the beef; Champagne with dessert.

Do-It-Yourself Parties for All Ages for Sunday Night Supper

A Pizza Party
From Julia Child's Kitchen

Your Own Homemade Pizza, page 484
Tomato topping, page 484
Niçoise topping (onions, anchovies, olives, and cheese), page 486
Tranches d'Aubergine à l'Italienne, Pizza with an Eggplant Base instead of dough, page 398
Caesar Salad, page 433 (As Caesar made it)
Le Gâteau des Trois Mages, Le Gâteau Deblieux, Cake in a Cage, page 553 (A layer cake with whipped cream and fruits, enclosed by a floor and a dome of hard caramel)

An Omelette Party from *The French Chef*

Two-egg omelettes, each serving one person
Sliced sautéed mushrooms, a cheese sauce, and grated cheese, to use separately or combine for an *Omelette gratinée aux Champignons,* page 105
Pipérade for filling, page 419 (A mixture of tomatoes, peppers, onions, and ham)
To make some of the classic fillings listed by Escoffier, you could set forth bowls of:
Minced parsley and herbs (*omelette aux fines herbes*)
Minced parsley and minced sautéed onion (*omelette à la Lyonnaise*)
Diced ham (*omelette à la fermière*)
Diced sautéed potato with onions and chopped parsley (*omelette Parmentier*)
Diced sautéed chicken livers (in this book) (*omelette aux foies de volaille*)
Skewered Salad (in this book)
Croquembouche, A Tower of Cream Puffs, filled or not, stuck together with cara-

mel, page 359 (You could set out a tray of puffs, a bowl of whipped cream for filling, and keep the caramel stickily warm on a heating tray, so your guests can build the tower together.)

A Buffet for 19 from *Mastering the Art of French Cooking, Volume One*

Gratins, which can be prepared in advance and presented in baking dish
Gratin of Potatoes, with Ham and Eggs and Onions, page 153
with Onions and Anchovies, page 154
with Onions and Sausages, page 155
Gratin of Leeks and Ham, page 155
Gratin of Endives and Ham, page 156
Gratins of creamed mixtures, of fish, chicken, brains, or sweetbreads, pages 156–57
Gratins of *quenelles* made of fish, shellfish, veal, chicken, or turkey, pages 188–89
Gratins of canned salmon or tuna, or fish leftovers, page 189
Thon à la Provençale, Tuna or Swordfish Steaks with Wine, Tomatoes, and Herbs, page 219
Coq au Vin, page 263
Beef stews
à la Bourguignonne (in red wine), page 315; *Carbonnades à la Flamande* (with beer), page 317; *en Daube,* page 322; *Paupiettes de Boeuf* (Braised Stuffed Beef Rolls), page 318
Lamb in a *Navarin Printanier* or *Moussaka,* page 345 or 349
Veal, *Prince Orloff,* page 355; or *Sauté Marengo,* A Brown Stew with Tomatoes and Mushrooms, but not with last-minute fried eggs, page 360
Jambon Farci et Braisé, Ham Sliced, Stuffed, and Braised in Madeira, page 394 (This can be done in a pastry crust.)
Cassoulet, French Baked Beans with Pork, Sausages, Duck, etc., page 399
A useful list of cold main dishes
Poulet en Gelée à l'Estragon, Tarragon

Chicken in Aspic, page 549 (You can cut up the chicken after cooking, before jelling.)

Suprêmes de Volaille en Chaud-froid, Blanche Neige, Breast of Chicken in a Special Stock-and-Cream Jellied Sauce, page 551 (This is not made with the usual jellied *béchamel*.)

Crab or lobster *en Chaud-froid,* page 553

Volailles en Escabèche, Cold Fowl or, especially, Game in Lemon Jelly, page 554

Boeuf Mode en Gelée, Aspic of Sliced Cold Braised Beef, page 556

Cold jellied mousses of chicken, turkey, duck, game, ham, or fish, pages 558–64

Desserts

Among the many classic tarts, I recommend the lime or lemon (cold) soufflé-filled one, page 645. And among the cakes, the Savarin (a *baba* ring mold, soaked in rum and filled with fruit and whipped cream, page 662).

Charlotte Malakoff, page 607

Diplomate, Custard, unmolded, with Glacéed Fruits, page 612

Charlotte Chantilly, A Strawberry or Raspberry Cream, page 608

Crème Plombières Pralinée, Caramel Almond Cream, in a bowl not in a mold, with variations, page 594

Bavarian creams: orange, chocolate, strawberry or raspberry, pages 596–600

Riz à l'Impératrice, Molded Custard with Rice and Glacéed Fruits, page 601

Unmolded caramel custard, with variations, pages 610–11

Chocolate Mousse, page 604, and Orange Mousse, page 603

Charlotte aux Pommes, Apple Charlotte, page 623 (Don't forget to use Golden Delicious apples or another firm kind; see notes in this book.)

Pommes Normande en Belle Vue, An Applesauce Caramel Mold, page 624

Aspic de Pommes, Rum-flavored Apple Aspic, unmolded, page 627

Pêches Cardinal, A Compote of Fresh Peaches with Raspberry Purée, page 630

A Chafing-Dish Dinner Menu
From Julia Child's Kitchen

Potage Crème de haricots, White Bean Soup with Herbs and Lemon, page 14 (May be served hot or cold)

Truites Meunière, Whole Trout Sautéed in Butter, page 126

Zucchini en Pipérade, Grated Zucchini Sautéed with Onions, Peppers, and Herbs, page 427

Petits Pains: Galettes ou Champignons, Homemade French Rolls: Round or Top-Knotted (nicknamed "mushrooms"), pages 468 and 469

Pommes Rosemarie, Apples Rosie, page 494 (A version of apple Betty)

Suggested wines: Pouilly-Fuissé, Pouilly-Fumé, Chablis, dry Riesling, or Chardonnay with the trout; Vouvray Mousseux or a domestic sparkling white wine with dessert

An Indoor/Outdoor Barbecue Menu *From Julia Child's Kitchen*

Brandade de Morue, Purée of Salt Cod with Potatoes, Olive Oil, and Garlic, page 179 (Used as a dip for crackers or potato chips)

Les Crudités, Assorted Raw Vegetables

Crevettes à la Grecque, Shrimp, either boiled in salted water or simmered in court bouillon, page 163

Homemade Mayonnaise (in this book)

Brochettes (skewers) of scallops or chicken breasts and livers, page 211, or beef tenderloin, page 287, or lamb, page 294

Pommes de Terre Sautées à l'Ail, Potatoes Sautéed with Garlic and Herbs, page 417

Courgette Géante en Barquette, Belle-soeur, A Giant Cooked Zucchini as a Container for a Vegetable Mixture, page 427

Bombe Glacée au Chocolat, Molded Vanilla and Chocolate Ice Cream, homemade or best-quality store-bought, page 543

Suggested wines: red and white jug wines

Practical Dishes for Big Parties

*Page references for recipes from *Julia Child & Company*
**"Expandable" means you can increase recipe quantities proportionately without changing timing or temperatures.

		No Last-Minute Jobs	Expandable Recipes **	Easy to Serve	Can Be Reheated	Can Be Frozen	Can Be Made Mostly by Machine	Relatively Little Handwork	Reasonable Price
Appetizers:									
267	Beet and Cucumber Soup (hot or cold)	●	●	●	○		●	●	●
422	Brandades (dips)	●	●	●			●	●	○
251	Celery Root Rémoulade	●	●	●			○	○	○
403	Chicken Liver Aspic	●	●	●					○
414	Chicken Liver Pâté	●	●	●			●	●	○
284	Consommé	○	●	○	●	○			○
465	Fish Dogs	○	●	○	●				○
369	Fish Terrine	●	●	○			●	●	○
233	Mediterranean Platter (with feta cheese)	●	●	○					●
226	Mussel Salad	●	●	○					○
224	Mussel Soup	○	●	○	○				○
423	Pissaladière (onion tart)	○	○	○		○	○		○
421	Sausage Nuggets	○	●	●	○				○
*103	*Cheese Appetizers (puff pastry)*	○	●	●	●	●	○	○	●
*104	*Gravlaks (dilled salmon)*	●	●	●				○	
*105	*Minimeatballs*	○	●	●	●	○		○	○
Main Courses:									
463	Baked Beans	○	●	●	●		●	●	●
426	Beef, Braised Pot Roast (bottom round)	○		○	○			○	
289	Cassoulet (bean and meat casserole)	○	○	○	○				○
340	Crêpe and Vegetable Gâteau	○		○	○				●
322	French Onion Soup	○	●	○	●	○			●
305	Hen Bonne Femme and Variations (chicken)	○		○	○				○
268	Monkfish en Pipérade	○	●	○	○				○
269	Monkfish Variations (cold)	●	●	●					○
372	Pâté en Croûte	●		○					
254	Pork, Butterflied Loin	○		○				○	
235	Rabbit Pie, Stew, and Variations	○	○	○	○				○
414	Salmon Gratin (casserole)	○	●	●	○			○	
405	Salmon Steaks (cold)	●	●	●				○	
*140	*Boiled Dinner*	○	○	○				○	○
*173	*Chicken Livers, Sautéed*	○	●	○	○				○
*172	*Corned Beef Hash*	○	●	○					○
*443	*Eggs in Aspic (ring of)*	●	●	○					●
*70	*Fish Chowder*	○	●	○	●		○	○	○
*197	*Lamb, Butterflied Leg of*	○		○				○	
*64	*Paëlla (rice and meat casserole)*	○	●	○	○				○
*106	*Peking Wings (chicken)*	○	●	○	○			○	●

The table below lists a selection of recipes from this book and its predecessor, and rates each dish as to how practical it is to prepare and serve at a large party. A solid dot (●) in any category means "highly recommended," an outline dot (○) means "manageable," and a blank space means either that the category doesn't apply or that the recipe may pose problems in this particular respect. I've skipped dishes that must be eaten as soon as made, but included those involving a lot of handwork (like Gazpacho Salad), provided you can do them well in advance, or have friendly help in your kitchen.

		No Last-Minute Jobs	Expandable Recipes**	Easy to Serve	Can Be Reheated	Can Be Frozen	Can Be Made Mostly by Machine	Relatively Little Handwork	Reasonable Price
Main Courses:									
*100	Pithiviers (ham tart)	○		○	○	●	○	○	○
*447	Turkey Casserole	○	●	●	●				●
*152	Turkey Orloff (more elaborate casserole)	○	●	○	○		●		○
*447	Turkey Salad	●	●	●					●
*215	Turkey Wine Stew	○	●	●	●				●
*174	Scrapple	○	●	○	○				○
Vegetables:									
304	Asparagus (boiled, cold)	●	●	●					
256	Butternut Squash with Ginger and Garlic	○	●	●	●			○	●
432	Beans, White, with Herbs	○	●	●	●			○	●
338	Eggplant Persillade	○	●	○	○			○	●
339	Eggplant with Sesame Seeds	○	●	○	○			○	●
367	Gazpacho Salad	●	●	●					○
428	Potato Gnocchi (dumplings)	○	●	○	○	○			●
391	Potato Gratin	○	●	○	○			○	●
292	Red Cabbage Slaw	●	●	●			●	●	●
467	Rice, Steamed	○	○	●	●			○	●
338	Spaghetti Squash	○	●	●	●				●
Desserts:									
310	Bombe aux Trois Chocolats, Chocolate Mousse, & Brownies	●	●	○		●			
272	Cream Cheese and Lemon Flan	●		○			○		●
258	Gâteau of Apples and Crêpes	●	○	○	○				●
392	Hazelnut Cookies (flat)	●	○	●		●			○
344	Ice Cream and Flaming Mincemeat		●	○		●		●	●
359	Macaroons	●	●	●		●	●	○	○
240	Meringue Cases with Ice Cream (vacherins)	●	●	●		●			●
435	Orange Bavarian Torte	●		○		●			○
293	Pineapple, Fresh	●	●	○					
377	Plantation Spice Cookies	●	●	●		●	○		●
409	Savarin and Rum Babas	●	○	○		○			○
*29	Apple Turnover	●	●	○	○	○	○	○	●
*441	Chocolate-Chip Cake	●		●		●			○
*130	Chocolate Truffles	●	●	●		●			
*58	Floating Island	●	○	●		●			●
*72	Indian Pudding	●	●		○				●
*155	Jamaican Ice Cream Goblet		●	●		●		●	●
*11	Los Gatos Gâteau Cake (meringue-apricot)	●	●	●		●			○
*205	Zabaione Batardo Veneziano	●	●	●		●			○

Q&A
Culinary Gazetteer

This is not only a culinary gazetteer; it is a catchall of miscellaneous information to answer questions that often come up about topics like the proper beating of egg whites, flour measuring, and so forth. I've also included here certain base recipes (some repeats from other books) for such items as mayonnaise and vinaigrettes, pie dough, tomato sauces, rice cooking methods, and other processes that reappear so frequently throughout this book it seems sensible to put them all in one place.

Subjects are listed alphabetically. If you do not find what you are looking for here please consult the index, because that particular topic may well have been discussed in one of the menus.

Almonds

To blanch and peel almonds
Drop shelled almonds into a large saucepan of rapidly boiling water and boil 1 minute, to loosen the skins. Slip the skins off 2 by 2 (using both hands), squeezing the nuts between your fingers. There appears to be no faster or easier way.

To toast almonds
Spread blanched almonds in a jelly-roll or roasting pan and set in the middle level of a preheated 350°F/180°C oven, rolling them about with a spatula every 5 minutes, until they are a light toasty brown. Be careful they do not burn; they will take 15 to 20 minutes to toast. (Even if the almonds are to be ground, they have better flavor if you toast them whole first.)

To grind or pulverize almonds
Grind them ½ cup (1 dL) at a time in an electric blender, or 1 cup (¼ L) at a time in a food processor using the on-off flick technique. Be careful that the almonds do not grind too fine and turn oily. It is always safer, if you are using them in a dessert recipe, to grind them with part of the sugar usually called for—they are less likely to turn into an oily mass.

Baked Beans

Baked Beans in a Slow-cooking Electric Pot (revised system):
Since the publication of the first volume, *J.C. & Co.*, I have revised my slow-cooker bean recipe to one that is so simple I can hardly believe it, following a suggestion from a reader in Oregon. "Why go to all the trouble you do?" she writes, and goes on to say she just dumps everything in and starts the cooking. Here's my new recipe.

For about 2 quarts (2 L) baked beans

1 pound (2 cups; 450 g) small white beans
5 cups (1¼ L) water
6 ounces (¾ cup; 180 g) sliced or diced salt pork (optional), simmered 10 minutes in 1 quart (1 L) water
1½ tsp salt
1 cup (¼ L) finely sliced onion
1 to 2 cloves garlic, minced (optional)
3 Tb dark unsulfured molasses
2 Tb Dijon-type prepared mustard
½ tsp dried thyme
2 imported bay leaves
½ Tb grated fresh ginger (optional)
Pepper to taste

Pick over and wash the beans. Mix everything up in the cooker, put on the lid, and turn the heat to high until contents are bubbling. Turn to low, and cook 14 to 16 hours or longer (turn to high once or twice if beans do not seem to be cooking); beans are not done until they have turned a nice darkish reddish brown. Correct seasoning.

Bread

Bread for Cooking—Bread for Crumbs:
There is quite a bit of bread used in these recipes: hard-toasted bread rounds as a topping for onion soup, fresh white crumbs in the stuffing for the poached chicken, crumbs in the fish pâté, on the Cornish hens, in the gazpacho salad, and so forth. Do get yourself the right kind of white bread for all of this: it should not be sweet-ish squashy bread, the kind you can grab with your hand and press into a sticky lump. It should be bread with natural body, of the Italian, Viennese, or French type; the sandwich bread put out by Pepperidge Farm and Arnold (unless they change their formulas) will also do for crumbs.

Bread crumbs
Cut the crusts off the bread and tear the bread into smallish pieces. Pulverize it a handful at a time either in an electric blender or with the grating disk of a food processor. It's a good idea to do a whole loaf at a time, bag what you don't use, and store it in the freezer.

Bread crusts toasted
If you are making crumbs out of a long loaf, cut the crusts off in neat fairly wide strips. Toast them in the oven with a sprinkling of melted butter and cheese and herbs, if you wish. Good with soups, or to use with dips.

Butter

Butter substitutes
There is no substitute for the taste of good butter in cookery. However, if you are using other spreads, they usually react in the same manner as butter, and you can use them interchangeably.

Clarified Butter:
Since butter is made from cream, a certain residue of milk particles remains in it after churning—more or less, depending on the quality of the butter. It is this milky residue that blackens when the butter is overheated, giving the butter itself and anything that cooks with it a speckled look and a burned taste. Therefore, if you are to brown anything in butter alone, you must clarify it, meaning that you rid the butter of its milky residue. Although you can clarify it by letting it melt and spooning the clear yellow liquid off the residue, which sinks to the bottom of the pan, you are getting only a partial clarification because much of the yellow liquid remains suspended in the residue. You are far better off actually cooking the butter, which coagulates the milk solids and evaporates the water content. Here is how to go about it.

To clarify butter
For about 1 ½ cups (3 ½ dL)

1 pound (450 g) butter

Equipment:

A 2-quart (2-L) saucepan; a small sieve lined with 3 thicknesses of washed cheesecloth; a screw-topped storage jar

For even melting, cut the butter into smallish pieces and place in the saucepan over moderate heat. When butter has melted, let it boil slowly, watching that it does not foam up over rim of pan. Listen to it crackle and bubble, and in a few minutes the crackling will almost cease—at this point, too, the butter may rise up in a foam of little bubbles. The clarification has been accomplished: the water content of the milky residue has evaporated, and if you continue to boil it, the butter will start to brown. Remove from heat at once and let cool a few minutes. Then strain through lined sieve into jar. You should have a beautifully clear deep yellow liquid, which will congeal and whiten slightly as it cools.

🕐 Clarified butter will keep for months in the refrigerator in a closed container. Scoop out what you want to use, and you may want to heat and liquefy it before using. (This clarified butter is the same as the *ghee* used in Indian cookery.)

Hot Butter Sauces:

The following 2 sauces are delicious with fish, shellfish, fish mousses, soufflés, asparagus, and broccoli. Both are given in detail in *J.C. & Co.*, and are simply outlined here for convenience.

Lemon Butter Sauce:
For about ¾ cup (1 ¾ dL)

2 Tb fresh lemon juice

3 Tb dry white French vermouth

Salt

1 stick (4 ounces or 115 g) chilled butter, cut into 12 pieces

White pepper

This sauce takes only minutes to make, and should be served at once. Boil the lemon juice, vermouth, and ¼ teaspoon salt in a small saucepan until reduced to 1 tablespoon. A piece or 2 at a time, over lowest heat, start beating in the chilled butter, adding a fresh piece just as the previous piece is almost melted. You should have a creamy ivory-colored sauce. Remove from heat, season to taste, and serve immediately.

White Butter Sauce—Beurre Blanc:
For 1 ½ to 1 ¾ cups (3 ½ to 4 dL)

4 Tb wine vinegar, preferably white

2 Tb lemon juice

4 Tb dry white French vermouth

2 Tb very finely minced shallots or scallions

Salt and white pepper

2 ½ sticks (10 ounces or 285 g) chilled butter, cut into 30 pieces

Optional additions: 4 to 8 Tb heavy cream, minced parsley and/or dill

Simmer the vinegar, lemon juice, vermouth, shallots or scallions, ½ teaspoon salt, and a big pinch of pepper in a smallish enameled or stainless-steel saucepan until reduced to about 1 ½ tablespoons. Then start beating in the butter and continue as directed in the preceding recipe, to make a thick ivory-colored sauce. Remove from heat; beat in optional cream by spoonfuls, then the herbs.

🕐 You can make the sauce somewhat ahead: omit the cream, and keep sauce barely warm near a gas pilot light or warm burner, just to keep it from congealing. Heat the cream shortly before serving and beat by driblets into the butter sauce to warm it.

Cheese

Storing and freezing cheese

Always store ripe and ready-to-eat cheese in a cool place or the refrigerator, wrapping up each kind of cheese individually.

Grate leftover hard cheeses like Cheddar, Swiss, and Parmesan, and store them together in a plastic bag in the freezer. A mixture makes a fine topping when dishes are to be gratinéed in the oven, and it is wonderfully convenient to have a ready hoard on hand.

Chocolate

Chocolate Sauce:
For about 1 ¾ cups (4 dL)

2 ½ ounces (70 g) best-quality semisweet chocolate

½ ounce (15 g) unsweetened chocolate

¾ cup (1 ¾ dL) water

3 to 4 Tb heavy cream

A small pinch of salt

Bring the chocolate and water to the simmer in a 4-cup (1-L) saucepan, and cook, stirring, for 4 to 5 minutes, until chocolate has melted and liquid is smoothly blended. Set chocolate pan in another pan of slowly simmering water, cover, and let cook for 15 to 20 minutes, stirring occasionally. Sauce will be quite thick; thin out with tablespoons of cream, and stir in a pinch of salt—to bring out the best chocolate flavor. Serve at room temperature.

🕐 May be cooked ahead, and refrigerated. Reheat either gently over direct heat while stirring, or over simmering water, stirring occasionally.

Cream

Lightly Whipped Cream—Crème Chantilly:
For about 2 cups (½ L)

1 cup (¼ L) heavy cream, chilled

½ cup (1 dL) confectioners sugar (optional)

½ tsp pure vanilla extract (optional)

Equipment:

A 2 ½-quart (3-L) round-bottomed metal mixing bowl; a larger bowl containing a tray of ice cubes and water to cover them; a large balloon-shaped wire whip, or a hand-held electric beater

Pour cream into metal bowl and set over ice. If you are using a whip, beat with an up-and-down circular motion, to beat as much air into the cream as possible. Or rotate an electric beater around the bowl to achieve the same effect. In 3 or 4 minutes cream will begin to thicken, and has reached the Chantilly or lightly whipped stage when the beater leaves light traces on the surface of the cream—a bit lifted in a spoon will hold its shape softly.

🕐 May be whipped in advance and kept over ice, then whipped lightly again before serving. Or you may refrigerate the cream in a sieve lined with damp washed cheesecloth, set over a bowl; liquid will exude into the bowl as the cream sits—will keep reasonably well for several hours.

If you are serving the cream for dessert, sift on the sugar, add the vanilla, and fold in with a rubber spatula just before using.

Variation:
See the whipped cream lightened with beaten egg whites, on page 187, in the rack of lamb chapter.

Dough

Dough for Pies, Quiches, Tarts, Tartlets, and Flans:
For an 8-inch (20-cm) shell

1 ¾ cups (8 ounces or 225 g) all-purpose flour, preferably unbleached (measure by scooping dry-measure cups into flour and sweeping off excess)

1 tsp salt

1 ¼ sticks (5 ounces or 140 g) chilled unsalted butter

2 Tb (1 ounce or 30 g) chilled lard or shortening

5 to 8 Tb iced water

Equipment:

A mixing bowl and rubber spatula; or bowl and pastry blender or 2 knives and spatula; or food processor with steel blade

Measure the flour and salt into the mixing bowl or bowl of processor. Quarter the chilled butter lengthwise, cut crosswise into ⅜-inch (1-cm) pieces, and add to the bowl or container along with the chilled lard or shortening, cut into small pieces.

Dough by hand

Rapidly, so fat will not soften, either rub it with the flour between the balls of your fingers until the fat is broken into pieces the size of small oatmeal flakes, or cut with pastry blender or knives until fat is the size of very coarse meal. (If fat softens during this process, refrigerate bowl or container for 20 minutes, then continue.) Then, with a rubber spatula, blend in 5 tablespoons iced water, pressing mixture against side of bowl to make a mass. Lift out massed pieces of dough onto your work surface, sprinkle droplets of water on the unmassed bits, press together, and add to rest of dough. Finish as in the final paragraph.

Dough in a food processor

The preceding proportions are right for machines with a 2-quart or 2-liter container; a large container will take double the amount. Turn machine on and off 4 or 5 times to break up the fat. Measure out 5 tablespoons iced water, turn the machine on, and pour it in. Turn machine on and off 5 or 6 times, and dough should begin to mass on blade; if not, dribble in another tablespoon water and repeat. Repeat again if necessary. Dough is done when it has begun to mass; it should not be overmixed. Remove dough to your work surface.

Finishing the dough

With the heel, not the warm palm, of your hand rapidly and roughly smear dough out 6 to 8 inches (15 to 20 cm) on your work surface by 3-spoonful bits, to make a final blending of fat and flour. If pastry seems stiff, you can at this time sprinkle on droplets more water as you smear. It should be pliable, but not damp and sticky. Knead and press it rapidly into a rough cake, flour lightly, and wrap in a sheet of plastic and a plastic bag. Chill for 1 hour—preferably 2 hours—before using, which will allow dough to relax while the flour particles absorb the liquid.

❶ Will keep under refrigeration for a day or 2, but if you have used unbleached flour it will gradually turn gray; it is best to store it in the freezer, where it will keep perfectly for several months. Let thaw overnight in the refrigerator, or at room temperature and then rechill.

Dough for Pâtés and Meat Pies:

The following proportions are for ½ pound (225 g) flour, to keep them in line with the previous doughs, but you will undoubtedly want more if you are making a *pâté en croûte*—like the fine pâté baked in a pastry crust in "Picnic." There the amount is tripled, and the dough is made in a heavy-duty machine, which is useful indeed for large amounts. The proportions and recipe

are on page 164, but here is the smaller amount suitable for making it as in the preceding directions.

1 ¾ cups (8 ounces or 225 g) all-purpose flour
1 ¼ tsp salt
½ stick (2 ounces or 60 g) chilled unsalted butter
3 Tb (1 ½ ounces or 45 g) chilled lard
2 egg yolks plus enough iced water to make 6 to 8 Tb liquid

Egg Whites

To Beat Egg Whites:
Preliminaries

Be sure your beating bowl and beater are perfectly clean and free of oil or grease, which will prevent them from mounting. Before you begin it is useful to wipe bowl and beater with 1 tablespoon each of salt and vinegar, which seem to provide a proper mounting atmosphere. If the egg whites are chilled, set beating bowl in hot water and stir for a few minutes until tepid.

Bowls and beaters

Egg whites mount best when almost the entire mass of them can be kept in motion at once. A beater on a stand should be equipped with a large whip that rotates as it circulates rapidly about the bowl, and the bowl should be narrow, and rounded at the bottom. A hand-held beater works well in a stainless-steel or unlined copper bowl—egg whites collapse down the slippery sides of glass and porcelain; again, choose a bowl with a rounded bottom, and not too big a bowl or you cannot keep the mass of whites circulating as you beat. A giant balloon whip beats egg whites beautifully in an unlined copper bowl, but be sure you have a big enough whip for your bowl.

Beating

Besides having a very clean, grease-free bowl, and room-temperature or tepid egg whites, you must also be sure that there is no particle of yolk in the whites, since this also will prevent them from rising.

For table-model beaters
Start at slow speed until egg whites are foaming throughout, then add a pinch of salt and a large pinch of cream of tartar for

every 3 egg whites—these help stabilize the whites after they have risen. Gradually increase your speed to fast, standing right over the mixer to be sure you don't overbeat the whites. Continue until egg whites form little mountains on the surface; stop and test them—the whites should stand up in stiff shining peaks as illustrated. If you are using the whites in a dessert, beat in ½ tablespoon sugar per egg white, which will also help stabilize them. Use the egg whites at once. Time: with an efficient beater, about 3 minutes.

For hand-held electric beaters
Use the same system as for table-model beaters, pretending you are an efficient whirling and rotating electric whip that circulates rapidly all about the bowl. Time: 3 to 4 minutes.

Beating by hand in a copper bowl
Start at slow speed until egg whites are foaming, then beat in a pinch of salt per 3 egg whites. Gradually increase speed to fast, using an up-and-down circular motion alternating at times with several round-the-bowl beats, and continue until the egg whites form stiff shining peaks. Beat in ½ tablespoon sugar per egg white, if you are doing a dessert. Time: 2 to 3 minutes.

Fish

Fish Mousse in Sausage Casings—
Fish Dogs—Boudins:

When you are making a fish mousse, such as that for the terrine on page 161, put the leftovers into sausage casings for an amusing first course or luncheon dish. Ask your butcher for a few lengths of small hog casings; if you don't plan to use them right away, you can store them by packing them in layers surrounded by coarse salt in a screw-topped jar in the refrigerator.

An hour before you plan to stuff the casings, wash off the salt, and soak them in cold water. Then attach one end of a 3-foot (90-cm) length to the end of your cold water faucet, and run a thin stream of water through it to be sure it is whole and unpierced. Attach the end, then, to the end of a wet pastry tube or sausage horn, and slip the rest of the length up onto the tube, leaving a free end of 4 inches (10 cm).

However you beat them, egg whites should form shining peaks.

Fish dogs, despite their name, make an elegant luncheon dish.

In the illustration here, the sausage mixture is in a pastry bag with tube attached, and the second tube with the casing on it is being held by hand onto the first—not the easiest way to stuff a sausage, but it works. Be sure to keep the filling coming constantly into the casing, to avoid air bubbles. Fill the length of the casing, then tie the free end; twist the casing at 4-inch (10-cm) intervals and tie, to form the sausages.

⊘   May be frozen raw, and cooked after thawing.

To cook them prick in 4 or 5 places with a pin, to prevent the casing from bursting as the sausages swell. Place in simmering salted water and cook at below the simmer for 15 minutes. Serve with melted butter or a sauce such as hollandaise or white butter sauce, or the sour cream sauce on page 163.

Flour

Measuring:

Be serious when you measure your flour because you can get into real trouble doing cakes and pastries if you get too much or too little; baking recipes are designed for quite accurate amounts. All flour in this book is measured as follows, in dry-measure cups:

Dip dry-measure cup into flour container until cup is overflowing; sweep off excess with the straight edge of a spatula or knife, as illustrated below.

Garlic

To peel and purée

I think the garlic press is a great invention but sometimes I want to do it by hand, and here is an easy way to peel, mince, or purée garlic. Lay a whole garlic clove on your work surface, set the flat of your big knife upon it, and smash down on the knife with your fist. The garlic will split, loosening the peel, which you can then easily pluck off from the flesh. To purée the garlic, mince finely with your big knife, and when in small pieces, sprinkle with salt. Continue mincing, and then press against

Always take the trouble to measure your flour this way.

the garlic with the flat of the knife, drawing it back and forth across the surface 2 or 3 times; continue mincing, then pressing, and in a few seconds the garlic will be a fine purée. (The salt seems to help soften the garlic, so that it purées quickly.)

Mayonnaise

Mayonnaise:

For a little more than 2 cups (½ L)
Mayonnaise couldn't be easier to make if you just remember these points: beat up the yolks well before you begin, add the oil by droplets at first until the sauce begins to thicken; don't exceed the proportions of 2 cups (½ L) oil to 3 egg yolks; and remember that a turned or thinned-out mayonnaise is very easy to bring back. Here are directions for making mayonnaise by hand, and in a food processor.

3 egg yolks (for a processor, 1 egg and 2 yolks)

¼ tsp dry mustard

½ tsp salt

Fresh lemon juice and/or wine vinegar to taste

2 cups (½ L) best-quality olive oil or a combination of olive oil and salad oil

More salt, and white pepper

Equipment:

Either a 2-quart (2-L) mixing bowl with rounded bottom and a large wire whip or hand-held electric mixer, or a food processor with steel blade; a rubber spatula

By hand

Set the bowl on a wet potholder to keep it from slipping about. Beat the egg yolks in the bowl for a good 2 minutes, until they turn pale yellow and thicken into a cream. Beat in the mustard and the salt, and 1 teaspoon of lemon juice or vinegar; continue beating a minute longer. Then, by ½-teaspoon driblets, start beating in the oil, making sure it is being constantly absorbed by the egg yolks—stop pouring for a moment every once in a while, and continue beating until about ½ cup (1 dL) oil has gone in and sauce has thickened into a heavy cream. Then add the oil by larger dollops, beating to absorb each addition before adding another. When sauce becomes too thick and heavy, thin out with droplets of lemon juice or vinegar, then continue with as much of the additional oil as you wish. Taste carefully for seasoning, adding more salt, pepper, lemon juice or vinegar.

By food processor

Place the whole egg and 2 yolks in the container and process for 1 minute. Then, with machine running, add the mustard, salt, and 1 teaspoon lemon juice or vinegar. Start adding the oil in a stream of droplets, and continue until you have used half, and

sauce is very thick. Thin out with 1 teaspoon of lemon juice or vinegar; continue with the oil. Add seasonings to taste, and if sauce is too thick add more lemon juice or vinegar, or droplets of water.

⊘   **Storing mayonnaise**
Scrape mayonnaise into a screw-topped jar and store in the refrigerator—7 to 10 days.

Turned or thinned-out mayonnaise
If you have added the oil too quickly and the sauce will not thicken, or if it has been refrigerated for some time and the chilled yolks have released the oil from suspension and the mayonnaise has curdled like the example in the photograph, the problem is easily remedied. Place 1 tablespoon prepared Dijon-type mustard and a ½ tablespoon of the sauce in a bowl and beat vigorously with a wire whip or hand-held mixer until mustard and sauce have creamed together; then, by droplets, beat in the turned sauce—it is important that you add it very slowly at first for the rethickening to take place.

Garlic Mayonnaise—Aïoli:

For about 2 cups (½ L)
This marvelous sauce goes well with fish soups, boiled fish, fish in cold sauces (like the monkfish *pipérade* on page 61), with boiled chicken (like our stewing hen on page 97), with poached egg dishes, with boiled potatoes—in fact with anything that could use a strong garlic mayonnaise to perk it up. And how do you get all that garlic off your breath? Everybody eat it and no one will notice a thing.

4 to 8 large cloves garlic

½ tsp salt

1 slice homemade-type French or Italian white bread

2 Tb wine vinegar

2 egg yolks

1½ cups (3½ dL) strong olive oil

More salt and vinegar to taste

White pepper and/or drops of hot pepper sauce

Equipment:

A mortar and pestle or heavy bowl and pounding instrument of some sort; a wire whip or hand-held electric mixer

A splendid example of horridly turned mayonnaise—but it's easy to fix.

Either purée the garlic into the mortar or bowl with a garlic press, or mince very fine and add to the bowl. Pound to a very fine paste with the salt—a most important step, taking a good minute or more. Cut the crust off the bread, tear bread into pieces and add to the bowl with the vinegar, and pound with the garlic into a paste; then pound in the egg yolks to make a thick sticky mass. By driblets, as though making a mayonnaise, start pounding and stirring in the oil; when thickened, begin adding it a little faster and beat it in with a whip or mixer. Sauce should be thick and heavy. Season to taste with more salt and droplets of vinegar as needed, and pepper and/or hot pepper sauce. Store as described for mayonnaise; if it turns, give it the same treatment.

Napkin Folding

Just a simple trick like the folding of napkins can make a most attractive decoration for your table. You'll want them made of a somewhat heavy material so that they will stand up in shape.

1)Fold the napkin in half, to make a triangle, its point away from you. *2*)Bring the 2 bottom corners from the folded side up to the point at the top, to make a diamond shape. *3*)Fold the napkin in half, making a smaller triangle, then fold the top corner down as shown. *4*)Turn the napkin over, and roll a lower corner to the middle of the bottom fold. *5*)Bring the other corner around to the front of the napkin and tuck it under a front fold flap as shown. *6*)Stand the napkin upright, and bend down the 2 top corners.

Rice

Cooking Methods:

Plain raw white rice is so easy to cook and to reheat that I see no reason for paying extra money to buy processed rice. Here are 2 methods I use all the time, to produce rice with separate, nongummy grains.

Amounts: 1 cup or ¼ L raw rice makes 3 cups or ¾ L cooked rice.

Steamed Rice:

Steaming is the simplest method and works for long, short, and fat-grain Italian rice. An advantage is that you can cook it ahead and reheat it.

For 6 cups (1½ L) cooked rice

2 cups (½ L) plain raw unwashed white rice
4 quarts (3¾ L) rapidly boiling water
2 Tb salt
Equipment:
A large saucepan or kettle; a colander that will fit into it (see notes in recipe); a well washed and rinsed kitchen towel

Sprinkle the rice into the rapidly boiling water, and add the salt. Boil slowly, uncovered, for 8 to 9 minutes or more, just until the rice is almost but not quite tender—bite into several grains to be sure. Drain in the colander; wash briefly under hot water to remove starch so that rice grains will not stick together. Pour 2 inches (5 cm) water into the kettle and set the colander with the rice in the kettle; cover with the damp towel. (*Note:* if colander does not fit into kettle down to the level of the rice, turn the rice into the towel and fold it up over, to keep rice from drying out.) About 10 minutes before serving, steam the rice to finish cooking.

May be completed hours in advance, and may even be steamed in advance, but be careful not to overcook the rice in that case. Leftovers may be rewarmed by steaming, or may be warmed in a saucepan with butter and seasonings.

Overcooked rice

You can tell it is overcooked because the rice grains will have splayed ends rather than rounded ones. You can still use it, but the taste and texture will have suffered.

Plain Boiled Rice:

This produces rice with a little more flavor than steamed rice.

For 6 cups (1½ L) cooked rice

2 cups (½ L) plain raw unwashed white rice, long-grain type
4 cups (1 L) water
3 Tb butter (optional)
2 to 3 tsp salt
Pepper
Equipment:
A heavy-bottomed 2-quart (2-L) saucepan with cover; a wooden fork or chopsticks

1

2

3

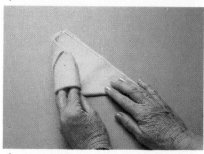

4

5

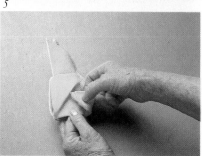

6

Bring the rice to the boil with the water, optional butter, and salt; when boil is reached, stir once with fork or chopsticks. Reduce heat, cover the pan, and let rice simmer over moderately low heat, undisturbed, for 12 to 15 minutes, or until it has absorbed the liquid and is just tender. Note the steam holes (I call them clam holes, the kind you find in the wet sand indicating clams are below), showing that the liquid has been absorbed; tilt pan and lift a lower side to be sure. Simmer, covered, a few minutes more if necessary.

Correct seasoning, after you have lifted and fluffed up the rice, and fold in more butter if you wish.

❶ If you are serving shortly, set pan in another pan of almost simmering water to keep warm. Fluff up again, before serving. Or set the rice aside, and reheat over simmering water several hours later, fluffing and turning the rice several times for even heating, and you may need to fold in a little water if rice seems dry.

Salad Dressings

Vinaigrette:
Basic French dressing for salads, cold vegetables, and so forth
For ½ cup (1 dL), enough for 6

1 to 2 Tb excellent wine vinegar and/or lemon juice

¼ tsp salt

¼ tsp dry mustard

6 to 8 Tb best-quality olive oil or salad oil or a combination of both

Several grinds of fresh pepper

Optional: 1 tsp finely minced shallots or scallions and/or fresh or dried herbs, such as chives, tarragon, basil

Either beat the vinegar, salt, and mustard in a bowl until dissolved, then beat in the oil and seasonings. Or place all ingredients in a screw-topped jar and shake vigorously to blend. Dip a piece of lettuce into the dressing and taste; correct seasoning.

Variations for Cold Fish Salads, Eggs, and Vegetables:
Garlic and lemon dressing
Purée a clove of garlic into a bowl, using a garlic press, then mash into a fine paste with the ¼ teaspoon salt and grated peel of ½ lemon. Proceed with vinaigrette as usual.
Vinaigrette with sesame paste
Make the garlic and lemon dressing, and beat in 1 teaspoon or so of sesame paste after you have added the lemon peel.
A creamy dressing
Make the dressing as usual, but also beat in an egg white or an egg yolk, or a tablespoon or 2 heavy cream or sour cream before adding the oil.

Vinaigrette for a Crowd of 30:
For about 3 ½ cups (almost 1 L)

4 Tb minced shallots or scallions

2 Tb dry mustard

5 or 6 shakes of hot pepper sauce

Grinds of fresh pepper to taste

About 1 Tb salt, or to your taste

5 Tb wine vinegar; more if needed

2 Tb fresh lemon juice

3 cups (¾ L) best-quality olive oil or salad oil or a combination of both

Herbs, such as tarragon, basil, or chives

Prepare the dressing as described previously, but you may want to beat it up in an electric mixer.

Spices

Special Spice Mixture:
Here is a special homemade spice mixture that I find wonderfully convenient to have on hand for seasoning pork chops and roasts, pâtés, and so forth. Saves you a lot of trouble, and it will keep for months in a screw-topped jar. If you don't have a special grinder, use an electric blender for those herbs and spices that are not already pulverized.

2 Tb each ground imported bay leaves, cloves, mace, nutmeg, paprika, thyme

1 Tb each ground dried basil (if fragrant, or else oregano), cinnamon, and savory

5 Tb ground white peppercorns

Tomatoes

Raw Tomato Garnish:
Cold chopped tomatoes, particularly in full tomato season, are a delicious accompaniment to many another cold dish, and you may use the tomato garnish as is, or add to it other chopped vegetables as suggested here.
For about 2 cups (½ L)

2½ to 3 cups (½ to ¾ L) fresh tomato pulp (tomatoes peeled, seeded, juiced, and neatly diced; page 119)

2 Tb minced shallots or scallions

1 tsp or so wine vinegar

Salt and pepper

Fresh minced herbs if available, such as parsley, basil, dill, and tarragon (or dried herbs)

1 to 2 Tb olive oil (optional)

Toss the tomato pulp in a bowl with the shallots or scallions, vinegar, and salt and pepper to taste. Let stand 10 minutes, then pour into a sieve set over a bowl. Drain several minutes; turn into a serving bowl and fold with the herbs, optional olive oil, and more seasonings to taste.

Tomato Fondue:
Fresh tomato lightly cooked in butter, herbs, and shallots
For about 1 ½ cups (3 ½ dL)

So often one needs a little something to go with a vegetable custard, a soufflé, or a boiled fish—something a little bit tart, something not too insistent in flavor, something with a bright color—this very simple accompaniment often fills just these requirements. (If you're doing the sauce in full tomato season, when they're bursting with flavor, of course you don't need the help of the canned plum tomatoes for extra taste and color, as suggested below.)

2 Tb minced shallots or scallions

2 Tb butter

2½ cups (6 dL), more or less, fresh tomato pulp, chopped (page 119)

4 Tb or more drained and seeded canned Italian plum tomatoes, if needed

Salt and pepper

Fresh herbs, such as fresh basil and parsley, or tarragon; or dried herbs to taste (tarragon, oregano, thyme)

Cook the minced shallots or scallions in butter, in a small frying pan or saucepan, for a minute or 2 without browning. Then add the tomato and cook over moderately high heat for several minutes until juices have exuded and tomato pulp has thickened enough to hold its shape lightly in a spoon. Season carefully to taste. Just before serving, fold in the herbs.

Tomato Sauce—with Fresh Tomatoes:
For use with meats, baked custards, fish, pizza toppings, pastas, etc.
For 2 ½ to 3 cups (½ to ¾ L)

1 cup (¼ L) minced onion

2 Tb olive oil

4 cups (1 L) tomato pulp (See Note)

1 imported bay leaf

½ tsp Italian or Provençal herb mixture

1 or more cloves garlic, puréed

Big pinch saffron threads (optional)

A 2-inch (5-cm) piece dried orange peel

Salt and pepper to taste

Cook the onion and olive oil in a heavy-bottomed saucepan, stirring frequently, until onion is limp and translucent but not browned (5 to 7 minutes). Stir in the tomato pulp, herbs, and seasonings, bring to the simmer, then cover and simmer slowly for 30 minutes, stirring occasionally. Taste, and carefully correct seasoning; if too thin, boil down rapidly, stirring.

Note: Out of tomato season, add a judicious amount of strained canned Italian-style plum tomatoes for color and flavor.

Metric Conversions

Some day we shall convert from our illogical system of pounds, ounces, feet, and inches to metrics, where all will be in easy divisions of 10 rather than a mishmash of 2's, 4's, 12's, 16's. In anticipation of that happy metric day, all the recipes in this book give both versions, and clumsy though this is at times, at least it will remind us that 350°F is 180°C, that 1 cup is ¼ liter, and that 9 inches is 23 centimeters.

At this writing there seems to be some agreement among metric consultants about some of the terms and abbreviations that should be used in this country. However, there is disagreement about whether the metric cup measure should be ¼ of a liter (250 milliliters) or 240 milliliters to correspond to our present 8-ounce cup. Should the tablespoon and teaspoon be retained as terms? Or should those measurements be expressed in milliliters? But why use milliliters at all? say I. The Europeans, who have been cooking in metrics for generations, don't ever use any milliliters in cooking, only the large fractions of the liter down to deciliters (1/10 of a liter) and centiliters (1/100 of a liter). I suppose our metric people want to be utterly logical, and if we are using grams, which are 1/1000 of a kilogram, we must then use milliliters, which are 1/1000 of a liter. However, is it logical to launch out on a new system when the rest of the metric users do not agree? After all, the point of our going metric is that we be able to communicate with the rest of the world.

Since, then, there is as yet no established plan, I am using the European system for liquid measures. No milliliters! I think the large fractions of the liter are far easier; besides, ¼ liter is just about the same as our 1 cup. And why use milliliters for our easy-to-measure tablespoon and teaspoon? You will note, in the charts to follow, that there is not always perfection in conversion since the deciliter does not fit as easily into our cup measures as could be wished—for instance, while ½ cup makes for convenience 1 deciliter, 1 cup makes 2½ deciliters, or ¼ liter. However, these slight discrepancies make no appreciable difference in home cooking. What I am looking for is reasonable accuracy and easy measurement.

By the way, there have been worry rumors that once we convert to metrics all of us will have to buy kitchen scales. Not so! Everything will be measured in cups and spoons as before; it is up to the recipe writers to figure out how many cups of flour 140 or 190 grams make, how many prunes fit into a ½ liter, how much sugar to a deciliter, and so forth and so on. In addition, recipes and cookbooks will have to include both systems, as this one does, for many years to come.

Liquid Measure Conversions

Cups and Spoons	Liquid Ounces	Approximate Metric Term	Approximate Centiliters	Actual Milliliters
1 tsp	1/6 oz	1 tsp	½ cL	5 mL
1 Tb	½ oz	1 Tb	1½ cL	15 mL
¼ c; 4 Tb	2 oz	½ dL; 4 Tb	6 cL	59 mL
⅓ c; 5 Tb	2⅔ oz	¾ dL; 5 Tb	8 cL	79 mL
½ c	4 oz	1 dL	12 cL	119 mL
⅔ c	5⅓ oz	1½ dL	15 cL	157 mL
¾ c	6 oz	1¾ dL	18 cL	178 mL
1 c	8 oz	¼ L	24 cL	237 mL
1¼ c	10 oz	3 dL	30 cL	296 mL
1⅓ c	10⅔ oz	3¼ dL	33 cL	325 mL
1½ c	12 oz	3½ dL	35 cL	355 mL
1⅔ c	13⅓ oz	3¾ dL	39 cL	385 mL
1¾ c	14 oz	4 dL	41 cL	414 mL
2 c; 1 pt	16 oz	½ L	47 cL	473 mL
2½ c	20 oz	6 dL	60 cL	592 mL
3 c	24 oz	¾ L	70 cL	710 mL
3½ c	28 oz	4/5 L; 8 dL	83 cL	829 mL
4 c; 1 qt	32 oz	1 L	95 cL	946 mL
5 c	40 oz	1¼ L	113 cL	1134 mL
6 c; 1½ qt	48 oz	1½ L	142 cL	1420 mL
8 c; 2 qt	64 oz	2 L	190 cL	1893 mL
10 c; 2½ qt	80 oz	2½ L	235 cL	2366 mL
12 c; 3 qt	96 oz	2¾ L	284 cL	2839 mL
4 qt	128 oz	3¾ L	375 cL	3785 mL
5 qt		4¾ L		
6 qt		5½ L (or 6 L)		
8 qt		7½ L (or 8 L)		

To convert:

Ounces to *milliliters:*
multiply *ounces* by 29.57
Quarts to *liters:*
multiply *quarts* by 0.95
Milliliters to *ounces:*
multiply *milliliters* by 0.034
Liters to *quarts:*
multiply *liters* by 1.057

Temperatures

Fahrenheit degrees are here converted to the most convenient Celsius term, with actual Celsius degrees in parentheses. (Note that by international agreement the term "Celsius" has been substituted for the term "Centigrade"; however, the degrees are the same whichever term you use. This decision was evidently made because both Celsius and Fahrenheit were men, which is not the case with Centigrade. We must be logical!

Fahrenheit°/Celsius°	(Actual Celsius°)
−5°F/−20°C	(−20.6°C)
32°F/0°C	(0°C)
37°F/3°C	(2.8°C)
50°F/10°C	(10°C)
60°F/16°C	(15.6°C)
70°F/21°C	(21.1°C)
75°F/24°C	(23.9°C)
80°F/27°C	(26.7°C)
85°F/29°C	(29.4°C)
100°F/38°C	(37.8°C)
105°F/41°C	(40.6°C)
110°F/43°C	(43.3°C)
115°F/46°C	(46.1°C)
120°F/49°C	(48.9°C)
125°F/52°C	(51.7°C)
130°F/54°C	(54.4°C)
135°F/57°C	(57.2°C)
140°F/60°C	(60°C)
150°F/66°C	(65.6°C)
160°F/71°C	(71.1°C)
165°F/74°C	(73.9°C)
170°F/77°C	(76.7°C)
180°F/82°C	(82.2°C)
190°F/88°C	(87.8°C)
200°F/95°C	(93.3°C)
205°F/96°C	(96.1°C)
212°F/100°C	(100°C)
225°F/110°C	(107.2°C)
228°F/109°C	(108.9°C)

Fahrenheit°/Celsius°	(Actual Celsius°)
238°F/115°C	(114.4°C)
250°F/120°C	(121.1°C)
275°F/135°C	(135°C)
285°F/140°C	(140.6°C)
300°F/150°C	(148.9°C)
325°F/165°C	(162.8°C)
350°F/180°C	(176.7°C)
375°F/190°C	(190.6°C)
400°F/205°C	(204.4°C)
425°F/220°C	(218.3°C)
450°F/230°C	(232.2°C)
475°F/245°C	(246.1°C)
500°F/260°C	(260°C)
525°F/275°C	(273.9°C)
550°F/290°C	(287.8°C)

To convert:
Fahrenheit to *Celsius:*
subtract 32, multiply by 5, divide by 9.
Celsius to *Fahrenheit:*
multiply by 9, divide by 5, add 32.

Inches to Centimeters

Inches ("in")	Centimeters ("cm") (Nearest equivalent)
1/16 in	¼ cm
⅛ in	½ cm
3/16 in	"less than ¼ in/¾ cm"
¼ in	¾ cm
⅜ in	1 cm
½ in	1½ cm
⅝ in	1½ cm
¾ in	2 cm
1 in	2½ cm
1½ in	4 cm
2 in	5 cm
2½ in	6½ cm
3 in	8 cm
3½ in	9 cm
4 in	10 cm
5 in	13 cm
6 in	15 cm
7 in	18 cm
8 in	20 cm
9 in	23 cm
10 in	25 cm
12 in	30 cm
14 in	35 cm
15 in	38½ cm
16 in	40 cm
18 in	45 cm
20 in	50 cm
24 in	60 cm
30 in	75 cm

To convert:
Inches to *centimeters:*
multiply *inches* by 2.54
Centimeters to *inches:*
multiply *centimeters* by 0.39

Ounces to Grams

Ounces	Convenient Equivalent	Actual Weight
1 oz	30 g	(28.35 g)
2 oz	60 g	(56.7 g)
3 oz	85 g	(85.05 g)
4 oz	115 g	(113.4 g)
5 oz	140 g	(141.8 g)
6 oz	180 g	(170.1 g)
8 oz	225 g	(226.8 g)
9 oz	250 g	(255.2 g)
10 oz	285 g	(283.5 g)
12 oz	340 g	(340.2 g)
14 oz	400 g	(396.9 g)
16 oz	450 g	(453.6 g)
20 oz	560 g	(566.99 g)
24 oz	675 g	(680.4 g)

To convert:
Ounces to *grams:*
multiply *ounces* by 28.35
Grams to *ounces:*
multiply *grams* by 0.035

Pounds to Grams and Kilograms

Pounds	Convenient Equivalent	Actual Weight
¼ lb	115 g	(113.4 g)
½ lb	225 g	(226.8 g)
¾ lb	340 g	(340.2 g)
1 lb	450 g	(453.6 g)
1¼ lb	565 g	(566.99 g)
1½ lb	675 g	(680.4 g)
1¾ lb	800 g	(794 g)
2 lb	900 g	(908 g)
2½ lb	1125 g; 1¼ kg	(1134 g)
3 lb	1350 g	(1360 g)
3½ lb	1500 g; 1½ kg	(1588 g)
4 lb	1800 g	(1814 g)
4½ lb	2 kg	(2041 g)
5 lb	2¼ kg	(2268 g)
5½ lb	2½ kg	(2495 g)
6 lb	2¾ kg	(2727 g)
7 lb	3¼ kg	(3175 g)
8 lb	3½ kg	(3629 g)
9 lb	4 kg	(4028 g)
10 lb	4½ kg	(4536 g)
12 lb	5½ kg	(5443 g)
14 lb	6¼ kg	(6350 g)
15 lb	6¾ kg	(6804 g)
16 lb	7¼ kg	(7258 g)
18 lb	8 kg	(8165 g)
20 lb	9 kg	(9072 g)
25 lb	11¼ kg	(11,340 g)

Flour and Sugar Measurements

Flour equivalents are for flour scooped and leveled: scooped into cup; leveled off even with lip by knife-edge sweep.

Flour Measurements	Ounces	Nearest equivalents
1 Tb	¼ oz	7½ g
¼ c; 4 Tb	1¼ oz	35 g
⅓ c; 5 Tb	1½ oz	50 g
½ c	2½ oz	70 g
⅔ c	3¼ oz	100 g
¾ c	3½ oz	105 g
1 c	5 oz	140 g
1¼ c	6 oz	175 g
1⅓ c	6½ oz	190 g
1½ c	7½ oz	215 g
2 c	10 oz	285 g
3½ c	16 oz; 1 lb	454 g
3¾ c	17½ oz	500 g

Sugar Measurements	Ounces	Nearest equivalents
1 tsp	1/6 oz	5 g
1 Tb	½ oz	12-15 g
¼ c; 4 Tb	1¾ oz	50 g
⅓ c; 5 Tb	2¼ oz	65 g
½ c	3½ oz	100 g
⅔ c	4½ oz	125 g
¾ c	5 oz	145 g
1 c	7 oz (6¾ oz)	190-200 g
1¼ c	8½ oz	240 g
1⅓ c	9 oz	245 g
1½ c	9½ oz	275 g
1⅔ c	11 oz	325 g
1¾ c	11¾ oz	240 g
2 c	13½ oz	380-400 g

Index

A Note About the Author

Julia Child was born in Pasadena, California. She was graduated from Smith College and worked for the OSS during World War II in Ceylon and China. Afterwards she lived for several years in Paris, studied at the Cordon Bleu, and taught cooking with Simone Beck and Louisette Bartholle, with whom she wrote the first volume of *Mastering the Art of French Cooking*, published in 1961.

In 1963 Boston's WGBH launched "The French Chef" television series, which made Julia Child a national celebrity, earning her the Peabody award in 1965 and an Emmy in 1966; subsequent public television shows were "Julia Child & Company" (1978) and "Julia Child & More Company" (1980), both accompanied by the cookbooks that we've combined in this new hardcover edition, and "Dinner at Julia's" (1983). She has also appeared frequently on "Good Morning America." In 1970 Volume II of *Mastering the Art of French Cooking*, written with Simone Beck, was published, and in 1975 *From Julia Child's Kitchen* followed. For four years in the early 80's, Mrs. Child wrote a monthly feature for *Parade* magazine. In 1989 Julia Child's magnum opus, *The Way to Cook*, was published.

Julia Child is married to Paul Child, who has worked closely with her as an artist and photographer. The Childs live in Cambridge, Massachusetts, and in Santa Barbara, California.